COLLINS MINIGEM ENGLISH DICTIONARY

With the compliments of
Ariel

Collins
London and Glasgow

© Wm. Collins Sons & Co. Ltd. 1981

First published 1981
Reprinted 1983 (twice), 1984 (twice), 1986
ISBN 0 00 458375 2

EDITORIAL STAFF

Managing Editor
William T. McLeod

Editors
Marian Makins, Margaret Martin,
Pamela Breckenridge, Diana Adams,
Michael Munro

Assistants
Danielle McGrath, Kay Cullen,
Nancy McGuire

Printed in Great Britain
Collins Clear-Type Press

ARRANGEMENT OF ENTRIES

All main entries are arranged in a single alphabetical listing, including abbreviations, foreign words, and combining forms or prefixes. Each such entry consists of a paragraph, with a main, or core, word at the head of it in large bold type. Derived or related words, in smaller bold type, appear later in the paragraph in alphabetical order, with phrases included at the end. Thus, **'labourer'** and **'laborious'** will be found under **'labour'**, **'abide by'** under **'abide'**, and so on. Alternative spellings are shown by bracketing optional letters, eg **'judg(e) ment'** or by placing the variants side by side (**accurs'ed, accurst'**); but if the divergence in spelling is very great there is a separate entry.

The part of speech is shown by an abbreviation placed after the word (or its pronunciation), eg **'dog** *n.,*' for noun. Words which are used as more than one part of speech are only written out once, the change being indicated by a new part of speech label, eg **'ravage** *vt.* plunder – *n.* destruction.' In the case of very short, simple entries, parts of speech may be combined, eg **'jest** *n./vi.* joke.' Spelling of verb parts is indicated in brackets after the verbal definitions, eg **'jab** ... stab (**-bb-**)'.

When a derived word is included within an entry, its meaning may be understood from the meaning of the headword or another derived word from within the paragraph.

Field labels and usage notes are added in italic type and abbreviated where there will be no confusion.

Although only '-ize' and '-ization' spellings are shown, the reader should understand that spellings in '-ise' and '-isation' are equally acceptable.

PRONUNCIATION

The pronunciation of many words is adequately shown simply by placing an accent (') immediately after the syllable that carries the main stress. All headwords are stressed except those that have only one syllable.

The position of the stress mark in a headword generally indicates the length of the stressed vowel: if it comes immediately after the vowel, the vowel is usually long (**sa'vour**); if it comes after a consonant, the vowel is usually short (**sav'age**). But there are some exceptions (like **recite'**, **voli'tion**, **colli'sion**).

Where the stress mark alone is insufficient to clarify some peculiarity of pronunciation or misleading spelling, a simple phonetic respelling of the whole or part of the word is given in square brackets immediately after the headword.

The special letters used in the phonetic respelling are listed below. All letters *not* listed have their normal pronunciation.

ā mate	o͞o food	ch church
ah calm	yoo sinuous	ng ring
aw law	yo͞o few	th thin
ē freeze	oi boil	TH this
ī bite	ow how	y yes
ō rope	ə *ago*	H loch
oo book		

Where a headword is stressed only and not pronounced by respelling, the following values are assumed for certain letters and letter combinations.

rai'sin	[-ā-]	**cord'ial**	[-awr-]
carp'et	[-ah-]	**board**	[-awr-]
laud'able	[-aw-]	**aloud'**	[-ow-]
fea'ture	[-ē-]	**tu'na**	[-yo͞o-]
foam	[-ō-]		

Whenever these letters are pronounced differently, this pronunciation is shown.

ABBREVIATIONS USED IN THE DICTIONARY

a.	adjective	*m*	metre(s)
abbrev.	abbreviation	*masc.*	masculine
adv.	adverb	*mm*	millimetre(s)
Afr.	Africa (n)	N	North
Amer.	America(n)	*n.*	noun
Aust.	Australia(n)	N.Z.	New Zealand
Brit.	Britain, British	*obs.*	obsolete, obsolescent
Canad.	Canada, Canadian	*offens.*	offensive
cent.	century	*oft.*	often
cm	centimetre(s)	*orig.*	originally
comb.	combining	*pers.*	person
comp.	comparative	*pert.*	pertaining
conj.	conjunction	*pl.*	plural
cu.	cubic	*pl.n.*	plural noun
dial.	dialect	*poss.*	possessive
dim.	diminutive	*pp.*	past participle
eg	for example	*prep.*	preposition
esp.	especially	*pres.t.*	present tense
fem.	feminine	*pron.*	pronoun
fig.	figuratively	*pr.p.*	present participle
Fr.	French	*pt.*	past tense
g	gram(s)	R.C.	Roman Catholic
Ger.	German	*refl.*	reflexive
Gr.	Greek	S	South
ie	that is	*sing.*	singular
impers.	impersonal	*sl.*	slang
ind.	indicative	Sp.	Spanish
inf.	informal	sq.	square
interj.	interjection	*sup.*	superlative
intr.	intransitive	*tr.*	transitive
It.	Italian	*usu.*	usually
k	kilogram(s)	*v.*	verb
km	kilometre(s)	*v.aux.*	auxiliary verb
l	litre(s)	*vi.*	intransitive verb
Lat.	Latin	*vt.*	transitive verb
lit.	literally		

R	Registered Trade Mark
A	Australia(n)
UK	United Kingdom
US	United States
C	Canadian
SA	South African

A

a, an *a.* the indefinite article meaning one; *an* is used before vowels

AA Alcoholics Anonymous; Automobile Association

aard'vark *n.* S African ant bear

aback' *adv.* -**taken aback** startled

ab'acus *n.* counting device of beads on wire frame

abalo'ne [-ō'ni] *n.* edible shellfish

aban'don *vt.* desert; give up -*n.* freedom from inhibitions *etc.* -**aban'doned** *a.* deserted; uninhibited; wicked

abase' *vt.* humiliate, degrade

abash' *vt.* make ashamed

abate' *v.* make or become less

ab'attoir *n.* slaughterhouse

abb'ey *n.* community of monks or nuns; abbey church

abb'ot *n.* head of monastery

abbre'viate *vt.* shorten -**abbrevia'tion** *n.* shortened word or phrase

ab'dicate *v.* give up (throne *etc.*)

ab'domen *n.* belly -**abdom'inal** *a.*

abduct' *vt.* carry off, kidnap

aberra'tion *n.* deviation from normal; lapse

abet' *vt.* help *esp.* in doing wrong -**abett'er,** -or *n.*

abey'ance *n.* -**in abeyance** not in use

abhor' *vt.* loathe -**abhor'rence** *n.* -**abhor'rent** *a.* hateful

abide' *vt.* endure -*vi. obs.* reside (abode, abi'ded, abi'ding) -**abide by** obey

abil'ity *n.* competence, power

ab'ject *a.* wretched; servile

abjure' *vt.* (swear to) renounce

ablaze' *a.* burning

a'ble *a.* capable, competent -**a'bly** *adv.*

ablu'tion *n.* (*usu. pl.*) act of washing (oneself)

ab'negate *vt.* give up

abnor'mal *a.* not usual or typical; odd -**abnormal'ity** *n.*

aboard' *adv.* on, onto ship, train, or aircraft

abode' *n.* home; dwelling

abol'ish *vt.* do away with -**aboli'tion** *n.*

A-bomb *n.* atomic bomb

abom'inate *vt.* detest -**abom'-inable** *a.* -**abomina'tion** *n.* loathing; the object loathed

Aborig'ine [-in-ē] *n.* early inhabitant of Aust. -**Aborig'inal** *a.*

abor'tion *n.* operation to terminate pregnancy -**abor'tionist** *n.* -**abor'tive** *a.* unsuccessful

abound' *vi.* be plentiful

about' *adv.* on all sides; nearly; astir -*prep.* round; near; concerning; ready to

above' *adv.* higher up -*prep.* over; higher than, more than; beyond

abra'sion *n.* place scraped (*eg* on skin); a wearing down -**abra'sive** *n.* substance for grinding, polishing *etc.* -*a.* causing abrasion; grating

abreast' *adv.* side by side; keeping up with

abridge' *vt.* shorten -**abridg(e)'-ment** *n.*

abroad' *adv.* to or in a foreign country; at large

ab'rogate *vt.* cancel, repeal

abrupt' *a.* sudden; blunt; steep

ab'scess [-ses] *n.* gathering of pus

abscond' [-sk-] *vi.* leave secretly

ab'sent *a.* away; missing -*vt.* [-sent'] keep away -**ab'sence** *n.* -**absentee'** *n.* one who stays away -**absentee'ism** *n.* persistent absence -**ab'sently** *adv.*

ab'solute *a.* complete; unrestricted; pure -**ab'solutely** *adv.* -*interj.* [-lōōt-] certainly

absolve' *vt.* free from, pardon

absorb' *vt.* suck up; engross; assimilate -**absorb'ent** *a.* -**absorp'tion** *n.*

abstain' *vi.* refrain -**absten'tion** *n.* -**ab'stinence** *n.*

abste'mious *a.* sparing in eating and drinking

ab'stract *a.* existing only in the mind; not concrete -*n.* summary -*vt.* [ab-strakt'] remove; summarize -**abstract'ed** *a.* preoccupied -**abstrac'tion** *n.*

abstruse' *a.* hard to understand

absurd' *a.* ridiculous -**absurd'ity** *n.*

abun'dance *n.* great amount -**abun'dant** *a.* plentiful

abuse' [-byōōz'] *vt.* misuse; address rudely -*n.* [-byōōs'] -**abu'sive** *a.* -**abu'sively** *adv.*

abut' vi. adjoin (-tt-) -**abut'ment** n. support

abys'mal [-z'-] a. immeasurable, very great; inf. extremely bad

abyss' n. very deep gulf or pit

AC alternating current

A/C account

aca'cia [-kā'shǝ] n. gum-yielding tree or shrub

acad'emy n. society to advance arts or sciences; institution for specialized training; secondary school -**academ'ic** a. of a place of learning; theoretical

acan'thus n. prickly plant; carved ornament (pl. -**thuses, -thi** [-thī])

accede' [aks-] vi. agree; attain (office etc.)

accel'erate [aks-] v. (cause to) increase speed -**accelera'tion** n. -**accel'erator** n. mechanism to increase speed

ac'cent [ak's-] n. stress or pitch in speaking; mark to show this; style of pronunciation -vt. [-sent']

accen'tuate [aks-] vt. emphasize -**accen'tual** a. -**accentua'tion** n.

accept' [ǝks-] vt. take, receive; admit, believe; agree to -**accept'able** a. -**accept'ance** n.

ac'cess [ak's-] n. right or means of entry -**access'ible** a. easy to approach

access'ion n. attaining of office, right etc.; addition

access'ory n. supplementary part of car, woman's dress etc.; person assisting crime

ac'cident [ak's-] n. event happening by chance; mishap, esp. causing injury -**acciden'tal** a.

acclaim' vt. applaud, praise -n. applause -**acclama'tion** n.

accli'matize vt. accustom to new climate or environment

acc'olade n. public approval; honour; token of knighthood

accomm'odate vt. supply, esp. with lodging; oblige; adapt -**accomm'odating** a. obliging -**accommoda'tion** n. lodgings

accom'pany vt. go with; supplement; occur with; play music to support a soloist (-**panied, -panying**) -**accom'paniment** n. -**accom'panist** n.

accom'plice [-plis] n. one assisting another in crime

accom'plish vt. carry out; finish -**accom'plished** a. complete; proficient -**accom'plishment** n.

accord' n. (esp. in accord with) agreement, harmony -v. (cause to) be in accord with -vt. grant -**accord'ingly** adv. as the circumstances suggest; therefore

accor'dion n. musical instrument with bellows and reeds

accost' vt. approach and speak to

account' n. report; importance; statement of moneys received, paid, or owed; person's money held in bank -v. regard as -v. give reason, answer (for) -**account'able** a. responsible -**account'ancy** n. keeping, preparation of business accounts -**account'ant** n. -**account'ing** n.

accou'trements [-trǝ-] pl.n. equipment, esp. military; trappings

accred'ited a. authorized, officially recognized

accrue' vi. be added; result

accu'mulate v. gather; collect -**accumula'tion** n. -**accu'mulator** n. type of rechargeable battery

acc'urate a. exact, correct

accurs'ed, accurst' a. under a curse; detestable

accuse' vt. charge with wrong doing; blame -**accusa'tion** n.

accus'tom vt. make used to, familiarize -**accus'tomed** a. usual; used (to); in the habit (of)

ace n. the one at dice, cards, dominoes; Tennis winning serve; inf. an expert

acerb'ity n. severity; sour taste

ac'etate rayon synthetic textile fibre

ac'etone [as'-] n. colourless liquid used as a solvent

acet'ylene [-set'-] n. colourless flammable gas

ache [ak] n. continuous pain -vi. to be in pain -a'ching a.

achieve' vt. accomplish; gain -achieve'ment n.

ac'id [as'-] a. sharp, sour -n. Chem. compound which combines with bases to form salts

acknowl'edge [ǝk-nol'ij] vt. admit, recognize; say one has received -**acknowl'edg(e)ment** n.

ac'me n. highest point

ac'ne n. pimply skin disease

ac'olyte n. follower or attendant, esp. of priest

a'corn [ā'-] n. fruit of oak tree

acou'stics pl.n. science of sounds; features of room or building as regards sounds heard in it

acquaint' vt. make familiar, inform -acquaint'ance n. person known; personal knowledge

acquiesce' [a-kwi-es'] vi. agree, consent -acquies'cence n.

acquire' vt. gain, get -acquisi'tion n. act of getting; material gain -acquis'itive a. desirous of gaining

acquit' vt. declare innocent; settle (a debt); behave (oneself) (-tt-) -acquit'tal n. declaration of innocence in court

a'cre [-kar] n. measure of land, 4840 square yards -a'creage n.

ac'rid a. pungent, sharp

ac'rimony n. bitter feeling or language -acrimo'nious a.

ac'robat n. one skilled in gymnastic feats, esp. in circus etc. -acrobat'ic a. -acrobat'ics pl.n.

ac'ronym n. word formed from initial letters of other words

acrop'olis n. citadel, esp. in ancient Greece

across' adv./prep. crosswise; from side to side; on or to the other side

acros'tic n. word puzzle in which the first, middle, or last letters of each line spell a word or words

acryl'ic [-kril'-] n. synthetic fibre

act n. thing done, deed; doing; law or decree; section of a play -v. perform, as in a play -vi. exert force, work, as mechanism; behave -ac'ting n. a temporary -ac'tion n. operation; deed; gesture; expenditure of energy; battle; lawsuit -ac'tivate vt. to make active -ac'tive a. in operation; brisk, energetic -activ'ity n. -ac'tor n. one who acts in a play, film etc. (fem. -tress)

ac'tual a. existing in the present; real -actual'ity n. -ac'tually adv. really, indeed

ac'tuary n. expert in insurance statistics -actua'rial a.

ac'tuate vt. activate; motivate

acu'men n. keen discernment

ac'upuncture n. medical treatment by insertion of needles into the body

acute' a. shrewd; sharp; severe -n. accent (') over a letter -acute'ly adv.

AD anno Domini

ad n. abbrev. of ADVERTISEMENT

ad'age n. proverb

adag'io [-dahzh'-] adv./n. Mus. slow (passage)

ad'amant a. unyielding

Adam's apple projecting part at front of the throat

adapt' v. alter for new use; modify; change -adapt'able a. -adapta'tion n. -adapt'er, -or n. esp. appliance for connecting two parts (eg electrical)

add v. join; increase by; say further -addi'tion n. -addi'tional a. -add'itive n. something added, esp. to foodstuffs

adden'dum n. thing to be added (pl. -da)

add'er n. small poisonous snake

ad'dict n. one who has become dependent on something -vt. [ə-dikt'] (usu. passive) -addic'tion n.

ad'dle v. make or become rotten, muddled

address' n. direction on letter; place where one lives; speech -vt. mark destination; speak to; direct

adduce' vt. offer as proof; cite

ad'enoids pl.n. tissue at back of nose

adept' a. skilled -n. [ad'-] expert

ad'equate [-kwət] a. sufficient, suitable; not outstanding -ad'equacy n.

adhere' vi. stick to; be firm in opinion etc. -adhe'rent n./a. -adhe'sion n. -adhe'sive n./a.

adieu' [-dyōō'] interj. farewell

ad'ipose a. of fat, fatty

adja'cent a. lying near, next (to)

ad'jective n. word which qualifies a noun

adjoin' v. be next to; join

adjourn' [ə-jurn'] v. close (meeting etc.) temporarily; inf. move elsewhere -adjourn'ment n.

adjudge' vt. declare; decide

adju'dicate v. judge; sit in judgment -adju'dicator n.

ad'junct n. person or thing added or subordinate

adjure' vt. earnestly entreat

adjust' vt. adapt; alter slightly, regulate -adjust'able a. -adjust'ment n.

ad'jutant n. military officer who assists superiors

ad' lib v. improvise -n./a./adv.

admin'ister vt. manage; dispense, as justice etc. -administra'tion n. -admin'istrator n.

ad'miral n. naval officer of highest sea rank -Admiralty (Board) department in charge of Royal Navy

admire' vt. regard with approval,

respect, or wonder **-ad'mirable** a. **-admira'tion** n.

admit' vt. confess; accept as true; allow; let in (**-tt-**) **-admiss'ible** a. **-admiss'ion** n. permission to enter; entrance fee; confession **-admitt'-ance** n. **-admitt'edly** adv.

admix'ture n. mixture; ingredient

admon'ish vt. reprove; exhort **-admoni'tion** n.

ad nau'seam [nawz-] Lat. to a boring or disgusting extent

ado' [a-dōō'] n. fuss

ado'be [-bi] n. sun-dried brick

adoles'cence n. period of life just before maturity **-adoles'cent** n. a youth **-a**.

adopt' vt. take as one's child; take up, as principle, resolution **-adop'tion** n.

adore' v. love intensely; worship **-ador'able** a. **-adora'tion** n.

adorn' vt. decorate

adre'nal a. near the kidney **-adren'alin(e)** n. hormone secreted by adrenal glands

adrift' a./adv. drifting; inf. detached; inf. off course

adroit' a. skilful; clever

adula'tion [-dyoo-] n. flattery

adult' a. grown-up, mature **-n**. mature person, animal or plant

adul'terate vt. make impure by addition **-adultera'tion** n.

adul'tery n. sexual unfaithfulness of a husband or wife **-adul'terous** a.

advance' [-vah-] vt. bring forward; suggest; lend (money) **-vi**. go forward; improve in position or value **-n**. progress; movement forward; improvement; a loan **-a**. ahead in time or position **-advanced'** a. at a late stage; not elementary; ahead of the times **-advance'ment** n. promotion

advan'tage n. more favourable position or state **-advanta'geous** a.

ad'vent n. a coming; (**A-**) the four weeks before Christmas **-the Advent** the coming of Christ

adventi'tious a. added by chance

adven'ture n. exciting undertaking or happening **-adven'turous** a.

ad'verb n. word added to verb etc. to modify meaning **-adverb'ial** a.

ad'verse a. hostile; unfavourable **-ad'versary** n. enemy **-adver'sity** n. distress, misfortune

ad'vert n. inf. advertisement

ad'vertise vt. publicize; give notice of, esp. in newspapers etc. **-vi**. make

public request (for) **-advert'-isement** [-iz-] n.

advice' n. counsel; notification

advise' vt. offer advice; give notice (of) **-advi'sable** a. expedient **-advi'ser, -or** n. **-advi'sory** a.

ad'vocate n. one who pleads the cause of another, esp. in court of law; barrister **-vt**. recommend **-ad'-vocacy** n.

adze [adz] n. tool like axe

ae'gis [e'jis] n. sponsorship

ae'on [e'-] n. long period of time

a'erate vt. charge liquid with gas; expose to air

a'erial a. operating in the air; pertaining to aircraft **-n**. part of radio etc. receiving or sending radio waves

a'ero- (comb. form) air or aircraft as in **aeroengine**

aerobat'ics pl.n. stunt flying

a'erodrome n. airfield

aerodynam'ics pl.n. (with sing. v.) study of air flow, esp. round moving solid bodies

aeronau'tics pl.n. (with sing. v.) science of air navigation and flying in general

a'eroplane n. heavier-than-air flying machine

a'erosol n. (substance dispensed from) pressurized can

a'erospace n. earth's atmosphere and space beyond **-a**.

aesthet'ic [es-] a. relating to principles of beauty **-aesthet'ics** pl.n. study of beauty **-aes'thete** n.

afar' adv. from, at, or to, a great distance

aff'able a. polite and friendly

affair' n. thing done or attended to; business; happening; sexual liaison **-pl**. personal or business interests; matters of public interest

affect' vt. act on; move feelings; make show of **-affecta'tion** n. show, pretence **-affect'ed** a. making a pretence; moved; acted upon **-affec'tion** n. fondness, love **-affec'tionate** a.

affida'vit n. written statement on oath

affil'iate v./n. (join as an) associate **-affilia'tion** n.

affin'ity n. natural liking; resemblance; chemical attraction

affirm' v. assert positively; make solemn declaration **-affirma'tion** n. **-affirm'ative** a./n. positive (statement)

affix' vt. fasten (to)

afflict' vt. cause to suffer -**afflic'tion** n.

aff'luent a. wealthy; abundant -**aff'luence** n.

afford' vt. to be able to (buy, do); provide

affront' vt./n. insult

afield' adv. away from home

afloat' adv. floating; at sea

afoot' adv. astir; on foot

afore'said a. previously mentioned

afraid' a. frightened; regretful

afresh' adv. again, anew

Africand'er n. breed of humpbacked S Afr. cattle

aft adv. towards stern of ship

af'ter [ahf-] adv. later; behind -prep. behind; later than; on the model of; pursuing -conj. later than -**af'ters** pl.n. dessert

af'terbirth n. membrane expelled after a birth

af'tereffect n. subsequent effect

af'termath n. result, consequence

afternoon' n. time from noon to evening

af'terthought n. idea occurring later

af'terward(s) adv. later

Ag Chem. silver

again' adv. once more; in addition

against' prep. in opposition to; in contact with; opposite; in readiness for

agape' a./adv. open-mouthed

ag'ate n. semiprecious quartz

age [aj] n. length of time person or thing has existed; time of life; period of history; long time -v. make or grow old -**aged** [ajd or a'jid] a. -pl.n. [a'jid] old people

agen'da [-jen'-] pl.n. (with sing. v.) list of things to be attended to

a'gent [-j-] n. one authorized to act for another; person or thing producing effect -**a'gency** n. instrumentality; business, premises of agent

agglom'erate v. gather into a mass

aggr'andize vt. make greater in size, power, or rank

agg'ravate vt. make worse or more severe; inf. annoy

agg'regate vt. gather into mass -a. gathered thus -n. mass, sum total; gravel etc. for concrete

aggres'sion n. unprovoked attack; hostile activity -**aggres'sive** a. -**aggress'or** n.

aggrieve' vt. pain, injure -**aggrieved'** a.

aghast' [-gahst'] a. appalled

ag'ile [-jīl] a. nimble; quick -**ag'ilely** adv. -**agil'ity** n.

ag'itate [-j-] vt. stir, shake up; trouble -vi. stir up public opinion (for or against) -**ag'itator** n.

aglow' a. glowing

AGM Annual General Meeting

agnos'tic n. one who holds that we know only the material world

ago' adv. in the past

agog' a./adv. eager, astir

ag'ony n. extreme suffering -**ag'onize** vi. suffer agony; worry greatly -**ag'onizing** a.

agorapho'bia n. fear of open spaces

agra'rian a. of agriculture, land or its management

agree' v. be of same opinion; consent; harmonize; approve (**agreed'**, **agree'ing**) -**agree'able** a. willing; pleasant -**agree'ment** n.

ag'riculture n. (the science of) farming -**agricul'tural** a.

aground' adv. (of boat) touching bottom

ahead' adv. in front; onwards

ahoy' interj. ship's hailing cry

aid vt./n. help, support

aide n. assistant

ail vt. trouble -vi. be ill -**ail'ing** a. sickly -**ail'ment** n. illness

ai'leron [ā'-] n. movable flap on aircraft wing

aim v. direct (weapon etc.); intend -n. -**aim'less** a. without purpose

ain't nonstandard am not; is not; are not; has not; have not

air n. (gases of) earth's atmosphere; breeze; tune; manner -pl. affected manners -vt. expose to air -**air'less** a. stuffy -**air'y** a. -**air bed** -**air brake** brake worked by compressed air -**air conditioning** control of temperature and humidity in building -**air'craft** n. flying machines generally; aeroplane -**air'field** n. landing and taking-off area for aircraft -**air force** strength of country in aircraft -**air gun** gun discharged by compressed air -**air'line** n. company operating aircraft -**air'lock** n. air bubble obstructing pipe; airtight chamber -**air mail** -**air'man** n. -**air pocket** less dense air where aeroplane drops suddenly -**air'port** n. station for civilian aircraft -**air raid** attack by aircraft

-air'ship n. lighter-than-air flying machine with means of propulsion **-air'speed** n. speed of aircraft relative to air **-air'strip** n. small airfield with only one runway **-air'tight** a. not allowing passage of air **-air'worthy** a. fit to fly

aisle [īl] n. passage between rows of seats

ajar' adv. partly open

akim'bo adv. with hands on hips

akin' a. related by blood; alike

al'abaster n. white, decorative stone

à la carte Fr. selected freely from the menu

alac'rity n. eager willingness

alarm' n. fright; apprehension; danger signal -vt. frighten; alert

alas' interj. cry of grief

al'batross n. large oceanic bird

albi'no [-ē-] n. individual lacking pigmentation (pl. -nos)

al'bum n. book for photographs, stamps etc.; collection of items in book or record form

al'bumen [-byoo-] n. egg white

al'bumin, -en [-byoo-] n. a protein found in egg white

al'chemy [-k-] n. medieval chemistry **-al'chemist** n.

al'cohol n. intoxicating fermented liquor; class of organic chemical substances **-alcohol'ic** a. -n. one addicted to alcoholic drink **-al'coholism** n.

al'cove n. recess

al'der [awl'-] n. tree related to the birch

al'derman [awl'-] n. formerly, senior local councillor

ale n. beer, orig. without hops

alert' a. watchful; brisk -n. warning -vt. warn; draw attention to

alfres'co adv./a. in the open air

al'gae [-jē] pl.n. (sing. **al'ga** [-gə]) various water plants

al'gebra n. method of calculating, using symbols to represent quantities **-algebra'ic(al)** a.

a'lias adv. otherwise -n. assumed name (pl. -liases)

al'ibi [-bī] n. plea of being elsewhere at time of crime

a'lien a. foreign; different in nature; repugnant (to) -n. foreigner **-a'lienate** vt. estrange; transfer

alight' vi. get down; land

alight' a. burning; lit up

align' [-līn'] vt. bring into line or agreement **-align'ment** n.

alike' a./adv. similar(ly)

aliment'ary canal food passage in body

al'imony n. allowance paid to separated or divorced spouse

alive' a. living; active; aware; swarming

al'kali [-lī] n. substance which combines with acid and neutralizes it, forming a salt (pl. -li(e)s) **-al'kaline** a.

all [awl] a. the whole of, every one of -adv. entirely -n. the whole; everything, everyone

allay' vt. relieve, soothe

allege' vt. state without proof **-allega'tion** n. **-alleg'edly** [-lej'id-] adv.

alle'giance n. loyalty, esp. to one's country

al'legory n. symbolic story, poem etc.

alle'gro [-lā'-] adv./a./n. Mus. fast (passage)

aller'gy n. abnormal sensitivity to a specific substance **-aller'gic** a.

alle'viate vt. ease, lessen

al'ley n. narrow street; enclosure for skittles (pl. -eys)

alli'ance n. union, eg by treaty, agreement, or marriage

al'ligator n. animal of crocodile family found in America

allitera'tion n. beginning of successive words with same sound

all'ocate vt. assign as a share

allot' vt. allocate (-tt-) **-allot'ment** n. distribution; portion of land rented for cultivation; portion allotted

allow' vt. permit; set aside -vi. (usu. with for) take into account **-allow'able** a. **-allow'ance** n.

al'loy n. metallic mixture

allude' [-lōōd] vi. refer (to) **-allu'sion** n.

allure' [-loor'] vt. entice -n. attractiveness **-allu'ring** a.

ally' vt. join by treaty, friendship etc. (allied' [-līd'], ally'ing) **-allied'** [or -īd'] a. **-al'ly** n. (pl. allies)

al'manac [awl'-] n. calendar of tides, events etc.

almi'ghty a. all-powerful; inf. very great **-The Almighty** God

al'mond [ahm'-] n. tree of peach family; its edible seed

al'most [awl'-] adv. very nearly

alms [ahmz] pl.n. gifts to the poor

al'oe n. African plant yielding laxative

aloft' adv. on high; overhead

alone' a./adv. by oneself, by itself; only

along' adv. lengthwise; together (with); forward -prep. over the length of -**along'side** adv./prep. beside

aloof' adv. apart -a. uninvolved

aloud' adv. loudly; audibly

alp n. high mountain -**al'pine** a.

al'phabet n. set of letters used in writing a language -**alphabet'ic(al)** a. in the standard order of the letters

alread'y [awl-red'i] adv. previously; sooner than expected

Alsa'tian [al-sā'shən] n. large dog of wolfhound breed

al'so [awl'-] adv. besides, moreover

al'tar [awl'-] n. Communion table; sacrificial table

al'ter [awl'-] v. change, make or become different -**al'terable** a. -**altera'tion** n.

alterca'tion [awl-] n. quarrel

al'ternate [awl'-] v. (cause to) occur by turns -**alter'nate** a. in turn; every second -**alter'native** n. one of two choices -a. -**alter'nately** adv. -**al'ternator** n. dynamo

although' [awl-THŌ'] conj. despite the fact that

altim'eter n. instrument for measuring height

al'titude n. height, elevation

al'to n. Mus. male singing voice or instrument above tenor; contralto (pl. -tos)

altogeth'er [awl-] adv. entirely; in total

al'truism n. unselfish concern for others

al'um n. mineral salt, used in dyeing etc.

alumin'ium [-lyoo-] n. light nonrusting silvery metal -**alu'minous** [-lōō-] a.

al'ways [awl'-] adv. at all times; for ever

al'yssum n. garden plant with small yellow or white flowers

AM, am amplitude modulation; ante meridiem

am first person sing. of BE

amal'gamate v. mix, (cause to) combine -**amalgama'tion** n.

amass' v. collect in quantity

am'ateur [-tər] n. one who does something for interest not money; unskilled practitioner -**am'ateurish** a. inexpert

amaze' vt. surprise greatly, astound -**amaze'ment** n.

ambass'ador n. senior diplomatic representative overseas

am'ber n. yellow fossil resin

am'bergris [-grēs] n. wax secreted by sperm whale

ambidex'trous a. able to use both hands with equal ease

ambig'uous a. having more than one meaning; obscure -**ambigu'ity** n.

ambi'tion [-bish'-] n. desire for success; goal, aim -**ambi'tious** a.

ambiv'alence n. simultaneous existence of conflicting emotions

am'ble vi./n. (move at an) easy pace

am'bulance [-byoo-] n. conveyance for sick or injured

am'bush vt. attack from hiding -n.

ame'liorate v. improve

amen' [ā-, ah-] interj. so be it

ame'nable a. easily controlled; answerable

amend' vt. correct; alter -**amend'ment** n.

ame'nity n. (oft. pl.) useful or pleasant facility or service

Amer'ican a. of, relating to, the American continent or the United States of America

am'ethyst n. bluish-violet gem

a'miable a. friendly, kindly

am'icable a. friendly

amid', amidst' prep. among -**amid'ship(s)** adv. near, towards, middle of ship

ami'no acid [-mē'-] organic compound found in protein

amiss' a. wrong -adv. faultily

am'ity n. friendship

amm'eter n. instrument for measuring electric current

ammo'nia n. pungent alkaline gas

ammuni'tion [-nish'-] n. projectiles that can be discharged from a weapon: also fig.

amne'sia n. loss of memory

am'nesty n. general pardon

amoe'ba [-mē'-] n. microscopic single-celled animal (pl. -bas, -bae [-bē])

among' [-mu-], **amongst'** prep. in the midst of, of the number of, between

amor'al [a-mor'al] a. nonmoral, having no moral qualities

am'orous a. inclined to love

amorph'ous a. without distinct shape

amount' vi. come, be equal (to) -n. quantity; sum total

amp. amperage; ampere(s)

am'pere *n.* unit of electric current

am'persand *n.* the sign & (and)

amphet'amine [-mēn] *n.* synthetic medicinal stimulant

amphib'ian *n.* animal that lives first in water then on land; vehicle, plane adapted to land and water **-amphib'ious** *a.*

am'phitheatre *n.* arena surrounded by rising tiers of seats

am'ple *a.* big enough; large, spacious **-am'ply** *adv.*

am'plify *vt.* increase; make bigger, louder *etc.* **(-fied, -fying) -am'plifier** *n.*

am'plitude *n.* spaciousness, width

am'putate [-pyoo-] *vi.* cut off (limb *etc.*) **-amputa'tion** *n.*

amuck', amok' *adv.* **-run amuck** rush about in murderous frenzy

amuse' [-myōōz'] *vt.* entertain; cause to laugh or smile **-amuse'ment** *n.* entertainment, pastime

anach'ronism [-k'-] *n.* something put in wrong historical period

anacon'da *n.* large snake which kills by constriction

anae'mia [-nē'-] *n.* deficiency of red blood cells **-anae'mic** *a.* pale, sickly

anaesthet'ic [-nis-] *n./a.* (drug) causing loss of sensation **-anaesthe'sia** *n.* **-anaes'thetist** [-nēs'-] *n.*

an'agram *n.* word(s) whose letters can be rearranged to make new word(s)

anal *see* ANUS

analge'sic *a./n.* (drug) relieving pain

anal'ogy [-ji] *n.* likeness in certain respects **-anal'ogous** [-gəs] *a.* similar

anal'ysis *n.* separation into elements or components (*pl.* **-yses** [-sēz]) **-an'alyse** *vt.* examine critically; determine constituent parts **-an'alyst** *n.* **-analyt'ic(al)** *a.*

an'archy [-k-] *n.* absence of government and law; disorder **-an'archist** *n.* one who opposes all government

anath'ema *n.* anything detested; curse of excommunication or denunciation (*pl.* **-s**)

anat'omy *n.* (study of) bodily structure; detailed analysis **-anatom'ical** *a.* **-anat'omist** *n.*

an'cestor *n.* person from whom another is descended; forerunner **-ances'tral** *a.* **-an'cestry** *n.*

an'chor [-ng'k-] *n.* heavy implement dropped to stop vessel drifting; any similar device **-vt.** **-an'chorage** *n.* act, place of anchoring

an'chovy [-ch-] *n.* small savoury fish of herring family

an'cient [ān'shənt] *a.* belonging to former age; old; timeworn

ancill'ary *a.* subordinate, auxiliary

and *conj.* used to join words and sentences, introduce consequence *etc.*

andan'te *adv./n. Mus.* moderately slow (passage)

an'ecdote *n.* short account of a single incident

anemom'eter *n.* wind gauge

anem'one [-ni] *n.* flower related to buttercup

an'eroid *a.* (barometer) that does not use mercury

anew' *adv.* afresh, again

an'gel [ān'j-] *n.* divine messenger; guardian spirit; person with such qualities **-angel'ic** [an-] *a.*

angel'ica [-j-] *n.* aromatic plant; its candied stalks

an'ger [-ng'g-] *n.* extreme annoyance; wrath **-vt.** make angry **-an'grily** *adv.* **-an'gry** *a.*

angi'na (**pec'toris**) [-j-] *n.* severe pain accompanying heart disease

an'gle [ang'gl] *n.* meeting of two lines or surfaces; point of view **-vt.** bend at an angle

an'gler *n.* one who fishes for sport

An'glican [ang'gli-] *a./n.* (member) of the Church of England

ango'ra *n.* goat with long white silky hair; cloth or wool of this

an'guish [ang'gw-] *n.* great mental or bodily pain

an'gular *a.* (of people) bony; having angles; measured by an angle

an'iline [-lin, -lēn] *n.* dye product of coal tar

animadvert' *vi.* (with (up)on) criticize **-animadver'sion** *n.*

an'imal *n.* living creature that can move at will; beast **-a.** of animals; sensual

an'imate *vt.* give life to; enliven; inspire; actuate; make cartoon film of **-an'imated** *a.* **-anima'tion** *n.* **-an'imator** *n.*

animos'ity *n.* hostility, enmity

an'imus *n.* hatred; animosity

an'ise [-is] *n.* plant with liquorice-flavoured seeds **-an'iseed** *n.*

an'kle [ang'kl] *n.* joint between foot and leg

ann'als pl.n. yearly records

anneal' vt. toughen by heating

annex' vt. append, attach; take possession of

ann'exe n. supplementary building

anni'hilate [-nʒ'əl-] vt. reduce to nothing, destroy utterly

anniver'sary n. yearly return of a date; celebration of this

ann'o Dom'ini Lat. in the year of our Lord

ann'otate vt. make notes upon

announce' vt. make known, proclaim **-announce'ment** n. **-announ'cer** n. broadcaster who announces items

annoy' vt. vex; irritate **-annoy'ance** n.

ann'ual a. yearly -n. plant which completes its life-cycle in a year; book published each year **-ann'ually** adv.

annu'ity n. fixed sum paid yearly

annul' vt. make void, cancel, abolish (-ll-) **-annul'ment** n.

an'ode n. Electricity the positive electrode

anoint' vt. smear with oil or ointment; consecrate with oil

anom'alous a. irregular, abnormal **-anom'aly** n.

anon' obs. adv. soon

anon. anonymous

anon'ymous a. without (author's) name **-anonym'ity** n.

an'orak n. warm, waterproof, usu. hooded jacket

anorex'ia n. loss of appetite

anoth'er [-UTH'-] pron./a. one other; a different one; one more

ans. answer

an'swer [ahn'sər] v. reply (to); be accountable (for, to); match; suit -n. reply; solution **-an'swerable** a.

ant n. small social insect **-ant'eater** n. animal which feeds on ants

antag'onist n. opponent **-antag'onism** n. **-antagonis'tic** a. **-antag'onize** vt. arouse hostility in

Antarc'tic a./n. (of) south polar regions

ante- (comb. form) before, as in **an'techamber** n.

antece'dent a./n. going before

antedilu'vian [-loo'-] a. before the Flood; ancient

an'telope n. deer-like animal

an'te merid'iem Lat. before noon

antena'tal a. of care etc. during pregnancy

antenn'a n. insect's feeler; aerial (pl. **-ae** [-ē])

ante'rior a. to the front; before

an'them n. song of loyalty; sacred choral piece

an'ther n. pollen sac of flower

anthol'ogy n. collection of poems

an'thracite n. slow-burning coal

an'thropoid a./n. man-like (ape)

anthropol'ogy n. study of origins, development of human race

anti-, ant- (comb. form) against Makes compounds as **anti-aircraft** a. **-antispasmod'ic** a./n. etc.

antibiot'ic n. any of various chemical, fungal or synthetic substances used against bacterial infection -a.

an'tibody n. substance which counteracts bacteria

antic'ipate [-tis'-] vt. expect; look forward to; foresee **-anticipa'tion** n.

anticli'max n. sudden descent to the trivial or ludicrous

an'tics pl.n. absurd behaviour

anticy'clone n. high-pressure area and associated winds

an'tidote n. counteracting remedy

an'tifreeze n. liquid added to water to prevent freezing

an'tigen [-j-] n. substance stimulating production of antibodies in the blood

antihis'tamine n. drug used esp. to treat allergies

an'timony n. brittle, bluish-white metal

antip'athy n. dislike, aversion

antiper'spirant n. substance used to reduce sweating

antip'odes [-dēz] pl.n. regions on opposite side of the globe

antique' [-ēk'] n. object valued because of its age -a. ancient; old-fashioned **-an'tiquated** a. out-of-date **-antiq'uity** n. great age; former times

antirrhi'num [-rī'-] n. garden plant, snapdragon

anti-Semit'ic a. discriminating against Jews **-anti-Sem'itism** n.

antisep'tic n./a. (substance) preventing infection -a. free from infection

antith'esis n. direct opposite; contrast (pl. **-eses**)

antitox'in n. serum used to neutralize disease poisons

ant'ler n. branching horn of certain deer

an'tonym *n.* word of opposite meaning to another

a'nus *n.* open end of rectum **-a'nal** *a.*

an'vil *n.* heavy iron block on which a smith hammers metal

anx'ious [angk'shəs] *a.* uneasy; concerned **-anxi'ety** [ang-zī'-] *n.*

an'y [en'i] *a./pron.* one indefinitely; some; every **-an'ybody** *n.* **-an'yhow** *adv.* **-an'yone** *n.* **-an'ything** *n.* **-an'yway** *adv.* **-an'ywhere** *adv.*

aor'ta [ā-aw'-] *n.* main artery carrying blood from the heart

apace' *adv.* swiftly

apart' *adv.* separately, aside; in pieces

apart'heid [-hīt, -hāt] *n.* (*esp.* in S Africa) official policy of racial segregation

apart'ment *n.* room; a flat

ap'athy *n.* indifference; lack of emotion **-apathet'ic** *a.*

ape *n.* tailless monkey; imitator **-vt.** imitate

aper'itif *n.* alcoholic appetizer

ap'erture *n.* opening, hole

a'pex *n.* top, peak; vertex (*pl.* **a'pexes**, **a'pices**)

aph'orism *n.* maxim, pithy saying

aphrodis'iac *a./n.* (substance) exciting sexual desire

a'piary *n.* place where bees are kept

apiece' *adv.* for each

aplomb' [-plom'] *n.* assurance

apoc'alypse *n.* prophetic revelation, *esp.* of the end of the world

apoc'ryphal *a.* spurious

apol'ogy *n.* expression of regret for a fault; poor substitute (for) **-apologet'ic** *a.* **-apol'ogize** *vi.*

ap'oplexy *n.* paralysis caused by broken or blocked blood vessel in the brain

Apos'tle [-sl] *n.* one of the first disciples of Jesus; (l-) leader of reform

apos'trophe [-trə-fi] *n.* mark (') showing omission of letter(s)

apoth'ecary *n.* old name for chemist

appal' [-awl'] *vt.* dismay, terrify (-ll-) **-appall'ing** *a.* inf. terrible

appara'tus *n.* equipment for performing any experiment, operation *etc.*

appar'el [-pa'-] *n.* clothing

appar'ent [-pa'-] *a.* seeming, obvious; acknowledged

appari'tion [-rish'-] *n.* ghost

appeal' *vi.* (with to) make earnest request; be attractive; apply to higher court **-n.** **-appeal'ing** *a.* attractive

appear' *vi.* become visible or present; seem, be plain; be seen in public **-appear'ance** *n.* an appearing; aspect; pretence

appease' *vt.* pacify, satisfy

appella'tion *n.* name

append' *vt.* join on, add

appendici'tis *n.* inflammation of appendix

appen'dix *n.* supplement; *Anatomy* small worm-shaped part of the intestine (*pl.* **-dices** [-di-sēz], **-dixes**)

appertain' *vi.* belong, relate to

app'etite *n.* desire, inclination, *esp.* for food **-app'etizer** *n.* something stimulating to appetite **-app'etizing** *a.*

applaud' *vt.* praise by hand-clapping; praise loudly **-applause'** *n.*

ap'ple *n.* round, firm, fleshy fruit; tree bearing it

appli'ance *n.* piece of equipment *esp.* electrical

appliqué [-plē'kā] *n.* decoration applied to surface of material

apply' *vt.* utilize; lay or place on; devote **-vi.** have reference (to); make request (to) (**-lied'**, **-ly'ing**) **-app'licable** *a.* relevant **-app'licant** *n.* **-applica'tion** *n.* request for a job *etc.*; diligence **-applied'** *a.* put to practical use

appoint' *vt.* assign to a job or position; fix; equip **-appoint'ment** *n.* engagement to meet; (selection for a) job

appor'tion *vt.* divide in shares

app'osite [-zit] *a.* appropriate

apprais'e *vt.* estimate value of **-apprais'al** *n.*

appre'ciate [-shi-] *vt.* value at true worth; be grateful for; understand **-vi.** rise in value **-appre'ciable** *a.* noticeable **-apprecia'tion** *n.*

apprehend' *vt.* arrest; understand; dread **-apprehen'sible** *a.* **-apprehen'sion** *n.* anxiety **-apprehen'sive** *a.*

appren'tice *n.* person learning a trade; novice

apprise' *vt.* inform

appro' *n.* inf. approval

approach' *v.* draw near (to); set about; address request to; approximate to **-n.** a drawing near;

means of reaching or doing; approximation **-approach'able** a.

approba'tion n. approval

appro'priate vt. take for oneself; allocate **-a.** suitable, fitting

approve' vt. think well of, commend; authorize **-appro'val** n.

approx. approximate(ly)

approx'imate a. nearly correct; inexact **-v.** come or bring close; be almost the same as **-approxima'tion** n.

appur'tenance n. accessory

Apr. April

a'pricot n. orange-coloured stone-fruit related to plum

A'pril n. the fourth month

a'pron n. covering worn in front to protect clothes; in theatre, strip of stage before curtain; on airfield, tarmac area where aircraft stand are loaded etc.

apropos' [-pô'] adv. with reference to **-a.** appropriate

apse n. arched recess

apt a. suitable; likely; quick-witted **-apt'itude** n.

aq'ualung n. breathing apparatus used in underwater swimming

aquamarine' n. precious stone **-a.** greenish-blue

aqua'rium n. tank for water animals or plants (pl. **-riums, -ria**)

aquat'ic a. living, growing, done in or on water

aq'ueduct n. artificial channel for water, esp. one like a bridge

aq'uiline a. like an eagle's beak

ar'able [a-] n. ploughland

arach'nid [-k'-] n. spider, scorpion etc.

ar'biter n. judge, umpire **-ar'bitrary** a. despotic; random **-ar'bitrate** v. settle (dispute) impartially **-arbitra'tion** n. **-ar'bitrator** n.

arb'our n. leafy glade

arc n. part of circumference of circle or similar curve

arcade' n. row of arches on pillars; covered walk or avenue

arch' n. curved structure spanning an opening; a curved shape; curved part of sole of the foot **-v.** form, make into, an arch

arch' a. chief; knowing, coyly playful

arch- (comb. form) chief, as in **archan'gel** [-k'-] n., **archen'emy** n. etc.

archaeology [-k'-] n. study of ancient times from remains

archa'ic [-k'-] a. old, primitive

-arch'aism n. obsolete word

archbish'op n. chief bishop

arch'ery n. skill, sport of shooting with bow and arrow **-arch'er** n.

arch'etype [-k'-] n. prototype; perfect specimen **-arch'etypal** a.

archipel'ago [-k-] n. group of islands (pl. **-agoes**)

arch'itect [-k'-] n. one qualified to design buildings; contriver **-arch'itecture** n.

ar'chives [-kîvz] pl.n. collection of records, documents etc.

Arc'tic a. of north polar regions; (a-) very cold **-n.**

ar'dent a. fiery; passionate

ard'our n. enthusiasm; zeal

ard'uous a. hard to accomplish

are' pres. ind. pl. of BE

are' n. 100 square metres

a'rea n. surface extent; two-dimensional expanse enclosed by boundary; region; part; field of activity

are'na n. space in middle of amphitheatre or stadium

ar'gon n. gas, constituent of air

ar'gue v. quarrel; offer reasons (for); debate **-ar'guable** a. **-arg'ument** n. **-argumen'tative** a.

ar'ia n. song in opera etc.

ar'id [a-] a. dry; dull

arise' vi. come about; get up; rise (up) (**arose', aris'en, aris'ing**)

aristoc'racy n. upper classes; country governed by these **-ar'istocrat** n. **-aristocrat'ic** a.

arith'metic n. science of numbers

ark n. Noah's vessel

arm' n. upper limb from shoulder to wrist; anything similar, as branch of sea, supporting rail of chair etc.; sleeve **Compounds** as **arm'chair** n. **-arm'ful** n. **-arm'hole** n. **-arm'pit** n. hollow under arm at shoulder

arm' vt. supply with weapons, furnish **-vi.** take up arms **-n.** branch of army **-pl.** weapons; war

armad'a [-mahd'-] n. large fleet

armadill'o n. Amer. animal protected by bony plates (pl. **-os**)

arm'ature n. revolving coil in electric motor, generator

arm'istice n. truce

arm'our n. defensive covering; plating of tanks, warships etc.; armoured fighting vehicles **-arm'oury** n.

ar'my n. military land force; great number

aro'ma n. sweet smell **-aromat'ic** a.

around' prep./adv. on all sides (of); somewhere in or near; approximately (of time); in a circle; here and there

arouse' vt. awaken, stimulate

arr. arranged; arrival, arrive

arraign' [-ān'] vt. accuse, indict

arrange' v. set in order; make agreement; plan; adapt, as music **-arrange'ment** n.

array' n. order, esp. military; dress; imposing show -vt. set out; dress richly

arrears' pl.n. amount unpaid or undone

arrest' vt. detain by legal authority; stop; catch attention -n. seizure by warrant **-arrest'ing** a. striking

arrive' vi. reach destination; (with at) reach, attain; inf. succeed **-arri'val** n.

arr'ogance n. conceit **-arr'ogant** a. proud; overbearing

arr'ow n. shaft shot from bow

ars'enal n. store for guns etc.

ars'enic n. soft, grey, very poisonous metallic element

ars'on n. crime of intentionally setting property on fire

art n. human skill as opposed to nature; creative skill in painting, poetry, music etc.; any of the works produced thus; craft; knack -pl. branches of learning other than science; wiles **-art'ful** a. wily **-art'ist** n. one who practises fine art, esp. painting **-artiste'** [-tēst'] n. professional entertainer **-artis'tic** a. **-art'istry** n. **-art'less** a. natural, frank **-art'y** a. ostentatiously artistic

ar'tery n. tube carrying blood from heart; any main channel of communications **-arterial road** major highway

arte'sian well a. one in which water rises by internal pressure

arthri'tis n. painful inflammation of joint(s) **-arthrit'ic** a./n.

ar'tichoke n. thistle-like plant with edible flower

art'icle n. item, object; short written piece; Grammar words the a, an; clause in a contract -vt. bind as apprentice

artic'ulate a. fluent; clear, distinct -v. utter distinctly **-artic'ulated** a. jointed

art'ifice n. contrivance, trick **-artifi'cial** a. synthetic; insincere

artill'ery n. large guns on wheels; troops who use them

art'isan [-z-] n. craftsman

artiste' see ART

as adv./conj. denoting: comparison; similarity; equality; identity; concurrence; reason

asap as soon as possible

asbes'tos n. fibrous mineral which does not burn

ascend' [ə-send'] v. go, come up; climb **-ascend'ancy** n. dominance **-ascen'sion** n. **-ascent'** n.

ascertain' [as-ər-] v. find out

ascet'ic [-set'-] n. one who practises severe self-denial -a.

ascribe' vt. attribute, assign

ash n. remains of anything burnt **-ash'en** a. pale

ash n. deciduous tree; its wood

ashamed' [-āmd'] a. feeling shame

ashore' adv. on shore

A'sian a. pert. to continent of Asia -n. native of Asia or descendant of one

aside' adv. to, on one side; privately -n. words spoken so as not to be heard by all

as'inine a. stupid, silly

ask [ah-] v. make request or inquiry; invite; require

askance' adv. with mistrust

askew' adv. awry

asleep' a./adv. sleeping

asp n. small venomous snake

aspar'agus [-pa'rə-] n. plant with edible young shoots

as'pect n. appearance; outlook; side

as'pen n. type of poplar tree

asper'ity n. harshness

asper'sion n. (usu. pl.) malicious remarks

as'phalt n. bitumen, used for road surfaces etc.

asphyx'iate v. suffocate

as'pic n. jelly used to coat meat, eggs, fish etc.

aspire' vi. have great ambition **-aspira'tion** n. **-aspi'ring** a.

as'pirin n. (a tablet of) drug used to allay pain and fever

ass n. donkey; fool

assail' vt. attack, assault **-assail'able** a. **-assail'ant** n.

assass'in n. one who kills for money or political reasons **-assass'inate** vt.

assault' n./vt. attack

assay' vt. test, esp. alloy and ore **-n.**

assem'ble v. meet, bring together;

put together **-assem'bly** n.

assent' vi. agree *-n*.

assert' vt. declare strongly, insist upon **-asser'tion** n. **-asser'tive** a.

assess' vt. fix value or amount of; evaluate **-assess'able** a. **-assess'ment** n. **-asses'sor** n.

ass'et n. valuable or useful person, thing *-pl*. things that can be used to raise money

assid'uous a. persevering

assign' [-īn'] vt. appoint; allot; transfer **-assigna'tion** [-ig-nā'-] n. secret meeting **-assign'ment** n.

assim'ilate vt. take in; incorporate; (cause to) become similar

assist' v. give help; aid **-assist'ance** n. **-assist'ant** n.

assoc. associated; association

asso'ciate vt. link, connect; join *-vi*. keep company; combine, unite *-n*. partner; friend; subordinate member *-a*. affiliated **-associa'tion** n.

assort'ed a. mixed **-assort'ment** n. mixture

asst. assistant

assuage' [-sw-] vt. soothe

assume' vt. take for granted; pretend; take on **-assump'tion** n.

assure' vt. tell positively, promise; make sure; insure against loss, *esp*. of life **-assur'ance** n. **-assured'** a. sure

AST US, C Atlantic Standard Time

as'ter n. plant with star-like flowers

as'terisk n. star (*) used in printing

astern' adv. in, behind the stern; backwards

as'teroid n. small planet *-a*.

asth'ma [as'mə] n. illness in which one has difficulty in breathing **-asthmat'ic** a./n.

astig'matism n. inability of lens (*esp*. of eye) to focus properly

astir' adv. on the move; out

aston'ish vt. amaze, surprise **-aston'ishment** n.

astound' vt. astonish greatly

astrakhan' [-kan'] n. lambskin with curled wool

as'tral a. of the stars

astray' adv. off the right path

astride' adv. with legs apart

astrin'gent [-j-] a. sharp; styptic *-n*.

astrol'ogy n. foretelling of events by stars **-astrol'oger** n.

as'tronaut n. one trained for travel in space

astron'omy n. scientific study of

heavenly bodies **-astron'omer** n. **-astronom'ical** a. very large; of astronomy

astute' a. perceptive, shrewd

asun'der adv. apart; in pieces

asy'lum n. refuge, sanctuary, place of safety; old name for mental hospital

at prep./adv. denoting: location in space or time; rate; condition or state; amount; direction; cause

a'theism [ā'-] n. belief that there is no God **-a'theist** n.

ath'lete n. one trained for athletics **-athlet'ic** a. **-athlet'ics** pl.n. sports such as running, jumping, throwing *etc.*

at'las n. volume of maps

at'mosphere n. gases surrounding earth *etc.*; prevailing mood **-atmospher'ic** a.

at'oll n. ring-shaped coral island enclosing lagoon

at'om n. smallest unit of matter which can enter into chemical combination; any very small particle **-atom'ic** a. of, arising from atoms **-at'omizer** n. instrument for discharging liquids in a fine spray **-atom(ic) bomb** one whose immense power derives from nuclear fission or fusion **-atomic energy** nuclear energy **-atomic reactor** *see* REACTOR

atone' vi. make amends (for); expiate **-atone'ment** n.

atro'cious [-shəs] a. extremely cruel; horrifying; *inf*. very bad **-atroc'ity** [-tros'-] n.

at'rophy n. wasting away *-vi*. waste away (-phied, -phying)

attach' v. (mainly t.) join, fasten; attribute **-attached'** a. (with to) fond of **-attach'ment** n.

attaché [a-tash'ā] n. specialist attached to diplomatic mission

attack' vt. take action against; criticize; set about with vigour; affect adversely *-n*. attacking action; bout

attain' vt. arrive at; achieve **-attain'able** a. **-attain'ment** n.

att'ar n. a fragrant oil made *esp*. from rose petals

attempt' vt./n. try

attend' vt. be present at; accompany v. (with to) take care of; pay attention to **-attend'ance** n. an attending; persons attending **-attend'ant** n./a. **-atten'tion** n. notice; heed; care; courtesy

atten'uate v. make or become weaker, thinner

attest' v. bear witness to

att'ic n. space within roof

attire' vt./n. dress, array

att'itude n. mental view, opinion; posture, pose; disposition, behaviour

attor'ney [-tur-] n. one legally appointed to act for another, esp. a lawyer (pl. -neys)

attract' v. draw (attention etc.); arouse interest of; cause to come closer (as magnet etc.) **-attrac'tion** n. **-attrac'tive** a.

attrib'ute vt. regard as belonging to or produced by –n. [at'-] quality or characteristic **-attrib'utable** a. **-attribu'tion** n.

attri'tion [-trish'-] n. wearing away

attune' vt. tune; adjust

Au Chem. gold

au'bergine [ō'bar-zhēn] n. edible, purple fruit of the egg-plant

au'burn a./n. reddish brown

auc'tion n. public sale in which goods are sold to the highest bidder –v. **-auctioneer'** n.

auda'cious a. bold; impudent

au'dible a. able to be heard

au'dience n. people assembled to listen or watch; formal interview

au'dio- (comb. form) relating to sound or hearing **-au'dio** n.

audiovis'ual a. involving both sight and hearing

au'dit n. formal examination of accounts –vt. **-au'ditor** n.

audi'tion n. test of prospective performer; hearing –vt. **-auditor'ium** n. place where audience sits; hall (pl. -s, -ia)

Aug. August

au'ger n. tool for boring holes

augment' v. increase, enlarge

au'gur v. foretell

august' a. majestic, dignified

Au'gust n. the eighth month

aunt [ahnt] n. father's or mother's sister, uncle's wife

au pair' [ō-] n. young foreigner who receives board and lodging in return for housework etc. –a.

au'ra n. atmosphere considered distinctive of person or thing

au'ral a. of, by ear

aure'ola, aur'eole n. halo

au'ricle n. outside ear; an upper cavity of heart

auror'a n. lights in the sky radiating from polar regions; dawn (pl. -ras)

aus'pices [-pi-siz] pl.n. patronage

-auspi'cious a. favourable

austere' [os-] a. severe; without luxury **-auster'ity** n.

authen'tic a. genuine **-authen'ticate** vt. make valid **-authentic'ity** [-tis'-] n.

au'thor n. writer; originator (**-ess** fem.)

author'ity [-tho'ri-] n. legal power or right; delegated power; influence; permission; expert; board in control **-author'itative** a. **-auth'orize** vt. empower; permit

autis'tic a. withdrawn and divorced from reality

au'to- (comb. form) self, as in autograph, autosuggestion etc.

autobiog'raphy n. life of person written by himself

au'tocrat n. absolute ruler; despotic person **-autocrat'ic** a.

au'tograph n. signature –vt. sign

automat'ic a. operated or controlled mechanically; done without conscious thought **-also** n. self-loading (weapon) **-automa'tion** n. use of automatic devices in industrial production

au'tomobile n. motor car

auton'omy n. self-government **-auton'omous** a.

au'topsy n. post-mortem

au'tumn n./a. (of) the season after summer **-autum'nal** a.

auxil'iary a./n. (one) helping, subsidiary

avail' v. be of use, advantage –n. benefit **-avail'able** a. obtainable; accessible **-avail oneself of** make use of

av'alanche n. mass of snow, ice, sliding down mountain; any great quantity

av'arice [-ris] n. greed for wealth **-avari'cious** a.

Ave. Avenue

avenge' vt. take vengeance for

av'enue n. wide street; approach; double row of trees

aver' vt. affirm, assert (-rr-)

av'erage n. mean value –a. ordinary –vt. calculate a mean –vi. form a mean

averse' a. disinclined **-aver'sion** n. (object of) dislike

avert' vt. turn away; ward off

a'viary [ā'vyə-ri] n. enclosure for birds

avia'tion [ā-] n. art of flying aircraft **-a'viator** n.

av'id a. keen; greedy (for)

avocad'o [-kahd'-] *n.* tropical pear-shaped fruit

avoid' *vt.* keep away from; refrain from; not allow to happen **-avoid'able** *a.*

avoirdupois' [av-ər-də-poiz'] *n./a.* system of weights based on pounds and ounces

avow' *vt.* declare; admit **-avow'al** *n.* **-avowed'** *a.*

await' *vt.* wait or stay for; be in store for

awake', **awa'ken** *v.* emerge or rouse from sleep; (cause to) become alert (**awoke'** *or* **awaked'** **-awa'king**) **-a.** not sleeping; alert

award' *vt.* to give formally **-n.**

aware' *a.* informed, conscious

away' *adv.* absent, apart, at a distance, out of the way

awe *n.* dread mingled with reverence **-awe'some** *a.*

aw'ful *a.* dreadful; *inf.* very great **-aw'fully** *adv.* in an unpleasant way; *inf.* very much

awk'ward *a.* clumsy; difficult; inconvenient; embarrassed

awl *n.* tool for boring wood *etc.*

awn'ing *n.* (canvas) roof to protect from weather

awry' [-rī'] *adv.* crookedly; amiss **-a.** crooked; wrong

axe *n.* tool for chopping; *inf.* dismissal from employment **-vt.**

ax'iom *n.* accepted principle

ax'is *n.* (imaginary) line round which body spins (*pl.* **ax'es** [-sēz]) **-ax'ial** *a.*

aye *adv.* yes **-n.** affirmative answer or vote

aza'lea *n.* genus of shrubby flowering plants

az'ure [azh'-] *n.* sky-blue colour; sky **-a.** sky-blue

B

BA Bachelor of Arts

baas [bahs] *n.* SA boss

bab'ble *v.* speak foolishly, incoherently **-n.**

babe *n.* baby; guileless person

baboon' *n.* large monkey

ba'by *n.* infant **-baby-sit** *vi.* **-baby-sitter** *n.* one who cares for children when parents are out

bacc'hanal [-k'ən-] *n.* drunken, riotous celebration

bach'elor *n.* unmarried man

bacill'us [-sil'-] *n.* minute organism sometimes causing disease (*pl.* **bacill'i**)

back *n.* hinder part of anything, *eg* human body; part opposite front; part further away or less used; (position of) player in ball games **-a.** situated behind; earlier **-adv.** at, to the back; in, into the past; in return **-vt.** move backwards **-vt.** support; put wager on; provide with back **-back'er** *n.* **-back'ward(s)** *adv.* to rear, past, worse state **-back'ward** *a.* behind in education **-back'wardness** *n.* **-back'bite** *vt.* slander absent person **-back'bone** *n.* spinal column **-back'cloth**, **back'drop** *n.* painted cloth at back of stage **-backdate'** *vt.* make effective from earlier date **-backfire'** *vi.* (of plan, scheme, *etc.*) fail to work; ignite wrongly **-back'gammon** *n.* game played with draughtsmen and dice **-back'ground** *n.* space behind chief figures of picture *etc.*; past history of person **-back'hand** *n.* stroke with hand turned backwards **-back'lash** *n.* sudden adverse reaction **-back'log** *n.* accumulation of work *etc.* **-backside'** *n.* rump

ba'con *n.* cured pig's flesh

bacte'ria *pl.n.* (*sing.* **bacte'rium**) microscopic organisms **-bacte'rial** *a.* **-bacteriol'ogy** *n.*

bad *a.* faulty; evil; severe; rotten (**worse** *comp.*, **worst** *sup.*)

badge *n.* distinguishing emblem

badg'er *n.* burrowing night animal **-vt.** pester, worry

bad'minton *n.* game like tennis, played with shuttlecocks

baf'fle *vt.* check, frustrate, bewilder **-n.** device to regulate flow of liquid *etc.*

bag *n.* sack; measure of quantity; woman's handbag **-vi.** bulge; sag **-vt.** put in bag; kill as game, *etc.* **-(-gg-)** **-bagg'y** *a.* loose

bagatelle' *n.* trifle; game like pinball

bagg'age *n.* suitcases, luggage

bag'pipes *pl.n.* musical wind-instrument

bail¹ *n.* Law security given for person's reappearance in court **-vt.** (obtain) release on security

bail² *n.* Cricket crosspiece on wicket

bail³, **bale** *vt.* empty water from

boat -ball out parachute

bai'liff [-li-] n. land steward, agent

bait n. food to entice fish; any lure -vt. lure; persecute

baize n. smooth woollen cloth

bake vt. cook or harden by dry heat -vi. make bread, cakes etc. -**ba'ker** n. -**ba'kery** n. -**baking powder** raising agent used in cooking

Ba'kelite R type of plastic

balalai'ka [-li-] n. Russian musical instrument, like guitar

bal'ance n. pair of scales; equilibrium; surplus; sum due on an account; difference between two sums -vt. weigh; bring to equilibrium

bal'cony n. platform outside window; upper seats in theatre

bald [bawld] a. hairless; plain; bare -**bald'ing** a. becoming bald

bale n./vt. bundle, package

bale'ful a. menacing

balk [bawk, bawlk] vi. swerve, pull up -vt. thwart; shirk -n. hindrance

ball¹ [bawl] n. anything round; globe, sphere, esp. as used in games -vi. gather into a mass -**ball bearings** steel balls used to lessen friction -**ball point (pen)** pen with ball bearing nib

ball² [bawl] n. assembly for dancing -**ball'room** n.

bal'lad n. narrative poem; simple song

ball'ast n. heavy material put in ship to steady it -vt.

ball'et [-ā] n. theatrical presentation of dancing and miming -**balleri'na** [-ē-] n.

ballis'tics pl.n. (with sing. v.) scientific study of motion of projectile

balloon' n. large bag filled with air or gas -vi. puff out

ball'ot n. voting, usually by ballot paper -v. vote

balm [bahm] n. healing or soothing (ointment)

bal'sa [bawl-] n. Amer. tree with light but strong wood

bal'sam [bawl-] n. resinous aromatic substance

bal'ustrade n. row of short pillars surmounted by rail

bamboo' n. large tropical treelike reed (pl. **bamboos'**)

bamboo'zle vt. mystify, hoax

ban vt. prohibit, forbid, outlaw (**-nn-**) -n. prohibition; proclamation

banal' [-nahl'] a. commonplace, trite -**banal'ity** n.

banan'a [-nahn'-] n. tropical treelike plant; its fruit

band¹ n. strip used to bind; range of frequencies -**ban'dage** n. strip of cloth for binding wound

band² n. company; company of musicians -v. bind together

bandann'a n. handkerchief

B & B bed and breakfast

ban'dit n. outlaw; robber (pl. **ban'-dits, bandit'ti**)

band'wagon n. -**climb, jump, get on the bandwagon** join something that seems assured of success

ban'dy vt. toss from one to another (**ban'died, ban'dying**) -**bandy-legged** a. curving outwards

bane n. person or thing causing misery or distress -**bane'ful** a.

bang n. sudden loud noise; heavy blow -vt. make loud noise; beat; slam

ban'gle [bang'gəl] n. ring worn on arm or leg

ban'ish vt. exile; drive away

ban'isters pl.n. railing and balusters on staircase

ban'jo n. musical instrument like guitar (pl. **-jo(e)s**)

bank¹ n. mound of earth; edge of river etc. -v. enclose with ridge; pile up

bank² n. establishment for keeping, lending, exchanging etc. money -vt. put in bank -vi. keep with bank -**bank'er** n. -**bank on** rely on

bank'rupt n. one who fails in business, insolvent debtor -a. financially ruined -vt. make bankrupt -**bank'ruptcy** n.

bann'er n. placard; flag

ban'quet [bang'kwit] n./v. feast

ban'tam n. dwarf fowl; very light boxing weight

ban'ter vt. make fun of -n. light, teasing language

ba'obab n. Afr. tree with thick trunk

baptise' [-īz'] vt. immerse in, sprinkle with water ceremonially; christen -**bap'tism** n.

bar n. rod or block of any substance; obstacle; rail in law court; body of lawyers; counter where drinks are served; unit of music -vt. fasten; obstruct; exclude (**-rr-**) -prep. except

barb n. sharp point curving backwards; cutting remark -**barbed** a.

bar'barous a. savage, brutal, uncivilized -**barba'rian** n. -**barbar'-**

ic a. -**bar'barism** n. -**barbar'ity** n.

bar'becue n. meal cooked outdoors over open fire -vt.

bar'ber n. one who shaves beards and cuts hair

barbit'urate n. derivative of barbituric acid used as drug

bard n. Celtic poet

bare a. uncovered; naked; plain; scanty -vt. make bare -**bare'ly** adv. only just -**bare'backed** a. on unsaddled horse -**bare'faced** a. shameless

bar'gain [-gin] n. something bought at favourable price; agreement -vi. haggle, negotiate

barge n. flat-bottomed freight boat -vi. inf. bump (into), push

bari'tone [ba'ri-] n. (singer with) second lowest adult male voice -a.

ba'rium n. white metallic element

bark[1] n./v. (utter) sharp loud cry of dog etc.

bark[2] n. outer layer of tree -vt. strip bark from; rub off (skin)

bar'ley n. grain used for food and making malt

barn n. building to store grain, hay etc. -**barn'yard** n.

bar'nacle n. shellfish which adheres to rocks and ships

barom'eter n. instrument to measure pressure of atmosphere -**baromet'ric** a.

bar'on [ba'ron] n. member of lowest rank of peerage; powerful businessman (fem. -**ess**) -**baro'nial** a.

bar'onet [ba'rə-] n. lowest British hereditary title

baroque' [-ok', -ōk'] a. extravagantly ornamented

barque [bahrk] n. sailing ship

barr'ack n. (usu. in pl.) building for lodging soldiers

barracou'ta, barracu'da n. type of large, predatory fish

barr'age [-ahzh] n. heavy artillery fire; continuous heavy delivery of questions etc.; dam across river

barr'el n. round wooden vessel; tube of gun etc.

barr'en a. sterile; unprofitable

barricade' n. improvised barrier -vt. block

barr'ier n. fence, obstruction

barr'ister n. advocate in the higher law courts

barr'ow n. small wheeled handcart; wheelbarrow

bart'er v. trade by exchange of goods -n.

bas'alt [-awlt] n. dark-coloured, hard, compact, igneous rock

base[1] n. bottom, foundation; starting point; centre of operations -vt. found, establish -**base'less** a. -**base'ment** n. lowest storey of building

base[2] a. low, mean; despicable

base'ball n. game played with bat and ball

bash inf. v. strike violently -n. blow; attempt

bash'ful a. shy, modest

ba'sic a. relating to, serving as base; fundamental; necessary

bas'il [baz'-] n. aromatic herb

ba'sin n. deep circular dish; harbour; land drained by river

ba'sis n. foundation; principal constituent (pl. -**ses** [-sēz])

bask [-ah-] vi. lie in warmth and sunshine (often fig.)

bask'et [-ah-] n. vessel made of woven cane, straw etc. -**bask'etball** n. ball game played by two teams

bas-relief' n. sculpture slightly raised from background

bass[1] [bās] n. lowest part in music; bass singer or voice -a.

bass[2] [bas] n. sea perch

bass'et [bas] n. type of smooth-haired dog

bassoon' n. woodwind instrument of low tone

bas'tard n. child born of unmarried parents; inf. person -a. illegitimate; spurious

baste[1] vt. moisten (meat) during cooking with hot fat

baste[2] vt. sew loosely, tack

bas'tion n. projecting part of fortification; defence

bat[1] n. of various types of club used to hit ball in cricket etc. -v. strike with bat

bat[2] n. nocturnal mouselike flying animal

bat[3] vt. flutter (one's eyelids)

batch n. group or set of similar objects

ba'ted a. -with **bated breath** anxiously

bath [-ah-] n. vessel or place to bathe in; water for bathing; act of bathing -vt. wash

bathe [-ǎTH-] v. swim; apply liquid; wash; immerse in water (**bathed**, **ba'thing**) -n. -**ba'ther** n.

bat'ik n. dyeing process using wax

bat'on n. stick, esp. of policeman, conductor, marshal

battal'ion n. military unit of three companies

batt'en[1] n. strip of wood -vt. (esp. with down) fasten

batt'en[2] vi. (usu. with on) thrive at someone's expense

batt'er vt. strike continuously -n. mixture of flour, eggs, milk, used in cooking

batt'ery n. connected group of electrical cells; accumulator; number of similar things occurring together; Law assault by beating; number of guns

bat'tle n. fight between armies -vi. fight

batt'lement n. parapet on fortification with openings

batt'leship n. heavily armed and armoured fighting ship

batt'y a. inf. crazy, silly

bau'ble n. showy trinket

baux'ite n. clay yielding aluminium

bawd'y a. obscene, lewd

bawl vi. cry; shout -n.

bay[1] n. wide inlet of sea; space between two columns; recess -bay window

bay[2] n./v. bark -at bay cornered; at a distance

bay[3] n. laurel tree -pl. honorary crown of victory

bay[4] a. reddish-brown

bay'onet n. stabbing weapon fixed to rifle -vt. stab with this (bay'oneted, bay'oneting)

bazaar' [-zahr'] n. market (esp. in Orient); sale for charity

BB Boys' Brigade

BBC British Broadcasting Corporation

BC before Christ; British Columbia

be vi. live; exist; have a state or quality (I am, he is; we, you, they are, pr. ind. -was, pl. were, pt. -been pp. -be'ing pr.p.)

beach n. shore of sea -vt. run boat on shore

beac'on n. signal fire; lighthouse, buoy; (radio) signal

bead n. little ball pierced for threading; drop of liquid -bead'ed a. -bead'y a.

bead'le n. Hist. church or parish officer

bea'gle n. small hound

beak n. projecting horny jaws of bird; anything similar; sl. magistrate

beak'er n. large drinking cup; glass vessel used by chemists

beam n. long squared piece of wood; ship's width; ray of light etc.; broad smile -vt. aim light, radio waves etc. (to) -vi. shine; smile benignly

bean n. edible seed of various leguminous plants

bear[1] [bār] vt. carry; support; produce; endure; press (upon) (bore pt., born or borne pp., bear'ing pr.p.) -bear'er n.

bear[2] [bār] n. heavy carnivorous quadruped

beard n. hair on chin -vt. oppose boldly

bear'ing n. support for mechanical part; relevance; behaviour; direction; relative position

beast n. four-footed animal; brutal man -beast'ly a.

beat vt. strike repeatedly; overcome; surpass; stir vigorously; flap (wings); make, wear (path) -vi. throb (beat pt., beat'en pp.) -n. stroke; pulsation; appointed course; basic rhythmic unit of music -a. sl. exhausted -beat'er n.

beau [bō] n. suitor (pl. beaux [bō(z)])

beau'ty [byōō'-] n. loveliness, grace; beautiful person or thing -beau'tiful a.

bea'ver n. amphibious rodent; its fur

becalmed' [-kahmd'] a. (of ship) motionless through lack of wind

because' adv./conj. by reason of, since

beck'on v. summon by signal

become' [-kum'] vi. come to be -vt. suit (became' pt., become' pp., becom'ing pr.p.) -becom'ing a. suitable

bed n. piece of furniture for sleeping on; garden plot; bottom of river; layer, stratum -vt. lay in a bed; plant (-dd-) -bedd'ing n. -bed'pan n. container used as lavatory by bedridden people -bed'ridden a. confined to bed -bed'room n. -bed'sitter n. one-roomed flat -bed'stead n.

bed'lam n. noisy confused scene

bedrag'gled a. messy and wet

bee n. insect that makes honey

beech n. European tree with smooth greyish bark and small nuts

beef n. flesh of cattle for eating; inf. complaint -vi. inf. complain

-beeves pl.n. cattle **-beef'y** a. fleshy, stolid

beer n. fermented alcoholic drink made from hops and malt **-beer parlour** C licensed place where beer is sold to the public

beet n. any of various plants with root used for food

bee'tle n. class of insect with hard upper-wing cases

befall' [-awl'] v. happen (to) (**befell', befall'en**)

befit' vt. be suitable to (**-tt-**)

before' prep. in front of; in presence of; in preference to; earlier than **-adv.** earlier; in front **-conj.** sooner than **-before'hand** adv. previously

beg vt. ask earnestly **-vi.** ask for alms (**-gg-**) **-begg'ar** n.

beget' vt. produce, generate (**begot', begat'** pt., **begott'en, begot'** pp., **begett'ing** pr.p.)

begin' v. (cause to) start (**began', begun', begin'ning**) **-beginn'er** n. novice **-begin'ning** n.

bego'nia n. tropical plant

begrudge' vt. grudge, envy anyone the possession of

beguile' [-gīl'] vt. charm, fascinate; amuse; deceive

behalf' [-hahf'] n. interest, esp. in on behalf of

behave' vi. act in particular way **-beha'viour** n. conduct

behead' vt. cut off head

behest' n. charge, command

behind' prep. further back or earlier than; in support of **-adv.** in the rear

behold' [-hō-] vt. watch, see (**beheld'** pt., **beheld', behold'en** pp.)

behold'en a. bound in gratitude

beige [bāzh] n. undyed woollen cloth; its colour

be'ing n. existence; that which exists; creature **-pr.p.** of BE

bel n. unit for comparing two power levels

bela'ted a. late; too late

belch vi. void wind by mouth **-vt.** eject violently **-n.**

bel'fry n. bell tower

believe' vt. regard as true **-vi.** have faith **-belief'** n. **-believ'able** a. credible

Belish'a bea'con [-lēsh'-] flashing light in orange globe marking a pedestrian crossing

belit'tle vt. regard, speak of, as having little worth

bell n. hollow metal instrument giving ringing sound when struck; electrical device emitting ring **-bell'boy** n. pageboy in hotel

belladon'na n. deadly nightshade

belle n. beautiful woman

bell'icose a. warlike

bellig'erent [-ij-] a. aggressive; making war **-n.**

bell'ow vi./n. roar; shout

bell'ows pl.n. instrument for creating stream of air

bell'y n. stomach **-v.** swell out (**bell'ied, bell'ying**)

belong' vi. be property of; be member of; have an allotted place; pertain to **-belong'ings** pl.n. personal possessions

belov'ed [-luv'id or -luvd'] a. much loved **-n.** dear one

below' [-ō'] adv. beneath **-prep.** lower than

belt n. band; girdle; zone **-vt.** inf. thrash

bemoan' vt. grieve over

bemuse' v. confuse, bewilder

bench n. long seat; seat or body of judges etc. **-vt.**

bend v. (cause to) form a curve (**bent** pt./pp.) **-n.**

beneath' prep. under, lower than **-adv.** below

benedic'tion n. blessing

ben'efit n. advantage, profit; money paid to unemployed etc. **-vt.** do good to **-vi.** receive good (**ben'efited, ben'efiting**) **-ben'efactor** n. one who helps or does good to others; patron (**ben'efactress** fem.) **-benef'icent** a. doing good; kind **-benefi'cial** a.

benev'olent a. kindly, charitable **-benev'olence** n.

benight'ed [-nīt'-] a. ignorant

benign' [-nīn'] a. kindly, favourable **-benig'nant** a.

bent a. curved; resolved (on); inf. corrupt; inf. deviant **-n.** inclination

benumb' [-m] vt. make numb

ben'zene, ben'zine n. one of group of flammable liquids used as solvents etc.

bequeath' [-ēTH'] vt. leave property etc. by will **-bequest'** n. bequeathing; legacy

berate' vt. scold harshly

bereave' vt. deprive of, esp. by death (**-reaved', -reft'** pt./pp.) **-bereave'ment** n.

ber'et [-rā] n. round, closefitting hat

beriberi' n. tropical disease caused by vitamin B deficiency

ber'ry n. small juicy stoneless fruit

berserk' a. frenzied

berth n. ship's mooring place; place to sleep in ship -vt. moor

ber'yl n. variety of crystalline mineral eg aquamarine, emerald

beseech' vt. entreat, implore (**besought** pt./pp.)

beset' vt. surround with danger, problems (**beset'**, **besett'ing**)

beside' prep. by the side of, near; distinct from -**besides'** adv./prep. in addition (to)

besiege' vt. surround

besott'ed a. drunk; foolish; infatuated

bespeak' vt. engage beforehand (**bespoke'** pt., **bespoke'**, **bespo'ken** pp.)

best a./adv. sup. of GOOD or WELL -vt. defeat

bes'tial a. like a beast, brutish

bestir' vt. rouse to activity

bestow' [-stō'] vt. give, confer

bet v. agree to pay money if wrong in guessing result of contest (**bet** or **bett'ed** pt./pp., **bett'ing** pr.p.) -n. money so risked

betray' vt. be disloyal to; reveal, divulge; show signs of -**betray'al** n.

betroth' [-ō'TH'] vt. promise to marry -**betroth'al** n.

bett'er a./adv. comp. of GOOD and WELL -v. improve -**bett'erment** n.

between' prep./adv. in the intermediate part, in space or time; indicating reciprocal relation or comparison

bev'el n. angled surface -vi. slope, slant (**-ll-**)

bev'erage n. drink

bev'y n. flock or group

bewail' vt. lament

beware' vi. be on one's guard

bewil'der vt. puzzle, confuse

bewitch' vt. charm, fascinate

beyond' adv. farther away -prep. on the farther side of; out of reach of

bi'as n. slant; inclination (-**ss-** or -**s-**) -**bi'ased**, **bi'assed** a. prejudiced

bib n. cloth put under child's chin when eating; top of apron

Bi'ble n. sacred writings of Christian religion -**bib'lical** a.

bibliog'raphy n. list of books on a subject

bi'ceps n. two-headed muscle, esp. of upper arm

bick'er vi./n. quarrel over petty things -**bick'ering** n.

bi'cycle n. vehicle with two wheels -**bi'cyclist** n.

bid vt. offer; say; command; invite (**bade**, **bid**, **bidd'en**) -n. offer, esp. of price; try; Card Games call -**bidd'er** n.

bide vi. remain; dwell -vt. await -**bi'ding** n.

bi'det [bē'dā] n. low basin for washing genital area

bienn'ial [bī-en'-] a. every two years; lasting two years -n. plant living two years

bier [bēr] n. frame for coffin

bifo'cal [bī-] a. having two focal lengths -**bifo'cals** pl.n. spectacles having bifocal lenses

big a. of great size, height, number, power etc. (**bigg'er** comp., **bigg'est** sup.) -**big'ness** n.

big'amy n. crime of marrying a person while one is still legally married to someone else

bight [bīt] n. curve or loop in rope; long curved shoreline

big'ot n. person intolerant of ideas of others -**big'otry** n.

bike n. short for BICYCLE or MOTOR BIKE

biki'ni [-kē'-] n. woman's brief two-piece swimming costume

bilat'eral [bī-] a. two-sided

bil'berry n. small moorland plant with edible blue berries

bile n. fluid secreted by the liver; ill-temper -**bil'ious** a. nauseous, nauseating

bilge [-j] n. bottom of ship's hull; dirty water collecting there; inf. nonsense

biling'ual [bī-ling'gwəl] a. speaking, or written in, two languages

bill' n. written account of charges; draft of Act of Parliament; poster; commercial document -vt. present account of charges; announce by advertisement

bill' n. bird's beak

bill'et n./vt. (provide) civilian quarters for troops

bill'iards n. game played on table with balls and cues

bill'ion n. million millions

bill'ow n. swelling wave -vi.

bill'y, **bill'ycan** n. can used for boiling water on open fire

bin n. receptacle for corn, refuse etc.

bi'nary a. composed of, characterized by, two; dual

bind [-t] vt. tie fast; tie round; oblige; seal; constrain; bandage; cohere; put (book) into cover (**bound** pt./pp.) **-bind'er** n. **-bind'ing** n. cover of book; tape for hem etc.

binge [-nj] n. inf. spree

bing'o [-ng'gō] n. game of chance in which numbers drawn are matched with those on a card

binoc'ulars pl.n. telescope made for both eyes

bio- [bī-ō-] (comb. form) life, living, as in **biochem'istry** n.

biodegra'dable a. capable of decomposition by natural means

biog'raphy [bī-] n. story of one person's life **-biog'rapher** n. **-biograph'ical** a.

biol'ogy [bī-] n. study of living organisms **-biolog'ical** a. **-biol'ogist** n.

bion'ic a. having physical functions augmented by electronic equipment

bi'opsy n. examination of tissue from a living body

bi'oscope n. SA cinema

bipartisan' [bī-pahrt-i-zan' or -pahrt'-] a. consisting of or supported by two political parties

bi'ped n. two-footed animal

birch n. tree with silvery bark; rod for punishment **-vt.** flog

bird n. feathered animal

birett'a n. square cap worn by Catholic clergy

birth n. bearing, or the being born, of offspring; parentage, origin **-birth'day** n.

bis'cuit [-kit] n. dry, small, thin variety of cake

bisect' [bī-] vt. divide into two equal parts **-bisect'or** n.

bish'op n. clergyman governing diocese; chess piece

bi'son n. large wild ox; Amer. buffalo

bi'stro [bē'-] n. small restaurant

bit[1] n. fragment, piece; biting, cutting part of tool; mouthpiece of horse's bridle

bit[2] n. Computers smallest unit of information

bitch n. female dog, fox or wolf; offens. sl. spiteful woman

bite vt. cut into esp. with teeth; grip; rise to bait; corrode (**bit** pt., **bit**, **bitt'en** pp., **bi'ting** pr.p.) **-n.** act of biting; wound so made; mouthful

bitt'er a. sour tasting; (of person) resentful; sarcastic

bitt'ern n. wading bird like heron

bit'umen n. viscous substance occurring in asphalt, tar etc.

biv'ouac n. temporary encampment of soldiers, hikers etc. **-vi.** camp (**biv'ouacked**, **biv'ouacking**)

bizarre' a. unusual, weird

blab v. reveal secrets; chatter idly (**-bb-**) **-n.**

black a. of the darkest colour; without light; dark; evil **-n.** darkest colour; black dye, clothing etc.; (**B-**) person of dark-skinned race **-vt.** boycott in industrial dispute **-black'en** v. **-black'ball** vt. vote against, exclude **-black'berry** n. plant with dark juicy berries, bramble **-black'bird** n. common European songbird **-black'board** n. dark surface for writing on with chalk **-black box** inf. name for FLIGHT RECORDER **-black'head** n. dark, fatty plug blocking pore in skin **-black'leg** n. strikebreaker **-black'list** n. list of people considered suspicious **-vt.** **-black market** illegal buying and selling of goods **-black spot** dangerous place, esp. on a road

black'guard [blag'ahrd] n. scoundrel **-black'guardly** a.

black'mail vt. extort money by threats **-n.** **-black'mailer** n.

black'out n. complete failure of electricity supply; state of temporary unconsciousness; obscuring of lights as precaution against night air attack **-v.**

black'smith n. smith who works in iron

bladd'er n. membranous bag to contain liquid

blade n. edge, cutting part of knife or tool; leaf of grass etc.; sword

blame n. censure; culpability **-vt.** find fault with; censure **-blam(e)'able** a. **-blame'less** a.

blanch [-ah-] v. whiten, bleach; turn pale

blancmange' [blə-monzh'] n. jellylike milk dessert

bland a. devoid of distinctive characteristics; mild

bland'ish vt. coax; flatter

blank a. without marks or writing; empty; vacant, confused **-n.** empty space; cartridge containing no bullet

blank'et n. thick bed cover; concealing cover **-vt.** cover, stifle

blare v. sound loudly and harshly –n. such sound

blar'ney n. flattering talk

blas'é [blah'zā] a. indifferent through familiarity; bored

blaspheme' v. show contempt for God esp. in speech –**blas'phemous** a. –**blas'phemy** n.

blast [-ahst] n. explosion; shock wave; gust of wind; loud sound –vt. blow up; blight

bla'tant a. obvious –**bla'tancy** n.

blaze¹ n. strong fire or flame; brightness; outburst –vi. burn strongly; be very angry

blaze² v. (mark trees to) establish trail –n. mark on tree; white mark on horse's face

bla'zer n. type of jacket worn esp. for sports

bla'zon vt. make public; depict (arms) –n. coat of arms

bleach v. make or become white –n. bleaching substance

bleak a. cold; exposed

blear'y(-eyed) a. with eyes dimmed, as with tears, sleep

bleat v. cry, as sheep; say plaintively –n. sheep's cry

bleed vi. lose blood –vt. draw blood from (**bled** pt./pp.)

bleep n. short high-pitched sound

blem'ish n. defect –vt. make defective –**blem'ished** a.

blend vt. mix –n. mixture –**blend'er** n. esp. electrical appliance for mixing food

bless vt. consecrate; ask God's favour for; make happy (**bless'ed**, **blest** pp.) –**bless'ed** a. –**bless'ing** n.

blight [blīt] n. plant disease; harmful influence –vt. injure

blimp n. small airship

blind [-ī-] a. unable to see; heedless; closed at one end –vt. deprive of sight –n. window screen; pretext –**blind'ness** n. –**blind'fold** vt. cover the eyes –n./a.

blink vi. wink; twinkle –vt. shut eyes momentarily –n. gleam –**blink at** ignore –**on the blink** inf. not working

blip n. repetitive sound or visible pulse, eg on radar screen

bliss n. perfect happiness –**bliss'ful** a.

blis'ter n. bubble on skin; surface swelling –v. form blisters (on)

blithe [blīтн] a. happy

blitz n. concentrated attack

blizz'ard n. blinding storm of wind and snow

bloat v. swell out –**bloat'ed** a. swollen –**bloat'er** n. smoked herring

blob n. soft mass, drop of liquid

bloc n. (political) grouping of people or countries

block n. solid (rectangular) piece of wood, stone etc.; obstacle; pulley with frame; large building of offices, flats etc. –vt. obstruct, stop up; shape –**block'age** n. obstruction

blockade' n. physical prevention of access, esp. to port –vt.

bloke n. inf. fellow, chap

blond a. (of hair) light-coloured –n. (**blonde** fem.)

blood [blud] n. red fluid in veins; kindred –vt. initiate (into hunting, war etc.) –**blood'less** a. –**blood'y** a. covered in blood –a./adv. sl. a common intensifier –vt. make bloody –**blood'hound** n. large hound noted for keen powers of scent –**blood'shed** n. slaughter –**blood'shot** a. inflamed (of eyes) –**blood'thirsty** a. cruel

bloom n. flower; prime; glow –vi. be in flower; flourish

bloom'er n. inf. mistake

bloom'ers pl.n. wide, baggy knickers

bloss'om n./vi. flower

blot n. spot, stain –vt. spot, stain; obliterate; soak up ink (**-tt-**) –**blott'er** n.

blotch n. dark spot –vt. make spotted –**blotch'y** a.

blouse [-owz] n. light, loose upper garment

blow¹ [blō] vi. make a current of air; pant; emit sound –vt. drive air upon or into; drive by current of wind; sound; sl. squander (**blew**, **blown**) –n. blast; gale –**blow'er** n. –**blow'fly** n. fly which infects food etc. –**blow'lamp** n. small burner with very hot flame –**blow-out** n. sudden puncture in tyre; uncontrolled escape of oil, gas, from well; sl. large meal

blow² [blō] n. stroke, knock; sudden misfortune

blowz'y a. slovenly, sluttish

blubb'er v. weep –n. whale fat

bludg'eon [bluj'ən] n. short thick club –vt. strike with one; coerce

blue a. of the colour of sky; depressed; indecent –n. the colour; dye or pigment –vt. make blue (**blued** pt./pp.) –**blues** pl.n. inf. depression; form of jazz music –**blu'-**

ish *a.* **-blue'bell** *n.* wild spring flower **-blue'bottle** *n.* blowfly **-blue-pencil** *vt.* alter, censor **-blue'print** *n.* copy of drawing; original plan

bluff¹ *n.* cliff, steep bank; C clump of trees *-a.* hearty; blunt

bluff² *vt./n.* (deceive by) pretence

blun'der *n./vi.* (make) clumsy mistake

blunt *a.* not sharp; (of speech) abrupt *-vt.* make blunt

blur *v.* make, become less distinct (**-rr-**) *-n.* something indistinct

blurb *n.* statement advertising, recommending book *etc.*

blurt *vt.* utter suddenly

blush *vi.* become red in face; be ashamed *-n.* this effect

blus'ter *vi./n.* (indulge in) noisy, aggressive behaviour **-blus'tery** *a.* (of wind) gusty

bo'a *n.* large, nonvenomous snake; long scarf of fur or feathers

boar *n.* male pig; wild pig

board *n.* broad, flat piece of wood, card *etc.*; table; meals; group of people who administer authority, cover with planks; supply food daily; enter ship *etc.* *-vi.* take daily meals **-board'er** *n.*

boast *vi.* speak too much in praise of oneself *-vt.* brag of; have to show *-n.* thing boasted (of) **-boast'ful** *a.*

boat *n.* small open vessel; ship *-vi.* sail about in boat **-boat'ing** *n.* **-boat'swain** [bō'son] *n.* ship's officer in charge of boats, sails *etc.*

bob *vi.* move up and down *-vt.* move jerkily; cut (women's) hair short (**-bb-**) *-n.* jerking motion; short hair style; weight on pendulum *etc.*

bobbejaan' [-ə-yahn'] *n.* SA baboon

bobb'in *n.* reel for thread

bob'ble *n.* small, tufted ball

bob'cat *n.* Amer. bay lynx

bode *vt.* be an omen of

bod'ice [-is] *n.* upper part of woman's dress

bod'kin *n.* large blunt needle

bod'y *n.* whole frame of man or animal; corpse; main part; substance; group of persons **-bod'ily** *a./adv.* **-bod'yguard** *n.* escort to protect important person

Boer [boor] *n.* a S Afr. of Dutch or Huguenot descent *-a.*

bog *n.* wet, soft ground **-bogg'y** *a.* **-bog down** stick as in a bog

bo'gan *n.* C sluggish side stream

bog'gle *vi.* stare, be surprised

bo'gie *n.* low truck on wheels

bo'gus *a.* sham, false

boil¹ *vi.* change from liquid to gas, *esp.* by heating; become cooked by boiling; *inf.* be hot; *inf.* be angry *-vt.* cause to boil; cook by boiling *-n.* boiling state

boil² *n.* inflamed suppurating swelling on skin

bois'terous *a.* wild; noisy

bold *a.* daring; presumptuous; prominent

bole *n.* trunk of a tree

bole'ro [-ā'-] *n.* Spanish dance; [bol'ə-rō] short loose jacket

boll [-ō-] *n.* seed capsule of cotton

boll'ard *n.* post to secure mooring lines; post in road as barrier

bol'ster *vt.* support, uphold *-n.* long pillow; pad, support

bolt [bō-] *n.* bar or pin (*esp.* with thread for nut); rush; lightning; roll of cloth *-vt.* fasten; swallow hastily *-vi.* rush away

bomb [bom] *n.* explosive projectile; any explosive device **-the bomb** nuclear bomb *-vt.* attack with bombs **-bombard'** *vt.* shell; attack (verbally)

bom'bast *n.* pompous language

bo'na fi'de [-di] *Lat.* genuine(ly)

bonan'za *n.* sudden wealth

bond *n.* that which binds; link; written promise *-vt.* bind

bond'age *n.* slavery

bone *n.* hard substance forming skeleton; piece of this *-vt.* take out bone **-bo'ny** *a.*

bon'fire *n.* large outdoor fire

bon'go *n.* small drum (*pl.* **-go(e)s**)

bonn'et *n.* hat with strings; cap; cover of motor vehicle engine

bonn'y *a.* beautiful, handsome **-bonn'ily** *adv.*

bon'sai [-sī] *n.* (art of growing) dwarf trees, shrubs

bo'nus *n.* extra (unexpected) payment or gift (*pl.* **bo'nuses**)

boo *interj.* expression of disapproval; exclamation to surprise *esp.* child *-v.*

boob'y *n.* fool **-booby trap** harmless-looking object which explodes when disturbed

book *n.* sheets of paper bound together; literary work *-vt.* reserve room, ticket *etc.*; charge with legal offence; enter name in book **-book'keeping** *n.* systematic recording of business transactions **-book'maker** *n.* one who takes bets (*inf.* **book'ie**)

boom[1] *n.* sudden commercial activity; prosperity -*vi.*

boom[2] *vi./n.* (make) deep sound

boom[3] *n.* long spar for bottom of sail; barrier across harbour

boo'merang *n.* curved wooden missile of Aust. Aborigines, which returns to the thrower

boon *n.* something helpful, favour

boor *n.* rude person -**boor'ish** *a.*

boost *n.* encouragement; upward push; increase -*vt.* **boost'er** *n.*

boot[1] *n.* covering for the foot and ankle; luggage receptacle in car; *inf.* kick -*vt. inf.* kick

booth [-TH] *n.* stall; cubicle

boot'leg *v.* make, carry, sell illicit goods, *esp.* alcohol -*a.* -**boot'legger** *n.*

boo'ty *n.* plunder, spoil

booze *n./vi. inf.* (consume) alcoholic drink

bor'ax *n.* white soluble substance, compound of boron -**borac'ic** *a.*

bord'er *n.* margin; frontier; limit; strip of garden -*v.* provide with border; adjoin

bore[1] *vt.* pierce hole -*n.* hole; calibre of gun

bore[2] *vt.* make weary by repetition -*n.* tiresome person or thing -**bore'dom** *n.* -**bor'ing** *a.*

bor'on *n.* chemical element used in hardening steel, *etc.*

bor'ough [bur'ə] *n.* town

borr'ow *vt.* obtain on loan

bor'stal *n.* reformatory for young criminals

bor'zoi *n.* breed of tall hound with long, silky coat

bos'om [booz'-] *n.* human breast

boss[1] *n.* person in charge of or employing others -*vt.* be in charge of; be domineering over -**boss'y** *a.* overbearing

bot'any *n.* study of plants -**botan'ic(al)** *a.* -**bot'anist** *n.*

botch *vt.* spoil by clumsiness

both [bōth] *a./pron.* the two -*adv./conj.* as well

both'er [-TH-] *vt.* pester; perplex -*vi./n.* fuss, trouble

bot'tle *n.* vessel for holding liquid; its contents -*vt.* put into bottle; restrain -**bot'tleneck** *n.* narrow outlet which impedes smooth flow

bott'om *n.* lowest part; bed of sea *etc.*; buttocks -*vt.* put bottom to; base (upon); get to bottom of

bou'doir [bōō'dwahr] *n.* lady's private sitting-room; bedroom

bough [bow] *n.* branch of tree

boul'der [bōl'-] *n.* large rock

boule'vard [bōōl'vahr, -vahrd] *n.* broad street or promenade

bounce *v.* (cause to) rebound on impact -*n.* rebounding; quality causing this; *inf.* vitality -**bounc'ing** *a.* vigorous

bound[1] *n./vt.* limit -**bound'ary** *n.* -**bound'less** *a.*

bound[2] *vi./n.* spring, leap

bound[3] *a.* on a specified course

bound[4] *a.* committed; certain; tied

boun'ty *n.* liberality; gift; premium -**boun'teous, boun'tiful** *a.*

bouquet[1] [bōō-kā'] *n.* bunch of flowers; aroma; compliment

bour'bon [bur'-] *n. US* whisky made from maize

bour'geois [boor'zhwah] *n./a.* middle class

bout *n.* period of time spent doing something; contest, fight

boutique[1] [bōō-tēk'] *n.* small shop, *esp.* one selling clothes

bo'vine *a.* of the ox or cow

bow[1] [bō] *n.* weapon for shooting arrows; implement for playing violin *etc.*; ornamental knot; bend -*v.* bend

bow[2] [bow] *vi.* bend body in respect, assent *etc.*; submit -*vt.* bend downwards; crush -*n.*

bow[3] [bow] *n.* fore end of ship

bow'el [-ō-] *n.* (*oft. pl.*) part of intestine; inside of anything

bow'er [-ō-] *n.* shady retreat

bowl[1] [-ō-] *n.* round vessel, deep basin; drinking cup; hollow

bowl[2] [-ō-] *n.* round ball -*pl.* game played with such balls -*v.* roll or throw ball in various ways -**bowl'er** *n.*

bowl'er [-ō-] *n.* man's low-crowned stiff felt hat

box[1] *n.* (wooden) container, usu. rectangular; its contents; any boxlike cubicle or receptacle -*vt.* put in box; confine -**box lacrosse** C indoor lacrosse

box[2] *v.* fight with fists, *esp.* with padded gloves on -*vt.* strike -*n.* blow -**box'er** *n.* one who boxes; large dog resembling bulldog

box[3] *n.* evergreen shrub used for hedges

boy *n.* male child; young man

boy'cott *vt.* refuse to deal with or participate in -*n.*

BP British Petroleum

BR British Rail

brace *n.* tool for boring; clamp; pair;

support –*pl.* straps to hold up trousers –*vt.* steady (oneself) as before a blow; support **-bra'cing** *a.* invigorating **-brace'let** *n.* ornament for the arm

brack'en *n.* large fern

brack'et *n.* support for shelf *etc.*; group –*pl.* marks [ ], ( ) used to enclose words *etc.* –*vt.* enclose in brackets; connect

brack'ish *a.* (of water) slightly salty

brad *n.* small nail

brag *vi.* boast (**-gg-**) –*n.* boastful talk **-bragg'art** *n.*

braid *vt.* interweave; trim with braid –*n.* anything plaited; ornamental tape

braille [brāl] *n.* system of printing for blind, with raised dots

brain *n.* mass of nerve tissue in head; intellect –*vt.* kill by hitting on head **-brain'y** *a.* **-brain'wave** *n.* sudden, clever idea

braise [-āz] *vt.* stew in covered pan

brake *n.* instrument for retarding motion of wheel on vehicle –*vt.* apply brake to

bram'ble *n.* prickly shrub

bran *n.* sifted husks of corn

branch [-ah-] *n.* limb of tree; offshoot –*vi.* bear branches; diverge; spread

brand *n.* trademark; class of goods; particular kind; mark made by hot iron; burning piece of wood –*vt.* burn with iron; mark; stigmatize

bran'dish *vt.* flourish, wave

bran'dy *n.* spirit distilled from wine

brash *a.* bold, impudent

brass [-ah-] *n.* alloy of copper and zinc; group of brass wind instruments; *inf.* money; *inf.* (army) officers –*a.*

brass'iere *n.* woman's undergarment, supporting breasts

brava'do [-vahd-] *n.* showy display of boldness

brave *a.* courageous; splendid –*vt.* warrior –*vt.* defy, meet boldly **-bra'very** *n.*

bra'vo! [brah-] *interj.* well done!

brawl *vi.* fight noisily –*n.*

brawn *n.* muscle; strength; pickled pork **-brawn'y** *a.*

bray *n.* donkey's cry –*vi.* utter such

bra'zen *a.* of, like brass; shameless –*vt.* (*usu. with out*) face, carry through with impudence

bra'zier *n.* pan for burning coals

breach *n.* opening; breaking of rule *etc.* –*vt.* make a gap in

bread [-ed] *n.* food made of flour baked; food; *sl.* money

breadth [-edth] *n.* extent across, width; largeness of view, mind

break [brāk] *vt.* part by force; shatter; burst, destroy; fail to observe; disclose; interrupt; surpass; mitigate; accustom (horse) to being ridden; decipher (code) –*vi.* become broken; open, separate; come suddenly; give way; part (**broke, bro'ken**) –*n.* fracture; gap; opening; separation; interruption; respite; interval; *inf.* opportunity **-break'able** *a.* **-break'age** *n.* **-break'down** *n.* collapse; failure to function; analysis **-break'fast** [brek'-] *n.* first meal of the day **-break'through** *n.* important advance **-break'water** *n.* barrier to break force of waves

bream *n.* broad, thin fish

breast [brest] *n.* human chest; milk-secreting gland on woman's chest; seat of the affections –*vt.* face, oppose; reach summit of **-breast'stroke** *n.* stroke in swimming

breath [breth] *n.* air used by lungs; life; respiration; slight breeze **-breathe** [brēTH] *v.* inhale and exhale (air); live; rest; whisper **-brea'ther** [-TH-] *n.* short rest **-breath'less** *a.* **-breath'taking** *a.* causing awe or excitement

Breath'alyser R device that estimates amount of alcohol in breath **-breath'alyse** *vt.*

breech *n.* buttocks; hinder part of anything **-breech'es** [brich'iz] *pl.n.* trousers

breed *vt.* generate; bring up; produce; be with young (**bred** *pt./pp.*) –*n.* offspring produced; race, kind

breeze *n.* gentle wind **-breez'ily** *adv.* **-breez'y** *a.* windy; lively; casual

breeze block light building brick made of ashes bonded by cement

brev'ity *n.* conciseness of expression; short duration

brew [-oo] *vt.* prepare liquor, as beer; make drink, as tea; plot –*vi.* be in preparation –*n.* beverage produced by brewing **-brew'er** *n.* **-brew'ery** *n.*

bri'ar, bri'er *n.* prickly shrub

bribe *n.* anything offered or given to gain favour –*vt.* influence by bribe **-bri'bery** *n.*

brick *n.* oblong mass of hardened

clay used in building -vt. build, block etc. with bricks -**brick'layer** n.

bride n. woman about to be, or just, married (**bride'groom** masc.) -**brides'maid** n.

bridge[1] n. structure for crossing river etc.; something joining or supporting other parts; raised narrow platform on ship; upper part of nose -vt. make bridge over, span

bridge[2] n. card game

bri'dle n. headgear of horse; curb -vt. put on bridle; restrain -vi. show resentment

brief a. short in duration; concise; scanty -n. summary of case for counsel's use; instructions -pl. underpants; panties -vt. give instructions

bri'er see BRIAR

brig n. two-masted, square-rigged ship

brigade' n. subdivision of army; organized band -**brigadier'** n. high-ranking army officer

bright [brīt] a. shining; full of light; cheerful; clever -**bright'en** v.

brill n. European food fish

brill'iant a. shining; sparkling; splendid; very clever; distinguished -**brill'iance, brill'iancy** n.

brim n. margin, edge, esp. of river, cup, hat -**brim'ful** a.

brim'stone n. sulphur

brin'dle(d) a. spotted, streaked

brine n. salt water; pickle

bring vt. fetch; carry with one; cause to come (**brought** pt./pp.)

brink n. edge of steep place

brisk a. active, vigorous

brisk'et n. meat from breast

bris'tle [-is'l] n. short stiff hair -vi. stand erect; show temper -**bris'tly** a.

Brit. Britain; British

britt'le a. easily broken; curt

broach vt. pierce (cask); open

broad [-aw-] a. wide, spacious; open; obvious; coarse; general -**broad'en** vt. -**broad'cast** vt. transmit by radio or television; make widely known -n. radio or television programme -**broad'caster** n. -**broad'side** n. discharge of guns; strong (verbal) attack

brocade' n. rich woven fabric with raised design

brocc'oli n. type of cauliflower

bro'chure [-sha] n. pamphlet

brogue [-ōg] n. stout shoe; dialect, esp. Irish accent

broil n. noisy quarrel

bro'ker n. one employed to buy and sell for others -**bro'kerage** n. payment to broker

bro'mide n. chemical compound used in medicine and photography

bro'mine [-mēn] n. liquid element used in production of chemicals

bronch'ial [-ng'k-] a. of branches of the windpipe -**bronch'itis** n. inflammation of bronchial tubes

bronze n. alloy of copper and tin -a. made of, or coloured like, bronze -vt. give appearance of bronze to

brooch [-ō-] n. ornamental pin

brood [-ōō-] n. family of young, esp. of birds -v. sit, as hen on eggs; fret over

brook[1] [-ōō-] n. small stream

brook[2] [-ōō-] vt. put up with

broom [-ōō-] n. brush for sweeping; yellow-flowered shrub

bros. brothers

broth n. thick soup

broth'el n. house of prostitution

broth'er [-uTH-] n. son of same parents; one closely united with another -**broth'erhood** n. relationship; company -**brother-in-law** n. brother of husband or wife; husband of sister

brow n. ridge over eyes; forehead; eyebrow; edge of hill

brown a. of dark colour inclining to red or yellow -n. the colour -v. make, become brown

browse vi. look through (book etc.) in a casual manner; feed on shoots and leaves

bruise [-ōōz] vt. injure without breaking skin -n. contusion, discolouration caused by blow

brum'by n. Aust. wild horse

brunette' n. woman of dark complexion and hair -a. dark brown

brunt n. chief shock of attack

brush n. device with bristles, hairs etc. used for cleaning, painting etc.; act of brushing; brief contact; skirmish; bushy tail; brushwood -v. apply, remove, clean, with brush; touch lightly

brusque [-oosk] a. curt

brute n. any animal except man; crude, vicious person -a. animal; sensual, stupid; physical -**bru'tal** a.

BSc Bachelor of Science

BST British Summer Time

bub'ble n. hollow globe of liquid, blown out with air; something insubstantial -vi. rise in bubbles -**bub'bly** a.

bubon'ic plague [byōō-] *n.* acute infectious disease

buccaneer' *n.* pirate

buck *n.* male deer, or other male animal; act of bucking; *US, A sl.* dollar –*v.* of horse, attempt to throw rider –**buck'shot** *n.* lead shot in shotgun shell

buck'et *n.* vessel, round with arched handle, for water *etc.*

buck'le *n.* metal clasp for fastening belt, strap *etc.* –*vt.* fasten with buckle –*vi.* warp, bend

buck'ram *n.* coarse stiff cloth

buckshee' *a. sl.* free

bucol'ic [byōō-] *a.* rustic

bud *n.* shoot containing unopened leaf, flower *etc.* –*vi.* begin to grow (-**dd**-)

budge *vi.* move, stir

budg'erigar *n.* small Aust. parakeet (*also* **budg'ie**)

budg'et *n.* annual financial statement; plan of systematic spending –*vi.*

buff *n.* leather from buffalo hide; light yellow colour; polishing pad –*vt.* polish

buff'alo *n.* large ox (*pl.* **-lo(e)s**)

buff'er *n.* contrivance to lessen shock of concussion

buff'et¹ *n.* blow, slap –*vt.* strike with blows; contend against

buff'et² [boofā] *n.* refreshment bar; meal at which guests serve themselves; sideboard

buffoon' *n.* clown; fool

bug *n.* any small insect; *inf.* disease, infection; concealed listening device

bug'bear *n.* object of needless terror; nuisance

bugg'er *n.* sodomite; *vulg. sl.* unpleasant person or thing

bu'gle *n.* instrument like trumpet

build [bild] *v.* construct by putting together parts (built *pt./pp.*) –*n.* make, form –**build'er** *n.* –**build'ing** *n.*

bulb *n.* modified leaf bud emitting roots from base, *eg* onion; globe surrounding filament of electric light –**bulb'ous** *a.*

bulge *n.* swelling; temporary increase –*vi.* –**bulg'y** *a.*

bulk *n.* size; volume; greater part; cargo –*vi.* be of weight or importance –**bulk'y** *a.*

bull *n.* male of cattle; male of various other animals –**bull'dog** *n.* thickset breed of dog –**bull'dozer** *n.* powerful tractor for excavating *etc.* –**bu'llock** *n.* castrated bull

bull'et *n.* projectile discharged from rifle, pistol *etc.*

bull'etin *n.* official report

bull'ion *n.* gold or silver in mass

bull'y *n.* one who hurts or intimidates weaker people –*vt.* (**bull'ied, bull'ying**)

bul'rush *n.* tall reedlike marsh plant

bul'wark *n.* rampart; any defence

bum *sl. n.* buttocks, anus

bum'ble *v.* perform clumsily

bump *n.* knock; thud; swelling –*vt.* strike or push against –**bump'er** *n.* horizontal bar on motor vehicle to protect against damage –*a.* abundant

bun *n.* small, round cake; round knot of hair

bunch *n.* number of things tied or growing together; group, party –*v.* gather together

bun'dle *n.* package; number of things tied together –*vt.* tie in bundle; send (off) without ceremony

bun'du [boon'doo] *n.* **SA** wild uninhabited country

bung *n.* stopper for cask –*vt.* stop up; *inf.* sling

bun'galow [bung'gə-lō] *n.* one-storeyed house

bun'gle [bung'gl] *vt./n.* botch

bun'ion *n.* inflamed swelling on foot or toe

bunk *n.* narrow, shelflike bed

bunk'er *n.* large storage container for coal *etc.*; sandy hollow on golf course; underground defensive position

bunt'ing *n.* material for flags

buoy [boi] *n.* floating marker anchored in sea; lifebuoy –*vt.* –**buoy'ancy** *n.* –**buoy'ant** *a.*

bur(r) *n.* head of plant with prickles or hooks

burd'en *n.* load; weight; cargo; anything difficult to bear –*vt.* load, encumber –**burd'ensome** *a.*

bu'reau [-rō] *n.* writing desk; office; government department (*pl.* **-reaus, -reaux**) –**bureau'cracy** [-ok'-] *n.* government by officials; body of officials –**bu'reaucrat** *n.*

bur'geon [-jən] *vi.* bud; flourish

burgh [bur'ə] *n.* Scottish borough

burg'lar *n.* one who enters building to commit crime, *esp.* theft –**burg'lary** *n.* –**bur'gle** *vt.*

bur'gundy *n.* name of various wines, white and red

burlesque' [-esk'] *n./vt.* caricature

bur'ly *a.* sturdy, stout, robust

burn *vt.* destroy or injure by fire *-vi.* be on fire, *lit.* or *fig.*; be consumed by fire (**burned** or **burnt** *pt./pp.*) *-n.* injury, mark caused by fire

burn'ish *vt./n.* polish

burr'ow [-ō] *n.* hole dug by rabbit *etc.* *-vt.*

burs'ar *n.* official managing finances of college *etc.*

burst *vi.* break into pieces; break suddenly into some expression of feeling *-vt.* shatter, break violently *-n.* bursting; explosion; outbreak; spurt

bur'y [ber'i] *vt.* put underground; inter; conceal (**bur'ied, bur'ying**) *-bur'ial n./a.*

bus *n.* (orig. omnibus) large motor vehicle for passengers

bus'by [-z'-] *n.* tall fur hat worn by certain soldiers

bush [-oo-] *n.* shrub; uncleared country *-bush'y a.* shaggy *-bush'baby n.* tree-living, nocturnal Afr. animal *-bush line* C airline operating in bush country *-bush'veld* [-felt] *n.* SA bushy countryside

bush'el [-oo-] *n.* dry measure of eight gallons

bus'iness [biz'nis] *n.* occupation; commercial or industrial establishment; trade; responsibility; work *-bus'inesslike a.*

busk'er *n.* one who makes money by singing, dancing *etc.* in the street

bust[1] *n.* sculpture of head and shoulders; woman's breasts

bust[2] *inf.* v. burst; make, become bankrupt *-vt.* raid; arrest *-a.* broken; bankrupt

bus'tle [-səl] *vi.* be noisily busy *-n.* fuss, commotion

bus'y [biz'i] *a.* actively employed; full of activity *-vt.* occupy (**bus'ied, bus'ying**) *-bus'ily adv.*

but *prep./conj.* without; except; only; yet; still; besides

bu'tane [byōō'-] *n.* gas used for fuel

butch'er [-oo-] *n.* one who kills animals for food, or sells meat; savage man *-vt.* slaughter

but'ler *n.* chief male servant

butt[1] *n.* thick end; target; object of ridicule; unused end *-vi.* lie, be placed end on to

butt[2] *v.* strike with head *-n.*

butt'er *n.* fatty substance got from cream by churning *-vt.* spread with butter; flatter

butt'ercup *n.* plant with glossy, yellow flowers

butt'erfly *n.* insect with large wings

butt'ermilk *n.* milk that remains after churning

butt'erscotch *n.* kind of hard, brittle toffee

butt'ock *n.* rump, protruding hinder part (*usu. pl.*)

butt'on *n.* knob, stud for fastening dress; knob that operates doorbell, machine *etc.* *-vt.* fasten with buttons *-butt'onhole n.* slit in garment to pass button through as fastening; flower, spray worn on lapel *etc.* *-vt.* detain (unwilling) person in conversation

butt'ress *n.* structure to support wall; prop *-vt.*

bux'om *a.* full of health, plump

buy [bī] *vt.* get by payment, purchase; bribe (**bought** *pt./pp.*) *-buy'er n.*

buzz *vi./n.* (make) humming sound

buzz'ard *n.* bird of prey

by *prep.* near; along; past; during; not later than; through use or agency of; in units of *-adv.* near; aside; past *-by and by* soon *-by and large* on the whole

by- (*comb. form*) subsidiary, near, as in **by'product, by'stander**

bye *n.* Sport situation where player, team, wins by default of opponent

by(e)'law *n.* law, regulation made by local subordinate authority

by'gone *a.* past, former *-n.* (*oft. pl.*) past occurrence

by'pass *n.* road for diversion of traffic from crowded centres

byre [bīr] *n.* cowshed

byte *n.* Computers sequence of bits processed as single unit of information

C

C Chem. carbon; Celsius; Centigrade

c. circa

CA chartered accountant

cab *n.* taxi; driver's compartment on lorry *etc.*

cabal' *n.* small group of intriguers; secret plot

cab'aret [-rā] *n.* floor show at a nightclub

cabb'age *n.* green vegetable

cab'in *n.* hut, shed; small room *esp.* in ship

cab'inet *n.* piece of furniture with drawers or shelves; outer case of television, radio *etc.*; committee of politicians

ca'ble *n.* strong rope; wires conveying electric power, telegraph signals *etc.*; message sent by this; nautical unit of measurement (100-120 fathoms) –*v.* telegraph by cable

caboose' *n.* ship's galley

caca'o [-kah'-] *n.* tropical tree from the seeds of which chocolate and cocoa are made

cache [kash] *n.* secret hiding place; store of food *etc.*

cack'le *vi./n.* (make) chattering noise, as of hen

cacoph'ony *n.* disagreeable sound; discord of sounds

cac'tus *n.* spiny succulent plant (*pl.* **cac'tuses, cac'ti** [-tī])

cad *n.* unchivalrous person

cadav'er *n.* corpse –**cadav'erous** *a.* corpselike; gaunt

cadd'ie, -y *n.* golfer's attendant

cadd'y *n.* small box for tea

ca'dence *n.* fall or modulation of voice in music or verse

caden'za *n. Mus.* elaborate solo passage

cadet' *n.* youth in training, *esp.* for armed forces

cadge [kaj] *v.* get (food, money *etc.*) by begging –**cadg'er** *n.*

cad'mium *n.* metallic element

Caesa'rean section surgical operation to deliver a baby

café [-ā] *n.* small restaurant serving light refreshments –**cafete'ria** *n.* self-service restaurant

caff'eine [-ēn] *n.* stimulating alkaloid in tea and coffee

caf'tan *n. see* KAFTAN

cage *n.* enclosure, box with bars or wires, *esp.* for keeping animals or birds –*vt.* put in cage, confine –**ca'gey** *a.* wary

cairn *n.* heap of stones, *esp.* as monument or landmark

cajole' *vt.* persuade by flattery, wheedle –**cajo'lery** *n.*

cake *n.* baked, sweet, bread-like food; compact mass –*v.* harden (as of mud)

cal'amine *n.* soothing ointment

calam'ity *n.* disaster –**calam'itous** *a.*

cal'cium *n.* metallic element, the

basis of lime –**cal'cify** *v.* convert, be converted, to lime

cal'culate *vt.* estimate; compute –*vi.* make reckonings –**cal'culable** *a.* –**cal'culating** *a.* shrewd; scheming –**calcula'tion** *n.* –**cal'culator** *n.* electronic device for making calculations

cal'endar *n.* table of months and days in the year; list of events

calf [kahf] *n.* young of cow and other animals; leather of calf's skin (*pl.* **calves** [kahvz])

calf [kahf] *n.* fleshy back of leg below knee (*pl.* **calves** [kahvz])

cal'ibre [-bər] *n.* size of bore of gun; capacity, character –**cal'ibrate** *vt.*

cal'ico *n.* cotton cloth

call [kawl] *vt.* speak loudly to attract attention; summon; telephone; name –*vi.* shout; pay visit –*n.* shout; animal's cry; visit; inner urge; demand –**call'er** *n.* –**call'ing** *n.* vocation, profession –**call up** summon to serve in army; imagine

callig'raphy *n.* handwriting

cal'lipers *pl.n.* instrument for measuring diameters

callisthen'ics [-is-then'-] *pl.n.* light gymnastic exercises

call'ous *a.* hardened, unfeeling

call'ow *a.* inexperienced

call'us *n.* area of hardened skin

calm [kahm] *a./v.* (make, become) still, tranquil –*n.* absence of wind –**calm'ly** *adv.* –**calm'ness** *n.*

cal'orie, -ory *n.* unit of heat; unit of energy from foods –**calorif'ic** *a.* heat-making

calum'ny *n.* slander

calyp'so *n.* (West Indies) improvised song

ca'lyx *n.* covering of bud (*pl.* **ca'lyxes, ca'lyces** [-sēz])

cam *n.* device to change rotary to reciprocating motion

camarad'erie [-rahd'-] *n.* spirit of comradeship, trust

cam'ber *n.* convexity on upper surface of road

cam'bric *n.* fine white linen or cotton cloth

cam'el *n.* animal of Asia and Africa, with humped back

came'llia *n.* ornamental shrub

cam'eo *n.* medallion, brooch *etc.* with design in relief

cam'era *n.* apparatus used to make photographs

cam'isole *n.* underbodice

c(h)am'omile *n.* aromatic creeping plant, used medicinally

cam'ouflage [-ahzh] n. disguise, means of deceiving enemy observation -vt. disguise

camp n. (place for) tents of hikers, army etc.; group supporting political party etc.; SA field, pasture -a. inf. homosexual; consciously artificial -vi. form or lodge in a camp

campaign' [-pān'] n./vi. (organize) series of coordinated activities for some purpose, eg political, military

cam'phor n. solid essential oil with aromatic taste and smell

camp'us n. grounds of university

can' vi. be able; have the power; be allowed (could pt.)

can' n. container, usu. metal, for liquids, foods -v. put in can (-nn-) -canned a. preserved in can; (of music) previously recorded

Canada Day July 1st, anniversary of day in 1867 when Canada received dominion status

Canada goose large greyish-brown N Amer. goose

Cana'dian n./a. (native) of Canada -Cana'dianize v. make, become Canadian

canal' n. artificial watercourse; duct in body

can'apé [-pē] n. small piece of toast etc. with savoury topping

cana'ry n. yellow singing bird

canas'ta n. card game played with two packs

can'can n. high-kicking dance

can'cel vt. cross out; annul; call off (-ll-) -cancella'tion n.

can'cer n. malignant growth or tumour -can'cerous a.

can'did a. frank, impartial -can'-dour n. frankness

can'didate n. one who seeks office etc.; person taking examination -can'didature n.

can'dle n. stick of wax with wick; light -candela'brum [-lahb'-] n. large, branched candle holder (pl. -bra) -can'dlestick n. -can'dlewick n. cotton fabric with tufted surface

can'dy n. crystallized sugar; US confectionery in general -vt. preserve with sugar (can'died, can'dying)

cane n. stem of small palm or large grass; walking stick -vt. beat with cane

ca'nine a. like, pert. to, dog

can'ister n. container, usu. of

metal, for storing dry food

cank'er n. eating sore; thing that destroys, corrupts

cann'abis n. hemp plant; drug derived from this

cannello'ni n. tubular pieces of pasta filled with meat etc.

cann'ibal n. one who eats human flesh -a. -cann'ibalism n.

cann'on' n. large gun (pl. -ons or -on)

cann'on' n. billiard stroke -vi. make this stroke; rebound, collide

cann'ot negative form of CAN'

cann'y a. shrewd; cautious

canoe' [-noo'] n. very light boat propelled with paddle(s) (pl. -oes') -canoe'ist n.

can'on n. law or rule, esp. of church; standard; list of saints -canoniza'-tion n. -can'onize vt. enrol in list of saints

can'opy n. covering over throne, bed etc. -vt. cover with canopy (-opied, -opying)

cant n. hypocritical speech; technical jargon; slang, esp. of thieves -vi. use cant

can'taloupe, -loup, -lope n. variety of musk melon

cantank'erous a. quarrelsome

canta'ta [-taht'-] n. choral work

canteen' n. place in factory, school etc. where meals are provided

can'ter n./v. (move at) easy gallop

Can'terbury bell plant with bell-shaped flowers

can'tilever n. beam, girder etc. fixed at one end only

Canuck' n./a. C inf. Canadian

can'vas n. coarse cloth used for sails, painting on etc.

can'vass vt. solicit votes, contributions etc.; discuss

can'yon n. deep gorge

cap n. covering for head; lid, top -vt. put a cap on; outdo (-pp-)

ca'pable a. able; competent; having the power -capabil'ity n.

capac'ity [-pas'-] n. power of holding; room; volume; character; ability -capa'cious a. roomy

cape' n. covering for shoulders

cape' n. headland -Cape salmon SA the geelbek -Cape sparrow common S Afr. bird

ca'per' n. skip; frolic; escapade -vi. skip, dance

ca'per' n. pickled flower bud of Sicilian shrub

capill'ary a. hairlike -n. small blood vessel

cap'ital n. chief town; money; large-sized letter -a. involving or punishable by death; chief; excellent -cap'italism n. economic system based on private ownership of industry -cap'italist n./a. -cap'italize v. convert into capital; (with on) turn to advantage

capit'ulate vi. surrender

ca'pon n. castrated cock fowl fattened for eating

caprice' [-ēs'] n. whim, freak -capri'cious a.

cap'sicum n. sweet pepper

capsize' v. (of boat) (be) upset

cap'stan n. machine to wind cable

cap'sule [-syool] n. case for dose of medicine

Capt. Captain

cap'tain [-tin] n. commander of vessel or company of soldiers; leader -vt. be captain of

cap'tion n. heading, title of article, picture etc.

cap'tive n. prisoner -a. taken, imprisoned -cap'tivate vt. fascinate -captiv'ity n.

cap'ture vt. seize, make prisoner -n. seizure, taking -cap'tor n.

car n. self-propelled road vehicle; passenger compartment

carafe' [-raf'] n. glass water-bottle for the table, decanter

car'amel [ka'rə-] n. burnt sugar for cooking; chewy sweet

car'at [ka'rət] n. weight used for gold, diamonds etc.; proportional measure of twenty-fourths used to state fineness of gold

car'avan [ka'rə-] n. large vehicle for living in, pulled by car etc.; company of merchants travelling together

car'away [ka'rə-] n. plant with spicy seeds used in cakes etc.

carb'ide n. compound of carbon with an element, esp. calcium carbide

carbohy'drate n. any of compounds containing carbon, hydrogen and oxygen, esp. sugars and starches

carbol'ic (acid) disinfectant derived from coal tar

carb'on n. nonmetallic element, substance of pure charcoal, found in all organic matter -carb'onate n. salt of carbonic acid -carbonic acid compound formed by carbon dioxide and water -carbon dioxide colourless gas exhaled in respiration -carbon paper paper used for duplicating

car'buncle n. inflamed ulcer, boil or tumour

carburett'or [-byoo-] n. device for mixing petrol with air in engine

carc'ass, carc'ase n. dead animal body

carcin'ogen [-sin'-] n. substance producing cancer

card n. thick, stiff paper; piece of this giving identification etc.; illustrated card sending greetings etc.; playing card -pl. any card game -card'board n. thin, stiff board made of paper pulp

car'diac a. pert. to the heart -n. heart stimulant -car'diograph n. instrument which records movements of the heart

card'igan n. knitted jacket

card'inal a. chief, principal -n. highest rank, next to the Pope in R.C. church -cardinal numbers 1, 2, 3, etc.

care vi. be anxious; have regard or liking (for); look after; be disposed to -n. attention; protection; anxiety; caution -care'free a. -care'ful a. -care'less a. -care'taker n. person in charge of premises

career' n. course through life; profession; rapid motion -vi. run or move at full speed

caress' vt. fondle, embrace, treat with affection -n.

car'et [ka'rit] n. mark (∧) showing where to insert word(s) etc.

car'go n. load, freight, carried by ship, plane etc. (pl. -goes)

car'ibou [ka'ri-bōō] n. reindeer

car'icature [ka'ri-] n. likeness exaggerated to appear ridiculous -vt. portray in this way

ca'ries [kā'ri-ēz] n. decay of tooth or bone

carill'on [-yən or kā'-] n. set of bells played by keys, pedals etc.; tune so played

car'mine n. brilliant red colour -a. of this colour

carn'age n. slaughter

carn'al a. fleshly, sensual

carna'tion n. cultivated flower

carn'ival n. festive occasion; travelling fair

carniv'orous a. flesh-eating -carn'ivore n.

car'ol [ka'rəl] n./vi. (sing) song or hymn of joy (-ll-)

carouse' [-owz'] *vi.* have merry drinking spree -*n.* **carou'sal** *n.*

carousel' [-r-sel'] *n.* US merry-go-round

carp *vi.* find fault; nag

carp'enter *n.* worker in timber -**carp'entry** *n.* this art

carp'et *n.* heavy fabric for covering floor

carr'iage [-ij] *n.* railway coach; bearing; horse-drawn vehicle -**carr'iageway** *n.* part of a road along which traffic passes in a single line

carr'ion *n.* rotting dead flesh

carr'ot *n.* plant with orange-red edible root; inducement

carr'y *vt.* convey, transport; capture, win; effect; behave -*vi.* (of projectile, sound) reach (**carr'ied, carr'ying**) -**carr'ier** *n.*

cart *n.* open (two-wheeled) vehicle -*vt.* convey in cart; carry with effort

cartel' *n.* industrial combination for fixing prices *etc.*

cart'ilage *n.* firm elastic tissue in the body; gristle

cartog'raphy *n.* map making

cart'on *n.* cardboard or plastic container

cartoon' *n.* drawing, *esp.* humorous or satirical; sequence of drawings telling story -**cartoon'ist** *n.*

cart'ridge *n.* case containing charge for gun; container for film *etc.*; unit in gramophone pick-up

carve *vt.* cut; hew; sculpture; engrave; cut in pieces or slices (meat) -**carv'ing** *n.*

cascade' *n.* waterfall

case¹ *n.* instance; circumstance; question at issue; arguments supporting particular action *etc.*; *Med.* patient; law suit

case² *n.* box, sheath, covering; receptacle; box and contents -*vt.* put in a case

case'ment [kās'-] *n.* window opening on hinges

cash *n.* money, banknotes and coin -*vt.* turn into or exchange for money -**cashier'** *n.* one in charge of receiving and paying of money

cashier' *vt.* dismiss from office

cash'mere *n.* fine soft fabric made from goat's wool

casi'no [-sē'-] *n.* building, institution for gambling (*pl.* -**os**)

cask *n.* barrel

cask'et [-ah-] *n.* small case for jewels *etc.*

cass'erole *n.* fireproof cooking dish; stew

cassette' *n.* plastic container for film, magnetic tape *etc.*

cass'ock *n.* clergyman's long tunic

cast [kah-] *v.* throw or fling; shed; deposit (a vote); allot, as parts in play; mould -*n.* throw; squint; mould; that which is shed or ejected; set of actors; type or quality

castanets' *pl.n.* two small curved pieces of wood clicked together in hand

caste [kah-] *n.* section of society in India; social rank

cast'er **sugar** [kah-] finely powdered sugar (also **castor sugar**)

cas'tigate *vt.* rebuke severely

cas'tle [kahs'l] *n.* fortress; chess piece

cast'or [kah-] *n.* bottle with perforated top; small swivelled wheel on table leg *etc.*

castor oil vegetable medicinal oil

cas'trate *vt.* remove testicles

cas'ual [-z'-] *a.* accidental; unforeseen; occasional; unconcerned; informal -**cas'ualty** *n.* person killed or injured in accident, war *etc.* (*pl.* -**ties**)

cat *n.* any of various feline animals, including, *eg* small domesticated furred animal, and lions, tigers *etc.* -**catt'y** *a.* spiteful -**cat'call** *n.* derisive cry -**cat'kin** *n.* drooping flower spike -**cat'nap** *vi./n.* doze -**cat's-eye** *n.* glass reflector set in road to indicate traffic lanes

cat'aclysm *n.* [-kli-zəm] (disastrous) upheaval; deluge

cat'acomb [-kōōm, -kōm] *n.* underground gallery for burial

cat'alogue [-log] *n.* descriptive list -*vt.* make such list of

cat'alyst *n.* substance causing or assisting a chemical reaction without taking part in it

catamaran' *n.* type of sailing boat with twin hulls

cat'apult *n.* small forked stick with sling for throwing stones; launching device -*vt.*

cat'aract *n.* waterfall; downpour; disease of eye

catarrh' *n.* inflammation of a mucous membrane

catas'trophe [-fi] *n.* great disaster -**catastroph'ic** *a.*

catch *vt.* take hold of; hear; contract disease; be in time for; detect -*vi.* be contagious; get entangled; begin to

burn (caught *pt./pp.*) -n. seizure; thing that holds, stops *etc.*; what is caught; *inf.* snag, disadvantage -**catch'er** n. -**catch'ing** a.

cat'echism [-kizm] n. instruction by questions and answers

cat'egory n. class, order -**categor'ical** [-go'ri-] a. positive

ca'ter vi. provide, *esp.* food -**ca'terer** n.

cat'erpillar n. hairy grub of moth or butterfly

cathe'dral n. principal church of diocese

cath'ode n. negative electrode

cath'olic a. universal; including whole body of Christians; (C-) relating to R.C. Church -n. (C-) adherent of R.C. Church -**Cathol'icism** n.

cat'tle pl.n. beasts of pasture, *esp.* oxen, cows -**cat'tleman** n.

caul'dron n. large pot used for boiling

caul'iflower [kol'-] n. variety of cabbage with edible white flowering head

caulk [kawk] vt. stop up cracks with waterproof filler

cause [-z] n. that which produces an effect; reason; motive; charity, movement; lawsuit -vt. bring about, make happen

cause'way [-z-] n. raised way over marsh *etc.*

caus'tic a. burning; bitter -n. corrosive substance

cau'terize vt. burn with caustic or hot iron

cau'tion n. heedfulness, care; warning -vt. warn -**cau'tionary** a. -**cau'tious** a.

cavalcade' n. procession

cavalier' a. careless, disdainful -n. courtly gentleman; *obs.* horseman; (C-) adherent of Charles I

cav'alry n. mounted troops

cave n. hollow place in the earth; den -**cav'ern** n. deep cave -**cav'ernous** a. -**cav'ity** n. hollow

caviar(e) n. salted sturgeon roe

cav'il vi. make trifling objections (-ll-)

cavort' vi. prance, frisk

caw n. crow's cry -vi. cry so

cayenne' (pepper) [kā-] n. pungent red pepper

CB Companion of the Order of the Bath

CBE Commander of the British Empire

CBI Confederation of British Industry

cc cubic centimetre(s)

cease v. bring or come to an end -**cease'less** a.

ce'dar n. large evergreen tree

cede vt. yield, give up, transfer

cei'lidh [kā'li] n. informal social gathering *esp.* in Scotland

cei'ling [sē'-] n. inner, upper surface of a room

cel'ebrate v. have festivities to mark (happy day, event *etc.*); observe (birthday *etc.*); perform (religious ceremony *etc.*); praise publicly -**cel'ebrated** a. famous -**cele'bra'tion** n. -**celeb'rity** n. famous person; fame

cel'ery n. vegetable with long juicy edible stalks

celes'tial a. heavenly, divine

cel'ibacy n. unmarried state -**cel'ibate** n.

cell n. small room in prison; small cavity; minute, basic unit of living matter; device converting chemical into electrical energy -**cell'ular** a.

cell'ar n. underground room for storage; stock of wine

cell'o [ch-] n. stringed instrument of violin family

Cell'ophane R transparent wrapping

Cell'uloid [-yoo-] R synthetic plastic substance

cell'ulose [-yoo-] n. fibrous carbohydrate

Cel'sius a./n. (of) scale of temperature from 0° to 100°

cement' n. fine mortar; glue -vt. unite as with cement

cem'etery n. burial ground

cen'otaph n. monument to one buried elsewhere

cen'ser n. incense burner

cen'sor n. one authorized to examine films, books *etc.* and suppress part(s) considered unacceptable -vt. -**censor'ious** a. faultfinding -**cen'sorship** n.

cen'sure n./vt. blame

cen'sus n. official counting of people, things *etc.*

cent n. hundredth part of dollar *etc.*

cen'taur n. mythical creature, half man, half horse

cen'tenary n. 100 years; celebration of hundredth anniversary -a. pert. to a hundred

cen'tigrade a. another name for Celsius

cent'imetre n. hundredth part of metre

cent'ipede n. small segmented animal with many legs

cen'tre n. midpoint; pivot; place for specific organization or activity **-cen'tral** a. **-cen'tralize** vt. bring to a centre; concentrate under one control **-cen'trally** adv. **-centrif'ugal** a. tending from centre

centu'rion n. Roman commander of 100 men

cen'tury n. 100 years; any set of 100

ceram'ics pl.n. (with sing. v.) art, techniques of making clay, porcelain objects

ce'real n. any edible grain; (breakfast) food -a.

cer'ebral a. pert. to brain

cer'emony n. formal observance; sacred rite; courteous act **-ceremo'nial** a./n.

cerise' [sǝ-rēz'] n./a. clear, pinkish red

cer'tain a. sure; inevitable; some, one; of moderate (quantity, degree etc.) **-cer'tainly** adv. **-cer'tainty** n.

cer'tify vt. declare formally; guarantee **(-fied, -fying) -certif'icate** n. written declaration

cer'vix n. neck, esp. of womb

cessa'tion n. stop, pause

cess'ion n. yielding up

cess'pool n. pit for sewage

cf. confer (Lat., compare)

cgs units metric system of units based on centimetre, gram, second

chafe vt. make sore by rubbing; warm; vex

chaff [-ah-] n. husks of corn; worthless matter -v. tease

chaff'inch n. small songbird

chag'rin [sh-] n. vexation, disappointment -vt. embarrass

chain n. series of connected rings; thing that binds; connected series of things or events; surveyor's measure -vt. fasten with a chain; restrain

chair n. movable seat, with back, for one person; seat of authority -vt. preside over; carry in triumph **-chair'man** n. one who presides over meeting **-chair'manship** n.

chal'et [shal'ā] n. Swiss wooden house

chal'ice n. Poet. cup

chalk [chawk] n. white substance, carbonate of lime; crayon -v. mark with chalk **-chalk'y** a.

chall'enge vt. call to fight or account; dispute; stimulate -n.

cha'mber n. (room for) assembly; compartment; cavity -pl. office or apartment of barrister **-cha'mbermaid** n. servant with care of bedrooms

chame'leon [kǝ-] n. lizard with power of changing colour

cham'fer n./vt. groove

cham'ois [sham'wah] n. goatlike mountain antelope; [sham'i] a soft pliable leather

champ v. munch noisily; be impatient

champagne' [sham-pān'] n. light, sparkling white wine

cham'pion n. one that excels all others; defender of a cause -vt. fight for **-cham'pionship** n.

chance [-ah-] n. unpredictable course of events; luck; opportunity; possibility; risk; probability -vt. risk -vi. happen -a. casual, unexpected **-chan'cy** a.

chan'cel [-ah-] n. part of a church where altar is

chan'cellor [-ah-] n. high officer of state; head of university

chandelier' [sh-] n. hanging frame with branches for lights

chand'ler [-ah-] n. dealer in ropes, ships' supplies etc.

change v. alter, make or become different; put on (different clothes, fresh coverings) -vt. put or give for another; exchange -n. alteration; variety; coins; balance received on payment **-change'able** a.

chann'el n. bed of stream; strait; deeper part of strait; groove; means of conveying; band of radio frequencies; television broadcasting station -vt. groove; guide

chant [-ah-] n. simple song or melody; rhythmic slogan -v. utter chant; speak monotonously

cha'os [kā'-] n. disorder, confusion **-chaot'ic** a.

chap' v. of skin, become raw and cracked **(-pp-) -chapped** a.

chap' n. inf. fellow, man

chap'el n. division of church with its own altar; Nonconformist place of worship

chap'eron(e) [sh-] n. one who attends young unmarried lady in public -vt. attend in this way

chap'lain [-lin] n. clergyman attached to regiment etc.

chap'ter n. division of book; assembly of clergy; organized branch of society

char vt. scorch (-rr-)

char'acter [ka-] n. nature; qualities making up individuality; moral qualities; an eccentric; fictional person **-characteris'tic** a. **-char'-acterize** vt. mark out; describe

charade' [shə-rahd'] n. absurd act -pl. word-guessing game

char'coal n. charred wood

charge vt. ask as price; bring accusation against; lay task on; attack; fill (with electricity) vi. make onrush, attack -n. price; accusation; attack; command; accumulation of electricity **-charge'able** a. **-char'ger** n. that which charges, esp. electrically; warhorse

char'iot [cha-] n. two-wheeled car used in ancient fighting; state carriage **-charioteer'** n.

charis'ma [kə-riz'-] n. special power of individual to inspire fascination, loyalty etc.

char'ity [cha-] n. giving of help, money to needy; organization for this; love, kindness **-char'itable** a.

char'latan [sh-] n. impostor

charm n. attractiveness; anything that fascinates; amulet; magic spell -vt. bewitch; delight **-charm'ing** a.

chart n. map of sea; tabulated statement -vt. map

char'ter n. document granting privileges etc. -vt. let or hire; establish by charter

char'woman n. woman paid to clean office, house etc.

cha'ry a. cautious, sparing

chase vt. hunt, pursue; drive from, away, into etc. -n. pursuit, hunting

chasm [kazm] n. deep cleft

chass'is [shas'i] n. framework of motor vehicle

chaste a. virginal; pure; modest; virtuous **-chas'tity** n.

cha'sten [-sən] vt. correct by punishment; subdue **-chastise'** [chas-tīz'] vt. inflict punishment on

chat vi. talk idly, or familiarly (-tt-) -n. such talk

chat'eau [shat'ō] n. (esp. in France) castle, country house (pl. -teaux [-tō] or -teaus)

chatt'el n. any movable property

chatt'er vi. talk idly or rapidly; rattle teeth -n. idle talk

chau'ffeur [shō'fər], n. paid driver of motorcar

cheap a. low in price; of little value; inferior **-cheap'en** vt.

cheat vt. deceive -vi. practise deceit to gain advantage -n. fraud

check vt. stop; control; examine -n. stoppage; restraint; brief examination; pattern of squares; threat to king at chess **-check'mate** n./vt. Chess (make) final winning move **-check'out** n. counter in supermarket where customers pay **-check'up** n. examination (esp. medical) to see if all is in order

cheek n. side of face below eye; inf. impudence **-cheek'y** a.

cheep vi./n. (utter) high-pitched cry, as of young bird

cheer n. comfort; gladden; encourage by shouts -vi. shout applause -n. shout of approval; happiness; mood **-cheer'ful** a. **-cheer'ily** adv. **-cheer'less** a. **-cheer'y** a.

cheese n. food made from solidified curd of milk **-chees'y** a. **-cheese'-cloth** n. loosely woven cotton cloth

chee'tah n. large, swift, spotted feline animal

chef [sh-] n. head cook

chem'istry [k-] n. science concerned with properties of substances and their combinations and reactions **-chem'ical** n./a. **-chem'ist** n. dispenser of medicines; shop that sells medicines etc.; one trained in chemistry

chenille' [shə-nēl'] n. soft cord, fabric of silk or worsted

cheque [-ek] n. written order to banker to pay money from one's account; printed slip of paper used for this **-cheque'book** n. book of cheques **-cheque card** banker's card

cheq'uer [-ər] n. marking as on chessboard; marble, peg etc. used in games -vt. mark in squares; variegate **-cheq'uered** a.

cher'ish vt. treat tenderly

cheroot' [sh-] n. cigar

cher'ry n. small red fruit with stone; tree bearing it

cher'ub n. winged creature with human face; angel (pl. cher'ubim, cher'ubs) **-cheru'bic** a.

cher'vil n. a herb

chess n. game of skill played by two on chequered board

chest n. upper part of trunk of body; large, strong box **-chest of drawers** piece of furniture containing drawers **-chest'erfield** n. padded sofa

chest'nut [-s'n-] n. tree bearing

large nut in prickly husk; *inf.* old joke -a. reddish-brown

chev'ron [sh-] *n. Mil.* V-shaped braid designating rank

chew [-ōō] *v.* grind with teeth -n.

chian'ti [ki-] *n.* It. wine

chic [shēk] *a.* stylish -n.

chica'nery [shi-] *n.* quibbling

chick, chick'en *n.* young of birds, *esp.* of hen; *sl.* girl, young woman -**chick'enpox** *n.* infectious disease

chic'ory *n.* salad plant whose root is used instead of coffee

chide *vt.* scold (**chid** *pt.*, **chidd'en**, **chid** *pp.*), **chi'ding** *pr.p.*)

chief *n.* head or principal person -a. principal, foremost -**chief'ly** *adv.*

chiff'on [sh-] *n.* gauzy material

chi'gnon [shē'nyon] *n.* roll of hair worn at back of head

chihua'hua [chi-wah'wah] *n.* breed of tiny dog

chil'blain *n.* inflamed sore on hands, legs *etc.*, due to cold

child [-ī-] *n.* young human being; offspring (*pl.* **child'ren** [-i-]) -**child'ish** [-ī-] *a.* silly -**child'like** *a.* of or like a child; innocent -**child'hood** *n.*

chill *n.* coldness; cold with shivering; anything that discourages -v. make, become cold -**chill'y** *a.*

chill'i *n.* small red hot-tasting seed pod

chime *n.* sound of bell -vi. ring harmoniously; agree -vt. strike (bells)

chim'ney *n.* passage for smoke (*pl.* -neys)

chimpanzee' *n.* ape of Africa

chin *n.* part of face below mouth

chi'na *n.* fine earthenware, porcelain; cups, saucers *etc.*

chincherinchee' *n.* S Afr. plant with white or yellow flower spikes

chinchill'a *n.* S Amer. rodent with soft, grey fur

Chinese lantern Asian plant cultivated for its orange-red inflated calyx

chink *n.* cleft, crack

chintz *n.* cotton cloth printed in coloured designs

chip *n.* splinter; place where piece has been broken off; thin strip of potato, fried; tiny wafer of silicon forming integrated circuit -vt. chop into small pieces; break small pieces from -vi. break off (**pp.** -**pp-**) -**chip** in interrupt; contribute

chip'munk *n.* small, striped N Amer. squirrel

chipolat'a [-lah'-] *n.* small sausage

chirop'odist [ki-] *n.* one who treats disorders of feet -**chirop'ody** *n.*

chirp, chirr'up *n./vi.* (make) short, sharp cry -**chir'py** *a. inf.* happy

chis'el [-z'-] *n.* cutting tool -vt. cut with chisel; *sl.* cheat (-**ll**-)

chit *n.* informal note

chiv'alry [sh-] *n.* bravery and courtesy; medieval system of knighthood -**chiv'alrous** *a.*

chive *n.* herb with onion flavour

chlor'ine [kl-] *n.* nonmetallic element, yellowish-green poison gas -**chlor'ide** *n.* bleaching agent -**chlor'inate** *vt.* disinfect

chlor'oform [kl-] *n.* volatile liquid formerly used as anaesthetic

chlor'ophyll [kl-] *n.* green colouring matter in plants

chock *n.* block or wedge

choc'olate *n.* confectionery, drink made from ground cacao seeds

choice *n.* act or power of choosing; alternative; thing or person chosen -a. select, fine

choir [kwīr] *n.* band of singers

choke *vt.* hinder, stop the breathing of; smother, stifle; obstruct -vi. suffer choking -n. act, noise of choking; device to increase richness of petrol-air mixture

chol'era [k-] *n.* deadly infectious disease

choles'terol [kol-] *n.* substance found in animal tissue and fat

choose *vt.* pick out, select; take by preference -vi. decide, think fit (**chose**, **cho'sen**, **choo'sing**) -**choo'sy** *a.* fussy

chop *vt.* cut with blow; hack (-**pp**-) -n. hewing blow; cut of meat with bone -**chopp'er** *n.* short axe; *inf.* helicopter -**chopp'y** *a.* (of sea) having short, broken waves

chop'sticks *pl.n.* implements used by Chinese for eating food

chor'al [k-] *a.* of, for a choir

chorale' [-rahl'-] *n.* slow, stately hymn tune

chord [k-] *n.* simultaneous sounding of musical notes

chore *n.* (unpleasant) task

choreog'raphy [ko-ri-] *n.* art of arranging dances, *esp.* ballet -**choreog'rapher** *n.*

chor'tle *vi.* chuckle happily -n.

chor'us [k-] *n.* (music for) band of singers; refrain -vt. sing or say together

chow[1] n. inf. food

chow[2] n. thick-coated dog with curled tail, orig. from China

Chris'tian [kris'chən] n. follower of Christ -a. -**chris'ten** [kris'n] vt. baptize, give name to -**Christian'ity** n. religion of Christ

Christ'mas [kris'-] n. festival of birth of Christ

chromat'ic [krə-] a. of colour; Mus. of scale proceeding by semitones

chrome, chro'mium [krō'-] n. metal used in alloys and for plating

chro'mosome [krō'-] n. microscopic gene-carrying body in the tissue of a cell

chron'ic [-kr-] a. lasting a long time; habitual; inf. serious; inf. of bad quality

chron'icle [kr-] n./vt. (write) record of historical events

chronolog'ical a. arranged in order of time

chronom'eter [kr-] n. instrument for measuring time exactly; watch

chrys'alis [kris'-] n. resting stage of insect; case enclosing it (pl. **chrys'alises, chrysal'ides** [-idēz])

chrysan'themum [kri-] n. garden flower of various colours

chubb'y a. plump

chuck inf. vt. throw; pat affectionately (under chin); give up

chuck'le vi. laugh softly -n. such laugh

chum n. inf. close friend -**chumm'y** a.

chunk n. thick, solid piece

church n. building for Christian worship; (C-) whole body or sect of Christians; clergy

churl'ish a. rude or surly

churn n. large container for milk; vessel for making butter -v. shake up, stir

chute [shōōt] n. slide for sending down parcels, coal etc.

chut'ney n. pickle of fruit, spices etc.

CIA US Central Intelligence Agency

CID Criminal Investigation Department

ci'der n. fermented drink made from apples

cigar' n. roll of tobacco leaves for smoking -**cigarette'** n. finely-cut tobacco rolled in paper for smoking

C-in-C Commander-in-Chief

cinch n. inf. easy task

cin'der n. remains of burned coal

cin'ema n. building used for showing of films; films generally -**cin'ematograph** n. combined camera, printer and projector

cinn'amon n. spice got from bark of Asian tree

ci'pher, cy'pher n. secret writing; arithmetical symbol; person of no importance

cir'ca Lat. about, approximately

cir'cle n. perfectly round figure; ring; Theatre section of seats above main level of auditorium; group, society with common interest -vt. surround -vi. move round -**cir'clar** a. round -n. letter sent to several persons -**cir'culate** vi. move round; pass round -vt. send round -**circula'tion** n. flow of blood; act of moving round; extent of sale of newspaper etc.

cir'cuit [-kit] n. complete round or course; area; path of electric current; round of visitation -**circu'itous** a. indirect

cir'cumcise [-z] vt. cut off foreskin of -**circumcis'ion** n.

circum'ference n. boundary line, esp. of circle

cir'cumscribe [or -skrīb'] vt. confine, bound, limit

cir'cumspect a. cautious

cir'cumstance n. detail; event -pl. state of affairs; condition in life, esp. financial; surroundings or things accompanying an action -**circumstan'tial** a.

circumvent' vt. outwit, evade, get round

cir'cus n. (performance of) acrobats, clowns, performing animals etc. (pl. **-es**)

cirrho'sis [si-rō'-] n. disease of liver

cis'tern n. water tank

cit'adel n. city fortress

cite vt. quote; bring forward as proof -**cita'tion** n. quoting; commendation for bravery etc.

cit'izen n. member of state, nation etc.; inhabitant of city -**cit'izenship** n.

cit'ron n. fruit like lemon -**cit'ric** a. of the acid of lemon or citron -**citrus** fruit lemons, oranges etc.

cit'y n. a large town

civ'et n. strong, musky perfume -**civet-cat** n. catlike animal producing it

civ'ic a. pert. to city or citizen -**civ'ics** pl.n. (with sing. v.) study of the rights and responsibilities of citizenship

civ'il a. relating to citizens; not military; refined, polite; Law not criminal **-civil'ian** n. nonmilitary person **-civil'ity** n.

civ'ilize vt. bring out of barbarism; refine **-civiliza'tion** n. **-civ'ilized** a.

clack n. sound, as of pieces of wood striking together -n.

claim vt. demand as right; assert; call for -n. demand for thing supposed due; right; thing claimed **-claim'ant** n.

clairvoy'ance [-voi'-] n. power of seeing things not present to senses **-clairvoy'ant** n./a.

clam n. edible mollusc

clam'ber vi. to climb awkwardly

clamm'y a. moist and sticky

clam'our n./vi. (make) loud outcry **-clam'orous** a.

clamp n. tool for holding -vt. fasten with or as with clamp

clan n. collection of families of common ancestry; group

clandes'tine a. secret; sly

clang v. (cause to) make loud ringing sound -n. this sound

clank n. metallic sound -v. cause, move with, such sound

clap v. (cause to) strike with noise; strike (hands) together; applaud -vt. pat; place or put quickly (-pp-) -n. hard, explosive sound; slap

clar'et [kla'rət] n. a dry red wine

clar'ify [kla'ri-] v. make or become clear (-fied, -fying) **-clarifica'tion** n. **-clar'ity** n. clearness

clarinet' n. woodwind instrument

clash n. loud noise; conflict, collision -vi. make clash; come into conflict -vt. strike together

clasp [-ah-] n. hook or fastening; embrace -vt. fasten; embrace, grasp

class [-ah-] n. any division, order, kind, sort; rank; group of school pupils; division by merit; quality -vt. assign to proper division **-class'ify** [klas'-] vt. arrange methodically in classes (-fied, -fying) **-classifica'tion** n.

class'ic a. of highest rank esp. of art; typical; famous -n. (literary) work of recognized excellence **-pl.n.** ancient Latin and Greek literature **-class'ical** a.

clatt'er n. rattling noise -v. (cause to) make clatter

clause [-z] n. part of sentence; article in formal document

claustropho'bia n. abnormal fear of confined spaces

clav'icle n. collarbone

claw n. sharp hooked nail of bird or beast -vt. tear with claws

clay n. fine-grained earth, plastic when wet, hardening when baked; earth **-clay'ey** a.

clean a. free from dirt; pure; guiltless; trim -adv. so as to leave no dirt; entirely -vt. free from dirt **-clean'liness** [klen'-] n. **-clean'ly** [klen'] adv. -a. [klen'-] clean **-cleanse** [klenz] vt. make clean

clear a. pure, bright; free from cloud; transparent; plain, distinct; without defect; unimpeded -adv. brightly; wholly, quite -vt. make clear; acquit; pass over; make as profit; free from obstruction, difficulty -vi. become clear, bright, free, transparent **-clear'ance** n. **-clear'ing** n. land cleared of trees

cleat n. wedge; device round which ropes are made fast

cleave[1] v. (cause to) split (clove, cleft pp. clo'ven, cleft pp. cleav'ing pr.p.) **-cleav'age** n. **-cleav'er** n. short chopper

cleave[2] vi. stick, adhere; be loyal (cleaved, cleav'ing)

clef n. Mus. mark to show pitch

cleft n. crack, fissure, chasm

cleg n. horsefly

clem'atis [or -a'tis] n. climbing plant

clem'ent a. merciful; gentle; mild **-clem'ency** n.

clench [-ch, -sh] vt. set firmly together; grasp, close (fist)

cler'gy n. body of ministers of Christian church **-cler'gyman** n.

cler'ical [kler'ik-] a. of clergy; of office work

clerk [-ark, US -erk] n. subordinate who keeps files etc.; officer in charge of records, correspondence etc.

clev'er a. intelligent; able, skilful, adroit

cli'ché [clē'shā] n. stereotyped hackneyed phrase (pl. -s)

click n./vi. (make) short, sharp sound

cli'ent n. customer **-cliente'tele'** [klē-on-tel'] n. clients

cliff n. steep rock face

cli'mate n. condition of country with regard to weather

cli'max n. highest point, culmination **-climac'tic** a.

climb [klīm] v. go up or ascend

clinch vt. conclude (agreement)

cling vi. adhere; be firmly attached to (**cling** pt./pp.)

clin'ic n. place for medical examination, advice, or treatment —**clin'ical** a.

clink n. sharp metallic sound —v. (cause to) make this sound

clip' vt. cut with scissors; cut short (-**pp**-) —n. inf. sharp blow

clip' n. device for holding

clipp'er n. fast sailing ship

clique [-ēk] n. small exclusive set; faction, group of people

clit'oris n. small erectile part of female genitals

cloak n./vt. (cover with) loose outer garment; disguise

clobb'er inf. vt. beat, batter

clock n. instrument for measuring time —**clock'wise** adv./a. in the direction that the hands of a clock rotate

clod n. lump of earth

clog vt. hamper, impede, choke up (-**gg**-) —n. obstruction, impediment; wooden-soled shoe

clois'ter n. covered pillared arcade; monastery or convent —**clois'tered** a. secluded

clone n. cells of same genetic constitution as another, derived by asexual reproduction —v.

close' [-s] a. near; compact; crowded; intimate; almost equal; searching; confined; secret; unventilated; niggardly; restricted —adv. nearly, tightly —n. shut-in place; precinct of cathedral —**close'up** n. close view

close' [-z] vt. shut; stop up; prevent access to; finish —vi. come together, grapple —n. end

clot n. mass or lump (of blood); inf. fool —v. (cause to) form into lumps (-**tt**-)

cloth [-th] n. woven fabric —**clothes** [-TH] pl.n. dress; bed coverings —**clothe** vt. put clothes on (**clothed** [klōTHd] or **clad** pt./pp.) —**clo'thing** n.

cloud n. vapour floating in air; state of gloom —vt. darken —vi. become cloudy —**cloud'y** a.

clout n. inf. blow; influence, power —vt. strike

clove n. pungent spice

clo'ver n. forage plant

clown n. circus comic

cloy vt. weary by sweetness

club n. thick stick; bat; association; suit at cards —vt. strike —vi. join (-**bb**-)

cluck vi./n. (make) noise of hen

clue n. indication, esp. of solution of mystery or puzzle

clump' n. cluster of plants

clump' vi. tread heavily —n.

clum'sy [-z-] a. awkward —**clums'ily** adv.

clus'ter n./v. group, bunch

clutch v. grasp eagerly; snatch (at) —n. grasp, tight grip; device enabling two revolving shafts to be (dis)connected at will

clutt'er v./n. disorder

cm centimetre(s)

Co. Company; County

c/o care of; carried over

coach n. long-distance bus; large four-wheeled carriage; railway carriage; tutor, instructor —vt. instruct

coag'ulate v. curdle, clot

coal n. mineral used as fuel; glowing ember

coalesce' [-les'] vi. unite

coali'tion n. alliance

coarse a. rough; unrefined; indecent —**coarse'ly** adv.

coast n. sea shore —v. move under momentum; sail by the coast —**coast'er** n. small ship

coat n. sleeved outer garment; animal's fur; covering layer —vt. cover

coax [kōks] vt. persuade

cob n. short-legged stout horse; male swan; head of corn

co'balt n. metallic element; blue pigment from it

cobb'le vt. patch roughly; mend shoes —n. round stone

co'bra n. venomous, hooded snake

cob'web n. spider's web

cocaine' [-kān'] n. addictive narcotic drug used medicinally

cochineal' n. scarlet dye

cock n. male bird, esp. of domestic fowl; tap; hammer of gun —v. draw back to firing position; raise, turn —**cock'eye(d)** a. crosseyed; askew

cockade' n. rosette for hat

cockatoo' n. crested parrot

cock'le n. shellfish

cock'pit n. pilot's seat, compartment in small aircraft

cock'roach n. insect pest

cock'tail n. mixed drink of spirits; appetizer

cock'y a. conceited, pert

co'coa [-kō] n. powdered seed of cacao; drink made from this

co'conut n. large, hard nut

cocoon' n. sheath of insect in chrysalis stage

co'copan n. SA small truck on rails used esp. in mines

COD cash on delivery

cod n. large sea fish

co'da n. Mus. final part of musical composition

cod'dle vt. overprotect

code n. system of letters, symbols to transmit messages secretly; scheme of conduct; collection of laws —**co'dify** vt. (-**fied, -fying**)

co'deine [-dēn] n. alkaline sedative, analgesic drug

cod'icil n. addition to will

coeduca'tional a. of education of boys and girls together —**co-ed** n. coeducational school etc. —a.

coeffi'cient [-fish-] n. Maths. numerical or constant factor

coerce' [kō-ers'] vt. compel, force —**coer'cion** n.

coexist' vt. exist together

C of E Church of England

coff'ee n. seeds of tropical shrub; drink made from these

coff'er n. chest for valuables

coff'in n. box for corpse

cog n. one of series of teeth on rim of wheel —**cog'wheel** n.

co'gent a. convincing

cog'itate [koj'-] v/i. think, reflect, ponder —**cogita'tion** n.

cogn'ac [kon'yak] n. French brandy

cog'nate a. related, kindred

cog'nizance [or kon'-] n. knowledge —**cog'nizant** a.

cohab'it v/i. live together as husband and wife

cohere' v/i. stick together, be consistent —**cohe'rent** a. capable of logical speech, thought; connected, making sense

co'hort n. troop; associate

coiffure' [kwah-fyoor'] n. hairstyle

coil v. twist in winding shape —n. series of rings; anything coiled

coin n. piece of money; money —vt. stamp; invent —**coin'age** n.

coincide' [kō-in-] v/i. happen together —**coin'cidence** n.

coit'ion [kō-ish'-] n. sexual intercourse (also **co'itus** [kō'it-])

coke' n. residue left from distillation of coal, used as fuel

coke' sl. n. Coca-Cola; cocaine

Col. Colonel

col'ander, cull'ender n. culinary strainer

cold a. lacking heat; indifferent, un-

moved; unfriendly —n. lack of heat; illness, marked by runny nose etc. —**cold'ly** adv. —**cold-blooded** a. lacking pity —**cold war** nonmilitary hostility

cole'slaw n. cabbage salad

col'ic n. severe pains in the intestines

collab'orate v/i. work with another —**collabora'tion** n. —**collab'orator** n.

collage' [-ahzh'] n. (artistic) composition of bits and pieces stuck together on background

collapse' v/i. fall; fail —n. act of collapsing; breakdown —**collaps'ible, -able** a.

coll'ar n. band, part of garment, worn round neck —vt. seize

collate' vt. compare carefully

collat'eral n. security pledged for loan —a. side by side; of same stock but different line

coll'eague [-ēg] n. fellow worker

collect' v. gather, bring, come together —**collec'tion** n. —**collec'tion** n. —**collec'tive** n. factory, farm etc., owned by the workers —a. —**collec'tor** n.

coll'ege [-lij] n. place of higher education —**colle'giate** a.

collide' v/i. crash together —**colli'sion** [-lizh'un] n.

coll'ie n. breed of sheepdog

coll'ier n. coal miner

coll'oid n. suspension of particles in a solution

collo'quial a. pert. to, or used in, informal conversation —**collo'quialism** n.

collu'sion [-loo'-] n. secret agreement for a fraudulent purpose

cologne' [kə-lōn'] n. perfumed liquid

co'lon n. mark (:) indicating break in a sentence

co'lon n. part of large intestine

colonel [kur'nəl] n. commander of regiment or battalion

colonnade' n. row of columns

col'ony n. body of people who settle in new country; country so settled —**colo'nial** a. —**col'onist** n. —**col'onize** vt.

col'ophon n. publisher's imprint or device

coloss'us n. huge statue (pl. **coloss'i** [-ī], **-suses**) —**coloss'al** a. huge, gigantic

col'our [kul'ər] n. hue, tint; complexion; paint; pigment; fig. semblance, pretext; timbre, quality -pl. flag; Sport distinguishing badge, symbol -vt. stain, paint; disguise; influence or distort -vi. blush -col'ourded a. non-White; in S Africa, of mixed descent -col'ourful a.

colt [-ō-] n. young male horse

col'umbine n. flower with five spurred petals

col'umn [-m] n. long vertical pillar; division of page; body of troops -col'umnist n. journalist writing regular feature

co'ma n. unconsciousness

comb [kōm] n. toothed instrument for tidying hair; cock's crest; mass of honey cells -vt. use comb on; search

com'bat vt./n. fight, contest -com'batant n. -com'bative a.

combine' v. join together -n. [kom¹-] syndicate, esp. of businesses -combina'tion n. -combine har'vester machine to harvest and thresh grain

combus'tion n. process of burning -combus'tible a.

come [kum] vi. approach, arrive, move towards; reach; occur; originate (from); become (came, come, com'ing) -come'back n. inf. return to active life; inf. retort

com'edy n. light, amusing play; humour -come'dian n. entertainer who tells jokes (comedienne' fem.)

come'ly [kum¹-] a. good-looking

com'et n. luminous heavenly body

com'fort [kum¹-] n. ease; (means of) consolation -vt. soothe; console -com'fortable a. -com'forter n.

com'ic a. relating to comedy; funny -n. comedian; magazine of strip cartoons -com'ical a.

comm'a n. punctuation mark (,)

command' [-mahnd¹] vt. order; rule; compel; have in one's power -n. order; power of controlling; mastery; post of one commanding; jurisdiction -comm'andant n. -commandeer' vt. seize for military use -command'er n. -command'ment n.

comman'do [-mahn¹dō] n. (member of) special military unit (pl. -dos)

commem'orate vt. keep in memory by ceremony

commence' v. begin

commend' vt. praise; entrust -commend'able a. -commenda'tion n.

commen'surate a. equal; in proportion

comm'ent n./vi. remark; gossip; note -comm'entary n. explanatory notes; spoken accompaniment to film etc. -comm'entate vi. -comm'entator n.

comm'erce n. trade -commer'cial a. of business, trade etc. -n. advertisement, esp. on radio or television

commis'erate [-miz¹-] vt. sympathize with

commiss'ariat n. military department of food supplies

commiss'ion [-sh¹-] n. authority; (body entrusted with) some special duty; agent's payment by percentage; document appointing to officer's rank; committing -vt. charge with duty; Mil. confer a rank; give order for -commiss'ioner n.

commissionaire' n. doorkeeper

commit' vt. give in charge; be guilty of; pledge; send for trial (-tt-) -commit'ment n. -committ'al n.

committ'ee n. body appointed, elected for special business

commode' n. chest of drawers; stool containing chamber pot

commod'ity n. article of trade

comm'on a. shared by all; public; ordinary; inferior -n. land belonging to community -pl. ordinary people; (C-) House of Commons -comm'oner n. one not of the nobility -comm'only adv. -comm'onwealth n. republic; (C-) federation of self-governing states

commo'tion n. stir, disturbance

commune'¹ [-myōo-] vi. converse intimately -commu'nion n. sharing of thoughts, feelings; body with common faith; (C-) (participation in) sacrament of the Lord's Supper

comm'une² n. group living together and sharing property, responsibility etc. -comm'unal a. for common use

commu'nicate vt. impart, convey; reveal -vi. give or exchange information; have connecting door -commu'nicable a. -communica'tion n. giving information; message; (usu. pl.) passage or means of exchanging messages

communiqué [-ni-kā] n. official announcement

comm'unism n. doctrine that all means of production etc., should be property of community -comm'unist n./a.

commu'nity n. body of people

living in one district; the public; joint ownership; similarity

commute[1] [-myōō] vi. travel daily some distance to work -vt. exchange; reduce (punishment) **-commut'er** n.

compact[1] a. closely packed; solid; terse -v. make, become compact

com'pact[2] n. small case to hold face powder etc.

com'pact[3] n. agreement

compan'ion n. comrade

compan'ionway n. staircase from deck to cabin

com'pany [kum-] n. gathering of persons; companionship; guests; business firm; division of regiment

compare[1] vt. notice likenesses and differences; liken -vi. be like; compete with **-comparabil'ity** n. **-com'parable** a. **-compar'ative** [-pa'rə-] a. relative -n. **-compar'ison** [-pa'ri-] n. act of comparing

compart'ment n. part divided off

com'pass [kum-] n. instrument for showing north; (usu. pl.) instrument for drawing circles; scope -vt. surround; comprehend; attain

compas'sion [-sh-] n. pity, sympathy **-compas'sionate** a.

compat'ible a. agreeing with

compat'riot n. fellow countryman

compel' vt. force (-ll-)

compen'dium n. collection of different games; summary (pl. -s, -ia)

com'pensate vt. make up for; recompense **-compensa'tion** n.

com'père [kom'per] n. one who introduces cabaret, television shows etc. -vt.

compete' vi. (oft. with with) strive in rivalry, contend for **-competi'tion** n. **-compet'itive** a. **-compet'itor** n.

com'petent a. able; properly qualified; sufficient **-com'petence** n. efficiency

compile' vt. make up from various sources

compla'cent a. self-satisfied **-compla'cence** n. **-cency** n.

complain' vt. grumble; make known a grievance; (with of) make known that one is suffering from **-complaint'** n. grievance; illness

complai'sance n. affability

com'plement n. something making up a whole -vt. add to, make complete **-complemen'tary** a.

complete' a. perfect; ended; entire; thorough -vt. make whole; finish **-complete'ly** adv. **-comple'tion** n.

com'plex a. intricate, compound, involved -n. group of related buildings; obsession **-complex'ity** n.

complex'ion [-ek'shən] n. look, colour, of skin, esp. of face; aspect, character

com'plicate vt. make involved, difficult **-complica'tion** n.

complic'ity [-plis'-] n. partnership in wrongdoing

com'pliment n. expression of regard, praise -pl. formal greetings -vt. praise **-complimen'tary** a. expressing praise; free of charge

comply' vi. do as asked (complied', comply'ing) **-compli'ance** n. **-compli'ant** a.

compo'nent n. part, constituent of whole

compose' vt. put in order; write, invent; make up; calm **-compo'ser** n. one who composes, esp. music **-com'posite** a. made up of distinct parts **-composi'tion** n. **-compo'sure** n. calmness

com'post n. decayed vegetable matter for fertilizing soil

com'pound[1] n. substance, word, made up of parts -a. not simple; composite -vt. [kam-pownd'] mix, make up; make worse; compromise

com'pound[2] n. enclosure containing houses etc.

comprehend' vt. understand; include **-comprehen'sible** a. **-comprehen'sion** n. **-comprehen'sive** a. taking in much

compress' vt. squeeze together; make smaller -n. [kom'-] pad of lint applied to wound, inflamed part etc. **-compres'sible** a. **-compres'sion** [-sh'-] n. **-compres'sor** n.

comprise' vt. include, contain

com'promise [-tz] n. coming to terms by giving up part of claim -v. settle by making concessions -vt. expose to suspicion

comptom'eter R a calculating machine

compul'sion n. act of compelling **-compul'sive** a. **-compul'sory** a. not optional

compunc'tion n. regret

compute' [-pyōō] vt. calculate **-computa'tion** n. **-compu'ter** n. electronic machine for processing information **-compu'terize** v. equip with, perform by computer

com'rade n. friend

con[1] v. inf. swindle

con[2] n. against

con'cave [*or* -kāv'] a. rounded inwards

conceal' [-sēl'] vt. hide

concede' [-sēd'] vt. admit truth of; grant

conceit' [-sēt'] n. vanity **-conceit'ed** a.

conceive' [-sēv'] v. imagine; believe; become pregnant **-conceiv'able** a.

con'centrate vt. focus (one's efforts *etc.*); increase in strength *etc.*); devote all attention to. concentrated substance **-concentra'tion** n.

concen'tric a. having the same centre

con'cept n. abstract idea

concep'tion n. idea, notion; act of conceiving

concern' vt. relate to; affect; (*with* in *or* with) involve (oneself) -n. affair; worry; business, enterprise **-concerned'** a. worried; involved **-concern'ing** prep. about

con'cert n. musical entertainment; agreement **-concert'ed** a. mutually planned **-concerti'na** [-sǝr-tē'-] n. musical instrument with bellows **-concert'o** [-cher'-] n. composition for solo instrument and orchestra (pl. -tos)

concess'ion [-sh-] n. act of conceding; thing conceded

conch [kongk *or* konch] n. seashell

concil'iate vt. win over from hostility **-concilia'tion** n. **-concil'iatory** a.

concise' [-sīs'] a. brief, terse

con'clave n. private meeting

conclude' [-ōōd'] vt. finish; deduce; settle -vi. come to end; decide **-conclu'sion** n. **-conclu'sive** a. decisive

concoct' vt. make mixture; contrive **-concoc'tion** n.

con'cord n. agreement; harmony

con'course n. crowd; large, open place in public area

con'crete n. mixture of sand, cement *etc.* -a. specific; actual; solid

con'cubine [-ngk'yoo-] n. woman cohabiting with man; secondary wife

concur' vi. agree; happen together (-rr-) **-concurr'ent** a. **-concurr'ently** adv. at the same time

concuss'ion n. brain injury

condemn' vt. blame; find guilty; doom; declare unfit

condense' vt. concentrate; turn from gas to liquid **-condensa'tion** n.

condescend' vi. treat graciously one regarded as inferior; stoop **-condescen'sion** n.

con'diment n. seasoning for food

condi'tion [-dish-] n. state or circumstances; thing on which something else depends; prerequisite; physical fitness -vt. accustom; regulate; make fit **-condi'tional** a. dependent on events

condo'lence n. sympathy

con'dom n. sheathlike rubber contraceptive device worn by man

condone' vt. overlook, forgive

condu'cive [-dyŏŏs'-] a. leading (to)

con'duct n. behaviour; management -vt. [kən-dukt'] guide; direct; manage; transmit (heat *etc.*) **-conduc'tion** n. **-conduc'tor** n. person in charge of bus *etc.*; director of orchestra; substance capable of transmitting heat *etc.*

con'duit [-dit] n. channel or pipe for water, cables *etc.*

cone n. tapering figure with circular base; fruit of pine, fir *etc.* **-con'ic(al)** a.

confec'tionery n. sweets, cakes *etc.*

confed'erate [-rit] n. ally; accomplice -v. [-rāt] unite **-confedera'tion** n. alliance of political units

confer' vt. grant -vi. talk with (-rr-) **-con'ference** n. meeting for consultation

confess' vt. admit -vi. declare one's sins orally to priest **-confess'ion** n. **-confess'ional** n. confessor's box **-confess'or** n. priest who hears confessions

confett'i pl.n. bits of coloured paper thrown at weddings

confide' vi. (*with* in) tell secrets -vt. entrust **-con'fidence** n. trust; assurance; intimacy; secret **-con'fident** a. **-confiden'tial** a. private; secret

configura'tion n. shape

confine' vt. keep within bounds; shut up **-con'fines** pl.n. limits **-confine'ment** n. esp. childbirth

confirm' vt. make sure; strengthen; make valid; admit as member of church **-confirma'tion** n. **-confirmed'** a. long-established

con'fiscate vt. seize by authority **-confisca'tion** n.

conflagra'tion n. great destructive fire

con'flict n. struggle; disagreement -vi. [-flikt'] be at odds with; clash

conform' v. comply with accepted standards etc.; adapt to rule, pattern, custom etc. **-conform'ist** n. **-conform'ity** n.

confound' vt. perplex; confuse

confront' [-unt'] vt. face; bring face to face with **-confronta'tion** n.

confuse' [-fyōō-'] vt. bewilder; jumble; make unclear; mistake **-confu'sion** n.

confute' [-fyōō-'] vt. prove wrong

congeal' [-j-'] v. solidify

conge'nial [-je'-] a. pleasant

congen'ital [-jen'-] a. existing at birth; dating from birth

con'ger [-ng'g-] n. sea eel

congest' [-jest'] v. overcrowd or clog **-conges'tion** n.

conglom'erate n. substance composed of smaller elements; business organization comprising many companies **-a. -conglomera'tion** n.

congrat'ulate vt. express pleasure at good fortune, success etc. **-congratula'tion** n.

con'gregate [-ng'gr-] v. assemble; flock together **-congrega'tion** n. assembly, esp. for worship

con'gress [-ng'gr-] n. formal assembly; legislative body **-con'gressman** n.

congruent [-ng'gr-] a. suitable, accordant; fitting together

co'nifer [or kon'-] n. cone-bearing tree

conjec'ture n./v. guess

conjug'al a. of marriage

con'jugate v. inflect verb in its various forms

conjunc'tion n. union; simultaneous happening; part of speech joining words, phrases etc. **-conjunc'tive** a.

conjunctivi'tis n. inflammation of membrane of eye

con'jure [kun'j-or] v. produce magic effects; perform tricks **-con'jurer**, **-or** n.

con'ker n. inf. horse chestnut

connect' v. join together, unite; associate in the mind **-connec'tion**, **connex'ion** n. association; connecting thing; relation

connive' vi. conspire

connoisseur' [kon-i-sur'] n. expert in fine arts

connote' vt. imply, mean in addition **-connota'tion** n.

con'quer [kong'kor] vt. overcome; defeat **-con'queror** n. **-con'quest** [kon'kwest] n.

con'science [-shons] n. sense of right or wrong **-conscien'tious** a. scrupulous

con'scious [-shos] a. aware; awake; intentional **-con'sciousness** n.

con'script n. one compulsorily enlisted for military service **-conscript'** vt. **-conscrip'tion** n.

con'secrate vt. make sacred

consec'utive a. in unbroken succession **-consec'utively** adv.

consen'sus n. widespread agreement

consent' vi. agree to **-n.** permission; agreement

con'sequence n. result, outcome; importance **-con'sequent** a. **-consequen'tial** a. important **-con'sequently** adv. therefore

conserve' vt. keep from change etc.; preserve **-n.** [also kon'-] jam **-conserva'tion** n. protection of environment **-conserv'ative** a. tending to conserve; moderate **-n. -conserv'atory** n. greenhouse

consid'er vt. think over; examine; make allowance for; be of opinion that **-consid'erable** a. important; large **-consid'erate** a. thoughtful for others' feelings **-considera'tion** n. act of considering; recompense

consign' [-īn'] vt. hand over; entrust **-consign'ment** n. goods consigned **-consign'or** n.

consist' vi. be composed of **-consist'ency, consist'ence** n. agreement; degree of firmness **-consist'ent** a.

console' vt. comfort, cheer in distress **-consola'tion** n.

con'sole n. bracket; keyboard etc., of organ; cabinet for television, radio etc.

consol'idate vt. combine; make firm

consomm'é [-ā] n. clear meat soup

con'sonant n. sound, letter other than a vowel **-a.** agreeing with, in accord **-con'sonance** n.

consort' vi. associate **-n.** [kon'-] husband, wife, esp. of ruler **-consort'ium** n. association of banks, companies etc.

conspic'uous a. noticeable

conspire' vi. plot together **-conspir'acy** n. **-conspir'ator** n.

con'stable [kun'-] n. policeman

con'stant a. unchanging; steadfast; continual **-n.** quantity that does not vary **-con'stancy** n. loyalty

constella'tion n. group of stars

consterna'tion n. alarm, dismay

constipa'tion n. difficulty in emptying bowels

constit'uent a. making up whole -n. component part; elector -con**stit'uency** n. body of electors; parliamentary division

con'stitute vt. form; found -con**stitu'tion** n. composition; health; principles on which state is governed -constitu'tional a.

constrain' vt. force -constraint' n.

constric'tion n. squeezing together -constrict' vt.

construct' vt. build; put together -construc'tion n. -construc'tive a. positive

construe' vt. interpret

con'sul n. government representative in a foreign country

consult' vt. seek advice, information from -consul'tant n. specialist, expert -consulta'tion n.

consume' [-syōōm'] vt. eat or drink; engross; use up; destroy -con**su'mer** n.

con'summate vt. perfect; complete -a. [-sum'-]

cont. continued

con'tact n. touching; being in touch; useful acquaintance -vt.

conta'gious a. communicable by contact, catching

contain' vt. hold; have room for; comprise; restrain -contain'er n.

contam'inate vt. pollute

con'template vt. meditate on; gaze upon; intend

contem'porary n./a. (one) existing at same time -contempora'neous a.

contempt' n. scorn, disgrace; wilful disrespect of authority -con**tempt'ible** a. -contempt'uous a. showing contempt

contend' vi. strive; dispute -vt. maintain (that) -conten'tion n. -conten'tious a.

con'tent' n. that contained -pl. index of topics

content'² a. satisfied; willing (to) -vt. satisfy -n. satisfaction -con**tent'ed** a.

con'test n. competition -vt. [-test'] dispute; compete for -contest'ant n.

con'text n. words coming before, after a word or passage

con'tinent n. large continuous mass of land -continent'al a.

contin'gent [-j-] a. depending (on) -n. group part of larger group -con**tin'gency** n.

contin'ue v. remain; carry on; resume; prolong -contin'ual a. -continua'tion n. continuance; logical sequence -contin'uous a.

contort' vt. twist out of normal shape -contor'tion n.

con'tour [-oor] n. outline, shape, esp. mountains, coast etc.

contra- (comb. form) against

con'traband n. smuggled goods

contracep'tion n. prevention of conception -contracep'tive a./n.

contract' v. make or become smaller; [or kon'-] enter into agreement -vt. incur -n. [kon'-] agreement -contrac'tion n. -contract'or n. one making contract, esp. builder -contract'ual a.

contradict' vt. deny; be inconsistent with -contradic'tory a.

contral'to n. lowest of three female voices (pl. -s)

contrap'tion n. gadget; device

con'trary a. opposed; [kon-trār'-] perverse -n. the exact opposite -adv. in opposition

con'trast [-ah-] v. bring out, show difference -n. [kon'-] striking difference

contravene' vt. infringe

contrib'ute v. give, pay to common fund; help to occur; write for the press -contribu'tion n. -contrib'utor n.

con'trite [or -trīt'] a. remorseful -contri'tion n.

contrive' vt. manage; devise, invent -contri'vance n.

control' [-ōl'] vt. command; regulate; direct, check (-ll-) -n. power to direct or determine; curb, check -pl.n. instruments to control car, aircraft etc. -control'ler n.

con'troversy [or -trov'-] n. debate -controver'sial a.

contu'sion [-yōō-zh-] n. bruise

conun'drum n. riddle

convalesce' [-es'] vi. recover health after illness, operation etc. -convales'cence n. -convales'cent a.

convec'tion n. transmission of heat by currents

convene' vt. call together, assemble -conven'tion n. assembly; treaty; accepted usage -conven'tional a. (slavishly) observing customs of society; customary; (of weapons, war etc.) not nuclear

conve'nient a. handy; favourable to needs, comfort -**conve'nience** n. ease, comfort, suitability; a (public) lavatory -a. (of food) quick to prepare

con'vent n. religious community, esp. of nuns

converge' vi. tend to meet -**conver'gence**, -**gency** n.

conver'sant a. familiar (with), versed in

converse'[1] vi. talk (with) -n. [kon'-] talk -**conversa'tion** n. -**conversa'tional** a.

con'verse[2] a. opposite, reversed -n. the opposite

convert' vt. apply to another purpose; change; transform; cause to adopt (another) religion, opinion -n. [kon'-] converted person -**conver'sion** n. -**conver'tible** n. car with folding roof -a.

con'vex [or -veks'] a. curved outwards

convey' vt. transport; impart; Law transfer -**convey'ance** n. -**convey'ancer** n. one skilled in legal forms of transferring property -**convey'ancing** n. this work

convict' vt. prove or declare guilty -n. [kon'-] criminal serving prison sentence -**convic'tion** n. verdict of guilty; being convinced, firm belief

convince' vt. firmly persuade -**convin'cing** a.

convivi'ial a. sociable

convoca'tion n. assembly

con'voluted a. involved; coiled -**convolu'tion** n.

con'voy n. party (of ships etc.) travelling together for protection -vt. escort

convulse' vt. shake violently; affect with spasms -**convul'sion** n.

co'n(e)y n. rabbit

coo n./vi. (make) cry of doves (**cooed** [kōōd], **coo'ing**)

cook vt. prepare (food) esp. by heat -vi. undergo cooking; act as cook -n. one who prepares food -**cook'ery** n. -**cook'ie** n. (esp. US) biscuit

cool a. moderately cold; calm; lacking friendliness -v. make, become cool

coop[1] n./vt. (shut up in) cage

co'op[2], **co-op** [kō'op] n. cooperative society or shop run by cooperative

coop'erate [kō-op'-] vi. work together -**coopera'tion** n. -**coop'erative** a. willing to cooperate; (of an enterprise) owned collectively (also n.)

coord'inate [kō-awrd'-] vt. bring into order, harmony -a. equal in degree, status etc.

coot n. small black water fowl

cop sl. n. policeman; a capture

cope[1] vi. deal successfully (with)

co'ping n. sloping top course of wall

co'pious a. abundant

copp'er n. reddish-brown metal; coin

copse n. small wood

cop'ulate vi. unite sexually

cop'y n. imitation; single specimen of book -vt. make copy of, imitate (**cop'ied**, **cop'ying**) -**cop'yright** n. legal exclusive right to print and publish book, work of art etc. -vt. protect by copyright

coquette' [-ket'] n. flirt

cor'al [ko'ral] n. hard substance made by sea polyps

cord n. thin rope or thick string; ribbed fabric

cord'ial a. sincere, warm -n. fruit-flavoured drink -**cordial'ity** n.

cor'don n. chain of troops or police

cor'duroy [-də-] n. cotton fabric with velvety, ribbed surface

core n. seed case of apple; innermost part -vt. take out core

co-respond'ent n. one cited in divorce case, alleged to have committed adultery with the respondent

cor'gi n. a small Welsh dog

corian'der n. herb

cork n. bark of an evergreen Mediterranean oak tree; stopper for bottle etc. -vt. stop up with cork -**cork'-screw** n. tool for pulling out corks

corm n. underground stem like a bulb

cor'morant n. large voracious sea bird

corn[1] n. grain, fruit of cereals -vt. preserve (meat) with salt -**corn'y** a. inf. trite, oversentimental -**corn'crake** n. brown bird with harsh call -**corn'flakes** pl.n. breakfast cereal -**corn'flour** n. finely ground maize -**corn'flower** n. blue flower growing in cornfields

corn[2] n. horny growth on foot

cor'nea n. transparent membrane covering front of eye

cor'ner n. part where two sides meet; remote or humble place; Business monopoly; Sport free kick or shot -vt. drive into position of no escape; establish monopoly –*vi.* move round corner

cor'net *n.* trumpet with valves; cone-shaped ice cream wafer

cor'nice *n.* moulding below ceiling

cornuco'pia *n.* horn overflowing with fruit and flowers

corol'lary *n.* inference from a preceding statement; deduction

cor'onary [kol'ro] *a.* of blood vessels surrounding heart –*n.* coronary thrombosis –**coronary thrombosis** disease of the heart

corona'tion *n.* ceremony of crowning a sovereign

cor'oner [kol'ro] *n.* officer who holds inquests on unnatural deaths

cor'onet [kol'ro] *n.* small crown

corp'oral¹ *a.* of the body

corp'oral² *n.* noncommissioned officer below sergeant

corpora'tion *n.* body of persons legally authorized to act as an individual –**corp'orate** *a.*

corps [kawr] *n.* military force; any organized body of persons (*pl.* **corps** [kawrz])

corpse *n.* dead body

corp'ulent *a.* fat –**corp'ulence** *n.*

cor'pus *n.* main part or body of something

corp'uscle [-usl] *n.* minute particle, *esp.* of blood

corral' [-rahl'] *n.* US enclosure for cattle

correct' *vt.* set right; indicate errors in; punish –*a.* right, accurate –**correc'tion** *n.* –**correc'tive** *n./a.*

cor'relate *vt.* bring into reciprocal relation

correspond' *vi.* be similar (to); exchange letters –**correspond'ence** *n.* –**correspond'ent** *n.* writer of letters; one employed by newspaper *etc.* to report on particular topic

cor'ridor *n.* passage

corrob'orate *vt.* confirm

corrode' *vt.* eat into –**corro'sion** *n.* –**corro'sive** *a.*

corr'ugated *a.* ridged

corrupt' *a.* lacking integrity; involving bribery; wicked –*vt.* make evil; bribe; make rotten –**corrup'tion** *n.*

corsage' [-sahzh'] *n.* (flower worn on) bodice of woman's dress

cors'et *n.* close-fitting undergarment to support the body

cortege' [-tāzh'] *n.* formal (funeral) procession

cor'tisone *n.* synthetic hormone used medically

cosh *n.* blunt weapon –*vt.* strike with one

cosmet'ic [-z-] *n./a.* (preparation) to improve appearance only

cos'mic [koz'-] *a.* relating to the universe; vast

cos'monaut [-z'l-] *n.* Soviet astronaut

cosmopol'itan [-z-] *a./n.* (person) familiar with many countries

cos'mos [-z'l-] *n.* the universe considered as an ordered system

coss'et *vt.* pamper, pet

cost *n.* price; expenditure of time, labour *etc.* –*vt.* have as price; entail payment, or loss of –**cost'ly** *a.* valuable; expensive

cos'tume *n.* style of dress of particular place or time

co'sy [-z-] *a.* snug, comfortable

cot *n.* child's bed

co'terie *n.* social clique

cott'age *n.* small house –**cottage cheese** mild, soft cheese

cott'on *n.* plant with white downy fibres; cloth of this

couch *n.* piece of furniture for reclining on –*vt.* put into (words)

couch grass [*or* -ठठ-] type of creeping grass

cou'gar [kठठ'-] *n.* puma

cough [kof] *vi.* expel air from lungs with sudden effort and noise –*n.* act of coughing

coun'cil *n.* deliberative or administrative body; local governing authority of town *etc.* –**coun'cillor** *n.*

coun'sel *n.* advice; barrister's –*vt.* advise, recommend (-**ll**-) –**coun'sellor** *n.*

count¹ *vt.* reckon, number; consider to be –*vi.* be reckoned in; depend (on); be of importance –*n.* reckoning; total number; act of counting –**count'less** *a.* too many to be counted

count² *n.* nobleman –**count'ess** *n. fem.*

count'enance *n.* face, its expression –*vt.* support, approve

count'er¹ *n.* horizontal surface in bank, shop *etc.*, on which business is transacted

count'er² *adv.* in opposite direction –*vi.* oppose

counter- (*comb. form*) reversed, opposite, rival, retaliatory, as in **count'erclaim** *n.* –**count'ermarch** *vi.*

counteract' *vt.* neutralize

count'erfeit [-fit] *a.* a sham, forged

-n. imitation, forgery -vt. imitate with intent to deceive; forge

coun'terfoil n. part of cheque, receipt etc. kept as record

countermand' [-mahnd'] vt. cancel (previous order)

coun'terpart n. something complementary to another

coun'terpoint n. melody added as accompaniment to given melody

coun'tersign [-sīn] vt. sign document already signed by another

coun'tersink v. enlarge top of hole to take head of screw, bolt etc. below surface

coun'try [kun'-] n. region; nation; land of birth; rural districts -**coun'tryside** n.

coun'ty n. division of country

coup [koo] n. successful stroke; (short for coup d'état) sudden, violent seizure of government

coupé [koo'pā] n. sporty style of motor car

coup'le [kup'l] n. two, pair; husband and wife -vt. connect, fasten together -vi. join, associate

coup'on [koo'-] n. ticket entitling holder to discount, gift etc.

cour'age [ku-] n. bravery, boldness -coura'geous a.

courgette' [-zhet'] n. type of small vegetable marrow

cour'ier [koor'-] n. messenger; person who guides travellers

course [-aw-] n. movement in space or time; direction; sequence; line of action; series of lectures etc.; any of successive parts of meal; area where golf is played; racetrack -vt. hunt -vi. run swiftly; (of blood) circulate

court [-aw-] n. space enclosed by buildings, yard; area for playing various games; retinue of sovereign; body with judicial powers, place where it meets, one of its sittings -vt. woo; seek, invite -**court'ier** n. one who frequents royal court -**court'ly** a. ceremoniously polite; characteristic of a court -**court card** king, queen or jack at cards -**court mar'tial** court of naval or military officers for trying naval or military offences (pl. **court martials, courts martial**) -**court'yard** n.

cour'tesy [kur'-] n. politeness -**court'eous** [kurt'-] a. polite

court'ship [-aw-] n. wooing

cous'in [kuz'n] n. son or daughter of uncle or aunt

cove n. small inlet of coast

cov'en [ku-] n. gathering of witches

cov'enant [ku-] n. agreement; compact -v. agree to a covenant

cov'er [ku-] vt. place over; extend, spread; bring upon (oneself); protect; travel over; include; be sufficient; report -n. lid, wrapper, envelope, anything which covers -**cov'erage** n. -**cov'erlet** n. top covering of bed

cov'ert [ku-] a. secret, sly

cov'et [ku-] vt. long to possess, esp. what belongs to another -**cov'etous** a. avaricious

cow¹ n. female of bovine and other animals (pl. **cows**)

cow² vt. frighten, overawe

cow'ard n. one who lacks courage -**cow'ardice** n. -**cow'ardly** a.

cow'er vi. crouch in fear

cowl n. monk's hooded cloak; hooded top for chimney

cow'ling n. covering for aircraft engine

cow'slip n. wild primrose

cox'swain [kok'sən], **cox** n. steersman of boat

coy a. (pretending to be) shy, modest -**coy'ly** adv.

coyo'te [-ōti] n. prairie wolf

coy'pu [-poo] n. aquatic rodent

crab n. edible crustacean -**crabb'ed** a. of handwriting, hard to read -**crabb'y** a. bad-tempered

crab apple wild sour apple

crack vt. split partially; break with sharp noise; break down, yield; inf. tell (joke); solve, decipher -vi. make sharp noise; split -n. sharp explosive noise; split; flaw; inf. joke; chat -a. inf. of great reputation for skill -**crack'er** n. decorated paper tube, pulled apart with a bang, containing toy etc.; explosive firework; thin dry biscuit -**crack'le** n./vi. (make) sound of repeated small cracks

cra'dle n. infant's bed -vt. hold or rock as in a cradle; cherish -**cra'dling** n.

craft¹ [-ah-] n. skill, esp. manual ability; cunning -**craft'y** a. cunning, shrewd -**crafts'man** n. -**crafts'manship** n.

craft² [-ah-] n. vessel; ship

crag n. steep rugged rock

cram vt. stuff; prepare quickly for examination (-mm-)

cramp n. painful muscular contraction -vt. restrict

cran'berry n. edible red berry

crane n. wading bird with long legs;

machine for moving heavy weights
-vi. stretch neck

cra'nium n. skull (pl. **-niums, -nia**)
-**cra'nial** a.

crank n. arm at right angles to axis, for turning main shaft; inf. eccentric person -v. start (engine) by turning crank -**crank'y** a. eccentric

crash v. (cause to) make loud noise; (cause to) fall with crash -vi. smash; collapse; cause (aircraft) to hit land or water; collide with; move noisily -n. loud, violent fall or impact; collision; uncontrolled descent of aircraft; sudden collapse; bankruptcy

crass a. grossly stupid

crate n. large (usu. wooden) container for packing goods

cra'ter n. mouth of volcano; bowl-shaped cavity

cravat' n. man's neckcloth

crave v. have very strong desire for -vt. beg

cra'ven a./n. coward(ly)

craw n. bird's crop

crawl vi. move on hands and knees; move very slowly; ingratiate oneself; swim with crawl-stroke; be overrun (with) -n. crawling motion; racing stroke at swimming

cray'fish n. edible freshwater crustacean

cray'on n. stick or pencil of coloured wax etc.

craze n. short-lived fashion; strong desire; madness -**cra'zy** a. insane; very foolish; madly eager (for)

creak n./vi. (make) grating noise

cream n. fatty part of milk; various foods, dishes; cosmetic etc.; yellowish-white colour; best part -vt. take cream from; take best part from; beat to creamy consistency -**cream'y** a.

crease [-s] n. line made by folding; wrinkle -v. make, develop creases

create' [krē-āt'] vt. bring into being; make -vi. inf. make a fuss -**crea'tion** n. -**crea'tor** n.

crea'ture [krēch-] n. living being

crèche [kresh, krāsh] n. day nursery for very young children

creden'tials pl.n. testimonials; letters of introduction

cred'ible a. worthy of belief

cred'it n. commendation; source of honour; trust; good name; system of allowing customers to pay later; money at one's disposal in bank etc. -vt. attribute; believe; put on credit side of account -**cred'itable** a.

bringing honour -**cred'itor** n. one to whom debt is due

cred'ulous a. too easy of belief, gullible -**credu'lity** n.

creed n. statement of belief

creek n. narrow inlet on coast

creel n. angler's fishing basket

creep vi. move slowly, stealthily; crawl; act in servile way; of flesh, feel shrinking sensation (**crept** pt./pp.) -n. creeping; sl. repulsive person -pl. feeling of fear or repugnance -**creep'er** n. creeping or climbing plant -**creep'y** inf. a. uncanny

crema'tion n. burning of corpses -**cremate'** vt.

cre'osote n. oily liquid used for preserving wood

crepe [krāp] n. fabric with crimped surface; crape

Cres. Crescent

crescen'do [-sh-] n. Mus. gradual increase of loudness

cres'cent [krez'ənt] n. (shape of) moon in first or last quarter

cress n. various plants with edible pungent leaves

crest n. tuft on bird's or animal's head; top of mountain, wave etc.; badge above shield of coat of arms

cret'in n. person afflicted by retardation; inf. stupid person

crev'ice [-is] n. cleft, fissure

crew [-ōō] n. ship's, aircraft's company; inf. gang

crib n. child's cot; rack for fodder; plagiarism

cribb'age n. card game

crick n. cramp esp. in neck

crick'et' n. chirping insect

crick'et² n. game played with bats, ball and wickets

crime n. violation of law; wicked act -**crim'inal** a./n.

crim'son [-z-] a./n. (of) rich deep red -v. turn crimson

cringe vi. shrink, cower; behave obsequiously

crin'kle [-ng'k-] v./n. wrinkle

crin'oline [-lin] n. hooped petticoat or skirt

crip'ple n. disabled person -vt. disable

cri'sis n. turning point; time of acute danger (pl. **cri'ses** [-sēz])

crisp a. brittle; brisk; clear-cut; fresh -n. very thin, fried slice of potato

crite'rion [krī-] n. standard of judgment (pl. **-ria**)

crit'ical a. fault-finding; discerning;

skilled in judging; crucial, decisive **-crit'ic** n. one who passes judgment; writer expert in judging works of literature, art *etc.* **-crit'icism** n. **-crit'icize** vt.

croak v./n. (utter) deep hoarse cry; talk dismally

cro'chet [-sha] n./v. (do) handicraft like knitting

crock n. earthenware pot **-crock'ery** n. earthenware dishes *etc.*

croc'odile [krok'-] n. large amphibious reptile

cro'cus n. small bulbous plant

croiss'ant [krwahs'ong] n. crescent-shaped bread roll

crone n. witchlike old woman

cro'ny n. intimate friend

crook n. hooked staff; *inf.* swindler; criminal **-crook'ed** a. twisted; deformed; dishonest

croon v. sing in soft tone

crop n. produce of cultivated plants; harvest; pouch in bird's gullet; whip; short haircut -v. cut short; produce crop; (of animals) bite, eat down; cut or clip (-pp-) **-cropp'er** n. heavy fall; disastrous failure **-crop up** *inf.* happen unexpectedly

cro'quet [-ka] n. lawn game played with balls and hoops

croquette' [-ket'] n. fried ball of minced meat, fish *etc.*

cross n. structure or symbol of two intersecting lines or pieces; such a structure as means of execution; symbol of Christian faith; any thing in shape of cross; affliction; hybrid -v. move or go across (something); intersect; meet and pass -vt. mark with lines across; (*with* out) delete; place in form of cross; make sign of cross; breed by intermixture; thwart -a. angry; transverse; contrary **-cross'ing** n. intersection of roads, rails *etc.*; part of street where pedestrians are expected to cross **-cross-examine** vt. examine witness already examined by other side **-crosseyed** a. having eye(s) turning inward **-cross-ply** a. (of tyre) having fabric cords in outer casing running diagonally **-cross-reference** n. reference within text to another part of text **-cross'roads** n. **-crossword puzzle** puzzle built up of intersecting words, indicated by clues **-The Cross** cross on which Jesus Christ was executed

crotch n. angle between legs

crotch'et n. musical note

crouch vi. bend low; huddle down close to ground; stoop

croup [-ōō-] n. throat disease of children, with cough

croup'ier [-ōō-] n. person dealing cards, collecting money *etc.* at gambling table

crow[1] [-ō] n. large black carrion-eating bird

crow[2] [-ō] vi. utter cock's cry; boast -n. cock's cry

crow'bar [-ō-] n. iron bar

crowd n. throng, mass -vi. flock together -vt. cram, pack; fill with people

crown n. monarch's headdress; royal power; various coins; top of head; summit, top; perfection of thing -vt. put crown on; occur as culmination; *inf.* hit on head

cru'cial [krōō'shəl] a. decisive, critical; *inf.* very important

cru'cible [-ōō-] n. small melting-pot

cru'cifix [-ōō-] n. cross; image of (Christ on the) Cross (*pl.* **-es**) **-crucifix'ion** n. **-cru'cify** vt.

crude [-ōō-] a. vulgar; in natural or raw state; rough **-cru'dity** n.

cru'el [-ōō-] a. causing pain or suffering **-cru'elty** n.

cru'et [-ōō-] n. small container for salt, pepper *etc.*

cruise [-ōōz] vi. travel about in a ship -n. voyage **-cruis'er** n. ship that cruises; warship

crumb [krum] n. fragment of bread

crum'ble v. break into small fragments **-crum'bly** a.

crum'pet n. flat, soft cake eaten with butter; *sl.* sexually desirable woman or women

crum'ple v. (cause to) collapse; make or become creased

crunch n. sound made by chewing crisp food, treading on gravel; *inf.* critical situation -v. make crunching sound

crusade' n. medieval Christian war; concerted action to further a cause -vi. **-crusa'der** n.

crush vt. compress so as to break; break to small pieces; defeat utterly -n. act of crushing; crowd of people *etc.*

crust n. hard outer part of bread; similar casing

crusta'cean [-shən] n. hard-shelled animal, *eg* crab, lobster

crutch n. staff with crosspiece to go under armpit of lame person; support; crotch

crux *n.* that on which a decision turns (*pl.* **crux'es, cru'ces** [krōō'sez])

cry *vi.* weep; utter call; shout; beg (for) –*vt.* proclaim (**cried, cry'ing**) –*n.* loud utterance; call of animal; fit of weeping

crypt [kript] *n.* vault, *esp.* under church –**cryp'tic** *a.* secret, mysterious

crys'tal *n.* transparent mineral; very clear glass; cut-glass ware; form with symmetrically arranged plane surfaces –**crys'talline** *a.* –**crys'tallize** *v.* form into crystals; become definite

CSE Certificate of Secondary Education

CST *US, C* Central Standard Time

cu. cubic

cub *n.* young of fox and other animals;

cube [kyōōb] *n.* solid figure with six equal square sides; cube-shaped block; product obtained by multiplying number by itself twice –*vt.* multiply thus –**cu'bic(al)** *a.*

cu'bicle *n.* enclosed section of room

cuck'oo [kook'ōō] *n.* migratory bird; its call

cu'cumber *n.* long fleshy green fruit used in salad

cud *n.* food which ruminant animal brings back into mouth to chew again

cud'dle *vt.* hug –*vi.* lie close and snug, nestle –*n.*

cudg'el *n.* short thick stick –*vt.* beat with cudgel (**-ll-**)

cue[1] [kyōō] *n.* signal to act or speak; hint

cue[2] [kyōō] *n.* long tapering rod used in billiards

cuff[1] *n.* ending of sleeve

cuff[2] *vt.* strike with open hand –*n.* blow with hand

cuisine' [kwi-zēn'] *n.* style of cooking; food cooked

cul'-de-sac' *n.* street open only at one end (*pl.* **culs-de-sac**)

cul'inary *a.* of, for, suitable for, cooking or kitchen

cull *vt.* select; take out animals from herd

cul'minate *vi.* reach highest point; come to a head

culottes' [kyōō-] *pl.n.* women's trousers flared like skirt

cul'pable *a.* blameworthy

cul'prit *n.* one guilty of usu. minor offence

cult *n.* system of worship; devotion to some person, thing

cul'tivate *vt.* till and prepare (ground); develop, improve; devote attention to

cul'ture *n.* state of manners, taste, and intellectual development; cultivating –**cul'tural** *a.*

cul'vert *n.* drain under road

cum'bersome *a.* unwieldy

cum(m)'in *n.* herb

cu'mulative [-iv] *a.* becoming greater by successive additions

cunn'ing *a.* crafty, sly –*n.* skill in deceit or evasion

cup *n.* small drinking vessel with handle; various cup-shaped formations; cup-shaped trophy as prize; portion or lot –*vt.* shape as cup (hands *etc.*) –**cup'ful** *n.* (*pl.* **cup'fuls**) –**cup'board** [kub'ərd] *n.* piece of furniture with door, for storage

cu'pola *n.* dome

cur *n.* dog of mixed breed; contemptible person

cu'raçao [kyoor'ə-sō] *n.* orange-flavoured liqueur

cu'rate [kyoor'ət] *n.* parish priest's appointed assistant

cura'tor [kyoo-rā'-] *n.* custodian, *esp.* of museum

curb *n.* check, restraint –*vt.* restrain; apply curb to

curd *n.* coagulated milk –**cur'dle** *v.* turn into curd, coagulate

cure [kyoor] *vt.* heal, restore to health; remedy; preserve (fish, skins *etc.*) –*n.* remedy; course of medical treatment; restoration to health

curette' [-tahzh'] *n.* removal of dead tissue *esp.* in uterus

cur'few *n.* official regulation prohibiting movement of people, *esp.* at night; deadline for this

cu'rio [kyoor'-] *n.* rare or curious thing sought for collections (*pl.* **cu'rios**)

cu'rious [kyoor'-] *a.* eager to know, inquisitive; puzzling; odd –**curios'ity** *n.*

curl *v.* take, bend into, spiral or curved shape –*n.* spiral lock of hair; spiral –**curl'y** *a.*

cur'lew *n.* large long-billed wading bird

curr'ant *n.* dried type of grape; fruit of various plants allied to gooseberry

curr'ent *a.* of immediate present; in general use –*n.* body of water or air in motion; transmission of electricity

-curr'ency n. money in use; state of being in use

curric'ulum n. specified course of study (pl. **-lums, -ia**)

curr'y¹ n. highly-flavoured, pungent condiment; dish flavoured with it -vt. prepare, flavour dish with curry (**curr'ied, curr'ying**)

curr'y² vt. groom (horse) with comb; dress (leather) (**curr'ied, curr'ying**)

curse n. profane or obscene expression of anger etc.; affliction -v. utter curse, swear (at); afflict

curs'ory a. hasty, superficial

curt a. rudely brief, abrupt

curtail' vt. cut short

cur'tain [-tən] n. hanging drapery at window etc. -vt. provide, cover with curtain

curt'se(y) n. woman's bow -vi.

curve n. line of which no part is straight -v. bend into curve

cush'ion [-oo-] n. bag filled with soft stuffing or air, to support or ease body -vt. provide, protect with cushion; lessen effects of

cus'tard n. dish made of eggs and milk; sweet sauce of milk and cornflour

cus'tody n. guardianship, imprisonment -**custo'dian** n. keeper, curator

cus'tom n. habit; practice; usage; business patronage -pl. duties levied on imports -**cus'tomary** a. usual, habitual -**cus'tomer** n. one who enters shop to buy, esp. regularly; purchaser

cut vt. sever, wound, divide; pare, detach, trim; intersect; reduce, decrease; abridge; inf. ignore (person) (**cut, cutt'ing**) -n. act of cutting; stroke; blow, wound; reduction; fashion, shape; inf. share

cute [kyōōt] a. appealing, pretty

cu'ticle n. dead skin, esp. at base of fingernail

cut'lery n. knives, forks etc.

cut'let n. small piece of meat

cut'tle n. sea mollusc like squid

cwt. hundredweight

cy'anide [sī'-] n. extremely poisonous chemical compound

cybernet'ics [sī-] pl.n. (with sing. v.) comparative study of control mechanisms of electronic and biological systems

cyc'lamen [sik'-] n. plant with flowers having turned-back petals

cy'cle [sī'-] n. recurrent, complete series or period; bicycle -vi. move in cycles; ride bicycle -**cy'clic(al)** a.

-cy'clist n. bicycle rider

cy'clone [sī'-] n. circular storm

cy'clotron [sī'-] n. powerful apparatus which accelerates the circular movement of subatomic particles

cyg'net [sig'-] n. young swan

cyl'inder [sil'-] n. roller-shaped body, of uniform diameter -**cylin'drical** a.

cym'bal [sim'-] n. one of two brass plates struck together to produce clashing sound

cyn'ic [sin'-] n. one who believes the worst about people or outcome of events -**cyn'ical** a. -**cyn'icism** n. being cynical

cy'press n. coniferous tree with very dark foliage

cyst [si-] n. sac containing liquid secretion or pus -**cysti'tis** n. inflammation of bladder

Czar, Tzar, Tsar [zahr] n. emperor esp. of Russia 1547-1917

D

dab vt. apply with momentary pressure -n. small mass

dab'ble vi. splash about; be amateur (in) -**dabb'ler** n.

dachs'hund [daks'hoond] n. short-legged long-bodied dog

dad, dadd'y n. inf. father -**dad-dy-longlegs** n. inf. crane fly

da'do [dā'dō] n. lower part of room wall (pl. **-do(e)s**)

daff'odil n. spring flower, yellow narcissus

daft [-ah-] a. foolish, crazy

dagg'er n. short stabbing weapon

dahl'ia [dāl'-] n. garden plant of various colours

dai'ly a./adv. (done) every day -n. daily newspaper; charwoman

dain'ty a. delicate; choice; fastidious -n. delicacy -**dain'tiness** n.

dai'ry n. place for processing milk and its products

da'is [dā'-] n. raised platform

dai'sy [-z-] n. flower with yellow centre and white petals

dale n. valley

dall'y vi. trifle; loiter (**dall'ied, dal-l'ying**)

Dalma'tian n. large dog, white with black spots

dam¹ n./vt. (barrier to) hold back flow of waters (**-mm-**)

dam[^1] n. female parent (of animals)

dam'age n. injury, harm –pl. compensation for injury –vt. harm

dam'ask n. figured woven material; velvety red

dame n. obs. lady; (D-) title of lady in Order of the British Empire; sl. woman

damn [-m] vt. condemn –vi. curse (**damned** [damd], **damn'ing** [dam'ing]) –interj. expression of annoyance etc. –**dam'nable** a. –**dam-na'tion** n.

damp a. moist –n. moisture; in mines, dangerous gas –vt. make damp; deaden Also **damp'en** –**damp'er** n. anything that discourages; plate in a flue

dam'son [-z-] n. small dark-purple plum

dance [-ah-] vi. move with rhythmic steps, to music; bob up and down –vt. perform (dance) –n. rhythmical movement; social gathering –**danc'er** n.

D & C dilation and curettage (of womb)

dan'delion n. yellow-flowered wild plant

dan'druff n. dead skin in small scales among the hair

dan'dy n. man excessively concerned with smartness of dress –a. inf. excellent

dan'ger [dān'j-] n. exposure to harm; peril –**dan'gerous** a.

dan'gle [-ng'gal] v. hang loosely

dank a. damp and chilly

dapp'er a. neat, spruce

dap'ple v. mark with spots –**dap'pled** a. spotted; mottled

dare [dār] vt. have courage (to); challenge –n. challenge –**da'ring** a./n. –**dare'devil** a./n. reckless (person)

dark a. without light; gloomy; deep in tint; unenlightened –n. absence of light –**dark'en** v. –**dark'ness** n. –**dark horse** person, thing about whom little is known

dar'ling a./n. beloved (person)

darn vt. mend (hole) by sewing

dart n. small pointed missile; darting motion; small seam –pl. indoor game played with numbered target –v. cast, go rapidly

dash vt. smash, throw; cast down; mix –vi. move, go with great speed –n. rush; smartness; small quantity; stroke (-) between words –**dash'er** n. C ledge along top of boards at ice

hockey rink –**dash'ing** a. spirited, showy –**dash'board** n. in car etc., instrument panel

da'ta pl.n. (oft. with sing. v.) series of facts; information

date[^1] n. day of the month; time of occurrence; appointment –vt. mark with date; reveal age of –vi. exist (from); become old-fashioned

date[^2] n. fruit of palm

daub vt. paint roughly

daught'er [dawt'-] n. one's female child –**daughter-in-law** n. son's wife

daunt vt. frighten into giving up purpose

dav'it n. crane, usu. one of pair, at ship's side

daw'dle vi. idle, loiter

dawn n. daybreak; beginning –vi. begin to grow light; (begin) to be understood

day n. period of 24 hours; time when sun is above horizon; time period –**day'break** n. dawn –**day'dream** n. idle fancy –vi. –**day'light** n. natural light; dawn

daze vt. stun, bewilder –n. bewildered state –**dazed** a.

daz'zle v. blind, confuse with brightness

dB decibel(s)

DC direct current

de- (comb. form) removal of, from, reversal of, as in **delouse**, **desegregate**

dea'con [dē'kən] n. one who assists in a church –**dea'coness** fem.

dead [ded] a. no longer alive; obsolete; numb; lacking vigour; complete –n. dead person(s) (oft. in pl., the dead) –adv. utterly –**dead'en** vt. –**dead'ly** a. fatal; deathlike –adv. as if dead –**dead'head** n. US, C log sticking out of water as hindrance to navigation –**dead'line** n. limit of time allowed –**dead'lock** n. standstill –**dead'pan** a. expressionless

deaf [def] a. without hearing; unwilling to listen –**deaf'en** vt. make deaf

deal[^1] v. distribute –vi. act; treat; do business (with, in) (**dealt** pt./pp.) –n. agreement; treatment; share –**deal'er** n.

deal[^2] n. (plank of) pine wood

dean n. university official; head of cathedral chapter

dear a. beloved; precious; expensive –n. beloved one

dearth [derth] n. scarcity

death [deth] n. dying; end of life; end –**death'ly** a./adv.

debacle [dā-bahk'l] n. utter collapse, rout, disaster

debar' vt. shut out from (-rr-)

debase' vt. lower in value

debate' v. argue, esp. formally –n. formal discussion –**deba'table** a. –**deba'ter** n.

debauch' [-bawch'] vt. lead into a life of depraved self-indulgence –n. orgy –**debauch'ery** n.

debil'ity n. feebleness –**debil'itate** vt. weaken

deb'it Accounting n. entry in account of sum owed –vt. enter as due

debonair' a. suave, genial

debrief' v. report result of mission

de'bris [dā'brē, deb'-] n. sing. and pl. rubbish

debt [det] n. what is owed; state of owing –**debt'or** n.

debunk' vt. expose falseness of, esp. by ridicule

de'but [dā'byōō] n. first appearance in public –**deb'utante** n. girl making society debut

Dec. December

deca- (comb. form) ten, as in **dec'alitre**

dec'ade n. period of ten years

dec'adent a. deteriorating; morally corrupt –**dec'adence** n.

decamp' vi. make off, break camp

decant' vt. pour off (wine) –**decant'er** n. stoppered bottle

decay' v. rot; decline –n. rotting

decease' [-sēs'] n. death –vi. die –**deceased'** a. dead –n.

deceive' [-sēv'] vt. mislead, delude –**deceit'** n. fraud; duplicity –**deceit'ful** a.

decel'erate [-sel'-] v. slow down

Decem'ber n. twelfth month

de'cent a. respectable; fitting; adequate; inf. kind –**de'cency** n.

decep'tion n. deceiving; trick –**decep'tive** a. misleading

dec'ibel [des'-] n. unit for measuring intensity of a sound

decide' vt. settle; give judgment –vi. come to a decision –**deci'ded** a. unmistakable; resolute –**deci'sion** [-zhən] n. –**deci'sive** a.

decid'uous a. of trees, losing leaves annually

dec'imal [des'-] a. relating to tenths –n. decimal fraction –**decimaliza'tion** n.

dec'imate vt. destroy or kill a tenth of, large proportion of

deci'pher vt. make out meaning of; decode

deck n. floor, esp. one covering ship's hull; turntable of record player –vt. decorate

declaim' v. speak rhetorically

declare' vt. announce formally; state emphatically –**declara'tion** n.

decline' vi. refuse; slope downwards; deteriorate; diminish –vt. deterioration; diminution; downward slope

décolleté [dā-kol'tā] a. (of dress) having a low-cut neckline

decompose' [-ōz'] v. rot

decompress' vt. free from pressure –**decompress'ion** n.

deconge'stant [-j-] a./n. (drug) relieving (esp. nasal) congestion

dé'cor, de'cor [dā'-] n. decorative scheme

dec'orate vt. beautify; paint room etc.; to invest (with medal etc.) –**decora'tion** n. –**dec'orative** a.

deco'rum n. propriety, decency –**dec'orous** a.

de'coy n. bait, lure –v. [di-koi'] lure, be lured as with decoy

decrease' v. diminish, lessen –n. [dē'-] lessening

decree' n./v. (give) order having the force of law; edict

decrep'it a. old; worn out

decry' vt. disparage (**decried'**, **decry'ing**)

ded'icate vt. commit wholly to special purpose; inscribe or address; devote –**dedica'tion** n.

deduce' vt. draw as conclusion –**deduct'** vt. subtract –**deduc'tion** n. deducting; amount subtracted; conclusion

deed n. action; exploit; legal document

deem vt. judge, consider, regard

deep a. extending far down; at, of given depth; profound; hard to fathom; of colour, dark; of sound, low –n. deep place; the sea –adv. far down etc. –**deep'en** vt.

deer n. ruminant animal typically with antlers in male (pl. **deer**)

deface' vt. spoil or mar surface

defame' vt. speak ill of –**defama'tion** n. –**defam'atory** a.

default' n. failure to act, appear or pay –v. fail (to pay)

defeat' vt. vanquish; thwart –n. overthrow

def'ecate vt. empty the bowels

de'fect [or -fekt'] n. lack, blemish

-vi. [-fekt'] desert **-defec'tion** n. **-defec'tive** a. faulty

defend' vt. protect, ward off attack; support by argument **-defence'** n. **-defend'ant** n. person accused in court **-defens'ible** a. **-defen'sive** a. serving for defence -n. attitude of defence

defer'¹ vt. postpone (-rr-)

defer'² vi. submit to opinion or judgment of another (-rr-) **-def'erence** n. respect

defi'cient [-ish'ənt] a. lacking in something **-defi'ciency** n. **-def'icit** n. amount by which sum of money is too small

defile' vt. soil; sully

define' vt. state meaning of; mark out **-defini'tion** n. **-def'inite** [-it] a. exact; clear; certain **-defin'itive** a. conclusive

deflate' v. (cause to) collapse by release of gas from **-defla'tion** n. Economics reduction of economic and industrial activity

deflect' v. (cause to) turn from straight course

deform' vt. spoil shape of; disfigure **-deform'ity** n.

defraud' vt. cheat, swindle

defray' vt. provide money for

defrost' v. make, become free of frost, ice; thaw

deft a. skilful, adroit

defunct' a. dead, obsolete

defuse' vt. remove fuse of bomb, etc.; remove tension

defy' vt. challenge, resist successfully (defied, defy'ing) **-defi'ance** n. resistance **-defi'ant** a. aggressively hostile

degen'erate vi. deteriorate to lower level -a. fallen away in quality -n. degenerate person

degrade' vt. dishonour; debase; reduce **-** decompose chemically **-degra'dable** a. **-degrada'tion** n.

degree' n. step, stage in process; university rank; unit of measurement

dehy'drate vt. remove moisture from

de'ify [or dā'-] vt. make god of (de'ified, de'ifying)

deign [dān] vt. condescend

de'ity [or dā'-] n. a god

deject'ed a. miserable

dekk'o n. sl. look

delay' vt. postpone -vi. linger (delayed', delay'ing) -n. a delaying

delect'able a. delightful

del'egate n. representative **-**vt.

send as deputy; entrust **-delega'tion** n.

delete' vt. remove, erase

delib'erate [-it] a. intentional; well-considered; slow -v. [-āt] consider

del'icate a. exquisite; fragile; requiring tact **-del'icacy** n.

delicatess'en n. shop selling esp. imported or unusual foods

deli'cious [-ish'əs] a. delightful, pleasing to taste

delight' vt. please greatly -vi. take great pleasure (in) -n. great pleasure **-delight'ful** a. charming

delin'eate vt. portray by drawing or description

delin'quent n. someone guilty of delinquency -a. **-delin'quency** n. (minor) offence or misdeed

delir'ium n. disorder of mind, esp. in feverish illness; violent excitement **-delir'ious** a.

deliv'er vt. carry to destination; hand over; release; give birth or assist in birth (of); utter **-deliv'erance** n. rescue **-deliv'ery** n.

dell n. wooded hollow

del'ta n. alluvial tract at river mouth; Greek letter (Δ)

delude' [-lōōd'] vt. deceive; mislead **-delu'sion** n.

del'uge n. flood, downpour -vt. flood, overwhelm

de luxe [-looks'] a. rich, sumptuous; superior in quality

delve v. (with into) search intensively; dig

dem'agogue [-og] n. mob leader or agitator **-dem'agogy** n.

demand' [-ah-] vt. ask as giving an order; call for as due, necessary -n. urgent request; call for

de'marcate vt. mark boundaries or limits of **-demarca'tion** n.

demean' vt. degrade, lower

demean'our n. conduct, bearing

dement'ed a. mad, crazy

demera'ra n. kind of brown cane sugar

demer'it n. undesirable quality

demi- (comb. form) half, as in demigod

dem'ijohn n. large bottle

demil'itarize vt. prohibit military presence

demise' [-īz'] n. death; conveyance by will or lease

demo'bilize vt. disband (troops); discharge (soldier)

democ'racy n. government by the people or their elected representatives; state so governed –**democrat'ic** a.

demol'ish vt. knock to pieces; destroy utterly –**demoli'tion** n.

de'mon n. devil, evil spirit

dem'onstrate vt. show by reasoning, prove; describe, explain –vi. make exhibition of support, protest etc. –**demon'strable** a. –**demonstra'tion** n. –**demon'strative** a. expressing feelings; pointing out; conclusive –**dem'onstrator** n. one who demonstrates equipment etc.; one who takes part in a public demonstration; assistant in laboratory etc.

demor'alize vt. deprive of courage; undermine morally

demote' vt. reduce in rank –**demo'tion** n.

demur' [-mur'] vi. make difficulties, object (-rr-)

demure' [-myoor'] a. reserved

demurr'age n. charge for keeping ship etc. beyond time agreed

den n. hole of wild beast; small room, esp. study

den'ier n. unit of weight of silk, rayon and nylon yarn

den'igrate vt. belittle

den'im n. strong cotton drill

den'izen n. inhabitant

denomina'tion n. particular sect or church; name, esp. of class or group –**denom'inator** n. divisor in vulgar fraction

denote' vt. stand for; show

denoue'ment [dā-nōō'mon] n. unravelling of plot

denounce' vt. speak violently against; accuse –**denuncia'tion** n.

dense a. thick, compact; stupid –**dens'ity** n.

dent n./vt. (make) hollow or mark by blow or pressure

den'tal a. of, pert. to teeth or dentistry –**den'tist** n. surgeon who attends to teeth –**den'ture** n. (usu. pl.) set of false teeth

denude' vt. strip, make bare

deny' vt. declare untrue; contradict; reject; refuse to give (**denied'**, **deny'ing**) –**deni'al** n.

deo'dorant n. substance to mask odour

De'o volen'te [dā'o-vo-len'ti] Lat. God willing

DEP Department of Employment and Productivity

dep. depart(s); departure

depart' vi. go away; start out; vary; die –**depart'ure** n.

depart'ment n. division; branch

depend' vi. (usu. with on) rely entirely; live; be contingent –**depend'able** a. reliable –**depend'ant** n. one for whose maintenance another is responsible –**depend'ent** a. depending on –**depend'ence** n.

depict' vt. give picture of; describe

deplete' vt. empty; reduce

deplore' vt. lament, regret –**deplor'able** a.

deploy' vt. of troops (cause to) adopt battle formation

depop'ulate v. (cause to) be reduced in population

deport' vt. expel, banish

deport'ment n. behaviour

depose' vt. remove from office –vi. make statement on oath

depos'it [-poz'-] vt. set down; give into safe keeping; let fall –n. thing deposited; money given in part payment; sediment –**deposi'tion** n. statement written and attested; act of deposing or depositing –**depos'itor** n. –**depos'itory** n.

dep'ot [-ō] n. storehouse

deprave' vt. make bad, corrupt

dep'recate vt. express disapproval of

depre'ciate [-shi-] v. (cause to) fall in value, price –vt. belittle

depreda'tion n. plundering

depress' vt. affect with low spirits; lower –**depres'sion** n. hollow; low spirits; low state of trade

deprive' vt. dispossess –**deprived'** a. lacking adequate food, care, amenities etc.

dept. department

depth n. (degree of) deepness; deep place; intensity

dep'uty [-yoo-] n. assistant; delegate –**deputa'tion** n.

derange' vt. put out of place, order; make insane

der'elict a. abandoned; falling into ruins

deride' vt. treat with contempt, ridicule –**deris'ion** [-zh-] n. –**deri'sive** a. –**deri'sory** a.

derive' vt. get, come from –**deriva'tion** n. –**deriv'ative** a./n.

dermati'tis n. inflammation of skin

derog'atory a. belittling

derr'ick n. hoisting machine

derv n. diesel oil for road vehicles (diesel engine road vehicle)

des'cant n. Mus. decorative variation to basic melody

descend' [-send'] vi. come or go down; spring from; be transmitted; attack -vt. go or come down -descend'ant n. person descended from an ancestor -descent' n.

describe' vt. give detailed account of -descrip'tion n.

descry' vt. catch sight of (des'cried', descry'ing)

des'ecrate vi. violate sanctity of; profane

des'ert' [-z-] n. uninhabited and barren region

desert' [-z-] vt. abandon, leave -vi. run away from service

desert' [-z-] n. (usu. pl.) what is due as reward or punishment

deserve' [-z-] vt. show oneself worthy of

design' [-zīn'] vt. sketch; plan; intend -n. sketch; plan; decorative pattern; project

des'ignate [dez'ig-] vt. name, appoint -a. appointed but not yet installed

desire' [-zīr'] vt. wish, long for; ask for -n. longing; expressed wish; sexual appetite -desi'rable a. -desi'rous a.

desist' [-zist'] vt. cease, stop

desk n. writing table

des'olate a. uninhabited; neglected; solitary; forlorn -vt. lay waste; overwhelm with grief -desola'tion n.

despair' vi. lose hope -n. loss of all hope; cause of this

des'perate a. reckless from despair; hopelessly bad -despera'do [-rahd'-] n. reckless, lawless person (pl. -do(e)s)

despise' [-īz'] vt. look down on as inferior -des'picable [or -spik'-] a. base, contemptible, vile

despite' prep. in spite of

despoil' vt. plunder, rob

despond'ent a. dejected, depressed

des'pot n. tyrant, oppressor -despot'ic a. -des'potism n.

dessert' [-z-] n. sweet course, or fruit, served at end of meal

destina'tion n. place one is bound for

des'tine [-tin] vt. ordain beforehand; set apart

des'tiny n. fate

des'titute a. in absolute want

destroy' vt. ruin; put an end to; demolish -destroy'er n. small, swift warship -destruct'ible a. -destruc'tion n. ruin -destruct'ive a.

des'ultory a. aimless; unmethodical

detach' vt. unfasten, separate -detach'able a. -detached' a. standing apart; disinterested -detach'ment n. aloofness; detaching; body of troops on special duty

de'tail n. particular; small or unimportant part; treatment of anything item by item; soldier(s) assigned for duty -vt. relate in full; appoint

detain' vt. keep under restraint; keep waiting -deten'tion n.

detect' vt. find out or discover -detec'tion n. -detec'tive n. policeman detecting crime -detec't'or n.

détente' [dé-tahnt'] n. lessening of international tension

deter' vt. discourage; prevent (-rr-) -deter'rent a./n.

deter'gent n. cleansing substance

deteriorate v. become or make worse

deter'mine vt. decide; fix; be deciding factor in -vi. come to an end; come to decision -determina'tion n. determining; resolute conduct; resolve -deter'mined a. resolute

detest' vt. hate, loathe -detest'-able a.

det'onate v. (cause to) explode -det'onator n.

de'tour n. roundabout way -vi.

detract' v. take away (a part) from, diminish -detrac'tor n.

det'riment n. harm done, loss, damage -detrimen'tal a.

deuce [dyōōs] n. card with two spots; Tennis forty all; in exclamatory phrases, the devil

deval'ue, deval'uate v. reduce in value -devalua'tion n.

dev'astate vt. lay waste; ravage

devel'op vt. bring to maturity; elaborate; evolve; treat photographic film to bring out image; improve or change use (of land) -vi. grow to maturer state (devel'oped, devel'-oping) -devel'opment n.

de'viate vi. leave the way -de'viant n./a. (person) deviating from normal esp. in sexual practices -de'vious a. deceitful; roundabout

device' n. contrivance; scheme

dev'il n. personified spirit of evil; person of great wickedness, cruelty etc.; inf. fellow; inf. something difficult or annoying -vt. do work that passes for employer's; grill with hot condiments **-dev'ilish** a. **-dev'ilment** n. **-dev'ilry** n. **-devil-may-care** a. happy-go-lucky

devise' [-ɪz'] vt. plan

devoid' a. (usu. with of) empty

devolve' v. (cause to) pass on to another **-devolu'tion** [-lōō'-] n. devolving

devote' vt. give up exclusively (to person, purpose etc.) **-devo'ted** a. loving **-devotee'** n. ardent enthusiast **-devo'tion** n. deep affection; dedication -pl. prayers

devour' vt. eat greedily

devout' a. pious; sincere

dew n. moisture from air deposited as small drops at night **-dew-worm** n. C large earthworm used as bait

dexter'ity n. manual skill **-dex'terous** a.

dex'trose n. sweet-tasting crystalline solid found in fruit, honey, animal tissue

DHSS Department of Health and Social Security

dia- [dɪ-ə-] (comb. form) through

diabe'tes [-bē'tēz] n. various disorders characterized by excretion of abnormal amount of urine **-diabet'ic** n./a.

diabol'ic(al) a. devilish

diacrit'ic n. sign above letter indicating phonetic value

di'adem n. a crown

diagno'sis n. identification of disease from symptoms (pl. **diagno'ses**) **-di'agnose** vt.

diag'onal a./n. (line) from corner to corner

di'agram n. drawing, figure, to illustrate something

di'al n. face of clock etc.; plate marked with graduations on which a pointer moves; numbered disc on front of telephone -vt. operate telephone **(-ll-)**

di'alect n. characteristic speech of district

di'alogue n. conversation

dial'ysis n. Med. filtering of blood through membrane to remove waste products

diaman'té n. (fabric covered with) glittering particles

diam'eter n. (length of) straight line through centre of circle

di'amond n. very hard and brilliant precious stone; rhomboid figure; suit at cards

diaph'anous a. transparent

di'aphragm [-am] n. muscular partition dividing two cavities of body, midriff; disc wholly or partly closing tube; any thin dividing membrane

diarrhoe'a [-rē'ə] n. excessive looseness of the bowels

di'ary n. daily record of events; book for this

diaton'ic a. Mus. pert. to regular major and minor scales

di'atribe n. violently bitter verbal attack

dice pl.n. (also functions as sing., orig. sing. **die**) cubes with sides marked one to six for games of chance -vi. gamble with dice -vt. Cookery cut vegetables into small cubes

dichot'omy [-kot'-] n. division into two parts

dick'y, dick'ey n. false shirt front (pl. **dick'ies, dick'eys**)

dictate' v. say or read for another to transcribe; prescribe; impose -n. [dik'-] bidding **-dicta'tion** n. **-dicta'tor** n. absolute ruler **-dictato'rial** a. **-dicta'torship** n.

dic'tion n. choice and use of words; enunciation

dic'tionary n. book listing, alphabetically, words with meanings etc.

dic'tum n. pronouncement (pl. **dic'ta**)

did pt. of DO

didac'tic a. designed to instruct

diddle vt. inf. cheat

die[1] [dī] vi. cease to live; end; inf. look forward (to) (**died, dy'ing**)

die[2] [dī] n. shaped block to form metal in forge, press etc.

die'sel [dēz'l] a. pert. to internal-combustion engine using oil as fuel -n. this engine; the fuel

di'et n. restricted or regulated course of feeding; kind of food lived on -vi. follow a dietary regimen, as to lose weight **-di'etary** a.

diff'er vi. be unlike; disagree **-diff'erence** n. unlikeness; point of unlikeness; disagreement; remainder left after subtraction **-diff'erent** a.

differen'tial a. varying with circumstances -n. mechanism in car etc. allowing back wheels to revolve at different speeds; difference between rates of pay **-differen'tiate**

vt. serve to distinguish between, make different -*vi.* discriminate

diff'icult *a.* requiring effort, skill *etc.*, not easy; obscure -**diff'iculty** *n.* difficult task, problem; embarrassment; hindrance; trouble

diff'ident *a.* lacking confidence

diffrac'tion *n.* deflection of ray of light

diffuse' [-fyōōz'] *vt.* spread abroad -*a.* [-fyōōs'] widely spread; loose, wordy

dig *vi.* work with spade -*vt.* turn up with spade; excavate; thrust into (dug, digg'ing) -*n.* piece of digging; thrust; jibe -*pl.* *inf.* lodgings

digest' [-j-] *vt.* prepare (food) in stomach *etc.* for assimilation; bring into handy form by summarizing -*vi.* of food, undergo digestion -*n.* [dī'-] methodical summary -**digest'ible** *a.* -**diges'tion** *n.*

dig'it [-j-] *n.* finger or toe; any of the numbers 0 to 9 -**dig'ital** *a.* of digits; performed with fingers; displaying information by numbers ·

dig'nity *n.* stateliness, gravity; worthiness -**dig'nify** *vt.* give dignity to (-fied, -fying) -**dig'nitary** *n.* holder of high office

digress' [dī-] *vi.* deviate from subject -**digres'sion** *n.*

dik'tat *n.* arbitrary decree

dilap'idated *a.* in ruins

dilate' [dī-] *vt.* widen, expand -**dil-(at)a'tion** *n.*

dil'atory *a.* tardy, slow

dilemm'a *n.* position offering choice only between unwelcome alternatives

dilettan'te [-tahn'ti] *n.* person who enjoys fine arts as pastime; dabbler (*pl.* dilettan'ti)

dil'igent *a.* hard-working -**dil'igence** *n.*

dill *n.* herb with medicinal seeds

dilly-dall'y *vi.* *inf.* loiter

dilute' [-lōōt'] *vt.* reduce (liquid) in strength, often by adding water

dim *a.* faint, not bright; mentally dull; unfavourable (dimm'er *comp.*, dimm'est *sup.*) -*v.* make, grow dim (-mm-)

dime *n.* 10-cent piece

dimen'sion *n.* measurement, size

dimin'ish *v.* lessen -**dimin'utive** *a.* very small

diminuen'do *a./adv.* *Mus.* of sound, dying away

dim'ple *n.* small hollow in surface of skin, *esp.* of cheek

din *n.* continuous roar of confused noises -*vt.* ram (fact, opinion *etc.*) into (-nn-)

dine *vi.* eat dinner -*vt.* give dinner to -**di'ner** *n.*

din'ghy [ding'gi] *n.* small open boat; collapsible rubber boat

din'gy [-j-] *a.* dirty-looking, dull

dinn'er *n.* chief meal of the day; official banquet

di'nosaur *n.* extinct reptile, often of gigantic size

dint *n.* **-by dint of** by means of

di'ocese [dī'ə-sis] *n.* district, jurisdiction of bishop

dip *vt.* plunge or be plunged partly or for a moment into liquid; take up in ladle, bucket *etc.*; direct headlights of vehicle downwards -*vi.* go down; slope downwards (-pp-) -*n.* act of dipping; bathe; downward slope; hollow

diphthe'ria [dip-thē'-] *n.* infectious disease of throat

diph'thong [dif'-] *n.* union of two vowel sounds

diplo'ma *n.* document vouching for person's proficiency

diplo'macy *n.* management of international relations; tactful dealing -**dip'lomat** *n.*

dipp'er *n.* a ladle, scoop; bird (water ouzel)

dipsoma'nia *n.* uncontrollable craving for alcohol

dire *a.* terrible; urgent

direct' *vt.* control, manage, order; point out the way; aim -*a.* frank; straight; immediate; lineal -**direc'tion** *n.* directing; aim; instruction -**direc'tive** *a./n.* -**direct'ly** *adv.* -**direc'tor** *n.* one who directs, *esp.* a film; member of board managing company -**direc'tory** *n.* book of names, addresses, streets *etc.*

dirge *n.* song of mourning

dir'igible [-j-] *n.* airship

dirk *n.* short dagger

dirn'dl [durn'-] *n.* full, gathered skirt

dirt *n.* filth; soil; obscene material -**dirt'y** *a.* unclean; obscene; unfair; dishonest

dis- (*comb. form*) negation, opposition, deprivation; in many verbs indicates undoing of the action of simple verb In the list that follows, the meaning may be inferred from the word to which *dis* is prefixed

disa'ble *vt.* make unable; cripple, maim -**disabil'ity** *n.*

disabuse' [-byōōz'] *vt.* undeceive,

disillusion; free from error

disadvant'age [-vahnt'-] n. drawback; hindrance –vt. handicap –**disadvant'aged** a. deprived, discriminated against –**disadvanta'geous** a.

disaffect'ed a. ill-disposed

disagree' vi. be at variance; conflict; (of food etc.) have bad effect on –**disagree'ment** n. –**disagree'able** a.

disappear' vi. vanish; cease to exist; be lost –**disappear'ance** n.

disappoint' vt. fail to fulfil (hope) –**disappoint'ment** n.

disarm' v. deprive of weapons; win over –**disarm'ament** n.

disarray' v. throw into disorder –n. disorderliness

disas'ter [-zahs'-] n. sudden or great misfortune –**disas'trous** a.

disbar' vt. Law expel from the bar

disburse' vt. pay out money

disc n. thin, flat, circular object; gramophone record –**disc jockey** announcer playing records

discard' v. reject; cast off

discern' [-sern'] vt. make out; distinguish –**discern'ible** a. –**discern'ing** a. discriminating

discharge' v. release; dismiss; emit; perform (duties); fulfil (obligations); fire off; unload; pay –n. discharging; being discharged

disci'ple [-sī'-] n. follower of a teacher

dis'cipline [-si-plin] n. training that produces orderliness, obedience, self-control; system of rules, etc. –vt. train; punish –**dis'ciplinary** a.

disclaim' vt. deny, renounce

disclose' [-ōz'] vt. make known

dis'co n. short for DISCOTHEQUE

discol'our [-kul'-] vt. stain

discom'fit [-um'-] vt. embarrass

disconcert' vt. ruffle, upset

discon'solate a. very unhappy

dis'cord n. strife; disagreement of sounds –**discord'ant** a.

dis'cotheque [-tek] n. club etc. for dancing to recorded music

dis'count [or -kount'] vt. reject as unsuitable; deduct from usual price –n. [dis'-] amount deducted from cost

discour'age [-kur'-] vt. reduce confidence of; deter; show disapproval of

dis'course n. conversation; speech –vi. [-kaws'] speak, converse

discov'er [-kuv'-] vt. (be the first to) find; make known –**discov'erable** a. –**discov'ery** n.

discred'it vt. damage reputation of; cast doubt on; reject as untrue –n. disgrace; doubt

discreet' a. prudent, circumspect

discrep'ancy n. variation, as between figures

discrete' a. separate

discre'tion [-kresh'on] n. quality of being discreet; freedom to act as one chooses –**discre'tionary** a.

discrim'inate vi. show prejudice; distinguish between –**discrimina'tion** n.

discur'sive a. rambling

dis'cus n. disc-shaped object thrown in athletic competition

discuss' vt. exchange opinions about; debate –**discus'sion** n.

disdain' n./vt. scorn

disease' n. illness

disembod'ied a. (of spirit) released from bodily form

disenchant'ed [-ah-] a. disillusioned

disfig'ure vt. mar appearance of

disgorge' vt. vomit

disgrace' n. shame, dishonour –vt. bring shame upon –**disgrace'ful** a.

disgrun'tled a. vexed; put out

disguise' [-gīz'] vt. change appearance of, make unrecognizable; conceal –n. device to conceal identity

disgust' n./vt. (affect with) violent distaste, loathing

dish n. shallow vessel for food; portion or variety of food -vt. serve (up)

dishev'elled a. [-sh-] untidy

disillu'sion [-loo-] vt. destroy ideals of -n.

disinfect'ant n. substance that prevents or removes infection -**disinfect'** vt.

disingen'uous a. not sincere

disinher'it vt. to deprive of inheritance

disin'tegrate v. fall to pieces

disin'terested a. free from bias or partiality

disjoint' vt. put out of joint; break the natural order of -**disjoint'ed** a. (of discourse) incoherent; disconnected

dislike' vt. consider unpleasant or disagreeable -n. feeling of not liking

dis'locate vt. put out of joint

dislodge' vt. drive out from previous position

dis'mal [-z-] a. depressing

disman'tle vt. take apart

dismay' vt. dishearten, daunt -n. consternation

dismem'ber vt. tear limb from limb

dismiss' vt. discharge from employment; send away; reject -**dismiss'al** n.

disobey' [-bā'] v. refuse or fail to obey -**disobe'dience** n. -**disobe'dient** a.

disor'der n. confusion; ailment -vt. -**disor'derly** a. unruly

disor'ientate vt. cause (someone) to lose his bearings, confuse

disown' vt. refuse to acknowledge

dispar'age [-pa'rij] vt. belittle

dispar'ity n. inequality; incongruity

dispas'sionate a. impartial

dispatch', despatch' vt. send off promptly; finish off -n. speed; official message

dispel' vt. drive away (-ll-)

dispense' vt. deal out; make up (medicine); administer (justice) -**dispens'able** a. -**dispens'ary** n. place where medicine is made up -**dispensa'tion** n. -**dispense with** do away with; manage without

disperse' vt. scatter

dispir'ited a. dejected

displace' vt. move from its place; take place of

display' vt./n. show

displease' v. offend; annoy

dispose' [-ōz'] vt. arrange; distribute -vi. deal with -**dispo'sable** a. designed to be thrown away after

use -**disposi'tion** n. temperament; arrangement -**dispose of** sell, get rid of

dispute' vi. debate, discuss -vt. call in question; contest -**dispu'table** a. -**dispu'tant** n.

disqual'ify vt. make ineligible

disqui'et n. anxiety, uneasiness

disregard' vt. ignore -n. lack of attention, respect

disrepair' n. state of bad repair, neglect

disrupt' vt. throw into disorder

dissect' vt. cut up (body) for detailed examination

dissem'ble v. pretend; disguise

dissem'inate vt. spread abroad

dissent' vi. differ in opinion; express such difference -**dissen'sion** n.

disserta'tion n. written thesis

disser'vice n. ill turn, wrong

dis'sident n./a. (one) not in agreement, esp. with government

diss'ipate vt. scatter; waste, squander -**diss'ipated** a.

disso'ciate v. separate, sever

diss'olute a. lax in morals

dissolu'tion [-loo-] n. break up; termination

dissolve' [-z-] vt. absorb or melt in fluid; annul -vi. melt in fluid; disappear; scatter -**dissol'vable** a. -**dissol'uble** a.

diss'onant a. jarring

dissuade' [-sw-] vt. advise to refrain, persuade not to

dis'taff [-ahf] n. stick to hold wool etc., for spinning

dis'tance n. amount of space between two things; remoteness; aloofness -**dis'tant** a.

distaste' n. dislike

distem'per n. disease of dogs; paint

distend' v. swell out -**disten'sible** a. -**disten'sion** n.

distil' vt. vaporize and recondense a liquid; purify (-ll-) -**distill'ery** n.

distinct' a. easily seen; definite; separate -**distinc'tion** n. point of difference; act of distinguishing; repute, high honour -**distinc'tive** a. characteristic

distin'guish [-ng'gw-] vt. make difference in; recognize; honour -vi. (usu. with between or among) draw distinction, grasp difference -**distin'guished** a.

distort' vt. put out of shape; misrepresent

distract' vt. draw attention away; divert; perplex, drive mad –**distrac'-tion** n.

distraught' [-awt'] a. frantic, distracted

distress' n. trouble, pain –vt. afflict

distrib'ute vt. deal out; spread –**distribu'tion** n. –**distrib'utor** n.

dis'trict n. region, locality; portion of territory

disturb' vt. trouble, agitate, unsettle –**disturb'ance** n.

disuse' [-s'] n. state of being no longer used –**disused'** [-zd'] a.

ditch n. long narrow hollow dug in ground for drainage etc.

dith'er vi. be uncertain or indecisive –n. this state

ditt'o n. same, aforesaid

ditt'y n. simple song

diur'nal [dī-ur'-] a. daily

divan' n. bed, couch without back or head

dive vi. plunge under surface of water; descend suddenly; go deep down into –n. act of diving; sl. disreputable bar or club –**div'er** n.

diverge' [dī-] vi. get farther apart; separate

diverse' [dī-] a. different, varied –**divers'ify** vt. make varied (-**ified, ifying**) –**divers'ity** n.

divert' [dī-] vt. turn aside; amuse –**diver'sion** n.

divest' [dī-] vt. unclothe

divide' vt. make into parts, split up; distribute, share –vi. become separated –n. watershed –**div'idend** n. share of profits; number to be divided by another

divine' a. of, pert. to God; sacred –n. clergyman –v. guess; predict –**divin'-ity** n.

divi'sion [-vizh'-] n. act of dividing; part of whole; barrier; section; difference in opinion etc.; *Math.* method of finding how many times one number is contained in another; army unit –**divis'ible** a. –**divi'sor** n. *Math.* number which divides dividend

divorce' n./vt. (make) legal dissolution of marriage; separation

div'ot n. piece of turf

divulge' [dī-] vt. reveal

DIY do-it-yourself

dizz'y a. feeling dazed, unsteady –**dizz'iness** n.

DJ disc jockey

DNA n. abbrev. for **deoxyrib-onucleic acid**, main constituent of the chromosomes of all organisms

do [dōō] vt. perform, effect, finish; work at; solve; suit; provide; sl. cheat –vi. act; fare; suffice –v. aux. makes negative and interrogative sentences and expresses emphasis (**did, done, do'ing**) –n. inf. celebration –**do away with** destroy –**do up** fasten; renovate

do. *ditto* lt. the same

do'cile a. willing to obey, submissive –**docil'ity** n.

dock' n. artificial enclosure for loading or repairing ships –v. put or go into dock –**dock'er** n. –**dock'-yard** n.

dock' n. solid part of tail; stump –vt. cut short; deduct (an amount) from

dock' n. enclosure in criminal court for prisoner

dock' n. coarse weed

dock'et n. piece of paper sent with package etc.

doc'tor n. medical practitioner; one holding university's highest degree –vt. treat medically; repair; falsify (accounts etc.)

doc'trine [-in] n. what is taught; belief, dogma

doc'ument n. piece of paper etc. providing information –vt. furnish with proofs –**document'ary** a./n. esp. (of) type of film dealing with real life

dodd'er vi. totter, as with age

dodge [doj] v. (attempt to) avoid by moving quickly; evade –n. trick; act of dodging –**dodg'y** inf. a. dangerous

Dodg'em [doj'-] R car used for bumping other cars in rink at funfair

do'do n. large extinct bird (pl. **do'-do(e)s**)

doe [dō] n. female of deer, hare, rabbit

doek [dook] n. SA inf. head cloth worn esp. by Afr. women

does [duz] third pers. sing., pres. ind. active of DO

doff vt. take off

dog n. domesticated carnivorous four-legged mammal; male of wolf, fox and other animals; person (in contempt, abuse or playfully) –vt. follow closely (-**gg**-) –**dogg'ed** a. persistent, tenacious –**dog-ear** n. turned-down corner of page in book –vt. –**dog-end** inf. n. cigarette end; rejected piece of anything –**dog train C** sleigh drawn by dog team

dogg'erel n. trivial verse

dog'ma n. article of belief (pl. -**s,**

-ata) **-dogmat'ic** a. asserting opinions with arrogance

doi'ly, doy'l(e)y n. small lacy mat to place under cake, dish etc.

dol'drums pl.n. state of depression; region of light winds and calms near the equator

dole n. inf. payment under unemployment insurance -vt. (usu. with out) deal out sparingly

dole'ful a. dreary, mournful

doll n. child's toy image of human being

dol'lar n. standard monetary unit of many countries, esp. USA

dol'lop n. inf. semisolid lump

dol'ly n. doll; wheeled support for film, TV camera

dol'our n. grief, sadness, distress **-dol'orous** a.

dol'phin n. sea mammal with beaklike snout

doit [-ɔ-] n. stupid fellow

domain' n. lands held or ruled over; sphere of influence

dome n. rounded roof; something of this shape

domes'tic a. of, in the home; homeloving; (of animals) tamed; of, in one's own country -n. house servant **-domes'ticate** vt. tame

dom'icile n. person's regular place of abode

dom'inate vt. rule, control; of heights, overlook -vi. be most influential **-domina'tion** n. **-domineer'** vi. act imperiously, tyrannize

dom'inee n. SA minister of Dutch Reformed Church

domin'ion n. sovereignty, rule; territory of government

Dominion Day see CANADA DAY

dom'inoes pl.n. game played with 28 oblong flat pieces marked with spots

don' vt. put on (clothes) (-nn-)

don' n. fellow or tutor of college; Spanish title, Sir

donate' [dō-] vt. give **-dona'tion** n. gift to fund **-do'nor** n.

done pp. of DO

don'ga [-ng'ə] n. SA deep gully

donk'ey n. ass (pl. -eys)

doo'dle vi./n. scribble

doom n. fate; ruin; judicial sentence -vt. condemn; destine

door [dawr] n. hinged barrier to close entrance **-door'way** n.

dope n. kind of varnish; narcotic drug; inf. stupid person -vt. drug **-do'p(e)y** a.

dorm'ant a. not active; sleeping

dorm'er n. upright window set in sloping roof

dorm'itory n. sleeping room with many beds

dor'mouse n. small hibernating mouselike rodent

dorp n. SA small town

dor'sal a. of, on back

dose n. amount (of drug etc.) -vt. give doses to

doss inf. n. temporary bed -vi. sleep

doss'ier [-i-ā, -yə] n. set of papers on particular subject

dot n. small spot, mark -vt. mark with dots; sprinkle

dote vi. (with on or upon) be passionately fond of **-do'tage** n. senility

doub'le [dub'l] a. of two parts, layers etc.; twice as much as many; designed for two users -adv. twice; to twice the amount or extent; in a pair -n. person or thing exactly like another; quantity twice as much as another; sharp turn; running pace -v. make, become double; increase twofold; fold in two; turn sharply **-doub'ly** adv. **-double-cross** v. betray **-double-quick** a./adv. very fast

doub'let [dub-] n. close-fitting body garment formerly worn by men

doubloon' [dub-] n. ancient Spanish gold coin

doubt [dowt] vt. hesitate to believe; call in question; suspect -vi. be wavering in belief or opinion -n. (state of) uncertainty **-doubt'ful** a. **-doubt'less** adv.

douche [dōōsh] n. jet of water applied to (part of) body

dough [dō] n. flour or meal kneaded with water; sl. money **-dough'nut** n. sweetened and fried piece of dough

dour [dōōr] a. grim; severe

douse [dows] vt. thrust into water; extinguish (light)

dove [duv] n. bird of pigeon family **-dove'tail** v. fit closely, neatly together

dow'ager [-j-] n. widow with title or property from husband

dow'dy a. shabbily dressed

dow'el n. wooden, metal peg

dow'er n. widow's share of husband's estate -vt. endow **-dow'ry** n. property wife brings to husband

down' adv. to, in, or towards, lower position; below the horizon; (of payment) on the spot -prep. from higher to lower part of; along -a. depressed -v.t. knock, pull, push down; inf. drink -**down′ward** a./adv. -**down′wards** adv. -**down′cast** a. dejected; looking down -**down′right** a. straightforward -adv. quite, thoroughly

down[1] n. soft underfeathers, hair; fluff -**down′y** a.

down′land n. open high land: also **downs** pl.n.

doz. dozen

doze vi./n. sleep, nap

doz′en [duz′-] n. (set of) twelve

Dr. Doctor; Drive

drab a. dull, monotonous

drachm [dram] n. 1/8 of fluid ounce

Draco′nian a. (also d-) very harsh, cruel

draft[1] [-ah-] n. sketch; rough copy of document; order for money; detachment of troops -vt. make sketch of; make rough copy; send detached party

draft[2] US vt. select for compulsory military service; see DRAUGHT -n.

drag vt. pull along with difficulty; trail; sweep with net; protract -vi. lag, trail; be tediously protracted (-gg-) -n. check on progress; checked motion -**drag′net** n. fishing net to be dragged along sea floor; comprehensive search, esp. by police

dragée′ [-zhā′] n. sugar-coated sweet, nut or pill

drag′on n. mythical fire-breathing monster -**drag′onfly** n. long-bodied insect with gauzy wings

dragoon′ n. cavalryman -vt. coerce

drain vt. draw off (liquid) by pipes, ditches etc.; dry; empty; exhaust -vi. flow off or away; become rid of liquid -n. channel; sewer; depletion, strain -**drain′age** n.

drake n. male duck

dram n. small draught of strong drink; drachm

dram′a [-ahm′-] n. stage play; art or literature of plays; playlike series of events -**dramat′ic** a. pert. to drama; exciting -**dram′atist** n. writer of plays -**dram′atize** vt. adapt for acting

drape vt. cover, adorn with cloth -**dra′per** n. dealer in cloth, linen etc. -**dra′pery** n.

dras′tic a. extreme; severe

draught US **draft** [drahft] n. current of air; act of drawing; act of drinking; quantity drunk at once;

depth of ship in water -pl. game played on chessboard with flat round "men" -a. for drawing; drawn -vt. see DRAFT -**draught′y** a. full of air currents -**draughts′man** n. one who makes drawings, plans etc.

draw vt. pull, haul; inhale; entice; portray with pencil etc.; write; attract; get by lot; of ship, require (depth of water); take from (well, barrel etc.); receive (money) -vi. pull, shrink; attract; make, admit current of air; make pictures with pencil etc.; of game, tie; write orders for money; come (near) (**drew** pt., **drawn** pp.) -n. event that attracts; casting of lots; tie -**draw′er** n. one or that which draws; sliding box in table or chest -pl. two-legged undergarment -**draw′ing** n. art of depicting in line; sketch so done; action of verb -**draw′back** n. snag -**draw′bridge** n. hinged bridge to pull up -**drawing room** living room, sitting room -**draw up** arrange; stop

drawl v. speak slowly -n. such speech

drawn a. haggard

dread [dred] vt. fear greatly -n. awe, terror -a. feared, awful -**dread′ful** a. disagreeable, shocking or bad

dream [drēm] n. vision during sleep; fancy, reverie, aspiration -vi. have dreams -vt. see, imagine in dreams; think of as possible (**dreamt** [dremt] or **dreamed** [drēmd] pt./pp.) -**dream′y** a.

drear′y a. dismal, dull

dredge[1] v. bring up mud etc., from sea bottom -n. scoop

dredge[2] vt. sprinkle with flour etc.

dregs pl.n. sediment, grounds

drench vt. wet thoroughly, soak

dress vt. clothe; array for show; prepare; put dressing on (wound) -vi. put on one's clothes -n. one-piece garment for woman; clothing; evening wear -**dress′er** n. one who dresses; kitchen sideboard -**dress′ing** n. something applied, as sauce to food, ointment to wound etc. -**dress′y** a. stylish

dress′age [-ahzh-] n. method of training horse

drey n. squirrel's nest

drib′ble v. flow in drops, trickle; run at the mouth -n. trickle, drop

drift vi. be carried as by current of air, water -n. process of being driven by current; tendency; meaning; windheaped mass of snow, sand etc.

-drift'er n. **-drift'wood** n. wood washed ashore by sea

drill[1] n. boring tool; exercise of soldiers; routine teaching -vt. bore hole; exercise in routine -v. practise routine

drill[2] vt./n. (machine to) sow seed in furrows

drink v. swallow liquid (**drank** pt., **drunk** pp.) -n. liquid for drinking; intoxicating liquor **-drink'able** a. **-drink'er** n.

drip v. fall or let fall in drops (-pp-) -n. act of dripping; drop; Med. intravenous administration of solution; inf. insipid person **-drip'ping** n. melted fat from roasting meat -a. very wet **-drip-dry** a. (of fabric) drying free of creases if hung up while wet

drive vt. urge in some direction; make move and travel (vehicle, animal etc.); hit with force -vi. keep machine, animal, going, steer it; be conveyed in vehicle (**drove**, **driv'en**, **driv'ing**) -n. act, action of driving; journey in vehicle; united effort, campaign; energy; forceful stroke **-driv'er** n.

driv'el vi. run at the mouth; talk nonsense -n. silly nonsense

driz'zle vi./n. rain in fine drops

droll [-ō-] a. funny, odd

drom'edary n. one-humped camel

drone n. male bee; lazy idler; deep humming -v. hum; talk in monotonous tone

drool vi. to slaver, drivel

droop vi. hang down; wilt, flag -vt. let hang down **-droop'y** a.

drop n. globule of liquid; very small quantity; fall, descent; distance of fall -vt. let fall; utter casually; set down; discontinue -vi. fall; lapse; come or go casually (-pp-) **-drop'pings** pl.n. dung of rabbits, sheep, birds etc. **-drop'out** n. person who fails to complete course of study or one who rejects conventional society

drop'sy n. disease causing watery fluid to collect in the body

dross n. scum of molten metal; impurity, refuse

drought [-owt] n. long spell of dry weather

drove n. herd, flock, esp. in motion

drown v. die or be killed by immersion in liquid; make sound inaudible by louder sound

drow'sy [-z-] a. half-asleep; lulling; dull **-drowse** vi.

drub vt. thrash, beat (-bb-) **-drubb'-ing** n. beating

drudge vi. work at menial or distasteful tasks -n. one who drudges **-drudg'ery** n.

drug n. medical substance; narcotic -vt. mix drugs with; administer drug to (-gg-)

dru'id [-ōō-] n. (also D-) Celtic priest

drum n. percussion instrument of skin stretched over round hollow frame; various things shaped like drum; part of ear -v. play drum; tap, thump continuously (-mm-) **-drum'm'er** n. **-drum major** leader of military band **-drum'stick** n. stick for beating drum; lower joint of cooked fowl's leg

drunk a. overcome by strong drink **-drunk'ard** n. **-drunk'en** a. **-drunk'enness** n.

dry a. without moisture; not yielding liquid; unfriendly; caustically witty; uninteresting; lacking sweetness -vt. remove water, moisture -vi. become dry; evaporate (**dried**, **dry'ing**) **-dri'ly** adv. **-dry'er**, **dri'er** n. person or thing that dries; apparatus for removing moisture **-dry-clean** v. clean clothes with solvent **-dry ice** solid carbon dioxide

DSO Distinguished Service Order

du'al a. twofold; of two, double, forming pair

dub vt. confer knighthood on; give title to; provide film with soundtrack (-bb-)

du'bious a. causing doubt

du'cal a. of, like a duke

duc'at [duk'-] n. former gold coin of Italy etc.

duch'ess n. duke's wife or widow

duch'y n. territory of duke

duck[1] n. common swimming bird (**drake** masc.) -v. plunge (someone) under water; bob down **-duck'ling** n.

duck[2] n. strong cotton fabric

duct n. channel, tube **-duct'ile** a. capable of being drawn into wire; flexible and tough **-duct'less** a.

dud n. futile, worthless person or thing -a. worthless

dudg'eon [-j'on] n. anger

due a. owing; proper; expected; timed for -adv. (with points of compass) exactly -n. person's right; (usu. pl.) charge, fee etc. **-du'ly** adv. properly; punctually **-due to** attributable to; caused by

du'el n. arranged fight with deadly

weapons, between two persons -*vi.* fight in duel (-**ll**-)

duet' [dyōō'-] *n.* piece of music for two performers

duff'el, duff'le *n.* coarse woollen cloth; coat of this

duff'er *n.* stupid inefficient person

dug'out *n.* covered excavation to provide shelter; canoe of hollowed-out tree; *Sport* bench for players when not on the field

duke *n.* peer of rank next below prince -**duke'dom** *n.*

dul'cet [-sit] *a.* (of sounds) sweet, melodious

dul'cimer [-sim-] *n.* stringed instrument played with hammers

dull *a.* stupid; sluggish; tedious; overcast -*v.* make or become dull -**dull'ard** *n.* -**dull'y** *adv.*

dumb [dum] *a.* incapable of speech; silent; *inf.* stupid -**dumb'bell** *n.* weight for exercises -**dumbfound'** *vt.* confound into silence

dumm'y *n.* tailor's or dressmaker's model; imitation object; baby's dummy teat -*a.* sham, bogus

dump *vt.* throw down in mass; deposit; unload -*n.* rubbish heap; temporary store of stores -*pl.* low spirits -**dump'ling** *n.* small round pudding of dough -**dumpy** *a.* short, stout

dun[1] *vt.* persistently demand payment of debts (-**nn**-)

dun[2] *a.* of dull greyish brown

dunce *n.* stupid pupil

dun'derhead *n.* blockhead

dune *n.* sandhill

dung *n.* excrement of animals

dungaree' *n.* coarse cotton fabric -*pl.* overalls of this

dun'geon [-jan] *n.* underground cell for prisoners

dunk *vt.* dip bread *etc.* in liquid before eating it

du'o *n.* pair of performers

duode'num *n.* upper part of small intestine -**duode'nal** *a.*

dupe *n.* victim of delusion or sharp practice -*vt.* deceive

du'plex *a.* twofold

du'plicate *vt.* make exact copy of -*a.* double -*n.* exact copy -**duplica'tion** *n.* -**du'plicator** *n.* -**duplic'ity** [-plis'-] *n.* deceitfulness, double-dealing

du'rable *a.* lasting, resisting wear -**durabil'ity** *n.*

dura'tion *n.* time thing lasts

duress' [dyoo-] *n.* compulsion

du'ring *prep.* throughout, in the time of, in the course of

dusk *n.* darker stage of twilight -**dusk'y** *a.*

dust *n.* fine particles, powder of earth or other matter; ashes of the dead -*vt.* sprinkle with powder; rid of dust -**dust'er** *n.* cloth for removing dust -**dust'y** *a.* covered with dust -**dust'bin** *n.* container for household rubbish

Dutch *a.* pert. to the Netherlands, its inhabitants, its language

du'ty *n.* moral or legal obligation; that which is due; tax on goods -**du'teous** *a.* -**du'tiful** *a.*

du'vet [dōō'va] *n.* quilt filled with down or artificial fibre

dux [duks] *n.* head pupil of school or class, leader

DV *Deo volente*

dwarf *n.* very undersized person; mythological, small, manlike creature (*pl.* dwarfs, dwarves) -*a.* unusually small -*vt.* make seem small; make stunted

dwell *vi.* live, make one's abode (in); think, speak at length (on) (dwelt *pt./pp.*) -**dwell'ing** *n.* house

dwin'dle *vi.* waste away

dye [dī] *vt.* impregnate (cloth *etc.*) with colouring matter; colour thus (dyed [dīd], dye'ing [dī'ing]) -*n.* colouring matter in solution

dyke *n.* embankment to prevent flooding; ditch

dynam'ics [dī-] *pl.n.* (with *sing. v.*) branch of physics dealing with force as producing or affecting motion -**dynam'ic** *a.* energetic and forceful

dy'namite *n.* high explosive mixture -*vt.* blow up with this

dy'namo *n.* machine to convert mechanical into electrical energy, generator of electricity (*pl.* -mos)

dyn'asty [din'-] *n.* line, family of hereditary rulers

dys'entery *n.* infection of intestine causing severe diarrhoea

dysfunc'tion [dis-] *n.* abnormal, impaired functioning

dyslex'ia [dis-] *n.* impaired ability to read -**dyslex'ic** *a.*

dyspep'sia [dis-] *n.* indigestion -**dyspep'tic** *a./n.*

dys'trophy *n.* wasting of body tissues, esp. muscles

E

E East; Eastern; English

each *a./pron.* every one taken separately

ea'ger [e'-] *a.* having a strong wish; keen, impatient

ea'gle [e'gl] *n.* large bird of prey

ear[1] *n.* organ of hearing; sense of hearing; sensitiveness to sounds; attention **-ear'mark** *vt.* assign for definite purpose **-ear'phone** *n.* receiver for radio etc. held to or put in ear **-ear'ring** *n.* ornament for lobe of the ear **-ear'shot** *n.* hearing distance **-ear'wig** *n.* small insect with pincer-like tail

ear[1] *n.* spike, head of corn

earl [erl] *n.* British nobleman

ear'ly [erl'-] *a./adv.* before expected or usual time; in first part, near beginning

earn [ern] *vt.* obtain by work or merit; gain **-earn'ings** *pl.n.*

earn'est [ern'-] *a.* serious, sincere **-in earnest** serious, determined

earth [er-] *n.* planet we live on; ground; soil; electrical connection to earth **-vt.** cover, connect with earth **-earth'ly** *a.* possible **-earth'y** *a.* of earth; uninhibited **-earth'enware** *n.* (vessels of) baked clay **-earth'quake** *n.* convulsion of earth's surface **-earth'worm** *n.*

ease [ez] *n.* comfort; freedom from constraint, awkwardness or trouble; idleness **-v.** reduce burden; give ease to; slacken; (cause to) move carefully **-eas'ily** *adv.* **-eas'y** *a.* not difficult; free from pain, care, or anxiety; compliant; comfortable **-easy going** *a.* not fussy; indolent

eas'el [ez'l] *n.* frame to support picture etc.

east *n.* part of horizon where sun rises; eastern lands, orient **-a.** on, in, or near, east; coming from east **-adv.** from, or to, east **-east'erly** *a./n.* **-east'ern** *a.* **-east'ward** *a./n.*

East'er *n.* movable festival of the Resurrection of Christ

eas'y *see* EASE

eat *v.* chew and swallow; destroy; gnaw; wear away (ate *pt.*, **eat'en** *pp.*) **-eat'able** *a.*

eau de Cologne [ō-də-kə-lōn'] Fr. a light perfume

eaves [evz] *pl.n.* overhanging edges of roof **-eaves'drop** *v.* listen secretly

ebb *vi.* flow back; decay **-n.** flowing back of tide; decline, decay

eb'ony *n.* hard black wood **-a.**

ebull'ient *a.* exuberant

eccen'tric [eks-] *a.* odd, unconventional; irregular; not placed centrally **-n.** odd, unconventional person **-eccentric'ity** [-is'-] *n.*

ecclesias'tic [-klēz-] *n.* clergyman **-a.** of the Christian Church **-ecclesias'tical** *a.*

ECG electrocardiogram; electrocardiograph

ech'elon [esh'-] *n.* level of command; formation of troops, planes etc.

ech'o [ek'ō] *n.* repetition of sounds by reflection; imitation (*pl.* **ech'oes**) **-vt.** repeat as echo; imitate **-vi.** resound; be repeated (**ech'oed**, **ech'oing**)

éclair [ā-klār'] *n.* finger-shaped, iced cake filled with cream

eclec'tic *a.* selecting from various sources

eclipse *n.* blotting out of sun, moon etc. by another heavenly body; obscurity **-vt.** obscure; surpass

ecol'ogy *n.* science of plants and animals in relation to their environment **-ecolog'ical** *a.* **-ecol'ogist** *n.*

econ'omy *n.* careful management of resources to avoid unnecessary expenditure; system of interrelationship of money, industry and employment **-econom'ic** *a.* **-econom'ical** *a.* frugal **-econom'ics** *pl.n.* (*with sing.* -*v.*) study of economies of nations; (*used as pl.*) financial aspects **-econ'omist** *n.* **-econ'omize** *v.*

ec'stasy *n.* exalted state of feeling **-ecstat'ic** *a.*

ecumen'ic(al) [ē-kyoo-] *a.* of the Christian Church, *esp.* its unity **-ecumen'icism** *n.*

ec'zema *n.* skin disease

edd'y *n.* small whirl in water, smoke etc. **-vi.** move in whirls (**edd'ied**, **edd'ying**)

edge *n.* border, boundary; cutting side of blade; sharpness; advantage **-vt.** sharpen, give edge or border to; move gradually **-vi.** advance gradually **-edg'y** *a.* irritable **-on edge** nervy; excited

ed'ible *a.* eatable

e'dict *n.* order, decree

ed'ifice [-fis] *n.* building

ed'ify vt. improve morally, instruct (-fied, -fying)

ed'it vt. prepare book, film, tape etc. **-edi'tion** n. form in which something is published; number of copies **-ed'itor** n. **-editor'ial** a. of editor **-n.** article stating opinion of newspaper etc.

ed'ucate vt. provide schooling for; teach; train **-educa'tion** n. **-educa'tional** a. **-educa'tion(al)ist** n. **-ed'ucator** n.

EEC European Economic Community

eel n. snakelike fish

ee'rie, ee'ry a. weird, uncanny

efface' vt. wipe or rub out

effect' n. result; efficacy; impression; condition of being operative **-pl.** property; lighting, sounds etc. **-vt.** bring about **-effect'ive** a. **-effect'ual** a.

effem'inate a. womanish, unmanly

effervesce' [-es'] vi. give off bubbles **-efferves'cent** a.

effica'cious a. effective

effi'cient [-fish'ənt] a. capable, competent **-effi'ciency** n.

eff'igy n. image, likeness

eff'luent n. liquid discharged as waste

eff'ort n. exertion, endeavour, attempt or something achieved

effront'ery [-un-] n. impudence

effu'sive a. gushing

e.g. exempli gratia (Lat., for example)

egalita'rian n. a believing that all people should be equal

egg¹ n. oval or round object from which young emerge

egg² vt. **-egg on** urge

eg'o [or ē'-] n. the self **-eg'otism** n. selfishness; self-conceit **-eg'otist** n. **-egotis'tic(al)** a. **-egocen'tric** a. self-centred

egre'gious [-jəs] a. blatant

e'gress n. way out; departure

e'gret n. lesser white heron

ei'der [ī-] n. Arctic duck **-ei'derdown** n. its breast feathers; quilt

eight [āt] n. cardinal number one above seven; eight-oared boat; its crew **-a.** **-eight'een** a./n. eight more than ten **-eight'eenth** a./n. **-eighth** [āt-th] a./n. **-eight'ieth** a./n. **-eight'y** a./n. ten times eight

ei'ther [ī-, ē-] a./pron. one or the other; one of two; each **-adv./conj.** bringing in first of alternatives

ejac'ulate v. eject (semen); exclaim **-ejacula'tion** n.

eject' vt. throw out; expel

eke out make (supply) last

elab'orate [-it] a. detailed; complicated **-vi.** [-āt] expand (upon) **-vt.** work out in detail

e'land n. largest S Afr. antelope, resembling elk

elapse' vi. of time, pass

elas'tic a. springy; flexible **-n.** tape containing strands of rubber

ela'tion n. high spirits **-elate'** vt. (usu. passive) make happy

el'bow [-bō] n. joint between fore and upper parts of arm; part of sleeve covering this **-vt.** shove with elbow

el'der a. older, senior **-comp.** of OLD **-n.** person of greater age; official of certain churches **-el'derly** a. **-el'dest** a. oldest **-sup.** of OLD

elect' vt. choose by vote; choose **-a.** appointed but not yet in office; chosen **-elec'tion** n. **-elec'tive** a. appointed by election **-elec'tor** n. **-elec'toral** a. **-elec'torate** n. body of electors

electric'ity [-is'-] n. form of energy electric current **-elec'tric** a. of, transmitting or powered by electricity **-elec'trical** a. **-electri'cian** n. one trained in installation etc. of electrical devices **-elec'trify** vt. (-fied, -fying)

electro- (comb. form) by, caused by electricity, as in **electrother'apy** n.

electrocar'diograph n. instrument for recording electrical activity of heart **-electrocar'diogram** n. tracing produced by this

elec'trocute vt. kill by electricity

elec'trode n. conductor of electric current

elec'trolyse vt. decompose by electricity **-electrol'ysis** n.

elec'tron n. one of fundamental components of atom, charged with negative electricity **-electron'ic** a. **-electron'ics** pl.n. (with sing. v.) physical science of electrons

elec'troplate vt. coat with silver etc. by electrolysis

el'egant a. graceful, tasteful; refined **-el'egance** n.

el'egy [-ji] n. lament for the dead in poem **-elegi'ac** a.

el'ement n. substance which cannot be separated by ordinary chemical techniques; component part;

trace; heating wire in electric kettle *etc.*; proper sphere -*pl.* powers of atmosphere; rudiments -**element'**ary *a.* rudimentary, simple

el'ephant *n.* huge animal with ivory tusks and long trunk

el'evate *vt.* raise, exalt -**eleva'tion** *n.* raising; height, *esp.* above sea level; drawing of one side of building *etc.* -**el'evator** *n.* US lift

elev'en *n.* number next above 10; team of 11 persons -*a.* -**elev'enth** *a.*

elf *n.* fairy (*pl.* **elves**) -**elf'in**, **elv'ish** *a.*

elic'it [-is'-] *vt.* draw out

elig'ible *a.* qualified; desirable

elim'inate *vt.* remove, get rid of, set aside -**elimina'tion** *n.*

elite [i-lēt', ā-] *n.* the pick or best part of society

elix'ir [-iks'ǝ] *n.* sovereign remedy

elk *n.* large deer

ellipse' *n.* oval -**ellip'tic(al)** *a.*

elm *n.* tree with serrated leaves

elocu'tion *n.* art of public speaking

el'ongate *vt.* lengthen

elope' *vi.* run away from home with lover -**elope'ment** *n.*

el'oquence *n.* fluent, powerful use of language -**el'oquent** *a.*

else *adv.* besides, instead; otherwise -**elsewhere'** *adv.* in or to some other place

elu'cidate [-lōō'-] *vt.* explain

elude' [-lōōd'] *vt.* escape; baffle -**elu'sive** *a.* difficult to catch

ema'ciate *v.* make or become abnormally thin -**emacia'tion** *n.*

em'anate *vi.* issue, proceed from -**emana'tion** *n.*

eman'cipate *vt.* set free -**emancipa'tion** *n.*

emas'culate *vt.* castrate; enfeeble, weaken

embalm' *vt.* preserve corpse

embank'ment *n.* artificial mound carrying road, railway, or to dam back water

embar'go *n.* order stopping movement of ships; ban (*pl.* -**goes**) -*vt.* put under embargo; requisition

embark' *v.* board ship, aircraft *etc.*; (*with on* or *upon*) commence new project *etc.* -**embarka'tion** *n.*

embarr'ass *vt.* disconcert; abash; confuse

em'bassy *n.* office or official residence of ambassador

embed', **imbed'** *vt.* fix fast (in)

embell'ish *vt.* adorn, enrich

em'ber *n.* glowing cinder

embez'zle *vt.* misappropriate (money in trust *etc.*) -**embezz'ler** *n.*

embitt'er *vt.* make bitter

em'blem *n.* symbol; badge

embod'y *vt.* represent, include, be expression of (**embod'ied**, **embod'ying**) -**embod'iment** *n.*

em'bolism *n.* Med. obstruction of artery

emboss' *vt.* carve in relief

embrace' *vt.* clasp in arms, hug; accept; comprise -*n.*

embroca'tion *n.* lotion for rubbing limbs *etc.* to relieve pain

embroi'der *vt.* ornament with needlework -**embroi'dery** *n.*

em'bryo [-bri-ō] *n.* undeveloped offspring, germ (*pl.* -**os**) -**embryon'ic** *a.*

emend' *vt.* to remove errors from, correct -**emenda'tion** *n.*

em'erald *n.* bright green gem

emerge' *vi.* come up, out; rise to notice -**emer'gence** *n.*

emer'gency *n.* sudden unforeseen event needing prompt action

em'ery *n.* hard mineral used for polishing

emet'ic *n./a.* (medicine) causing vomiting

em'igrate *vt.* go and settle in another country -**em'igrant** *n.*

em'inent *a.* distinguished -**em'inence** *n.* fame; rising ground

em'issary *n.* agent, representative sent on mission

emit' *vt.* give out, put forth (-**tt**-) -**emis'sion** *n.*

emoll'ient *a.* softening, soothing -*n.* ointment

emol'ument *n.* salary, pay

emo'tion *n.* excited state of feeling, as joy, fear *etc.* -**emo'tional** *a.*

em'peror *n.* ruler of an empire (**em'press** *fem.*)

em'phasis *n.* importance attached; stress on words (*pl.* -**ses** [-sēz]) -**em'phasize** -**emphat'ic** *a.* forceful -**emphat'ically** *adv.*

em'pire *n.* aggregate of states under supreme ruler

empir'ical *a.* relying on experiment or experience

employ' *vt.* provide work in return for money; keep busy; use (**employed'**, **employ'ing**) -**employ'ee** *n.* -**employ'er** *n.* -**employ'ment** *n.* an employing, being employed; work; occupation

empow'er *vt.* authorize

em'press *see* EMPEROR

emp'ty a. containing nothing; un-occupied; senseless -v. make, become devoid of content; discharge (contents) into (**emp'tied, emp'-tying**) -**emp'ties** pl.n. empty bottles etc. -**emp'tiness** n.

e'mu [ē'myōō] n. large Aust. flightless bird like ostrich

em'ulate vt. strive to equal or excel; imitate -**emula'tion** n.

emul'sion n. light-sensitive coating of film; liquid with oily particles in suspension

en- (also **em-** before labials) (comb. form) put in, into, on, as **enrage'** vt.

ena'ble vt. make able

enact' vt. make law; act part

enam'el n. glasslike coating applied to metal etc.; coating of teeth; any hard coating -vt. (**-ll-**)

enam'our vt. inspire with love

enchant' [-ah-] vt. bewitch, delight

encir'cle vt. surround; enfold

enclose' vt. shut in; surround; place in with letter -**enclo'sure** [-zha] n.

encom'pass vt. surround, contain

en'core [ong'kawr] interj. again -n. (call for) repetition of song etc.

encoun'ter vt. meet unexpectedly; meet in conflict -n.

encour'age [-kur'-] vt. inspire with hope; embolden -**encour'agement** n.

encroach' vi. intrude (on)

encrust', incrust' v. form a crust, or hard covering

encum'ber vt. hamper; burden -**encum'brance** n.

encyc'lical [-sik'-] n. circular letter, esp. from Pope

encyclop(a)e'dia [-pēd'-] n. book, set of books of information on one or all subjects

end n. limit; extremity; conclusion; fragment; latter part; death; event; aim -v. put an end to; come to an end, finish -**end'ing** n.

endear' vt. to make beloved -**endear'ment** n. loving word

endeav'our [-dev'ər] vi. try, make after -n. attempt

endem'ic a. regularly occurring in a country or district

en'docrine [-īn] a. of those glands which secrete hormones directly into bloodstream

endorse' vt. sanction; confirm; sign back of; record conviction on driving licence -**endorsa'tion** n. C approval, support -**endorse'ment** n.

endow' vt. provide permanent income for; furnish (with)

endure' vt. undergo; tolerate, bear -vi. last -**endu'rable** a. -**endu'rance** n.

enem'a n. medicine, liquid injected into rectum

en'emy n. hostile person; opponent; armed foe

en'ergy n. vigour, force, activity; source(s) of power, as oil, coal etc.; capacity of machine, battery etc. for work -**energet'ic** a.

en'ervate vt. weaken

enforce' vt. compel obedience to; impose (action) upon -**enforce'able** a. -**enforce'ment** n.

enfran'chise vt. give right of voting to; give parliamentary representation to; set free

engage' [-gāj'] vt. employ; reserve; betroth; undertake; attract; occupy; bring into conflict; interlock -vi. employ oneself (in); promise; begin to fight -**engaged'** a. -**engage'ment** n.

engen'der [-jen'-] vt. give rise to

en'gine [-jin] n. any machine to convert energy into mechanical work; railway locomotive -**engineer'** n. one who is in charge of engines, machinery etc.; one who originates, organizes -vt. construct as engineer; contrive -**engineer'ing** n.

engrave' vt. cut in lines on metal for printing; carve, incise; impress deeply

engross' [-ō-] vt. absorb (attention); occupy wholly

engulf' v. swallow up

enhance' [-ah-] vt. intensify value or attractiveness

enig'ma n. puzzling thing or person -**enigmat'ic(al)** a.

enjoin' vt. command; prescribe

enjoy' vt. delight in; have benefit of -v. refl. be happy -**enjoy'able** a. -**enjoy'ment** n.

enlarge' vt. make bigger -vi. grow bigger; talk in greater detail -**enlarge'ment** n.

enligh'ten vt. give information to

enlist' v. engage as soldier or helper

enli'ven vt. animate

en'mity n. ill will, hostility

enor'mous a. very big, vast -**enor'mity** n. a gross offence

enough' [i-nuf'] a./n./adv. as much as need be

enquire' see INQUIRE

enrich vt. make rich; add to

enrol [-ōl] vt. write name of on roll; enlist (-ll-) -vi. become member -**enrol'ment** n.

en route' [on-root'] Fr. on the way

ensem'ble [on-som'bal] n. all parts taken together; woman's complete outfit; Mus. group of soloists performing together

enshrine' vt. preserve with sacred affection

en'sign [-sīn] n. naval or military flag; badge

enslave' vt. make into slave

ensnare' vt. trap; entangle

ensue' vi. follow, happen after

ensure' vt. make certain

entail' vt. necessitate

entan'gle vt. ensnare; perplex

entente' [on-tont'] n. friendly understanding between nations

en'ter vt. go, come into; penetrate; join; write in -vi. go, come in, join, begin -**en'trance** n. going, coming in; door, passage; right to enter; fee -**en'trant** n. one who enters -**en'try** n.

enteri'tis n. bowel inflammation

en'terprise n. bold undertaking; bold spirit; business -**en'terprising** a.

entertain' vt. amuse; receive as guest; consider -**entertain'ment** n.

enthral' vt. captivate (-ll-)

enthu'siasm n. ardent eagerness -**enthu'siast** n. -**enthusias'tic** a.

entice' vt. allure, attract

entire' a. whole, complete -**entire'ly** adv. -**enti'rety** n.

enti'tle vi. qualify; style

enti'ty n. thing's being or existence; reality

entomol'ogy n. study of insects

en'trails pl.n. intestines

entrance'¹² [-ah-] vt. delight

entrance'¹ see ENTER

entreat' vt. ask earnestly; beg, implore -**entreat'y** n.

en'trée [on'trā] n. main course of meal; right of access

entrench' vt. establish firmly

entrepreneur' [on-trə-prə-nur'] n. businessman who attempts to profit by risk and initiative

entrust' vt. commit, charge with

entwine' vt. plait, interweave

enu'merate vt. mention one by one

enun'ciate vt. state clearly

envel'op vt. wrap up, surround

en'velope n. cover of letter

envi'ronment n. surroundings; conditions of life or growth -**environmen'tal** a. -**envi'rons** pl.n. outskirts

envis'age [-z'-] vt. visualize

en'voy n. diplomat

en'vy vt. grudge another's good fortune (**en'vied, en'vying**) -n. (object of) this feeling -**en'viable** a. -**en'vious** a.

en'zyme [-zīm] n. any of group of proteins produced by living cells and acting as catalysts

ep-, eph-, epi- (comb. form) upon, during, as in ephemeral, epitaph, epoch etc.

ep'aulette n. shoulder ornament on uniform

ephem'eral a. short-lived

ep'ic n. long poem telling of achievements of hero -a.

ep'icure n. one delighting in eating and drinking -**epicure'an** [-ē'-] a./n.

epidem'ic n. (esp. of disease) prevalent and spreading rapidly -n.

epider'mis n. outer skin

ep'igram n. witty saying

ep'ilepsy n. disorder of nervous system causing fits -**epilep'tic** n./a.

ep'ilogue [-og] n. closing speech

epis'copal a. of, ruled by bishop

ep'isode n. incident; section of (serialized) book etc.

epis'tle [-sl] n. letter

ep'itaph n. inscription on tomb

ep'ithet n. descriptive word

epit'ome [-o-mi] n. typical example (pl. -s) -**epit'omize** vt.

EPNS electroplated nickel silver

ep'och [-ok] n. period, era

e'quable a. even-tempered, placid

e'qual a. the same in number, size, merit etc.; fit -n. one equal to another -vt. be equal to -**equal'ity** [-ol-] n. -**e'qualize** v.

equanim'ity n. composure

equate' vt. make equal -**equa'tion** n. equating of two mathematical expressions

equa'tor n. imaginary circle round earth equidistant from the poles

eques'trian a. of horse-riding

equi- (comb. form) equal, at equal, as in **equidis'tant** a.

equilat'eral a. having equal sides

equilib'rium n. state of steadiness (pl. -riums, -ria)

e'quine a. of, like a horse

e'quinox n. time when sun crosses equator and day and night are equal

equip' vt. supply, fit out (-pp-) -**equip'ment** n.

eq'uitable a. fair, reasonable, just -**eq'uity** n.

equiv'alent a. equal in value

equiv'ocal a. of double or doubtful meaning -**equiv'ocate** vi.

ER Elizabeth Regina

e'ra n. period of time

erad'icate vt. wipe out

erase' vt. rub out; remove

ere [ar] prep./conj. Poet. before

erect' a. upright -vt. set up; build -**erec'tion** n.

erg n. cgs unit of work

er'mine [-min] n. stoat in northern regions

Ern'ie n. computer that randomly selects winning numbers of Premium Bonds (Electronic Random Number Indicating Equipment)

erode' vt. wear away; eat into -**ero'sion** n.

erot'ic a. of sexual pleasure

err vi. make mistakes; be wrong; sin -**errat'ic** a. irregular -**erro'neous** a. wrong -**err'or** n. mistake

err'and n. short journey for simple business

err'ant a. wandering

erst'while a. former

er'udite a. learned -**erudi'tion** n.

erupt' vi. burst out -**erup'tion** n.

es'calate v. increase, be increased, in extent, intensity etc.

es'calator n. moving staircase

escall'op see SCALLOP

escape' vi. get free; get off safely; find way out -vt. elude -n. escaping -**es'capade** [-or -pād'] n. wild adventure -**esca'pism** n. taking refuge in fantasy

escarp'ment n. steep hillside

eschew' vt. avoid, shun

es'cort n. person(s) accompanying another to guard, guide etc. -**es-cort'** vt.

esoter'ic [-ō-] a. obscure

ESP extrasensory perception

espe'cial [is-pesh'al] a. pre-eminent; particular -**espe'cially** adv.

es'pionage [-nahzh] n. spying

es'planade n. promenade

espouse' [-owz'] vt. support; obs. marry -**espous'al** n.

espy' vt. catch sight of (**espied'**, **espy'ing**)

Esq. Esquire, title used on letters

ess'ay n. prose composition; at-
tempt -**essay'** vt. try (**essayed'**, **essay'ing**)

ess'ence n. all that makes thing what it is; extract got by distillation -**essen'tial** a./n. (something) necessary

EST C, US Eastern Standard Time

estab'lish vt. set up; settle; prove -**estab'lishment** n.

estate' n. landed property; person's property; area of property development

esteem' vt./n. regard, respect

es'ter n. Chem. organic compound

es'timate vt./n. (form) approximate idea of (amounts, measurements etc.) -**estima'tion** n. worthy of regard -**estima'tion** n. opinion

estrange' vt. lose affection of

es'tuary n. mouth of river

etc., &c. et cetera

et cet'era [-set-] Lat. and the rest, and others, and so on

etch vt. make engraving on metal plate using acids etc.

eter'nal a. everlasting -**eter'nity** n.

e'ther [-th-] n. colourless volatile liquid used as anaesthetic; the clear sky -**ethe'real** a. airy; heavenly

eth'ics pl.n. science of morals -**eth'ic(al)** a.

eth'nic a. of race or relating to classification of humans into social, cultural etc., groups

e'thos n. distinctive spirit etc. of people, culture etc.

et'iquette [-ket] n. conventional code of conduct

é'tude [ā'- or -tyōōd'] n. short musical composition, exercise

etymol'ogy n. tracing, account of word's origin, development

eu-, ev- (comb. form) well, as in eugenic, evangelist etc.

Eu'charist [-k-] n. Christian sacrament of the Lord's Supper

eugen'ics [-j-] pl.n. (with sing. v.) science of improving the human race by selective breeding

eu'logy n. praise

eu'nuch [-k] n. castrated man

eu'phemism n. substitution of mild term for offensive one

eupho'ria n. sense of elation

euthana'sia n. painless putting to death to relieve suffering

evac'uate vt. empty; withdraw from -**evacua'tion** n. -**evacuee'** n.

evade' vt. avoid; elude -**eva'sion** n. -**eva'sive** a.

eval'uate vt. find or judge value of –**evalua'tion** n.

evangel'ical [-jel'-] a. of, or according to, gospel teaching –**evan'gelism** n. –**evan'gelist** n.

evap'orate v. turn into vapour –**evapora'tion** n.

eva'sion see EVADE

eve [ev] n. evening before; time just before

e'ven a. flat, smooth; uniform, equal; divisible by two; impartial –vt. smooth; equalize –adv. equally; simply; notwithstanding

e'vening [-vn-] n. close of day

event' n. happening; notable occurrence; result; any one contest in sporting programme –**event'ful** a. full of exciting events –**event'ual** a. resulting in the end –**eventual'ity** n. possible event

ev'er adv. always; at any time –**evergreen** n./a. (tree or shrub) bearing foliage throughout year –**ev'ery** [-vri] a. each of all; all possible –**ev'erybody** n. –**ev'eryday** a. usual, ordinary –**ev'eryone** n. –**ev'erything** n. –**ev'erywhere** adv. in all places

evict' vt. expel by legal process, turn out –**evic'tion** n.

ev'ident a. plain, obvious –**ev'idence** n. ground of belief; sign; testimony –vt. indicate, prove

e'vil a./n. (what is) bad or harmful –**e'villy** adv.

evince' vt. show, indicate

evoke' vt. call to mind –**evoca'tion** n. –**evoc'ative** a.

evolve' v. (cause to) develop gradually –vi. undergo slow changes –**evolu'tion** [-lōō'-] n. development of species from earlier forms –**evolu'tionary** a.

ewe [yōō] n. female sheep

ew'er [yōō'-] n. pitcher

ex-, e-, ef- (comb. form) out from, from, out of, formerly, as in exclaim, evade, effusive, exodus

exac'erbate [ig-zas'-] vt. aggravate, make worse

exact' [igz-] a. precise, strictly correct –vt. demand, extort –**exact'ing** a. making rigorous demands

exagg'erate [ig-zaj'-] vt. magnify beyond truth, overstate

exalt' [igza-awlt'] vt. raise up; praise

exam'ine [-gz-] vt. investigate; look at closely; ask questions of; test knowledge of –**examina'tion** n.

exam'ple [ig-zahm'-] n. specimen; model

exas'perate [ig-zahs'-] vt. irritate –**exaspera'tion** n.

ex'cavate vt. hollow out; dig; unearth –**ex'cavator** n.

exceed' vt. be greater than; go beyond –**exceed'ingly** adv. very

excel' vt. surpass –vi. be very good (-ll-) –**ex'cellence** n. –**ex'cellent** a. very good

except' prep. not including –vt. exclude –**excep'tion** n. thing not included in a rule; objection –**excep'tional** a. above average

ex'cerpt n. passage from book etc. –**excerpt'** vt. extract, quote

excess' n. too great amount; intemperance –**excess'ive** a.

exchange' vt. give (something) in return for something else; barter –n. giving one thing and receiving another; thing given; building where merchants meet for business; central telephone office –**exchange'able** a.

exchequ'er [-k'ər] n. government department in charge of revenue

ex'cise [-īz] n. duty charged on home goods

excite' vt. arouse to strong emotion, stimulate; set in motion –**exci'table** a. –**excite'ment** n. –**exci'ting** a.

exclaim' v. speak suddenly, cry out –**exclama'tion** n.

exclude' vt. shut out; debar from; reject, not consider –**exclu'sion** n. –**exclu'sive** a. excluding; only; select

excommu'nicate vt. to cut off from the sacraments of the Church

ex'crement n. waste matter from bowels –**ex'crete'** vi. discharge from the system –**excre'tion** n. –**excre'tory** a.

excru'ciating [-krōō'shi-] a. unbearably painful

excur'sion n. trip for pleasure

excuse' [-skyōōz'] vt. overlook; try to clear from blame; gain exemption; set free –n. [-skyōōs'] that which serves to excuse; apology –**excu'sable** [-z-] a.

ex'ecrable a. hatefully bad

ex'ecute vt. inflict capital punishment on, kill; carry out, perform; make –**exe'cution** n. –**exec'utive** n. person(s) in administrative position –a. esp. of branch of government enforcing laws –**exec'utor** n. person appointed to carry out provisions of a will (**exec'utrix** fem.)

exem'plary a. serving as example

exem'plify vt. serve as example of (-fied, -fying)

exempt' [igz-] vt. free from; excuse -a. freed from, not liable for -exemp'tion n.

ex'ercise [-z] vt. use; give exercise to; carry out -vi. take exercise -n. use of limbs for health; practice; task; use

exert' [igz-] vt. make effort -exer'tion n.

exhale' v. breathe out

exhaust' [ig-zawst'] vt. tire out; use up; empty -n. waste gases from engine; passage for this -exhaust'ible a. -exhaus'tion n. state of extreme fatigue -exhaust'ive a. comprehensive

exhib'it [igz-] vt. show, display -n. thing shown -exhibi'tion [eks-] n. display; public show -exhibi'tionist n. one with compulsive desire to draw attention to himself -exhib'itor n.

exhil'arate [igz-] vt. enliven, gladden -exhilara'tion n.

exhort' [igz-] vt. urge

ex'igency [-j-] n. urgency

ex'ile [egz'-] n. banishment, expulsion from one's own country; one banished -vt. banish

exist' [igz-] vi. be, have being, live -exist'ence n. -exist'ent a.

ex'it n. way out; going out -vi. go out

ex'odus n. departure

exon'erate vt. free, declare free, from blame

exorb'itant [igz-] a. excessive

ex'orcise [-z] vt. cast out (evil spirits) by invocation -ex'orcism n. -ex'orcist n.

exot'ic [igz-] a. foreign; unusual

expand' v. increase, spread out -expand'able, -ible a. -expanse' n. wide space -expan'sion n. -expan'sive a. extensive; friendly

expa'tiate [-shi-] vi. speak or write at great length (on)

expat'riate vt. exile -a./n.

expect' vt. regard as probable; look forward to -expect'ant a. -expecta'tion n.

expect'orate v. spit out

expe'dient a. fitting; politic; convenient -n. something suitable, useful -expe'diency n.

ex'pedite [-it] vt. help on, hasten -expedi'tion [-ish'-] n. journey for definite purpose; people, equipment comprising expedition

expel' vt. drive out; exclude (-ll-) -expul'sion n.

expend' vt. spend, pay out; use up -expend'able a. likely to be used up -expend'iture n. -expense' n. cost -pl. charges incurred -expen'sive a.

expe'rience n. observation of facts as source of knowledge; being affected by event; the event; knowledge, skill gained -vt. undergo, suffer, meet with

exper'iment [-pe'ri-] n./vi. test to discover or prove something

ex'pert n./a. (one) skilful, knowledgeable, in something -expertise' [-tēz'] n.

ex'piate vt. make amends for

expire' vi. come to an end; give out breath; die -vt. breathe out -expi'ry n. end

explain' vt. make clear, intelligible; account for -explana'tion n.

exple'tive n. exclamation; oath

explic'able [or ex'-] a. explainable

explic'it [-is'-] a. clearly stated

explode' vi. burst violently; (of population) increase rapidly -vt. make explode; discredit -explo'sion n. -explo'sive a.

ex'ploit n. brilliant feat, deed -vt. [-ploit'] turn to advantage; make use of for one's own ends

explore' vt. investigate; examine (country etc.) by going through it -explora'tion n.

expo'nent see EXPOUND

export' vt. send (goods) out of the country -ex'port n./a.

expose' [-ōz'] vt. reveal; lay open (to); leave unprotected -expo'sure n.

expo'sé [-zā] n. disclosure of scandal, crime etc.

expos'tulate vi. remonstrate

expound' vt. explain, interpret -expo'nent n. one who expounds or promotes (idea, cause etc.); performer -exposi'tion n. explanation; exhibition of goods etc.

express' vt. put into words; make known or understood -a. definitely stated; specially designed; speedy -adv. with speed -n. express train; rapid parcel delivery service -express'ible a. -expres'sion n. expressing; word, phrase; look -express'ive a.

expro'priate vt. dispossess

ex'purgate vt. remove objectionable parts (from book etc.)

exquis'ite [-kwiz'- or eks'-] a. of extreme beauty or delicacy

extant' a. still existing

extem'pore [-pə-ri] a./adv. without previous preparation **-extem'porary** a. **-extem'porize** vt.

extend' vt. stretch out; prolong; widen; accord, grant -vi. reach; cover area; have range or scope; become larger or wider **-exten'dible, -dable, exten'sible** a. **-exten'sion** n. an extending; additional part **-exten'sive** a. wide **-extent'** n. space, scope; size

exten'uate vt. make less blameworthy, lessen; mitigate

exte'rior n. the outside -a. outer, external

exterm'inate vt. destroy utterly **-extermina'tion** n.

extern'al a. outside, outward

extinct' a. having died out; quenched **-extinc'tion** n.

extin'guish [-ng'gw-] vt. put out, quench; wipe out

extol' [-tōl'] vt. praise highly (**-ll-**)

extort' vt. get by force or threats **-extor'tion** n. **-extor'tionate** a. excessive

ex'tra a./adv. additional(ly); more than usual(ly) -n. extra person or thing; something charged as additional

extra- (comb. form) beyond, as in extradition, extramural etc.

extract' vt. take out, esp. by force; get by distillation etc.; derive; quote -n. [eks'-] passage from book, film etc.; concentrated solution **-extrac'tion** n. extracting; ancestry

extradi'tion [-dish'-] n. delivery of foreign fugitive **-ex'tradite** vt.

extramur'al [-myoor'-] a. outside normal courses etc. of university or college

extra'neous a. not essential; added from without

extraor'dinary [-trawd'-] a. very unusual **-extraor'dinarily** adv.

extrasen'sory a. of perception apparently gained without use of known senses

extrav'agant a. wasteful; exorbitant **-extrav'agance** n. **-extrava'ganza** n. elaborate entertainment

ex'travert see EXTROVERT

extreme' a. of high or highest degree; severe; going beyond moderation; outermost -n. utmost degree; thing at either end **-extreme'ly** adv. **-extrem'ity** n. end -pl. hands and feet

ex'tricate vt. disentangle

ex'trovert n. one who is interested in other people and things rather than his own feelings

extrude' vt. squeeze, force out

exu'berant [ig-zyōō'-] a. high-spirited **-exu'berance** n.

exude' [ig-zyōōd'] vi. ooze out -vt. give off

exult' [igz-] vi. rejoice, triumph **-exult'ant** a. triumphant **-exulta'tion** n.

eye [ī] n. organ of sight; look, glance; attention; aperture; thing resembling eye -vt. look at; observe **-eye'brow** n. fringe of hair above eye **-eye'lash** n. hair fringing eyelid **-eye'let** n. small hole **-eye'lid** n. **-eye'sore** n. ugly object **-eye'tooth** n. canine tooth **-eye'witness** n. one who saw something for himself

ey'rie [er'-, ĭr'-] n. nest of bird of prey, esp. eagle

F

F Fahrenheit; Fellow

f. Mus. forte

FA Football Association

fa'ble n. short story with moral **-fab'ulous** a. amazing; inf. extremely good

fab'ric n. cloth; structure **-fab'ricate** v. construct; invent (lie etc.)

façade [fə-sahd'] n. front of building; outward appearance

face [fās] n. front of head; distorted expression; outward appearance; chief side of anything; dignity -vt. look or front towards; meet (boldly); give a covering surface -vi. turn **-fac'et** [fas'-] n. one side of cut gem; one aspect **-fa'cial** [fā'shl] n. cosmetic treatment for face -a. **-face'less** a. anonymous

face'tious [fə-sē'shəs] a. given to jesting

fa'cia [-sh-] n. see FASCIA

fac'ile [fas'-] a. easy; superficial **-facil'itate** [-sil'-] vt. make easy **-facil'ity** n. easiness, dexterity -pl. opportunities, good conditions; means, equipment for doing something

facsim'ile [fak-sim'i-li] n. an exact copy

fact n. thing known to be true; reality **-fac'tual** a.

fac'tion n. (dissenting) minority group; dissension

fac'tor n. something contributing to a result; one of numbers which multiplied together give a given number; agent

fac'tory n. building where things are manufactured

fac'ulty n. inherent power; ability, aptitude; department of university

fad n. short-lived fashion

fade vi. lose colour, strength -vt. cause to fade

fae'ces [fē'sēz] pl.n. excrement

fag n. inf. boring task; sl. cigarette -v. inf. (esp. with out) tire (-gg-)

fagg'ot n. bundle of sticks

Fah'renheit [fa'rən-hīt] a. measured by thermometric scale with freezing point of water 32°, boiling point 212°

fail vi. be unsuccessful; stop working; be below the required standard; be insufficient; become bankrupt -vt. disappoint, give no help to; neglect, forget to do; judge (candidate) to be below required standard -**fail'ing** n. deficiency; fault -prep. in default of -**fail'ure** n. -**without fail** certainly

faint a. feeble, dim, pale; weak; dizzy -vi. lose consciousness temporarily

fair[1] a. just; according to rules; blond; beautiful; of moderate quality or amount; favourable -adv. honestly -**fair'ly** adv. -**fair'ness** n.

fair[2] n. travelling entertainment with sideshows etc.; trade exhibition -**fair'ground** n.

fair'y n. imaginary small creature with powers of magic; sl. male homosexual -a. of fairies; delicate, imaginary

fait accom'pli [fe-ta-kon'plī] Fr. something already done that cannot be altered

faith n. trust; belief (without proof); religion; loyalty -**faith'ful** a. constant, true -**faith'fully** adv. -**faith'less** a.

fake vt. touch up; counterfeit n. fraudulent object, person, act -a.

fa'kir n. member of Islamic religious order; Hindu ascetic

fal'con [fawl'-, faw'-] n. small bird of prey, esp. trained in hawking for sport

fall [fawl] vi. drop; become lower; hang down; cease to stand; perish; collapse; be captured; become; happen (**fell** pt., **fall'en** pp.) -n. falling;

amount that falls; decrease; collapse; drop; (oft. pl.) cascade; yielding to temptation; US autumn -**fall'out** n. radioactive particles spread as result of nuclear explosion

fall'acy [fal'-] n. incorrect opinion or argument -**falla'cious** a. -**fall'ible** a. liable to error

fall'ow [fal'ō] a. ploughed but left without crop

false [-aw-] a. wrong; deceptive; faithless; artificial -**false'ly** adv. -**fal'sify** vt. alter fraudulently (**fal'sified, fal'sifying**) -**false'hood** n. lie

falsett'o n. forced voice above natural range (pl. -os)

fal'ter [-aw-] vi. hesitate; waver; stumble

fame n. renown -**famed** a. -**fa'mous** a. widely known

famil'iar a. well-known; customary; intimate; acquainted; impertinent -n. friend; demon -**famil'iar'ity** n. -**fam'iliarize** vt.

fam'ily n. parents and children, relatives; group of allied objects

fam'ine [-in] n. extreme scarcity of food; starvation -**fam'ish** vi. be very hungry

fan[1] n. instrument for producing current of air; folding object of paper etc., for cooling the face -vt. blow or cool with fan -v. spread out (-nn-)

fan[2] inf. devoted admirer

fanat'ic a./n. (person) filled with abnormal enthusiasm -**fanat'ical** a. -**fanat'icism** n.

fan'cy a. ornamental -n. whim; liking; imagination; mental image -vt. imagine; be inclined to believe; inf. have a liking for (**fan'cied, fan'cying**) -**fan'cier** n. one with special interest in something -**fan'ciful** a.

fan'fare n. a flourish of trumpets; ostentatious display

fang n. snake's poison tooth; long, pointed tooth

fan'tail n. kind of bird (esp. pigeon) with fan-shaped tail

fan'tasy n. power of imagination; mental image; fanciful invention -**fan'tasize** v. -**fantas'tic** a. quaint, extremely fanciful; wild; inf. very good; inf. very large -**fantas'tically** adv.

far adv. at or to a great distance or a remote time; by very much (**far'ther, fur'ther** comp.; **far'thest, fur'thest** sup.) -a. distant; more distant **-far-fetched** *a.* incredible **-Far North** Arctic and sub-Arctic regions

farce *n.* comedy of boisterous humour; absurd and futile proceeding **-far'cical** *a.*

fare *n.* charge for transport; passenger; food **-vi.** get on; happen **-farewell'** *interj.* goodbye **-n.** leavetaking

farm *n.* tract of land for cultivation or rearing livestock **-v.** cultivate (land); rear livestock (on farm) **-farm'er** *n.* **-farm'house** *n.* **-farm'yard** *n.*

farr'ier *n.* one who shoes, cares for horses

fart *vulg. n.* (audible) emission of gas from anus **-vi.**

far'ther [-TH-] *adv./a.* further; *comp.* of FAR **-far'thest** *adv./a.* furthest; *sup.* of FAR

far'thing [-TH-] *n.* formerly, coin worth a quarter of a penny

fa'scia, fa'cia [-sh-] *n.* flat surface above shop window; dashboard (*pl.* **fa'(s)ciae** [-ē])

fas'cinate *vt.* attract and delight **-fascina'tion** *n.*

fas'cism [-sh-] *n.* authoritarian political system opposed to democracy and liberalism **-fas'cist** *a./n.*

fash'ion *n.* (latest) style, *esp.* of dress *etc.*; manner; type **-vt.** shape, make **-fash'ionable** *a.* **-fash'ionably** *adv.*

fast' [-ah-] *a.* (capable of) moving quickly; ahead of true time; *obs.* dissipated; firm, steady **-adv.** rapidly; tightly

fast' [-ah-] *vi.* go without food **-n.** **-fast'ing** *n.*

fast'en [fahs'n] *vt.* attach, fix, secure **-vi.** become joined

fastid'ious *a.* hard to please

fat *n.* oily animal substance; fat part **-a.** having too much fat; greasy; profitable (**fatt'er** *comp.*, **fatt'est** *sup.*) **-fatt'en** *v.* **-fatt'y** *a.*

fate *n.* power supposed to predetermine events; destiny; person's appointed lot; death or destruction **-vt.** preordain **-fa'tal** *a.* ending in death **-fa'talism** *n.* belief that everything is predetermined **-fa'talist** *n.* **-fatal'ity** *n.* accident resulting in death **-fa'tally** *adv.* **-fate'ful** *a.*

fath'er [fahTH'-] *n.* male parent; ancestor; (F-) God; originator; priest **-vt.** beget; originate **-fath'erhood** *n.*

-father-in-law *n.* husband's or wife's father

fath'om [faTH'-] *n.* measure of six feet of water **-vt.** sound (water); understand

fatigue' [-tēg'] *n.* weariness; toil; weakness of metals *etc.*

fat'uous *a.* very silly, idiotic

fault *n.* defect; misdeed; blame **-v.** find fault in; (cause to) commit fault **-fault'ily** *adv.* **-fault'less** *a.* **-faul'ty** *a.*

faun *n.* mythological woodland being with tail and horns

faun'a *n.* animals of region collectively (*pl.* **-s, -ae** [-ē])

faux pas' [fō-pah'] *n.* social blunder or indiscretion

fa'vour [-vər] *n.* goodwill; approval; especial kindness; partiality **-vt.** regard or treat with favour; oblige; treat with partiality; support **-fa'vourable** *a.* **-fa'vourite** [-it] *n.* favoured person or thing **-a.** chosen, preferred **-fa'vouritism** *n.* practice of showing undue preference

fawn' *n.* young deer **-a.** light yellowish brown

fawn' *vi.* cringe, court favour servilely

FBI *US* Federal Bureau of Investigation

FC Football Club

Fe *Chem.* iron

fear *n.* unpleasant emotion caused by coming danger **-vi.** be afraid **-vt.** regard with fear; revere **-fear'ful** *a.* **-fear'fully** *adv.* **-fear'less** *a.* **-fear'some** *a.*

fea'sible [-z-] *a.* able to be done **-feasibil'ity** *n.*

feast *n.* banquet; religious anniversary **-vi.** partake of banquet **-vt.** regale with feast; delight

feat *n.* notable deed

feath'er [feTH'-] *n.* one of the barbed shafts which form covering of birds; anything resembling this **-vt.** provide with feathers **-vi.** grow feathers **-feath'ery** *a.*

fea'ture *n.* (*usu. pl.*) part of face; notable part of anything; main or special item **-vt.** portray **-vi.** be prominent (in) **-fea'tureless** *a.* without striking features

Feb. February

fe'brile *a.* of fever

Feb'ruary *n.* second month

fe'cund [*or* fek'-] *a.* fertile

fed'eral *a.* of the government of states which are united but retain internal independence -**fed'erate** v. form into, become, a federation -**federa'tion** n. league; federal union

fee n. payment for services

fee'ble a. weak; lacking effectiveness -**fee'bly** adv.

feed vt. give food to; supply, support -vi. take food (**fed** pt./pp.) -n. feeding; fodder

feel v. touch; experience; find (one's way) cautiously; be sensitive to; show emotion (for); believe, consider -n. feeling; impression perceived by feeling; sense of touch -**feel'er** n. -**feel'ing** n. sense of touch; sensation; emotion; sympathy; opinion -pl. susceptibilities -a. sensitive, sympathetic -**feel like** have an inclination for

feet see FOOT

feign [fān] v. pretend, sham

feint [fānt] n. sham attack; pretence -vi. make feint

felic'ity [-is'-] n. great happiness; apt wording -**felic'itous** a.

fe'line a. of cats; catlike

fell[1] vt. knock down; cut down (tree) -**fell'er** n.

fell[2] n. mountain, moor

fell'ow n. inf. man, boy; associate; counterpart; member (of society, college etc.) -a. of the same class, associated -**fell'owship** n.

fel'on n. one guilty of felony -**fel'ony** n. serious crime

felt n. soft, matted fabric -vt. make into, or cover with, felt -vi. become matted

fe'male a. of sex which bears offspring; relating to this sex -n. one of this sex

fem'inine [-in] a. of women; womanly -**fem'inism** n. advocacy of equal rights for women -**fem'inist** n./a. -**feminin'ity** n.

fe'mur [fē'mo] n. thigh-bone

fen n. tract of marshy land

fence n. structure of wire, wood etc. enclosing an area; sl. dealer in stolen property -v. erect fence; fight with swords; sl. deal in stolen property -**fen'cing** n. art of swordplay

fend vt. ward off, repel -vi. provide (for oneself etc.) -**fend'er** n. low metal frame in front of fireplace

fer'ment n. leaven, substance causing thing to ferment; excitement -v. [-ment'] (cause to) undergo chemical change with effervescence and alteration of properties; (cause to) become excited -**fermenta'tion** n.

fern n. plant with feathery fronds

fero'cious [-shəs] a. fierce, savage, cruel -**feroc'ity** n.

ferr'et n. tamed animal like weasel -vt. drive out with ferrets; search out -vi. search about

ferr'ic, ferr'(e)ous a. pert. to, containing iron

ferr'y n. boat for transporting people, vehicles, across water -v. carry, travel, by ferry (**ferr'ied, ferr'ying**)

fer'tile a. (capable of) producing offspring, bearing crops etc.; producing abundantly -**fertil'ity** n. -**fer'tilize** vt. make fertile -**fer'tilizer** n.

fer'vent, fer'vid a. ardent, intense -**fer'vour** [-vər] n.

fes'ter v. (cause to) form pus -vi. rankle; become embittered

fes'tival n. day, period of celebration; organized series of events, performances etc. -**fes'tive** a. joyous, merry -**festiv'ity** n. gaiety; rejoicing -pl. festive proceedings

festoon' n. loop of flowers, ribbons etc. -vt. form, adorn with festoons

fetch vt. go and bring; draw forth; be sold for -n. trick -**fetch'ing** a. attractive

fete, fête [fāt] n. gala, bazaar etc., esp. one held out of doors -vt. honour with festive entertainment

fet'id, foet'id [-ē-] a. stinking

fet'ish n. object believed to have magical powers; object, activity, to which excessive devotion is paid

fett'er n. chain for feet; check -pl. captivity -vt. chain up; restrain

fet'tle n. state of health

feu [fyoo] n. in Scotland, tenure of land in return for fixed annual payment

feud [fyood] n. bitter, lasting, mutual hostility; vendetta -vi. carry on feud

feu'dal [fyood'-] a. of, like, medieval system of holding land from superior in return for service -**feu'dalism** n.

fe'ver n. condition of illness with high body temperature; intense nervous excitement -**fe'vered** a. -**fe'verish** a.

few a. not many -n. small number

fez n. red, brimless tasselled cap (pl. **fezz'es**)

fian'cé [-on'sā] n. man engaged to be married (**fian'cée** fem.)

fias'co n. breakdown, total failure (pl. -**co(e)s**)

fi'at n. decree

fib n./vt. (tell) trivial lie (**-bb-**)

fi'bre n. filament forming part of

animal or plant tissue; substance that can be spun -**fi'brous** a. -**fi'breglass** n. material made of fine glass fibres

fic'kle a. changeable

fic'tion n. literary works of the imagination -**fic'tional** a. -**ficti'tious** a. false; imaginary

fid'dle n. violin; inf. fraudulent arrangement -vi. play fiddle; fidget -v. sl. cheat -**fidd'ling** a. trivial -**fidd'ly** a. small, awkward to handle

fidel'ity n. faithfulness

fidg'et vi. move restlessly -n. (oft. pl.) restless mood; one who fidgets -**fidg'ety** a.

field n. area of (farming) land; tract of land rich in specified product; players in a game or sport collectively; battlefield; sphere of knowledge -v. Cricket etc., stop and return ball; send player, team, on to sportsfield -**field day** day of outdoor activities; important occasion -**field glasses** binoculars

fiend n. devil; person addicted to something -**fiend'ish** a.

fierce a. savage, wild, violent; intense -**fierce'ly** adv.

fi'ery a. consisting of, or like, fire; irritable (**fi'erier** comp., **fi'eriest** sup.) -**fi'erily** adv.

fies'ta n. carnival

fife n. high-pitched flute

fif'teen', fifth', fif'ty see FIVE

fig n. soft, pear-shaped fruit; tree bearing it

fight [fīt] v. contend with in battle; maintain against opponent; settle by combat (**fought** pt./pp.) -n. -**fight'er** n.

fig'ment n. imaginary thing

fig'ure [-ər] n. numerical symbol; amount, number; (bodily) shape; (conspicuous) appearance; space enclosed by lines; diagram, illustration -v. calculate -vi. (oft. with in) show -**figurine'** [-ēn'] n. statuette -**fig'urehead** n. nominal leader

fil'ament n. fine wire; threadlike body

filch vt. steal, pilfer

file' n. (box, folder etc. holding) papers for reference; orderly line -vt. arrange (papers etc.) and put them away for reference -vi. march in file -**fi'ling** n.

file' n./vt. (use) roughened tool for smoothing or shaping -**fi'ling** n. scrap of metal removed by file

fil'ial a. of, befitting, son or daughter -**fil'ially** adv.

fil'igree n. fine tracery or openwork of metal

fill vt. make full; occupy completely; discharge duties of; stop up; satisfy; fulfil -vi. become full -n. full supply; as much as desired -**fill'ing** n.

fill'et n. boneless slice of meat, fish; narrow strip -vt. cut into fillets, bone -**fill'eted** a.

fill'ip n. stimulus

fill'y n. young female horse

film n. sequence of images projected on screen, creating illusion of movement; sensitized celluloid roll used in photography, cinematography; thin skin or layer -a. connected with cinema -vt. photograph with cine camera; make cine film of -v. cover, become covered, with film -**film'y** a. gauzy

fil'ter n. device permitting fluid to pass but retaining solid particles; anything similar -vt. act as filter, or as if passing through filter -vi. pass slowly (through)

filth [-th] n. disgusting dirt; obscenity -**filth'ily** adv. -**filth'iness** n. -**filth'y** a.

fin n. propelling organ of fish; anything like this

fi'nal a. at the end; conclusive -n. game, heat, examination etc., coming at end of series -**final'e** [fi-nahl'i] n. closing part of musical composition -**fi'nally** adv.

finance' [fi-, fī-, or fī'-] n. management of money; money resources (also pl.) -vt. find capital for -**finan'cial** a. -**finan'cier** n.

finch n. one of family of small singing birds

find [fī-] vt. come across; experience, discover; Law give a verdict -n. (valuable) thing found (**found** pt./pp.) -n.

fine' a. of high quality; delicate, subtle; pure; in small particles; slender; excellent; inf. healthy, at ease; free from rain -vt. make clear or pure -**fi'nery** n. showy dress -**finesse'** [fin-] n. skilful management -**fine art** art produced for its aesthetic value

fine' n. sum fixed as penalty -vt. punish by fine

fin'ger [-ng'g-] n. one of the jointed branches of the hand; various things like this -vt. touch with fingers -**fin'gerprint** n. impression of tip of finger

fin'ish v. (mainly tr.) bring, come to an end, conclude; complete; perfect -n. end; way in which thing is finished; final appearance

fi'nite a. bounded, limited

fiord see FJORD

fir n. coniferous tree

fire n. state of burning; mass of burning fuel; destructive burning; device for heating a room etc.; ardour -vt. discharge (firearm); inf. dismiss from employment; bake; make burn; inspire; explode -vi. discharge firearm; begin to burn; become excited -**fire'arm** n. gun, rifle, pistol etc. -**fire brigade** organized body of men and appliances to put out fires -**fire'damp** n. explosive hydrocarbon gas forming in mines -**fire engine** vehicle with apparatus for extinguishing fires -**fire escape** means, esp. stairs, for escaping from burning buildings -**fire'guard** n. protective grating in front of fire -**fire hall** C fire station -**fire'man** n. member of fire brigade; stoker -**fire'place** n. recess in room for fire -**fire'work** n. (oft. pl.) device to give spectacular effects by explosions and coloured sparks -pl. outburst of temper

firm a. solid, fixed, stable -v. make, become firm -n. commercial enterprise

firm'ament n. expanse of sky

first a. earliest in time or order; foremost in rank or position -a. beginning; first occurrence of something -adv. before others in time, order etc. -**first aid** help given to injured person before arrival of doctor -**first-hand** a. obtained directly from the first source -**first'rate** a. of highest class or quality

firth n. river estuary

fis'cal a. of government finances

fish n. vertebrate cold-blooded animal with gills, living in water (pl. fish, fish'es) -v. (attempt to) catch fish; try to get information indirectly -**fish'y** a. of, like, or full of fish; open to suspicion -**fish'erman** n.

fiss'ure [-sh'-] n. cleft, split -**fiss'ion** n. splitting; reproduction by division of living cells; splitting of atomic nucleus -**fiss'ionable** a.

fist n. clenched hand -**fist'icuffs** pl.n. fighting

fit' vt. be suited to; be properly adjusted to; adjust; supply -vi. be correctly adjusted or adapted (-tt-) -a.

well-suited; proper; in good health (**fitt'er** comp., **fitt'est** sup.) -n. way anything fits -**fit'ness** n. -**fit'ter** n. -**fit'ing** a. appropriate -n. fixture; apparatus; action of fitting

fit' n. seizure with convulsions; passing state, mood -**fit'ful** a. spasmodic

five a./n. cardinal number after four -**fifth** a./n. ordinal number -**fif'teen** a./n. ten plus five -**fif'teenth** a./n. -**fif'tieth** a./n. -**fif'ty** a./n. five tens -**five'pins** n. bowling game played esp. in Canada

fix vt. fasten, make firm; determine; repair; inf. influence unfairly -vi. become firm; determine -n. difficult situation; position of ship, aircraft ascertained by radar, observation etc.; sl. dose of narcotic drug -**fixa'tion** n. obsession -**fix'edly** [-id-li] adv. intently -**fix'ture** n. thing fixed in position; (date for) sporting event

fizz vi. hiss -n. hissing noise; effervescent liquid -**fiz'zle** vi. splutter weakly -n. fizzling noise; fiasco -**fizzle out** inf. fail

fjord, flord [fyord] n. (esp. in Norway) long, narrow inlet of sea

flabb'ergast [-gahst] vt. overwhelm with astonishment

flabb'y a. limp; too fat; feeble -**flabb'iness** n.

flacc'id [flas'-, flak's-] a. flabby, lacking firmness

flag' n. banner, piece of bunting as standard or signal -vt. inform by flag signals (-gg-)

flag' n. iris plant

flag' n. flat slab of stone -**flag'stone** n.

flag' vi. lose vigour (-gg-)

flag'on n. large bottle

fla'grant a. blatant

flail n. instrument for threshing corn by hand -v. beat with, move as, flail

flair n. natural ability

flake n. small, thin piece; piece chipped off -v. (cause to) peel off in flakes -**fla'ky** a.

flamboy'ant a. showy

flame n. burning gas, esp. above fire -vi. give out flames

flamin'go [-ng'g-] n. large pink bird with long neck and legs (pl. -s, -es)

flamm'able a. liable to catch fire

flan n. open sweet or savoury tart

flank n. part of side between hips and ribs; side of anything -vt. be at, move along either side of

flann'el n. soft woollen fabric; small piece of cloth for washing face

flap v. move (wings, arms *etc.*) as bird flying (**-pp-**) -n. act of flapping; broad piece of anything hanging from one side; *inf.* state of panic

flare [-âr] vi. blaze with unsteady flame; spread outwards -n. instance of flaring; signal light

flash n. sudden burst of light or flame; very short time -vi. break into sudden flame; gleam; move very fast -vt. cause to gleam; emit (light *etc.*) suddenly -**flash**, **flash'y** a. showy, sham -**flash'back** n. break in narrative to introduce what has taken place previously

flask [-ah-] n. type of bottle

flat a. level; at full length; smooth; downright; dull; *Mus.* below true pitch; (of tyre) deflated; (of battery) dead (**flatt'er** comp., **flatt'est** sup.) -n. what is flat; *Mus.* note half tone below natural pitch -**flatt'en** vt. -**flat'fish** n. type of fish with broad, flat body -**flat rate** the same in all cases -**flat out** a. with maximum speed or effort

flat n. suite of rooms in larger building

flatt'er vt. praise insincerely; gratify -**flatt'ery** n.

flat'ulent a. suffering from, generating (excess) gases in intestines -**flat'ulence** n.

flaunt v. show off

fla'vour [-var] n. distinctive taste, savour -vt. give flavour to -**fla'vouring** n.

flaw n. defect, blemish

flax n. plant grown for its fibres, spun into linen thread -**flax'en** a. of flax; light yellow

flay vt. strip skin off; criticize severely

flea [-ê] n. small, wingless, jumping, blood-sucking insect

fleck n./vt. (make) small mark(s)

fledg(e)'ling n. young bird; inexperienced person

flee v. run away from (**fled, flee'ing**)

fleece n. sheep's wool -vt. rob -**flee'cy** a.

fleet[1] n. number of warships organized as unit; number of ships, cars *etc.*

fleet[2] a. swift, nimble -**fleet'ing** a. passing quickly

flesh n. soft part, muscular substance, between skin and bone; in plants, pulp; fat; sensual appetites -**flesh'ily** adv. -**flesh'ly** a. carnal

-**flesh'y** a. plump, pulpy -**in the flesh** in person, actually present

flex n. flexible insulated electric cable -v. bend, be bent -**flex'ible** a. easily bent; manageable; adaptable

flick vt. strike lightly, jerk -n. light blow; jerk -pl. sl. cinema

flick'er vi. burn, shine, unsteadily -n. unsteady light or movement

flight [-ît] n. act or manner of flying through air; Air Force unit of command; power of flying; stairs between two landings; running away -**flight recorder** electronic device in aircraft storing information about its flight

flim'sy [-zi] a. weak, thin

flinch vi. draw back, wince

fling v. (*mainly tr.*) throw, send, move, with force (**flung** pt./pp.) -n. throw; spell of indulgence; vigorous dance

flint n. hard steel-grey stone

flip v. flick lightly; turn over (**-pp-**) -**flipp'ant** a. treating serious things lightly -**flipp'er** n. limb, fin for swimming

flirt vi. play with another's affections -n. person who flirts

flit vi. pass lightly and rapidly (**-tt-**)

float vi. rest on surface of liquid; be suspended freely -vt. of liquid, support, bear alone; in commerce, get (company) started; obtain loan -n. anything small that floats; small delivery vehicle; motor vehicle carrying tableau *etc.*; sum of money used to provide change

flock n. number of animals of one kind together; religious congregation -vi. gather in a crowd

floe [-ô] n. floating ice

flog vt. beat with whip, stick *etc.*; *sl.* sell (**-gg-**)

flood [flud] n. inundation, overflow of water; rising of tide; outpouring -vt. inundate; cover, fill with water; arrive, move *etc.* in great numbers -**flood'light** n. broad, intense beam of artificial light -**flood'lit** a.

floor [flawr] n. lower surface of room; set of rooms on one level; (right to speak in) legislative hall -vt. supply with floor; knock down; confound -**floor'ing** n. material for floors

flop vi. bend, fall, collapse loosely, carelessly; fall flat on water *etc.*; *inf.* fail (**-pp-**) -n. flopping movement or sound; *inf.* failure -**flopp'y a**

flor'a n. plants of a region (*pl.* **-ras,**

-rae [-rē]) -flor'al a. of flowers
-flor'ist [-o-] n. dealer in flowers

flor'id [-o-] a. with red, flushed complexion; ornate

floss n. mass of fine, silky fibres

flotill'a n. fleet of small vessels; group of destroyers

flot'sam n. floating wreckage

flounce¹ vi. go, move abruptly and impatiently -n. fling, jerk of body or limb

flounce² n. ornamental gathered strip on woman's garment

floun'der¹ vi. plunge and struggle, esp. in water or mud

floun'der² n. flatfish

flour n. powder prepared by sifting and grinding wheat etc.

flour'ish [flu'-] vi. thrive -vt. brandish; wave about -n. ornamental curve; showy gesture; fanfare

flout vt. show contempt for

flow [flō] vi. glide along as stream; circulate, as the blood; hang loose; be present in abundance -n. act, instance of flowing; quantity that flows; rise of tide

flow'er n. coloured (not green) part of plant from which fruit is developed; bloom, blossom; choicest part -pl. chemical sublimate -vi. produce flowers; come to prime condition -flow'ery a.

fl. oz. fluid ounce(s)

flu n. short for INFLUENZA

fluc'tuate v. vary, rise and fall, undulate -fluctua'tion n.

flue [floo] n. chimney

flu'ent [floo'-] a. speaking, writing easily and well

fluff n. soft, feathery stuff -v. make or become soft, light; inf. make mistake -fluff'y a.

flu'id [floo'-] a. flowing easily -n. gas or liquid -fluid ounce unit of capacity 1/20 of pint

fluke¹ [flook] n. flat triangular part of anchor

fluke² [flook] n. stroke of luck

flumm'ox vt. bewilder, perplex

fluores'cent a. giving off a special type of bright light

fluor'ide n. salt containing fluorine -fluor'idate vt. -fluor'ine n. nonmetallic element, yellowish gas

flurr'y n. gust; bustle; fluttering -vt. agitate (flur'ried, flur'rying)

flush v. blush; flow suddenly or violently; be excited -vt. cleanse (eg toilet) by rush of water; excite -n. blush; rush of water; excitement;

freshness -a. full; well supplied; level with surrounding surface

flus'ter v. make or become nervous, agitated -n.

flute [floot] n. wind instrument with blowhole in side; groove -vi. play on flute -vt. make grooves in -fluted a.

flutt'er v. flap (as wings) rapidly; quiver; be or make agitated -n. flapping movement; agitation; inf. modest wager

flux n. discharge; constant succession of changes; substance mixed with metal in soldering etc.

fly¹ v. move through air on wings or in aircraft; pass quickly; float loosely; run away -vt. operate aircraft; cause to 'ly; set flying -vi. run from (flew pt., flown pp.) -n. (zip or buttons fastening) opening in trousers -fly'ing n. a hurried, brief -flying colours conspicuous success -flying squad special detachment of police, soldiers etc., ready to act quickly -fly'over n. road passing over another by bridge -fly'wheel n. heavy wheel regulating speed of machine

fly² n. two-winged insect, esp. common housefly

FM frequency modulation

foal n. young of horse

foam n. collection of small bubbles on liquid; light cellular solid -v. (cause to) produce foam -foam'y a.

fob off ignore, dismiss in offhand manner (-bb-)

fo'c's'le [fōk'səl] n. contracted form of FORECASTLE

fo'cus n. point at which rays meet; state of optical image when it is clearly defined; point on which interest, activity is centred (pl. fo'cuses, fo'ci [-sī]) -vt. bring to focus; concentrate -vi. come to focus; converge (fo'cused, fo'cusing) -fo'cal a.

fodd'er n. bulk food for livestock

foe [fō] n. enemy

foe'tus, fe'tus [-ē-] n. fully-developed young in womb or egg

fog n. thick mist -vt. cover in fog; puzzle (-gg-) -fogg'y a.

fo'g(e)y n. old-fashioned person

foi'ble n. minor weakness, idiosyncrasy

foil¹ vt. baffle, frustrate -n. blunt sword for fencing

foil² n. metal in thin sheet; anything which sets off another thing to advantage

foist vt. (usu. with off or on) sell,

pass off inferior or unwanted thing as valuable

fold [-ō-] *vt.* double up, bent part of; interlace (arms); clasp (in arms); *Cooking* mix gently —*vi.* become folded; admit of being folded; *inf.* fail —*n.* folding; line made by folding —**fold'er** *n.* binder, file for loose papers

fo'liage *n.* leaves collectively

fo'lio *n.* sheet of paper folded in half to make two leaves of book; book of largest common size (*pl.* -**lios**)

folk [fōk] *n.* people in general family, relatives; race of people —**folk'lore** *n.* tradition, customs, beliefs popularly held

foll'icle *n.* small sac

foll'ow *v.* go or come after —*vt.* accompany, attend on; keep to; take as guide; have a keen interest in; be consequent on; grasp meaning of —*vi.* come next; result —**foll'ower** *n.* disciple, supporter —**foll'owing** *a.* about to be mentioned —*n.* body of supporters

foll'y *n.* foolishness

foment' *vt.* foster, stir up

fond *a.* tender, loving —**fond of** having liking for

fon'dle *vt.* caress

font *n.* bowl for baptismal water usu. on pedestal

fontanel(le)' *n.* soft, membraneous gap between bones of baby's skull

food [-ōō-] *n.* solid nourishment; what one eats

fool [-ōō-] *n.* silly, empty-headed person; *Hist.* jester —*vt.* delude; dupe —*vi.* act as fool —**fool'hardy** *a.* foolishly adventurous —**fool'ish** *a.* silly, stupid —**fool'proof** *a.* proof against failure

foot [-oo-] *n.* lowest part of leg, from ankle down; lowest part of anything, base, stand; end of bed *etc.*; infantry; measure of twelve inches (*pl.* **feet**) —*v.* (*usu. tr.*) dance; walk; pay cost of —**foot'ing** *n.* basis, foundation —**foot'ball** *n.* game played with large blown-up ball; the ball —**foot'baller** *n.* —**foot'hold** *n.* place affording secure grip for the foot —**foot'lights** *pl.n.* lights across front of stage —**foot'note** *n.* note of reference or explanation printed at foot of page —**foot'print** *n.* mark left by foot

fop *n.* man excessively concerned with fashion —**fopp'ery** *n.*

for *prep.* directed to; because of; instead of; towards; on account of; in favour of; respecting; during; in

search of; in payment of; in the character of; in spite of —*conj.* because

for- (*comb. form*) from, away, against, as in *forswear, forbid*

for'age [fo'rij] *n.* food for cattle and horses —*v.* collect forage; make roving search

for'ay [fo'rā] *n.* raid, inroad

for(e)'bear [-bār] *n.* ancestor

forbear' [-bār'] *v.* (*esp. with* from) cease; refrain (from); be patient (**forbore'** *pt.*, **forborne'** *pp.*) —**forbear'ance** *n.*

forbid' *vt.* prohibit; refuse to allow (**forbade'** [-bad'] *pt.*, **forbidd'en** *pp.*, **forbidd'ing** *pr.p.*) —**forbidd'ing** *a.* uninviting, threatening

force *n.* strength, power; compulsion; that which tends to produce a change in a physical system; body of troops, police *etc.*; group of people organized for particular task; operative force; violence —*vt.* compel; produce by effort, strength; break open; hasten maturity of —**forced** *a.* compulsory; unnatural —**force'ful** *a.* powerful, persuasive —**for'cible** *a.* done by force

for'ceps *pl.n.* surgical pincers

ford *n.* shallow place where river may be crossed —*vt.*

fore *a.* in front (**form'er**, **fur'ther** *comp.*, **fore'most, first, fur'thest** *sup.*) —*n.* front part

fore- (*comb. form*) previous, before, front

fore-and-aft *a.* placed in line from bow to stern of ship

fore'arm *n.* arm between wrist and elbow —*vt.* [-ârm'] arm beforehand

forebode' *vt.* indicate in advance —**forebo'ding** *n.* anticipation of evil

fore'cast *vt.* estimate beforehand (*esp.* weather) —*n.* prediction

fore'castle [fōk'sel] *n.* forward raised part of ship

foreclose' *vt.* take away power of redeeming (mortgage)

fore'father *n.* ancestor

fore'finger *n.* finger next to thumb

forego'ing *a.* going before, preceding —**fore'gone** *a.* determined beforehand

fore'ground *n.* part of view nearest observer

fore'hand *a.* of stroke in racquet games made with inner side of wrist leading

fore'head [*or* fo'rid] *n.* part of face

above eyebrows and between temples

for'eign [fo'rin] a. not of, or in, one's own country; relating to other countries; strange **-for'eigner** n.

fore'man n. one in charge of work; leader of jury

fore'most a./adv. first in time, place, importance etc.

fore'noon n. morning

foren'sic a. of courts of law **-forensic medicine** application of medical knowledge in legal matters

fore'runner n. one who goes before, precursor

foresee' vt. see beforehand (**-saw'** pt., **-seen'** pp.)

foreshad'ow vt. show, suggest beforehand, be a type of

fore'sight n. foreseeing; care for future

fore'skin n. skin that covers the glans penis

for'est [fo'rist] n. area with heavy growth of trees and plants **-for'estry** n.

forestall' vt. prevent, guard against in advance

foretell' vt. prophesy (**foretold'** pt./pp.)

fore'thought n. thoughtful consideration of future events

forev'er adv. always; eternally; inf. for a long time

forewarn' vt. warn, caution in advance

fore'word n. preface

for'feit [-fit] n. thing lost by crime or fault; penalty, fine **-a.** lost by crime or fault **-vt.** lose by penalty

forge[1] [-j] n. place where metal is worked, smithy **-vt.** shape (metal) by heating and hammering; counterfeit **-for'ger** n. **-for'gery** n.

forge[2] [-j] vi. advance steadily

forget' vt. lose memory of, neglect, overlook (**forgot'** pt., **forgot'ten** pp., **forget'ting** pr.p.) **-forget'ful** a. liable to forget

forgive' [-giv'] v. cease to blame or hold resentment against; pardon **-forgive'ness** n.

forgo' vt. go without; give up (**-went'** pt., **-gone'** pp., **-go'ing** pr.p.)

fork n. pronged instrument for eating food; pronged tool for digging or lifting; division into branches **-vi.** branch **-vt.** dig, lift, throw, with fork; make forkshaped

forlorn' a. forsaken; desperate

form n. shape, visible appearance; structure; nature; species, kind; regularly drawn up document; condition; class in school; customary way of doing things; bench **-vt.** shape, organize; conceive; make part of **-vi.** come into existence or shape **-forma'tion** n. forming; thing formed; structure **-for'mative** a. **-form'less** a.

for'mal a. ceremonial, according to rule; of outward form; stiff **-formal'ity** n. observance required by custom; condition of being formal **-for'mally** adv.

for'mat n. size and shape of book etc.

for'mer a. earlier in time; of past times; first named **-pron.** first named thing or person or fact **-for'merly** adv. previously

for'midable a. to be feared; overwhelming; likely to be difficult

for'mula [-myoo-] n. set form of words, rule; Science, Math. rule, fact expressed in symbols and figures (pl. **-ulae** [-ē], **-s**) **-for'mulate** v.

fornica'tion n. sexual intercourse outside marriage **-for'nicate** vi.

forsake' vt. abandon, desert; give up (**forsook'**, **forsa'ken**, **forsa'king**)

forswear' vt. renounce, deny **-refl.** perjure (**-swore'** pt., **-sworn'** pp.)

fort n. stronghold

forte[1] [or for'tā] n. one's strong point, that in which one excels

forte[2] [-ti] adv. Mus. loudly

forth adv. onwards, into view **-forthcom'ing** a. about to come; ready when wanted; willing to talk **-forthwith'** adv. at once

forth'right a. outspoken

for'tify vt. strengthen (**for'tified**, **for'tifying**) **-fortifica'tion** n.

for'titude n. endurance

fort'night [-nīt] n. two weeks

for'tress n. fortified place

fortu'itous a. accidental

for'tune n. good luck; wealth; chance **-for'tunate** a. **-for'tunately** adv.

for'ty see FOUR

fo'rum n. (place or medium for) meeting, discussion or debate

for'ward a. lying in front of; onward; presumptuous; advanced; relating to the future **-n.** player in various team games **-adv.** towards the future; towards the front, to the front, into view **-vt.** help forward; send, dispatch -for'wards adv.

foss'il n. remnant or impression of animal or plant, preserved in earth -foss'ilize v. turn into fossil; petrify

fos'ter vt. promote development of; bring up child, esp. not one's own

foul a. loathsome, offensive; stinking; dirty; unfair; obscene -n. act of unfair play; the breaking of a rule -v. (mainly tr.) make, become foul; jam; collide with -foul'ly adv.

found¹ vt. establish; lay base of; base -founda'tion n. basis; lowest part of building; founding; endowed institution etc.

found³ vt. melt and run into mould; cast -found'ry n. place for casting

found'er vi. collapse; sink

found'ling n. deserted infant

fount n. fountain

foun'tain [-in] n. jet of water, esp. ornamental one; spring; source

four [-aw-] n./a. cardinal number next after three -fourth a. the ordinal number -for'tieth a. -for'ty n./a. four tens -four'teen n./a. four plus ten -four'teenth a. -four'some n. group of four people -a.

fowl n. domestic cock or hen; bird, its flesh

fox n. red bushy-tailed animal; its fur; cunning person -vt. perplex -n. act craftily -fox'y a. -fox'glove n. tall flowering plant -fox'trot n. (music for) ballroom dance -v.

foy'er [-â] n. entrance-hall in theatres, hotels etc.

fra'cas [-k'ah] n. noisy quarrel

frac'tion n. numerical quantity not an integer; fragment

frac'tious [-shəs] a. irritable

frac'ture n. breakage; breaking of bone -v. break

frag'ile [-aj-] a. breakable; delicate -fragil'ity n.

frag'ment n. piece broken off -v. [-ment'] -frag'mentary a.

fra'grant a. sweet-smelling -fra'grance n.

frail a. fragile; in weak health -frail'ly adv. -frail'ty n.

frame n. that in which thing is set, as square of wood round picture etc.; structure; build of body -vt. make; put into words; put into frame; bring false charge against -frame'work n. supporting structure

franc [-angk] n. monetary unit of France, Switzerland etc.

fran'chise n. right of voting; citizenship; privilege or right

frank a. candid, outspoken; sincere -n. official mark on letter either cancelling stamp or ensuring delivery without stamp -vt. mark letter thus

frank'furter n. smoked sausage

frank'incense n. aromatic gum resin burned as incense

fran'tic a. distracted with rage, grief, joy etc.; frenzied -fran'tically adv.

frater'nal a. of brother, brotherly -frater'nity n. brotherliness; brotherhood -frat'ernize vi. to associate, make friends

fraud n. criminal deception; imposture -fraud'ulent a.

fraught [-awt] a. filled (with), involving

fray¹ n. fight; noisy quarrel

fray³ v. make, become ragged at edge

fraz'zle inf. v. make or become exhausted -n. exhausted state

freak n. abnormal person, animal, thing -a.

freck'le n. light brown spot on skin, esp. caused by sun

free a. able to act at will, not under compulsion or restraint; not restricted or affected by; not subject to cost or tax; not in use; (of person) not occupied; loose, not fixed -vt. set at liberty; remove (obstacles, pain etc.); rid (of) (freed, free'ing) -free'dom n. -free-for-all n. brawl -free'hand a. drawn without guiding instruments -free'hold n. tenure of land without obligation of service or rent -free'lance [-ah-] a./n. (of) self-employed person -free-range a. kept, produced in natural, nonintensive conditions -free speech right to express opinions publicly

free'sia [-zi-ə] n. plant with fragrant, tubular flowers

freeze v. change (by reduction of temperature) from liquid to solid, as water to ice -vt. preserve (food etc.) by extreme cold; fix (prices etc.) -vi. feel very cold; become rigid (froze, fro'zen, free'zing) -free'zer n. insulated cabinet for long-term storage of perishable foodstuffs

freight [-āt] n. commercial transport (esp. by railway, ship); cost of this; goods so carried -vt. send as or by freight -freight'er n.

French n. language spoken by people of France -a. of, or pertaining to France -French dressing salad dressing –**French horn** musical wind instrument

frenet'ic a. frenzied

fren'zy n. violent mental derangement; wild excitement –**fren'zied** a.

fre'quent a. happening often; common; numerous –vt. [-kwent'] go often to –**fre'quency** n. rate of occurrence; in radio etc. cycles per second of alternating current

fres'co n. (method of) painting on wet plaster (pl. -co(e)s)

fresh a. not stale; new; additional; different; recent; inexperienced; pure; not pickled, frozen etc.; not faded; not tired; of wind, strong –**fresh'en** v. –**fresh'man, fresh'er** n. first-year student

fret[1] v. be irritated, worry (-tt-) –n. irritation –**fret'ful** a.

fret[2] n. repetitive geometrical pattern –vt. ornament with carved pattern (-tt-) –**fret'work** n.

fri'able a. easily crumbled

fri'ar n. member of mendicant religious order

fricassee' [or frik'-] n. dish of stewed pieces of meat

fric'tion n. rubbing; resistance met with by body moving over another; clash of wills etc.

Fri'day n. the sixth day of the week

fridge n. inf. refrigerator

friend [frend] n. one well known to another and regarded with affection and loyalty –**friend'ly** a. kind; favourable –**friend'ship** n.

frieze [frēz] n. ornamental band, strip (on wall)

frig'ate n. old (sailing) warship; fast destroyerlike warship

fright [frīt] n. sudden fear; shock; alarm; grotesque or ludicrous person or thing –**fright'en** vt. cause fear, fright in –**fright'ful** a. terrible, calamitous; shocking; inf. very great, very large

frig'id [-ij'-] a. formal; (sexually) unfeeling; cold

frill n. strip of fabric gathered at one edge; ruff of hair, feathers around neck of dog, bird etc.; unnecessary words; superfluous thing; adornment

fringe n. ornamental edge of hanging threads, tassels etc.; hair cut in front and falling over brow; edge –a. (of theatre etc.) unofficial

frisk vi. move, leap, playfully –vt. wave briskly; inf. search (person)

fritt'er[1] vt. waste

fritt'er[2] n. piece of food fried in batter

friv'olous a. not serious, unimportant; flippant –**frivol'ity** n.

frizz vt. crisp, curl into small curls –n. frizzed hair –**frizz'y** a.

fro adv. away, from (only in to and fro)

frock n. woman's dress; various similar garments

frog n. tailless amphibious animal developed from tadpole

frol'ic n. merrymaking –vi. behave playfully (frol'icked, frol'icking)

from prep. expressing point of departure, source, distance, cause, change of state etc.

frond n. plant organ consisting of stem and foliage esp. ferns

front [-unt] n. fore part; position directly before or ahead; seaside promenade; outward aspect; inf. something serving as a respectable cover –v. look, face; inf. be a cover for –a. of, at, the front –**front'age** n. façade of building; extent of front –**front'ier** n. part of country which borders on another

frost n. frozen dew or mist; act or state of freezing –v. cover, be covered with frost or something similar in appearance –**frost'y** a. accompanied by frost; chilly; cold; unfriendly

froth [-th] n. collection of small bubbles, foam –v. (cause to) foam –**froth'y** a.

frown vi. wrinkle brows –n.

frow'zy n. dirty, unkempt

FRS Fellow of the Royal Society

fru'gal [-ōō-] a. sparing, thrifty, economical; meagre

fruit [-ōō-] n. seed and its envelope, esp. edible one; vegetable products; (usu. in pl.) result, benefit –vi. bear fruit –**fruit'ful** a. –**frui'tion** [-ōō-ish'-] n. enjoyment; realization of hopes –**fruit'less** a.

frump n. dowdy woman

frustrate' vt. thwart; disappoint –**frustra'tion** n.

fry[1] vt. cook with fat –vi. be cooked thus (fried, fry'ing)

fry[2] n. young fishes

ft. feet; foot

fu'chsia [fyōō'sha] n. shrub with purple-red flowers

fud'dle v. (cause to) be intoxicated, confused

fuddy-duddy n. inf. (elderly) dull person

fudge n. soft, variously flavoured sweet

fu'el n. material for burning as source of heat or power -vt. provide with fuel

fug n. stuffy indoor atmosphere -**fugg'y** a.

fu'gitive n. one who flees, esp. from arrest -a. elusive

fugue [fyōōg] n. musical composition in which themes are repeated in different parts

ful'crum n. point on which a lever is placed for support (pl. **ful'cra**)

fulfil' [fool-] vt. satisfy; carry out (-ll-) -**fulfil'ment** n.

full [fool] a. containing as much as possible; abundant; complete; ample; plump -adv. very; quite; exactly -**full'y** adv. -**full'ness, ful'ness** n. -**fullblown'** a. fully developed -**full stop** punctuation mark (.) at end of sentence

ful'minate vi. (esp. with against) criticize harshly

fum'ble v. grope about; handle awkwardly -n. awkward attempt

fume [fyōōm] vi. be angry; emit smoke or vapour -n. smoke; vapour -**fu'migate** vt. apply fumes or smoke to, esp. for disinfection -**fu'migator** n.

fun n. anything enjoyable, amusing etc. -**funn'ily** adv. -**funn'y** a. comical; odd

func'tion [-ngk'-] n. work a thing is designed to do; (large) social event; duty; profession -vi. operate, work -**func'tional** a.

fund n. stock or sum of money; supply -pl. money resources -vt. provide or obtain fund(s)

fundament'al a. of, affecting, or serving as, the base; essential, primary -n. basic rule or fact

fu'neral n. (ceremony associated with) burial or cremation of dead -**fune'real** [-nē-] a. like a funeral; dark; gloomy

fun'gus [-ng'g-] n. plant without leaves, flowers, or roots, as mushroom, mould (pl. -**gi** [-ji], -**guses**)

funn'el n. cone-shaped vessel or tube; chimney of locomotive or ship -v. (cause to) move as through funnel

funn'y a. see FUN

fur n. soft hair of animal; garment of this -**furr'ier** n. dealer in furs -**fur'ry** a.

fur'ious [fyoor'-] a. extremely angry; violent

furl vt. roll up and bind

fur'long n. eighth of mile

fur'nace n. apparatus for applying great heat to metals

fur'nish vt. fit up house with furniture; supply -**fur'niture** n.

furore [fyoo-] n. public outburst; sudden enthusiasm

furr'ow [-ō] n. trench; groove -vt. make furrows in

fur'ther [-TH-] adv. more; in addition; at or to a greater distance or extent -a. more distant; additional -comp. of FAR, FORE[1] -vt. promote -**fur'thermore** adv. besides -**fur'thest** a. sup. of FAR, FORE[1] -adv. -**fur'thermost** a.

fur'tive a. stealthy, sly, secret -**fur'tively** adv.

fur'y [fyoor'-] n. wild rage; violence

fuse [fyōōz] n. blend by melting; melt with heat; (cause to) fail as a result of blown fuse -n. soft wire used as safety device in electrical systems; device for igniting bomb etc. -**fu'sion** n.

fu'selage [-ahzh] n. body of aircraft

fuss n. needless bustle or concern; complaint; objection -vi. make fuss -**fuss'y** a.

fus'ty a. mouldy; smelling of damp; old-fashioned

fu'tile a. useless, ineffectual, trifling -**futil'ity** n.

fu'ture n. time to come; what will happen -a. that will be; of, relating to, time to come

fuzz n. fluff; frizzed hair; blur; sl. police(man) -**fuzz'y** a.

G

g gram(s)

gab'ble v. talk, utter inarticulately or too fast (**gab'bled, gab'bling**)

gab'erdine, gab'ardine [-ēn] n. fine twill cloth like serge

ga'ble n. triangular upper part of wall at end of ridged roof

gad vi. (esp. with about) go around in search of pleasure (-dd-)

gad'fly n. cattle-biting fly

gadg'et n. small mechanical device

gaff n. stick with iron hook for landing fish

gaffe n. tactless remark

gaff'er n. old man; inf. foreman, boss

gag[1] vt. stop up (person's mouth) -vi.

sl. retch, choke (**-gg-**) –*n.* cloth etc. tied across mouth

gag¹ *n.* joke, funny story

gage [gājʹ] *n.* pledge, thing given as security

gag'gle *n.* flock of geese

gain *vt.* obtain (as profit); earn; reach –*vi.* increase, improve; get nearer –*n.* profit; increase, improvement –**gain'fully** *adv.* profitably

gainsay' *vt.* deny, contradict (**gain-said, gainsaying**)

gait [gāt] *n.* manner of walking

gal'a [gahlʹə] *n.* festive occasion; show; sporting event

gal'axy *n.* system of stars –**galac'tic** *a.*

gale *n.* strong wind; *inf.* outburst, *esp.* of laughter

gal(l)'ivant, gal'avant *vi.* gad about

gall¹ [gawl] *n.* *inf.* impudence; bitterness –**gall bladder** sac for bile

gall² [gawl] *vt.* make sore by rubbing; irritate

gall'ant *a.* fine, stately, brave; [*also* -lantʹ] chivalrous –*n.* suitor; fashionable young man –**gall'antry** *n.*

gall'eon *n.* large sailing ship

gall'ery *n.* projecting upper floor in church, theatre *etc.*; room(s) for showing works of art

gall'ey *n.* one-decked vessel with sails and oars; kitchen of ship or aircraft

gall'on *n.* liquid measure of eight pints (4.55 litres)

gall'op *v.* go, ride at gallop; move fast –*n.* horse's fastest pace; ride at this pace

gall'ows [-ōz] *n.* structure for hanging criminals

galore' *adv.* in plenty

galosh'es *pl.n.* waterproof overshoes

gal'vanize *vt.* stimulate to action; coat (iron *etc.*) with zinc

gam'bit *n.* opening move, comment *etc.* intended to secure an advantage

gam'ble *vi.* play games of chance to win money; act on expectation of –*n.* risky undertaking; bet

gam'bol *vi.* skip, jump playfully (**-ll-**) –*n.*

game¹ *n.* pastime; jest; contest for amusement; scheme; animals or birds hunted; their flesh –*a.* brave; willing –**game'keeper** *n.* man employed to breed game, prevent poaching

game², **gamm'y** *a.* lame

gamm'on *n.* cured or smoked ham

gam'ut *n.* whole range or scale

gan'der *n.* male goose

gang *n.* (criminal) group; organized group of workmen –*vi.* (*esp. with* together) form gang

gan'gling [-ngʹg-] *a.* lanky

gang'plank *n.* portable bridge for boarding or leaving vessel

gan'grene [-ngʹg-] *n.* death or decay of body tissue as a result of disease or injury

gang'ster *n.* member of criminal gang

gang'way *n.* bridge from ship to shore; anything similar; passage between row of seats

gan'net *n.* predatory sea bird

gan'try *n.* structure to support crane, railway signals *etc.*

gaol [jāl] *n.* *see* JAIL.

gap *n.* opening, interval

gape *vi.* stare in wonder; open mouth wide; be, become wide open –*n.*

gar'age [gaʹrahzh, -rij] *n.* (part of) building to house cars; refuelling and repair centre for cars

garb *n./vt.* dress

gar'bage [-ij] *n.* rubbish

gar'ble *vt.* jumble or distort story, account *etc.*

gar'den *n.* ground for cultivation –*vi.* cultivate garden –**gar'dener** *n.* –**gar'dening** *n.*

gargan'tuan *a.* immense

gar'gle *v.* wash throat with liquid kept moving by the breath –*n.* gargling; preparation for this purpose

gar'ish *a.* showy; gaudy

gar'land *n.* wreath of flowers as decoration

gar'lic *n.* (bulb of) plant with strong smell and taste, used in cooking and seasoning

gar'ment *n.* article of clothing

gar'ner *vt.* store up, collect

gar'net *n.* red semiprecious stone

gar'nish *vt.* decorate (*esp.* food) –*n.* material for this

garr'et *n.* attic

garr'ison *n.* troops stationed in town, fort *etc.*; fortified place –*vt.* occupy with garrison

garr'ulous *a.* talkative

gar'ter *n.* band worn round leg to hold up sock or stocking

gas *n.* air-like substance; fossil fuel in form of gas; gaseous anaesthetic; gaseous poison or irritant; *inf.* (*esp.* US) petrol (*pl.* **-es**) –*vt.* poison with

gas -vi. inf. talk idly, boastfully (**-ss-**) -**gas'eous** a. of, like gas

gash n. gaping wound, slash -vt. cut deep

gas'ket n. seal between metal faces, esp. in engines

gasp [-ah-] vi./n. catch of breath as in exhaustion or surprise

gas'tric a. of stomach -**gastron'-omy** n. art of good eating

gate n. opening in wall, fence etc.; barrier for closing it; any entrance or way out -**gate-crash** v. enter social function etc. uninvited

gât'eau [-ô] n. elaborate, rich cake (pl. **-x**)

gath'er [GATH-] v. (cause to) assemble; increase gradually; draw together -vt. collect; learn, understand -**gath'ering** n. assembly

gauche [gōsh] a. tactless

gaud'y a. showy in tasteless way

gauge [gāj] n. standard measure, as of diameter of wire etc.; distance between rails of railway; instrument for measuring -vt. measure; estimate

gaunt [-aw-] a. lean, haggard

gaunt'let [-aw-] n. (armoured) glove covering part of arm

gauze [-aw-] n. thin transparent fabric of silk, wire etc. -**gauz'y** a.

gav'el n. auctioneer's mallet

gaw'ky a. clumsy, awkward

gawp v. sl. stare stupidly

gay a. merry; lively; bright; given to pleasure; inf. homosexual -**gai'ety** n. -**gai'ly** adv.

gaze vi. look fixedly -n.

gazelle' n. small graceful antelope

gazette' n. official newspaper for government announcements -**gazet-teer'** n. geographical dictionary

GB Great Britain

GC George Cross

GCE General Certificate of Education

gear n. set of wheels working together, esp. by engaging cogs; equipment; clothing -vt. adapt (one thing) so as to conform with another -**gear'box** n. case protecting gearing of bicycle, car etc.

geel'bek [chēl'-] n. edible S Afr. marine fish

geese pl. of GOOSE

gei'sha [gā'-] n. in Japan, professional female companion for men

gel [jel] n. jelly-like substance

gel'atin(e) [jel'-] n. substance prepared from animal bones etc., producing edible jelly

geld vt. castrate -**geld'ing** n. castrated horse

gel'ignite [jel-] n. powerful explosive consisting of dynamite in gelatin form

gem n. precious stone, esp. when cut and polished

gen [j-] n. inf. information

gen'der [j-] n. sex, male or female

gene [jēn] n. biological factor determining inherited characteristics

geneal'ogy [jē-] n. study or account of descent from ancestors

gen'eral [j-] a. widespread; not particular or specific; usual; miscellaneous -n. army officer of rank above colonel -**gen'eralize** vi. draw general conclusions -**general prac-titioner** doctor serving local area

gen'erate [j-] vt. bring into being; produce -**genera'tion** n. bringing into being; all persons born about same time; time between generations (about 30 years) -**gen'erator** n. apparatus for producing (steam, electricity etc.)

gen'erous [j-] a. free in giving; abundant -**generos'ity** n.

gen'esis [j-] n. origin; mode of formation (pl. **-eses**)

genet'ics [j-] pl.n. (with sing. v.) scientific study of heredity -**genet'ic** a.

ge'nial [jē'-] a. cheerful; mild

ge'nie [jē'-] n. in fairy tales, servant appearing by, and working, magic (pl. **ge'nii**)

gen'ital [j-] a. relating to sexual organs or reproduction -**gen'itals** pl.n. the sexual organs

ge'nius [jē'-] n. (person with) exceptional power or ability

gent [j-] inf. n. gentleman -pl. men's public lavatory

genteel' [j-] a. well-bred; affectedly proper

gen'tile [j-] a. of race other than Jewish -n.

gen'tle [j-] a. mild, not rough or severe; moderate; well-born -**gentil'ity** n. respectability -**gen'tleness** n. quality of being gentle -**gen'tleman** n. chivalrous well-bred man; man (used as a mark of politeness)

gen'uine [j-] a. real; sincere

ge'nus [jē'-] n. class, order, group (esp. of insects, animals etc.) with common characteristics (pl. **gen'-era**)

geog'raphy [j-] n. science of earth's form, physical features, climate, population etc. -geog'rapher n. -geograph'ic(al) a.

geol'ogy [j-] n. science of earth's crust, rocks, strata etc. -geol'ogist n.

geom'etry [j-] n. science of properties and relations of lines, surfaces etc. -geomet'rical a.

geophys'ics [j-] n. science of physics of the earth

gera'nium [j-] n. plant with red, pink or white flowers

ger'bil [j-] n. desert rodent of Asia and Africa

geria'trics [j-] n. science of old age and its diseases -geriat'ric a./n. old (person)

germ [j-] n. microbe, esp. causing disease; rudiment

germ'inate [j-] v. (cause to) sprout or begin to grow

gesta'tion [j-] n. carrying of young in womb

gestic'ulate [j-] vi. use expressive movements of hands and arms when speaking

ges'ture [j-] n./vi. (make) movement to convey meaning

get vt. obtain; catch; cause to go or come; bring into position or state; induce; be in possession of, have (to do) -vi. reach; become (got, gett'ing)

gey'ser [gē'z-] n. hot spring throwing up spout of water; water heater

ghast'ly [gah-] a. deathlike; inf. horrible -adv. sickly

gher'kin [ger'-] n. small cucumber used in pickling

ghett'o [get'-] n. densely populated (esp. by one racial group) slum area (pl. -tos)

ghost [gō-] n. dead person appearing again; spectre; faint trace

ghoul [gōōl] n. malevolent spirit; person with morbid interests

GHQ General Headquarters

gi'ant [jī'-] n. mythical being of superhuman size; very tall person, plant etc. -a. huge -gigan'tic a. enormous, huge

gibb'er [j-] vi. make meaningless sounds with mouth -gibb'erish n. meaningless speech or words

gibb'et [j-] n. gallows; post on which executed criminal was hung

gibb'on n. type of ape

gibe [j-], jibe v. jeer -n.

gib'lets [j-] pl.n. internal edible parts of fowl

gidd'y a. dizzy; liable to cause dizziness; flighty

gift n. thing given, present; faculty, power -gift'ed a. talented

gigan'tic [j-] see GIANT

gig'gle vi. laugh nervously, foolishly -n. such a laugh

gild vt. put thin layer of gold on (gilded pt. -gilt or gilded pp.) -gilt n. thin layer of gold put on

gill¹ [g-] n. breathing organ in fish

gill² [j-] n. liquid measure, quarter of pint (0.142 litres)

gim'let n. boring tool, usu. with screw point

gimm'ick n. stratagem etc., esp. designed to attract attention or publicity

gin¹ [j-] n. spirit flavoured with juniper berries

gin² [j-] n. snare, trap

gin'ger [j-] n. plant with hot-tasting spicy root; the root -vt. stimulate -gin'gerbread n. cake flavoured with ginger

gin'gerly [j-] adv. cautiously

ging'ham [-ng'əm] n. cotton cloth, usu. checked

Gip'sy n. see GYPSY

giraffe' [ji-rahf'] n. Afric. animal, with very long neck

gird vt. put belt round; prepare (oneself) (girt, gird'ed pt./pp) -gird'er n. large beam

gir'dle n. corset; waistband

girl n. female child; young (unmarried) woman -girl'hood n.

gi'ro [jī'-] n. system operated by banks and post offices for the transfer of money

girth n. measurement round thing; band put round horse to hold saddle

gist [j-] n. substance, main point of remarks etc.)

give [giv] vt. make present of; deliver; assign; utter -vi. yield, give way (gave, giv'en, giv'ing) -n. yielding, elasticity

gizz'ard n. part of bird's stomach

glacé [glas'i] a. crystallized, iced

glac'ier [-as'-, -ā'-] n. slow-moving river of ice

glad a. pleased; happy -gladd'en vt. make glad

glade n. grassy space in forest

glad'iator n. trained fighter in Roman arena

gladio'lus n. kind of iris, with sword-shaped leaves

glam'our n. alluring charm, fascination -**glam'orous** a.

glance [-ah-] vi. look rapidly or briefly; glide off something struck -n. brief look

gland n. organ controlling different bodily functions by chemical means -**gland'ular** a.

glare [-ār] vi. look fiercely; shine intensely -n.

glass [-ah-] n. hard transparent substance; things made of it; tumbler; its contents -pl. spectacles -**glass'y** a. like glass; expressionless

glauco'ma n. eye disease

glaze vt. furnish with glass; cover with glassy substance -vi. become glassy -n. transparent coating; substance used for this -**gla'zier** n. one who glazes windows

gleam n./vi. (give out) slight or passing beam of light

glean v. pick up; gather

glee n. mirth, merriment

glen n. narrow valley

glib a. fluent but insincere or superficial

glide vi. pass smoothly and continuously -n. smooth, silent movement -**gli'der** n. aircraft without engine

glimm'er vi. shine faintly -n.

glimpse n. brief view -vt. catch glimpse of

glint v. flash -n.

glis'ten [-is'n] vi. gleam by reflecting light

glitt'er vi. shine with bright quivering light, sparkle -n. lustre; sparkle

gloat vi. regard with smugness or malicious satisfaction

globe n. sphere with map of earth or stars; ball -**glo'bal** a. of globe; relating to whole world

gloom n. darkness; melancholy -**gloom'y** a.

glor'y n. renown; splendour; heavenly bliss -vi. take pride (in) (**glor'ied, glor'ying**) -**glor'ify** vt. make glorious (**-ified, -ifying**) -**glor'ious** a. illustrious; splendid; delightful -**glor'iously** adv.

gloss[1] n. surface shine, lustre -vt. put gloss on; (esp. with over) (try to) cover up, pass over (fault, error) -**gloss'y** a. smooth, shiny

gloss[2] n. marginal interpretation of word; comment -vt. interpret; comment -**gloss'ary** n. dictionary of special words

glove [-uv] n. covering for the hand

-vt. cover as with glove -**the gloves** boxing gloves; boxing

glow [-ō] vi. give out light and heat without flames; be or look hot -n. shining heat -**glow-worm** n. insect giving out light

glow'er [-ow'-] vi. scowl

glu'cose [gloo'-] n. type of sugar found in fruit etc.

glue [gloo] n./vt. (fasten with) sticky substance -**glu'ey** a.

glum a. sullen, gloomy

glut n. surfeit, excessive amount -vt. feed, gratify to the full or to excess (-tt-)

glutt'on[1] n. greedy person; one with great liking or capacity for something -**glutt'ony** n.

glutt'on[2] n. wolverine

glyc'erine(e), **glyc'erol** [glis'-] n. colourless sweet liquid

GMT Greenwich Mean Time

gnarled [narld] a. knobby, twisted

gnash [n-] v. grind (teeth) together as in anger or pain

gnat [n-] n. small, biting fly

gnaw [n-] v. bite or chew steadily

gnome [n-] n. legendary creature like small old man

gnu [noo] n. oxlike antelope

go vi. move along; depart; function; fail; elapse; be able to be put; become (**went** pt., **gone** pp.) -n. going; energy; attempt; turn

goad n. spiked stick for driving cattle; anything that urges to action -vt. urge on; torment

goal n. end of race; object of effort; posts through which ball is to be driven in football etc.; the score so made

goat n. animal with long hair, horns and beard

gob'ble[1] vt. eat hastily, noisily or greedily

gob'ble[2] n./vi. (make) cry of the turkey-cock

gob'let n. drinking cup

gob'lin n. Folklore small, usu. malevolent being

god n. superhuman being worshipped as having supernatural power; object of worship; idol; (G-) the Supreme Being, creator and ruler of universe (**godd'ess** fem.) -**god'ly** a. devout, pious -**god'child** n. one considered in relation to godparent -n. -**god'father** n. sponsor at baptism (fem. **god'mother**) -**god'send** n. something unexpected but welcome

gog'gle vi. (of eyes) bulge; stare

-pl.n. protective spectacles

goi'tre [-tə] n. enlargement of thyroid gland

go-kart (or **cart**) n. miniature, low-powered racing car

gold [-ō] n. yellow precious metal; coins of this; colour of gold -a. of, like gold -**gold'en** a. -**gold'finch** n. bird with yellow feathers -**gold'fish** n. any of various ornamental pond or aquarium fish

golf n. outdoor game in which small hard ball is struck with clubs into a succession of holes -vi. play this game -**golf'er** n.

goll'iwog n. black-faced doll

gon'dola n. Venetian canal boat -**gondolier'** n. rower of gondola

gong n. metal plate which resounds as bell when struck with soft mallet

good a. commendable; right; beneficial; well-behaved; virtuous; sound; valid (**bett'er** comp., **best** sup.) -n. benefit; wellbeing; profit -pl. property; wares -**good'ly** a. large, considerable -**good'ness** n. -**good sort** inf. agreeable person

goodbye' interj./n. form of address on parting

goo'ey a. inf. sticky, soft

goon n. inf. stupid fellow

goose n. web-footed bird; its flesh; simpleton (pl. **geese**)

goose'berry [gooz'-] n. thorny shrub; its hairy fruit

go'pher n. various species of Amer. burrowing rodents

gore[1] n. (dried) blood from wound -**go'ry** a.

gore[2] vt. pierce with horns

gorge [-j] n. ravine; disgust, resentment -vi. feed greedily

gor'geous [-jəs] a. splendid, showy

gorill'a n. largest anthropoid ape, found in Afr.

gor'mandize vt. eat hurriedly or like a glutton

gorm'less a. inf. stupid

gorse n. prickly shrub

gos'ling [-z-] n. young goose

gos'pel n. unquestionable truth; (G-) any of first four books of New Testament

goss'amer n. filmy substance like spider's web

goss'ip n. idle (malicious) talk about other persons; one who talks thus -vi. engage in gossip

gouge [gowj] vt. scoop out; force out -n. chisel with curved cutting edge

gou'lash [gōō'-] n. stew seasoned with paprika

gourd [goord] n. large fleshy fruit; its rind as vessel

gour'mand [goor'-] n. glutton

gour'met [goor'mā] n. connoisseur of wine, food; epicure

gout [-ow-] n. disease with inflammation, esp. of joints

gov'ern [guv-] vt. rule, control; determine -**gov'ernable** a. -**gov'erness** n. woman teacher, esp. in private household -**gov'ernment** n. exercise of political authority in directing a people, state etc.; system by which community is ruled; governing group; control -**gov'ernor** n. one who governs; chief administrator of an institution; member of committee responsible for an organization or institution; regulator for speed of engine

gown n. loose flowing outer garment; woman's (long) dress; official robe

GP General Practitioner

GPO General Post Office

grab vt. grasp suddenly; snatch (-**bb**-) -n. sudden clutch; quick attempt to seize

grace n. charm, elegance; goodwill, favour; sense of propriety; postponement granted; short thanksgiving for meal -vt. add grace to, honour -**grace'ful** a. -**gra'cious** a. kind; condescending

grade n. step, stage; class; rating; slope -vt. arrange in classes; assign grade to -**grada'tion** n. series of steps; each of them

gra'dient n. (degree of) slope

grad'ual a. taking place by degrees; slow and steady; not steep

grad'uate vi. take university degree -vt. divide into degrees -n. holder of university degree -**gradua'tion** n.

graffi'ti [-fē'tē] pl.n. (oft. obscene) writing, drawing on walls

graft[1] [-ah-] n. shoot of plant set in stalk of another; the process; surgical transplant of skin, tissue -vt. insert (shoot) in another stalk; transplant (living tissue in surgery)

graft[2] [-ah-] inf. n. hard work; self-advancement, profit by unfair means

grain n. (seed, fruit of) cereal plant; small hard particle; very small unit of weight; arrangement of fibres; any very small amount

gram(me) *n.* one thousandth of a kilogram

gramm'ar *n.* science of structure and usages of language; use of words -**grammat'ical** *a.* -**grammar school** state-maintained secondary school providing academic education

gram'ophone *n.* instrument for reproducing sounds on discs, record-player

gram'pus *n.* type of dolphin

gran, grann'y *n. inf.* grandmother

gran'ary *n.* storehouse for grain

grand *a.* magnificent; noble; splendid; eminent -**gran'deur** [-jə] *n.* nobility; magnificence; dignity -**grand'iose** *a.* imposing; affectedly grand -**grand'child** [-ch-] *n.* child of one's child (**grand'son** *or* **grand'daughter**) -**grand'parent** [-d(ə)'-] *n.* parent of parent (**grand'father** *or* **grand'mother**) -**grand'stand** [-n-](d)'-] *n.* structure with tiered seats for spectators

gran'ite [-it] *n.* hard crystalline rock

grant [-ah-] *vt.* consent to fulfil (request); permit; admit -*n.* sum of money provided as education; gift; allowance, concession -**grantee'** *n.* -**grantor'** *n.*

gran'ule *n.* small grain -**gran'ular** *a.* of or like grains -**gran'ulate** *vt.* form into grains

grape *n.* fruit of vine

grape'fruit *n.* subtropical citrus fruit

graph *n.* drawing depicting relation of different numbers, quantities *etc.*

graph'ic *a.* vividly descriptive; of writing, drawing, painting *etc.* -**graph'ite** *n.* form of carbon (used in pencils)

grap'nel *n.* hooked iron instrument for seizing anything

grap'ple *v.* wrestle

grasp [-ah-] *v.* (try, struggle to) seize hold; understand -*n.* grip; comprehension -**grasp'ing** *a.* greedy, avaricious

grass [-ah-] *n.* common type of plant with jointed stems and long narrow leaves; such plants grown as lawn; pasture; *sl.* marijuana; *sl.* informer -**grass hockey C** hockey played on field -**grass'hopper** *n.* jumping, chirping insect

grate¹ *n.* framework of metal bars for holding fuel in fireplace -**gra'ting** *n.* framework of bars covering opening

grate² *vt.* rub into small bits on rough surface -*vi.* rub with harsh noise; irritate -**gra'ter** *n.* utensil with rough surface for reducing substance to small particles -**gra'ting** *a.* harsh; irritating

grate'ful *a.* thankful; appreciative; pleasing -**grat'itude** *n.* sense of being thankful

grat'ify *vt.* satisfy; please -**gratifica'tion** *n.*

gra'tis [-ā'-, -a'-, -ah'-] *adv./a.* free, for nothing

gratu'itous *a.* given free; uncalled for -**gratu'ity** *n.* gift of money for services rendered; tip

grave¹ *n.* hole dug to bury corpse

grave² *a.* serious; solemn

grav'el *n.* small stones; coarse sand -**grav'elly** *a.*

gra'ven *a.* carved, engraved

grav'itate *vi.* move by gravity; tend (towards) centre of attraction; sink, settle down

grav'ity *n.* force of attraction of one body for another, *esp.* of objects to the earth; heaviness; importance; seriousness

gra'vy *n.* juices from meat in cooking; sauce made from these

graze¹ *v.* feed on grass, pasture

graze² *vt.* touch lightly in passing, scratch, scrape -*n.* grazing; abrasion

grease [-ēs] *n.* soft melted fat of animals; thick oil as lubricant -*vt.* [*or* -ez] apply grease to -**greas'y** *a.*

great [-āt] *a.* large; important; pre-eminent; *inf.* excellent -*prefix* indicates a degree further removed in relationship, *eg* great-grand'father *n.*

greed *n.* excessive consumption of, desire for, food, wealth -**greed'y** *a.* -**greed'iness** *n.*

green *a.* of colour between blue and yellow; grass-coloured; unripe; inexperienced; envious -*n.* colour; area of grass, *esp.* for playing bowls *etc.* -*pl.* green vegetables -**green'fly** *n.* aphid, small green garden pest -**green'grocer** *n.* dealer in vegetables and fruit -**green'house** *n.* glasshouse for rearing plants

greet *vt.* meet with expressions of welcome; salute; receive -**greet'ing** *n.*

grega'rious *a.* sociable

grenade' *n.* bomb thrown by hand or shot from rifle -**grenadier'** *n.* soldier of Grenadier Guards

grenadine¹ [-ēn'] *n.* syrup made from pomegranate juice, for sweetening and colouring drinks

grey [grā] a. between black and white; clouded; turning white; aged; intermediate, indeterminate -n. grey colour

grey'hound n. swift slender dog

grid n. network of horizontal and vertical lines, bars etc.; any inter-connecting system of links

grid'dle, gir'dle n. flat iron plate for cooking

grid'iron n. frame of metal bars for grilling

grief [-ēf] n. deep sorrow **-grie'vance** n. real or imaginary ground of complaint **-grieve** vi. feel grief -vt. cause grief to **-grie'vous** a. painful, oppressive; very serious

grill n. device on cooker to radiate heat downwards; food cooked under grill; gridiron -v. cook (food) under grill; subject to severe questioning

grill(e) n. grating

grim a. stern; relentless; joyless

grimace' n./vi. (pull) wry face

grime n. ingrained dirt, soot **-gri'my** a.

grin vi./n. (give) broad smile (-nn-)

grind [-ī-] v. crush to powder; make sharp, smooth; grate (**ground** pt./pp.) -n. inf. hard work; action of grinding

grip n. firm hold; mastery; handle; travelling bag -vt. hold tightly; hold attention of (-pp-)

gripe vi. inf. complain (persistently) -n. intestinal pain (esp. in infants); inf. complaint

gris'ly [-z-] a. causing terror

grist n. corn to be ground **-grist for one's mill** something which can be turned to advantage

gris'tle [grisʹl] n. cartilage, tough flexible tissue

grit n. rough particles of sand; courage -vt. clench (teeth) (-tt-)

griz'zle inf. vi. whine

griz'zled, griz'zly a. grey (haired)

groan vi. make low, deep sound of grief or pain -n.

gro'cer n. dealer in foodstuffs **-gro'ceries** pl.n. commodities sold by a grocer **-gro'cery** n. trade, premises of grocer

grog n. spirit (esp. rum) and water **-grog'gy** a. inf. shaky, weak

groin n. fold where legs meet abdomen; euphemism for genitals

groom n. person caring for horses; bridegroom -vt. tend or look after;

brush or clean (esp. horse); train

groove n. narrow channel; routine -vt. cut groove in

grope vi. feel about, search blindly

gross [-ōs] a. very fat; total, not net; coarse; flagrant; -n. twelve dozen

grotesque' [-teskʹ] a. (horribly) distorted; absurd

grott'o n. cave (pl. -o(e)s)

grouch inf. n. persistent grumbler; discontented mood -vi. grumble

ground n. surface of earth; soil, earth; reason; special area -pl. dregs; enclosed land round house -vt. establish; instruct; place on ground -vi. run ashore **-ground'ed** a. of aircraft, unable or not permitted to fly **-ground'less** a. without reason

ground'sel n. yellow flowered plant

group [-ōō-] n. number of persons or things together; small musical band; class -v. place, fall into group

grouse' [-ows] n. game bird; its flesh (pl. **grouse**)

grouse' [-ows] vi. grumble, complain -n. complaint

grout n. thin fluid mortar -vt. fill up with grout

grove n. small group of trees

grov'el vi. abase oneself; lie face down (-ll-)

grow [-ō] v. develop naturally; increase; be produced; become by degrees -vt. produce by cultivation (**grew** pt., **grown** pp.) **-growth** n. growing; increase; what has grown or is growing **-grown-up** a./n. adult

growl vi. make low guttural sound of anger -n.

grub v. dig; root up rummage (-bb-) -n. larva of insect; sl. food **-grubb'y** a. dirty

grudge vt. be unwilling to give, allow -n. ill will

gru'el [grōō-] n. food of oatmeal etc., boiled in milk or water **-gru'elling** a. exhausting

grue'some [grōō-] a. horrible, grisly

gruff a. rough-voiced, surly **-gruff'ly** adv.

grum'ble vi. complain; rumble -n. complaint

grump'y a. ill-tempered, surly

grunt vi./n. (make) sound characteristic of pig

G-string n. very small covering for genitals; Mus. string tuned to G

guarantee' [ga-] n. formal assurance (esp. in writing) that product *etc.* will meet certain standards, last for given time *etc.* –*vt.* give guarantee; secure (against risk *etc.*) (**guaranteed'**, **guarantee'ing**) –**guarantor'** *n.*

guard [gah-] *vt.* protect, defend –*vi.* take precautions (against) –*n.* person, group that protects; sentry; official in charge of train; protection –**guard'ian** *n.* keeper, protector; person having custody of infant *etc.*

guava [gwahv'-] *n.* tropical tree with fruit used to make jelly

guer(r)ill'a [g∂-] *n.* member of irregular armed force

guess [ges] *vt.* estimate; conjecture US think –*vi.* form conjectures –*n.*

guest [gest] *n.* one entertained at another's house; one living in hotel

guffaw' *n.* burst of boisterous laughter –*vi.*

guide [gīd] *n.* one who shows the way; adviser; book of instruction or information –*vt.* lead, act as guide to –**gui'dance** *n.*

g(u)ild [gi-] *n.* organization for mutual help, or with common object

guile [gīl] *n.* cunning, deceit

guill'otine [gil'ə-tēn] *n.* machine for beheading; machine for cutting paper –*vt.* use guillotine on

guilt [gilt] *n.* fact, state of having done wrong; responsibility for offence –**guilt'less** *a.* innocent –**guilt'y** *a.* having committed an offence

guin'ea [gin'ī] *n.* formerly, sum of 21 shillings –**guinea pig** rodent originating in S Amer.; *inf.* person or animal used in experiments

guise [gīz] *n.* external appearance, *esp.* one assumed

guitar' [git-] *n.* 6-stringed instrument played by plucking or strumming

gulch *n.* ravine; gully

gulf *n.* large inlet of the sea; chasm; large gap

gull[1] *n.* long-winged web-footed sea bird

gull[2] *n.* dupe, fool –**gull'ible** *a.* easily imposed on, credulous

gull'et *n.* food passage from mouth to stomach

gull'y *n.* channel or ravine worn by water

gulp *vt.* swallow eagerly –*vi.* gasp, choke –*n.*

gum[1] *n.* firm flesh in which teeth are set

gum[2] *n.* sticky substance issuing from certain trees; an adhesive; chewing gum –*vt.* stick with gum

(**-mm-**) –**gumm'y** *a.* –**gum'boots** *pl.n.* boots of rubber –**gum'tree** *n.* any species of eucalypt

gump'tion *n.* resourcefulness; shrewdness, sense

gun *n.* weapon with metal tube from which missiles are discharged by explosion; cannon, pistol *etc.* –*v.* shoot; pursue, as with gun –**gunn'er** *n.* –**gun'powder** *n.* explosive mixture of saltpetre, sulphur, charcoal –**gun'shot** *n.* shot or range of gun –*a.* caused by missile from gun –**gun'wale** [gun'əl], **gunn'el** *n.* upper edge of ship's side

gunge *n. inf.* any sticky, unpleasant substance

gupp'y *n.* small colourful aquarium fish

gur'gle *n./vi.* (make) bubbling noise

gur'u [goo'roo] *n.* a spiritual teacher, *esp.* in India

gush *vi.* flow out suddenly and copiously, spurt –*n.* sudden and copious flow

guss'et *n.* triangle or diamond-shaped piece of material let into garment

gust *n.* sudden blast of wind; burst of rain, anger, passion *etc.*

gust'o *n.* enjoyment, zest

gut *n.* (*oft. pl.*) intestines; material made from guts of animals, *eg* for violin strings *etc.* –*pl. inf.* courage –*vt.* remove guts from (fish *etc.*); remove, destroy contents of (house)

gutt'er *n.* shallow trough for carrying off water from roof or side of street

gutt'ural *a.* harsh-sounding, as if produced in the throat

guy[1] [gī] *n.* effigy of Guy Fawkes burnt on Nov. 5th; *inf.* person (*usu.* male) –*vt.* make fun of; ridicule

guy[2] [gī] *n.* rope, chain to steady, secure something, *eg* tent

guz'zle *v.* eat or drink greedily –*n.*

gym [jim] *n.* short for GYMNASIUM *or* GYMNASTICS

gymkhan'a [jim-kahn'-] *n.* competition or display of horse riding

gymna'sium [jim-] *n.* place equipped for muscular exercises, athletic training (*pl.* **-s**, **-na'sia**) –**gymnas'tics** *pl.n.* muscular exercises

gynaecol'ogy [gīn-] *n.* branch of medicine dealing with functions and diseases of women

gyp'sum [jip'-] *n.* chalklike mineral, used for making plaster

Gyp'sy [jip'-] *n.* one of wandering

race originally from NW India, Romany

gyrate[1] [jī-] *vi.* move in circle, spiral

H

H *Chem.* hydrogen

hab'erdasher *n.* dealer in articles of dress, ribbons, pins, needles *etc.* -**hab'erdashery** *n.*

hab'it *n.* settled tendency or practice; customary apparel *esp.* of nun or monk -**habit'ual** *a.* formed or acquired by habit; usual, customary -**habit'uate** *vt.* accustom -**habit'ué** [-yoo-ā] *n.* constant visitor

hab'itable *a.* fit to live in -**hab'itant** *n.* C (descendant of) original French settler -**hab'itat** *n.* natural home (of animal *etc.*) -**habita'tion** *n.* dwelling place

hack[1] *vt.* cut, chop (at) violently; *inf.* utter harsh, dry cough -*n.*

hack[1] *n.* horse for ordinary riding; literary drudge

hac'kles *pl.n.* hairs on back of neck of dog and other animals which are raised in anger

hack'ney *n.* harness horse, carriage, coach kept for hire (*pl.* -**neys**)

hack'neyed *a.* (of words *etc.*) stale, trite because of overuse

hack'saw *n.* handsaw for cutting metal

hadd'ock *n.* large, edible seafish

ha'dedah [hah'di-dah] *n.* S Afr. ibis

haema-, haemo- (*comb. form*) blood

haemoglo'bin [hē-] *n.* colouring and oxygen-bearing matter of red blood corpuscles

haem'orrhage [hem'ə-rij] *n.* profuse bleeding

haem'orrhoids [hem'ə-roidz] *pl.n.* swollen veins in rectum (*also called* **piles**)

haft [-ah-] *n.* handle (of knife *etc.*) -*vt.* fit with one

hag *n.* ugly old woman; witch

hagg'ard *a.* anxious, careworn

hagg'le *vi.* bargain over price

hail[1] *n.* (shower of) pellets of ice; barrage -*vi.* pour down as shower of hail -**hail'stone** *n.*

hail[1] *vt.* greet; acclaim; call -*vi.* come (from)

hair *n.* filament growing from skin of animal, as covering of man's head; such filaments collectively -**hair'y** *a.* -**hair'do** *n.* way of dressing hair -**hair'dresser** *n.* one who attends to and cuts hair -**hair'pin** *n.* pin for keeping hair in place -**hairpin bend** U-shaped turn of road

hale *a.* robust, healthy

half [hahf] *n.* either of two equal parts of thing (*pl.* **halves** [hahvz]) -*a.* forming half -*adv.* to the extent of half -**half-baked** *a. inf.* silly -**half-breed, half-caste** *n.* person with parents of different races -**half-brother, -sister** *n.* brother (sister) by one parent only -**half-hearted** *a.* unenthusiastic

hal'ibut *n.* large edible flatfish

halito'sis *n.* bad-smelling breath

hall [hawl] *n.* (entrance) passage; large room or building used for *esp.* public assembly

hallelu'jah [-loo'yə] *n./interj.* exclamation of praise to God

hall'mark *n.* mark used to indicate standard of tested gold and silver; mark of excellence; distinguishing feature

hallo[1] *interj. see* HELLO

halloo[1] *n.* call to spur on hunting dogs -*v.* shout loudly to

hall'ow [-ō] *vt.* make, or honour as holy

hallu'cinate [-lōō'si-] *vi.* suffer illusions -**hallucina'tion** *n.* -**hallu'cinatory** *a.* -**hallu'cinogen** *n.* drug inducing hallucinations

ha'lo *n.* circle of light (*pl.* -**lo(e)s**)

halt[1] [hawlt] *n.* interruption or end to progress *etc.* (*esp.* as command to stop marching) -*v.* (cause to) stop

halt[1] [hawlt] *vi.* falter, fail -**halt'ing** *a.* hesitant, lame

hal'ter [hawlt-] *n.* rope with headgear to fasten horse; low-cut dress style with strap passing behind neck; noose for hanging person

halve [hahv] *vt.* cut in half; reduce to half; share

hal'yard, hall'iard *n.* rope for raising sail, flag *etc.*

ham *n.* meat (*esp.* salted or smoked) from thigh of pig; actor adopting exaggerated style; amateur radio enthusiast -**ham-fisted** *a.* clumsy

ham'burger *n.* fried cake of minced beef

ham'let *n.* small village

hamm'er *n.* tool usu. with heavy head at end of handle, for beating, driving nails etc. -v. strike as with hammer

hammock n. bed of canvas etc., hung on cords

hamper [-¹] n. large covered basket

hamper [²] vt. impede, obstruct

hamster n. type of rodent, sometimes kept as pet

hamstrung a. crippled; thwarted

hand n. extremity of arm beyond wrist; side; style of writing; cards dealt to player; manual worker; help; pointer on dial; applause -v. pass; deliver; hold out -**hand'ful** n. small quantity; inf. person, thing causing problems (pl. -**fuls**) -**hand'iness** n. dexterity; state of being near, available -**hand'y** a. convenient; clever with the hands -**hand'bag** n. woman's bag -**hand'book** n. small instruction book -**hand'cuff** n. fetter for wrist, usu. joined in pair -vt. secure thus -**hand'icraft** n. manual occupation or skill -**hand'iwork** n. thing done by particular person -**hand'kerchief** [hang'kə-chif] n. small square of fabric for wiping nose etc. -**hand'writing** n. way person writes -**hand'yman** n. man employed to do various tasks

hand'icap n. something that hampers or hinders; race, contest in which chances are equalized; any physical disability -vt. hamper; impose handicaps on (**-pp-**)

han'dle n. part of thing to hold it by -vi. touch, feel with hands; manage; deal with; trade

hand'some [han's-] a. of fine appearance; generous; ample

hang vt. suspend; kill by suspension by neck (hanged etc. /pp./); attach, set up (wallpaper, doors etc.) -vi. be suspended, cling (hung etc. /pp./) -**hang'er** n. frame on which clothes etc. can be hung -**hang'dog** a. sullen, dejected -**hang'over** n. after-effects of too much drinking

hang'ar n. large shed for aircraft

hank n. skein, length of yarn

hank'er vi. crave

haphaz'ard a. random, careless

hap'less a. unlucky

happ'en vi. come about, occur; chance to do -**happ'ening** n. occurrence, event

happ'y a. glad, content; lucky -**happ'ily** adv. -**happ'iness** n.

harangue' [-ang'] n. vehement speech; tirade -v.

har'ass [ha'rəs] vt. worry, torment -**har'assment** n.

harb'inger [-j-] n. forerunner

har'bour [-bər] n. shelter for ships -v. give shelter; maintain (secretly)

hard a. firm, resisting pressure; solid; difficult to do, understand; unfeeling; heavy -adv. vigorously; with difficulty; close -**hard'en** v. -**hard'ly** adv. unkindly, harshly; scarcely, not quite; only just -**hard'ship** n. ill-luck; severe toil, suffering; instance of this -**hard-headed** a. shrewd -**hard'ware** n. tools, implements; Computers mechanical and electronic parts -**hard'wood** n. wood from deciduous trees

hard'y a. robust, vigorous; bold; of plants, able to grow in the open all the year round

hare n. animal like large rabbit -**hare'bell** n. round-leaved bell-flower -**hare'brained** a. rash, wild -**hare'lip** n. fissure of upper lip

ha'rem [or hah-rēm'] n. women's part of Mohammedan dwelling; one man's wives

har'icot [ha'ri-kō] n. type of French bean

hark vi. listen

har'lequin n. masked clown in diamond-patterned costume

har'lot n. whore, prostitute

harm n./v. damage -**harm'ful** a. -**harm'less** a. unable or unlikely to hurt

harm'ony n. agreement; combination of notes to make chords; melodious sound -**harmon'ic** a. of harmony -**harmon'ica** n. esp. mouth organ -**harmo'nious** a. -**har'monize** vt. bring into harmony; cause to agree; reconcile -vi. be in harmony

harn'ess n. equipment for attaching horse to cart, plough etc. -vt. put on, in, harness; utilize energy or power of

harp n. musical instrument of strings played by hand -vi. play on harp; dwell on continuously -**harp'er**, **harp'ist** n. -**harp'sichord** n. stringed instrument like piano

harpoon' n./vt. (use) barbed spear for catching whales

harr'idan n. shrewish old woman

harr'ier n. hound used in hunting hares; falcon

harr'ow [-ō] n. implement for smoothing, levelling or stirring up soil -vt. draw harrow over; distress greatly -**harr'owing** a. distressful

harr'y vt. harass; ravage (**harr'ied**, **harr'ying**)

harsh a. rough, discordant; severe; unfeeling

hart n. male deer

harv'est n. (season for) gathering in grain; gathering; crop –vt. reap and gather in –**harv'ester** n.

has third person sing. pres. indicative of HAVE

hash n. dish of hashed meat etc. –vt. cut up small, chop; mix up

hash'ish [-ēsh], **hash'eesh** n. resinous extract of Indian hemp, esp. used as hallucinogen

hasp [-ah-] n. clasp for fastening door etc.

has'sle inf. n. quarrel; a lot of bother, trouble –v.

hass'ock n. kneeling-cushion

haste [hāst] n. speed, hurry –vi. hasten –**has'ten** [-sən] v. (cause to) hurry –**has'tily** adv. –**has'ty** a.

hat n. head-covering, usu. with brim

hatch¹ v. of young, esp. of birds, (cause to) emerge from egg; contrive, devise –**hatch'ery** n.

hatch² n. hatchway; trapdoor over it; opening in wall, to facilitate service of meals etc. –**hatch'way** n. opening in deck of ship etc.

hatch'et n. small axe

hate vt. dislike strongly; bear malice towards –n. this feeling; that which is hated –**hate'ful** a. detestable –**ha'tred** n.

haughty [hawt'-] a. proud, arrogant –**haught'ily** adv.

haul vt. pull, drag with effort –n. hauling; what is hauled –**haul'age** n. –**haul'ier** n.

haunch n. human hip or fleshy hindquarter of animal

haunt vt. visit regularly; visit in form of ghost; recur to –n. esp. place frequently visited –**haunt'ed** a. frequented by ghosts; worried

have [hav] vt. hold, possess; be affected with; be obliged (to do); cheat; obtain; contain; allow; cause to be done; give birth to; (as auxiliary, forms perfect and other tenses) (pres. tense: I have, thou hast, he has, we, you, they have) (**had**, **hav'ing**)

ha'ven n. place of safety

hav'ersack n. canvas bag for provisions etc. carried on back

hav'oc n. devastation, ruin; inf. confusion, chaos

hawk¹ n. bird of prey smaller than eagle

hawk² vt. offer (goods) for sale, as in street –**hawk'er** n.

haw'ser [-z-] n. large cable

haw'thorn n. thorny shrub or tree

hay n. grass mown and dried –**hay fever** allergic reaction to pollen, dust etc. –**hay'stack** n. large pile of hay –**hay'wire** a. crazy; disorganized

haz'ard n. chance; risk, danger –vt. expose to risk; run risk of –**haz'ardous** a. risky

haze n. mist; obscurity –**ha'zy** a. vague

ha'zel n. bush bearing nuts –a. light brown

H bomb short for HYDROGEN BOMB

he pron. (third person masculine) n. pron, animal already referred to; (comb. form) male, as **he-goat**

head [hed] n. upper part of body, containing mouth, sense organs and brain; upper part of anything; chief of organization, school etc.; chief part; aptitude, capacity; crisis; person, animal considered as unit –a. chief, principal; of wind, contrary –vt. be at the top; lead; provide with head; hit (ball) with head –vi. make for; form a head –**head'ing** n. title –**head'y** a. apt to intoxicate or excite –**head'ache** [-āk] n. continuous pain in head –**head'light** n. powerful lamp on front of vehicle etc. –**head'line** n. news summary, in large type in newspaper –**head'long** adv. in rush –**head'quarters** pl.n. centre of operations –**head'strong** a. self-willed –**head'way** n. progress

heal v. make or become well –**health** [helth] n. soundness of body; condition of body; toast drunk in person's honour –**health'y** a.

heap n. pile; great quantity –vt. pile, load with

hear vt. perceive by ear; listen to; Law try (case); heed –vi. perceive sound; learn (**heard** [herd] pt./pp.) –**hear'ing** n. ability to hear; earshot; audience –**hear'say** n. rumour –a.

hear'ken [hahr'-] vi. listen

hearse [hurs] n. funeral carriage for coffin

heart [-ah-] n. organ which makes blood circulate; seat of emotions and affections; mind, soul, courage; central part –**heart'en** v. make, become cheerful –**heart'less** a. unfeeling –**heart'y** a. friendly; vigorous; in good health; satisfying –**heart**

attack sudden severe malfunction of heart **-heart-rending** a. agonizing **-by heart** by memory

hearth [-ah-] n. part of room where fire is made; home

heat n. hotness; sensation of this; hot weather; warmth of feeling, anger etc.; sexual excitement in female animals; one of many eliminating races etc. **-v.** make, become hot **-heat'ed** a. esp. angry

heath n. tract of waste land

hea'then [-TH-] a./n. (one) not adhering to a religious system; pagan (pl. **hea'thens, hea'then**)

heath'er [heTH'-] n. shrub growing on heaths and mountains

heave vt. lift (and throw) with effort; utter (sigh) **-vi.** swell, rise; feel nausea **-n.**

heav'en [hev'n] n. abode of God; place of bliss; sky (also pl.) **-heav'enly** a.

heav'y [hev'-] a. weighty; dense; sluggish; severe; sorrowful; serious; dull **-heav'ily** adv.

heck'le [hek'l] v. interrupt (speaker) by questions, taunts etc.

hect-, hecto- (comb. form) one hundred, esp. in metric system, as in **hec'tolitre, hec'tometre**

hec'tare [-tahr] n. one hundred ares or 10 000 square metres (2.471 acres)

hec'tic a. rushed, busy

hec'tor v. bully, bluster

hedge n. fence of bushes **-vt.** surround with hedge; obstruct; bet on both sides **-vi.** trim hedges; be evasive; secure against loss **-hedge'-hog** n. small animal covered with spines **-hedge sparrow** small brownish songbird

heed vt. take notice of **-heed'less** a. careless

heel' n. hinder part of foot; part of shoe supporting this; sl. undesirable person **-vt.** supply with heel

heel' v. of ship, (cause to) lean to one side

hef'ty a. bulky; weighty; strong

heif'er [hef'-] n. young cow

height [hīt] n. measure from base to top; quality of being high; elevation; highest degree; (oft. pl.) hilltop **-height'en** vt. make higher; intensify

hei'nous [hā'-] a. atrocious, extremely wicked, detestable

heir [ār] n. person entitled to inherit property or rank (**heir'ess** fem.)

-heir'loom n. thing that has been in family for generations

hel'copter n. aircraft made to rise vertically by pull of airscrew revolving horizontally

he'lium n. very light, nonflammable gaseous element

hell n. abode of the damned; abode of the dead generally; place of torture **-hell'ish** a.

hello' (also **hallo', hullo'**) interj. expression of greeting

helm n. tiller, wheel for turning ship's rudder

helm'et n. defensive or protective covering for head

help vt. aid, assist; support; remedy, prevent **-n.** **-help'er** n. **-help'ful** a. **-help'ing** n. single portion of food taken at a meal **-help'less** a. incompetent; unaided; unable to help

hel'ter-skel'ter adv./a./n. (in) hurry and confusion **-n.** high spiral slide at fairground

hem n. edge of cloth, folded and sewn down **-vt.** sew thus; confine, shut in (**-mm-**)

hem'isphere n. half sphere; half of the earth

hem'lock n. poisonous plant

hemp n. Indian plant; its fibre used for rope etc.; any of several narcotic drugs

hen n. female of domestic fowl and others

hence adv. from this point; for this reason **-henceforward, hence'-forth** adv. from now onwards

hench'man n. trusty follower

henn'a n. flowering shrub; reddish dye made from it

hepat'itis n. inflammation of the liver

hep'tagon n. figure with seven angles

her a. form of SHE used after verb or preposition or to show possession **-hers** pron. of her **-herself'** pron.

her'ald [he'rəld] n. messenger, envoy **-vt.** announce **-herald'ic** a. **-her'aldry** n. study of (right to have) heraldic bearings

herb n. plant with soft stem which dies down after flowering; plant used in cookery or medicine **-herba'ceous** [-shəs] a. of, like herbs; perennial flowering **-herb'icide** n. chemical which destroys plants **-herbiv'orous** a. feeding on plants

hercule'an a. requiring great strength, courage

herd n. company of animals feeding together -v. crowd together -vt. tend (herd) -**herds'man** n.

here adv. in this place; at or to this point -**here'af'ter** adv. in time to come -n. future existence

hered'ity n. tendency of organism to transmit its nature to its descendants -**hered'itary** a. descending by inheritance or heredity

her'esy [her'ə-] n. unorthodox opinion or belief -**her'etic** n.

her'itage [her'i-] n. what may be or is inherited

hermaph'rodite n. person or animal with characteristics, or reproductive organs, of both sexes

hermet'ic a. sealed so as to be airtight -**hermet'ically** adv.

her'mit n. one living in solitude

her'nia n. projection of organ through lining (pl. -**ias**, -**iae** [-i-ē])

he'ro n. one greatly regarded for achievements or qualities; principal character in story (pl. **he'roes** -**her'oine** fem.) -**hero'ic** [hi-] a. -**her'oism** [he'rō-] n.

her'oin [he'rō-] n. highly addictive narcotic

her'on [he'rən] n. long-legged wading bird

her'ring n. important food fish

hertz n. SI unit of frequency (pl. **hertz**)

hes'itate [hez'-] vi. hold back; feel, or show indecision; be reluctant -**hes'itancy**, **hesita'tion** n. -**hes'itant** a.

hes'sian n. coarse jute cloth

hetero- (comb. form) other or different

het'erodox a. not orthodox

heteroge'neous a. composed of diverse elements -**heterogene'ity** n.

heterosex'ual n. person sexually attracted to members of the opposite sex

hew v. chop, cut with axe (**hewn**, **hewed** pp.) -**hew'er** n.

hex'agon n. figure with six angles -**hexag'onal** a.

hey'day n. bloom, prime

hia'tus [hī-ā'-] n. break or gap (pl. **hia'tuses**, **hia'tus**)

hi'bernate vi. pass the winter, esp. in a torpid state

hicc'up, hicc'ough [hik'up] n./vi. (have) spasm of the breathing organs with an abrupt sound

hick'ory n. N Amer. nut-bearing tree; its tough wood

hide' vt. put, keep out of sight -vi. conceal oneself (hid pt., **hidd'en** or hid pp., **hi'ding** pr.p.)

hide' n. skin of animal -**hi'ding** n. sl. thrashing -**hide'bound** a. restricted; narrow-minded

hid'eous a. repulsive, revolting

hi'erarchy [-ki] n. system of persons or things arranged in graded order -**hierarch'ical** a.

hieroglyph'ic a. of picture writing, as used in ancient Egypt -n. symbol representing object, concept or sound

hi'-fi [hī'fī] a. short for HIGH-FIDELITY -n. high-fidelity equipment

high [hī] a. tall, lofty; far up; of sound, acute in pitch; expensive; of great importance, quality, or rank; inf. in state of euphoria -adv. at, to a height -**high'ly** adv. -**high'ness** n. quality of being high; (H-) title of prince and princess -**high'brow** n./a. sl. intellectual -**high-fidel'ity** a. of high-quality sound reproducing apparatus -**high-handed** a. domineering -**high'light** n. outstanding feature -**highly strung** excitable, nervous -**high-rise** a. of building that has many storeys -**high time** latest possible time -**high'way** n. main road; ordinary route

hi'jack vt. divert or wrongfully take command of a vehicle (esp. aircraft) -**hi'jacker** n.

hike vi. walk a long way (for pleasure) in country -vt. pull (up), hitch -n. -**hi'ker** n.

hilar'ity [-la'ri-] n. cheerfulness, gaiety -**hila'rious** a.

hill n. natural elevation, small mountain; mound -**hill'ock** n. little hill -**hill'y** a.

hilt n. handle of sword etc.

him pron. form of HE used after verb or preposition -**himself'** pron. emphatic form of HE

hind' [hīnd] n. female of deer

hind' [hīnd], **hind'er** a. at the back, posterior

hin'der vt. obstruct, impede, delay -**hin'drance** n.

Hin'du [-ōō] n. person who adheres to Hinduism, the dominant religion of India

hinge [-j] n. movable joint, as that on which door hangs -vt. attach with hinge -vi. depend on

hint n./v. (give) slight indication

hint'erland n. district lying behind coast, port etc.

hip n. either side of body below waist and above thigh; fruit of rose

hippopot'amus n. large Afr. animal living in rivers (pl. -amuses, -ami [-mī])

hire vt. obtain temporary use of by payment; engage for wage -n. hiring or being hired; payment for use of thing

hir'sute [-syōōt] a. hairy

his pron./a. belonging to him

hiss vi. make sharp sound of letter S -vt. express disapproval thus -n.

his'tory n. (record of) past events; study of these -histor'ian n. -histor'ic [-to'rik] a. -histor'ical a.

histrion'ic a. excessively theatrical, insincere, artificial in manner -histrion'ics pl.n. behaviour like this

hit vt. strike with blow or missile; affect injuriously; find -vi. strike; light (upon) (hit, hit'ting) -n. blow; success -hit'ter n.

hitch vt. fasten with loop etc.; raise with jerk -vi. be caught or fastened -n. difficulty; knot; jerk -hitch'- (hike) vi. travel by begging free rides

hith'er [hɪTHˈ] adv. to this place -hitherto' adv. up to now

hive n. structure in which bees live -hive off transfer

hives pl.n. eruptive skin disease

HM His (or Her) Majesty

HMCS His (or Her) Majesty's Canadian Ship

HMS His (or Her) Majesty's Service or Ship

HMSO His (or Her) Majesty's Stationery Office

hoard [-aw-] n. store, esp. hidden -vt. amass and hide

hoard'ing [-aw-] n. large board for displaying advertisements

hoarse [-aw-] a. sounding husky

hoar'y [hawrˈ-] a. grey with age; greyish-white; very old -hoar'frost n. frozen dew

hoax [hōks] n. practical joke -vt. play trick upon

hob n. top area of cooking stove

hob'ble vi. walk lamely -vt. tie legs together -n. limping gait

hobb'y n. favourite occupation as pastime

hobgob'lin n. mischievous fairy

hob'nob vi. drink together; be familiar (with) (-bb-)

ho'bo n. shiftless, wandering person (pl. -bos)

hock¹ n. backward-pointing joint on leg of horse etc.

hock² n. dry white wine

hock'ey n. team game played on a field with ball and curved sticks; US, C ice hockey

ho'cus-po'cus n. trickery

hod n. small trough for carrying bricks etc.; coal scuttle

hoe n. tool for weeding, breaking ground etc. -vt. (hoed, hoe'ing)

hog n. pig; greedy person -vt. inf. eat, use (something) selfishly

hoist vt. raise aloft, raise with tackle etc.

hold¹ [-ō-] vt. keep in hands; maintain in position; contain; occupy; carry on; detain -vi. cling; keep (to); be in force; occur (held pt./pp.) -n. grasp; influence -hold'er n. -hold'ing n. (oft. pl.) property -hold'up n. armed robbery; delay

hold² n. space in ship or aircraft for cargo

hole n. hollow place; perforation; opening; inf. unattractive place -ho'ley a.

hol'iday n. day(s) of rest from work etc., esp. spent away from home

holl'ow [-ō] a. having a cavity, not solid; empty; insincere -n. cavity, hole, valley -vt. make hollow; excavate

holl'y n. evergreen shrub with prickly leaves and red berries

holl'yhock n. tall plant bearing many large flowers

hol'ocaust n. great destruction of life, esp. by fire

hol'ster [hōlˈ-] n. leather case for pistol, hung from belt etc.

ho'ly a. belonging, devoted to God; free from sin; divine; consecrated -ho'lily adv.

hom'age n. tribute, respect

home n. dwelling-place; residence -a. of home; native -adv. to, at one's home; to the point -v. direct or be directed onto a point or target -home'less a. -home'ly a. plain -home'ward a./adv. -home'wards adv. -home'sick a. depressed by absence from home -home'sick-ness n. -home'spun a. domestic; simple -home'stead [-sted] n. house with outbuildings, esp. on farm

hom'icide n. killing of human being; killer -homici'dal a.

hom'ily n. sermon

homo- (comb. form) same, as in homosexual etc.

homoge'neous [-j-] a. formed of uniform parts; similar **-homog'en-ize** vt. break up fat globules in milk and cream to distribute them evenly

hom'onym n. word of same form as another, but of different sense

Hon. Honourable; (also h-) honorary

hone n. whetstone **-vt.** sharpen on one

hon'est [on¹-] a. not cheating, lying, stealing etc.; genuine **-hon'esty** n.

hon'ey [hun¹i] n. sweet fluid made by bees **-hon'eycomb** n. wax structure in hexagonal cells **-vt.** fill with cells or perforations **-hon'eymoon** n. holiday taken by newly-wedded pair **-hon'eysuckle** n. climbing plant

honk n. call of wild goose; sound of motor-horn **-vi.** make this sound

hon'our [on¹ə] n. personal integrity; renown; reputation **-vt.** respect highly; confer honour on; accept or pay (bill etc.) when due **-hon'ourable** a. **-hon'ourably** adv. **-hon'orary** a. conferred for the sake of honour only

hood n. covering for head and neck; hood-like thing **-hood'wink** vt. deceive

hood'lum [-ठ्ठ-] n. gangster

hoof [-ठ्ठ-] n. horny casing of foot of horse etc. (pl. **hoofs** or **hooves**)

hoo'-ha [-ठ्ठ-] n. needless fuss

hook n. bent piece of metal etc., for catching hold, hanging up etc.; something resembling hook in shape or function **-vt.** grasp, catch, hold, as with hook **-hooked** a. shaped like hook; caught; sl. addicted to **-hook-up** n. linking of radio, television stations

hoo'ligan n. violent, irresponsible (young) person

hoop [-ठ्ठ-] n. rigid circular band of metal, wood etc.

hoot [-ठ्ठ-] n. owl's cry or similar sound; cry of derision; sl. funny person or thing **-vi.** utter hoot **-hoot'er** n. device (eg horn) to emit hooting sound

Hoo'ver [hठ्ठ-] R vacuum cleaner **-v.** (h-) vacuum

hop¹ vi. spring on one foot (**-pp-**) **-n.** leap, skip

hop¹ n. climbing plant with bitter

cones used to flavour beer etc. **-pl.** the cones

hope n. expectation of something desired; thing that gives, or object of, this feeling **-v.** feel hope (for) **-hope'ful** a. **-hope'fully** adv. (esp. now) inf. it is hoped **-hope'less** a.

hopp'er n. one who hops; device for feeding material into mill; SA see COCOPAN

horde n. large crowd

hori'zon n. boundary of part of the earth seen from any given point; lines where earth and sky seem to meet **-horizon'tal** a. parallel with horizon, level

hor'mone n. substance secreted by certain glands which stimulates organs of the body

horn n. hard projection on heads of certain animals; various things made of, or resembling it; wind instrument; device (esp. in car) emitting sound **-horned** a. having horns **-horn'y** a. **-horn'pipe** n. sailor's lively dance

hor'net n. large insect of wasp family

hor'oscope [horə-] n. telling of person's fortune by studying disposition of planets etc. at his birth

horren'dous a. horrific

horr'or n. terror; loathing, fear of; its cause **-horr'ible** a. exciting horror, hideous, shocking **-horr'ibly** adv. **-horr'id** a. unpleasant, repulsive; inf. unkind **-horr'ify** vt. move to horror **-(-ified, -ifying) -horrif'ic** a. particularly horrible

hors d'oeu'vre [aw-dur'vr] n. small dish served before main meal

horse n. four-footed animal used for riding and draught; cavalry; frame for support etc. **-horse chestnut** tree with conical clusters of white or pink flowers and large nuts **-horse'-man** n. (**horse'woman** fem.) rider on horse **-horse'power** n. unit of power of engine etc. **-horse'radish** n. plant with pungent root **-horse'-shoe** n. protective U-shaped piece of iron nailed to horse's hoof

hor'ticulture n. art or science of gardening

hosann'a [-z-] n. cry of praise

hose n. flexible tube for conveying liquid or gas; stockings **-vt.** water with hose **-ho'siery** n. stockings etc.

hos'pital n. institution for care of sick

hospital'ity n. friendly and liberal

reception of strangers or guests -**hos'pitable** a.

host[1] [hō-] n. (**host'ess** fem.) one who entertains another; innkeeper; compere of show -vt. act as a host

host[2] [hō-] n. large number

hos'tage n. person taken or given as pledge or security

hos'tel n. building providing accommodation at low cost for students etc.

hos'tile a. antagonistic; warlike; of an enemy -**hostil'ity** n. enmity -pl. acts of warfare

hot a. of high temperature; angry; new; spicy (**hott'er** comp., **hott'est** sup.) -**hot'ly** adv. -**hot'bed** n. bed of heated earth for young plants; any place encouraging growth -**hot'-blooded** a. excitable -**hot dog** hot sausage in split bread roll -**hot'foot** v./adv. (go) quickly -**hot'head** n. intemperate person -**hot'house** n. forcing house for plants -**hot'plate** n. heated plate on electric cooker

hotch'potch n. medley; dish of many ingredients

hotel[1] [hō-] n. commercial establishment providing lodging and meals -**hotel'ier** [-yā] n.

hound n. hunting dog -vt. chase, urge, pursue

hour [owr] n. twenty-fourth part of day; sixty minutes; appointed time -pl. fixed periods for work etc. -**hour'ly** adv./a.

house [-s] n. building for human habitation; legislative assembly; family; business firm -vt. [-z] give or receive shelter, lodging or storage; cover or contain -**hous'ing** n. (providing of) houses; part designed to cover, protect, contain -**house'hold** n. inmates of house collectively -**house'keeper** n. person managing affairs of household

hov'el n. mean dwelling

hov'er vi. hang in the air; loiter; be in state of indecision -**hov'ercraft** n. type of craft which can travel over both land and sea on a cushion of air

how adv. in what way; by what means; in what condition; to what degree; (in direct or dependent question) -**howev'er** conj. nevertheless -adv. in whatever way, degree; all the same

howl vi. utter long loud cry -n. such cry -**howl'er** n. inf. stupid mistake

HP hire purchase

HQ headquarters

HRH His (or Her) Royal Highness

hub n. middle part of wheel; central point of activity

hubb'ub n. confused noise

hud'dle n. crowded mass; inf. impromptu conference -v. heap, crowd together; hunch

hue[1] [hyoō] n. colour

hue and cry public outcry

huff n. passing mood of anger -v. make or become angry -vi. blow -**huff'y** a.

hug vt. clasp tightly in the arms; keep close to (-**gg**-) -n. fond embrace

huge a. very big -**huge'ly** adv. very much

hulk n. body of abandoned vessel; offens. large, unwieldy person or thing -**hulk'ing** a.

hull n. frame, body of ship; calyx of strawberry etc. -vt. remove shell, hull

hullabaloo' n. uproar, clamour

hum vi. make low continuous sound as bee -vt. sing with closed lips (-**mm**-) -n. humming sound

hu'man a. of man, relating to, characteristic of, man's nature -**hu'mane'** a. kind; merciful -**hu'manism** n. belief in human effort rather than religion -**humanita'rian** n. philanthropist -a. -**human'ity** n. human nature; human race; kindliness -pl. study of literature, philosophy, the arts

hum'ble a. lowly, modest -vt. humiliate -**hum'bly** adv.

hum'bug n. impostor; sham, nonsense; sweet of boiled sugar

hum'drum a. commonplace, dull

hu'mid a. moist, damp -**humid'ifier** n. device for increasing amount of water vapour in air in room etc. -**humid'ity** n.

humil'iate [hyoō-] vt. lower dignity of, abase, mortify -**humilia'tion** n.

humil'ity [hyoō-] n. state of being humble; meekness

humm'ock n. low knoll, hillock

hu'mour n. faculty of saying or perceiving what excites amusement; state of mind, mood -vt. gratify, indulge -**hu'morist** n. person who acts, speaks, writes humorously -**hu'morous** a.

hump n. normal or deforming lump, esp. on back -vt. make hump-shaped; sl. carry or heave -**hump'back** n. person with hump

hu'mus n. decayed vegetable and animal mould

hunch *n. inf.* intuition; hump *-vt.* bend into hump **-hunch'back** *n.* humpback

hun'dred *n./a.* cardinal number, ten times ten **-hun'dredth** *a.* the ordinal number **-hun'dredfold** *a./ adv.* **-hun'dredweight** *n.* weight of 112 lbs. (50.8 kg), 20th part of ton

hun'ger *n.* discomfort from lack of food; strong desire *-vi.* **-hung'rily** *adv.* **-hung'gry** *a.* having keen appetite

hunk *n.* thick piece

hunt *v.* seek out to kill or capture for sport or food; search (for) *-n.* chase, search; (party organized for) hunting

hur'dle *n.* portable frame of bars for temporary fences or for jumping over; obstacle *-vt.* race over hurdles

hurl *vt.* throw violently

hurrah', hurray' *interj.* exclamation of joy or applause

hurr'icane *n.* very strong, violent wind or storm

hurr'y *v.* (cause to) move or act in great haste **(hurr'ied, hurr'ying)** *-n.* undue haste; eagerness **-hurr'iedly** *adv.*

hurt *vt.* injure, damage, give pain to *-vi. inf.* feel pain **(hurt** *pt./pp.***)** *-n.* wound, injury, harm **-hurt'ful** *a.*

hur'tle *vi.* rush violently

hus'band [-z-] *n.* married man *-vt.* economize; use to best advantage **-hus'bandry** *n.* farming; economy

hush *v.* make or be silent *-n.* stillness; quietness

husk *n.* dry covering of certain seeds and fruits *-vt.* remove husk from **-husk'y** *a.* rough in tone; hoarse

hus'ky *n.* Arctic sledgedog

hussar' [-z-] *n.* light armed cavalry soldier

huss'y *n.* cheeky young woman

hust'ings *pl.n.* political campaigning

hus'tle [hus'l] *v.* push about, jostle, hurry *-n.*

hut *n.* any small house or shelter

hutch *n.* box-like pen for rabbits *etc.*

hy'acinth *n.* bulbous plant with bell-shaped flowers

hy(a)e'na [hī-ē'nə] *n.* wild animal related to dog

hy'brid *n.* offspring of two plants or animals of different species *-a.* crossbred

hy'drant *n.* water-pipe with nozzle for hose

hydraul'ic *a.* concerned with, operated by, pressure transmitted through liquid in pipe

Hy'dro *n.* C hydroelectric power company

hydro- *(comb. form)* water, as *hydroelectric*

hydroelec'tric *a.* pert. to generation of electricity by use of water

hy'drofoil *n.* fast, light vessel with hull raised out of water at speed

hy'drogen *n.* colourless gas which combines with oxygen to form water **-hydrogen bomb** atom bomb of enormous power **-hydrogen perox'ide** colourless liquid used as antiseptic and bleach

hydropho'bia *n.* aversion to water, esp. as symptom of rabies

hydropon'ics *pl.n.* science of cultivating plants in water without using soil

hydrother'apy *n. Med.* treatment of disease by water

hy'giene [hī'jēn] *n.* (study of) principles and practice of health and cleanliness **-hygie'nic** *a.* **-hygie'nically** *adv.*

hy'men *n.* membrane partly covering vagina of virgin

hymn [him] *n.* song of praise, *esp.* to God *-vt.* praise in song **-hym'nal** *a.* of hymns *-n.* book of hymns *Also* **hymn book**

hype *sl. n.* hypodermic syringe; drug addict *-v.* (with up) inject (oneself) with drug

hyper- *(comb. form)* over, above, excessively, as in **hyperac'tive** *etc.*

hyper'bole [-bə-li] *n.* rhetorical exaggeration

hy'permarket *n.* huge self-service store

hyperten'sion *n.* abnormally high blood pressure

hy'phen *n.* short line (-) indicating that two words or syllables are to be connected **-hy'phenate** *vt.* **-hy'phenated** *a.*

hypno'sis [hip-] *n.* induced state like deep sleep in which subject acts on external suggestion **-hypnot'ic** *a.* **-hyp'notize** *vt.* affect with hypnosis

hypo-, hyph-, hyp- *(comb. forms)* under, below, less, as in *hypocrite, hyphen etc.*

hy'pocaust *n.* ancient Roman underfloor heating system

hypochon'dria [hī-pō-kon'-] *n.* morbid depression, without cause, about one's own health **-hypochon'driac** *a./n.*

hypoc'risy [hip-] *n.* assuming of false appearance of virtue; insincerity -**hyp'ocrite** *n.* -**hypocrit'ical** *a.*

hypoderm'ic [hī-] *a.* introduced, injected beneath the skin -*n.* hypodermic syringe or needle

hypot'enuse [hī-] *n.* side of a right-angled triangle opposite the right angle

hyperther'mia *n.* condition of having body temperature reduced to dangerously low level

hypoth'esis [hī-] *n.* suggested explanation of something; assumption as basis of reasoning (*pl.* -**eses** [-sēz]) -**hypothet'ical** *a.*

hysterec'tomy [his-] *n.* surgical operation for removing the uterus

hyste'ria [his-] *n.* mental disorder with emotional outbursts; fits of crying or laughing -**hyster'ical** [-te'ri-] *a.* -**hyster'ics** *pl.n.* fits of hysteria

Hz hertz

I

I *pron.* the pronoun of the first person singular

IBA Independent Broadcasting Authority

i'bex *n.* type of wild goat

i'bis *n.* storklike bird

IBM International Business Machines Corporation

ice *n.* frozen water; ice cream -*v.* cover, become covered with ice; cool with ice; cover with icing -**i'cicle** *n.* hanging spike of ice -**i'cily** *adv.* -**i'cing** *n.* mixture of sugar and water *etc.* used to decorate cakes -**i'cy** *a.* covered with ice; cold; chilling -**ice'-berg** *n.* large floating mass of ice -**ice cream** sweetened frozen dessert made from cream, eggs *etc.* -**ice hockey** team game played on ice with puck

ichthyol'ogy [ik-thi-] *n.* scientific study of fish

ICI Imperial Chemical Industries

i'cicle *see* ICE

i'con *n.* religious image -**icon'oclast** *n.* one who attacks established ideas

ide'a *n.* notion; conception; plan, aim -**ide'al** *n.* idea of perfection; perfect person or thing -*a.* perfect -**ide'alism** *n.* tendency to seek perfection in everything -**ide'alist** *n.* one who strives after the ideal; impractical person -**idealis'tic** *a.* -**idealiza'tion** *n.* -**ide'alize** *vt.* portray as ideal -**ide'ally** *adv.*

ident'ity *n.* individuality; state of being exactly alike -**ident'ical** *a.* very same -**ident'ifiable** *a.* -**identifica'tion** *n.* -**ident'ify** *v.* establish identity of; associate (oneself) with; treat as identical (**ident'ified,** **ident'ifying**)

ideol'ogy [ī-di-] *n.* body of ideas, beliefs of group, nation *etc.* -**ideolog'ical** *a.*

id'iom *n.* expression peculiar to a language or group -**idiomat'ic** *a.*

idiosyn'crasy *n.* peculiarity of mind

id'iot *n.* mentally deficient person; stupid person -**id'iocy** *n.* -**idiot'ic** *a.* utterly stupid

i'dle *a.* unemployed; lazy; useless; groundless -*vi.* be idle; run slowly in neutral gear -**i'dleness** *n.* -**i'dler** *n.* -**i'dly** *adv.*

i'dol *n.* image worshipped as deity; object of excessive devotion -**idol'ater** *n.* -**idol'atrous** *a.* -**idol'atry** *n.* -**i'dolize** *vt.* love or venerate to excess

id'yll *n.* (poem describing) picturesque or charming scene or episode -**idyll'ic** *a.* delightful

i.e. *Lat. id est,* that is

if *conj.* on condition or supposition that; whether; although

ig'loo *n.* Eskimo snow house

ignite' *v.* (cause to) burn -**igni'tion** *n.* act of kindling or setting on fire; car's electrical firing system

igno'ble *a.* mean, base; of low birth -**igno'bly** *adv.*

ig'nominy *n.* public disgrace; shameful act -**ignomin'ious** *a.*

ignore' *vt.* disregard, leave out of account -**ig'norance** *n.* lack of knowledge -**ig'norant** *a.* lacking knowledge; uneducated

iguan'a [i-gwahn'ə] *n.* large tropical American lizard

il- (*comb. form*) for *in-* before *l*: see IN- and listed words

ill *a.* not in good health; bad, evil; harmful -*n.* evil, harm -*adv.* badly; hardly -**ill'ness** *n.* -**ill-advised** *a.* imprudent -**ill-fated** *a.* unfortunate -**ill-gotten** *a.* obtained dishonestly -**ill-treat** *vt.* treat cruelly -**ill will** hostility

illegit'imate [-jit'-] *a.* born out of

wedlock; irregular **-illegit'imacy** n.

illic'it [-lis'-] a. illegal; prohibited, forbidden

illit'erate a. not literate; unable to read or write -n. illiterate person **-illit'eracy** n.

illu'minate [-loo'-] vt. light up; clarify; decorate with lights or colours **-illumina'tion** n.

illu'sion [-loo'-] n. deceptive appearance or belief **-illu'sionist** n. conjuror **-illu'sory** a.

ill'ustrate vt. provide with pictures or examples; exemplify **-illustra'tion** n. picture, diagram; example **-ill'ustrative** a. **-ill'ustrator** n.

illus'trious a. famous; glorious

im- (comb. form) for in- before m, b, and p: see IN- and listed words

im'age n. likeness; optical counterpart; double, copy; general impression; word picture

imag'ine [-maj'-] vt. picture to oneself; think; conjecture **-imag'inable** a. **-imag'inary** a. existing only in fancy **-imagina'tion** n. faculty of making mental images of things not present; fancy **-imag'inative** a.

imbal'ance n. lack of balance, proportion

im'becile [-sēl] n. idiot -a. idiotic

imbibe' v. drink (in)

imbue' [-byoo'] vt. instil, fill

IMF International Monetary Fund

im'itate vt. take as model; copy **-im'itable** a. **-imita'tion** n. act of imitating; copy; counterfeit **-im'itative** a. **-im'itator** n.

immac'ulate a. spotless; pure

imma'terial a. unimportant; not consisting of matter

imme'diate a. occurring at once; closest **-imme'diately** adv.

immense' a. huge, vast **-immense'ly** adv. **-immen'sity** n.

immerse' vt. submerge in liquid; involve; engross **-immer'sion** n. **-immersion heater, immer'ser** n. electric appliance for heating liquid

imm'igrant n. settler in foreign country -a. **-immigra'tion** n.

imm'inent a. liable to happen soon **-imm'inence** n.

imm'olate vt. kill, sacrifice

immor'al [-mo'ral] a. corrupt; promiscuous **-immoral'ity** n.

immor'tal a. deathless; famed for all time -n. **-immortal'ity** n. **-immor'talize** vt.

immune' [-myōōn'] a. protected (against a disease etc.); exempt **-im-**

mu'nity n. **-immuniza'tion** n. process of making immune to disease **-imm'unize** vt.

imp n. little devil; mischievous child

im'pact n. collision; profound effect **-impact'ed** a. wedged

impair' vt. weaken, damage **-impair'ment** n.

impale' vt. pierce with sharp instrument **-impale'ment** n.

impart' vt. communicate; give

impar'tial a. unbiased; fair **-impartial'ity** n.

impass'able a. blocked

impasse' [-pahs'] n. deadlock

impass'ioned [-sh-] a. full of feeling, ardent

impass'ive a. showing no emotion; calm **-impassiv'ity** n.

impeach' vt. charge, esp. with treason or crime in office; denounce **-impeach'able** a. **-impeach'ment** n.

impecc'able a. faultless

impecu'nious a. poor

impede' vt. hinder **-imped'iment** n. obstruction; defect

impel' vt. induce; drive (-ll-)

impen'ding a. imminent

imper'ative [-pe'rə-] a. necessary; peremptory; expressing command -n. imperative mood

impe'rial a. of empire, or emperor; majestic; denoting weights and measures established by law in Brit. **-impe'rialism** n. policy of acquiring empire **-impe'rialist** n.

imper'il vt. endanger (-ll-)

impe'rious a. domineering

imper'sonal a. objective

imper'sonate vt. pretend to be **-impersona'tion** n. **-imper'sonator** n.

impert'inent a. insolent, rude **-impert'inence** n.

impertur'bable a. calm, not excitable **-impertur'bably** adv.

imper'vious a. impenetrable (to feeling, argument etc.)

impeti'go [-tī'-] n. contagious skin disease

impet'uous a. rash **-impetuos'ity** n.

im'petus n. momentum

impinge' vi. encroach (upon); collide (with)

im'pious a. irreverent

implac'able a. not to be placated

implant' [-ah-] vt. insert firmly

im'plement n. tool, instrument -vt. carry out

im'plicate vt. involve **-implica'-**

tion n. something implied –**implic'it** [-plis'-] a. implied; absolute

implore' vt. entreat earnestly

imply' vt. hint; mean (**implied', im-ply'ing**)

import' vt. bring in –n. [im'] thing imported; meaning; **C** sl. sportsman not native to area where he plays –**importa'tion** n. –**import'er** n.

import'ant a. of great consequence –**import'ance** n.

importune' vt. request insistently –**importu'nity** n.

impose' vt. place (upon) –vi. take advantage (of) –**impos'ing** a. impressive –**imposi'tion** n. (unfair) burden

impossible a. not possible; unreasonable –**impossibil'ity** n. –**impos'sibly** adv.

impos'tor n. one who assumes false identity –**impos'ture** n.

im'potent [-pyoo-] a. powerless; (of males) incapable of sexual intercourse –**im'potence** n.

impound' vt. seize legally

impov'erish vt. make poor or weak –**impov'erishment** n.

impreg'nable a. proof against attack

im'pregnate vt. saturate; make pregnant

impresar'io n. organizer of public entertainment; manager of opera, ballet etc. (pl. **-s**)

impress' vt. affect deeply, usu. favourably; imprint, stamp; fix –**impres'sion** n. effect; notion, belief; imprint; a printing –**impres'sionable** a. susceptible –**impres'sive** a. making deep impression

im'print n. mark made by pressure –vt. [im-print'] stamp; fix in mind

impris'on [-z'-] vt. put in prison –**impris'onment** n.

impromp'tu [-tyoo] adv./a. extempore –n. improvisation

improve' [-oov'] v. make or become better –**improve'ment** n.

improv'ident a. thriftless

im'provise v. make use of materials at hand; perform, speak without preparation –**improvisa'tion** n.

im'pudent [-pyoo-] a. impertinent –**im'pudence** n.

impugn' [-pyoon'] vt. call in question, challenge

im'pulse n. sudden inclination to act; impetus –**impul'sive** a. rash

impu'nity n. exemption from consequences

impute' vt. attribute to –**imputa'tion** n. reproach

in prep. expresses inclusion within limits of space, time, circumstance, sphere etc. –adv. in or into some state, place etc.; inf. in vogue etc. –a. inf. fashionable

in. inch(es)

in- (comb. form) with its forms **il-**, **im-**, **ir-** negatives the idea of the simple word: also forms compounds with the meaning of in, into, upon, as inter The list below contains some compounds that will be understood if not or lack of is used with the meaning of the simple word

inadvert'ent a. unintentional

inane' a. foolish –**inan'ity** n.

inan'imate a. lifeless

inau'gurate [-yoo-rāt] vt. initiate; admit to office –**inau'gural** a. –**inaugura'tion** n. formal initiation (to office etc.)

inauspi'cious [-spish'-] a. unlucky

in'born a. existing from birth

inbreed' vt. breed from closely related individuals (**inbred'** pp.) –**in'bred'** a. produced by inbreeding; inborn –**inbreed'ing** n.

incal'culable a. beyond calculation; very great

incandes'cent a. glowing; produced by glowing filament

incanta'tion n. magic spell

incapac'itate [-pas'-] vt. disable; disqualify **-incapac'ity** n.

incar'cerate vt. imprison

incarn'ate a. in human form **-incarna'tion** n.

incen'diary a. designed to cause fires; inflammatory **-n.** fire-bomb

incense'[1] vt. enrage

in'cense[2] n. gum, spice giving perfume when burned; its smoke

incen'tive n. something that stimulates effort

incep'tion n. beginning

incess'ant a. unceasing

in'cest n. sexual intercourse between close relatives **-incest'uous** a.

inch n. one twelfth of foot, or .0254 metre **-v.** move very slowly

in'cident n. event, occurrence **-in'cidence** n. extent or frequency of occurrence **-incident'al** a. occurring as a minor, inevitable, or chance accompaniment **-incident'ally** adv. by chance; by the way **-incident'als** pl.n. accompanying items

incin'erate vt. burn up completely **-incin'erator** n.

incip'ient a. beginning

incise' [-sīz'] vt. cut into **-inci'sion** [-sizh'-] n. **-inci'sive** a. sharp

incite' vt. urge, stir up

inclem'ent a. severe

incline' v. lean, slope; (cause to) be disposed a. **-n.** [in'-] slope **-inclina'tion** n. liking, tendency; degree of deviation

include' [-klōōd'] vt. have as (part of) contents; add in **-inclu'sion** n. **-inclu'sive** a. including (everything)

incog'nito [-nē- or in-kog'-] adv./a. under assumed identity **-n.** assumed identity (pl. **-tos**)

incohe'rent a. lacking clarity; inarticulate **-incohe'rence** n.

in'come n. money received from salary, investments etc.

in'coming a. coming in; about to come into office; next

incon'gruous [-ng'g-] a. not appropriate **-incongru'ity** n.

inconsequen'tial a. trivial; haphazard

incontrovert'ible a. undeniable

incorp'orate vt. include; form into corporation

incorr'igible a. beyond correction or reform

increase' v. make or become greater in size, number etc. **-n.** [in'-] growth, enlargement **-increas'ingly** adv. more and more

incred'ible a. unbelievable; inf. amazing

incred'ulous a. unbelieving **-incredu'lity** n.

in'crement n. increase

incrim'inate vt. imply guilt of

in'cubate [-kyoo-] vt. provide eggs, bacteria etc. with heat for development **-vi.** develop in this way **-incuba'tion** n. **-in'cubator** n. apparatus for hatching eggs, for rearing premature babies

incul'cate vt. fix in the mind

incum'bent n. holder of office, esp. church benefice **-it is incumbent on** it is the duty of

incur' vt. bring upon oneself (-rr-) **-incur'sion** n. invasion

inda'ba [-dah'-] n. SA meeting; problem

indebt'ed a. owing gratitude or money

indeed' adv. really; in fact **-interj.** denoting surprise, doubt etc.

indefat'igable a. untiring

indefen'sible a. not justifiable or defensible

indel'ible a. that cannot be blotted out **-indel'ibly** adv.

indel'icate a. coarse, embarrassing

indem'nity n. compensation; security against loss **-indem'nify** vt. give indemnity to (**indem'nified, indem'nifying**)

indent' v. set in (from margin etc.); notch; place order for by indent **-n.** [in'-] notch; requisition **-indenta'tion** n.

indepen'dent a. not subject to others; self-reliant; free; valid in itself **-indepen'dence** n. being independent; self-reliance; self-support

indescrib'able a. beyond description

indeterm'inate a. uncertain

in'dex n. alphabetical list of references; indicator; Math. exponent; forefinger (pl. **in'dexes**, Math. **in'dices** [-sēz]) **-vt.** provide with, insert in index

in'dicate vt. point out; state briefly; signify **-indica'tion** n. **-indic'ative** a. pointing to; Grammar stating fact **-in'dicator** n.

indict [-dīt'] vt. accuse, esp. by legal process -**indict'able** a. -**indict'ment** n.

indiff'erent a. uninterested; inferior -**indiff'erence** n.

indig'enous [-dij'-] a. native

in'digent [-j-] a. poor, needy

indiges'tion [-jest'-] n. (discomfort caused by) poor digestion

indig'nant a. angered by injury or injustice -**indigna'tion** n. -**indig'-nity** n. humiliation, insult, slight

in'digo n. blue dye obtained from plant; the plant (pl. -**go(e)s**) -a. deep blue

indiscrim'inate a. lacking discrimination; jumbled

indispens'able a. essential

indisposed' a. unwell; disinclined

indissol'uble a. permanent

individ'ual a. single; distinctive -n. single person or thing -**individual'ity** n. distinctive personality -**individually** adv. singly

indoc'trinate vt. implant beliefs in the mind of

in'dolent a. lazy -**in'dolence** n.

indom'itable a. unyielding

in'door a. within doors; under cover -**indoors'** adv.

indu'bitable a. beyond doubt

induce' vt. persuade; bring on -**in-duce'ment** n. incentive

induct' vt. install in office -**induc'-tion** n. an inducting; general inference from particular instances; production of electric or magnetic state by proximity -**induc'tive** a.

indulge' vt. gratify; pamper -**in-dul'gence** n. an indulging; extravagance; favour, privilege -**indul'-gent** a.

indun'a [-dōōn'a] n. SA headman, overseer

in'dustry n. manufacture, processing etc. of goods; branch of this; diligence -**indus'trial** a. of industries, trades -**indus'trialize** vt. -**indus'trious** a. diligent

ine'briate vt. make drunk

ined'ible a. not eatable

ineff'able a. unutterable

inel'igible [-ji-] a. not fit or qualified (for something)

inept' a. absurd; out of place; clumsy -**inep'titude** n.

inert' a. without power of motion; sluggish; unreactive -**iner'tia** [-sha] n. inactivity; tendency to continue at rest or in uniform motion

ines'timable a. immeasurable

inev'itable a. unavoidable; sure to happen -**inevitabil'ity** n.

inex'orable a. relentless

infall'ible a. not liable to fail or err -**infallibil'ity** n.

in'famous a. notorious; shocking -**in'famy** n.

in'fant n. very young child -**in'-fancy** n. -**infan'tile** a. childish

in'fantry n. foot soldiers

infat'uated a. foolishly enamoured -**infatua'tion** n.

infect' vt. affect (with disease); contaminate -**infec'tion** n. -**infec'tious** a. catching

infer' vt. deduce, conclude (-rr-) -**in'ference** n.

infe'rior a. of poor quality; lower -n. one lower (in rank etc.) -**inferior'ity** n.

infer'nal a. devilish; hellish; inf. irritating, confounded

infer'no n. hell; conflagration

infest' vt. inhabit or overrun in dangerously or unpleasantly large numbers -**infesta'tion** n.

infidel'ity n. unfaithfulness; religious disbelief -**in'fidel** n. unbeliever

in'filtrate v. trickle through; gain access surreptitiously -**infiltra'tion** n.

in'finite [-it] a. boundless -**in'fin-itely** adv. exceedingly -**infinites'-imal** a. extremely small -**infin'ity** n. unlimited extent

infin'itive n. form of verb without tense, person, or number

infirm' a. weak; irresolute -**infirm'-ary** n. hospital, sick-quarters -**in-firm'ity** n.

inflame' v. rouse to anger, excitement; cause inflammation in -**in-flamm'able** a. easily set on fire; excitable -**inflamma'tion** n. painful infected swelling -**inflamm'atory** a.

inflate' v. blow up with air, gas; swell; raise price, esp. artificially -**infla'table** a. -**infla'tion** n. increase in prices and fall in value of money -**infla'tionary** a.

inflec'tion, inflex'ion n. modification of word; modulation of voice

inflex'ible a. incapable of being bent; stern -**inflexibil'ity** n.

inflict' vt. impose, deliver forcibly -**inflic'tion** n.

in'fluence n. power to affect other people, events etc.; person, thing possessing such power -vt. sway; induce; affect -**influen'tial** a.

influen'za n. contagious feverish catarrhal virus disease

in'flux n. a flowing in; inflow

in'fo n. inf. information

inform' v. give information (about) -**inform'ant** n. one who tells -**informa'tion** n. what is told, knowledge -**inform'ative** a. -**inform'er** n.

infrared' a. below visible frequency

in'frastructure n. basic structure or fixed capital items of an organization or economic system

infringe' vt. transgress, break -**fringe'ment** n.

infur'iate vt. enrage

infuse' v. soak to extract flavour etc.; instil -**infu'sion** n. an infusing; extract obtained

inge'nious [-jē'-] a. clever at contriving; cleverly contrived -**ingenu'ity** n.

ingen'uous [-jen'-] a. frank; innocent -**ingen'uously** adv.

in'got [ing'g-] n. brick of cast metal, esp. gold

ingrained' a. deep-rooted; inveterate

ingra'tiate v. refl. get (oneself) into favour

ingre'dient n. component part of a mixture

inhab'it vt. dwell in -**inhab'itable** a. -**inhab'itant** n.

inhale' v. breathe in (air etc.) -**inhala'tion** n. esp. medical preparation for inhaling

inher'ent a. existing as an inseparable part

inher'it [-he'rit] v. receive, succeed as heir; derive from parents -**inher'itance** n.

inhib'it vt. restrain; hinder -**inhibi'tion** n. repression of emotion, instinct

inhu'man a. cruel, brutal; not human -**inhuman'ity** n.

inim'ical a. unfavourable (to); unfriendly; hostile

inim'itable a. defying imitation

iniq'uity n. gross injustice; sin -**iniq'uitous** a. unjust; inf. outrageous

ini'tial [-ish'-] a. of, occurring at the beginning -n. initial letter, esp. of person's name -vt. mark, sign with one's initials (-ll-)

ini'tiate [-ish'-] vt. originate; admit into closed society; instruct -**initia'tion** n. -**ini'tiative** n. lead; ability to act independently

inject' vt. introduce (esp. fluid,

medicine etc. with syringe) -**injec'tion** n.

injunc'tion n. (judicial) order

in'jury n. physical damage; wrong -**in'jure** vt. do harm or damage to -**inju'rious** a.

injus'tice n. want of justice; wrong; unjust act

ink n. fluid used for writing or printing -vt. mark, cover with ink -**ink'y** a.

ink'ling n. hint, vague idea

inlaid' see INLAY

in'land a./adv. in, towards the interior; away from the sea

in'-law n. relative by marriage

in'lay vt. embed; decorate with inset pattern (**inlaid'** pt./pp.) -n. [in'-] inlaid piece or pattern

in'let n. entrance; mouth of creek; piece inserted

in'mate n. occupant, esp. of prison, hospital etc.

in'most a. most inward, deepest

inn n. public house providing food and accommodation; hotel -**inn'-keeper** n.

innate' a. inborn; inherent

inn'er a. lying within -**inn'ermost** a.

inn'ings n. Sport player's or side's turn of batting; turn

inn'ocent a. guiltless; harmless -n. -**inn'ocence** n.

innoc'uous a. harmless

inn'ovate vt. introduce new things -**innova'tion** n. -**inn'ovator** n.

innuen'do n. indirect accusation (pl. -does)

innu'merable a. countless

inoc'ulate vt. immunize by injecting vaccine -**inocula'tion** n.

inop'erable a. Med. that cannot be operated on -**inop'erative** a. not operative

inopp'ortune a. badly timed

inor'dinate a. excessive

inorgan'ic a. not organic; not containing carbon

in'put n. material, data, current etc. fed into a system

in'quest n. coroner's inquiry into cause of death; detailed inquiry

inquire', enquire' vi. seek information -**inqui'rer, enqui'rer** n. -**inqui'ry, enqui'ry** n. question; investigation

inquisi'tion [-zish'-] n. searching investigation; Hist. (I-) tribunal for suppression of heresy -**inquis'itor** n.

inquis'itive a. curious; prying

in'road n. incursion

insane' a. mentally deranged; crazy -**insane'ly** adv. madly; excessively -**insan'ity** n.

insa'tiable a. incapable of being satisfied

inscribe' vt. write, engrave (in or on something) -**inscrip'tion** n. words inscribed

inscru'table a. incomprehensible

in'sect n. small, usu. winged, animal with six legs -**in'secticide** n. preparation for killing insects

insecure' [-kyoor'] a. not safe or firm; anxious

insem'inate vt. implant semen into

insen'sible a. unconscious; without feeling; not aware -**insensibil'ity** n. -**insen'sibly** adv. imperceptibly

insert' vt. place or put (in, into, between) -n. [in'-] something inserted -**inser'tion** n.

in'set n. something extra inserted -**inset'** vt.

in'shore adv./a. near shore

inside' [or in'-] n. inner part -a./adv./prep. in, on, into the inside, within

insid'ious a. unseen but deadly

in'sight [-sīt] n. discernment

insig'nia pl.n. badges, emblems

insin'uate vt. hint; introduce subtly -**insinua'tion** n.

insip'id a. dull, tasteless

insist' vi. demand persistently; maintain; emphasize -**insist'ence** n. -**insist'ent** a.

in'solent a. impudent -**in'solence** n.

insom'nia n. sleeplessness -**insom'niac** a./n.

insomuch' adv. to such an extent

inspan' vt. SA harness, yoke (-nn-)

inspect' vt. examine closely or officially -**inspec'tion** n. -**inspec'tor** n.

inspire' vt. arouse creatively; give rise to -**inspira'tion** n. good idea; creative influence

inst. (instant) of the current month

instal(l)' [-awl'] vt. place in position -**installa'tion** n. act of installing; that which is installed

instal'ment [-awl-] n. part payment; one of a series of parts

in'stance n. example -vt. cite

in'stant n. moment -a. immediate; (of foods) requiring little preparation -**instanta'neous** a. happening in an instant -**in'stantly** adv. at once

instead' [-ed'] adv. in place (of)

in'step n. top of foot between toes and ankle

in'stigate vt. incite, urge -**instiga'tion** n. -**in'stigator** n.

instil' vt. implant; inculcate (-ll-)

in'stinct n. inborn impulse; unconscious skill -**instinc'tive** a.

in'stitute vt. establish; set going -n. society for promoting science etc.; its building -**institu'tion** n. an instituting; establishment for care or education; an established custom or law or (inf.) figure -**institu'tional** a. of institutions; routine

instruct' vt. teach; inform; order -**instruc'tion** n. teaching; order -pl. directions -**instruc'tive** a. informative -**instruc'tor** n.

in'strument n. tool, implement, means, person, thing used to make, do, measure etc.; mechanism for producing musical sound -**instrument'al** a. acting as instrument or means; produced by musical instruments

insubor'dinate a. mutinous, rebellious -**insubordina'tion** n.

in'sular [-syoo-] a. of an island; narrow-minded -**insular'ity** n.

in'sulate [-syoo-] vt. prevent or reduce transfer of electricity, heat, sound etc.; isolate, detach -**insula'tion** n. -**in'sulator** n.

in'sulin [-syoo-] n. hormone used in treating diabetes

insult' vt. behave rudely to; offend -n. [in'-] affront -**insult'ing** a.

insu'perable [-soo-] a. that cannot be overcome

insure' v. contract for payment in event of loss, death etc.; make safe (against) -**insur'ance** n.

insur'gent a. in revolt -n. rebel -**insur'gence, insurrec'tion** n. revolt

intact' a. untouched; uninjured

in'take n. thing, amount taken in; opening

in'teger [-j-] n. whole number

in'tegral [-g-] a. essential -**in'tegrate** vt. combine into one whole -**integra'tion** n.

integ'rity n. honesty

in'tellect n. power of thinking and reasoning -**intellec'tual** a. of, appealing to intellect; having good intellect -n.

intell'igent a. clever -**intell'igence** n. intellect; information, esp.

military **-intell'igently** adv. **-intell'igible** a. understandable

intemp'erate a. drinking alcohol to excess; immoderate

intend' vt. propose, mean

intense' a. very strong or acute; emotional **-intens'ify** v. increase (**intens'ified, intens'ifying**) **-inten'sity** n. **-inten'sive** a.

intent' n. purpose **-a.** concentrating (on); resolved **-inten'tion** n. purpose, aim **-inten'tional** a.

inter' vt. bury **(-rr-)** **-inter'ment** n.

inter- (comb. form) between, among, mutually eg **interfa'cial, interrela'tion**

interact' vi. act on each other **-interac'tion** n.

intercede' vi. plead in favour of, mediate **-interces'sion** n.

intercept' vt. cut off; seize, stop in transit **-intercep'tion** n.

interchange' v. (cause to) exchange places **-n.** [in'-] motorway junction **-interchange'able** a. able to be exchanged in position or value

intercity a. linking cities directly

intercontinen'tal a. connecting continents; (of missile) able to reach one continent from another

in'tercourse n. mutual dealings; sexual joining of two people; copulation

in'terdict n. formal prohibition **-interdict'** vt. prohibit

in'terest n. concern, curiosity; thing exciting this; sum paid for borrowed money (also fig.); right, advantage, share **-vt.** excite, cause to feel interest **-interesting** a.

in'terface n. area, surface, boundary linking two systems

interfere' vi. meddle, intervene; clash **-interfe'rence** n. act of interfering; Radio atmospherics

interfe'ron n. a cellular protein that stops the development of an invading virus

in'terim n. meantime **-a.** temporary

inte'rior a. inner; inland; indoors **-n.** inside; inland region

interject' vt. interpose (remark etc.) **-interjec'tion** n. exclamation; interjected remark

in'terlard v. intersperse

interlock' v. lock together firmly

in'terloper n. intruder

in'terlude n. interval; something filling an interval

intermarr'y vi. (of families, races, religions) become linked by marriage; marry within one's family **-intermarr'iage** n.

interme'diate a. coming between; interposed **-interme'diary** n.

intermin'able a. endless

intermiss'ion n. interval **-intermitt'ent** a. occurring at intervals

intern' vt. confine to special area or camp **-intern'ment** n.

inter'nal a. inward; interior; within (a country, organization)

interna'tional [-nash'-] a. of relations between nations **-n.** game or match between teams of different countries

interne'cine a. mutually destructive; deadly

interplan'etary a. of, linking planets

in'terplay n. mutual action and reaction

inter'polate vt. insert new matter; interject **-interpola'tion** n.

interpose' vt. insert; say as interruption; put in the way **-vi.** intervene **-interposi'tion** n.

inter'pret v. explain; translate, esp. orally; represent **-interpreta'tion** n. **-inter'preter** n.

interr'ogate vt. question, esp. closely or officially **-interroga'tion** n. **-interrog'ative** a. word used in asking question **-interr'ogator** n.

interrupt' v. break in (upon); stop; block **-interrup'tion** n.

intersect' vt. divide by passing across or through **-vi.** meet and cross **-intersec'tion** n.

intersperse' vt. sprinkle (something with or something among or in)

interstell'ar a. between stars

inter'stice n. slit, crevice

intertwine' v. twist together

in'terval n. intervening time or space; pause, break; difference (of pitch)

intervene' vi. come into a situation in order to change it; be, come between or among; occur in meantime; interpose **-interven'tion** n.

in'terview n. meeting, esp. one involving questioning **-vt.** have interview with **-interviewee'** n. **-in'terviewer** n.

intes'tate a. not having made a will

intes'tine n. (usu. pl.) lower part of alimentary canal between stomach and anus

in'timate [-it] a. closely acquainted,

familiar; private -n. **intimate friend** -**in'timacy** n.

in'timate² [-at] vt. announce; imply -**intima'tion** n. notice

intim'idate vt. frighten into submission -**intimida'tion** n.

in'to prep. expresses motion to a point within; indicates change of state; indicates coming up against, encountering; indicates arithmetical division

intone' vt. chant -**intona'tion** n. accent

intox'icate vt. make drunk -**intoxica'tion** n.

intra- (comb. form) within

intract'able a. difficult

intran'sigent a. uncompromising

intrau'terine [-a-yōō'-] a. within the womb

intrave'nous a. into a vein

intrep'id a. fearless, undaunted

in'tricate a. complex -**in'tricacy** n.

intrigue' [-trēg'] n. underhand plot; secret love affair -vi. carry on intrigue -vt. interest, puzzle

intrin'sic a. inherent, essential

intro- (comb. form) into, within, as in introduce, introvert

introduce' vt. make acquainted; present; bring in; insert -**introduc'tion** n. -**introduc'tory** a. preliminary

in'trovert n. Psychoanalysis one who looks inward -**in'troverted** a.

intrude' v. thrust (oneself) in -**intru'der** n. -**intru'sion** n. -**intru'sive** a.

intui'tion [-ish'-] n. spontaneous insight -**intu'itive** a.

In(n)uit n. C Eskimo of N Amer. or Greenland

in'undate n. flood; overwhelm -**inunda'tion** n.

inured' [-yoord'] a. hardened

invade' vt. enter by force; overrun -**inva'der** n. -**inva'sion** n.

in'valid [-lēd] n. one suffering from ill health -a. ill -vt. retire because of illness etc.

inval'uable a. priceless

inva'sion see INVADE

invec'tive n. bitter verbal attack

invei'gle [-vē'-, -vā'-] vt. entice

invent' vt. devise, originate; fabricate -**inven'tion** n. that which is invented; ability to invent -**invent'ive** a. resourceful; creative -**invent'or** n.

in'ventory n. detailed list

invert' vt. turn upside down; reverse

-**inverse'** [or in'-] a. inverted; opposite -n. -**inver'sion** n.

inver'tebrate n. animal without backbone -a.

invest' vt. lay out (money, time, effort etc.) for profit or advantage; install; endow -**inves'titure** n. formal installation in office or rank -**invest'ment** n. investing; money invested; stocks and shares bought -**invest'or** n.

invest'igate vt. inquire into; examine -**investiga'tion** n. -**invest'igator** n.

invet'erate a. deep-rooted; confirmed

invid'ious a. likely to cause ill will

invig'orate vt. give vigour to

invin'cible a. unconquerable -**invincibil'ity** n.

invi'olable a. not to be violated -**invi'olate** a. unviolated

invite' vt. request the company of; ask courteously; ask for; attract, call forth -**invita'tion** n.

in'voice n. a list of goods or services sold, with prices -vt. make or present an invoice

invoke' vt. call on; appeal to; ask earnestly for; summon -**invoca'tion** n.

invol'untary a. unintentional; instinctive

involve' vt. include; entail; implicate (person); concern; entangle -**involved'** a. complicated; concerned (in)

in'ward a. internal; situated within; mental -adv. (also **in'wards**) towards the inside; into the mind -**in'wardly** adv. in the mind; internally

i'odine [-ēn] n. nonmetallic element found in seaweed

i'on n. electrically charged atom or group of atoms -**ion'osphere** n. region of atmosphere 60 to 100 km above earth's surface

io'ta [ī-ō'-] n. (usu. with not) very small amount

I.O.U. n. signed paper acknowledging debt

IQ intelligence quotient

ir- (comb. form) for in- before r: see IN- and listed words

IRA Irish Republican Army

ire n. anger -**iras'cible** [-i-] a. hot-tempered -**irate'** [ī'-] a. angry

irides'cent a. exhibiting changing colours -**irides'cence** n.

i'ris n. circular membrane of eye containing pupil; plant with sword-shaped leaves and showy flowers

irk vt. irritate, vex **-irk'some** a. tiresome

i'ron n. common metallic element; tool etc., of this metal; appliance used to smooth cloth; metal-headed golf club -pl. fetters -a. of, like, iron; unyielding; robust -v. press **-i'ron-monger** n. dealer in hardware **-i'ronmongery** n. his wares **-i'ron-wood** n. various S Afr. trees

i'rony n. use of words to mean the opposite of what is said; event, situation opposite of that expected **-iron'ic(al)** a. of, using, irony

irra'diate vt. treat by irradiation; shine upon

irrep'arable a. not able to be repaired or remedied

irrespec'tive a. without taking account (of)

irrev'ocable a. not able to be changed

irr'igate vt. water by artificial channels, pipes etc. **-irriga'tion** n.

irr'itate vt. annoy; inflame **-irr'itable** a. easily annoyed **-irr'itant** a./n. (person or thing) causing irritation **-irrita'tion** n.

is third person singular, present indicative of BE

Is'lam [iz'lahm] n. Mohammedan faith or world **-Islam'ic** a.

i'sland [i'lənd] n. piece of land surrounded by water; anything like this **-i'slander** n. inhabitant of island

isle [il] n. island **-i'slet** [i'lit] n. little island

i'sobar n. line on map connecting places of equal mean barometric pressure

i'solate vt. place apart or alone **-isola'tion** n.

i'somer n. substance with same molecules as another but different atomic arrangement **-isomer'ic** a. **-isom'erism** n.

isomet'ric a. having equal dimensions; relating to muscular contraction without movement **-isomet'rics** pl.n. system of isometric exercises

isos'celes [-sos'i-lēz] a. of triangle, having two sides equal

i'sotherm n. line on map connecting points of equal mean temperature

i'sotope n. atom of element having a different nuclear mass and atomic weight from other atoms in same element

iss'ue [i'shyōō] n. sending or giving out; number or amount so given out; discharge; offspring; topic of discussion or dispute; outcome -vi. go out; result in; arise (from) -vt. give, send out; publish

isth'mus [is'məs] n. neck of land between two seas

it pron. neuter pronoun of the third person **-its** a. belonging to it **-it's** contraction of it is **-itself'** pron. emphatic form of it

ital'ic a. of type, sloping **-ital'ics** pl.n. this type, now used for emphasis etc. **-ital'icize** vt. put in italics

itch n./vi. (feel) irritation in the skin **-itch'y** a.

i'tem n. single thing; piece of information; entry -adv. also **-i'temize** vt.

itin'erant [i-, ī-] a. travelling from place to place; working in various places **-itin'erary** n. record, line of travel; route

ITV Independent Television

i'vory n. hard white substance of the tusks of elephants etc.

i'vy n. climbing evergreen plant

J

jab vt. poke roughly; thrust, stab (-bb-) -n. poke; inf. injection

jabb'er v. chatter; talk incoherently

jack n. device for lifting heavy weight, esp. motor car; lowest court card; Bowls ball aimed at; socket and plug connection in electronic equipment; small flag, esp. national, at sea -vt. (usu. with up) lift with a jack

jack'al [-awl] n. doglike scavenging animal of Asia and Africa

jack'ass n. the male of the ass; blockhead

jack'boot n. large riding boot

jack'daw n. small kind of crow

jack'et n. outer garment, short coat; outer casing, cover

jack'knife n. clasp knife -v. angle sharply, esp. the parts of an articulated lorry

jack'pot n. large prize, accumulated stake, as pool in poker

jade' n. ornamental semiprecious stone, usu. dark green; this colour

jade' n. worn-out horse **-ja'ded** a. tired; off colour

jagg'ed a. having sharp points

jag'uar n. large S Amer. feline carnivore

jail n. building for confinement of criminals or suspects -vt. send to, confine in prison -**jail'er** n.

jalop'y n. inf. old car

jam v. pack together; (cause to) stick and become unworkable; Radio block (another station) (-mm-) -n. fruit preserved by boiling with sugar; crush; hold-up of traffic; awkward situation

jamb [jam] n. side post of door, fireplace etc.

jamboree' n. large gathering or rally of Boy Scouts

Jan. January

jan'gle [-ng'gl] v. (cause to) sound harshly, as bell; (of nerves) irritate -n.

jan'itor n. caretaker; doorkeeper

Jan'uary n. first month

jape n./vi. joke

jar¹ n. round vessel of glass, earthenware etc.; inf. glass of esp. beer

jar² v. grate, jolt; have distressing effect on (-rr-) -n. jarring sound; shock etc.

jardinière' [zhar-din-yâr'] n. ornamental pot for growing plants

jar'gon n. special vocabulary for particular subject; pretentious language

jaun'dice n. disease marked by yellowness of skin -v. make, become prejudiced, bitter etc.

jaunt n. short pleasure excursion -vi. make one

jaunt'y a. sprightly; brisk

jav'elin n. spear, esp. for throwing in sporting events

jaw n. one of bones in which teeth are set -pl. mouth; gripping part of vice etc.

jay n. noisy bird of brilliant plumage -**jay'walker** n. careless pedestrian -**jay'walk** vi.

jazz n. syncopated music and dance -**jazz'y** a. flashy, showy

jeal'ous [jel'-] a. envious; suspiciously watchful -**jeal'ousy** n.

jeans pl.n. casual trousers, esp. of denim

jeep n. light four-wheel drive motor utility vehicle

jeer v./n. scoff, taunt

jell v. congeal; inf. assume definite form

jell'y n. sweet, preserve etc. becoming softly stiff as it cools; anything of like consistency -**jell'yfish** n. jellylike small sea animal

jemm'y n. short steel crowbar

jeop'ardy [jep'-] n. danger -**jeop'ardize** vt. endanger

jerk n. sharp push or pull; sl. stupid person -v. move or throw with a jerk -**jerk'ily** adv. -**jerk'iness** n. -**jerk'y** a. uneven, spasmodic

jer'kin n. sleeveless jacket

jer'sey [-z-] n. knitted jumper; machine-knitted fabric

jest n./vi. joke -**jest'er** n. joker, esp. Hist. court fool

jet¹ n. stream of liquid, gas etc.; spout, nozzle; aircraft driven by jet propulsion -v. throw out; shoot forth (-tt-) -**jet-black** a. glossy black -**jet propulsion** propulsion by jet of gas or liquid -**jet-propelled** a.

jet² n. hard black mineral

jet'sam n. goods thrown overboard -**jett'ison** vt. abandon; throw overboard

jett'y n. small pier, wharf

Jew n. one of Hebrew religion or ancestry; offens. inf. miser -**Jew'ess** n.fem. -**Jew'ish** a.

jew'el n. precious stone; ornament containing one; precious thing -**jew'eller** n. dealer in jewels -**jew'ellery** n.

jib n. triangular sail set forward of mast; arm of crane -vi. of horse, person, stop and refuse to go on (-bb-)

jibe see GIBE

jiff'y n. inf. moment

jig n. lively dance; music for it; guide for cutting etc. -vi. dance jig; make jerky up-and-down movements -**jig'saw** n. machine fretsaw

jig'gle v. move jerkily

jilt vt. cast off (lover)

jin'gle [-ng'gl] n. light metallic noise; catchy, rhythmic verse, song etc. -v. (cause to) make jingling sound

jinks pl.n. -**high jinks** boisterous merrymaking

jinx n. force, person, thing bringing bad luck -vt.

jitt'ers pl.n. worried nervousness, anxiety -**jitt'ery** a.

jive n. (dance performed to) rock and roll music, esp. of 1950's -vi.

job n. piece of work, task; post; inf. difficult task -**jobb'ing** a. doing single, particular jobs for payment -**job'less** a./pl.n. unemployed (people) -**job centre** government office in town centre providing information about vacant jobs -**job lot as-**

sortment sold together; miscellaneous collection

jock'ey n. rider in horse races (pl. -eys) -v. (esp. with for) manoeuvre (**jock'eyed, jock'eying**)

joc'ular a. joking; given to joking -**jocular'ity** n.

joc'und a. merry, cheerful

jodh'purs [jod'perz] pl.n. tight-legged riding breeches

jog vi. run slowly, trot, esp. for exercise -vt. nudge; stimulate (-gg-) -n. jogging -**jogg'er** n. -**jogg'ing** n.

join v. fasten, unite; become a member (of) become connected; (with up) enlist; take part (in) -n. (place of) joining -**join'er** n. maker of finished woodwork -**join'ery** n. joiner's work

joint n. arrangement by which two things fit together; place of this; meat for roasting, oft. with bone; sl. disreputable bar or nightclub; sl. marijuana cigarette -a. shared -vt. connect by joints; divide at the joints -**joint'ly** adv. -**out of joint** dislocated; disorganized

joist n. beam supporting floor or ceiling

joke n. thing said or done to cause laughter; something not in earnest, or ridiculous -vi. make jokes -**jo'ker** n. one who jokes; sl. fellow; extra card in pack

joll'y a. jovial; merry -vt. make person, occasion happier (**joll'ied, joll'ying**) -**jollifica'tion** n. -**joll'ity** n.

jolt [-ō-] n./v. jerk; jar; shock

joss stick stick of Chinese incense

jos'tle [-sl] v. knock or push

jot n. small amount -vt. note (-tt-) -**jott'er** n. notebook

joule [jool] n. Electricity unit of work or energy

jour'nal [jurnal] n. newspaper or other periodical; daily record -**jour'nalism** n. editing, writing in periodicals -**jour'nalist** n.

jour'ney [jur'-] n. going to a place, excursion; distance travelled -vi. travel

jour'neyman n. qualified craftsman

jo'vial a. convivial, merry, gay -**jovial'ity** n.

jowl n. cheek, jaw; dewlap

joy n. gladness, pleasure, delight; cause of this -**joy'ful** a. -**joy'less** a. -**joy ride** trip esp. in stolen car

-joy'stick n. inf. control column of aircraft

JP Justice of the Peace

Jr. Junior

ju'bilant a. exultant -**ju'bilantly** adv. -**jubila'tion** n.

ju'bilee n. time of rejoicing, esp. 25th or 50th anniversary

judge [juj] n. officer appointed to try cases in law courts; one who decides in a dispute, contest etc.; one able to form a reliable opinion -v. act as judge (of, for) -**judg(e)'ment** n. faculty of judging; sentence of court; opinion

judic'ial [-ish'-] a. of, by, a court or judge -**judi'cially** adv. -**judi'ciary** n. judges collectively -**judi'cious** a. well-judged, sensible

ju'do n. modern sport derived from jujitsu

jug n. vessel for liquids, with handle and small spout; its contents -vt. stew (esp. hare) in jug (-gg-)

jugg'ernaut n. large heavy lorry; any irresistible, destructive force

jug'gle v. keep several objects in the air simultaneously; manipulate to deceive -n. -**jugg'ler** n.

jug'ular vein one of three large veins of the neck returning blood from the head

juice [joos] n. liquid part of vegetable, fruit, or meat; inf. electric current; inf. petrol -**juic'y** a. succulent

jujit'su, jujut'su, jiujit'su n. the Japanese art of wrestling and self-defence

juke'box n. automatic, coin-operated record-player

July' n. the seventh month

jum'ble vt. mix in (a confused heap) -**jumble sale** sale of miscellaneous, usu. secondhand, items

jum'bo n. elephant; anything very large

jump v. (cause to) spring, leap (over); move hastily; pass or skip (over); rise steeply; start (with astonishment etc.); -n. act of jumping; obstacle to be jumped; distance, height jumped; -**jump'er** n. sweater, pullover -**jump'y** a. nervous

junc'tion n. place where routes meet; point of connection

junc'ture n. state of affairs

June [joon] n. the sixth month

jun'gle [-ng'gl] n. equatorial forest;

ju'nior a. younger; of lower standing -n. junior person

ju'niper n. evergreen shrub

junk[1] n. useless objects -**junk'ie, junk'y** n. sl. drug addict

junk[2] n. Chinese sailing vessel

junk'et n. flavoured curdled milk -vi. feast, picnic -**junk'eting** n.

jun'ta n. group holding power in a country

jurisdic'tion [joor-] n. authority; territory covered by it

jur'y [joor'i] n. body of persons sworn to render verdict in court of law; judges of competition -**jur'or, jur'yman** n.

just a. fair; upright; honest; right, equitable -adv. exactly; barely; at this instant; merely; really -**just'ice** [-s] n. moral or legal fairness; judge, magistrate -**just'ify** vt. prove right; vindicate (-**ified, ifying**) -**just'ifiable** a. -**just'ifiably** adv. -**justifica'tion** n. -**just'ly** adv.

jut vi. protect, stick out (-**tt-**)

jute n. plant fibre used for rope, canvas etc.

ju'venile a. of, for young children; immature -n. young person, child

juxtapose' [-pōz'] vt. put side by side -**juxtaposi'tion** n.

K

K Kelvin; Chess king

kaf'tan n. woman's long, loose dress with sleeves

kale, kail n. type of cabbage

kalei'doscope [-lī'-] n. optical toy producing changing patterns; any complex pattern -**kaleidoscop'ic** a.

kangaroo' n. Aust. marsupial with very strongly developed hind legs for jumping -**kangaroo court** irregular, illegal court

ka'olin n. a fine white clay used for porcelain and medicinally

ka'pok n. plant fibre used to stuff cushions etc.

karat'e [-raht'-] n. Japanese system of unarmed combat

karoo' n. SA high plateau

kay'ak [kī'-] n. Eskimo canoe; any similar canoe

KB Knight of the Bath

KBE Knight Commander (of the Order) of the British Empire

KC King's Counsel

KCB Knight Commander (of the Order) of the Bath

kebab' n. dish of small pieces of meat, tomatoes etc. grilled on skewers (also shish kebab)

kedg'eree n. dish of fish cooked with rice, eggs etc.

keel n. lowest longitudinal support on which ship is built -**keel over** turn upside down; inf. collapse suddenly

keen a. sharp; acute; eager; shrewd; (of price) competitive -**keen'ness** n.

keep vt. retain possession of, not lose; reserve; cause to remain; maintain -vi. remain good; remain; continue (kept pt./pp.) -n. maintenance; central tower of castle -**keep'er** n. -**keep'ing** n. harmony; care, charge

keg n. small barrel; container for beer

kelp n. large seaweed

Kelvin a. of thermometric scale starting at absolute zero (-273.15° Celsius) -n. SI unit of temperature

ken n. range of knowledge

kenn'el n. shelter for dog(s) -vt. put into kennel (-**ll-**)

kerb n. stone edging to footpath

kern'el n. inner seed of nut or fruit stone; central, essential part

ker'osene n. paraffin oil

kes'trel n. small falcon

ketch'up n. sauce of vinegar, tomatoes etc.

kett'le n. metal vessel with spout and handle, esp. for boiling water -**kett'ledrum** n. musical instrument made of membrane stretched over copper hemisphere

key n. instrument for operating lock, winding clock etc.; explanation, means of achieving an end etc.; Mus. set of related notes; operating lever of typewriter, piano, organ etc. -a. vital; most important -**key'board** n. set of keys on piano etc. -**key'note** n. dominant idea -**key'stone** n. central locking stone of arch

kg kilogram(s)

khak'i [kahk'-] a. dull yellowish-brown -n. khaki cloth; military uniform

kibbutz' [-oo'-] n. Jewish communal agricultural settlement in Israel

kick v. strike (out) with foot; recoil; inf. free oneself of (habit etc.) -n. foot blow; recoil; thrill

kid n. young goat; leather of its skin; inf. child -vt. inf. tease, deceive -vi. inf. behave, speak in fun (**-dd-**)

kid'nap vt. seize and hold to ransom (**-pp-**) -**kid'napper** n.

kid'ney n. either of the pair of organs which secretes urine; animal kidney used as food; nature, kind (pl. **-neys**)

kill vt. deprive of life; put an end to; pass (time); inf. cause pain -n. act of killing; animals etc. killed -**kill'er** n. -**kill'ing** inf. a. very tiring; very funny

kiln n. furnace, oven

ki'lo [kē¹-] n. short for KILOGRAM

kilo- (comb. form) one thousand, as in **kil'ometre** [or -lom'-] n. **kil'owatt** a.

kil'ogram(me) n. 1000 grams

kil'ohertz n. one thousand cycles per second

kilt n. pleated tartan skirt worn orig. by Scottish Highlanders

kimo'no n. loose Japanese robe

kin n. relatives -a. related -**kin'dred** n. relatives -a. similar; related -**kins'folk** n. -**kins'man** n. (**kins'woman** fem.)

kind [kīnd] n. sort, type, class -a. considerate; gentle -**kind'liness** n. -**kind'ly** a. kind, genial -adv. -**kind'ness** n. -**kind-hearted** a.

kin'dergarten n. class, school for children of about four to six years old

kin'dle vt. set alight; arouse -vi. catch fire -**kind'ling** n. small wood to kindle fires

kinet'ic a. relating to motion

king n. male ruler; principal chess piece; highest court card; Draughts crowned piece -**king'ship** n. -**king'dom** n. state ruled by king; realm; sphere -**king'fisher** n. small brightly-coloured bird -**king'pin** n. inf. chief thing or person

king'klip n. S Afr. marine fish

kink n. tight twist in rope, wire, hair etc. -v. make, become kinked -**kink'y** a. full of kinks; inf. deviant

ki'osk [kē¹-] n. small, sometimes movable booth; public telephone box

kip n./vi. inf. sleep

kipp'er n. a smoked herring

kirk n. in Scotland, church

kis'met [kiz¹-] n. fate, destiny

kiss n. touch or caress with lips; light touch -v. -**kiss of life** mouth-to-mouth resuscitation

kit n. outfit, equipment; personal effects, esp. of traveller; set of pieces of equipment sold ready to be assembled -**kit'bag** n. bag for soldier's or traveller's kit

kitch'en n. room used for cooking -**kitchenette'** n.

kite n. light papered frame flown in wind; large hawk

kith n. acquaintances

kitsch [kitch] n. vulgarized, pretentious art

kitt'en n. young cat

kitt'y n. short for KITTEN; in some card games, pool; communal fund

ki'wi [kē¹-] n. N.Z. flightless bird; inf. New Zealander

klax'on n. formerly, a powerful electric motor horn

kleptoma'nia n. compulsion to steal -**kleptoma'niac** n.

kloof n. SA mountain pass

km kilometre(s)

knack [n-] n. acquired facility or dexterity; trick; habit

knack'er [n-] n. buyer of worn-out horses etc., for killing -**knack'ered** a. sl. exhausted

knap'sack [n-] n. haversack

knave [nā-] n. jack at cards; obs. rogue -**kna'very** n. villainy -**kna'vish** a.

knead [nē-] vt. work into dough; massage

knee [n-] n. joint between thigh and lower leg -**knee'cap** n. bone in front of knee

kneel [n-] vi. fall, rest on knees (**knelt** pt./pp.)

knell [n-] n. death bell

knick'ers [n-] pl.n. woman's undergarment for lower half of body

knick'knack [nik'nak] n. trinket

knife [n-] n. cutting blade, esp. one in handle, used as implement or weapon -vt. cut or stab with knife

knight [nīt] n. man of rank below baronet; member of medieval order of chivalry; champion; piece in chess -vt. confer knighthood on -**knight'hood** n.

knit [n-] v. form (garment etc.) by linking loops of yarn; draw together; unite (**knitt'ed, knit** pt./pp. -**knitt'ing** pr.p.) -**knitt'er** n. -**knitt'ing** n. knitted work; act of knitting

knob [n-] n. rounded lump -**knobb'(l)y** a.

knock [n-] v. strike, hit; inf. disparage; rap suddenly; (of engine) make metallic noise -n. blow, rap -**knock'er** n. appliance for knocking on door -**knock-kneed** a. having incurved legs **-knock out** *inf.* render unconscious; *inf.* overwhelm, amaze **-knock'out** *n.*

knoll [nōl] *n.* small hill

knot [n-] *n.* fastening of strands by looping and pulling tight; cluster; hard lump, *esp.* in timber; nautical mile per hour **-vt.** tie with knot, in knots **(-tt-) -knot'ty** *a.* full of knots; puzzling, difficult

know [nō] *v.* be aware (of); have information (about); be acquainted with; understand; feel certain **(knew** *pt.*, **known** *pp.***) -know'ing** *a.* shrewd **-know'ingly** *adv.* shrewdly; deliberately **-knowl'edge** [nol-] *n.* knowing; what one knows; learning **-knowl'edg(e)able** *a.* well-informed

knuc'kle [nuk'l] *n.* bone at finger joint **-vt.** strike with knuckles **-knuckle down** get down (to work) **-knuckle under** submit

knurled [n-] *a.* serrated; gnarled

KO knockout

koal'a [kō-ahl'ə] *n.* marsupial Aust. animal, native bear

ko'matik *n.* C Eskimo sledge with wooden runners

kop'je, kopp'ie [kop'i] *n.* SA small hill

Koran' [-ahn'] *n.* sacred book of Muslims

ko'sher *a.* conforming to Jewish dietary law; *inf.* legitimate, authentic

kow'tow *vi.* prostrate oneself; be obsequious

krans [-ah-] *n.* SA cliff

kryp'ton [krip'-] *n.* rare atmospheric gas

ku'dos [kyōō'-] *n.* fame; credit

kung fu [fōō] *n.* Chinese martial art combining judo and karate

kW kilowatt

L

l litre

lab *n. inf.* short for LABORATORY

la'bel *n.* slip of paper, metal *etc.*, giving information; descriptive phrase **-vt.** (-**ll**-)

la'bial *a.* of the lips; pronounced with the lips **-n.**

labor'atory [-bo'-] *n.* place for scientific investigations or for manufacture of chemicals

la'bour [lā'bər] *n.* exertion of body

or mind; workers collectively; process of childbirth **-vi.** work hard; strive; move with difficulty **-vt.** stress to excess **-la'boured** *a.* uttered, done, with difficulty **-la'bourer** *n.* manual worker **-labor'ious** *a.* tedious

lab'rador *n.* breed of large, smooth-coated retriever dog

labur'num *n.* tree with yellow hanging flowers

lab'yrinth *n.* maze; perplexity

lace *n.* patterned openwork fabric; cord, usu. one of pair, to draw edges together **-vt.** fasten with laces; flavour with spirit **-lac'y** *a.* fine, like lace

la'cerate [las'-] *vt.* tear, mangle **-lacera'tion** *n.*

lach'rymose *a.* tearful

lack *n.* deficiency **-vt.** need, be short of

lackadai'sical [-dā'z-] *a.* languid

lack'ey *n.* servile follower; footman (*pl.* **-eys**)

lacon'ic [lə-kon'-] *a.* terse **-lacon'ically** *adv.*

lac'quer [lak'ər] *n.* hard varnish **-vt.** coat with this

lacrosse' *n.* ball game played with long-handled racket

lad *n.* boy, young fellow

ladd'er *n.* frame with rungs, for climbing; line of torn stitches, *esp.* in stockings

la'den *a.* heavily loaded

la'dle *n.* spoon with long handle and large bowl **-vt.** serve out liquid with a ladle

la'dy *n.* female counterpart of gentleman; *polite* term for a woman; title of some women of rank **-la'dybird** *n.* small beetle, usu. red with black spots **-la'dylike** *a.* gracious **-Our Lady** the Virgin Mary

lag[1] *vi.* go too slowly, fall behind **(-gg-) -lagg'ard** *n.* one who lags

lag[2] *vt.* wrap boiler, pipes *etc.* with insulating material **-lagg'ing** *n.* this material

lag[3] *n. sl.* convict (*esp.* **old lag**)

lag'er [lahg'-] *n.* a light-bodied beer

lagoon' *n.* saltwater lake, enclosed by atoll or sandbank

laid *pt./pp.* of LAY

lair *n.* den of animal

laissez-faire' [les-ā-fer'] *n.* principle of nonintervention

la'ity *n.* laymen (as opposed to clergy)

lake *n.* expanse of inland water

la'ma [lahm-] n. Buddhist priest in Tibet or Mongolia

lamb [lam] n. young of sheep; its meat; innocent or helpless creature -vi. give birth to lamb

lam'bent a. (of flame) flickering softly

lame a. crippled in a leg; limping; unconvincing -vt. cripple

lam'é [lahm-ā] n./a. (fabric) interwoven with gold or silver thread

lament' v. express sorrow (for) -n. expression of grief; song of grief -lam'entable a. deplorable -lamenta'tion n.

lam'inate v. make (sheet of material) by bonding together two or more thin sheets; cover with thin sheet -n. laminated sheet -lamina'tion n.

lammergei'er, lammergey'er [-gī-] n. type of rare vulture

lamp n. appliance (esp. electrical) that produces light, heat etc.

lampoon' n./vt. (make subject of) a satire

lamp'rey n. fish like an eel

lance' [-ah-] n. horseman's spear -vt. pierce with lance or lancet -lan'cet n. pointed two-edged surgical knife

land n. solid part of earth's surface; ground; country; estate -vi. come to land, disembark; arrive on ground; C be legally admitted as immigrant -vt. bring to land; inf. obtain; catch; inf. strike -land'ed a. possessing, consisting of lands -land'ing n. act of landing; platform between flights of stairs; a landing stage -land'locked a. enclosed by land -land'lord n., land'lady fem. person who lets land or houses etc.; master or mistress of inn, boarding house etc. -land'lubber n. person ignorant of the sea and ships -land'mark n. conspicuous object; event, decision etc. considered as important stage in development of something -land'scape n. piece of inland scenery; picture of it -v. create, arrange, garden, park etc. -land'slide, land'slip n. falling of soil, rock etc. down mountainside; overwhelming electoral victory -landing stage platform for embarkation and disembarkation

lane n. narrow road or street; specified air, sea route; area of road for one stream of traffic

lan'guage [lang'gwij] n. system of sounds, symbols etc. for communicating thought; style of speech or expression

lan'guish [-ng-gw-] vi. be or become weak or faint; droop, pine -lan'guid a. lacking energy; spiritless -lan'guidly adv. -lan'guor [-gər] n. want of energy; tender mood -lan'guorous a.

lank a. lean; limp -lank'y a.

lan'olin n. grease from wool used in ointments etc.

lan'tern n. transparent case for lamp or candle

lan'yard n. short cord for securing whistle; cord for firing cannon

lap' n. the part between waist and knees of a person when sitting; single circuit of track; stage or part of journey -vt. enfold, wrap round; overtake opponent to be one or more circuits ahead (-pp-)

lap' vt. drink by scooping up with tongue; (of waves etc.) beat softly (-pp-)

lapel' n. part of front of a coat folded back towards shoulders

lap'idary a. of stones; engraved on stone -n. cutter of stones

lapse' n. fall (in standard, condition, virtue etc.); slip; passing (of time etc.) -vi. fall away; end, esp. through disuse

lap'wing n. type of plover

lar'ceny n. theft

larch n. deciduous coniferous tree

lard n. prepared pig's fat -vt. insert strips of bacon in (meat); intersperse

lar'der n. storeroom for food

large a. great in size, number etc. -adv. in a big way -large'ly adv. -largess(e)' n. bounty; gift; donation -at large free; in general

lar'iat [la'ri-] n. lasso

lark' n. small, brown singing-bird, skylark

lark' n. frolic, spree -vi. indulge in lark -lark'y a.

larr'igan n. knee-high moccasin boot

lar'va n. immature insect (pl. -ae [-ē]) -lar'val a.

lar'ynx [la'ringks] n. part of throat containing vocal cords (pl. laryn'ges [-jēz]) -laryngi'tis n. inflammation of this

lasag'ne [lə-zan'yə] pasta formed in wide, flat sheets

lasciv'ious [lə-siv'-] a. lustful

la'ser [lāz-] n. device for concentrating electromagnetic radiation in an intense, narrow beam

lash[1] n. stroke with whip; flexible part of whip; eyelash -vt. strike with whip etc.; dash against; attack verbally, ridicule; flick, wave sharply to and fro -vi. (with out) hit, kick

lash[2] vt. fasten or bind tightly

lash'ings pl.n. inf. abundance

lass, lass'ie n. girl

lass'itude n. weariness

lass'o [-ōō'] n. rope with noose for catching cattle etc. (pl. lasso(e)s') -vt. (lassoed' [la-sōōd'], lasso'ing)

last[1] [-ah-] a./adv. after all others; most recent(ly) -a. only remaining -n. last person or thing -last'ly adv. finally

last[2] [-ah-] vi. continue, hold out

last[3] [-ah-] n. model of foot on which shoes are made, repaired

latch n. fastening for door -vt. fasten with latch

late a. coming after the appointed time; recent; recently dead; (la'ter comp., la'test, last sup.) -adv. after proper time; recently; at, till late hour -late'ly adv. not long since

la'tent a. existing but not developed; hidden

lat'eral a. of, at, from the side -lat'erally adv.

la'tex n. sap or fluid of plants, esp. of rubber tree

lath [lahth] n. thin strip of wood (pl. -s)

lathe [lāTH] n. machine for turning and shaping

lath'er [lahTH'-] n. soapy froth; frothy sweat -v. make frothy

Lat'in n. language of ancient Romans -a. of ancient Romans, their language

lat'itude n. angular distance N or S from equator; scope -pl. regions

latrine[1] [-ēn'] n. in army etc., lavatory

latt'er a. second of two; later; more recent -latt'erly adv.

latt'ice n. network of strips of wood, metal etc.; window so made -latt'iced a.

laud'able a. praiseworthy

laud'anum n. tincture of opium

laugh [lahf] vi. make sounds of amusement, merriment, or scorn -n. -laugh'able a. ludicrous -laugh'ter n. -laughing stock object of general derision

launch[1] vt. set afloat; set in motion; begin; propel (missile, spacecraft) into space

launch[2] n. large power-driven boat

laun'dry n. place for washing clothes; clothes etc. for washing -laun'der vt. wash and iron -Launderette' [-dret'] R shop with coin-operated washing, drying machines

lau'reate [-lawr'i-at] a. crowned with laurels -poet laureate poet with appointment to Royal Household

lau'rel [lo'-] n. glossy-leaved shrub, bay tree -pl. its leaves, emblem of victory or merit

la'va [lahv'-] n. molten matter thrown out by volcano

lav'atory n. toilet, water closet

lav'ender n. shrub with fragrant, pale-lilac flowers; this colour

lav'ish a. very generous -vt. spend, bestow, profusely

law n. rule binding on community; system of such rules; legal science; general principle deduced from facts -law'ful a. allowed by law -law'less a. ignoring laws; violent -law'yer n. professional expert in law -law'suit n. prosecution of claim in court

lawn[1] n. tended turf in garden etc.

lawyer see LAW

lax a. not strict; slack -lax'ative n. having loosening effect on bowels -n. -lax'ity, lax'ness n.

lay[1] pt. of LIE[1] -lay'about n. lazy person, loafer

lay[1] vt. deposit, set, cause to lie (laid, lay'ing) -lay'er n. single thickness, as stratum or coating; shoot of plant pegged down to encourage root growth -vt. propagate plants by making layers -lay-by n. stopping place for traffic beside road -lay-off n. dismissal of staff during slack period -lay'out n. arrangement, esp. of matter for printing

lay[3] a. not clerical or professional -lay'man n. ordinary person

layette' [lā-et'] n. clothes for new-born child

la'zy a. averse to work -laze vi. be lazy -la'zily adv. -la'ziness n.

lb. pound

l.b.w. leg before wicket

lead[1] [lēd] vt. guide, conduct; persuade; direct -vi. be, go, play first; result; give access to (led, lead'ing) -n. that which leads or is used to lead; example; front or principal place, role etc.; cable bringing current to electric instrument -lead'er n. one who leads; editorial article in newspaper (also leading article) -lead'ership n.

lead[2] [led] n. soft heavy grey metal;

plummet; graphite -*pl.* lead-covered piece of roof -*vt.* cover, weight with lead (**lead'ed, lead'ing**) -**lead'en** *a.* of, like lead; heavy; dull

leaf *n.* organ of photosynthesis in plants, consisting of a flat, usu. green blade on stem; two pages of book etc.; thin sheet (*pl.* **leaves**) -*vt.* turn through (pages etc.) cursorily -**leaf'less** *a.* -**leaf'let** *n.* small leaf; single printed and folded sheet, handbill -**leaf'y** *a.*

league [lēg] *n.* agreement for mutual help; parties to it; federation of clubs etc.; *inf.* class, level

leak *n.* defect that allows escape or entrance of liquid, gas, radiation etc.; disclosure -*vi.* let fluid etc. in or out; (of fluid etc.) find its way through leak -*vt.* let escape -*v.* (allow to) become known little by little -**leak'age** *n.* leaking; gradual escape or loss -**leak'y** *a.*

lean[1] *a.* lacking fat; thin; meagre -*n.* lean part of meat

lean[2] *v.* rest against; incline; tend (towards); rely (on) (**leaned** [lēnd] or **leant** [lent] *pt./pp.*) -**lean'ing** *n.* tendency -**lean'-to** *n.* room, shed built against existing wall

leap *vi.* spring, jump -*vt.* spring over (**leaped** [lept] or **leapt** [lept] *pt./pp.*) -*n.* jump

learn [lern] *vt.* gain skill, knowledge -*vi.* find out (**learnt** or **learned** [lernd] *pt./pp.*) -**learn'ed** *a.* showing much learning -**learn'edly** *adv.* -**learn'er** *n.* -**learn'ing** *n.* knowledge got by study

lease *n.* contract by which land or property is rented -*vt.* let, rent by lease -**lease'hold** *a.* held on lease

leash *n.* thong for holding a dog

least *a.* smallest -*sup.* of LITTLE -*n.* smallest one -*adv.* in smallest degree

leath'er [lETH'-] *n.* prepared skin of animal -**leath'ery** *a.* like leather, tough

leave[1] *vt.* go away from; allow to remain; entrust; bequeath -*vi.* go away, set out (**left, leav'ing**)

leave[2] *n.* permission *esp.* to be absent from duty; period of such absence; formal parting

leav'en [lev'-] *n.* yeast -*vt.* raise with leaven

lech'erous *a.* full of lust; lascivious -**lech'ery** *n.*

lec'tern *n.* reading desk

lec'ture *n.* instructive discourse; speech of reproof -*vi.* deliver dis-

course -*vt.* reprove -**lec'turer** *n.*

LED light-emitting diode

ledge *n.* narrow shelf sticking out from wall, cliff etc.; ridge below surface of sea

ledg'er *n.* book of debit and credit accounts

lee *n.* shelter; side *esp.* of ship, away from wind -**lee'ward** *a./adv.* on, towards lee side -*n.* -**lee'way** *n.* leeward drift of ship; room for movement within limits

leech *n.* species of bloodsucking worm; *Hist.* physician

leek *n.* plant like onion with long bulb and thick stem

leer *vi./n.* glance with malign or lascivious expression

lees [-z] *pl.n.* sediment; dregs

left[1] *a./adv.* on or to the west; opposite to the right -*n.* the left hand or part; *Politics* reforming or radical party (*also* **left wing**) -**left'ist** *n./a.* (person) of the political left

left[2] *pt./pp.* of LEAVE

leg *n.* one of limbs on which person or animal walks, runs, stands; part of garment covering leg; support, as leg of table; stage -**legg'ings** *pl.n.* covering of leather or other material for legs -**legg'y** *a.* long-legged

leg'acy *n.* bequest; thing handed down to successor

le'gal *a.* in accordance with law -**legal'ity** *n.* -**le'galize** *vt.* make legal -**le'gally** *adv.*

legatee' *n.* recipient of legacy

lega'tion *n.* diplomatic minister and his staff; his residence

leg'end [lej'-] *n.* traditional story; notable person or event; inscription -**leg'endary** *a.*

leg'erdemain [lej'-] *n.* sleight of hand

leghorn' [le-gorn'] *n.* breed of fowls

leg'ible [lej'-] *a.* readable -**legibil'ity** *n.*

le'gion [lē'jun] *n.* various military bodies; association of veterans; large number -**le'gionary** *a./n.*

leg'islator [lej'-] *n.* maker of laws -**leg'islate** *vi.* make laws -**legisla'tion** *n.* act of legislating; laws which are made -**leg'islative** *a.* -**leg'islature** *n.* body that makes laws -**leg'islative assembly** single-chamber legislature in most Canad. provinces

legit'imate [-j-] *a.* born in wedlock; lawful, regular -**legit'imacy** *n.*

-legit'imate, legit'imize vt. make legitimate

leg'uan [-oo-ahn] n. large S Afr. lizard

legu'minous [-gyōō-] a. (of plants) pod-bearing

lei'sure [lezh'ər] n. spare time **-lei'surely** a. unhurried **-adv.** slowly

lemm'ing n. rodent of arctic regions

lem'on n. pale yellow acid fruit; its colour; sl. useless person or thing **-lemonade'** n. drink made from lemon juice **-lemon curd** creamy spread made of lemons, butter etc.

le'mur [le'mər] n. nocturnal animal like monkey

lend vt. give temporary use of; let out at interest; bestow (**lent**, **lend'ing**) **-lend'er** n.

length n. measurement from end to end; duration; extent; piece of a certain length **-length'en** v. make, become, longer **-length'wise/** adv. **-length'y** a. (over)long **-at length** in full detail; at last

le'nient a. not strict **-le'nience, le'niency** n.

lens [-z] n. glass etc. shaped to converge or diverge light rays (pl. **lens'es**)

lent pt./pp. of LEND

Lent n. period of fasting from Ash Wednesday to Easter Eve

lent'il n. edible seed of leguminous plant

le'onine a. like a lion

leop'ard [lep'-] n. large, spotted, carnivorous cat (**leop'ardess** fem.)

le'otard [lē'ō-] n. tight-fitting garment covering most of body

lep'er n. one ill with leprosy; person shunned **-lep'rosy** n. ulcerous skin disease

lepidop'tera pl.n. insects with four wings as moths, butterflies

lep'rechaun [-kawn] n. mischievous Irish elf

les'bian n. a homosexual woman

le'sion n. harmful sore on bodily organ

less a. comp. of LITTLE; not so much **-n.** smaller part, quantity; a lesser amount **-adv.** to a smaller extent **-prep.** minus **-less'en** vt. diminish; reduce **-less'er** a. smaller; minor

lessee' n. one holding a lease

less'on n. instalment of course of instruction; content of this; experience that teaches; portion of Scripture read in church

less'or n. grantor of a lease

lest conj. for fear that

let[1] vt. allow, enable, cause; rent *-vi.* be leased (**let**, **lett'ing**)

let[2] n. hindrance; in some games, minor infringement or obstruction of ball

le'thal [lē'-] a. deadly

leth'argy n. apathy, want of energy **-lethar'gic** a. **-lethar'gically** adv.

lett'er n. alphabetical symbol; written message; strict meaning, interpretation **-pl.** literature *-vt.* mark with, in, letters

lett'uce [-tis] n. a salad plant

leukae'mia [lyōō-ke'-] n. a progressive blood disease

lev'ee n. river embankment

lev'el a. horizontal; even, flat *-n.* horizontal line or surface; instrument for establishing horizontal position; position on scale; grade *-v.* make, become level; knock down; aim (gun, or, fig., accusation etc.) **-level-headed** a. not apt to be carried away by emotion

le'ver n. bar pivoted so as to increase force applied to it; operating handle *-vt.* prise, move, with lever **-le'verage** n. action, power of lever; influence

lev'eret n. young hare

levi'athan n. sea monster; anything huge or formidable

levita'tion n. raising of a solid body into the air supernaturally **-lev'itate** v. (cause to) do this

lev'ity n. (undue) frivolity

lev'y vt. impose (tax); raise (troops) (**lev'ied, lev'ying**) *-n.*

lewd a. lustful; indecent

lex'icon n. dictionary **-lexicog'rapher** n. writer of dictionaries

li'able a. answerable; exposed (to); subject (to); likely (to) **-liabil'ity** n. state of being liable, obligation; hindrance, disadvantage **-pl.** debts

liai'son [lē-ā'zon] n. union; connection; intimacy, esp. secret **-liaise'** vi.

lian'a, liane' [-ah-] n. tropical climbing plant

liar n. one who tells lies

lib n. inf. short for LIBERATION

liba'tion [lī-] n. drink poured as offering to the gods

li'bel n. published statement falsely damaging person's reputation *-vt.* defame falsely (**-ll-**) **-li'bellous** a. defamatory

lib'eral a. (also L-) of political party

favouring democratic reform and individual freedom; generous; tolerant; abundant -n. one who has liberal ideas or opinions -**lib'erally** adv. -**lib'erally** adv.

lib'erate vt. set free -**libera'tion** n. -**lib'erator** n.

lib'ertine [-ēn] n. morally dissolute person -a. dissolute

lib'erty n. freedom -**at liberty** free; having the right -**take liberties** (with) to be presumptuous

libi'do [-bē-] n. psychic energy; sexual drive -**libid'inous** a. lustful

li'brary n. room, building where books are kept; collection of books, gramophone records etc. -**librar'ian** n. keeper of library

librett'o n. words of an opera (pl. -os, -i) -**librett'ist** n.

lice pl.n. see LOUSE

li'cence, US li'cense n. permit; permission; excessive liberty; dissoluteness -**li'cense** vt. grant licence to -**licensee'** n. holder of licence

licen'tious [-⌐-] a. dissolute

li'chen [līk'-, lich'-] n. small flowerless plants on rocks, trees etc.

lick vt. pass the tongue over; touch lightly; sl. defeat -n. act of licking; small amount (esp. of paint etc.); inf. speed -**lick'ing** n. sl. beating

lic'orice n. see LIQUORICE

lid n. movable cover; eyelid

li'do [lē'-] n. pleasure centre with swimming and boating

lie¹ vi. be horizontal, at rest; be situated; be in certain state; exist (**lay, lain, lying**) -n. state (of affairs etc.)

lie² vi. make false statement (**lied, ly'ing**) -n. deliberate falsehood -**li'ar** n. person who tells lies

lieu [lyōō] n. place -**in lieu of** instead of

lieuten'ant [lef'-] n. deputy; Army rank below captain; Navy [lə-ten'-] rank below commander

life n. active existence of existence, animate existence; time of its lasting; story of person's life; way of living; vigour, vivacity (pl. **lives**) -a. dead; dull -**life'long** a. lasting a lifetime -**life'time** n. time person, animal, or object lives or functions

lift vt. raise in position, status, mood, volume etc.; take up and remove; inf. steal -vi. rise -n. cage in vertical shaft for raising and lowering people or goods; act of lifting; ride in car etc., as passenger

lig'ament n. band of tissue joining bones -**lig'ature** n. anything which binds; thread for tying up artery

light¹ [līt] a. of, or bearing, little weight; not severe; easy; trivial; (of industry) producing small, usu. consumer goods, using light machinery -adv. in light manner -vi. come by chance (upon) (**light'ed, lit** pt./pp.) -**light'en** vt. reduce, remove (load etc.) -**light'ly** adv. -**light'ness** n. -**lights** pl.n. lungs of animals -**light'headed** a. dizzy; delirious -**light'hearted** a. carefree -**light'weight** n./a. (person) of little weight or importance

light² [līt] n. electromagnetic radiation by which things are visible; source of this, lamp; window; means or act of setting fire to; understanding -pl. traffic lights -a. bright; pale, not dark -vt. set burning; give light to -vi. take fire; brighten (**light'ed** or **lit** pt./pp.) -**light'en** vt. give light to -**light'ing** n. apparatus for supplying artificial light -**light'ning** n. visible discharge of electricity in atmosphere -**light'house** n. tower with a light to guide ships

light'er n. device for lighting cigarettes etc.; flat-bottomed boat for unloading ships

like¹ a. resembling; similar; characteristic of -adv. in the manner of -pron. similar thing -**like'lihood** n. probability -**like'ly** a. probable; promising -adv. probably -**li'ken** vt. compare -**like'ness** n. resemblance; portrait -**like'wise** adv. in like manner

like² vt. find agreeable, enjoy, love -**like'able** a. -**lik'ing** n. fondness; inclination, taste

li'lac n. shrub bearing pale mauve or white flowers

lilt n. rhythmical swing -**lilt'ing** a.

lil'y n. bulbous flowering plant -**lily of the valley** small garden plant with fragrant, white bell-like flowers

limb [lim] n. arm or leg; wing; branch of tree

lim'ber a. pliant, lithe -**limber up** loosen stiff muscles by exercises

lim'bo n. region between Heaven and Hell for the unbaptized; indeterminate place or state (pl. **-bos**)

lime n. calcium oxide etc., used in fertilizer, cement -vt. treat (land) with lime -**lime'light** n. glare of publicity -**lime'stone** n. sedimentary rock used in building

lime¹ *n.* small acid fruit like lemon –**lime-juice** *n.*

lime² *n.* tree

lim'erick *n.* humorous verse of five lines

lim'it *n.* utmost extent or duration; boundary –*vt.* restrict, restrain, bound –**limita'tion** *n.* –**limited company** one whose shareholders' liability is restricted

lim'ousine [-zēn] *n.* large, luxurious car

limp¹ *a.* without firmness or stiffness –**limp'ly** *adv.*

limp² *vi.* walk lamely –*n.* limping gait

limp'et *n.* shellfish which sticks tightly to rocks

limp'id *a.* clear; translucent

linch'pin *n.* pin to hold wheel on its axle; essential person or thing

linc'tus *n.* syrupy cough medicine

line *n.* long narrow mark; row; series, course; telephone connection; progeny; of activity; shipping company; railway track; any class of goods; cord –*v.* cover inside; mark with lines; bring into line –**lin'eage** [-i-idj] *n.* descent from, descendants of an ancestor –**lin'eament** [-i-ə-mənt] *n.* feature –**lin'ear** *a.* of, in lines –**lin'er** *n.* large ship or aircraft of passenger line

lin'en *n.* made of flax –*n.* linen cloth; linen articles collectively

ling *n.* heather

lin'ger [-ng'g-] *vi.* delay, loiter; remain long

lin'gerie [lan'zhə-rē] *n.* women's underwear or nightwear

lin'guist *n.* one skilled in languages or language study –**linguis'tic** *a.* of languages or their study –**linguis'tics** *pl.n.* (*with sing. v.*) study, science of language

lin'iment *n.* embrocation

li'ning *n.* covering for the inside of garment *etc.*

link *n.* ring of a chain; connection; measure, 1-100th part of chain –*vt.* join with, as with, link; intertwine –**link'age** *n.*

links *pl.n.* golf course

linn'et *n.* songbird of finch family

li'no *n.* short for LINOLEUM

lino'leum *n.* floor covering of powdered cork, linseed oil *etc.*, backed with hessian

lin'seed *n.* seed of flax plant

lint *n.* soft material for dressing wounds

lin'tel *n.* top piece of door or window

li'on *n.* large animal of cat family (**li'oness** *fem.*)

lip *n.* either edge of the mouth; edge or margin; *sl.* impudence –**lip ser'vice** insincere tribute or respect –**lip'stick** *n.* cosmetic for colouring lips

liqueur' [li-kyoor'] *n.* alcoholic liquor flavoured and sweetened

liq'uid *a.* fluid, not solid or gaseous; flowing smoothly; (of assets) easily converted into money –*n.* substance in liquid form –**liq'uefy, liq'uidize** *v.* make or become liquid (**liq'uefied, liq'uefying**) –**liquid'ity** *n.* state of being able to meet debts –**liq'uidizer** *n.*

liq'uidate *vt.* pay (debt); arrange affairs of, and dissolve (company); wipe out, kill –**liquida'tion** *n.* clearing up of financial affairs; bankruptcy –**liq'uidator** *n.* official appointed to liquidate business

liq'uor [lik'ər] *n.* liquid, *esp.* an alcoholic one

liq'uorice [-kər-is] *n.* black substance used in medicine and as a sweet

li'ra [lē-] *n.* monetary unit of Italy and Turkey (*pl.* **-re, -ras**)

lisp *v.* speak with faulty pronunciation of s and z –*n.*

list¹ *n.* inventory, register; catalogue –*vt.* place on list

list² *vi.* (of ship) lean to one side –*n.* inclination of ship

list'en [lis'ən] *vi.* try to hear, attend to –**list'ener** *n.*

list'less *a.* indifferent, languid –**list'lessly** *adv.*

lit'any *n.* prayer with responses

lit'eral *a.* according to the strict meaning of the words, not figurative –**lit'erally** *adv.*

lit'erate *a.* able to read and write; educated –**lit'eracy** *n.*

lit'erature *n.* books and writings of a country, period or subject –**lit'erary** *a.*

lithe [līTH] *a.* supple, pliant

lithog'raphy *n.* method of printing using the antipathy of grease and water –**lith'ograph** *n.* print so produced –*vt.* print thus

lit'igant *n./a.* (person) conducting a lawsuit –**litiga'tion** *n.* lawsuit

lit'mus *n.* blue dye turned red by acids and restored to blue by alkali –**litmus paper**

li'tre [lē'tər] *n.* measure of volume of

fluid, one cubic decimetre, about 1.75 pints

litt'er n. untidy refuse; young of animal produced at one birth; kind of stretcher for wounded -vt. strew with litter; bring forth

litt'le a. small, not much (**less, least**) -n. small quantity -adv. slightly

lit'urgy n. prescribed form of public worship -**litur'gical** a.

live¹ [liv] v. have life; pass one's life; continue in life; continue, last; dwell; feed -**liv'ing** n. condition of being in life; people now alive; means of living; church benefice

live² [līv] a. living, alive, active, vital; flaming; (of electrical conductor) carrying current; (of broadcast) transmitted during the actual performance -**live'ly** a. brisk, active, vivid -**live'liness** n. -**liv'en** vt. (esp. with up) make (more) lively

live'lihood n. means of living

live'long [liv-] a. lasting throughout the whole day

liv'er n. organ secreting bile; animal liver as food -**liv'erish** a. unwell, as from liver upset; touchy, irritable

liv'ery n. distinctive dress, esp. servant's

liv'id a. lead-coloured; discoloured, as by bruising; inf. angry, furious

liz'ard n. four-footed reptile

llam'a [lahm'ə] n. woolly animal of S Amer.

LL.B. Bachelor of Laws

load n. something carried; quantity carried; burden; amount of power used -vt. put load on or into; charge (gun); weigh down -**load'ed** a. carrying a load; (of dice) dishonestly weighted; (of question) worded as a trap; sl. wealthy; sl. drunk

load'star, -stone n. see LODE

loaf¹ n. mass of bread as baked; shaped mass of food (pl. **loaves**)

loaf² vi. idle, loiter -**loaf'er** n. idler

loam n. fertile soil

loan n. act of lending; thing lent; money borrowed at interest -vt. lend

lo(a)th [-th] a. unwilling -**loathe** [-TH] vt. abhor -**loath'ing** n. disgust -**loath'some** a.

lob n. in tennis etc., shot pitched high in air -v. throw, pitch shot thus (**-bb-**)

lobb'y n. corridor into which rooms open; group which tries to influence legislature -v. try to enlist support (of)

lobe n. soft, hanging part of ear; rounded segment

lob'ster n. shellfish with long tail and claws, turning red when boiled

lob'worm n. lugworm

lo'cal a. of, existing in; confined to one part of the body -n. person from district; inf. (nearby) pub -**locale'** [-ahl'] n. scene of event -local'ity n. district; site -**lo'calize** vt. assign, restrict to definite place -**lo'cally** adv.

locate' vt. find; situate -**loca'tion** n. placing; situation; site of film production away from studio

loch [loх, lok] n. Scottish lake or long narrow bay

lock¹ n. appliance for fastening door, lid etc.; arrangement for moving boats from one level of canal to another; extent to which vehicle's front wheels will turn; block, jam -v. fasten, make secure with lock; place in locked container; join firmly; jam; embrace closely -**lock'er** n. small cupboard with lock -**lock'jaw** n. tetanus -**lock'out** n. exclusion of workers by employers as means of coercion -**lock'smith** n. one who makes and mends locks -**lock'up** n. garage, storage area away from main premises

lock² n. tress of hair

lock'et n. small hinged pendant for portrait etc.

locomo'tive [lō-] n. engine for pulling carriages on railway tracks -a. -**locomo'tion** n. action, power of moving

lo'cum Lat. substitute, esp. for doctor or clergyman

lo'cus n. curve traced by all points satisfying specified mathematical condition (pl. **lo'ci** [-sī])

lo'cust n. destructive winged insect

lode n. a vein of ore -**lode'star** n. Pole Star -**lode'stone** n. magnetic iron ore

lodge n. house, cabin used seasonally or occasionally, eg for hunting, skiing; gatekeeper's house; branch of Freemasons etc. -vt. house; deposit; bring (a charge etc.) -vi. live in another's house at fixed charge; come to rest (in, on) -**lodg'er** n. -**lodg'ings** pl.n. rented room(s) in another person's house

loft n. space under the roof -**loft'ily** adv. haughtily -**loft'iness** n. -**loft'y** a. of great height; elevated; haughty

log¹ n. trimmed portion of felled tree; record of voyages of ship, aircraft

etc. -vt. enter in a log; record (-gg-)
-log'ger n. -log'book n.

log² n. logarithm

log'arithm [-Thəm] n. one of series of arithmetical functions tabulated for use in calculation

logg'erhead n. -at loggerheads quarrelling, disputing

log'ic [loj'-] n. science of reasoning; reasoned thought or argument; coherence of various facts, events etc. -log'ical a. of logic; according to reason; reasonable; apt to reason correctly

logis'tics pl.n. (with sing. or pl. v.) the handling of supplies and personnel

loin n. part of body between ribs and hip; cut of meat from this -pl. hips and lower abdomen -loin'cloth n. garment covering loins only

loi'ter vi. dawdle, hang about; idle -loi'terer n.

loll vi. sit, lie lazily; (esp. of the tongue) hang out

loll'ipop n. sweet on small wooden stick

loll'y n. inf. lollipop or ice lolly; sl. money

lone a. solitary -lone'ly a. sad because alone; unfrequented; solitary -lone'liness n. -lo'ner n. inf. one who prefers to be alone -lone'some a.

long¹ a. having length, esp. great length, in space or time; extensive; protracted -adv. for a long time -long'hand n. words written in full -long'playing a. (of record) for 10 to 30 minutes -long-range a. of the future; able to travel long distances without refuelling; (of weapons) designed to hit distant target -long shot competitor, undertaking, bet etc. with small chance of success -long ton the imperial ton (2240 lb) -long-winded a. tediously loquacious

long² vi. have keen desire, yearn (for) -long'ing n. yearning

longev'ity [-j-] n. long life

lon'gitude [-j-] n. distance east or west from standard meridian -longitu'dinal a. of length or longitude

loo n. inf. lavatory

look vi. direct eyes (at); face; seem; search (for); hope (for); (with after) take care of -n. looking; view; search; (oft. pl.) appearance -good looks beauty -look'out n. watchman;

place for watching; prospect

loom¹ n. machine for weaving

loom² vi. appear dimly; seem ominously close

loop n. made by curved line crossing itself -v. form loop

loop'hole n. means of evading rule without infringing it; vertical fortification slit in wall

loose a. slack; not fixed or restrained; vague; dissolute -vt. free; unfasten; slacken -vi. (with off) shoot, let fly -loose'ly adv. -loos'en vt. make loose -loose'ness n. -on the loose inf. on a spree

loot n./vt. plunder

lop vt. cut away twigs and branches; chop off (-pp-)

lope vi. run with long, easy strides

lop'sided a. with one side lower than the other

loqua'cious a. talkative

lord n. British nobleman, peer of the realm; God -vi. domineer -lord'ly a. imperious; fit for a lord

lore n. learning; body of facts and traditions

lorgnette' [lor-nyet'] n. spectacles with long handle

lor'is n. tree-dwelling, nocturnal Asian animal

lorr'y n. motor vehicle for heavy loads, truck

lose [lōōz] vt. be deprived of, fail to retain or use; fail to get; (of clock etc.) run slow; be defeated in -vi. suffer loss (lost pt./pp. -los'ing [lōōz'ing] pr.p.) -loss n. a losing; what is lost -lost a. unable to be found; unable to find one's way; bewildered; not won; not utilized

lot pron. great number -n. collection; large quantity; share; fate; item at auction; object used to make decision by chance; area of land -pl. great numbers or quantity -adv. inf. a great deal

lo'tion n. liquid for washing wounds, improving skin etc.

lott'ery n. method of raising funds by selling tickets and prizes by chance; gamble

lo'tus n. legendary plant whose fruits induce forgetfulness

loud a. strongly audible; noisy -loud'ly adv. -loudspeak'er n. instrument for converting electrical signals into sound audible at a distance

lounge vi. recline, move at ease -n. living room of house; public room, area for sitting **–lounge suit** man's suit for daytime wear

lour *see* LOWER

lou'rie *n.* S Afr. bird

louse [lows] *n.* a parasitic insect (*pl.* **lice**) **–lous'y** [-z'-] *a. sl.* bad; *sl.* nasty; *sl.* (too) generously provided (with); having lice

lout *n.* crude, oafish person **–lout'ish** *a.*

lou'vre [loo'vər] *n.* one of a set of slats slanted to admit air but not rain

love [luv] *n.* warm affection; benevolence; sexual passion; sweetheart; *Tennis etc.* score of nothing **–v.** admire passionately; delight in; be in love **–lov'(e)able** *a.* **–love'liness** *n.* **–love'ly** *a.* beautiful, delightful **–lov'er** *n.* **–lov'ing** *a.* affectionate; tender **–lov'ingly** *adv.* **–love-in-a-mist** *n.* plant with pale-blue flowers **–love-lies-bleeding** *n.* plant with long, drooping red flowers **–make love (to)** have sexual intercourse (with)

low¹ [lō] *a.* not tall, high or elevated; humble; vulgar; unwell; below what is usual; not loud **–low'er** *vt.* cause, allow to move down; diminish **–a.** below; at an early stage, period **–lowli'ness** *n.* **–low'ly** *a.* modest, humble **–low'brow** *n./a.* nonintellectual (person) **–a. –low'down** *n. inf.* inside information **–low-down** *a. inf.* mean, shabby **–low-key** *a.* not intense **–low'land** *n.* low-lying country **–low-tension** *a.* carrying, operating at low voltage

low² [lō] *vi./n.* of cattle, (utter) their cry, bellow

low'er, lour [low'ər] *vi.* look threatening, as sky; scowl

loy'al *a.* faithful, true to allegiance **–loy'alist** *n.* **–Loy'alist** *n.* C United Empire Loyalist **–loy'ally** *adv.* **–loy'alty** *n.*

loz'enge *n.* small sweet or tablet of medicine; diamond shape

LP long-playing (record)

L-plate *n.* sign on car driven by learner driver

LSD lysergic acid diethylamide (hallucinogenic drug); librae, solidi, denarii (*Lat.*, pounds, shillings, pence)

Lt. Lieutenant

Ltd. Limited (Liability)

lu'bricate [loo'-] *vt.* oil, grease; make slippery **–lu'bricant** *n.* substance used for this **–lubrica'tion** *n.*

lu'cid [loo'sid] *a.* clear; easily understood; sane **–lucid'ity** *n.*

luck *n.* fortune, good or bad; chance

–luck'ily *adv.* fortunately **–luck'less** *a.* having bad luck **–luck'y** *a.* having good luck

lu'crative *a.* very profitable

lu'dicrous [loo'-] *a.* ridiculous

lu'do [loo'-] *n.* game played with dice and counters on board

lug¹ *vt.* drag with effort (**-gg-**)

lug² *n.* projection serving as handle or support; *inf.* ear

lug'gage *n.* traveller's baggage

lugu'brious [loo-goo'-] *a.* doleful **–lugu'briously** *adv.*

lug'worm *n.* large worm used as bait, lobworm

luke'warm [look'-] *a.* tepid; indifferent

lull *v.* soothe, sing to sleep; calm; subside **–***n.* quiet spell **–lull'aby** [-bī] *n.* lulling song, *esp.* for children

lumba'go *n.* rheumatism in the lower part of the back

lum'ber *n.* disused articles, useless rubbish; sawn timber **–vi.** move heavily **–v.** *inf.* burden with something unpleasant **–lum'berjack** *n.* US, C man who fells trees and prepares logs

lu'minous [loo'-] *a.* shedding light; glowing **–luminos'ity** *n.*

lump *n.* shapeless piece or mass; swelling; large sum **–vt.** throw together **–lump'y** *a.* full of lumps; uneven

lu'nar [loo'-] *a.* relating to the moon

lu'natic [loo'-] *a./n.* insane (person) **–lu'nacy** *n.*

lunch *n.* meal taken in the middle of the day **–v.** eat, entertain to lunch **–lunch'eon** [-shən] *n.* a lunch

lung *n.* one of the two organs of respiration in vertebrates

lunge *vi.* thrust with sword *etc.* **–n.** such thrust; sudden movement of body, plunge

lu'pin [loo'-] *n.* leguminous plant with spikes of flowers

lurch *n.* sudden roll to one side **–vi.** stagger **–leave in the lurch** leave in difficulties

lure [lyoor] *n.* bait; power to attract **–vt.** entice; attract

lu'rid [loo'-] *a.* sensational; garish

lurk *vi.* lie hidden **–lurk'ing** *a.* (of suspicion) not definite

lus'cious [-shəs] *a.* sweet, juicy; extremely attractive

lush *a.* (of plant growth) luxuriant; luxurious

lust *n.* strong desire for sexual gratification; any strong desire **–vi.** have passionate desire -lust'ful a. -lust'ily adv. -lust'y a. vigorous, healthy

lus'tre n. gloss, sheen; renown; metallic pottery glaze -lus'trous a. shining

lute [loot] n. old stringed musical instrument played like a guitar -lu'tenist n.

lux'ury n. possession and use of costly, choice things for enjoyment; enjoyable, comfortable surroundings -luxu'riance n. abundance -luxu'riant a. growing thickly; abundant -luxu'riate vi. indulge in luxury; flourish profusely; take delight (in) -luxu'rious a. fond of luxury; self-indulgent; sumptuous

lymph n. colourless body fluid, mainly white blood cells -lymphat'ic a.

lynch vt. put to death without trial

lynx n. animal of cat family

lyre [līr] n. instrument like harp

lyr'ic a. songlike poem expressing personal feelings -pl. words of popular song -lyr'ical a. expressed in this style; enthusiastic

M

M Monsieur; Motorway

m metre(s)

MA Master of Arts

macab're [-kahb'ər] a. gruesome, ghastly

macad'am n. road surface of small broken stones -macad'amize vt.

macaro'ni n. pasta in long, thin tubes (pl. -ni(e)s)

macaroon' n. biscuit containing almonds

macaw' n. kind of parrot

mace¹ n. staff of office

mace² n. spice made of nutmeg shell

machete' [mə-shet'ē] n. broad, heavy knife

Machiavell'ian [mak-] a. (politically) unprincipled, crafty

machina'tion [-kin-] n. (usu. pl.) plotting, intrigue

machine' [-shēn'] n. apparatus with several parts to apply mechanical force; controlling organization; mechanical appliance -vt. shape etc. with machine -machin'ery n. parts of machine; machines -machin'ist n. -machine gun automatic gun firing repeatedly

mack'erel n. edible sea fish

mack'intosh n. waterproof raincoat

macram'é [-krahm'ē] n. ornamental work of knotted cord

mac'rocosm n. the universe

mad n. suffering from mental disease; foolish; enthusiastic (about); excited; inf. furious -madd'en vt. make mad

mad'am n. polite title for a woman

mad'cap n. reckless person

madd'er n. climbing plant; its root; red dye made from this

Madonn'a n. the Virgin Mary

mad'rigal n. unaccompanied part song

mael'strom [māl'-] n. great whirlpool

maes'tro [mī'-] n. outstanding musician, conductor; master of any art

magazine' [-zēn'] n. periodical publication; appliance for supplying cartridges to gun; storehouse for arms etc.

magen'ta [-j-] a. deep purplish-red

magg'ot n. grub, larva -magg'oty a.

mag'ic [-j-] n. art of supposedly invoking supernatural powers to influence events etc.; witchcraft, conjuring -a. -mag'ical a. -mag'ically adv. -mag'ician n. wizard, conjurer

mag'istrate [maj-] n. civil officer administering law -magiste'rial a. of magistrate; dictatorial

magnan'imous a. generous, not petty -magnanim'ity n.

mag'nate n. influential person

magne'sium n. metallic element -magne'sia n. white powder used in medicine

mag'net n. piece of iron, steel having properties of attracting iron, steel -magnet'ic a. of magnet; exerting powerful attraction -magnet'ically adv. -mag'netism n. -mag'netize vt. -magne'to n. apparatus for ignition in internal combustion engine (pl. -tos) -magnetic tape coated plastic strip for recording sound or video signals

magnif'icent a. splendid; imposing; excellent -magnif'icence n.

mag'nify [-fī] vt. increase apparent size of, as with lens; exaggerate (-fied, -fying) -magnifica'tion n.

mag'nitude n. importance; greatness

magno'lia n. tree with white, sweet-scented flowers

mag'num n. large wine bottle

mag'pie n. black-and-white bird

maharaʹjah [mah-hah-rahʹ-] n. former title of some Indian princes (**mahara'nee** fem.)

mahar'ishi [mah-hah-reʹ-] n. Hindu religious teacher or mystic

mahjong(g)' n. Chinese table game for four

mahog'any n. tree yielding reddish brown wood

maid'en n. Literary young unmarried woman -a. unmarried; first -**maid** n. Literary maiden; woman servant -**maid'enly** a. -**maid'enhead** n. virginity -**maiden name** woman's surname before marriage

mail[1] n. letters etc. transported and delivered by the post office; postal system; train etc. carrying mail -vt. -**mailed** a.

mail[2] n. armour of interlaced rings -**mailed** a.

maim vt. cripple, mutilate

main a. chief, principal -n. principal pipe, line carrying water etc.; power; obs. sea -**main'ly** adv. -**main'land** n. stretch of land which forms main part of a country -**main'spring** n. chief spring of clock; chief cause -**main'stay** n. chief support

maintain' vt. carry on; support; keep up; support by argument -**main'tenance** n. maintaining; means of support; upkeep of buildings etc.

maisonette' [mā-zən-etʹ] n. part of house fitted as self-contained dwelling

maize n. type of corn

maj'esty n. stateliness; sovereignty -**majes'tic** a. -**majes'tically** adv.

ma'jor n. army officer above captain; scale in music -a. greater in number, extent etc. -**major'ity** n. greater number; coming of age

make vt. construct; produce; create; establish; appoint; amount to; cause to do; reach; earn -vi. tend; contribute (**made, ma'king**) -n. brand, type -**make'shift** n. temporary expedient -**make-up** n. cosmetics; characteristics; layout -**make'weight** n. trifle added

mal-, male- (comb. form) ill, badly, as in **malforma'tion** n., -**malfunc'tion** n./vi.

maladjust'ed a. badly adjusted, as to society

maladroit' a. clumsy, awkward

mal'ady n. disease

malaise' [-āzʹ] n. vague feeling of bodily discomfort

mal'apropism n. ludicrous misuse of word

mala'ria n. infectious disease transmitted by mosquitoes

mal'content a./n. discontented (person)

male a. of sex that fertilizes female; of men or male animals -n.

maledic'tion n. curse

mal'efactor n. criminal

malev'olent a. full of ill will -**malev'olence** n.

mal'ice n. ill will; spite -**mali'cious** a. spiteful

malign' [-līnʹ] a. causing evil -vt. slander -**malig'nancy** n. -**malig'nant** a. feeling ill will; (of disease) resistant to therapy

maling'er [-ngʹg-] vi. feign illness to escape duty -**maling'erer** n.

mall [mawl, mal] n. shaded walk

mall'ard n. wild duck

mall'eable a. capable of being hammered into shape; adaptable -**malleabil'ity** n.

mall'et n. (wooden) hammer

malnutri'tion [-trishʹ-] n. inadequate nutrition

malo'dorous a. evil-smelling

malprac'tice n. immoral, illegal or unethical conduct

malt [mawlt] n. grain used for brewing -**malt'ster** n.

maltreat' vt. treat badly

mamm'al n. animal of type that suckles its young

mamm'ary a. of, relating to breast

mamm'on n. wealth regarded as source of evil

mamm'oth n. extinct animal like an elephant -a. colossal

man n. human being; human race; adult male; piece used in chess etc. (pl. **men**) -vt. supply with men (-**nn-**) -**man'ful** a. brave -**man'ly** a. -**man'handle** vt. treat roughly -**man'hole** n. opening through which man may pass to a sewer etc. -**man'kind'** n. human beings -**man'slaughter** n. unintentional homicide

Man. Manitoba

man'acle n./vt. fetter

man'age vt. be in charge of; succeed in doing; control; handle -**man'ageable** a. -**man'agement** n. those who manage; administration -**man'ager** n. -**manage'rial** a.

man'darin n. Hist. Chinese high-ranking bureaucrat; Chinese variety of orange

man'date *n.* command of, or commission to act for, another; instruction from electorate to representative or government **-man'datory** *a.* compulsory

man'dible *n.* lower jawbone

man'dolin(e) *n.* stringed musical instrument

mane *n.* long hair on neck of horse, lion *etc.*

man'ganese [-ng'g-] *n.* metallic element; black oxide of this

mange [mānj] *n.* skin disease of dogs *etc.* **-ma'ngy** *a.*

man'gelwurzel [mang'gəl-] *n.* variety of beet

man'ger [mānj'ər] *n.* eating trough in stable

man'gle[1] [mang'gəl] *n.* machine for rolling clothes *etc.* to remove water **-vt.** press in mangle

man'gle[1] [mang'gəl] *vt.* mutilate

man'go [-ng'gō] *n.* tropical fruit (*pl.* **-go(e)s**)

man'grove *n.* tropical tree which grows on muddy river banks

ma'nia *n.* madness; prevailing craze **-ma'niac** *a./n.* mad (person) **man'ic** *a.* affected by mania

man'icure *n.* treatment and care of fingernails and hands **-vt. -man'icurist** *n.*

man'ifest *a.* clear, undoubted **-vt.** make manifest **-manifesta'tion** *n.* **-manifes'to** *n.* declaration of policy by political party *etc.* (*pl.* **-to(e)s**)

man'ifold *a.* numerous and varied **-n.** in engine, pipe with several outlets

manil(l)'a *n.* fibre used for ropes; tough paper

manip'ulate *vt.* handle skilfully; manage; falsify **-manipula'tion** *n.*

mann'a *n.* food of Israelites in the wilderness; nourishment

mann'equin [-i-kin] *n.* woman who models clothes

mann'er *n.* way, style; sort, kind; custom **-pl.** social behaviour **-mann'erism** *n.* person's distinctive habit

manoeu'vre [-ōō'vər] *n.* complicated, perhaps deceptive plan or action **-v.** employ stratagems; (cause to) perform manoeuvres

man'or *n.* Hist. land belonging to a lord; feudal unit of land **-manor'ial** *a.*

manse *n.* house of minister in some religious denominations

man'sion *n.* large house

man'telpiece *n.* shelf at top of fireplace

man'tis *n.* large tropical insect (*pl.* **man'tes** [-tēz])

man'tle *n.* loose cloak; covering **-vt.** cover

man'ual *a.* done with the hands; by human labour, not automatic **-n.** handbook

manufac'ture *vt.* make (materials) into finished articles; concoct **-n.** making of articles *esp.* in large quantities **-manufac'turer** *n.*

manure' *n.* dung or chemical fertilizer used to enrich land

man'uscript *n.* book *etc.* written by hand; copy for printing

man'y [men'i] *a.* numerous (**more** comp., **most** sup.) **-n.** large number

map *n.* flat representation of the earth or heavens **-vt.** make map of; (with out) plan **(-pp-)**

ma'ple *n.* tree of sycamore family

mar *vt.* spoil **(-rr-)**

Mar. March

mar'abou [ma-] *n.* kind of stork; its soft white tail feathers

maraschi'no [mar-ə-skē'-] *n.* liqueur made from cherries

mar'athon [ma-] *n.* long-distance race; endurance contest

maraud' *v.* raid, plunder **-maraud'er** *n.*

mar'ble *n.* kind of limestone; small ball used in children's game

March *n.* third month

march *vi.* walk with military step; go, progress **-n.** act of marching; distance marched; marching tune

mar'chioness [-shən-] *n.* wife, widow of marquis

mare *n.* female horse

mar'garine [-j-, -g-] *n.* butter substitute made from vegetable fats

mar'gin [-j-] *n.* border, edge; space round printed page; amount allowed beyond what is necessary **-mar'ginal** *a.*

marguerite' [-ēt'] *n.* large daisy

mar'igold [ma-] *n.* plant with yellow flowers

marijua'na, marihua'na [mar-i-hwah'na] *n.* dried flowers and leaves of hemp plant, used as narcotic

mari'na [-rē'-] *n.* mooring facility for pleasure boats

marine' [-ēn'] *a.* of the sea or shipping **-n.** fleet; soldier trained for land or sea combat **-mar'iner** *n.* sailor

marionette' [ma-] n. puppet

mar'ital [ma'-] a. of marriage

mar'itime [ma'-] a. of seafaring; near the sea

mark[1] n. dot, scar etc.; sign, token; letter, number showing evaluation of schoolwork etc.; indication; target -vt. make mark on; distinguish; notice; assess; stay close to sporting opponent -**mark'er** n. -**marks'man** n. skilled shot

mark[2] n. German coin

mark'et n. place for buying and selling; demand for goods -vt. offer for sale -**mark'etable** a.

mar'malade n. preserve made of oranges, lemons etc.

marmor'eal a. of marble

mar'moset n. small bushy-tailed monkey

maroon[1] a./n. (of) brownish-crimson colour

maroon[2] vt. leave on deserted island etc.; isolate

marquee' [-kē'] n. large tent

mar'quetry [-kit-] n. inlaid work, wood mosaic

mar'quis, -quess n. nobleman of rank below duke

marr'ow [-rō] n. fatty substance inside bones; vital part; vegetable marrow

marr'y v. join as husband and wife; unite closely (**marr'ied, marr'ying**) -**marr'iage** [-ij] n. being married; wedding

marsh n. low-lying wet land -**mar'sh'y** a.

mar'shal n. high officer of state; US law enforcement officer; high-ranking officer in army, air force -vt. arrange; conduct with ceremony

marsu'pial n. animal that carries its young in pouch

mar'ten n. weasellike animal

mar'tial [-shəl] a. of war; warlike -court martial see COURT

mar'tin n. species of swallow

martinet' n. strict disciplinarian

mar'tyr [-tər] n. one who suffers or dies for his beliefs -vt. make martyr of -**mar'tyrdom** n.

mar'vel vi. wonder (-ll-) -n. wonderful thing -**mar'vellous** a.

mar'zipan n. paste of almonds, sugar etc.

mascar'a n. cosmetic for darkening eyelashes

mas'cot n. thing supposed to bring luck

mas'culine [-lin] a. relating to males; manly

mash n./vt. (crush into) soft mass or pulp

mask [-ah-] n. covering for face; disguise, pretence -vt.

mas'ochism [-kizm] n. abnormal condition where pleasure (esp. sexual) is derived from pain -**mas'ochist** n.

ma'son n. worker in stone -**ma'sonry** n. stonework

masquerade' n. masked ball -vi. appear in disguise

Mass n. service of the Eucharist, esp. in R.C. Church

mass n. quantity of matter; large quantity -v. form into mass -**mass'ive** a. large and heavy -**mass-produce'** vt. produce standardized articles in large quantities

mass'acre [-kər] n. indiscriminate, large-scale killing -vt.

mass'age [-ahzh] n. rubbing and kneading of muscles etc. as curative treatment -vt. -**masseur'** n. one who practises massage (**masseuse'** fem.)

mast [-ah-] n. pole for supporting ship's sails; tall support for aerial etc.

mastec'tomy n. surgical removal of a breast

mas'ter [mah'-] n. one in control; employer; owner; document etc. from which copies are made; expert; teacher -vt. overcome; acquire skill in -**mas'terful** a. domineering -**mas'tery** n. understanding (of); expertise; victory -**mas'termind** vt. plan, direct -n. -**mas'terpiece** n. outstanding work

mas'ticate vt. chew -**mastica'tion** n.

mas'tiff n. large dog

mas'toid n. prominence on bone behind human ear -**mastoidi'tis** n. inflammation of this area

mas'turbate v. stimulate (one's own) genital organs -**masturba'tion** n.

mat n. small rug; piece of fabric to protect another surface; thick tangled mass -v. form into such mass (-tt-)

mat(t) a. dull, lustreless

mat'ador n. man who slays bull in bullfights

match[1] n. contest, game; equal; person, thing corresponding to another; marriage -vt. get something corresponding to; oppose, put in competition (with) -vi. correspond -**match'less** a. unequalled

match [1] n. small stick with head which ignites when rubbed -**match'box** n. -**match'wood** n. small splinters

mate n. comrade; husband, wife; one of pair; officer in merchant ship -v. marry; pair

mate'rial n. substance from which thing is made; cloth -a. of body; affecting physical wellbeing; important -**mate'rialism** n. excessive interest in money and possessions; doctrine that nothing but matter exists -**materialis'tic** a. -**mate'rialize** vi. come into existence or view -**mate'rially** adv. appreciably

mater'nal a. of mother -**mater'nity** n. motherhood

mathemat'ics pl.n. (with sing. v.) science of number, quantity, shape and space -**mathemat'ical** a. -**mathemati'cian** [-tish'-] n.

mat'inée [-nā] n. afternoon performance in theatre

mat'ins pl.n. morning prayers

ma'triarch [-k] n. mother as head of family -**ma'triarchal** a.

matric'ulate v. enrol, be enrolled in a college or university

mat'rimony n. marriage -**matrimo'nial** a.

ma'trix n. substance, situation in which something originates, is enclosed; mould (pl. **ma'trices** [-sēz])

ma'tron n. married woman; former name for NURSING OFFICER; woman who superintends domestic arrangements of public institution

matt'er n. substance of which thing is made; affair, business; trouble; pus -vi. be of importance

matt'ock n. tool like pick with ends of blades flattened

matt'ress n. stuffed flat (sprung) case used as part of bed

mature' a. ripe, completely developed; grown-up -v. bring, come to maturity -**matu'rity** n.

maud'lin a. weakly sentimental

maul vt. handle roughly

mausole'um n. stately building as a tomb (pl. -**le'ums**, -**le'a**)

mauve [mōv] a./n. pale purple

mav'erick n. independent, unorthodox person

maw n. stomach, crop

mawk'ish a. maudlin; sickly

max'im n. general truth; rule of conduct

max'imum a./n. greatest (size or number)

May n. fifth month; (m-) hawthorn or its flowers

may v. aux. expresses possibility, permission, opportunity etc. (**might** pt.) -**may'be** adv. perhaps; possibly

may'hem n. violent maiming; any violent destruction

mayonnaise' n. creamy sauce, esp. for salads

may'or [mâr] n. head of municipality -**may'oress** n. mayor's wife; lady mayor

maze n. labyrinth; network of paths, lines

maz(o)ur'ka n. lively Polish dance

MBE Member of the Order of the British Empire

MC Master of Ceremonies; Military Cross

MCC Marylebone Cricket Club

me pron. form of I used after verb or preposition

mead n. alcoholic drink made from honey

mead'ow [med'-] n. piece of grassland

mea'gre [mē'gər] a. lean, scanty

meal [1] n. occasion when food is served and eaten; the food

meal [2] n. grain ground to powder -**meal'ie** n. SA maize

mean [1] vt. intend; signify -vi. have a meaning; have the intention of behaving (**meant** [ment] pt./pp.) -**mean'ing** pr.p.) -**mean'ing** n. -**mean'ingful** a. of great significance

mean [2] a. ungenerous, petty; miserly; callous; shabby

mean [3] n. middle point -pl. that by which thing is done; money; resources -a. intermediate; average -**mean'time**, **mean'while** adv./n. (during) time between one happening and another

mean'der [mē-and'-] vi. flow windingly; wander aimlessly

meas'les [mēz'lz] n. infectious disease producing rash of red spots

meas'ure [mezh'ər] n. size, quantity; unit, system of measuring; course of action; laws -vt. ascertain size, quantity of; be (so much) in size or quantity; indicate measurement of -**meas'urement** n. measuring; size

meat n. animal flesh as food; food -**meat'y** a.

mechan'ic [-k-] n. one who works with machinery -pl. scientific theory of motion -mechan'ical a. of, by machine; acting without thought -mechan'ically adv.

mech'anism [mek-] n. structure of machine; piece of machinery -mechaniza'tion n. -mech'anize vt. equip with machinery; make automatic

med'al n. piece of metal with inscription etc. used as reward or memento -medall'ion n. (design like) large medal -med'allist n.

med'dle vi. interfere -med'dlesome a.

me'dia n., pl. of MEDIUM, used esp. of the mass media, radio, television etc.

mediae'val see MEDIEVAL

me'dian a./n. middle (point or line)

me'diate vi. intervene to reconcile -media'tion n. -me'diator n.

med'icine [-sin] n. drug or remedy for treating disease; science of preventing, curing disease -med'ical a. -med'icate vt. impregnate with medicinal substances -medic'inal a. curative

medie'val, mediae'val a. of Middle Ages

medio'cre [mē-di-ō-kə] a. ordinary, middling; second-rate -medioc'rity n.

med'itate vi. be occupied in thought -vt. plan -medita'tion n. -med'itative a.

me'dium n. between two qualities, degrees etc. -n. middle quality; means; agency of communicating news etc. to public; surroundings (pl. me'diums, me'dia)

med'lar n. tree with fruit like small apple

med'ley n. mixture (pl. -leys)

meek a. submissive, humble

meet v. come face to face (with); satisfy; pay; converge; assemble; come into contact (met pt./pp.) -meet'ing n.

meg'alith n. great stone

megaloma'nia n. desire for, delusions of grandeur, power etc.

meg'aphone n. cone-shaped instrument to amplify voice

meg'aton n. explosive power of 1 000 000 tons of TNT

mel'ancholy [-k-] n. sadness, dejection -a. gloomy, dejected

mêl'ée [mel'ā] n. mixed fight

mellif'luous, -luent a. (of sound) smooth, sweet

mell'ow a. ripe; softened by age, experience; not harsh; genial -v. make, become mellow

mel'odrama n. play full of sensational situations -melodramat'ic a.

mel'ody n. series of musical notes which make tune; sweet sound -melo'dious a.

mel'on n. large, fleshy, juicy fruit

melt v. (cause to) become liquid by heat; dissolve; soften; disappear (melt'ed pt./pp., mol'ten [mōl'tən] pp.)

mem'ber n. individual making up body or society; limb; any part of complex whole -mem'bership n.

mem'brane n. thin flexible tissue in plant or animal body

memen'to n. reminder, souvenir (pl. -to(e)s)

mem'o n. short for MEMORANDUM

mem'oir [-wahr] n. autobiography, personal history

mem'ory n. faculty of recalling to mind; recollection; thing remembered; commemoration -memor'ial n. thing which serves to keep in memory -mem'orable a. worthy of remembrance -memoran'dum n. note to help the memory etc.; informal letter (pl. -dums, -da) -mem'orize vt. commit to memory

men n. pl. of MAN

men'ace n. threat -vt. threaten

ménage' [me-nahzh', mā-] n. household

menag'erie [-j-] n. collection of wild animals

mend v. repair; correct; put right; improve -n. repaired breakage, hole

menda'cious a. untruthful -mendac'ity n.

men'dicant a. begging -n. beggar

me'nial a. requiring little skill; servile -n. servant

meningi'tis [-jī-] n. inflammation of the membranes of the brain

men'opause n. final cessation of menstruation

menstrua'tion n. monthly discharge of blood from womb -men'struate vi.

mensura'tion [-sho-rā'-] n. measuring

ment'al a. of, by the mind; inf. mad -mental'ity n.

men'thol n. substance found in peppermint

men'tion vt. refer to briefly -n. acknowledgment; reference to

men'tor n. wise adviser

men'u n. list of dishes served

mer'cantile [-k-] a. of trade

mer'cenary [-s-] a. influenced by greed; working merely for reward –n. hired soldier

mer'chant n. one engaged in trade; wholesale trader –**mer'chandise** n. his wares –**merchant navy** ships engaged in a nation's commerce

mer'cury [-kyoor-] n. silvery metal, liquid at ordinary temperature –**mer'curial** a. lively, changeable

mer'cy n. refraining from infliction of suffering by one who has right, power to inflict it –**mer'ciful** a.

mere [mēr] a. only; nothing but –**mere'ly** adv.

meretric'ious [-ish-] a. superficially attractive

merge v. (cause to) lose identity or be absorbed –**mer'ger** [-j-] n. esp. combination of business firms

merid'ian n. circle of the earth passing through poles; highest point reached by star etc.; period of greatest splendour

meringue' [mə-rang'] n. baked mixture of white of eggs and sugar

mer'it n. excellence, worth; quality of deserving reward –vt. deserve –**merito'rious** a.

mer'maid n. imaginary sea creature half woman, half fish

merr'y a. joyous, cheerful –**merr'ily** adv. –**merr'iment** n. –**merry-go-round** n. roundabout

mesh n. (one of the open spaces of, or wires etc. forming) network, net –v. (cause to) entangle, engage

mes'merize vt. hypnotize

mess n. untidy confusion; trouble; (place where) group regularly eat together –vi. potter (about) –vt. muddle –**mess'y** a.

mess'age n. communication sent; meaning, moral –**mess'enger** n.

Messrs. [mes'əz] pl. of Mr.

met pt./pp. of MEET

meta- (comb. form) change, as in metamorphosis

metab'olism n. chemical process of living body –**metabol'ic** a.

met'al n. mineral substance, malleable and capable of conducting heat and electricity –**metall'ic** a. –**metall'urgist** n. –**metall'urgy** n. scientific study of metals

metamor'phosis n. change of shape, character etc. (pl. -phoses [-ēz])

met'aphor n. figure of speech in which term is transferred to something it does not literally apply to –**metaphor'ical** [-for'i-] a.

metaphys'ical a. abstract; abstruse

mete vt. –**mete out** distribute; allot

me'teor n. small, fast-moving celestial body, visible as streak of incandescence if it enters earth's atmosphere –**meteor'ic** [-o'rik] a. of meteor; brilliant but short-lived –**me'teorite** n. fallen meteor

meteorol'ogy n. study of climate, weather –**meteorolog'ical** a. –**meteorol'ogist** n.

me'ter n. instrument for recording, measuring

me'thane n. inflammable gas, compound of carbon and hydrogen

meth'od n. way, manner; technique; orderliness –**method'ical** a. orderly

meth'ylated spir'its alcoholic mixture used as fuel etc.

metic'ulous a. (over-)particular about details

Métis' [mē-tēs'] n. C person of mixed parentage

me'tre n. unit of length in decimal system; SI unit of length; rhythm of poem –**met'ric** a. of system of weights and measures in which metre is a unit

Met'ro n. C metropolitan city administration

met'ronome n. instrument which marks musical time by means of ticking pendulum

metrop'olis n. chief city of a region (pl. -lises) –**metropol'itan** a.

met'tle n. courage, spirit –**met'tlesome** a. high-spirited

mew n./vi. (utter) cry of cat, gull

mews pl.n. (used as sing.) yard, street orig. of stables, now oft. converted to houses

mezz'anine [mets'ə-nēn, mez'ə-] n. intermediate storey, balcony between two main storeys

mezz'o-sopra'no [mets'ō-] n. voice, singer between soprano and contralto (pl. -nos)

mg milligram(s)

MI Military Intelligence

mias'ma [-z-] n. unwholesome atmosphere (pl. -mata, -mas)

mi'ca n. mineral found as glittering scales, plates

mi'crobe n. minute organism; disease germ

mi'crocopy n. minute photographic replica

mi'crocosm n. miniature representation of larger system

mi'crofiche [-fēsh] n. microfilm in sheet form

mi'crofilm n. miniaturized recording of manuscript, book on roll of film

mi'cron n. unit of length, one millionth of a metre

mi'crophone n. instrument for amplifying, transmitting sounds

mi'croscope n. instrument by which very small body is magnified -microscop'ic a. very small

mid a. intermediate -mid'day n. noon -mid'land n. middle part of country -mid'night n. twelve o'clock at night -mid'way a./adv. halfway

mid'dle a. equidistant from two extremes -n. middle point or part -mid'dling a. mediocre; moderate -adv. -middle class social class of businessmen, professional people etc. -mid'dleman n. trader between producer and consumer

midge n. gnat or similar insect

midg'et [mij'it] n. very small person or thing

mid'riff n. middle part of body

midst prep. in the middle of -n. middle

mid'wife n. trained person who assists at childbirth -mid'wifery [-wif-əri] n.

mien [mēn] n. person's manner or appearance

might[1] [mīt] see MAY

might[2] [mīt] n. power, strength -might'ily adv. -might'y a.

mi'graine [mē'grān] n. severe headache

migrate[1] [mī-] vi. move from one place to another -mi'grant n./a. -migra'tion n.

mike n. inf. microphone

mild [-ī-] a. not strongly flavoured; gentle; temperate

mil'dew n. destructive fungus on plants or things exposed to damp

mile n. measure of length, 1760 yards, 1.609 km -mile'age n. travelling expenses per mile; miles travelled (per gallon of petrol) -mile'stone n. significant event

mi'lieu [mē'lyə] n. environment

mil'itary a. of, for, soldiers, armies or war -mil'itant a. aggressive, vigorous in support of cause; prepared to fight -mil'itarism n. enthu-

siasm for military force and methods -mili'tia [-ish'ə] n. military force of citizens for home service

mil'itate vi. (esp. with against) have strong influence, effect on

milk n. white fluid with which mammals feed their young; fluid in some plants -vt. draw milk from -milk'y a. -milk teeth first set of teeth in young mammals

mill n. factory; machine for grinding, pulverizing corn, paper etc. -vt. put through mill; cut fine grooves across edges of (eg coins) -vi. move in confused manner -mill'er n. -mill'stone n. flat circular stone for grinding

millenn'ium n. period of a thousand years; period of peace, happiness (pl. -iums, -ia)

mill'epede, mill'ipede n. small animal with many pairs of legs

mill'et n. a cereal grass

milli- (comb. form) thousandth, as in **mill'igram** n. thousandth part of a gram -**mill'ilitre** n. -**mill'imetre** n.

mill'iner n. maker of women's hats -mill'inery n.

mill'ion n. 1000 thousands -million-aire' n. owner of a million pounds, dollars etc. -mill'ionth a./n.

mime n. acting without words -v.

mim'ic vt. imitate esp. for satirical effect (mim'icked, mim'icking) -n. one who does this

mimo'sa n. plant with fluffy, yellow flowers

minaret' n. tall slender tower of mosque

mince vt. cut, chop small; soften (words etc.) -vi. walk, speak in affected manner -n. minced meat -min'cer n. -mince'meat n. mixture of currants, spices, suet etc.

mind [-ī-] n. intellectual faculties; memory; intention; taste; sanity -vt. take offence at; care for; attend to -vi. heed

mine[1] pron. belonging to me

mine[2] n. deep hole for digging out coal, metals etc.; hidden deposit of explosive to blow up ship etc. -vt. dig from mine; place explosive mines in, on -mi'ner n. -mine'field n. area of land or sea containing mines

min'eral n. naturally occurring inorganic substance -a. -mineralog'-ical a. -mineral'ogy n. science of minerals

min'gle [-ng'g-] v. mix, blend

min'i n. something small or miniature; short skirt -a.

min'iature [-it-] n. small painted portrait; anything on small scale -a.

min'ibus n. small bus

min'im n. unit of fluid measure Mus. note half the length of semibreve

min'imize vt. bring to, estimate at smallest possible amount -**min'imum** n. lowest size or quantity -a. (pl. -mums, -ma)

min'ion n. servile dependant

min'ister n. person in charge of department of State; diplomatic representative; clergyman -vi. take care of -**ministe'rial** a. -**ministra'tion** n. rendering help -**min'istry** n. office of clergyman; ministers forming government

mink n. variety of weasel

minn'ow [-ō] n. small freshwater fish

mi'nor a. lesser; under age -n. person below age of legal majority; scale in music -**minor'ity** n. lesser number, group; state of being a minor

min'ster n. cathedral, large church

min'strel n. medieval singer, musician, poet

mint'¹ n. place where money is coined -vt. coin, invent

mint'² n. aromatic plant

minuet' n. stately dance

mi'nus prep./a. less; lacking; negative -n. the sign of subtraction (-)

minute'¹ [mī-nyōōt'] a. very small; precise

min'ute'² [min'it] n. 60th part of hour or degree -pl. record of proceedings of meeting etc.

minx n. bold, flirtatious woman

mir'acle n. supernatural event; marvel -**mirac'ulous** a.

mir'age [-ahzh] n. deceptive image in atmosphere

mire n. swampy ground, mud

mirr'or n. glass or polished surface reflecting images

mirth n. merriment, gaiety

mis- (comb. form) wrong(ly), bad(ly), as in the list that follows

misadven'ture n. unlucky chance

mis'anthrope, misan'thropist n. hater of mankind

misappro'priate vt. put to dishonest use; embezzle

miscarr'y vi. bring forth young prematurely; fail -**miscarr'iage** n.

miscella'neous a. mixed -**miscell'any** n. medley

mischance' n. unlucky event

mis'chief [-chif] n. annoying behaviour; inclination to tease; harm, annoyance -**mis'chievous** a.

mis'creant n. evildoer

misdemea'nour n. minor offence

mi'ser n. hoarder of money

mis'erable [-z-] a. very unhappy; causing misery; worthless; squalid -**mis'ery** n.

misfire' vi. fail to fire, start etc.

mis'fit n. esp. person not suited to his environment

misgiv'ing n. (oft. pl.) feeling of fear; doubt etc.

misguid'ed a. foolish

mis'hap n. minor accident

mislay' vt. put in place which cannot later be remembered

mislead' vt. give false information to (**misled'** pt./pp.)

misno'mer n. wrong name or term

misog'yny [-oj'-] n. hatred of women -**misog'ynist** n.

Miss n. title of unmarried woman; (m-) girl

miss vt. fail to hit, reach, catch etc.; omit; notice or regret absence of; avoid -n. fact, instance of missing

miss'al n. book containing prayers etc. of the Mass

miss'ile n. that which may be thrown, shot, homed to damage, destroy

miss'ion [mish'ən] n. specific duty; delegation; those sent -**miss'ionary** n. one sent to a place, society to spread religion

miss'ive [-iv] n. letter

mist n. water vapour in fine drops -**mis'ty** a.

mistake' n. error -vt. fail to understand; take (person or thing) for another

mis'ter n. title of courtesy to man (abbrev. Mr.)

mis'tletoe [mis'əl-] n. evergreen parasitic plant

mis'tress n. object of man's illicit love; woman with mastery or control;

---

misbehave'   misfor'tune   misspell'
miscon'duct   misjudge'   misunderstand'
mis'deed   mis'print   misuse'
              missha'pen

woman teacher; *obs.* title given to married woman (*abbrev.* **Mrs.** [misˈiz])

mite *n.* very small insect; anything very small

mitˈigate *vt.* make less severe

miˈtre [-tər] *n.* bishop's headdress; right-angled joint

mitt *n.* glove leaving fingers bare; baseball glove

mittˈen *n.* glove with two compartments for thumb and fingers

mix *vt.* put together, combine, blend -*vi.* be mixed; associate -**mixed** *a.* of different elements, races *etc.* -**mixˈture** *n.*

ml millilitre(s)

MLA C Member of the Legislative Assembly

mm millimetre(s)

MNA C Member of the National Assembly

mnemonˈic [n-] *n.* something to help the memory

moan *v./n.* (utter) low murmur, usually of pain

moat *n.* deep wide ditch *esp.* round castle

mob *n.* disorderly crowd -*vt.* attack in mob, hustle (**-bb-**)

moˈbile *a.* capable of movement; easily changed -*n.* hanging structure designed to move in air currents -**mobilˈity** *n.*

moˈbilize *v.* prepare, *esp.* for military service -**mobilizaˈtion** *n.*

moccˈasin *n.* Amer. Indian soft shoe, usu. of deerskin

mock *vt.* ridicule; mimic -*a.* sham -**mockˈery** *n.* derision; travesty

mode *n.* manner; prevailing fashion -**moˈdish** *a.* fashionable

modˈel *n.* miniature representation; pattern; one worthy of imitation; person employed to pose, or display clothing -*vt.* make model of; mould; display (clothing) (**-ll-**)

modˈerate [-ər-et] *a.* not going to extremes -*n.* person of moderate views -*v.* [-ər-āt] make, become less excessive; preside over -**moderaˈtion** *n.*

modˈern *a.* of present or recent times; in current fashion -**modˈernity** *n.* -**modˈernize** *vt.* bring up to date

modˈest *a.* not overrating one's qualities or achievements; moderate; decent -**modˈesty** *n.*

modˈicum *n.* small quantity

modˈify [-fī] *v.* (mainly tr.) change

slightly (**-fied, -fying**) -**modificaˈtion** *n.*

modˈulate *vt.* regulate; vary in tone -**modulaˈtion** *n.*

modˈule *n.* (detachable) component with specific function

moˈgul *n.* powerful person

moˈhair *n.* cloth of goat's hair

Mohammˈedan *a./n.* Muslim

moist *a.* slightly wet -**moistˈen** [moiˈsən] *v.* -**moisˈture** *n.* liquid, *esp.* diffused or in drops

moˈlar *n./a.* (tooth) for grinding

molassˈes [-iz] *n.* syrup, by-product of sugar refining

mole[1] *n.* small dark protuberant spot on the skin

mole[2] *n.* small burrowing animal

mole[3] *n.* pier or breakwater

molˈecule *n.* simplest freely existing chemical unit -**molecˈular** *a.*

molest *vt.* pester, interfere with so as to annoy or injure -**molestaˈtion** *n.*

moll *sl. n.* gangster's female accomplice

mollˈify *vt.* calm down, placate (**-fied, -fying**) -**mollificaˈtion** *n.*

mollˈusc [-əsk] *n.* soft-bodied, usu. hard-shelled animal, *eg* snail

mollˈycoddle *v.* pamper

molten *see* MELT

moˈment *n.* short space of, (present) point in, time -**moˈmentarily** *adv.* -**moˈmentary** *a.* lasting only a moment

momenˈtous *a.* of great importance

momenˈtum *n.* force of a moving body; impetus gained from motion (*pl.* **-ta, -tums**)

monˈarch [-k] *n.* sovereign ruler -**monˈarchy** *n.* state ruled by sovereign; his rule

monˈastery *n.* house occupied by a religious order -**monasˈtic** *a.* -**monasˈticism** *n.*

Monˈday [munˈdi] *n.* second day of the week

monˈey [munˈi] *n.* banknotes, coin *etc.*, used as medium of exchange (*pl.* **-eys, -ies**) -**monˈetary** *a.* -**monˈeyed, monˈied** *a.* rich

monˈgolism [-ng·g-] *n.* form of physical and mental retardation -**monˈgol** *n./a.*

monˈgoose [-ng·g-] *n.* small animal of Asia and Africa (*pl.* **-gooses**)

monˈgrel [mungˈg-] *n.* animal of mixed breed; hybrid

monˈitor *n.* person or device which

checks, controls, warns, records; pupil assisting teacher with odd jobs; type of large lizard -vt. watch, check on

monk [munk] n. one of a religious community of men living apart under vows

monk'ey [munk'i] n. long-tailed primate -vi. meddle (with) -monkey puzzle coniferous tree with sharp stiff leaves

mono- (comb. form) single, as in monosyllab'ic a.

mon'ochrome n. of one colour

mon'ocle n. single eyeglass

mon'ogram n. design of letters interwoven

mon'ograph n. short book on single subject

mon'ologue [-log] n. long speech by one person

mon'oplane n. aeroplane with one pair of wings

monop'oly n. exclusive possession of trade, privilege etc. -monop'olize vt. claim, take exclusive possession of

mon'orail n. railway with cars running on single rail

mon'otone n. continuing on one note -monot'onous a. lacking variety, dull -monot'ony n.

monsoon' n. seasonal wind of SE Asia; very heavy rainfall season

mon'ster n. fantastic imaginary beast; huge or misshapen person, animal or thing -monstros'ity n. monstrous being; deformity -mon'strous a. enormous; horrible

month [munth] n. one of twelve periods into which the year is divided -month'ly a./adv. once a month

mon'ument n. anything that commemorates, esp. a building or statue -monument'al a.

moo vi./n. (make) cry of cow

mooch vi. sl. loaf, slouch

mood[1] n. state of mind and feelings -mood'y a. gloomy; changeable in mood

mood[2] n. Grammar form indicating function of verb

moon n. satellite which revolves round earth; any secondary planet -vi. go about dreamily -moon'light n.

moor[1] n. tract of open uncultivated land, often heather-clad

moor[2] v. secure (ship) with chains or ropes -moor'ings pl.n. ropes etc. for mooring

moose n. N Amer. deer

moot a. debatable -vt. bring for discussion

mop n. yarn, cloth etc. on end of stick, used for cleaning; tangle (of hair etc.) -vt. clean, wipe as with mop (-pp-)

mope vi. be gloomy, apathetic

mo'ped n. light motorized bicycle

moraine' n. accumulated mass of debris deposited by glacier

mor'al [mo'-] a. pert. to right and wrong conduct; of good conduct -n. practical lesson, eg of fable -pl. habits with respect to right and wrong -moral'ity n. good moral conduct; moral goodness or badness -mor'alize vi. write, think about moral aspect of things

morale' [-ahl'] n. degree of confidence, hope

morass' n. marsh; mess

morato'rium n. authorized postponement of payments etc. (pl. -ria)

mor'bid a. unduly interested in death; gruesome; diseased

mor'dant a. biting; corrosive

more a./pron. greater or additional (amount or number -comp. of MANY and MUCH -adv. to a greater extent; in addition -more'over adv. besides

mor'gen n. SA land unit, approx. two acres (0.8 hectare)

morgue [mawg] n. mortuary

mor'ibund [mo'ri-] a. dying

morn'ing n. early part of day until noon -morn n. Poet. morning

morocc'o n. goatskin leather

mor'on n. mentally deficient person

morose' [-ōs'] a. sullen, moody

morph'ia, morph'ine n. extract of opium used to relieve pain

morr'ow [mo'rō] n. Poet. next day

Morse n. telegraphic signalling in which letters are represented by dots and dashes

mor'sel n. small piece

mor'tal a. subject to death; causing death -n. mortal creature -mortal'ity n. state of being mortal; death rate

mor'tar n. mixture of lime, sand and water for holding bricks together; small cannon; vessel in which substances are pounded -mor'tarboard n. square academic cap

mort'gage [maw'gij] n. conveyance of property as security for debt -vt.

mor'tify vt. humiliate; subdue by self-denial -vi. (of flesh) be affected with gangrene (**-fled, -fying**) **-mor·ti·fi·ca'tion** n.

mor'tise [-tis] n. hole in piece of wood etc. to receive the tongue (tenon) and end of another piece

mor'tuary n. building where corpses are kept before burial

mo·sa'ic [mō-zā'ik] n. picture or pattern of small bits of coloured stone, glass etc.

mosque [mosk] n. Muslim temple

mosqui'to [-kē'tō] n. flying, biting insect (pl. **-toes**)

moss n. small plant growing in masses on moist surfaces **-moss'y** a.

moss'ie n. SA Cape sparrow

most [mō-] a./n. (of) greatest number, amount or degree **-sup.** of MUCH and of MANY **-adv.** in the greatest degree **-most'ly** adv. generally

MOT Ministry of Transport

mo'tel [mō-] n. roadside hotel for motorists

moth n. usu. nocturnal insect like butterfly **-moth'ball** n. small ball of chemical to repel moths from stored clothing etc. **-vt.** store, postpone etc. **-moth'eaten** a. damaged by grub of moth; scruffy

moth'er [muTH·] n. female parent; head of religious community of women **-a.** inborn **-vt.** act as mother to **-moth'erly** a. **-mother-in-law** n. mother of one's wife or husband **-mother of pearl** iridescent lining of certain shells

motif' [mō-tēf'] n. dominating theme

mo'tion n. process or action or way of moving; proposal in meeting **-vt.** direct by sign **-mo'tionless** a.

mo'tive n. that which makes person act in particular way **-mo'tivate** vt. incite **-motiva'tion** n.

mot'ley a. varied; multicoloured

mo'tocross n. motorcycle race over rough course

mo'tor n. that which imparts movement; machine to supply motive power **-vi.** travel by car **-mo'torist** n. **-mo'torbike, mo'torcycle -mo'torway** n. main road for fast-moving traffic

mot'tle vt. mark with blotches

mot'to n. saying adopted as rule of conduct (pl. **-es**)

mould¹ [mōld] n. hollow object in which metal etc. is cast; character; shape **-vt.** shape **-mould'ing** n. ornamental edging

mould² [mōld] n. fungoid growth caused by dampness **-mould'y** a.

mould³ [mōld] n. loose or surface earth **-mould'er** vi. decay

moult [mōlt] v. cast or shed fur, feathers etc. **-n.**

mound n. heap; small hill

mount vi. rise; increase; get on horseback **-vt.** get up on; frame (picture); set up **-n.** support; horse; hill

moun'tain n. hill of great size **-mountaineer'** n. one who lives among or climbs mountains **-moun'tainous** a.

moun'tebank [-ti-] n. charlatan, fake

mourn [-aw-] v. feel, show sorrow (for) **-mourn'er** n. **-mourn'ful** a. sad; dismal **-mourn'ing** n. grieving; clothes of mourner

mouse n. small rodent (pl. **mice**) **-mous'y** a. like mouse, esp. in colour

moustache¹ [mə-stahsh'] n. hair on the upper lip

mouth [-th; pl. -THZ] n. opening in head for eating, speaking etc.; opening, entrance **-vt.** [-TH] form (words) with lips without speaking **-mouth'piece** n. end of anything placed between lips

move [mōōv] vt. change position of; stir emotions of; incite; propose **-vi.** change places; change one's dwelling etc. **-n.** a moving; motion **-move(e)'able** a./n. **-move'ment** n. moving; moving parts; division of piece of music

mow [mō] v. cut (grass etc.) (**mown** pp.) **-mow'er** n.

MP Member of Parliament; Military Police; Mounted Police

mpg miles per gallon

mph miles per hour

Ms [miz] title used instead of Miss or Mrs.

MS(S) manuscript(s)

MST US, C Mountain Standard Time

much a. existing in quantity (**more** comp., **most** sup.) **-n.** large amount; important matter **-adv.** in a great degree; nearly

muck n. dung; dirt **-muck'y** a.

mu'cus n. fluid secreted by **mucous membrane**, lining of body cavities

mud n. wet and soft earth **-mudd'y** a.

mud'dle vt. (esp. with up) confuse; bewilder; mismanage **-n.**

muff¹ n. tube-shaped covering to keep the hands warm

muff² *vt.* bungle, fail in

muf'fle *vt.* wrap up, esp. to deaden sound -**muf'fler** *n.* scarf

mug¹ *n.* drinking cup

mug² *n. sl.* face; *sl.* fool, simpleton -*vt.* rob violently -**mug'ger** *n.*

mug³ *vi. inf.* (esp. *with* up) study hard

mug'gy *a.* damp and stifling

muk'luk *n.* C Eskimo's soft (sealskin) boot

mul'berry *n.* tree whose leaves are used to feed silkworms

mulch *n.* straw, leaves *etc.*, spread as protection for roots of plants -*vt.* protect thus

mule *n.* cross between horse and ass; hybrid -**mul'ish** *a.* obstinate

mull *vt.* heat (wine) with sugar and spices; think (over)

mul'lion *n.* upright dividing bar in window

multi-, mult- (*comb. form*) many, as in **multistor'ey** *a.*

multifa'rious *a.* of various kinds or parts

mul'tiple *a.* having many parts -*n.* quantity which contains another an exact number of times -**multiplica'tion** *n.* -**multiplic'ity** [-plis'-] *n.* variety, greatness in number -**mul'tiply** *v.* increase; add a number to itself a given number of times (-**plied,** -**plying**)

mul'titude *n.* great number -**multitu'dinous** *a.*

mum'ble *v.* speak indistinctly

mum'mer *n.* actor in dumb show -**mum'mery** *n.* dumb show acting

mum'my *n.* embalmed body -**mum'mify** *vt.* (-**fied,** -**fying**)

mumps *pl.n.* infectious disease marked by swelling in neck

munch *v.* chew vigorously

mundane' *a.* ordinary, everyday; earthly

munic'ipal [myōō-nis'-] *a.* belonging to affairs of city or town -**municipal'ity** *n.* city or town with local self-government

munif'icent [myōō-] *a.* very generous -**munif'icence** *n.*

muni'tion [myōō-nish'-] *n.* (usu. *pl.*) military stores

mur'al [myoor'-] *n.* painting on a wall

mur'der *n.* unlawful premeditated killing of human being -*vt.* kill thus -**mur'derer** *n.* -**mur'derous** *a.*

murk *n.* darkness -**murk'y** *a.*

mur'mur *n.* low, indistinct sound -*v.* make, utter such a sound; complain

mus'cle [mus'al] *n.* part of body which produces movement by contracting; system of muscles -**mus'cular** *a.* strong; of muscle

muse [myōōz] *vi.* ponder; be lost in thought -*n.* musing; reverie; goddess inspiring creative artist

muse'um [myōō-zē'-] *n.* (place housing) collection of historical *etc.* objects

mush *n.* soft pulpy mass -**mush'y** *a.*

mush'room *n.* fungoid growth, typically with stem and cap -*vi.* shoot up rapidly

mu'sic [-z-] *n.* art form using harmonious combination of notes; composition in this art -**mu'sical** *a.* of, like, interested in music -*n.* show, film in which music plays essential part -**musi'cian** [-zish'ən] *n.*

musk *n.* scent obtained from gland of musk deer -**musk'y** *a.* -**musk'rat** *n.* N Amer. rodent found near water; its fur

mus'keg *n.* C boggy hollow

mus'ket *n. Hist.* infantryman's gun

Mus'lim, Mos'lem *n.* follower of religion of Islam -*a.*

mus'lin [-z-] *n.* fine cotton fabric

muss'el *n.* bivalve shellfish

must *v. aux.* be obliged to, or certain to

mus'tang *n.* wild horse

mus'tard *n.* powder made from the seeds of a plant, used in paste as a condiment

mus'ter *v.* assemble -*n.* assembly, esp. for exercise, inspection

mus'ty *a.* mouldy, stale

mutate' [myōō-] *v.* (cause to) undergo mutation -**muta'tion** *n.* change, esp. genetic change causing divergence from kind or racial type

mute *a.* dumb; silent -*n.* dumb person; *Mus.* contrivance to soften tone of instruments -**mut'ed** *a.* muffled; subdued

mu'tilate *vt.* deprive of a limb *etc.*; damage -**mutila'tion** *n.*

mu'tiny *n.* rebellion against authority, esp. against officers of disciplined body -*vi.* commit mutiny (**mu'tinied, mu'tinying**) -**mu'tinous** *a.*

mutt'er *v.* speak, utter indistinctly; grumble -*n.*

mutt'on *n.* flesh of sheep used as food

mu'tual *a.* done, possessed *etc.*, by

each of two with respect to the other; *inf.* common

muz'zle *n.* mouth and nose of animal; cover for these to prevent biting; open end of gun -*vt.* put muzzle on

muzz'y *a.* indistinct, confused

MV motor vessel

my *a.* belonging to me -**myself'** *pron.* emphatic or reflexive form of I or ME

my'na(h) *n.* Indian bird related to starling

myo'pia *n.* short-sightedness -**myop'ic** *a.*

myr'iad [mir'-] *n.* large indefinite number

myrrh [mer] *n.* aromatic gum, formerly used as incense

myr'tle [mer'-] *n.* flowering evergreen shrub

myself' *see* MY

mys'tery [mis'-] *n.* obscure or secret thing; anything strange or inexplicable -**myste'rious** *a.*

mys'tic [mis'-] *n.* one who seeks divine, spiritual knowledge, *esp.* by prayer, contemplation *etc.* -**myst'ical** *a.* -**myst'icism** *n.*

myst'ify [mis'-] *vt.* bewilder, puzzle (-fied, -fying) -**mystifica'tion** *n.*

mystique' [mis-tēk'] *n.* aura of mystery, power *etc.*

myth [mith] *n.* tale with supernatural characters or events; imaginary person or object -**myth'ical** *a.* -**myth'ology** *n.* myths collectively

myxomato'sis [miks-] *n.* contagious, fatal disease of rabbits

N

N *Chem.* nitrogen

nab *inf. vt.* arrest criminal; catch suddenly (-bb-)

na'dir *n.* lowest point

nag' *v.* scold or trouble constantly (-gg-) -*n.* nagging; one who nags

nag' *n. inf.* horse; small horse for riding

nail [nāl] *n.* horny shield at ends of fingers, toes; small metal spike for fixing wood *etc.* -*vt.* fix with nails

naïve', **naïve'** [nah-ēv', nī-] *a.* simple, unaffected, ingenuous -**naïveté'**, **naïve'ty** *n.*

na'ked *a.* without clothes; exposed, bare; undisguised

name *n.* word by which person, thing *etc.* is denoted; reputation -*vt.* give name to; call by name; appoint; mention -**name'less** *a.* without a name; indescribable -**name'ly** *adv.* that is to say -**name'sake** *n.* person with same name as another

nann'y *n.* child's nurse -**nanny goat** she-goat

nap' *vi./n.* (take) short sleep (-pp-)

nap' *n.* downy surface on cloth made by projecting fibres

nape *n.* back of neck

nap'kin *n.* cloth, paper for wiping fingers or lips at table; nappy

napp'y *n.* towelling cloth to absorb baby's excrement

narciss'us *n.* genus of bulbous plants including daffodil, *esp.* one with white flowers (*pl.* -**cissi** [-ī])

narcot'ic *n.* any of a group of drugs producing numbness and stupor -*a.*

nark *vt. sl.* annoy, irritate

narrate' *vt.* tell (story) -**narra'tion** *n.* -**narr'ative** *n.* account, story -*a.* relating -**narra'tor** *n.*

narr'ow [-ō] *a.* of little breadth; limited -*v.* make, become narrow -**narrow-minded** *a.* illiberal; bigoted

na'sal [-z-] *a.* of nose -*n.* sound partly produced in nose

nastur'tium [-shəm] *n.* garden plant with red or orange flowers

nas'ty [nah-] *a.* foul, unpleasant

na'tal *a.* of birth

na'tion [-shən] *n.* people or race organized as a state -**na'tional** [nash'-] *a.* belonging to a nation -*n.* citizen -**na'tionalism** *n.* devotion to one's country; movement for independence -**na'tionalist** *n./a.* -**na'tionality** *n.* fact of belonging to particular nation -**nationaliza'tion** *n.* acquisition and management of industries by the State -**na'tionalize** *vt.* -**National Health Service** system of medical services financed mainly by taxation

na'tive *a.* inborn; born in particular place -*n.* native person, animal or plant

nativ'ity *n.* birth; (N-) birth of Christ

NATO North Atlantic Treaty Organization

natt'er *vi. inf.* talk idly

natt'y *a.* neat and smart

na'ture *n.* innate qualities of person or thing; class, sort; (*oft.* N-) power underlying all phenomena; natural unspoilt scenery -**na'tural** *a.* of nature; inborn; normal; unaffected -n. something, somebody well suited for something; *Mus.* character (♮) used to remove effect of sharp or flat preceding it -**nat'uralist** n. one who studies animals and plants -**nat'uralize** vt. admit to citizenship -**nat'urally** adv. -**na'turism** n. nudism

naugh'ty a. disobedient; *inf.* mildly indecent

nau'sea [-si-a, -zi-a] n. feeling that precedes vomiting -**nau'seate** vt. sicken -**nau'seous** a.

nau'tical a. of seamen or ships -**nautical mile** 1852 metres

nave n. main part of church

na'vel n. small depression in abdomen where umbilical cord was attached

nav'igate v. direct, plot path of ship etc.; travel -**nav'igable** a. -**naviga'tion** n. -**nav'igator** n.

navv'y n. labourer employed on roads, railways etc.

na'vy n. fleet; warships of country with their crews -**navy-blue** -**na'val** a. of the navy -**navy-blue** a. very dark blue

nay adv. *obs.* no

NB nota bene

N.B. New Brunswick

NCO noncommissioned officer

ne- (*comb. form*) not

near prep. close to -adv. at or to a short distance -a. close at hand; closely related; stingy -v. approach -**near'by** a. adjacent -**near'ly** adv. closely; almost

neat a. tidy, orderly; deft; undiluted

neb'ulous a. vague

nec'essary [nes'-] a. that must be done; inevitable -**nec'essarily** adv. -**necess'itate** vt. make necessary -**necess'ity** n. something needed; constraining power; compulsion; poverty

neck n. part of body joining head to shoulders; narrow part of anything -**neck'lace** n. ornament round the neck

nec'tar n. honey of flowers

nec'tarine [-rin] n. variety of peach

née, nee [nā] a. indicating maiden name of married woman

need vt. want, require -n. (state, instance of) want; requirement; necessity; poverty -**need'less** a. unnecessary -**need'y** a. poor, in want

nee'dle n. thin pointed piece of

metal for sewing, knitting; stylus for record player; leaf of fir -v. *inf.* goad, provoke

nefar'ious [-ār'-] a. wicked

negate' vt. deny, nullify -**nega'tion** n.

neg'ative a. expressing denial or refusal; lacking enthusiasm; not positive; of electrical charge having the same polarity as the charge of an electron -n. negative word or statement; *Photography* picture in which lights and shades are reversed

neglect' vt. take no care of; fail to do -n. fact of neglecting or being neglected

neg'ligee, -gé(e) [-zhā] n. woman's light dressing gown

neg'ligence [-jəns] n. carelessness -**neg'ligent** a. -**neg'ligible** a. very small or unimportant

nego'tiate vi. discuss with view to mutual settlement -vt. arrange by conference; transfer (bill, cheque etc.); get over (obstacle) -**nego'tiable** a. -**negotia'tion** n. -**nego'tiator** n.

Ne'gro n. member of black orig. Afr. race (pl. -es, *fem.* **Ne'gress**) -**Ne'groid** a.

neigh [nā] n./vi. (utter) cry of horse

neigh'bour [nā'bər] n. one who lives near another -**neigh'bourhood** n. district; people of a district -**neigh'bourly** a. friendly; helpful

nei'ther [nī'-, nē'-] a./pron. not the one or the other -adv. not on the one hand; not either -conj. nor yet

ne'o- (*comb. form*) new, later

neol'ogism [-j-] n. new-coined word or phrase

ne'on n. inert gas in the atmosphere, used in illuminated signs and lights

neph'ew [nev'-, nef'-] n. brother's or sister's son

nep'otism n. undue favouritism towards one's relations

nerve n. bundle of fibres conveying feeling, impulses to motion etc. to and from brain; assurance; coolness in danger; audacity -pl. sensitiveness to fear, annoyance etc. -vt. give courage to -**nerv'ous** a. excitable; apprehensive -**nerv'y** a. nervous; jumpy

nest n. place in which bird lays and hatches its eggs; animal's breeding place -vi. make, have a nest -**nest egg** (fund of) money in reserve

nes'tle [-sl] vi. settle comfortably close to something

net *n.* openwork fabric of meshes of cord *etc.* –*vt.* cover with, or catch in, net –(**-tt-**) –**net'ting** *n.* string or wire net –**net'ball** *n.* game in which ball has to be thrown through high ring of netting

net(t) *a.* left after all deductions –*vt.* gain, yield as clear profit

neth'er [-TH-] *a.* lower

net'tle *n.* plant with stinging hairs –*vt.* irritate

net'work *n.* system of intersecting lines, roads *etc.*; interconnecting group; linked broadcasting stations

neu'ral [nyoor'-] *a.* of the nerves

neural'gia [nyoor'-] *n.* pain in, along nerves

neuro'sis [nyoor'-] *n.* relatively mild mental disorder –**neurot'ic** *a./n.*

neut'er [nyōōt'-] *a.* neither masculine nor feminine –*vt.* castrate (animals)

neut'ral [nyōō'-] *a.* taking neither side in war, dispute *etc.*; without marked qualities –*n.* neutral nation or a subject of one; position of disengaged gears –**neutral'ity** *n.* –**neu'tralize** *vt.* make ineffective

neu'tron [nyōō'-] *n.* electrically neutral particle of the nucleus of an atom

nev'er *adv.* at no time –**nev'ertheless'** *adv.* for all that

new *a.* not existing before, fresh; unfamiliar –*adv.* (*usu.* **new'ly**) recently, fresh –**new'ly** *adv.* –**new'comer** *n.* recent arrival –**new'fang'led** [-ng'gld] *a.* of new fashion

news *n.* report of recent happenings; interesting fact not previously known –**news'cast** *n.* news broadcast –**news'paper** *n.* periodical publication containing news –**news'reel** *n.* cinema or television film giving news

newt *n.* small, tailed amphibian

next *a./adv.* nearest; immediately following

Nfld. Newfoundland

NHS National Health Service

nib *n.* (split) pen point

nib'ble *v.* take little bites of –*n.* little bite

nice *a.* pleasant; friendly; kind; subtle, fine; careful, exact –**nice'ly** *adv.* –**ni'cety** [-si-ti] *n.* minute distinction or detail

niche [nich, nēsh] *n.* recess in wall

nick *vt.* make notch in, indent; *sl.* steal –*n.* notch; exact point of time; *sl.* prison

nick'el *n.* silver-white metal much used in alloys and plating; *US, C* five cent piece

nick'name *n.* familiar name

nic'otine [-ēn] *n.* poisonous oily liquid in tobacco

niece *n.* brother's or sister's daughter

nif'ty *inf.* *a.* smart; quick

nigg'ard *n.* mean, stingy person –**nigg'ardly** *a./adv.*

nig'gle *vi.* find fault continually; annoy

nigh [nī] *a./adv./prep., obs.* or *Poet.* near

night [nīt] *n.* time of darkness between sunset and sunrise –**night'ie**, **night'y** *n.* woman's nightdress –**night'ly** *a./adv.* (happening, done) every night –**night'dress** *n.* woman's loose robe worn in bed –**night'ingale** [-ng-g-] *n.* small bird which sings *usu.* at night –**night'mare** *n.* very bad dream; terrifying experience –**night'shade** *n.* various plants of potato family, some with very poisonous berries –**night-time** *n.*

nil *n.* nothing, zero

nim'ble *a.* agile, quick, dexterous –**nim'bly** *adv.*

nim'bus *n.* rain or storm cloud; halo (*pl.* **-bi** [-bī], **-buses**)

nine *a./n.* cardinal number next above eight –**ninth** [-ī-] *a.* –**nine'teen'** *a./n.* nine more than ten –**nineteenth'** *a.* –**nine'ty** *a./n.* nine tens –**nine'tieth** *a.*

nip *vt.* pinch sharply; detach by pinching, bite; check growth (of plants) thus –*vi. inf.* hurry (**-pp-**) –*n.* pinch; sharp coldness of weather; short drink –**nip'per** *n.* thing that nips; *inf.* small child –*pl.* pincers –**nip'py** *inf. a.* cold; quick

nip'ple *n.* point of a breast, teat; anything like this

nit *n.* egg of louse or other parasite; *inf.* short for nitwit –**nit'wit** *n. inf.* fool

ni'trogen *n.* one of the gases making up the air –**ni'trate** *n.* compound of nitric acid and an alkali –**ni'tric** *a.* –**nitrogly'cerin(e)** [-s-] *n.* explosive liquid

no *a.* not any, not a; not at all –*adv.* expresses negative reply –*n.* refusal; denial; negative vote(r) (*pl.* **noes**) –**no-one, no one** nobody

no. number

no'ble *a.* of the nobility; having high

moral qualities; impressive –n. member of the nobility –n. class holding special rank; being noble –no'bleman n. –no'bly adv.

no'body n. no person; person of no importance

noctur'nal a. of, in, by, night

nod v. bow head slightly and quickly in assent, command etc.; let head droop with sleep (-dd-) –n. act of nodding

node n. knot or knob

nod'ule n. little knot; rounded irregular mineral mass

noise n. any sound, esp. disturbing one –vt. rumour –nois'ily adv. –nois'y a.

no'mad n. member of wandering tribe; wanderer –nomad'ic a.

nom'inal a. in name only; (of fee etc.) small

nom'inate vt. propose as candidate; appoint to office –nomina'tion n. –nom'inator n. –nominee' n. candidate

non- (comb. form) negatives the idea of the simple word, as in the list that follows

non'chalant [-sh-] a. casually unconcerned, indifferent –non'chalance n.

noncom'batant n. civilian during war; member of army who does not fight

noncommiss'ioned off'icer Mil. subordinate officer, risen from the ranks

noncommitt'al a. avoiding definite preference or pledge

nonconform'ist n. dissenter, esp. from Established Church

non'descript a. lacking distinctive characteristics

none [nun] pron. no-one, not any –a. no –adv. in no way –nonethe'less' adv. despite that, however

nonen'tity n. insignificant person, thing

nonflamm'able a. not easily set on fire

non'pareil [-rəl] n./a. (person or thing) unequalled or unrivalled

nonplus' vt. disconcert (-ss-)

non'sense n. absurd language; absurdity; silly conduct

noo'dle n. strip of pasta served in soup etc.

nook n. sheltered corner

noon [-ōō-] n. midday, twelve o'clock

noose [-ōō-] n. running loop; snare

nor conj. and not

norm n. average level; standard –nor'mal a. ordinary; usual; conforming to type –n. –normal'ity n. –nor'mally adv.

north [-th] n. direction to the right of person facing the sunset –adv./a. from, towards or in the north –nor'therly [-TH-] a. –n. wind from the north –nor'thern a. –north'wards adv.

nos. numbers

nose n. organ of smell, used also in breathing; any projection resembling a nose –v. (cause) to move forward slowly and carefully –vt. touch with nose; smell, sniff –vi. smell; pry –no'-s(e)y a. inf. inquisitive

nostal'gia [-j-] n. longing for past events –nostal'gic a.

nos'tril n. one of the two external openings of the nose

not adv. expressing negation, refusal, denial

no'ta be'ne [-ni] Lat. note well

no'table a./n. remarkable (person) –notabil'ity n. an eminent person –no'tably adv.

no'tary n. person authorized to draw up deeds, contracts

nota'tion n. representation of numbers, quantities, by symbols; C footnote, memorandum

notch n./vt. (make) V-shaped cut

note n. brief comment or record; short letter; banknote; symbol for musical sound; single tone; fame; notice –vt. observe, record; heed –no'ted a. well-known –note'book n. small book with blank pages for writing

noth'ing [nuth'-] n. no thing; not anything, nought –adv. not at all, in no way

no'tice [-tis] n. observation; attention; warning, announcement –vt.

observe, mention; give attention to -no'ticeable a.

no'tify vt. give notice of or to (-fied, -fying) -notifi'able a.

no'tion n. concept; opinion; whim

notor'ious a. known for something bad -notori'ety n.

notwithstand'ing prep. in spite of -adv. all the same -conj. although

nou'gat [noo'gah, nug'ət] n. chewy sweet containing nuts, fruit etc.

nought [nawt] n. nothing; cipher 0

noun [nown] n. word used as name of person, idea, or thing

nour'ish [nu'-] vt. feed; nurture -nour'ishment n.

Nov. November

nov'el[1] n. fictitious tale in book form -nov'elist n.

nov'el[2] a. new, recent; strange -nov'elty n. newness; something new; small trinket

Novem'ber n. the eleventh month

nov'ice n. beginner

now adv. at the present time; immediately; recently (oft. with just) -conj. seeing that, since -now'adays adv. in these times, at present

no'where adv. not in any place or state

nox'ious [-k'shəs] a. poisonous, harmful

noz'zle n. pointed spout, esp. at end of hose

N.S. Nova Scotia

NSPCC National Society for the Prevention of Cruelty to Children

NST Newfoundland Standard Time

nuance[1] [nyoo-ahns', nyoo-] n. delicate shade of difference

nub n. small lump; main point

nu'cleus n. centre, kernel; core of the atom -pl. -lei [-li-ī] -nu'clear [-i-ər] a. of, pert. to atomic nucleus -nuclear energy energy released by nuclear fission -nuclear fission disintegration of the atom -nuclear reactor see REACTOR

nude [nyood] n./a. naked (person) -nu'dism n. practice of nudity -nu'dist n. -nu'dity n.

nudge vt. touch slightly with elbow -n. such touch

nugg'et n. lump of native gold

nui'sance [nyoo-] n. something or someone annoying

null a. of no effect, void -null'ify vt. cancel; make useless (-fied, -fying)

numb [num] a. deprived of feeling -vt. make numb

num'ber n. sum or aggregate; word

or symbol saying how many; single issue of a paper etc.; company, collection; identifying number -vt. count; class, reckon; give a number to; amount to -num'berless a. countless

nu'meral n. sign or word denoting a number -nu'merate a. able to use numbers in calculations -vt. count -nu'merator n. top part of fraction -numer'ical a. of, in respect of, number or numbers -nu'merous a. many

num'skull n. dolt, dunce

nun n. woman living in (convent) under religious vows -nunn'ery n. convent of nuns

nup'tial a. of marriage -nup'tials pl.n. wedding

nurse n. person trained for care of sick or injured -vt. act as nurse to; suckle -nur'sery n. room for children; rearing place for plants -nursing officer administrative head of nursing staff of hospital

nur'ture n. bringing up; rearing -vt. bring up; educate

nut n. fruit consisting of hard shell and kernel; hollow metal collar into which a screw fits; inf. head; inf. crazy person (also nutt'er) -nut'meg n. aromatic seed of Indian tree

nu'trient a. nourishing -n. something nutritious

nu'triment n. nourishing food -nutri'tion [-trish'-] n. receiving foods; act of nourishing -nutri'tious, nu'tritive a.

nuz'zle vi. burrow, press with nose; nestle

N.W.T. Northwest Territories (of Canada)

ny'lon n. synthetic material used for fabrics etc. -pl. stockings of this

nymph n. legendary semidivine maiden of sea, woods etc.

O

O Chem. oxygen

oaf n. lout; dolt

oak n. common, deciduous forest tree -oak'en a. of oak -oak apple round gall on oak trees

OAP old age pensioner

oar n. wooden lever with broad blade worked by the hands to propel boat; oarsman -v. row

oa'sis [ō-ā'-] *n.* fertile spot in desert (*pl.* **oa'ses** [-sēz])

oat *n.* (*usu. pl.*) grain of cereal plant; the plant –**oat'meal** *n.*

oath *n.* confirmation of truth of statement by naming something sacred; curse

ob'durate *a.* stubborn, unyielding –**ob'duracy** *n.*

OBE Officer of the Order of the British Empire

obe'dience *n.* submission to authority –**obe'dient** *a.*

ob'elisk *n.* tapering rectangular stone column

obese' *a.* very fat, corpulent –**obe'sity** *n.*

obey' [-bā'] *v.* do the bidding of; do as ordered

obit'uary *n.* notice, record of death; biographical sketch of deceased person

ob'ject[1] *n.* material thing; that to which feeling or action is directed; end or aim; *Grammar* word dependent on verb or preposition

object[2] *v.* express or feel dislike or reluctance to something –**objec'tion** *n.* –**objec'tionable** *a.*

objec'tive *a.* external to the mind; impartial –*n.* thing or place aimed at –**objectiv'ity** *n.*

oblige' *vt.* bind; compel –**ob'ligate** bind *esp.* by legal contract –**obliga'tion** *n.* binding duty, promise; debt of gratitude –**oblig'atory** *a.* required; binding –**oblig'ing** *a.* ready to serve others, helpful

oblique' [-lēk'] *a.* slanting; indirect

oblit'erate *vt.* blot out, efface, destroy completely

obliv'ion *n.* forgetting or being forgotten –**obliv'ious** *a.* forgetful; unaware

ob'long *a.* rectangular, with adjacent sides unequal –*n.* oblong figure

obnox'ious [-nok'shəs] *a.* offensive, odious

o'boe [-bō] *n.* woodwind instrument –**o'boist** *n.*

obscene' *a.* indecent, repulsive –**obscen'ity** *n.*

obscure' *a.* unclear, indistinct; dark –*vt.* make unintelligible; dim; conceal –**obscu'rity** *n.* indistinctness; lack of intelligibility; darkness; obscure place or position

obse'quious *a.* servile, fawning

observe' [-z-] *vt.* notice, remark; watch; note systematically; keep, follow –*vi.* make a remark –**observ'ance** *n.* paying attention; keeping –**observ'ant** *a.* quick to notice –**observa'tion** *n.* –**observ'atory** *n.* place for watching stars *etc.*

obsess' *vt.* haunt, fill the mind –**obses'sion** *n.*

ob'solete *a.* disused, out of date –**obsoles'cent** [-ənt] *a.* going out of use

ob'stacle *n.* obstruction

obstet'rics *pl.n.* (*with sing. v.*) branch of medicine concerned with childbirth –**obstetri'cian** *n.*

ob'stinate *a.* stubborn; hard to overcome or cure –**ob'stinacy** *n.*

obstrep'erous *a.* unruly, noisy

obstruct' *vt.* block up; hinder; impede –**obstruc'tion** *n.* –**obstruc'tive** *a.*

obtain' *vt.* get; acquire –*vi.* be customary –**obtain'able** *a.*

obtrude' *vt.* thrust forward unduly –**obtru'sion** *n.* –**obtru'sive** *a.*

obtuse' [-tyōōs'] *a.* dull of perception; stupid; greater than right angle; not pointed

ob'verse *n.* complement; principal side of coin, medal *etc.* –*a.*

ob'viate *vt.* remove, make unnecessary

ob'vious *a.* clear, evident

ocari'na [-rē-] *n.* small, egg-shaped wind instrument

occa'sion *n.* time when thing happens; reason, need; opportunity; special event –*vt.* cause –**occa'sional** *a.* happening, found now and then

Oc'cident [oks'i-] *n.* the West –**oc'cidental** *a.*

occult' *a.* secret, mysterious; supernatural

occ'upy *vt.* inhabit, fill; employ; take possession of (-**pied**, -**pying**) –**occ'upancy** *n.* fact of occupying –**occ'upant** *n.* –**occupa'tion** *n.* employment; pursuit; occupying –**occupa'tional** *a.* –**occ'upier** *n.*

occur' *vi.* happen; come to mind (-**rr**-) –**occurr'ence** *n.* happening

o'cean [ō'shən] *n.* great body of water; large division of this; the sea –**ocean'ic** [ō-shi-, ō-si-] *a.*

o'chre [ō'kər] *n.* earth used as yellow or brown pigment

o'clock' *adv.* by the clock

oc'tagon *n.* plane figure with eight angles –**octag'onal** *a.*

oc'tave *n. Mus.* eighth note above or below given note; this space

octet' *n.* (music for) group of eight

Octo'ber *n.* the tenth month

octogena'rian *n.* person aged between eighty and ninety –*a.*

oc'topus *n.* mollusc with eight arms covered with suckers

oc'ular *a.* of eye or sight

odd *a.* strange, queer; incidental; random; left over or additional; not even; not part of a set –**odds** *pl.n.* advantage conceded in betting; likelihood –**oddity** *n.* odd person or thing; quality of being odd –**odds and ends** odd fragments or scraps

ode *n.* lyric poem

o'dium *n.* hatred, widespread dislike –**o'dious** *a.*

o'dour *n.* smell –**o'dorous** *a.* fragrant; scented

of *prep.* denotes removal, separation, ownership, attribute, material, quality

off *adv.* away –*prep.* away from –*a.* not operative; cancelled or postponed; bad, sour *etc.*; distant; of horses, vehicles *etc.*, right –**off'ing** *n.* formerly, part of sea visible to observer on ship or shore –**offhand'** *a./adv.* without previous thought; curt –**off-licence** *n.* place where alcoholic drinks are sold for consumption elsewhere –**off'set** *n.* that which counterbalances, compensates; method of printing –**offset'** *vt.* –**off'spring** *n.* children, issue

off'al *n.* edible entrails of animal; refuse

offend' *vt.* hurt feelings of, displease –*vi.* do wrong –**offence'** *n.* wrong; crime; insult –**offen'sive** *a.* causing displeasure; aggressive –*n.* position or movement of attack

off'er *vt.* present for acceptance or refusal; tender; propose; attempt –*vi.* present itself –*n.* offering, bid

off'ice *n.* room(s), building, in which business, clerical work *etc.* is done; commercial or professional organization; official position; service; duty; form of worship –*pl.* task; service –**off'icer** *n.* one in command in army, navy, ship *etc.*; official

offi'cial [-fish'-] *a.* with, by authority –*n.* one holding office –**Official Receiver Official Receiver** officer who manages estate of bankrupt

offi'ciate [-fish'-] *vi.* perform duties of office, ceremony

offi'cious [-fish'əs] *a.* importunate in offering service; interfering

offside' *a./adv.* Sport illegally forward

of'ten [ofn] *adv.* many times, frequently (*Poet.* oft)

o'gee arch pointed arch with S-shaped curve on both sides

o'gle *v.* stare, look (at) amorously –*n.* this look

o'gre [-gər] *n.* Folklore man-eating giant; monster

oh [o] *interj.* exclamation of surprise, pain *etc.*

ohm *n.* unit of electrical resistance

OHMS On His (*or* Her) Majesty's Service

oil *n.* any viscous liquid with smooth, sticky feel; petroleum –*vt.* lubricate with oil –**oil'y** *a.* –**oil'skin** *n.* cloth treated with oil to make it waterproof

oint'ment *n.* greasy preparation for healing or beautifying the skin

o.k., okay' *n. inf. a./adv.* all right

okap'i [-kahp'-] *n.* Afr. animal like short-necked giraffe

old [old] *a.* aged, having lived or existed long; belonging to earlier period (**old'er, eld'er** *comp.*, **old'est, eld'est** *sup.*) –**old'en** *a.* old –**old-fashioned** *a.* in style of earlier period, out of date; fond of old ways –**old maid** elderly spinster

olfac'tory *a.* of smelling

ol'igarchy [-ki] *n.* government by a few

ol'ive [-iv] *n.* evergreen tree; its oil-yielding fruit; its wood –*a.* greyish-green

Olym'piad *n.* four-year period between Olympic Games

OM Order of Merit

o'mega [ō'-] *n.* last letter of Greek alphabet; end

om'elet(te) *n.* dish of eggs beaten up and fried

o'men *n.* prophetic happening –**om'inous** *a.* boding evil, threatening

omit' *vt.* leave out; leave undone (-tt-) –**omiss'ion** *n.*

om'nibus *n.* large passenger-carrying road vehicle (*also* **bus**); book containing several works –*a.* serving, containing several objects

omnip'otent *a.* all-powerful –**omnip'otence** *n.*

on *prep.* above and touching, at, near, towards *etc.*; attached to; concerning; performed upon; during; taking regularly –*a.* operating; taking place –*adv.* so as to be on; forwards; continuously *etc.*; in progress

once [wuns] *adv.* one time; formerly;

ever -at once immediately

one [wun] *n.* lowest cardinal number; single; united; only, without others; identical *-n.* number or figure 1; unity; single specimen *-pron.* particular but not stated person; any person *-oneself* *pron.* **-one-sided** *a.* partial; uneven

on'erous *a.* burdensome

on'ion [un'yən] *n.* edible bulb of pungent flavour

on'ly [ō-] *a.* being the one specimen *-adv.* solely, merely, exclusively *-conj.* but then, excepting that

on'set *n.* attack; beginning

on'slaught [-slawt] *n.* attack

Ont. Ontario

on'to *prep.* on top of

o'nus *n.* responsibility, burden

on'ward *a.* advanced or advancing *-adv.* in advance, ahead, forward **-on'wards** *adv.*

on'yx [on'iks] *n.* variety of chalcedony

ooze *vi.* pass slowly out, exude *-n.* sluggish flow; wet mud

o'pal *n.* glassy gemstone displaying variegated colours

opaque' [ō-pāk'] *a.* not transparent **-opac'ity** [-pas'-] *n.*

OPEC Organization of Petroleum Exporting Countries

o'pen *a.* not shut or blocked up; without lid or door; bare; undisguised; not enclosed, covered or exclusive; spread out, accessible; frank *-v.* make or become open; begin *-n.* clear space, unenclosed country **-o'pening** *n.* hole, gap; beginning; opportunity *-a.* first; initial **-o'penly** *adv.* without concealment **-open-handed** *a.* generous **-open-minded** *a.* unprejudiced

op'era *n.* musical drama **-operat'ic** *a.* **-operett'a** *n.* light opera

opera'tion *n.* working, way things work; act of surgery **-op'erate** *vt.* cause to function *-vi.* work; produce an effect; perform act of surgery **-op'erative** *a.* working *-n.* worker **-op'erator** *n.*

ophthal'mic [of-thal'-] *a.* of eyes **-ophthalmol'ogist** *n.* **-ophthalmol'ogy** *n.* study of eye and its diseases

opin'ion *n.* what one thinks about something; belief, judgment **-opin'-ionated** *a.* stubborn in one's opinions

o'pium *n.* narcotic drug made from poppy **-o'piate** *n.* drug containing opium

oposs'um *n.* small Amer. and Aust. marsupial

oppo'nent *n.* adversary, antagonist

opp'ortune *a.* seasonable, well-timed **-opportu'nist** *n.* one who grasps opportunities regardless of principle *-a.* **-opportu'nity** *n.* favourable time or condition; good chance

oppose' [-z] *vt.* resist; set against **-opp'osite** [-zit] *a.* contrary; facing *-n.* the contrary *-prep./adv.* facing; on the other side **-opposi'tion** [-ish-] *n.* resistance; hostility; group opposing another

oppress' *vt.* govern with tyranny; weigh down **-oppres'sion** *n.* **-oppres'sive** *a.* tyrannical; hard to bear; (of weather) hot and tiring **-oppres'sor** *n.*

oppro'brium *n.* disgrace **-oppro'-brious** *a.* reproachful; shameful; abusive

opt *vi* make a choice

op'tic *a.* of eye or sight *-pl.* (with sing. v.) science of sight and light **-op'tical** *a.* **-opti'cian** [-ish-] *n.* maker of, dealer in spectacles, optical instruments

op'timism *n.* disposition to look on the bright side **-op'timist** *n.* **-op-timis'tic** *a.*

op'timum *a./n.* the best, the most favourable

op'tion *n.* choice; thing chosen **-op'tional** *a.* leaving to choice

optom'etrist *n.* person testing eyesight, prescribing corrective lenses

op'ulent *a.* rich; copious **-op'u-lence**

o'pus *n.* work; musical composition

or *conj.* introduces alternatives; if not

or'acle [o'rə-] *n.* divine utterance, prophecy given at shrine of god; the shrine; wise adviser **-orac'ular** *a.*

or'al *a.* spoken; by mouth *-n.* spoken examination

or'ange [o'rinj] *n.* bright reddish-yellow round fruit; tree bearing it; fruit's colour

orang-outang', **orang-utan'** *n.* large E. Indian ape

or'ator [o'rə-] *n.* maker of speech; skilful speaker **-ora'tion** *n.* formal speech **-or'atory** [o'rə-] *n.* speeches; eloquence

orb *n.* globe

orb'it *n.* track of planet, satellite, comet *etc.*, around another heavenly body; field of influence -v. move in, or put into, an orbit

orch'ard n. area for fruit trees; the trees

or'chestra [-k-] n. band of musicians; place for such band in theatre etc. -**orches'tral** a.

or'chid, or'chis [-k-] n. genus of various flowering plants

ordain' vt. confer holy orders upon; decree, enact; destine

ordeal' n. severe, trying experience

or'der n. regular, proper or peaceful arrangement or condition; class; command; request for something to be supplied; monastic society -vt. command; request (something) to be supplied; arrange -**or'derly** a. tidy; well-behaved -n. hospital attendant; soldier following officer, to carry orders

or'dinance n. decree, rule

or'dinary a. usual, normal; commonplace -n. -**or'dinarily** adv.

ord'nance n. artillery; military stores -**ordnance survey** official geographical survey of Britain

ore n. mineral which yields metal

or'gan n. musical wind instrument of pipes and stops, played by keys; member of animal or plant with particular function; medium of information -**organ'ic** a. of, derived from, living organisms; of bodily organs; Chem. of compounds formed from carbon; organized, systematic -**or'ganist** n. organ player

or'gandie n. light, transparent muslin

or'ganize vt. give definite structure; arrange; unite in a society -**or'ganism** n. plant, animal -**organiza'tion** n. organized society

or'gasm n. sexual climax

or'gy [-ji] n. drunken or licentious revel

or'ient n. (O-) East determine (one's) position (also **or'ientate**) -**orien'tal** a./n. -**orienta'tion** n.

or'ifice [o'ri-] n. opening, mouth

or'igin [o'ri-] n. beginning; source; parentage

orig'inal [-j-] a. earliest; new, not copied; thinking or acting for oneself -n. thing from which another is copied -**original'ity** n.

orig'inate v. come or bring into existence, begin -**orig'inator** n.

or'nament n. any object used to adorn or decorate -vt. adorn -**or'namen'tal** a.

ornate' a. highly decorated or elaborate

ornithol'ogy n. science of birds -**ornithol'ogist** n.

or'phan n. child bereaved of one or both parents -**or'phanage** n. institution for care of orphans

orthodox a. holding accepted views; conventional -**or'thodoxy** n.

orthopaed'ic [-pēd'-] a. for curing deformity, disorder of bones

os'cillate vi. swing to and fro; waver

o'sier [-z-] n. species of willow used for basketwork

os'prey n. fishing hawk

oss'ify v. turn into bone; grow rigid (-**fied, -fying**)

osten'sible a. apparent; professed

ostenta'tion n. show, pretentious display -**ostenta'tious**

osteop'athy n. art of treating disease by manipulation of bones -**os'teopath** n.

os'tracize vt. exclude, banish from society -**os'tracism** n.

os'trich n. large flightless bird

oth'er [UTH'-] a. not this; not the same; alternative -pron. other person or thing -**oth'erwise** adv. differently -conj. else, if not

ott'er n. furry aquatic fish-eating animal

ouch interj. exclamation of sudden pain

ought [awt] v. aux. expressing obligation or advisability or probability

ou'ma [ō'mah] n. SA grandmother; elderly woman

ounce n. a weight, sixteenth of pound (28.4 grams)

ou'pa [ō'pah] n. SA grandfather; elderly man

our a. belonging to us -**ours** pron. -**ourselves'** pl.pron. emphatic or reflexive form of 'we'

oust vt. put out, expel

out adv. from within, away; wrong; not burning; not allowed; Sport dismissed -out'er a. away from the inside -**out'ermost, out'most** a. on extreme outside -out'ing n. pleasure excursion -**out'ward** a./adv.

outbal'ance vt. exceed in weight

out'board a. of boat's engine, mounted on, outside stern

out'break n. sudden occurrence

out'cast n. someone rejected -a.

out'come n. result

outdoors' adv. in the open air -out'door a.

out'fit n. equipment; clothes and accessories; *inf.* group or association regarded as a unit

outland'ish a. queer, extravagantly strange

out'law n. one beyond protection of the law -vt. make (someone) an outlaw; ban

out'lay n. expenditure

out'let n. means of release or escape; market

out'line n. rough sketch; general plan; lines enclosing visible figure -vt. sketch; summarize

out'look n. point of view; probable outcome

out'lying a. remote

out'put n. quantity produced; *Computers* information produced

out'rage n. violation of others' rights; shocking act; anger arising from this -vt. commit outrage -out-ra'geous a.

out'right a. undisputed; downright -adv. completely

out'set n. beginning

outside' n. exterior -adv. not inside -a. on exterior; unlikely; greatest possible -outsid'er n. person outside specific group; contestant thought un-likely to win

out'skirts pl.n. outer areas, districts, esp. of city

out'span n. SA unyoking of oxen; area for rest

outspo'ken a. frank, candid

outstand'ing a. excellent; remarkable; unsettled, unpaid

outwit' vt. get the better of by cunning

o'val a./n. egg-shaped, elliptical (thing)

o'vary n. female egg-producing organ

ova'tion n. enthusiastic burst of applause

ov'en [uv⌐] n. heated chamber for baking in

o'ver adv. above; beyond; in excess; finished; in repetition; across; downwards etc. -prep. above; upon; more than; along etc. -n. Cricket delivery of agreed number of balls from one end

over- (comb. form) too, too much, in excess, above, as in the list that follows

o'verall n. loose garment worn as protection against dirt etc. (also pl.) -a. total

overbear'ing a. domineering

o'vercast a. cloudy

overcome' vt. conquer; surmount; make incapable or powerless

overhaul' vt. examine and set in order

overhead' a./adv. over one's head, above

o'verland a./adv. by land

overlook' vt. fail to notice; disregard

o'versea(s) a./adv. foreign; from or to a place over the sea

o'verseer n. supervisor -over-see' vt. supervise

o'versight n. failure to notice; mistake

o'vert a. open, unconcealed

overtake' vt. move past; catch up

overthrow' vt. overturn; defeat -n. [0⌐] ruin; fall

o'vertime n. time at work, outside normal working hours; payment for this time

o'vertone n. additional meaning

o'verture n. Mus. orchestral introduction; opening of negotiations; formal offer

overwhelm' vt. crush; submerge -overwhelm'ing a. irresistible

overwrought' a. over excited

o'void a. egg-shaped

owe [o] vt. be bound to repay, be indebted for -ow'ing a. owed, due -owing to caused by, as result of

owl n. night bird of prey

own [on] a. emphasizes possession -vt. possess; acknowledge -vi. to confess -own'er n. -own'ership n. possession

ox n. large cloven-footed and usu. horned farm animal; bull or cow (pl. ox'en)

Ox'fam Oxford Committee for Famine Relief

ox'ide n. compound of oxygen and one other element

ox'ygen n. gas in atmosphere essential to life

oy'ster [oi⌐] n. edible mollusc

oz. ounce

o'zone n. form of oxygen with pungent odour

overbal'ance
o'vercoat

overcrowd'
o'verdose
overflow'

overpow'er
overrule'

P

P (car) park

p page; pence; penny; *Mus.* piano (softly)

pace n. step; rate of movement; eg step -vt. set speed for; measure with steps

pach'yderm [pak'-] n. thick-skinned animal, eg elephant

pac'ify [pas'-] vt. calm (-ified, -ifying) -**pacif'ic** a. peaceable; calm -**pac'ifism** n. -**pac'ifist** n. advocate of abolition of war; one who refuses to help in war

pack n. bundle; band of animals; large set of people or things -vt. put together in suitcase etc.; make into a bundle; cram; fill; order off -**pack'-age** n. parcel; set of items offered together -vt. -**pack'et** n. small parcel; small container (and contents)

pact n. covenant, agreement

pad¹ n. soft stuff used as a cushion, protection etc.; block of sheets of paper; foot or sole of various animals -vt. make soft, fill in, protect etc., with pad (-dd-)

pad² vi./n. (walk with) soft step (-dd-)

pad'dle¹ n. short oar with broad blade -v. move by, as with, paddles

pad'dle² vt. walk with bare feet in shallow water -n.

pad'dock n. small grass enclosure

padd'y field field where rice is grown

pad'lock n. detachable lock with hinged hoop -vt. fasten top

pae'an [pē'-] n. song of triumph

paediat'rics [pē-] pl.n. branch of medicine dealing with diseases of children (also US **pediat'rics**) -**paediatri'cian** n.

pa'gan a./n. heathen

page¹ n. one side of leaf of book etc.

page² n. boy attendant -v. summon by loudspeaker announcement

pag'eant [paj'ənt] n. show of persons in costume in procession, dramatic scenes etc. -**pag'eantry** n.

pago'da n. pyramidal temple of Chinese or Indian type

pail n. bucket -**pail'ful** n.

pain n. bodily or mental suffering -pl. trouble -vt. inflict pain upon -**pain'ful** a. -**pain'less** a. -**pains'-taking** a. careful

paint n. colouring matter spread on a surface -vt. colour, coat, or make picture of, with paint -**paint'er** n. -**paint'ing** n.

pair n. set of two -v. arrange in twos

pal n. inf. friend

pal'ace n. residence of king, bishop etc.; stately mansion -**pala'tial** a.

palaeontol'ogy [-li-on-] n. study of fossils

pal'ate n. roof of mouth; sense of taste -**pal'atable** a. agreeable to eat

palav'er [-ahv'-] n. fuss

pale a. wan, whitish -vi. whiten; lose superiority

pal'ette n. artist's flat board for mixing colours on

pal'indrome n. word etc. that is the same backwards or forwards

palisade' n. fence of stakes

pall¹ [pawl] n. cloth spread over a coffin -**pall'bearer** n. one carrying coffin at funeral

pall² [pawl] vi. become tiresome; cloy

pall'et n. straw mattress; small bed

pall'iasse [pal'i-as] n. straw mattress

pall'iate vt. relieve without curing; excuse -**pall'iative** a./n.

pall'id a. pale -**pall'or** n.

palm [pahm] n. inner surface of hand; tropical tree; its leaf as symbol of victory -**palm'istry** n. fortune-telling from lines on palm of hand

palomi'no [-mē'-] n. golden horse with white mane and tail

pal'pable a. obvious

pal'pitate vi. throb

pal'sy [pawl'zi] n. paralysis

pal'try [pawl'-] a. worthless

pam'pas pl.n. vast grassy treeless plains in S Amer.

pam'per vt. overindulge, spoil

pamph'let n. thin unbound book

pan¹ n. broad, shallow vessel; bowl of lavatory; depression in ground -vt. inf. criticize harshly (-nn-) -**pan out** result

pan² v. move film camera slowly while filming (-nn-)

pan-, pant-, panto- (comb. form) all, as in panacea, pantomime

panace'a [-sē'ə] n. universal remedy

panache' [-ash'] n. dashing style

panama' [-mah'] n. straw hat

pan'cake n. thin cake of batter fried in pan

pan'creas [-ng-kri-əs] n. digestive gland behind stomach

pan'da n. large black and white bearlike mammal of China

pandemo'nium n. din and uproar
pan'der v. (esp. with to) give gratification to –n. pimp
p & p postage and packing
pane n. sheet of glass
panegyr'ic [-i-jir'-] n. speech of praise
pan'el n. compartment of surface, usu. raised or sunk, eg in door; team in quiz game etc.; list of jurors, doctors etc. –vt. adorn with panels (**-ll-**) **-pan'elling** n.
pang n. sudden pain
pan'ic n. sudden and infectious fear –a. of fear etc. –v. (cause to) feel panic (**-icked, -icking**) **-pan'icky** a.
pann'ier n. basket carried by beast of burden, bicycle etc.
pan'oply n. magnificent array
panora'ma [-ahm'-] n. wide view **-panoram'ic** [-ram'-] a.
pan'sy [-zi] n. flower, species of violet; inf. effeminate man
pant vi./n. gasp
pantech'nicon [-tek'-] n. large van, esp. for carrying furniture
pan'ther n. variety of leopard
pan'ties pl.n. women's undergarment
pan'tomime n. theatrical show, usu. at Christmas time, often founded on a fairy tale; dumbshow
pan'try n. room for storing food or utensils
pants pl.n. undergarment for lower trunk; US trousers
pap n. soft food; SA maize porridge
pa'pacy [-si] n. office of Pope **-pa'pal** a. of the Pope
pa'per n. material made by pressing pulp of rags, wood etc., into thin sheets; sheet of paper; newspaper; essay –pl. documents etc. –vt. cover with paper **-pa'perback** n. book with flexible covers
papier-mâché [pap-yā-mash'ā] n. paper pulp mixed with size, shaped and dried hard
pap'rika n. red pepper
papy'rus n. species of reed; paper made from this (pl. **papy'ri** [-rī])
par n. equality of value or standing; face value; Golf estimated standard score **-par'ity** [pa'ri-] n. equality; analogy
par'a-, par-, pa- (comb. form) beside, beyond, as in parallel, parody
par'able [pa'ra-] n. allegory, story with a moral lesson
par'achute [pa'ra-shoot] n. apparatus extending like umbrella used to

retard the descent of a falling body –v. drop by parachute
parade' n. display; muster of troops –v. march; display
par'adise [pa'ra-] n. Heaven; state of bliss; Garden of Eden
par'adox [pa'ra-] n. statement that seems self-contradictory **-paradox'ical** a.
par'affin [pa'ra-] n. waxlike or liquid hydrocarbon mixture used as fuel, solvent etc.
par'agon [pa'ra-] n. pattern or model of excellence
par'agraph [pa'ra-] n. section of chapter or book –vt. arrange in paragraphs
par'akeet [pa'ra-] n. small parrot
par'allel [pa'ra-] a./n. (line or lines) continuously at equal distances; (thing) precisely corresponding –vt. represent as similar **-parallel'ogram** n. four-sided plane figure with opposite sides parallel
paral'ysis n. incapacity to move or feel (pl. **-yses** [-sēz]) **-par'alyse** [pa'ra-] vt. affect with paralysis **-paralyt'ic** a./n.
par'amount [pa'ra-] a. supreme
par'amour [pa'ra-] n. formerly, illicit lover, mistress
paranoi'a [pa-ra-] n. mental disease with delusions of persecution etc. **-par'anoid** a./n.
par'apet [pa'ra-] n. low wall along edge of bridge etc.
paraphernа'lia pl.n. (used as sing.) belongings; equipment
par'aphrase [pa'ra-] n./vt. (express) in other words
paraple'gia [-j-] n. paralysis of lower body **-paraple'gic** n./a.
par'asite [pa'ra-] n. animal or plant living in or on another **-parasit'ic** a.
par'asol [pa'ra-] n. sunshade
par'atroops, -troopers [pa'ra-] pl.n. troops trained to descend by parachute
par'boil vt. boil until partly cooked
par'cel n. packet –vt. wrap up; divide into parts (**-ll-**)
parch v. make, become hot and dry
parch'ment n. sheep, goat, calf skin prepared for writing
par'don vt. forgive, excuse –n. forgiveness; release from punishment **-par'donable** a.
pare vt. peel, trim; decrease
pa'rent n. father or mother **-pa'rentage** n. descent, extraction **-pa'rental** a.

paren'thesis n. word(s) inserted in passage **-paren'theses** [-sēz] pl.n. round brackets, ( ), used to mark this

pari'ah n. social outcast

par'ish [-a-] n. district under one clergyman **-parish'ioner** n. inhabitant of parish

par'ity see PAR

park n. large area of land in natural state for recreational use -vt. leave for a short time; manoeuvre (car) into a suitable space

park'a n. warm waterproof coat

par'ley v./n. (hold) discussion about terms

par'liament n. the legislature of the United Kingdom **-parliament'ary** a.

par'lour n. sitting room

paro'chial [-k-] a. narrow, provincial; of a parish

par'ody [pa'rə-] n./vt. (write) satirical, amusing imitation of a work (-odied, -odying)

parole' [-rōl'] n./vt. release of prisoner on condition he is of good behaviour

par'oxysm [pa'raks-] n. sudden attack of pain, rage, laughter

par'quet [-kā] n. flooring of wooden blocks

parr'ot n. brightly coloured bird which can imitate speaking

parr'y vt. ward off, turn aside (**par'ried, par'rying**)

par'simony n. stinginess **-parsimo'nious** a. sparing

pars'ley n. herb used for seasoning, garnish etc.

pars'nip n. root vegetable

par'son n. clergyman

part n. portion; role; duty; (oft. pl.) region -v. divide; separate **-part'ing** n. division of hair on head; separation; leave-taking **-part'ly** adv. in part

partake' v. take or have share in; take food or drink (**partook', -ta'ken, -ta'king**)

parti'al [-shal] a. not complete; prejudiced; fond of **-partial'ity** n. **-par'tially** adv. partly

partic'ipate [-tis'-] v. share in; take part in **-partic'ipant** n.

par'ticiple n. verbal adjective

par'ticle n. minute portion

partic'ular a. relating to one; distinct; fastidious -n. detail, item -pl. items of information **-particular'ity** n.

partisan' [-zan'] n. adherent of a party; guerilla -a. adhering to faction; prejudiced

parti'tion [-tish'-] n. division; interior dividing wall -vt. divide into sections

part'ner n. ally or companion; associate **-part'nership** n.

part'ridge n. game bird

part'y n. social assembly; group of persons organized together; person

pass [-ah-] vt. go by, beyond, through etc.; exceed; spend; transfer -v. go; be transferred from one state or person to another; elapse; undergo examination successfully -n. way, esp. through mountains; permit; successful result **-pass'able** a. (just) acceptable **-pass'ing** a. transitory; casual

pass'age n. opening; corridor; part of book etc.; voyage, fare

pass'enger n. traveller, esp. by public conveyance

pass'ion [-sh'-] n. ardent desire; any strong emotion **-pass'ionate** a.

pass'ive a. submissive; inactive

pass'port [-ah-] n. official document granting permission to travel abroad etc.

pass'word [-ah-] n. word(s) to distinguish friend from enemy

past [-ah-] a. ended; gone by; elapsed -n. bygone times -adv. by; along -prep. beyond; after

pas'ta n. any of several preparations of dough, eg spaghetti

paste n. soft composition; adhesive -vt. fasten with paste **-pa'sty** a. like paste; white; sickly **-paste'board** n. stiff thick paper

pas'tel n. coloured crayon; drawing with crayons; pale, delicate colour -a.

pas'teurize vt. sterilize by heat **-pasteuriza'tion** n.

pas'til(le) n. lozenge

pas'time [-ah-] n. recreation

pas'tor [-ah-] n. clergyman **-pas'toral** a. of rural life; of pastor

pas'try n. article of food made chiefly of flour, fat and water

pas'ture [-ah-] n. ground on which cattle graze -v. (cause to) graze

pas'ty n. small pie of meat and crust, baked without a dish

pat' vt. tap (-tt-) -n. tap; small mass, as of butter

pat' adv. exactly; fluently

patch n. piece of cloth sewed on garment; spot; plot of ground -vt.

mend; repair clumsily -**patch'y** a. of uneven quality

pate n. head; top of head

pâté [pa'ta] n. spread of finely minced liver etc.

pa'tent n. exclusive right to invention -a. open; evident -vt. secure a patent -**pa'tently** adv. obviously -**patent leather** (imitation) leather with hard, glossy surface

pater'nal a. fatherly; of a father -**pater'nalism** n. -**pater'nity** n. fatherhood

path [-ah-] n. way or track; course of action

pathet'ic a. moving to pity -**pathet'ically** adv.

pathol'ogy n. science of diseases -**patholog'ical** a. -**pathol'ogist** n.

pa'thos n. power of exciting tender emotions

pa'tient [-shənt] a. bearing trials calmly -n. person under medical treatment -**pa'tience** n.

pat'ina n. fine layer on a surface; sheen of age on woodwork

pat'io n. paved area adjoining house

pa'triarch [-k-] n. father and ruler of family

patri'cian [-rish'-] n./a. (one) of noble birth

pat'rimony n. inheritance

pa'triot [or pat'-] n. one that loves his country -**patriot'ic** [pat-] a. -**pa'triotism** n.

patrol' [-ōl'] n. regular circuit by guard; person, small group patrolling -v. go round on guard (-ll-)

pa'tron n. one who aids artists, charities etc.; regular customer; guardian saint -**pat'ronage** n. support given by patron -**pat'ronize** vt. assume air of superiority towards; frequent as customer

patt'er n./vi. (make) quick succession of taps; inf. (utter) glib, rapid speech

patt'ern n. arrangement of repeated parts; design; plan for cutting cloth etc.; model -vt. (with on, after) model

patt'y n. a little pie

pau'city n. scarcity

paunch n. belly

pau'per n. very poor person

pause vi./n. stop or rest

pave vt. form surface with stone -**pave'ment** n. paved footpath

pavil'ion n. clubhouse on playing field etc.; building for for exhibition etc.; large tent

paw n. foot of animal -v. scrape with forefoot; maul

pawn' vt./n. deposit (article) as security for money borrowed -**pawn'-broker** n. lender of money on goods pledged

pawn' n. piece in chess; person used as mere tool

pay vt. give money etc., for goods or services rendered; give; be profitable to -vi. be profitable; (with out) spend; (paid, pay'ing) -n. wages -**pay'-able** a. justly due -**payee'** n. person to whom money is paid or due -**pay'-ment** n.

P.A.Y.E. pay as you earn

PC Police Constable; Privy Councillor; C Progressive Conservative

p.c. per cent; postcard

PE physical education

pea n. edible green seed of leguminous plant fruit, growing in pods, of climbing plant; the plant

peace n. freedom from war; harmony; calm -**peace'able** a. disposed to peace -**peace'ful** a.

peach n. stone fruit of delicate flavour

pea'cock n. male of bird (**pea'-fowl**) with fan-like tail (**pea'hen** fem.)

peak n. pointed end of anything, esp. hilltop; highest point -**peaked**, **peak'y** a. like, having a peak; sickly, wan

peal n. (succession of) loud sound(s) -vi. sound loudly

pea'nut n. pea-shaped nut -pl. inf. trifling amount of money

pear [pār] n. tree yielding sweet, juicy fruit; the fruit -**pear-shaped** a. shaped like a pear, heavier at the bottom than the top

pearl [purl] n. hard, lustrous structure found esp. in oyster and used as jewel

peas'ant [pez'-] n. member of low social class, esp. in rural district -**peas'antry** n.

peat n. decomposed vegetable substance

peb'ble n. small roundish stone

pecan' n. N Amer. tree; its edible nut

peccadillo' n. slight offence; petty crime (pl. -es, -s)

peck' n. fourth part of bushel, 2 gallons; great deal

peck' v. strike with or as with beak; inf. kiss quickly -n. -**peck'ish** a. inf. hungry

pec'tin n. gelatinizing substance in ripe fruits

pec'toral a. of the breast

pecu'liar a. strange; particular; belonging to -**pecular'ity** n. oddity; characteristic; distinguishing feature

pecu'niary a. of money

ped'agogue [-gog] n. schoolmaster; pedant -**pedagog'ic** a.

ped'al n. foot lever -v. propel bicycle by using its pedals; use pedal (-ll-)

ped'ant n. one who insists on petty details of book-learning, grammatical rules etc. -**pedant'ic** a. -**ped'antry** n.

ped'dle vt. go round selling goods -**peddler** n. one who sells narcotic drugs

ped'estal n. base of column

pedes'trian n. one who walks on foot -a. going on foot; commonplace; dull -**pedestrian crossing** place marked where pedestrians may cross road

ped'igree n. register of ancestors; genealogy

ped'lar n. one who sells; hawker

peek vi./n. peep, glance

peel vt. strip off skin, rind or covering -vi. come off, as skin, rind -n. rind, skin

peep[1] vi. look slyly or quickly -n. such a look

peep[2] vi./n. chirp, as chick

peer[1] n. nobleman; one of the same rank (**peer'ess** fem.) -**peer'age** n. -**peer'less** a. without match or equal

peer[2] vi. look closely

peeved a. inf. sulky, irritated

peev'ish a. fretful; irritable

pee'wit n. lapwing

peg n. pin for fixing, fastening, marking etc.; (mark of) level, standard etc. -vt. fasten with pegs; stabilize (prices) -vi. (with away) persevere (-gg-)

P.E.I. Prince Edward Island

pejor'ative [pi-jo'rə- or pēˈjər-] a. (of words etc.) with disparaging connotation

pekinese' [-ēzˈ], **peke** n. small Chinese dog

pelargo'nium n. plant with red, white or pink flowers

pel'ican n. waterfowl with large pouch beneath its bill

pell'et n. little ball

pell'-mell' adv. in utter confusion, headlong

pel'met n. ornamental drapery or board, concealing curtain rail

pelt[1] vt. strike with missiles -vi. throw missiles; fall persistently

pelt[2] n. raw hide or skin

pel'vis n. bony cavity at base of human trunk (pl. **pel'vises**, **-ves** [-vēz]) -**pel'vic** a.

pen[1] n. instrument for writing -vt. compose; write (-nn-)

pen[2] n./vt. (put in) enclosure (-nn-)

pe'nal a. of punishment -**pe'nalize** vt. impose penalty on -**pen'alty** n. punishment; forfeit; Sports handicap

pen'ance n. suffering submitted to as expression of penitence

pence n. pl. of PENNY

pen'chant [or pahn'shahn] n. inclination, decided taste

pen'cil n. instrument as of graphite, for writing etc. -vt. draw; mark with pencil (-ll-)

pend'ant n. hanging ornament -**pend'ent** a. hanging

pend'ing prep. during, until -a. awaiting settlement; imminent

pend'ulous a. hanging, swinging -**pend'ulum** n. suspended weight swinging to and fro

pen'etrate vt. enter into; pierce; arrive at meaning of -**pen'etrable** a. -**pen'etrating** a. sharp; easily heard; quick to understand -**pen-etra'tion** n.

pen'guin n. flightless bird

penicill'in [-sil'-] n. antibiotic drug

penin'sula n. portion of land nearly surrounded by water -**penin'sular** a.

pe'nis n. male organ of copulation and urination (pl. **pe'nises**, **pe'nes** [-nēz])

pen'itent a. affected by sense of guilt -n. one that repents -**pen'itence** n. sorrow for sin -**peniten'tiary** a. -n. US prison

penn'ant n. long narrow flag

penn'on n. small pointed flag

penn'y n. Brit. bronze coin, 100th part of pound (pl. **pence**, **penn'ies**) -**penn'iless** a. having no money

pen'sion n. regular payment to old people, soldiers etc. -vt. grant pension to -**pen'sioner** n.

pen'sive a. thoughtful

pent a. shut up, kept in

pent'agon n. plane figure having five angles

pent'house n. apartment, flat on top of building

penul'timate a. next before the last

pen'ury *n.* extreme poverty **-pen'u'rious** *a.* niggardly; scanty

pe'ony *n.* plant with showy red, pink, white flowers

peo'ple [pē'pl] *pl.n.* persons generally; nation; race; family **-vt.** populate

pep *n. inf.* vigour; energy **-vt.** impart energy to (**-pp-**)

pep'per *n.* pungent aromatic spice; slightly pungent vegetable **-vt.** season with pepper; sprinkle; pelt with missiles **-pepp'ermint** *n.* plant noted for aromatic pungent liquor distilled from it; a sweet flavoured with this

pep'tic *a.* of digestion

per *prep.* for each; by; in manner of

per-, par-, pel-, pil- (*comb. form*) through, thoroughly, as in *perfect*

peram'bulate *vt.* walk through or over **-vi.** walk about **-peram'bulator** *n.* pram

per an'num *Lat.* by the year

perceive' *vt.* obtain knowledge of through senses; understand **-percep'tible** *a.* **-percep'tion** *n.* **-percep'tive** *a.*

percent'age *n.* proportion or rate per hundred **-per cent** in each hundred

perch[1] *n.* freshwater fish

perch[2] *n.* resting place, as for bird **-vt.** place, as on perch **-vi.** alight; roost; balance on

per'colate *v.* pass through fine mesh as liquor; filter **-per'colator** *n.* coffeepot with filter

percuss'ion [-sh'-] *n.* vibratory shock

perdi'tion [-ish'-] *n.* spiritual ruin

per'egrine [pe'ri-] *n.* type of falcon

peremp'tory *a.* imperious

perenn'ial *a.* lasting through the years; perpetual **-n.** plant lasting more than two years

per'fect *a.* complete; unspoilt; correct, precise; excellent **-vt.** [-fect'] improve; make skilful **-perfect'able** *a.* **-perfec'tion** *n.*

per'fidy *n.* treachery, disloyalty **-perfid'ious** *a.*

per'forate *vt.* make holes in, penetrate **-perfora'tion** *n.*

perform' *vt.* fulfil **-vi.** function; act part; play, as on musical instrument **-perform'ance** *n.*

per'fume *n.* agreeable scent **-vt.** [-fyōōm'] imbue with an agreeable odour

perfunct'ory *a.* done indifferently

perhaps' *adv.* possibly

peri- (*comb. form*) round, as in *perimeter, period*

per'il [pe'ri-] *n.* danger; exposure to injury **-per'ilous** *a.*

perim'eter *n.* outer boundary of an area; length of this

pe'riod *n.* particular portion of time; a series of years; single occurrence of menstruation; full stop (.) at the end of a sentence **-a.** of furniture, dress *etc.,* belonging to particular time in history **-period'ic** *a.* recurring at regular intervals **-period'ical** *a./n.* (of) publication issued at regular intervals

peripatet'ic *a.* travelling about

periph'ery *n.* circumference; outside **-periph'eral** *a.* unimportant

per'iscope [pe'ri-] *n.* instrument used for giving view of objects on different level

per'ish [pe'ri-] *vi.* die; rot **-perish'able** *a.* that will not last long **-pl.n.** perishable food

per'jure *vt.* be guilty of perjury **-per'jury** *n.* crime of false testimony on oath

perk *n. inf.* PERQUISITE

per'ky *a.* lively, cheerful

per'manent *a.* continuing in same state; lasting **-per'manence** *n.*

per'meate *vt.* pervade; pass through pores of **-per'meable** *a.*

permit' *vt.* allow; give leave to (**-tt-**) **-n.** [per'-] warrant or licence to do something **-permiss'ible** *a.* **-permiss'ion** *n.* **-permiss'ive** *a.* (too) tolerant, *esp.* sexually

permuta'tion *n. Maths.* arrangement of a number of quantities in every possible order

perni'cious [-nish'-] *a.* wicked; harmful

pernick'ety *a. inf.* fussy

perox'ide *n.* short for HYDROGEN PEROXIDE

perpendic'ular *a./n.* (line) at right angles to another; exactly upright

per'petrate *vt.* perform or be responsible for (something bad) **-per'petrator** *n.*

perpet'ual *a.* continuous; lasting for ever **-perpet'uate** *vt.* make perpetual; not to allow to be forgotten **-perpetu'ity** *n.*

perplex' *vt.* puzzle; bewilder **-perplex'ity** *n.*

per'quisite [-it] *n.* any incidental

benefit from a certain type of employment

per'secute vt. oppress because of race, religion etc. **-persecu'tion** n. **-per'secutor** n.

persevere' vi. persist, maintain effort **-persever'ance** n.

persimm'on n. Amer. tree; its hard wood; its fruit

persist' vi. continue in spite of obstacles or objections **-persist'ence** n. **-persist'ent** a.

per'son n. individual (human) being; body of human being; Grammar classification of pronouns and verb forms according to the person speaking, spoken to, or of **-per'sonable** a. good-looking **-per'sonage** n. notable person **-per'sonal** a. individual, private; of grammatical person **-personal'ity** n. distinctive character; a celebrity **-per'sonally** adv.

person'ify vt. represent as person; typify **(-ified, -ifying)**

personnel' n. staff employed in a service or institution

perspec'tive [-iv] n. mental view; (art of) drawing on flat surface to give effect of relative distances and sizes

Per'spex n. R unbreakable plastic substitute for glass

perspica'cious a. having quick mental insight **-perspicac'ity** [-kas'-] n.

perspire' v. sweat **-perspira'tion** n.

persuade' [-sw-] vt. bring (one to do something) by argument, charm etc. **-persua'sion** n. art, act of persuading; belief **-persua'sive** a.

pert' a. forward, saucy

pertain' vi. belong, relate, have reference (to)

pertina'cious [-shas] a. persistent **-pertinac'ity** [-as'-] n.

pert'inent a. to the point **-pert'inence** n. relevance

perturb' vt. disturb; alarm

peruse' [-ōōz'] vt. read in careful or leisurely manner **-peru'sal** n.

pervade' vt. spread through **-perva'sive** a.

pervert' vt. turn to wrong use; lead astray **-n.** [per'-] one who practises sexual perversion **-perverse'** a. obstinately or unreasonably wrong; wayward **-perver'sion** n. **-perver'sity** n.

pese'ta n. Sp. monetary unit

pess'imism n. tendency to see worst side of things **-pess'imist** n. **-pessimist'ic** a.

pest n. troublesome or harmful thing, person or insect **-pest'icide** n. chemical for killing pests, esp. insects

pest'er vt. vex; harass

pes'tilence n. epidemic disease

pes'tle [pes'əl] n. instrument with which things are pounded

pet n. animal or person kept or regarded with affection **-vt.** make pet of; inf. fondle **(-tt-)**

pet'al n. white or coloured leaflike part of flower

pe'ter vi. **-peter out** inf. lose power gradually

petite' [-tēt'] a. small, dainty

peti'tion [-ish-] n. request, esp. to sovereign or parliament **-vt.** present petition to

pet'rel n. sea bird

pet'rify vt. turn to stone; make motionless with fear **(-ified, -ifying)**

petro'leum n. mineral oil **-pet'rol** n. refined petroleum as used in motorcars etc.

pett'icoat n. women's underskirt

pett'y a. unimportant; small-minded

pet'ulant a. irritable; peevish

pew n. fixed seat in church

pew'ter n. alloy of tin

phal'anx n. body of men formed in close array **(pl. phal'anxes, phalan'ges** [-jēz])

phall'us n. penis; symbol of it used in primitive rites **-phall'ic** a.

phan'tom n. apparition; ghost

Pha'raoh [fā'rō] n. title of ancient Egyptian kings

phar'isee [fa'ri-] n. sanctimonious person; hypocrite

pharmaceut'ical [-syoot'-] a. of drugs or pharmacy **-phar'macist** n. person qualified to dispense drugs **-pharmacol'ogy** n. study of drugs **-phar'macy** n. preparation and dispensing of drugs; dispensary

phar'ynx [fa'ringks] n. cavity forming back part of mouth **(pl. pharyn'ges** [-jēz]) **-pharyngi'tis** [-jī'-] n. inflammation of pharynx

phase [-z] n. distinct stage in a development

PhD Doctor of Philosophy

pheas'ant [fez'-] n. game bird

phenom'enon n. anything observed; remarkable person or thing **(pl. phenom'ena) -phenom'enal** a.

phi'al n. small bottle

phil- (*comb. form*) loving, as in *philanthropy, philosophy*

philan'thropy *n.* practice of doing good to one's fellow men -**philan'thropic** a. -**philan'thropist** *n.*

philat'ely *n.* stamp collecting -**philat'elist** *n.*

philharmon'ic *a.* musical

phil'istine *n.* ignorant person

philos'ophy *n.* study of realities and general principles; system of theories on nature of things or on conduct -**philos'opher** *n.* -**philosoph'ic(al)** a. of, like philosophy; wise, learned; calm, stoical

phlegm [flem] *n.* viscid substance formed in throat -**phlegmat'ic** [fleg-] *a.* not easily agitated

pho'bia *n.* fear or aversion

phoe'nix [fē-] *n.* legendary bird; unique thing

phone *n./a./vi. inf.* telephone

phonet'ic *a.* of vocal sounds -**phonet'ics** *pl.n.* science of vocal sounds

pho'ney *inf.* a. sham; suspect

pho'nograph *n.* instrument recording and reproducing sounds

phos'phorus *n.* nonmetallic element which appears luminous in the dark -**phos'phate** *n.* compound of phosphorus -**phosphores'cence** *n.* faint glow in the dark

pho'to *n. inf.* PHOTOGRAPH

pho'tocopy *n.* photographic reproduction -*vt.*

photoelectric'ity *n.* electricity produced or affected by light

photogen'ic *a.* capable of being photographed attractively

pho'tograph *n.* picture made by chemical action of light on sensitive film -*vt.* take photograph of -**photog'rapher** *n.* -**photograph'ic** *a.* -**photog'raphy** *n.*

Pho'tostat R apparatus for obtaining photographic reproductions of documents etc. -*vt.* take photostat copies of

photosyn'thesis *n.* process by which green plant uses sun's energy to make carbohydrates

phrase [-z] *n.* group of words; expression -*vt.* express in words -**phraseol'ogy** [fräz-i-] *n.* choice of words

phys'ic [-iz-] *n.* medicine, esp. cathartic -*pl.* science of properties of matter and energy -**phys'ical** a. bodily, as opposed to mental; material -**phys'ically** *adv.* -**physi'cian** *n.* qualified medical practitioner

-phys'icist *n.* one skilled in, or student of physics

physiog'nomy [-on'-] *n.* judging character by face; face

physiol'ogy *n.* science of living things -**physiol'ogist** *n.*

physiother'apy *n.* therapeutic use of physical means, as massage etc. -**physiother'apist** *n.*

physique' [-ēk'] *n.* bodily structure, constitution

pi *n. Maths.* ratio of circumference of circle to its diameter

pian'o *n.* (*orig.* pianoforte) musical instrument with keyboard (*pl.* pian'os) -a./adv. Mus. softly -**pi'anist** [pē'-] *n.* performer on piano

piazz'a [-at'sə] *n.* square

pic'ador *n.* mounted bullfighter with lance

picc'olo *n.* small flute (*pl.* -los)

pick' *vt.* choose, select carefully; pluck, gather; find occasion for -*n.* act of picking; choicest part -**pick-up** *n.* device for conversion of mechanical energy into electrical signals, as in record player etc.; small truck -**pick on** find fault with -**pick up** lift; collect; get better; accelerate

pick' *n.* tool with curved iron crossbar -**pick'axe** *n.* pick

pick'aback *n.* ride on the back

pick'et *n.* pointed stake; party of trade unionists posted to deter would-be workers during strike -*vt.* post as picket

pic'kle [pik'l] *n.* food preserved in brine, vinegar etc.; awkward situation -*vt.* preserve in pickle

pic'nic *n.* pleasure excursion including meal out of doors -*vi.* take part in picnic (**pic'nicked, pic'nicking**)

pic'ture *n.* drawing or painting; mental image -*pl.* cinema -*vt.* represent in, or as in, a picture -**pic'torial** a. of, with pictures -*n.* newspaper with pictures -**pictur'esque** [-esk'] a. visually striking, vivid

pidg'in *n.* language made up of two or more other languages

pie *n.* baked dish of meat, fruit etc., usu. with pastry crust

pie'bald *a.* irregularly marked with black and white -**pied** a. piebald; variegated

piece [pēs] *n.* bit, part, fragment; single object; literary or musical composition etc. -*vt.* mend, put together -**piece'meal** *adv.* by in, or into pieces, a bit at a time

pier n. structure running into sea; piece of solid upright masonry

pierce vt. make hole in; make a way through **-pierc'ing** a.

pi'ety n. godliness; devoutness

pig n. wild or domesticated mammal killed for pork, ham, bacon; inf. greedy, dirty person

pig'eon [pij'in] n. bird of wild and domesticated varieties **-pig'eon-hole** n. compartment for papers in desk etc. -vt. defer; classify

pigg'yback n. see PICKABACK

pig'ment n. colouring matter, paint or dye

pig'my see PYGMY

pike[1] n. predatory freshwater fish

pike[2] n. medieval spear

pilau' [-low], **pil'af(f)** n. Oriental dish of meat or fowl boiled with rice, spices etc.

pil'chard n. small sea fish like the herring

pile[1] n. heap -vt. heap (up) -vi. (with in, out, off etc.) crowd

pile[2] n. beam driven into the ground, esp. as foundation

pile[3] n. nap of cloth

piles pl.n. haemorrhoids

pil'fer v. steal small items

pil'grim n. one who journeys to sacred place **-pil'grimage** n.

pill n. small ball of medicine swallowed whole **-the pill** oral contraceptive

pill'age v./n. plunder

pill'ar n. upright support

pill'ion n. seat behind rider of motorcycle or horse

pill'ory n. frame with holes for head and hands in which offender was confined -vt. expose to ridicule and abuse (pill'oried, pill'orying)

pill'ow n. cushion for the head, esp. in bed

pi'lot n. person qualified to fly an aircraft or spacecraft; one qualified to take charge of ship entering or leaving harbour etc.; steersman; guide -a. experimental and preliminary -vt. act as pilot to; steer

pimen'to n. allspice; sweet red pepper: also **pimien'to** (pl. -tos)

pimp n. one who solicits for prostitute -vi. act as pimp

pim'pernel n. plant with small scarlet, blue, or white flowers

pim'ple n. small pus-filled spot on the skin **-pim'ply** a.

pin n. piece of stiff wire with point and head, for fastening; wooden or metal peg or rivet -vt. fasten with pin; seize and hold fast (-nn-) **-pin'-point** vt. mark exactly

pin'afore n. apron; dress with a bib top

pin'cers pl.n. tool for gripping; claws of lobster etc.

pinch vt. nip, squeeze; stint; inf. steal; inf. arrest -n. nip; small amount; emergency

pine[1] n. evergreen coniferous tree; its wood

pine[2] vi. yearn; waste away with grief etc.

pine'apple n. tropical plant bearing large edible fruit

pin'ion[1] n. bird's wing -vt. confine by binding wings, arms etc.

pin'ion[2] n. small cogwheel

pink n. pale red colour; garden plant; best condition -vt. pierce; cut indented edge -vi. of engine, knock

pinn'acle n. highest point; mountain peak; pointed turret

pint [-I-] n. liquid measure, 1/8 gallon (.568 litre)

pin'-up n. picture of sexually attractive person

pioneer' [-a-] n. explorer; early settler; originator -vi. act as pioneer

pi'ous a. devout; righteous

pip[1] n. seed in fruit

pip[2] n. high-pitched sound as time signal on radio; spot on cards, dice etc.; inf. star on junior officer's shoulder showing rank

pipe n. tube of metal or other material; tube with small bowl at end for smoking tobacco; musical instrument -pl. bagpipes -v. play on pipe; utter in shrill tone; convey by pipe; ornament with a piping **-pip'er** n. **-pip'ing** n. **-pipe'line** n. long pipe for transporting oil, water etc.

pip'it n. bird like lark

pipp'in n. kinds of apple

pi'quant [pe'kont] a. pungent

pique [pēk] n. feeling of injury -vt. hurt pride of; irritate

pi'rate n. sea robber; publisher etc. who infringes copyright -n./a. (person) broadcasting illegally -vt. use or reproduce (artistic work etc.) illicitly **-pi'racy** n.

pirouette' [pi-roo-] n. spinning round on the toe -vi. do this

pistach'io [-tahsh-] n. small hardshelled, sweet-tasting nut (pl. -os)

pis'til n. seed-bearing organ of flower

pis'tol n. small firearm for one hand

pist'on n. in engine, cylindrical part propelled to and fro in hollow cylinder

pit n. deep hole in ground; mine or its shaft; depression; part of theatre occupied by orchestra; servicing area on motor-racing track -vt. set to fight, match; mark with small dents (-tt-) -**pit'fall** n. any hidden danger; covered pit as trap

pitch[1] vt. throw; set up; set the key of (a tune) -vi. fall headlong -n. act of pitching; degree, height, intensity; slope; *Sport* field of play -**pitch'fork** n. fork for lifting hay etc. -vt. throw with, as with, pitchfork

pitch[2] n. dark sticky substance obtained from tar or turpentine

pitch'blende n. mineral composed largely of uranium oxide

pitch'er n. large jug

pith n. tissue in stems and branches of certain plants; essential part -**pith'y** a. terse, concise; consisting of pith

pitt'ance n. inadequate wages

pitu'itary a. of, pert. to, the endocrine gland at base of brain

pit'y n. sympathy for others' suffering; regrettable fact -vt. feel pity for (**pit'ied, pit'ying**) -**pit'eous** a. deserving pity -**pit'iable** a. -**pit'iful** a. woeful; contemptible -**pit'iless** a. feeling no pity; hard, merciless

piv'ot n. shaft or pin on which thing turns -vt. furnish with pivot -vi. hinge on one

pix'y, pix'ie n. fairy

pizz'a [pēt'sə] n. baked disc of dough covered with savoury topping

pl. place; plate; plural

plaas [-ah-] n. SA farm

plac'ard n. notice for posting up or carrying, poster

placate' vt. pacify, appease

place n. locality, spot; position; duty; town, village, residence, buildings; employment; seat, space -vt. put in particular place; identify; make (order, bet etc.)

placen'ta [-sen'-] n. organ formed in uterus during pregnancy, providing nutrients for foetus; afterbirth (pl. -tas, -tae [-tē])

plac'id [plas'-] a. calm

pla'giarism [-jə-] n. presenting another's ideas, writings as one's own -**pla'giarize** v.

plague [plāg] n. highly contagious disease; inf. nuisance -vt. trouble,

annoy -**pla'gu(e)y** [plā'gi] a. inf. annoying

plaice n. flat fish

plaid [plad, plād] n. long Highland cloak or shawl; tartan pattern

plain a. flat, level; not intricate; clear simple; ordinary; without decoration; not beautiful -n. tract of level country -adv. clearly -**plain'ly** adv. -**plain'ness** n.

plaint n. *Law* statement of complaint -**plaint'iff** n. *Law* one who sues in court -**plaint'ive** a. sad, mournful

plait [plat] n. braid of hair, straw etc. -vt. weave into plaits

plan n. scheme; way of proceeding; project; drawing; map -vt. make plan of; arrange beforehand (-nn-)

plane[1] n. smooth surface; a level; tool for smoothing wood -vt. make smooth with one -a. perfectly flat or level

plane[2] n. aeroplane

plane[3] n. tree with broad leaves

plan'et n. heavenly body revolving round sun -**plan'etary** a.

planeta'rium n. apparatus that shows movement of sun, moon, stars and planets by projecting lights on inside of dome

plank n. long flat piece of timber

plank'ton n. minute animal and vegetable organisms floating in ocean

plant [-ah-] n. living organism without power of locomotion; building and equipment for manufacturing purposes -vt. set in ground, to grow; establish; sl. hide

planta'tion n. estate for cultivation of tea, tobacco etc.; wood of planted trees

plaque [plak] n. ornamental tablet; plate of brooch; deposit on teeth

plas'ma [-az'-] n. clear, fluid portion of blood

plas'ter [-ah-] n. mixture of lime, sand etc. for coating walls etc.; adhesive dressing for cut, wound etc. -vt. apply plaster; apply like plaster

plas'tic n. synthetic product of casein, cellulose etc., easily moulded and extremely durable -a. made of plastic; easily moulded -**plastic'ity** [-s'-] n. ability to be moulded

Plas'ticine R a modelling material like clay

plate n. shallow round dish; flat thin sheet of metal, glass etc.; utensils of gold or silver; device for printing; illustration in book; device to straighten children's teeth; *inf.* denture *-vt.* cover with thin coating of metal

plat'eau [-ō] *n.* tract of level high land; period of stability

plat'form *n.* raised level surface, stage; raised area in station from which passengers board trains

plat'inum *n.* white heavy malleable metal

plat'itude *n.* commonplace remark

platon'ic *a.* (of love) purely spiritual, friendly

platoon' *n.* body of soldiers employed as unit

platt'eland [-ə'lant] *n.* SA rural district

platt'er *n.* flat dish

plau'dit *n.* act of applause

plau'sible [-z-] *a.* apparently reasonable; fair-spoken

play [plā] *v.* amuse oneself; contend with in game; take part in (game); trifle; act the part of; perform (music); perform on (instrument) *-n.* dramatic piece or performance; sport; amusement; activity; free movement; gambling **-play'er** *n.* **-play'ful** *a.* lively **-playing card** one of set of 52 cards **-playing fields** extensive piece of ground for open-air games **-play'wright** *n.* author of plays

plaz'a [-ahz'ə] *n.* open space or square

plea [plē] *n.* entreaty; statement of prisoner or defendant; excuse **-plead** *vi.* make earnest appeal; address court of law *-vt.* bring forward as excuse or plea (**plead'ed** *or* US, Scots **pled**, **plead'ing**)

please [-z-] *vt.* be agreeable to; gratify; delight *-vi.* like; be willing *-adv.* word of request **-pleas'ant** *a.* pleasing, agreeable **-pleas'antly** *adv.* **-pleas'antry** *n.* joke, humour **-pleas'urable** *a.* giving pleasure **-pleas'ure** *n.* enjoyment; satisfaction

pleat *n.* fold made by doubling material *-vi.* make pleats

plebe'ian [-bē'ən] *n./a.* (one) of the common people

pleb'iscite *n.* decision by direct voting of the electorate

plec'trum *n.* small implement for plucking strings of guitar *etc.*

pledge *n./vt.* promise; give (something) as security; toast

ple'nary *a.* complete

plenipoten'tiary *a./n.* (envoy) having full powers

plen'itude *n.* abundance

plen'ty *n.* abundance; quite enough **-plent'eous** *a.* ample **-plent'iful** *a.*

pleth'ora *n.* oversupply

pleur'isy [ploor'-] *n.* inflammation of membrane lining chest and covering lungs

pli'able *a.* easily bent or influenced **-pli'ant** *a.* pliable

pli'ers *pl.n.* tool with hinged arms and jaws for gripping

plight[1] [plīt] *n.* distressing state

plight[2] [plīt] *vt.* promise

plim'solls *pl.n.* rubber-soled canvas shoes

plinth *n.* slab as base of column *etc.*

plod *vi.* walk or work doggedly

plop *n.* sound of object falling into water without splash *-v.*

plot[1] *n.* secret plan, conspiracy; essence of story, play *etc.* *-vt.* devise secretly; mark position of; make map of *-vi.* conspire (**-tt-**)

plot[2] *n.* small piece of land

plough, US **plow** [plow] *n.* implement for turning up soil *-vt.* turn up with plough, furrow *-vi.* work at slowly **-plough'man** *n.*

plov'er [pluv'-] *n.* shore bird with straight bill and long pointed wings

pluck *vt.* pull, pick off; strip from; sound strings of (guitar *etc.*) with fingers, plectrum *-n.* courage; sudden pull or tug **-pluck'y** *a.* courageous

plug *n.* thing fitting into and filling a hole; *Electricity* device connecting appliance to electricity supply *-vt.* stop with plug (**-gg-**)

plum *n.* stone fruit; tree bearing it; choicest part, piece, position *etc.* *-a.* choice; plum-coloured

plumb [-m] *n.* ball of lead attached to string used for sounding, finding the perpendicular *etc.* *-a.* perpendicular *-adv.* perpendicularly; exactly *-vt.* set exactly upright; find depth of; equip with, connect to plumbing system **-plumb'er** *n.* worker who attends to water and sewage systems **-plumb'ing** *n.* trade of plumber; system of water and sewage pipes **-plumb'line** *n.* cord with plumb attached

plume [ploom] *n.* feather; ornament of feathers *etc.* *-vt.* furnish with plumes; pride oneself **-plu'mage** *n.* bird's feathers

plumm'et vi. plunge headlong –n. plumbline

plump[1] a. fat, rounded –v. make, become plump

plump[2] v. drop, fall abruptly; choose –adv. suddenly; directly

plun'der v. take by force; rob –n. booty, spoils

plunge v. put forcibly, throw (into); descend suddenly –n. dive –**plun'ger** n. suction cap to unblock drains

plur'al [ploor'-] a. of, denoting more than one –n. word in its plural form –**plural'ity** n. majority

plus prep. with addition of (usu. indicated by the sign +) –a. to be added; positive

plush n. fabric with long nap –a. luxurious

plu'tocrat n. powerful wealthy man

ply[1] vt. wield; work at; supply pressingly –vi. go to and fro regularly (-ied, -y'ing)

ply[2] n. fold or thickness; strand of yarn –**ply'wood** n. board of thin layers of wood glued together

PM prime minister

pm, PM post meridiem (Lat., after noon)

pneumat'ic [nyōō-] a. of, worked by, inflated with wind or air

pneumo'nia [nyōō-] n. inflammation of the lungs

PO postal order; Post Office

poach[1] vt. take (game) illegally –vi. encroach –**poach'er** n.

poach[2] vt. simmer (eggs, fish etc.) gently in water etc. –**poach'er** n.

pock'et n. small bag inserted in garment; cavity, pouch or hollow; isolated group or area –vt. put into one's pocket; appropriate –a. small

pod n. long seed vessel, as of peas, beans etc. –vi. form peas –vt. shell (-dd-)

podg'y a. short and fat

po'dium n. small raised platform

po'em n. imaginative composition in rhythmic lines –**po'et** n. writer of poems –**po'etry** n. art or work of poet, verse –**poet'ic(al)** a.

poign'ant [poin'yant] a. moving; keen –**poign'ancy** n.

point n. dot; punctuation mark; detail; unit of value, scoring; degree, stage; moment; gist; purpose; special quality; sharp end; headland; direction mark on compass; movable rail changing train to other rails; power etc. plug –vi. show direction or position by extending finger; direct attention

–vt. aim; direct; sharpen; fill up joints with mortar –**point'ed** a. sharp; direct –**point'edly** adv. –**point'er** n. indicating rod etc. used for pointing; indication –**point'less** a. blunt; futile –**point-blank** a./adv. aimed horizontally; at short range; blunt, direct

poise n. composure; self-possession; balance –v. (cause to be) balanced or suspended –vt. hold in readiness

poi'son [-z-] n. substance harmful or fatal to living organism –vt. give poison to; infect –**poi'sonous** a.

poke vt. push, thrust with finger, stick etc.; thrust forward –vi. make thrusts; pry –n. act of poking –**po'ker** n. metal rod for poking fire –**po'ky** a. small, confined, cramped

po'ker n. card game

pole[1] n. long rounded piece of wood etc. –vt. propel with pole

pole[2] n. each of the ends of axis of earth or celestial sphere; each of opposite ends of magnet, electric cell etc. –**po'lar** a.

pole'cat n. small animal of weasel family

police [pə-lēs'] n. the civil force which maintains public order –vt. keep in order –**police'man** n. member of police force (**police'woman** fem.)

pol'icy[1] n. course of action adopted, esp. in state affairs

pol'icy[2] n. insurance contract

pol'ish vt. make smooth and glossy; refine –vi. shine; polishing; substance for polishing; refinement

polite' a. showing regard for others in manners, speech etc.; refined, cultured

pol'itics a. wise, shrewd –**pol'itics** pl.n. art of government; political affairs –**polit'ical** a. of the state or its affairs –**politi'cian** n. one engaged in politics

pol'ka n. lively dance; music for it –**polka** dot one of pattern of bold spots on fabric etc.

poll [pōl] n. voting; counting of votes; number of votes recorded; survey of opinion –vt. receive (votes); take votes of –vi. vote –**polling booth** voting place

poll'en n. fertilizing dust of flower –**poll'inate** vt.

pollute' [-lōōt'] vt. make foul; corrupt –**pollu'tion** n.

po'lo n. game like hockey played on horseback

polyg'amy [-lig-] n. custom of being married to several persons at a time -**polyg'amist** n.

pol'yglot a. speaking, writing in several languages

pol'ygon n. figure with many angles or sides -**polyg'onal** a.

pol'yp n. sea anemone, or allied animal

polysty'rene n. synthetic material used esp. as white rigid foam for packing etc.

polytech'nic n. college dealing mainly with various arts and crafts -a.

pol'ythene n. tough light plastic material

pom'egranate n. tree; its fruit with thick rind containing many seeds in red pulp

pomm'el n. front of saddle; knob of sword hilt

pomp n. splendid display or ceremony

pom'pon, pom'pom n. decorative tuft of ribbon, wool, feathers etc.

pomp'ous a. self-important; ostentatious; of language, inflated, stilted -**pompos'ity** n.

pond n. small body of still water

pon'der v. muse, think over

pond'erous a. heavy, unwieldy; boring

pon'tiff n. Pope; bishop -**pontif'ical** a. -**pontif'icate** vi. speak dogmatically

pontoon'[1] n. flat-bottomed boat or metal drum for use in supporting temporary bridge

pontoon'[2] n. gambling card game (also **twenty-one**)

po'ny n. horse of small breed

poo'dle n. pet dog with long curly hair

pool' [-oo-] n. small body of still water; deep place in river or stream; puddle; swimming pool

pool'[2] [-oo-] n. common fund or resources; group of people, eg typists, shared by several employers; collective stakes in various games -vt. put in common fund

poop [-oo-] n. ship's stern

poor a. having little money; unproductive; inadequate; miserable, pitiable -**poor'ly** a. not in good health -adv.

poort n. SA narrow mountain pass

pop'[1] v. (cause to) make small explosive sound; put or place suddenly (-pp-) -n. small explosive sound

-**pop'corn** n. maize that puffs up when roasted

pop'[2] n. music of general appeal, esp. to young people -a.

Pope n. bishop of Rome and head of R.C. Church

pop'lar n. tree noted for its slender tallness

pop'lin n. corded fabric usu. of cotton

popp'y n. bright-flowered plant yielding opium

pop'ulace n. the common people

pop'ular a. finding general favour; of, by the people -**popular'ity** n. -**pop'ularize** vt. make popular

pop'ulate vt. fill with inhabitants -**popula'tion** n. inhabitants; their number -**pop'ulous** a. thickly populated

por'celain [-slin] n. fine earthenware, china

porch n. covered approach to entrance of building

porc'upine n. rodent covered with long, pointed quills

pore' vi. study closely

pore'[2] n. minute opening, esp. in skin -**por'ous** a. allowing liquid to soak through; full of pores

pork n. pig's flesh as food

pornog'raphy n. indecent literature, films etc. -**pornog'rapher** n. -**pornograph'ic** a.

por'poise [-pǝs] n. blunt-nosed sea mammal like dolphin

porr'idge n. soft food of oatmeal etc. boiled in water

port' n. (town with) harbour

port'[2] n. left side of ship

port'[3] n. strong red wine

port'[4] n. opening in side of ship -**port'hole** n. small opening or window in side of ship

port'able n./a. (something) easily carried

port'age n. (cost of) transport

por'tal n. large doorway or imposing gate

portend' vt. foretell; be an omen of -**port'ent** n. omen

port'er n. person employed to carry burden; door-keeper

portfo'lio n. flat portable case for loose papers

por'tion n. part, share, helping; destiny, lot -vt. divide into shares

port'ly a. bulky, stout

portman'teau [-tō] n. leather suitcase, esp. one opening into two compartments (pl. -s, -x [-ōz])

portray' vt. make pictures of, describe -por**trait** [-trit] n. likeness of (face) individual -por**traiture** n. -portray'al n. act of portraying

pose n. place in attitude; put forward -vi. assume attitude, affect or pretend to be a certain character -n. attitude, esp. one assumed for effect

poi'ser n. puzzling question

posi'tion [-zish'-] n. place; situation; attitude; status; employment -vt. place in position

pos'itive [poz'-] a. sure; definite; downright; confident; not negative -n. something positive -pos'itively adv.

possess' [-zes'] vt. own; have mastery of -possess'ion n. act of possessing; thing possessed; ownership -possess'ive a. of, indicating possession; with excessive desire to possess, control -possess'or n.

poss'ible a. that can, or may, be, exist, happen or be done; worthy of consideration -possibil'ity n. -poss'ibly adv. perhaps

poss'um n. see OPOSSUM

post¹ [pōst] n. upright pole to support or mark something -vt. display; stick up (on notice board etc.) -post'er n. large advertising bill

post² [pōst] n. official carrying of letters or parcels; collection or delivery of these; office; situation; place of duty; fort -vt. put into official box for carriage by post; station (soldiers etc.) in particular spot -post'age n. charge for carrying letter -post'al a. -postal order written order, available at post office, for payment of sum of money -post'card n. stamped card sent by post -post'man n. man who collects or delivers post -post'mark n. official mark with name of office etc. stamped on letters -post'master n. official in charge of post office, place where postal business is conducted

poste'rior [pos-] a. later, hinder -n. the buttocks

poster'ity [-te'ri-] n. later generations; descendants

pos'thumous [-tyoo-] a. occurring after death; born after father's death

postmor'tem n. medical examination of dead body

postpone' vt. put off to later time, defer -postpone'ment n.

post'script n. addition to letter, book

pos'tulate vt. take for granted -n. something postulated

pos'ture n. attitude, position of body -v. pose

po'sy n. bunch of flowers

pot n. round vessel; cooking vessel; -vt. put into, preserve in pot (-tt-) -pott'ed a.

po'table a. drinkable

potass'ium n. white metallic element

pota'to n. plant with tubers grown for food; one of these tubers (pl. -es)

po'tent a. powerful, influential -po'tency n.

po'tentate n. ruler

poten'tial a. latent, that may or might but does not now exist or act -n. possibility

po'tion n. dose of medicine or poison

pott'er¹ n. maker of earthenware vessels -pott'ery n. earthenware; where it is made; art of making it

pott'er² vi. work, act in feeble, unsystematic way

pouch n. small bag; pocket -vt. put into one

pouf(fe) [poof] n. large solid cushion

poult'ice [pōlt'is] n. soft composition of mustard, kaolin etc., applied hot to sore or inflamed parts of the body

poult'ry [pōl-] n. domestic fowls -poult'erer n. dealer in poultry

pounce vi. spring upon suddenly, swoop (upon) -n. swoop or sudden descent

pound¹ vt. beat, thump; crush to pieces or powder; walk, run heavily

pound² n. unit of troy weight; unit of avoirdupois weight equal to .454 kg; monetary unit in U.K.

pound³ n. enclosure for stray animals or officially removed vehicles

pour [pawr] vi. come out in a stream, crowd etc.; flow freely; rain heavily -vt. give out thus

pout v. thrust out (lips), look sulky -n. act of pouting

pov'erty n. state of being poor; poorness; scarcity

POW prisoner of war

pow'der n. solid matter in fine dry particles; medicine in this form; gunpowder; facepowder etc. -vt. apply powder to; reduce to powder -pow'dery a.

pow'er n. ability to do or act; strength; authority; control; person or thing having authority; mechanical energy; electricity supply -**pow'er-ed** a. having or operated by mechanical or electrical power -**pow'erful** a. -**pow'erless** a.

pp pages

PR public relations

prac'tical a. given to action rather than theory; useful; virtual -**prac'tically** adv. -**practicabil'ity** n. -**prac'ticable** a. that can be done, used etc.

prac'tise, US prac'tice vt. do repeatedly, work at to gain skill; do habitually; put into action -vi. exercise oneself; exercise profession -**prac'tice** n. habit; exercise of art or profession; action, not theory

pragmat'ic a. concerned with practical consequence

prair'ie n. large treeless tract of grassland -**prairie dog** small Amer. rodent

praise n. commendation; fact of praising -vt. express approval, admiration of -**praise'worthy** a.

pram n. carriage for baby

prance [-ah-] vi. swagger; caper -n.

prank n. mischievous trick

prat'tle vi. talk like child -n. trifling, childish talk

prawn n. edible sea shellfish like a shrimp but larger

pray vt. ask earnestly; entreat -vi. offer prayers esp. to God -**prayer** [prâr] n. action, practice of praying to God; earnest entreaty

preach vi. deliver sermon; give moral, religious advice -vt. set forth in religious discourse; advocate

pream'ble n. introductory part of story etc.

preca'rious a. insecure, unstable, perilous

precau'tion n. previous care to prevent evil or secure good -**precau'tionary** a.

precede' v. go, come before in rank, order, time etc. -**prec'edence** [or prê-sê'-] n. priority in position, rank, time etc. -**prec'edent** n. previous case or occurrence taken as rule

pre'cept n. rule for conduct

pre'cinct n. enclosed, limited area -pl. environs

prec'ious [presh'∂s] a. beloved, cherished; of great value -**prec'iousness** n.

prec'ipice [pres'-] n. very steep cliff or rockface -**precip'itous** a. sheer

precip'itate [-ât] vt. hasten happening of; throw headlong; Chem. cause to be deposited in solid form from solution -a. [-it] too sudden; rash -n. [-ât] substance chemically precipitated -**precip'itately** adv.

pré'cis [prâ'sê] n./vt. (make) summary (pl. **pré'cis** [-sêz])

precise' a. definite; exact; careful in observance -**precise'ly** adv. -**preci'sion** n.

preclude' vt. prevent

preco'cious a. developed, matured early or too soon

preconceive' vt. form an idea beforehand -**preconcep'tion** n.

precur'sor n. forerunner

pred'atory a. preying on other animals -**pred'ator** n.

pre'decessor n. one who precedes another in an office or position

predes'tine [-tin] vt. decree beforehand, foreordain -**predestina'tion** n.

predic'ament n. difficult situation

predict' vt. foretell, prophesy -**predict'able** a. -**predic'tion** n.

predispose' vt. incline, influence; make susceptible

predom'inate vi. be main or controlling element -**predom'inance** n. -**predom'inant** a.

pre-em'inent a. excelling all others -**pre-em'inence** n.

preen vt. trim (feathers) with beak, plume; smarten oneself

prefab'ricate vt. manufacture buildings etc. in shaped sections, for rapid assembly

pref'ace [-is] n. introduction to book etc. -vt. introduce

pre'fect n. person put in authority; schoolchild in position of limited power over others

prefer' vt. like better; promote (-rr-) -**pref'erable** a. more desirable -**pref'erence** n. -**prefer'ment** n. promotion

pre'fix n. preposition or particle put at beginning of word or title -vt. [-fiks'] put as introduction; put as prefix

preg'nant a. carrying foetus in womb; full of meaning, significant -**preg'nancy** n.

prehistor'ic [-to'rik] a. before period in which written history begins

prej'udice [-is] n. preconceived opinion; bias, partiality; injury to person or his rights -vt. influence; bias; injure -**prejudi'cial** a.

prel'ate n. clergyman of high rank

prelim'inary a./n. preparatory, introductory (action, statement)

prel'ude n. Mus. introductory movement; performance, event etc. serving as introduction

premature' [or prem'-] a. happening, done before proper time

premed'itate vt. consider, plan beforehand **-premedita'tion** n.

prem'ier n. prime minister -a. chief, foremost; first **-prem'iership** n.

première' [-mi-âr'] n. first performance of a play etc.

prem'ise [-is] n. Logic proposition from which inference is drawn -pl. house, building with its belongings

pre'mium n. bonus; sum paid for insurance; excess over nominal value; great value or regard (pl. -iums)

premoni'tion [-nish'-] n. presentiment

preocc'upy [-pî'] vt. occupy to the exclusion of other things **-preoccupa'tion** n.

prepare' v. make, get ready; make **-prepara'tion** n. making ready beforehand; something prepared, as a medicine **-prepar'atory** [-pa'rə-] a. serving to prepare; introductory **-prepa'redness** n.

prepon'derate vi. be of greater weight or power **-prepond'erance** n.

preposi'tion [-zish'-] n. word marking relation between noun or pronoun and other words

prepossess' [prē-] vt. impress, esp. favourably, beforehand **-prepossess'ing** a.

prepos'terous a. utterly absurd, foolish

prereq'uisite n./a. (something) required as prior condition

prerog'ative n. peculiar power or right, esp. as vested in sovereign -a.

prescribe' v. set out rules for; order use of (medicine) **-prescrip'tion** n. prescribing; thing prescribed; written statement of it

pres'ent [-z-] a. that is here; now existing or happening -n. present time or tense **-pres'ence** n. being present; appearance, bearing **-pres'ently** adv. soon; US at present

present' [-z-] vt. introduce formally; show; give **-pres'ent** n. gift **-present'able** a. fit to be seen **-presenta'tion** n.

present'iment [-z-] n. sense of something about to happen

preserve' [-z-] vt. keep from harm, injury or decay -n. special area; place where game is kept for private fishing, shooting **-preserva'tion** n. **-preserv'ative** n. preserving agent -a. preserving

preside' [-z-] vi. be chairman; superintend **-pres'ident** n. head of society, company, republic etc. **-pres'idency** n. **-presiden'tial** a.

press v. subject to push or squeeze; smooth; urge; throng; hasten -n. machine for pressing, esp. printing machine; printing house; newspapers and journalists collectively; crowd **-press'ing** a. urgent; persistent

press'ure [presh'-] n. act of pressing; compelling force; Physics thrust per unit area

prestige' [-êzh'] n. reputation; influence depending on it

presume' [-zyōōm'] vt. take for granted -vi. take liberties **-presump'tion** n. forward, arrogant opinion or conduct; strong probability **-presump'tive** a. that may be assumed as true or valid until contrary is proved **-presump'tuous** a. forward, impudent

presuppose' vt. assume or take for granted beforehand **-presupposi'tion** n.

pretend' vt. claim or allege (something untrue); make believe -vi. lay claim (to) **-pretence'** n. simulation **-pretend'er** n. claimant (to throne) **-preten'sion** n. **-preten'tious** a. making claim to special merit or importance; given to outward show

preternat'ural [prē-] a. out of ordinary way of nature

pre'text n. excuse; pretence

prett'y [priti'] a. appealing in a delicate way -adv. moderately

prevail' vi. gain mastery; be generally established **-prevail'ing** a. **-prev'alent** a. widespread; predominant

prevar'icate [-va'ri-] vi. tell lies or speak evasively **-prevar'icator** n.

prevent' vt. stop, hinder **-prevent'able** a. **-preven'tion** n. **-preven'tive** a./n.

pre'view n. advance showing; a showing of scenes from a forthcoming film

pre'vious a. preceding; happening before **-pre'viously** adv.

prey n. an animal hunted by another for food; victim -vi. treat as prey; afflict, obsess (with upon)

price n. that for which thing is bought or sold; cost -vt. fix, ask price for -**price'less** a. invaluable

prick vt. pierce slightly; cause to feel sharp pain -n. slight hole made by pricking; pricking; sting -**prick'le** n. thorn, spike -vi. feel pricking sensation -**prick'ly** a.

pride n. too high an opinion of oneself; worthy self-esteem; great satisfaction; something causing this -v.refl. take pride

priest n. official minister of religion (-**ess** fem.)

prig n. smug self-righteous person -**prigg'ish** a.

prim a. formally prudish

pri'macy n. supremacy

pri'mary a. chief; earliest; elementary

pri'mate[1] n. archbishop

pri'mate[2] n. one of order of mammals including monkeys and man

prime[1] a. fundamental; original; chief; best -n. first, best part of anything -vt. prepare for use -**Prime Minister** leader of government

prime[2] vt. prepare for paint with preliminary coating of oil, size etc. -**pri'mer** n. paint etc. for priming

prim'itive a. of an early undeveloped kind; crude

prim'rose n. pale yellow spring flower; this colour -a. of this colour

prince n. son or (in Britain) grandson of king or queen; ruler, chief (**princess'** fem.) -**prince'ly** a. generous; magnificent

prin'cipal a. chief in importance -n. person for whom another is agent; head of institution, esp. school or college; sum of money lent and yielding interest -**principal'ity** n. territory of prince

prin'ciple n. moral rule; settled reason of action; uprightness; fundamental truth

print vt. reproduce (words, pictures etc.) by pressing inked types on blocks to paper etc.; write in imitation of this; Photog. produce pictures from negatives; stamp (fabric) with design -n. printed matter; photograph; impression left by something pressing; printed cotton fabric -**print'er** n.

pri'or a. earlier -n. chief of religious house or order (-**ess** fem.) -**prior'ity**

[-o'ri-] n. precedence; something given special attention -**pri'ory** n. monastery, nunnery under prior, prioress -**prior** to before

prise vt. force open by levering

prism [-zam] n. transparent solid usu. with triangular ends and rectangular sides, used to disperse light into spectrum -**prismat'ic** a. of prism shape; (of colour) such as is produced by refraction through prism, rainbowlike, brilliant

pris'on [-iz'-] n. jail -**pris'oner** n. one kept in prison; captive

pri'vate a. secret, not public; not general, individual; personal; secluded; denoting soldier of lowest rank -n. private soldier -**pri'vacy** [or priv'-] n. -**pri'vately** adv.

priva'tion n. want of comforts or necessaries

priv'et n. bushy evergreen shrub used for hedges

priv'ilege [-lij] n. right, advantage granted or belonging only to few -**priv'ileged** a. enjoying privilege

priv'y a. admitted to knowledge of secret -n. lavatory

prize n. reward given for success in competition; thing striven for; thing won, eg in lottery etc. -a. winning or likely to win a prize -vt. value highly

pro[1] a./adv. in favour of

pro[2] n. professional

prob'able a. likely -**probabil'ity** n. likelihood; anything probable -**prob'ably** adv.

pro'bate n. proving of authenticity of will; certificate of this

proba'tion n. system of dealing with lawbreakers by placing them under supervision; trial period -**proba'tioner** n. person on probation

probe vt. search into, examine, question closely -n. that which probes, or is used to probe; thorough inquiry

prob'lem n. matter etc. difficult to deal with or solve; question set for solution -**problemat'ic(al)** a.

proceed' vi. go forward, continue; be carried on; go to law -**pro'ceeds** pl.n. profit -**proce'dure** n. act, manner of proceeding -**proceed'ing** n. act or course of action -pl. minutes of meeting; legal action

pro'cess n. series of actions or changes; method of operation; state of going on; action of law -vt. handle, treat, prepare by special method of manufacture etc. -**proces'sion** n.

train of persons in formal order

proclaim' vt. announce publicly, declare -**procla'mation** n.

procras'tinate vi. put off, delay -**procrastina'tion** n. -**procras'tinator** n.

procure' vt. obtain, acquire; bring about -vi. act as pimp -**procu'rable** a. -**procure'ment** n. -**procu'rer** n. one who procures; pimp (**procu'ress** fem.)

prod vt. poke -n. prodding; pointed instrument

prod'igal a. wasteful -n. spendthrift -**prodigal'ity** n.

prod'igy [-ji] n. person with some marvellous gift; thing causing wonder -**prodig'ious** a. very great; extraordinary

produce' vt. bring into existence; yield; bring forward; manufacture; present on stage, film, television -n. [prod'-] that which is yielded or made -**produ'cer** n. -**prod'uct** n. thing produced; number resulting from multiplication -**produc'tion** n. producing; things produced -**produc'tive** a. fertile; creative -**productiv'ity** n.

Prof. Professor

profane' a. irreverent, blasphemous; not sacred -vt. treat irreverently -**profan'ity** n. profane talk

profess' vt. affirm belief in; claim, pretend -**profess'edly** [-id-li] adv. avowedly -**profes'sion** n. calling or occupation, esp. learned, scientific or artistic; a professing -**profes'sional** a. engaged in a profession; engaged in a game or sport for money -n. paid player -**profes'sor** n. teacher of highest rank in university -**profess'orship** n.

proff'er vt./n. offer

profi'cient [-ish'-] a. skilled; expert -**profi'ciency** n.

pro'file n. outline, esp. of face, as seen from side; brief biographical sketch

prof'it n. money gained; benefit obtained -v. benefit -**prof'itable** a. yielding profit -**profiteer'** n. one who makes excessive profits at the expense of the public -vi. do this

profound' a. very learned; deep -**profun'dity** n.

profuse' [-fyoos'] a. abundant, prodigal -**profu'sion** n.

prog'eny [proj'-] n. children -**progen'itor** n. ancestor

pro'gramme n. plan of intended proceedings; broadcast on radio or television -**pro'gram** n. instructions for a computer -vt. feed program into (computer); arrange program (**-mm-**)

pro'gress n. onward movement; development -vi. [-gres'] go forward; improve -**progres'sion** n. moving forward; improvement -**progress'ive** a. progressing by degrees; favouring political or social reform

prohib'it vt. forbid -**prohibi'tion** [-bish'-] n. act of forbidding -**prohib'itive** a. tending to forbid or exclude

proj'ect n. plan, scheme -v. [-jekt'] plan; throw; cause to appear on distant background -vi. stick out -**projec'tile** n. heavy missile -**projec'tion** n. -**projec'tor** n. apparatus for projecting photographic images

proleta'riat n. working class -**proleta'rian** a./n.

prolif'erate v. grow or reproduce rapidly -**prolifera'tion** n.

prolif'ic a. fruitful; producing much

pro'logue [-log] n. preface, esp. speech before a play

prolong' vt. lengthen

promenade' [-ahd'] n. leisurely walk; place made or used for this -vi. take leisurely walk

prom'inent a. sticking out; conspicuous; distinguished -**prom'inence** n.

promis'cuous a. indiscriminate, esp. in sexual relations

prom'ise [-is] v. give undertaking or assurance -vi. be likely to -n. undertaking to do or not to do something; potential -**prom'ising** a. showing good signs, hopeful

prom'ontory n. high land jutting out into the sea

promote' vt. help forward; move up to higher rank or position; encourage sale of -**promo'ter** n. -**promo'tion** n.

prompt a. done at once; punctual -v. urge, suggest; help (actor or speaker) by suggesting next words

prom'ulgate vt. proclaim, publish -**promulga'tion** n.

prone a. lying face downwards; inclined (to)

prong n. one spike of fork or similar instrument

pro'noun n. word used to replace noun

pronounce' vt. utter (formally) -vi. give opinion -**pronounced'** a. strongly marked -**pronounce'ment**

n. declaration -**pronuncia'tion** *n.* way word *etc.* is pronounced

proof *n.* evidence; thing which proves; test, demonstration; trial impression from type or engraved plate; standard of strength of alcoholic drink -*a.* giving impenetrable defence against

prop *vt./n.* support (-**pp-**)

propagand'a *n.* organized dissemination of information to assist or damage political cause *etc.* -**propagan'dist** *n.*

prop'agate *v.* reproduce, breed; spread -**propaga'tion** *n.*

propel' *vt.* cause to move forward (-**ll-**) -**propel'ler** *n.* revolving shaft with blades for driving ship or aircraft -**propul'sion** *n.* act of driving forward

propen'sity *n.* inclination; tendency

prop'er *a.* appropriate; correct; conforming to etiquette; strict; (of noun) denoting individual person or place -**prop'erly** *adv.*

prop'erty *n.* that which is owned; quality, attribute

proph'et *n.* inspired teacher or revealer of Divine Will; foreteller of future (-**tess** *fem.*) -**proph'ecy** [-si] *n.* prediction, prophetic utterance -**proph'esy** [-sī] *vi.* foretell -**prophet'ic** *a.* -**prophet'ically** *adv.*

propor'tion *n.* relative size or number; due relation between connected things or parts; share -*pl.* dimensions -*vt.* arrange proportions of -**propor'tional, propor'tionate** *a.* having a due proportion -**proportionally** *adv.*

propose' *vt.* put forward for consideration; intend -*vi.* offer marriage -**propo'sal** *n.* -**propo'ser** *n.* -**proposi'tion** *n.* offer; statement

propound' *vt.* put forward for consideration

propri'etor *n.* owner (-**tress,** -**trix** *fem.*) -**propri'etary** *a.* belonging to owner; made by firm with exclusive rights of manufacture

propri'ety *n.* properness; correct conduct

propul'sion *see* PROPEL

prosa'ic *a.* commonplace, unromantic

proscribe' *vt.* outlaw, condemn

prose *n.* speech or writing not verse

pros'ecute *vt.* carry on, bring legal proceedings against -**pros-**

ecu'tion *n.* -**pros'ecutor** *n.* (-**trix** *fem.*)

pros'pect *n.* expectation, chance for success; view -*v.* [or -pekt'] explore, *esp.* for gold -**prospec'tive** *a.* anticipated; future -**prospec'tor** *n.*

pros'per *v.* (cause to) do well -**prosper'ity** [-pe'ri-] *n.* -**pros'perous** *a.* successful; well-off

pros'titute *n.* one who offers sexual intercourse in return for payment -*vt.* make a prostitute of; put to unworthy use -**prostitu'tion** *n.*

pros'trate *a.* lying flat; overcome -*vt.* [-trāt'] throw flat on ground; reduce to exhaustion -**prostra'tion** *n.*

protect' *vt.* keep from harm -**protec'tion** *n.* -**protec'tive** *a.* -**protec'tor** *n.* -**protec'torate** *n.* relation of state to territory it protects and controls; such territory

pro'tégé [-ti-zhā] *n.* one under another's patronage (-**ée** *fem.*)

pro'tein [-tēn] *n.* kinds of organic compound which form most essential part of food of living creatures

pro'test *n.* declaration or demonstration of objection -*vi.* [-test'] object; make declaration against; assert formally -**protesta'tion** *n.* strong declaration

pro'tocol *n.* diplomatic etiquette

pro'ton *n.* positively charged particle in nucleus of atom

pro'totype *n.* original, or model, after which thing is copied

protract' *vt.* lengthen; prolong

protrude' *vt.* stick out, project -**protru'sion** *n.*

protu'berant *a.* bulging out -**protu'berance** *n.* bulge

proud *a.* feeling or displaying pride; noble

prove [proov] *vt.* establish validity of; demonstrate, test -*vi.* turn out (to be *etc.*) (proved, proved [proov-] *pp.*) -**pro'ven** [proov-] *a.* proved

prov'ender *n.* fodder

prov'erb *n.* short, pithy saying in common use -**proverb'ial** *a.*

provide' *vi.* make preparation -*vt.* supply, equip -**provided that** on condition that

prov'ident *a.* thrifty; showing foresight -**prov'idence** *n.* kindly care of God or nature; foresight; economy -**providen'tial** *a.* strikingly fortunate

prov'ince *n.* division of a country; sphere of action -*pl.* any part of country outside capital -**provin'cial**

a. of a province; narrow in outlook -*n.* unsophisticated person; inhabitant of province

provi'sion [-vizh'-] *n.* a providing, *esp.* for the future; thing provided -*pl.* food -*vt.* supply with food -**pro-vi'sional** *a.* temporary

provi'so *n.* condition (*pl.* -os)

provoke' *vt.* anger; arouse; cause -**provoca'tion** *n.* -**provoc'ative** *a.*

prow *n.* bow of vessel

prow'ess *n.* bravery; skill

prowl *vi.* roam stealthily, *esp.* in search of prey or booty -*n.* -**prowl'-er** *n.*

prox'y *n.* authorized agent or substitute; writing authorizing one to act as this

prude *n.* one who affects excessive modesty or propriety -**pru'dery** *n.* -**pru'dish** *a.*

pru'dent *a.* careful, discreet; sensible -**pru'dence** *n.* -**pruden'tial** *a.*

prune[1] *n.* dried plum

prune[2] *vt.* cut out dead parts, excessive branches *etc.*; shorten, reduce

pry *vi.* make furtive or impertinent inquiries (**pried, pry'ing**)

PS postscript

psalm [sahm] *n.* sacred song -**psalm'ist** *n.* writer of psalms

pseu'donym [syōō-] *n.* false, fictitious name; pen name

psy'chic [sī'kik] *a.* sensitive to phenomena lying outside range of normal experience; of soul or mind -**psychi'atry** *n.* medical treatment of mental diseases -**psychoanal'-ysis** *n.* method of studying and treating mental disorders -**psy-choan'alyst** *n.* of psychology; of the mind -**psy-chol'ogist** *n.* -**psychol'ogy** *n.* study of mind; *inf.* person's mental make-up -**psy'chopath** *n.* person afflicted with severe mental disorder -**psy-chopath'ic** *a.* -**psycho'sis** *n.* severe mental disorder -**psy-chosomat'ic** *a.* of physical disorders thought to have psychological causes -**psychother'apy** *n.* treatment of disease by psychological, not physical, means

PT physical training

Pte. Private (soldier)

PTO please turn over

pub *n.* public house, building with bar(s) and licence to sell alcoholic drinks

pu'berty *n.* sexual maturity

pu'bic *a.* of the lower abdomen

pub'lic *a.* of or concerning the public as a whole; not private -*n.* the community or its members -**pub'-lican** *n.* keeper of public house -**pub'licly** *adv.* -**public house** *see* PUB

public'ity [-lis'-] *n.* process of attracting public attention; attention thus gained -**pub'licize** *vt.* advertise

pub'lish *vt.* prepare and issue for sale (books, music *etc.*); make generally known; proclaim -**publica'-tion** *n.* -**pub'lisher** *n.*

puck *n.* rubber disc used instead of ball in ice hockey

puck'er *v.* gather into wrinkles -*n.* crease, fold

pudd'ing [pood'-] *n.* sweet, cooked dessert, often made from suet, flour *etc.*; sweet course of meal; soft savoury dish with pastry or batter; kind of sausage

pud'dle *n.* small muddy pool

puer'ile [pyoor'-] *a.* childish

puff *n.* short blast of breath, wind *etc.*; type of pastry; laudatory notice or advertisement -*vi.* blow abruptly; breathe hard -*vt.* send out in a puff; inflate; advertise; smoke hard -**puff'y** *a.* swollen

puff'in *n.* sea bird with large brightly-coloured beak

pug *n.* small snub-nosed dog

pu'gilist [-j-] *n.* boxer -**pu'gilism** *n.* -**pugilist'ic** *a.*

pugna'cious *a.* given to fighting -**pugnac'ity** *n.*

pull [pool] *vt.* exert force on object to move it towards source of force; strain or stretch -*n.* act of pulling; force exerted by it

pull'et [-oo-] *n.* young hen

pull'ey [-oo-] *n.* wheel with groove in rim for cord, used to raise weights

pull'over *n.* jersey, sweater without fastening, to be pulled over head

pul'monary *a.* of lungs

pulp *n.* soft, moist, vegetable or animal matter; flesh of fruit; any soft soggy mass -*vt.* reduce to pulp

pul'pit [-oo-] *n.* (enclosed) platform for preacher

pulse[1] *n.* movement of blood in arteries corresponding to heartbeat, discernible to touch, *eg* in wrist; any regular beat or vibration -**pulsate'** *vi.* throb, quiver -**pulsa'tion** *n.*

pul'verize *vt.* reduce to powder

pu'ma *n.* large Amer. feline carnivore, cougar

pum'ice [-is] n. light porous variety of lava

pumm'el vt. strike repeatedly (-ll-)

pump[1] n. appliance for raising water, or putting in or taking out air or liquid etc. -vt. raise, put in, take out etc. with pump; empty by means of a pump -vi. work pump; work like pump

pump[2] n. light shoe

pump'kin n. edible gourd

pun n. play on words -vi. make one (-nn-) -**pun'ster** n.

punch[1] n. tool for perforating or stamping; blow with fist -vt. stamp, perforate with punch; strike with fist

punch[2] n. drink of spirits or wine with fruit juice etc.

punctil'ious a. making much of details of etiquette; very exact, particular

punc'tual a. in good time, not late, prompt -**punctual'ity** n.

punc'tuate vt. put in punctuation marks; interrupt at intervals -**punctua'tion** n. marks, eg commas, colons etc. put in writing to assist in making sense clear

punc'ture n. small hole made by sharp object -vt. prick hole in, perforate

pun'gent [-j-] a. acrid; bitter; biting; caustic -**pun'gency** n.

pun'ish vt. cause to suffer for offence; inflict penalty on; use or treat roughly -**pun'ishable** a. -**pun'ishment** n. -**pu'nitive** a. inflicting or intending to inflict punishment

punt n. flat-bottomed square-ended boat, propelled by pushing with pole -vt. propel thus

pu'ny a. small and feeble

pup n. young of certain animals, eg dog, seal

pu'pa n. stage between larva and adult in metamorphosis of insect, chrysalis (pl. **pu'pae** [-pē])

pu'pil[1] n. person being taught; opening in iris of eye

pupp'et n. small doll controlled by operator's hand -**puppeteer'** n. -**pupp'etry** n.

pupp'y n. young dog

pur'chase vt. buy -n. buying; what is bought; leverage, grip -**pur'chaser** n.

pure [pyoor] a. unmixed, untainted; simple; faultless; innocent; concerned with theory only -**pure'ly** adv. -**purifica'tion** n. -**pur'ify** vt. make, become pure, clear or clean (-**ified**, -**ifying**) -**pur'ity** n. state of being pure

pur'ée [pyoor'ā] n. pulp of cooked fruit or vegetables -vt.

purg'atory n. place or state of torment, pain or distress, esp. temporary

purge [-j] vt. make clean, purify; remove, get rid of; clear out -n. act, process of purging -**pur'gative** a./n.

purl n. stitch that forms ridge in knitting -vi. knit in purl

purloin' vt. steal; pilfer

pur'ple n./a. (of) colour between crimson and violet

purport' vt. claim to be (true etc.); signify, imply -n. [pur'-] meaning; apparent meaning

pur'pose [-pəs] n. reason, object; design; aim, intention -vt. intend -**pur'posely** adv. -**on purpose** intentionally

purr n. pleased noise which cat makes -vi. utter this

purse n. small bag for money; resources; money as prize -v. pucker -**pur'ser** n. ship's officer who keeps accounts

pursue' [-syōō'] v. chase; engage in; continue -**pursu'er** n. -**pursuit'** [-syōōt'] n. pursuing; occupation

purvey' vt. supply (provisions) -**purvey'or** n.

pus n. yellowish matter produced by suppuration

push [-oo-] vt. move, try to move away by pressure; drive or impel -vi. make thrust; advance with steady effort -n. thrust; persevering self-assertion; big military advance -**push'er** n. -**push'chair** n. (collapsible) chair-shaped carriage for baby

puss [poos] n. cat: also **puss'y**

pust'ule n. pimple containing pus

put [poot] vt. place; set; express; throw (esp. shot) (put, **putt'ing**) -n. throw -**put off** postpone; disconcert; repel

pu'trid a. decomposed; rotten -**pu'trefy** v. make or become rotten (-efied, -efying) -**putrefac'tion** n.

putt [put] vt. strike (golf ball) along ground -**putt'er** n. golf club for putting

putt'y n. paste used by glaziers

puz'zle v. perplex or be perplexed -n. bewildering, perplexing question, problem or toy -**puz'zlement** n.

PVC polyvinyl chloride

pyg'my, pig'my n. abnormally undersized person; (P-) member of one of dwarf peoples of Equatorial Africa -a.

pyjam'as [pə-jahm'-] *pl.n.* sleeping suit of trousers and jacket

py'lon *n.* towerlike erection *esp.* to carry electric cables

pyr'amid *n.* solid figure or structure with sloping sides meeting at apex, *esp.* ancient Egyptian -pyram'idal *a.*

pyre *n.* pile of wood for burning a dead body

pyroma'niac *n.* person with uncontrollable desire to set things on fire

pyrotech'nics [-k-] *n.* manufacture, display of fireworks

py'thon *n.* large nonpoisonous snake that crushes its prey -py'thon'ic *a.*

Q

QC UK Queen's Counsel

qt. quart; quantity

quack *n.* harsh cry of duck; pretender to medical or other skill -vi. (of duck) utter cry

quad'rangle [kwod'-] *a.* four-sided figure; four-sided courtyard in a building -quadrang'ular *a.*

quad'rant [kwod'-] *n.* quarter of circle

quadraphon'ic [kwod-] *a.* of a sound system using four independent speakers

quadrilat'eral [kwod-] *a./n.* four-sided (figure)

quad'ruped [kwod'-] *n.* four-footed animal

quad'ruple [kwod'-] *a.* fourfold -v. make, become four times as much

quad'ruplet [kwod'-] *n.* one of four offspring born at one birth

quaff [-o-, -ah-] *v.* drink heartily or in one draught

quag, quag'mire *n.* bog, swamp

quail[1] *n.* small bird of partridge family

quail[2] *vi.* flinch; cower

quaint *a.* interestingly old-fashioned or odd; curious

quake *vi.* shake, tremble

qual'ify *v.* make (oneself) competent; moderate; ascribe quality to (-fied, -fying) -qualifica'tion *n.* thing that qualifies; qualifying

qual'ity [kwol'-] *n.* attribute; (degree of) excellence

qualm [kwahm] *n.* misgiving; sudden feeling of sickness

quan'dary [kwon'-] *n.* state of perplexity, dilemma

quan'tity [kwon'-] *n.* (specified or considerable) amount

quar'antine [kwo'rən-tēn] *n./vt.* (place in) isolation to prevent spreading of infection

quar'rel [kwo'r-] *n.* angry dispute; argument -vi. argue; find fault with (-ll-)

quar'ry[1] [kwo'ri] *n.* object of hunt or pursuit; prey

quar'ry[2] [kwo'ri] *n.* excavation where stone *etc.* is dug for building *etc.* -v. get from quarry (quarr'ied, quarr'ying)

quart [kwort] *n.* liquid measure of gallon or 2 pints

quart'er [kwort'-] *n.* fourth part; region, district; mercy -pl. lodgings -vt. divide into quarters; lodge -quart'ermaster *n.* officer responsible for stores -quart'erly *a.* happening, due *etc.* each quarter of year

quartet' [kwort-] *n.* (music for) group of four musicians

quartz [kworts] *n.* hard glossy mineral

quash [kwosh] *vt.* annul; reject; subdue forcibly

qua'ver *vt.* say or sing in quavering tones -vi. tremble, shake, vibrate -n. musical note half length of crotchet

quay [kē] *n.* solid, fixed landing stage; wharf

Que. Quebec

queas'y *a.* inclined to, or causing, sickness

queen *n.* king's wife; female sovereign; piece in chess; fertile female bee, wasp *etc.*; court card

queer *a.* odd, strange

quell *vt.* crush, put down; allay

quench *vt.* slake; extinguish

quer'ulous [kwe'roo-] *a.* peevish, whining

que'ry *n./vt.* question (que'ried, que'rying)

quest *n./v.* search

ques'tion [-chən] *n.* sentence seeking for answer; problem; doubt -vt. ask questions of; dispute; doubt -ques'tionable *a.* doubtful -ques'tionnaire *n.* formal list of questions

queue [kyōō] *n.* line of waiting persons, vehicles -vi. wait in queue

quib'ble *n./v.* (make) trivial objection

quick *a.* fast; lively; hasty -*n.* sensitive flesh -*adv.* rapidly -**quick'en** *v.* make, become faster or more lively -**quick'ly** *adv.* -**quick'sand** *n.* loose wet sand that engulfs heavy objects -**quick'silver** *n.* mercury

ques'cent [kwi-es'-] *a.* inactive; silent

qui'et *a.* with little or no motion or noise; undisturbed; not showy or obtrusive -*n.* quietness *v.* make, become quiet -**qui'eten** *v.* -**qui'etness** *n.*

quill *n.* large feather; pen made from feather; spine of porcupine

quilt *n.* padded coverlet -*vt.* stitch (two pieces of cloth) with pad between

quince *n.* acid pear-shaped fruit; tree bearing it

quinine' [-ēn'] *n.* drug used to treat fever and as tonic

quintet' *n.* (music for) group of five musicians

quin'tuplet [-tyoo-] *n.* one of five offspring born at one birth

quip *n./v.* (utter) witty saying

quirk *n.* individual peculiarity of character; unexpected twist

quit *v.* stop doing (something); leave; give up (-**tt**-) -*a.* rid

quite *adv.* completely; somewhat -*interj.* of agreement, just so

quiv'er¹ *vi.* shake, tremble -*n.*

quiv'er² *n.* carrying case for arrows

quiz *n.* entertainment in which knowledge of players is tested by questions; examination, interrogation -*vt.* question, interrogate (-**zz**-) -**quizz'ical** *a.* questioning; mocking

quoit *n.* ring for throwing at peg as a game -*pl.* (*with sing. v.*) the game

quor'um *n.* least number that must be present to make a meeting valid

quo'ta *n.* share to be contributed or received

quote *vt.* repeat passages from; state price for -**quota'tion** *n.*

quo'tient [-shənt] *n.* number resulting from dividing one number by another

q.v. *quod vide* (*Lat.* which see)

R

R Regina (*Lat.* Queen); Rex (*Lat.* King); river

RA Royal Academy

rabb'i [-ī] *n.* Jewish learned man, spiritual leader (*pl.* **rabb'is** [-īz])

rabb'it *n.* small burrowing rodent

rab'ble *n.* crowd of vulgar, noisy people

rab'id *a.* of, having rabies; fanatical

ra'bies *n.* infectious disease transmitted by dogs *etc.*

RAC Royal Automobile Club

raccoon' *n.* small N Amer. mammal

race¹ *n.* contest of speed; rivalry; strong current -*pl.* meeting for horse racing -*v.* (cause to) run, move swiftly -**ra'cer** *n.*

race² *n.* group of people of common ancestry with distinguishing physical features; species -**ra'cial** *a.* -**ra'cialism, ra'cism** *n.* belief in superiority of particular race; antagonism towards members of different race based on this -**ra'cialist, ra'cist** *a./n.*

rack¹ *n.* framework for displaying or holding things; *Mechanics* straight bar with teeth on its edge, to work with pinion; instrument of torture -*vt.* torture

rack² *n.* destruction *esp.* in rack and ruin

rack³ *n.* thin, flying clouds

rack'et¹ *n.* uproar; occupation by which money is made illegally -**racketeer'** *n.* -**racketeer'ing** *n.*

rack'et² *n.* bat used in tennis *etc.* -*pl.* ball game

raconteur' [-kon-] *n.* skilled storyteller

rac'quet *see* RACKET¹

ra'cy *a.* lively; piquant

ra'dar *n.* device for locating objects by radio waves, which reflect back to their source

ra'dial *see* RADIUS

ra'diate *v.* emit, be emitted in rays; spread out from centre -**ra'diance** *n.* brightness; splendour -**radia'tion** *n.* transmission of heat, light *etc.* from one body to another; particles, rays, emitted in nuclear decay -**ra'diator** *n. esp.* heating apparatus for rooms; cooling apparatus of car engine

rad'ical *a.* fundamental; extreme; of

root -n. person of extreme (political) views -**rad'icalism** n.

ra'dio n. use of electromagnetic waves for broadcasting, communication etc.; device for receiving, amplifying radio signals; broadcasting of radio programmes -vt. transmit message etc. by radio

radioact'ive a. emitting invisible rays that penetrate matter -**radioactiv'ity** n.

radiog'raphy n. production of image on film by radiation

radiol'ogy n. science of use of rays in medicine

radiother'apy n. diagnosis and treatment of disease by x-rays

rad'ish n. pungent root vegetable

ra'dium n. radioactive metallic element

ra'dius n. straight line from centre to circumference of circle (pl. **ra'dii** [-di-î], **ra'diuses**) -**ra'dial** a.

RAF Royal Air Force

raff'ia n. prepared palm fibre for making mats etc.

raff'le n. lottery in which article is won by one of those buying tickets -vt. dispose of by raffle

raft,[-ah-] n. floating structure of logs, planks etc.

raft'er [-ah-] n. main beam of roof

rag[1] n. fragment of cloth; torn piece -pl. tattered clothing -**ragg'ed** a. -**rag'time** n. style of jazz piano music

rag[2] vt. tease; play jokes on

rag'amuffin n. ragged, dirty person

rage n. violent anger; fury -vi. speak, act with fury; proceed violently (as storm) -**all the rage** very popular

rag'lan a. of sleeves that continue in one piece to the neck

raid n. attack; foray -vt. make raid on

rail[1] n. horizontal bar -**rail'ing** n. fence, barrier made of rails supported by posts -**rail'way** n. track of iron rails on which trains run

rail[2] vi. utter abuse; scold -**rail'lery** n. banter

rai'ment [rā'-] n. obs. clothing

rain n. moisture falling in drops from clouds -v. pour down as, like rain -**rain'y** a. -**rain'bow** n. arch of prismatic colours in sky -**rain'coat** n.

raise [-z] vt. lift up; set up; build; increase; heighten, as voice; breed; collect

rai'sin [-z-] n. dried grape

raj'ah n. Indian prince

rake[1] n. tool with long handle and teeth for gathering leaves etc. -vt. gather, smooth with rake; search over; sweep with shot

rake[2] n. dissolute man

ra'kish a. dashing; speedy

rall'y vt. bring together, esp. what has been scattered -vi. come together; regain health or strength (**rall'ied**, **rall'ying**) -n. assembly, esp. outdoor; Tennis lively exchange of strokes

ram n. male sheep; hydraulic machine; battering engine -vt. force, drive; strike against with force; stuff (**-mm-**)

ram'ble vi. walk without definite route; talk incoherently; spread in random fashion -n. rambling walk -**ram'bler** n.

ram'ify v. spread in branches; become complex (**-ified**, **-ifying**) -**ramifica'tion** n.

ramp n. gradual slope joining two level surfaces

rampage[1] vi. dash about violently -n. [ram'-] angry or destructive behaviour

ram'pant a. violent; rife; rearing

ram'part n. wall for defence

ram'shackle a. rickety

ran pt. of RUN

ranch [-ah-] n. Amer. cattle farm -**ranch'er** n.

ran'cid a. smelling or tasting offensively, like stale fat

ran'cour [rang'kər] n. bitter hate -**ran'corous** a.

rand n. monetary unit of S Africa

ran'dom a. by chance, without plan -**at random** haphazard(ly)

rang pt. of RING[1]

range n. limits; row; scope; distance missile can travel; place for shooting practice; kitchen stove -vt. set in row; roam -vi. extend; roam; fluctuate -**rang'er** n. official patrolling park etc. -**rang'y** [rān'ji] a. with long, slender limbs

rank[1] n. row, line; place where taxis wait; order; status; relative position -pl. common soldiers; great mass of people (also **rank and file**) -vt. draw up in rank -vi. have rank, place

rank[2] a. growing too thickly; rancid; flagrant

ran'kle [-ng'kl] vi. continue to cause anger or bitterness

ran'sack vt. search thoroughly; pillage

ran'som n. release from captivity by payment; amount paid –vt. pay ransom for

rant vi. rave in violent language

rap v./n. (give) smart slight blow (-pp-)

rapa'cious a. greedy; grasping –rapac'ity [-pas'-] n.

rape[1] vt. force (woman) to submit to sexual intercourse –n.

rape[2] n. plant with oil-yielding seeds

rap'id a. quick, swift –n. (esp. in pl.) part of river with fast, turbulent current –rapid'ity n.

ra'pier n. fine-bladed sword

rap'ine n. plunder

rapport' [-paw'] n. harmony, agreement

rapscal'lion n. rascal

rapt n. engrossed –rap'ture n. ecstasy

rare[1] [rār] a. uncommon; infrequent –rare'ly adv. seldom –ra'rity n.

rare[2] [rār] a. (of meat) lightly cooked

ra'refy v. make, become thin or less dense (-fied, -fying)

ra'ring a. enthusiastically willing, ready

ras'cal n. rogue; naughty (young) person –rascal'ity n.

rash[1] a. hasty, reckless

rash[2] n. skin eruption; outbreak

rash'er n. slice of bacon

rasp [-ah-] n. harsh, grating noise; coarse file –v. scrape with rasp; make scraping noise; irritate

rasp'berry [rahz'b-] n. red edible berry; plant which bears it

rat n. small rodent –vi. inform (on); betray; desert (-tt-) –rat race continual hectic competitive activity

rate n. proportion between two things; charge; degree of speed etc. –pl. local tax on property –vt. value –rat(e)able a.

rath'er [rahTH'-] adv. to some extent; preferably; more willingly

rat'ify vt. confirm (-ified, -ifying) –ratifica'tion n.

ra'ting n. valuing; classification; sailor (naval rating)

ra'tio [-shi-ō] n. proportion; relation

ra'tion [rash'ən] n. fixed allowance of food etc. –vt. supply with, limit to certain amount

ra'tional [rash'ən-] a. reasonable; capable of reasoning –rationaliza'tion n. –ra'tionalize vt. justify by plausible reasoning; reorganize to improve efficiency etc.

rattan' n. climbing palm with jointed stems; cane of this

rat'tle v. (cause to) give out succession of short sharp sounds –n. such sound; instrument for making it; set of horny rings in rattlesnake's tail –rat'tlesnake n. poisonous snake

rau'cous [-aw'-] a. hoarse

rav'age n. plunder –n. destruction

rave vi. talk wildly in delirium or enthusiastically –n.

rav'el v. entangle; fray out (-ll-)

ra'ven n. black bird –a. jet-black

rav'enous a. very hungry

ravine' [-ēn'] n. narrow steep-sided valley

rav'ish vt. enrapture; rape –rav'ishing a. lovely

raw a. uncooked; not manufactured or refined; skinned; inexperienced; chilly –raw'hide n. untanned hide

ray[1] n. narrow beam of light, heat etc.; any of set of radiating lines –vi. radiate

ray[2] n. marine flatfish

ray'on n. synthetic fibre

raze vt. destroy completely

ra'zor n. sharp instrument for shaving

RC Roman Catholic

RCAF Royal Canad. Air Force

RCMP Royal Canad. Mounted Police

RCN Royal Canad. Navy

RE religious education

re prep. concerning

re-, red-, ren- (comb. form) again In the list that follows, the meaning may be inferred from the word to which re- is prefixed

reappear'	re-create'	reo'pen
rearm'	redec'orate	reprint'
rearrange'	redevel'op	reroute'
rebuild'	re-ech'o	reset'
recap'ture	re-em'phasize	restrain'
reconstruct'	refill'	reunite'
re-cov'er	reheat'	

reach vt. arrive at; extend; touch; attain to -vi. extend -n. act of reaching; grasp; range

react' vi. act in return, opposition or towards former state -**reac'tion** n. counter or backward tendency; inf. response; chemical or nuclear change -**reac'tionary** n./a. (person) opposed to change, esp. in politics etc. -**reac'tor** n. apparatus to produce nuclear energy

read [rēd] vt. understand written matter; learn by reading; read and utter; study; understand indicating instrument (read [red] pt./pp.) -**read'er** n. one who reads; university lecturer; school textbook -**read'ing** n.

read'y [red'ị] a. prepared for action; willing -**read'iness** n.

real a. happening; actual; genuine -**re'alism** n. regarding things as they are -**re'alist** n. -**realist'ic** a. -**real'ity** n. real existence -**re'ally** adv. -**real estate** landed property

re'alize vt. grasp significance of; make real; convert into money -**re'alization** n.

realm [relm] n. kingdom

ream¹ n. twenty quires of paper -pl. inf. large quantity of written matter

ream² vt. enlarge, as hole in metal

reap v. cut and gather harvest

rear¹ n. back part -**rear admiral** lowest flag rank in certain navies

rear² vt. care for and educate (children); breed -vi. rise on hind feet

reas'on [rēz'-] n. motive; ability to think; sanity; sensible thought -vi. think logically -vt. persuade by logical argument -**reas'onable** a. sensible; suitable; logical

reassure' vt. restore confidence to

re'bate n. discount, refund -vt. [-bāt'] deduct

rebel' vi. resist lawful authority (-ll-) -n. [reb'] one who rebels -**rebell'ion** n. organized resistance to authority -**rebell'ious** a.

rebound' vi. spring back; misfire, esp. so as to hurt perpetrator -n. [rē'] recoiling

rebuff' n./vt. repulse, snub

rebuke' n./vt. reprimand

rebut' vt. refute, disprove (-tt-) -**rebutt'al** n.

recal'citrant a. wilfully disobedient -**recal'citrance** n.

recall' vt. remember; call back; restore -n. summons; ability to remember

recant' vt. withdraw statement, opinion etc. -**recanta'tion** n.

recapit'ulate vt. state again briefly -**recapitula'tion** n.

recede' vi. go back; slope backwards

receipt' [-sēt'] n. written acknowledgment of money received; receiving

receive' [-sēv'] vt. accept; experience; greet (guests) -**receiv'er** n. officer appointed to take public money; one who knowingly takes stolen goods; equipment in telephone etc. to convert electrical signals into sound etc.

re'cent a. lately happened; new -**re'cently** adv.

recep'tacle n. vessel to contain anything

recep'tion n. receiving; formal party; area for receiving guests etc.; in broadcasting, quality of signals received -**recep'tionist** n. person who receives clients etc.

recep'tive a. quick, willing to receive new ideas

recess' n. alcove; hollow; suspension of business

reces'sion [-sesh'-] n. period of reduction in trade; act of receding

re'cipe [res'i-pi] n. directions for cooking a dish

recip'ient n. one that receives

recip'rocal a. complementary; mutual; moving backwards and forwards -**recip'rocate** vt. give and receive mutually

recite' vt. repeat aloud, esp. to audience -**recit'al** n. musical performance, usu. by one person; narration -**recita'tion** n.

reck'less a. incautious -**reck'lessness** n.

reck'on v. count; include; think

reclaim' vt. make fit for cultivation; bring back; reform; demand the return of -**reclama'tion** n.

recline' vi. sit, lie back

recluse' n. [-klōōs'] n. hermit

rec'ognize vt. know again; treat as valid; notice -**recogni'tion** n.

recoil' vi. draw back in horror; rebound -n. [or rē'] recoiling

recollect' vt. remember -**recollec'tion** n.

recommend' vt. advise; praise; make acceptable -**recommenda'tion** n.

rec'ompense vt. reward; compensate -n.

rec'oncile vt. bring back into friendship; adjust, harmonize -reconcilia'tion n.

recon'dite a. obscure

recondi'tion [-dish'-] vt. restore to good condition

reconnoi'tre [-tə] vt. make preliminary survey of -vi. make reconnaissance -reconn'aissance n. survey esp. for military purposes

recon'stitute vt. restore (food) to former state esp. by addition of water

rec'ord n. document that records; disc with indentations which gramophone transforms into sound; best achievement; known facts -vt. [-kord'] put in writing -v. preserve (sound etc.) on magnetic tape etc. for reproduction on playback device -record'er n. one that records; type of flute -record'ing n. process of making records; something recorded

recount' vt. tell in detail

recoup' vt. recover what has been expended or lost

recourse' n. (resorting to) source of help

recov'er [-kuv'-] vt. get back -vi. get back health -recov'ery n.

rec'reant a./n. cowardly, disloyal (person)

recrea'tion n. agreeable relaxation, amusement

recrimina'tion n. mutual abuse and blame

recruit' [-root'] n. newly-enlisted soldier; one newly joining -vt. enlist -recruit'ment n.

rect'angle n. oblong four-sided figure with four right angles -rectang'ular a.

rect'ify vt. correct (-fied, -fying) -rectifica'tion n.

rect'itude n. honesty

rect'or n. clergyman with care of parish; head of academic institution -rec'tory n. rector's house

rect'um n. final section of large intestine (pl. -ta) -rect'al a.

recum'bent a. lying down

recu'perate [-koo'-] v. restore, be restored from illness etc. -recupera'tion n.

recur' vi. happen again; go or come back in mind (-rr-) -recurr'ence n. -recurr'ent a.

recy'cle vt. reprocess a manufactured substance for use again

red a./n. (of) colour of blood; inf. communist -redd'en v. -redd'ish a. -red'breast n. robin -red'brick a. of provincial university -red flag emblem of communist party; danger signal -red-handed a. inf. (caught) in the act of committing crime -red herring topic introduced to divert attention -Red Indian N Amer. Indian -red tape excessive adherence to rules -red'wood n. giant coniferous tree of California

redeem' vt. buy back; set free; free from sin; make up for -redemp'tion n.

red'olent a. smelling strongly; reminiscent (of) -red'olence n.

redou'ble [-dub'-] v. increase, intensify

redoubt'able [-dowt'-] a. dreaded, formidable

redress' vt. make amends for -n. compensation

reduce' vt. lower; lessen; bring by necessity to some state; slim; simplify -reduc'tion n.

redun'dant a. superfluous; (of worker) deprived of job because no longer needed -redun'dancy n.

reed n. various water plants; tall straight stem of one; Mus. vibrating strip of certain wind instruments -reed'y a.

reef n. ridge of rock or coral near surface of sea; part of sail which can be rolled up to reduce area -reef'er n. sailor's jacket; sl. hand-rolled cigarette, esp. with cannabis

reek vi./n. (emit) strong (unpleasant) smell

reel n. spool on which film, thread etc. is wound; Cinema portion of film; lively dance -vt. wind on reel; draw (in) by means of reel -vi. stagger

reeve n. Hist. manorial steward; C president of local (rural) council

ref. referee; reference

refec'tory n. room for meals in college etc.

refer' vi. relate (to) -vt. send to for information; ascribe to; submit for decision (-rr-) -referee' n. arbitrator; umpire -v. act as referee -ref'erence n. act of referring; citation; appeal to judgment of another; testimonial; one to whom inquiries as to character etc. may be made -referen'dum n. submitting of question to electorate (pl. -dums, -da)

refine' vt. purify -refine'ment n.

subtlety; elaboration; fineness of taste or manners –**refi'nery** n. place where sugar, oil etc. is refined

refla'tion n. increase in economic activity of country etc.

reflect' vt. throw back, esp. light; cast (discredit etc.) upon –vi. meditate –**reflec'tion, reflex'ion** n. reflecting; image of object given back by mirror etc.; thought; expression of thought –**reflect'ive** a. –**reflec'tor** n.

re'flex n. reflex action –a. (of muscular action) involuntary; bent back –**reflex'ive** a. Grammar describes verb denoting agent's action on himself

reform' v. improve; abandon evil practices –n. improvement –**reforma'tion** n. –**reform'er** n.

refract' vi. change course of light etc. passing from one medium to another –**refrac'tion** n.

refract'ory a. unmanageable

refrain' vi. abstain (from)

refrain' n. chorus

refresh' vt. revive; renew; brighten –**refresh'ment** n. that which refreshes, esp. food, drink

refrig'erate [-frij'-] vt. freeze; cool –**refrig'erant** n./a. –**refrigera'tion** n. –**refrig'erator** n. apparatus in which foods, drinks are kept cool

ref'uge n. shelter, sanctuary –**refugee'** n. one who seeks refuge, esp. in foreign country

refund' vt. pay back –n. [re'-]

refuse'¹ [-z] vt. decline, deny, reject –**refu'sal** n.

ref'use² [-yōos] n. rubbish

refute' vt. disprove –**refuta'tion** n.

re'gal a. of, like a king –**rega'lia** pl.n. insignia of royalty; emblems of high office –**regal'ity** n.

regale' vt. give pleasure to; feast

regard' vt. look at; consider; relate to –n. look; attention; particular respect; esteem –pl. expression of good will –**regard'less** a. heedless –adv. in spite of everything

regatt'a n. meeting for boat races

regen'erate [-jen'-] v. reform; recreate; reorganize –**regenera'tion** n.

re'gent n. ruler of kingdom during absence, minority etc., of its monarch –**re'gency** n.

regg'ae [-gā] n. popular music with strong beat

regime' [rā-zhēm'] n. system of government

reg'imen [rej'-] n. prescribed system of diet etc.

reg'iment [rej'-] n. organized body of troops –vt. discipline (too) strictly –**regiment'al** a.

re'gion [-jon] n. area, district; part; sphere –**re'gional** a.

reg'ister [rej'-] n. list; catalogue; device for registering; range of voice or instrument –v. show, be shown on meter, face etc. –vt. enter in register; record –**regis'trar** n. keeper of a register; senior hospital doctor –**registra'tion** n. –**reg'istry** n. registering; place where registers are kept

reg'nant a. reigning

regorge' vt. vomit up

regress' vi. revert to former place, condition etc. –**regres'sion** n.

regret' vt. feel sorry, distressed for loss of or on account of (-tt-) –n. –**regret'ful** a. –**regrett'able** n.

reg'ular a. normal; habitual; according to rule; periodical; straight –n. soldier in standing army –**regular'ity** n.

reg'ulate vt. adjust; arrange; govern –**regula'tion** n. –**reg'ulator** n.

regur'gitate [-gurj'i-] v. vomit; bring back (swallowed food) into mouth –**regurgita'tion** n.

rehabil'itate [rē-] vt. help (person) to readjust to society after illness, imprisonment etc.; restore to former position –**rehabilita'tion** n.

rehash' n. old materials presented in new form

rehearse' [-hurs'] vt. practise (play etc.); repeat; train –**rehears'al** n.

reign [rān] n. period of sovereign's rule –vi. rule

reimburse' [rē-im-] vt. pay back

rein [rān] n. strap attached to bit to guide horse; instrument for governing

reincarna'tion [rē-in-] n. rebirth of soul in successive bodies

rein'deer [rān'-] n. deer of cold regions

reinforce' [rē-in-] vt. strengthen with new support, material, force –**reinforce'ment** n.

reinstate' [rē-in-] vt. replace, restore

reit'erate [rē-it'-] vt. repeat again –**reitera'tion** n.

reject' vt. refuse to accept; put aside; discard; renounce –n. [rē'-] person or thing rejected –**rejec'tion** n.

rejoice' v. make or be joyful

rejoin' vt. reply -**rejoin'der** n.

reju'venate vt. restore to youth -**rejuvena'tion** n.

relapse' vi. fall back into evil, illness etc. -n.

relate' vt. narrate; establish relation between; make reference to -vi. (with **to**) form sympathetic relationship

rela'tion n. relative condition; connection by blood or marriage; connection between things; narrative -**rela'tionship** n. -**rel'ative** a. dependent on relation to something else; having reference (to) -n. one connected by blood or marriage -**rel'ativity** n.

relax' v. make, become loose or slack; ease up make, become less strict -**relaxa'tion** n. recreation; abatement

re'lay n. fresh set of people or animals relieving others; Radio, Television broadcasting station receiving programmes from another station -vt. (-la') pass on, as message (relayed', re'laying) -**relay race** race between teams of which each runner races part of distance

release' vt. set free; permit showing of (film etc.) -n. releasing; permission to show publicly; film, record etc. newly issued

rel'egate vt. consign; demote -**relega'tion** n.

relent' vi. become less severe -**relent'less** a.

rel'evant a. having to do with the matter in hand -**rel'evance** n.

reli'able, reli'ance see RELY

rel'ic n. thing remaining

relief' n. alleviation of pain etc.; money, food given to victims of disaster; release from duty; one who relieves another; bus, plane etc. operating when a scheduled service is full; freeing of besieged city; projection of carved design from surface; prominence -**relieve'** vt.

relig'ion [-lij'-] n. system of belief in, worship of a supernatural power or god -**relig'ious** a.

relin'quish v. give up

rel'ish v. enjoy -n. liking; savoury taste

reluc'tant a. unwilling -**reluct'ance** n.

rely' vi. depend (on); trust (relied', rely'ing) -**reliabil'ity** n. -**reli'able** a. -**reli'ance** n. trust; confidence

remain' vi. be left behind; continue;

last -**remains'** pl.n. relics; dead body -**remain'der** n.

remand' [-ah-] vt. send back, esp. into custody

remark' v./n. (make) casual comment (on) -**remark'able** a. unusual

rem'edy n. means of curing -vt. put right (-edied, -edying)

remem'ber v. retain in, recall to memory -**remem'brance** n.

remind' [-mind'] vt. cause to remember -**remind'er** n.

rem'inisce [-is'] vi. talk, write of past times, experiences etc. -**rem'inis'cence** n. -**reminis'cent** a.

remiss' a. careless

remit' v. send money for goods etc.; refrain from exacting; give up; return; slacken -n. [rē-] area of authority -**remis'sion** n. abatement; reduction of prison term; pardon -**remitt'ance** n. sending of money

rem'nant n. fragment

remon'strate vi. protest -**remon'strance** n.

remorse' n. regret and repentance -**remorse'ful** a. -**remorse'less** a. pitiless

remote' a. distant; aloof

remove' [-mōōv'] v. take, go away; transfer; withdraw -**remo'val** [-ōō-] n.

remu'nerate vt. reward, pay -**remunera'tion** n. -**remu'nerative** a.

renais'sance [-nā'səns] n. revival, rebirth

re'nal a. of the kidneys

rend v. tear apart; burst (**rent**, **rend'ing**)

rend'er vt. submit; give in return; cause to become; represent; melt down; plaster

rend'ezvous [rond'i-vōō] n. meeting place; appointment

ren'egade n. deserter

reneg(u)e' [-nēg'] vi. go back (on) (promise etc.)

renew' vt. begin again; make valid again; make new; restore; replenish -**renew'al** n.

renounce' vt. give up, disown; resign, as claim -**renuncia'tion** n.

ren'ovate vt. restore, repair -**renova'tion** n.

renown' n. fame

rent' n. payment for use of land, buildings etc. -vt.

rent' n. -pt./pp. of REND

rep n. short for repertory or representative

repair' vt. make whole again; mend

-repara'tion n. compensation

repair'[1] vi. go (to)

repartee' n. witty retort; interchange of them

repast' [-ah-] n. meal

repat'riate vt. send (someone) back to his own country **-repatria'tion** n.

repay' vt. pay back; make return for (**repaid'**, **repay'ing**) **-repay'ment** n.

repeal' vt. revoke, cancel -n.

repeat' vt. say, do again -vi. recur -n. act, instance of repeating **-repeat'edly** [-id-li] adv. **-repeti'tion** n. act of repeating; thing repeated **-repet'itive** a.

repel' vt. drive back; be repulsive to (-ll-) **-repel'lent** a./n.

repent' v. feel regret for deed or omission **-repent'ance** n. **-repent'ant** a.

repercus'sion [-kush'-] n. indirect effect, oft. unpleasant; echo

rep'ertoire [-twar] n. stock of plays, songs etc. that player or company can give **-rep'ertory (theatre, company)** (theatre etc. with) permanent company producing succession of plays

repeti'tion see REPEAT

repine' vi. fret, complain

replace' vt. substitute for; put back **-replace'ment** n.

replen'ish vt. fill up again **-replen'ishment** n.

replete' a. filled, gorged **-reple'tion** n.

rep'lica n. exact copy

reply' v. answer (**replied'**, **reply'ing**) -n.

report' n. account; written statement of child's progress at school; rumour; repute; bang -vi. announce; give account of; complain about -vi. make report; present oneself (to) **-report'er** n.

repose' n. peace; composure; sleep -vi. rest -vt. place **-repos'itory** n. place where valuables are deposited for safekeeping

reprehen'sible a. deserving censure; unworthy

represent' [-zent'] vt. stand for; deputize for; act; symbolize; make out to be; describe **-representa'tion** n. **-represent'ative** n. one chosen to stand for group; salesman -a. typical

repress' vt. keep down or under **-repres'sion** n. **-repres'sive** a.

reprieve' vt. suspend execution of

(condemned person) -n. postponement or cancellation of punishment; respite

rep'rimand [-mahnd] n./vt. rebuke

repri'sal [-zal] n. retaliation

reproach' vt. blame, rebuke -n. scolding; thing bringing discredit **-reproach'ful** a.

rep'robate a./n. depraved (person)

reproduce' [re-] v. produce copy of; bring new individuals into existence **-reproduc'tion** n. **-reproduc'tive** a.

reprove' vt. censure, rebuke **-reproof'** n.

rep'tile n. cold-blooded, air breathing vertebrate, as snake

repub'lic n. state without monarch governed by elected representatives **-repub'lican** a./n.

repu'diate vt. reject authority or validity of **-repudia'tion** n.

repug'nant a. offensive; distasteful; contrary **-repug'nance** n.

repulse' vt. drive back; rebuff; repel -n. **-repul'sion** n. **-repul'sive** a. disgusting

repute' vt. consider -n. reputation **-rep'utable** a. of good repute **-reputa'tion** n. estimation in which person is held; character; good name

request' n. asking; thing asked for -vt. ask

Re'quiem [rek'wi-əm] n. Mass for the dead

require' vt. need; demand **-require'ment** n.

req'uisite [-zit] a./n. essential

requisi'tion [-zish'-] n. formal demand, eg for materials -vt. demand; press into service

requite' vt. repay **-requi'tal** n.

rescind' [-sind'] vt. cancel

res'cue vt. save, extricate -n. **-res'cuer** n.

research' n. investigation to discover facts -v.

resem'ble [-z-] vt. be like; look like **-resem'blance** n.

resent' [-z-] vt. show, feel indignation **-resent'ful** a. **-resent'ment** n.

reserve' [-z-] vt. hold back, set aside -n. (also pl.) something esp. troops kept for emergencies; area of land reserved for particular purpose or group (also reservation); reticence **-reserva'tion** n. reserving; thing reserved; doubt; limitation **-reserved'** a.

res'ervoir [rez'ər-vwahr] n. enclosed area for storage of water; receptacle for liquid, gas etc.

reside' [-z-] vi. dwell permanently -**res'idence** n. home -**res'ident** a./n. -**residen'tial** a.

res'idue [rez'-] n. remainder -**sid'ual** a.

resign' [-zīn'] v. give up (esp. office, job); reconcile (oneself) to -**resigna'tion** [-zig-nā'-] n. -**resigned'** a.

resil'ient [-z-] a. elastic; (of person) recovering quickly from shock etc. -**resil'ience** n.

res'in [rez'-] n. sticky substance from plants, esp. firs and pines -**res'inous** a.

resist' [-z-] v. withstand, oppose -**resist'ance** n. resisting; opposition -**resist'ant** a. -**resist'or** n.

res'olute [rez'-lōōt] a. determined -**resolu'tion** n. resolving; firmness; thing resolved; decision, vote

resolve' [-z-] v. decide; vote; separate component parts of; make clear -n. fixed purpose

res'onance [rez'-] n. echoing, esp. in deep tone -**res'onant** a.

resort' [-z-] vi. have recourse; frequent -n. place of recreation eg beach; recourse

resound' [-z-] vi. echo, go on sounding -**resound'ing** a.

resource' [-zawrs', -sawrs'] n. ingenuity; that to which one resorts for support; expedient -pl. stock that can be drawn on; funds -**resource'ful** a.

respect' n. esteem; aspect; reference -vt. treat with esteem; show consideration for -**respectabil'ity** n. -**respect'able** a. worthy of respect; fairly good -**respect'ful** a. -**respect'ing** prep. concerning -**respect'ive** a. relating separately to each; separate

respire' v. breathe -**respira'tion** n. -**res'pirator** n. apparatus worn over mouth and breathed through -**res'piratory** a.

res'pite n. pause; interval; reprieve

resplend'ent a. brilliant, shining

respond' vi. answer; react -**respond'ent** a. replying -n. one who answers; defendant -**response'** n. -**respon'sive** a. readily reacting

respon'sible a. liable to answer for; dependable; involving responsibility -**responsibil'ity** n.

rest' n. repose; freedom from exertion etc.; pause; support -v. take, give rest; support, be supported -**rest'ful** a. -**rest'less** a.

rest² n. remainder -vi. remain

rest'aurant [-ta-rong, -ront] n. commercial establishment serving food

restitu'tion n. giving back; compensation

rest'ive a. restless

restore' vt. repair, renew; give back -**restora'tion** n. -**restor'ative** a./n.

restrain' vt. hold back; prevent -**restraint'** n. restraining; self-control

restrict' vt. limit -**restric'tion** n.

result' [-z-] vi. follow as consequence; happen; end -n. outcome -**result'ant** a.

resume' [-z-] vt. begin again -**rés'umé** [rezyoo-mā] n. summary -**resump'tion** [-z-] n.

resur'gence n. rising again -**resur'gent** a.

resurrect' vt. restore to life, use -**resurrec'tion** n.

resus'citate vt. revive to life, consciousness -**resuscita'tion** n.

re'tail' n. sale in small quantities -adv. by retail -v. sell, be sold, retail; [-tāl'] recount -**re'tailer** n.

retain' vt. keep; engage services of -**retain'er** n. fee to retain esp. barrister; Hist. follower of nobleman etc. -**reten'tion** n. -**reten'tive** a.

retal'iate v. repay in kind -**retalia'tion** n.

retard' vt. make slow; impede development of -**retarda'tion** n. -**retard'ed** a.

retch vi. try to vomit

ret'icent a. reserved; uncommunicative -**ret'icence** n.

ret'ina n. light-sensitive membrane at back of eye

ret'inue n. band of followers

retire' vi. give up office or work; go away; go to bed -**retire'ment** n. -**retir'ing** a. unobtrusive, shy

retort' v. reply; retaliate -n. vigorous reply; vessel with bent neck used for distilling

retouch' vt. touch up, improve

retrace' vt. go back over

retract' v. draw back, recant -**tract'able, -ible** a. -**retrac'tion** n.

re'tread n. renovated tyre

retreat' vi. move back -n. withdrawal; place to which anyone retires; refuge

retrench' vt. reduce expenditure -**retrench'ment** n.

retribu'tion n. recompense, esp. for evil

retrieve' vt. fetch back again; regain -**retriev'al** n. -**retriev'er** n. dog trained to retrieve game

retroact'ive a. applying to the past

ret'rograde a. going backwards, reverting

ret'rospect n. survey of past -**retrospec'tive** a.

return' vi. go, come back -vt. give, send back; report officially; elect -n. returning; profit; report -**returning officer** one conducting election

reu'nion n. gathering of people who have been apart

Rev. Reverend

rev n. inf. revolution (of engine)

revalue v. adjust exchange value of currency upwards

revamp' vt. renovate, restore

reveal' vt. make known; show -**revela'tion** n.

reveille [-val'i] n. morning bugle call etc. to waken soldiers

rev'el vi. take pleasure (in); make merry (-ll-) -n. (usu. pl.) merry-making -**rev'elry** n.

revenge' n. retaliation for wrong done -v. avenge; make retaliation for -**revenge'ful** a.

rev'enue n. income, esp. of state

rever'berate v. echo, resound -**reverbera'tion** n.

revere' [-vēr'] vt. hold in great regard or religious respect -**rever'ence** n. -**rev'erend** a. (esp. as prefix to clergyman's name) worthy of reverence -**rev'erent** a.

rev'erie n. daydream

revers' [-vēr'] n. lapel

reverse' v. (of vehicle) (cause to) move backwards -vt. turn other way round; change completely -n. opposite; side opposite; defeat -a. -**rever'sal** n. -**revers'ible** a. -**reverse gear** mechanism enabling vehicle to move backwards

revert' vi. return to former state, subject -**rever'sion** n.

review' [-vyōō'] vt. examine; reconsider; hold, make, write review of -n. survey; critical notice of book etc.; periodical with critical articles; inspection of troops -**review'er** n.

revile' vt. abuse viciously

revise' [-vīz'] vt. look over and correct; restudy (work done previously); change -**revi'sion** n.

revive' v. bring, come back to life, vigour, use etc. -**revi'val** n.

revoke' vt. withdraw; cancel -**rev'ocable** a. -**revoca'tion** n.

revolt' [-ō-] n. rebellion -vi. rise in rebellion; feel disgust -vt. affect with disgust -**revolt'ing** a. disgusting

revolve' vt. turn round; be centred on -vt. rotate -**revolu'tion** [-lōō-] n. violent overthrow of government; great change; complete rotation -**revolu'tionary** a./n. -**revolu'tionize** vt.

revol'ver n. pistol with revolving magazine

revue' n. entertainment with sketches and songs

revul'sion n. repugnance or abhorrence

reward' vt. pay, make return for service, conduct etc. -n. -**reward'ing** a.

rhap'sody n. enthusiastic (musical) composition or utterance -**rhap'sodize** v.

rhe'buck n. brownish-grey S Afr. antelope

rhe'sus n. small, long-tailed monkey -**rhesus factor** (also **Rh factor**) feature distinguishing different types of human blood

rhet'oric n. art of effective speaking or writing; exaggerated language -**rhetor'ical** [-o'ri-] a. (of question) not requiring an answer

rheum [rōōm] n. watery discharge -**rheum'y** a.

rheum'atism [rōōm'-] n. painful inflammation of joints or muscles -**rheumat'ic** a./n.

rhinoc'eros [-os'-] n. large animal with one or two horns on nose

rhododen'dron n. evergreen flowering shrub

rhom'bus, rhomb [rom] n. diamond-shaped figure -**rhom'boid** a.

rhu'barb n. garden plant with edible fleshy stalks

rhyme, rime n. identity of sounds in words; word or syllable identical in sound to another; verse marked by rhyme

rhythm [rirH'əm] n. measured beat of words, music etc. -**rhyth'mic(al)** a. -**rhyth'mically** adv.

RI religious instruction

rib n. one of curved bones springing from spine and forming framework of upper part of body; raised series of rows in knitting etc. -vt. mark with ribs; knit to form a rib pattern (-**bb-**) -**ribb'ing** n.

rib'ald a. irreverent, scurrilous -**rib'aldry** n.

ribb'on *n.* narrow band of fabric; long strip of anything

ribofla'vin [-rī] *n.* form of vitamin B

rice *n.* Eastern cereal plant; its seeds as food

rich *a.* wealthy; fertile; abounding; valuable; containing much fat or sugar; mellow; amusing –**rich'es** *pl.n.* wealth

rick[1] *n.* stack of hay etc.

rick[2] *vt./n.* sprain, wrench

rick'ets *n.* disease of children marked by softening of bones –**rick'ety** *a.* shaky, unstable

ric'ochet [-shā] *vi.* (of bullet) rebound or be deflected –*n.*

rid *vt.* relieve of; free (**rid, ridd'ing**) –**ridd'ance** *n.*

ridd'en *pp.* of RIDE –*a.* afflicted, affected, as **disease-ridden**

rid'dle[1] *n.* question made puzzling to test one's ingenuity; puzzling thing, person

rid'dle[2] *vt.* pierce with many holes –*n.* coarse sieve

ride *v.* sit on and control or propel; be carried on or across –*vi.* go on horseback or in vehicle; lie at anchor (**rode, ridd'en, ri'ding**) –*n.* journey on horse, in vehicle; riding track –**ri'der** *n.* one who rides; supplementary clause; addition to a document

ridge *n.* long narrow hill; line of meeting of two sloping surfaces –*vt.* form into ridges

ridic'ulous *a.* deserving to be laughed at, absurd –**rid'icule** *vt.* laugh at, deride –*n.*

ri'ding *n.* former administrative district; C parliamentary constituency

rife *a.* prevalent, common

riff'raff *n.* rabble

ri'fle *vt.* search and rob –*n.* firearm with long barrel

rift *n.* crack, split

rig *vt.* provide (ship) with ropes etc.; equip; arrange in dishonest way (-**gg**-) –*n.* apparatus for drilling for oil –**rigg'ing** *n.* ship's spars and ropes

right [rīt] *a.* just; in accordance with truth and duty; true; correct; proper; of side that faces east when front is turned to north; *Politics* conservative; straight –*v.* make, become right –*n.* claim, title etc. allowed or due; what is right; conservative political party –*adv.* straight; properly; very; on or to right side –**right'ful** *a.* –**right'ly** *adv.* –**right angle** angle of 90 degrees

right'eous [rī'chas] *a.* virtuous; good –**right'eousness** *n.*

rig'id [rij-] *a.* inflexible; stiff –**rigid'ity** *n.*

rig'marole *n.* long, complicated procedure; nonsense

rig'or mor'tis stiffening of body after death

rig'our *n.* severity; hardship –**rig'orous** *a.*

rile *vt. inf.* anger

rill *n.* small stream

rim *n.* edge

rime *n.* hoarfrost

ri'mu [rēmōō] *n.* tall N.Z. tree, red pine; its valuable cabinet wood

rind [-ī-] *n.* outer coating of fruits etc.

ring[1] *n.* circular band for finger; circle of persons; enclosed area –*vt.* put ring round –**ring'er** *n.* –**ring'bark** *vt.* kill tree by cutting bark round trunk –**ring'leader** *n.* instigator of mutiny, riot etc. –**ring'let** *n.* curly lock of hair –**ring road** main road that bypasses a town (centre) –**ring'worm** *n.* skin disease

ring[2] *v.* (cause to) give out resonant sound, as bell; telephone (**rang** *pt.*, **rung** *pp.*) –*n.*

rink *n.* sheet of ice for skating

rink'hals [-hows] *n.* S Afr. ring-necked cobra

rinse [-s] *vt.* remove soap from by applying water; wash lightly –*n.* a rinsing; liquid to tint hair

ri'ot *n./vi.* (engage in) tumult, disorder –**ri'otous** *a.*

RIP requiescat in pace (*Lat.,* rest in peace)

rip *vt./n.* cut, slash (-**pp**-)

ripe *a.* ready to be reaped, eaten etc. –**ri'pen** *v.*

rip'ple *n.* slight wave; soft sound –*vi.* form into little waves; (of sounds) rise and fall gently

rise [rīz] *vi.* get up; move upwards; reach higher level; increase; rebel; have its source (**rose, ris'en, ri'sing**) –*n.* rising; upslope; increase –**ri'sing** *n.* revolt

risk *n.* chance of disaster or loss –*vt.* put in jeopardy; take chance of –**risk'y** *a.*

ris'qué [-kā] *a.* suggestive of indecency

rite *n.* formal practice or custom, esp. religious –**rit'ual** *n.* prescribed order of rites; stereotyped behaviour –*a.* concerning rites –**rit'ualism** *n.*

ri'val *n.* one that competes with

another -vt. vie with (**-ll-**) -**ri'valry** n.

riv'en a. split

riv'er n. large natural stream of water

riv'et n. bolt for fastening metal plates, the end being put through holes and then beaten flat -vt. fasten firmly

riv'ulet n. small stream

RL Rugby League

rly. railway

RM C Rural Municipality

RN Royal Navy

RNZAF Royal New Zealand Air Force

RNZN Royal New Zealand Navy

roach n. freshwater fish

road n. track, way prepared for passengers, vehicles etc.; direction, way; street -**road'side** n./a.

roam v. wander about, rove

roar [raw] v./n. (utter) loud deep hoarse sound

roast v. cook in oven or over open fire; make, be very hot -n. roasted joint -a. roasted

rob vt. steal from (**-bb-**) -**robb'er** n. -**robb'ery** n.

robe n. long outer garment -vt. dress -vi. put on robes

rob'in n. small brown bird with red breast

ro'bot n. automated machine, esp. performing functions in human manner; SA traffic lights

robust' a. sturdy, strong

rock[1] n. stone; mass of stone; hard sweet in sticks -**rock'y** a. -**rock bottom** lowest possible level

rock[2] v. (cause to) sway to and fro -n. style of pop music -**rock'er** n. curved piece of wood etc. on which thing may rock; rocking chair

rock'et n. self-propelling device powered by burning of explosive contents -vi. move fast, esp. upwards, as rocket

rod n. slender straight bar, stick; cane

ro'dent n. gnawing animal

ro'deo [or -dā'ō] n. US, A display of bareback riding, cattle handling etc.

roe[1] n. small species of deer

roe[2] n. mass of eggs in fish

rogue [rōg] n. scoundrel; mischief-loving person or child -**ro'guish** [-gish] a.

role, rôle n. actor's part; specific task or function

roll [rōl] v. move by turning over and over -vt. wind round; smooth out with roller -vi. move, sweep along; undulate -n. act of rolling; anything rolled up; list; bread baked into small round; continuous sound, as of drums, thunder etc. -**roll'er** n. cylinder of wood, stone, metal etc.; long wave of sea -**roller skate** skate with wheels instead of runner -**rolling pin** cylindrical roller for pastry -**rolling stock** locomotives, carriages etc. of railway

roll'icking a. boisterously jovial and merry

ro'ly-po'ly n. pudding of suet pastry -a. round, plump

Ro'man a. of Rome or Church of Rome -**Roman Catholic** member of that section of Christian Church which acknowledges supremacy of the Pope

romance' n. love affair; mysterious or exciting quality; tale of chivalry; tale remote from ordinary life -vi. exaggerate, fantasize -**roman'tic** a. characterized by romance; of love; of literature etc. of passion and imagination -n. -**roman'ticism** n.

Rom'any n. gypsy; gypsy language -a.

romp vi. play wildly -n. spell of romping -**rom'pers** pl.n. child's overall

rood [rōōd] n. crucifix

roof [rōōf] n. outside upper covering of building -vt. put roof on, over

rooi'bos [roi'-] n. S Afr. red-leafed tree

rooi'kat [roi'-] n. S Afr. lynx

rook n. bird of crow family -vt. sl. swindle, cheat

rook'ie n. inf. recruit

room [rōōm] n. space; division of house; scope -pl. lodgings -**room'y** a. spacious

roost [-ōō-] n./v. perch

root [rōōt] n. underground part of plant; source, origin; Anatomy embedded portion of tooth, hair etc. -v. (cause to) take root; pull by roots; dig, burrow

rope n. thick cord -vt. secure, mark off with rope

ro'sary n. series of prayers; string of beads for counting these prayers

rose n. shrub usu. with prickly stems and fragrant flowers; the flower; pink colour -**ro'seate** a. rose-coloured, rosy -**rosette'** n. rose-shaped bunch of ribbon -**ro'sy** a. flushed; promising -**rose-coloured** a. having colour of rose; unwarrantably optimistic

ro'sé [-zā] n. pink wine

rose'mary n. evergreen fragrant flowering shrub

ros'in [roz'-] n. resin

ros'ter n. list of turns of duty

ros'trum n. platform, stage (pl. -trums, -tra)

rot v. decompose naturally; corrupt (-tt-) -n. decay; any disease producing decomposition of tissue; inf. nonsense **-rott'en** a.

ro'ta n. roster, list

ro'tary a. (of movement) circular **-rotate'** v. (cause to) move round centre **-rota'tion** n.

rote n. mechanical repetition

ro'tor n. revolving portion of a dynamo motor or turbine

rotund' a. round; plump

rouge [roozh] n. red powder, cream used to colour cheeks

rough [ruf] a. not smooth; violent, stormy; rude; approximate; in preliminary form -n. make rough; plan; (with it) live without usual comforts etc. -n. rough state or area; sketch **-rough'en** vt. **-rough'age** n. unassimilated portion of food

round [-ow-] a. spherical, circular, curved; complete; roughly correct; considerable -adv. with circular course -n. thing round in shape; recurrent duties; stage in competition; customary course; game (of golf); period in boxing match etc.; cartridge for firearm -prep. about; on all sides of -v. make, become round -vt. move round **-round'ers** pl.n. ball game **-round'about** n. revolving circular platform on which people ride for amusement; road junction at which traffic passes round a central island -a. not straightforward **-round up** drive (cattle) together

rouse [rowz] vt. wake up, stir up, excite -vi. waken

rout [rowt] n. overwhelming defeat, disorderly retreat -vt. put to flight

route [root] n. road, chosen way

routine' [roo-tēn'] n. regularity of procedure -a. ordinary, regular

rove v. wander, roam **-ro'ver** n.

row' [rō] n. number of things in a straight line

row' [rō] v. propel boat by oars -n. spell of rowing **- rowing boat**

row' inf. n. dispute; disturbance -vi. quarrel noisily

row'an [or rō'-] n. tree producing bright red berries, mountain ash

rowd'y a./n. disorderly, noisy (person)

row'lock [rol'ok] n. device to hold oar on gunwale of boat

roy'al a. of king or queen **-roy'alist** n. supporter of monarchy **-roy'alty** n. royal power; royal persons; payment for right, use of invention or copyright

rpm revolutions per minute

RSPCA Royal Society for the Prevention of Cruelty to Animals

RSVP répondez s'il vous plaît (Fr. please reply)

RU Rugby Union

rub vt. apply pressure to with circular or backwards and forwards movement; clean, polish, dry; thus; abrade, chafe; remove by friction -vi. come into contact accompanied by friction; become frayed or worn by friction (-bb-) -n. rubbing; impediment

rubb'er n. elastic coagulated sap of certain tropical trees; piece of rubber etc. used for erasing -a.

rubb'ish n. refuse; anything worthless; nonsense

rub'ble n. fragments of stone

rubell'a n. mild contagious viral disease, German measles

ru'bicund [roo'-] a. ruddy

ru'by [roo'-] n. precious red gem; its colour -a. of this colour

ruck' n. crowd; common herd

ruck' n./v. crease

ruck'sack n. pack carried on back, knapsack

ruc'tion n. inf. noisy disturbance

rudd'er n. steering device for boat, aircraft

rudd'y a. of healthy red colour

rude a. impolite; coarse; vulgar; roughly made

ru'diments [roo'-] pl.n. elements, first principles **-rudimen'tary** a.

rue [roo] v. grieve for; regret **-rue'ful** a.

ruff n. frilled collar; natural collar of feathers, fur etc. on some birds and animals **-ruf'fle** vt. rumple; annoy; frill -n. frilled trimming

ruff'ian n. violent, lawless person

rug n. small floor mat; woollen coverlet

rug'by n. form of football in which the ball may be carried

rugg'ed a. rough; austere

ru'in [roo'-] n. destruction; downfall;

fallen or broken state; loss of wealth etc. -pl. ruined buildings etc. -vt. bring or come to ruin -ru'inous a.

rule n. principle; government; what is usual; measuring stick -vt. govern; decide; mark with straight lines -ru'ler n. one who governs; stick for measuring or ruling lines

rum n. spirit distilled from sugar cane

rum'ble vi./n. (make) noise as of distant thunder

ru'minate [rōō-] vi. chew cud; ponder over -ru'minant a./n. cud-chewing (animal)

rumm'age v. search thoroughly

rumm'y n. card game

ru'mour [rōōmə] n. hearsay, un-proved statement -vt. put round as rumour

rump n. tail end; buttocks

rum'ple v./n. crease, wrinkle

rum'pus n. disturbance

run vi. move with more rapid gait than walking; go quickly; flow; flee; compete in race, contest, election; -vt. cross by running; manage; operate (ran pt., run pp., runn'ing pr.p.) -n. act, spell of running; rush; tendency, course; enclosure for do-mestic fowls; ride in car; unravelled stitches; score of one at cricket -runn'er n. racer; messenger; curved piece of wood on which sleigh slides; stem of plant forming new roots; strip of cloth, carpet -runn'ing a. continuous; consecutive; flowing -n. act of moving or flowing quickly; management -runn'y a. -run'down n. summary -run-down a. exhausted -run down stop working; reduce; ex-haust; denigrate -run'way n. level stretch where aircraft take off and land

rung n. crossbar in ladder

runt n. unusually small animal

rup'ture n. breaking, breach; hernia -v. break; burst, sever

rur'al [roor'-] a. of the country; rustic

ruse [-z] n. stratagem, trick

rush[1] v. hurry or cause to hurry; move violently or rapidly -n. rushing -a. done with speed

rush[2] n. marsh plant with slender pithy stem

rusk n. kind of biscuit

russ'et a. reddish-brown

rust n. reddish-brown coating formed on iron; disease of plants -v. affect with rust -rust'y a.

rust'ic a. of country people; rural; of rude manufacture -n. countryman

rus'tle[1] [-sl] vi./n. (make) sound as of blown dead leaves etc.

rus'tle[2] [-sl] vt. US steal (cattle) -rus'tler n.

rut n. furrow made by wheel; settled habit

ruth'less [rōōth'-] a. merciless

rye n. grain; plant bearing it

S

s second(s)

Sabb'ath n. Jewish and Christian day of worship and rest; Sunday

sa'ble n. small weasellike Arctic animal; its fur

sab'otage [-tahzh] n. intentional damage done to roads, machines etc., esp. secretly in war -v. -saboteur' n.

sa'bre [-bər] n. curved cavalry sword

sac n. pouchlike structure in an ani-mal or vegetable body

sacc'harin [sak'ə-] n. artificial sweetener -sacc'harine a. lit./fig. excessively sweet

sach'et [sash'ā] n. small envelope or bag, esp. one holding liquid

sack[1] n. large bag, orig. of coarse material; pillaging; inf. dismissal -vt. pillage (captured town); inf. dismiss -sack'ing n. material for sacks -sack'cloth n. coarse fabric used for sacks

sac'rament n. one of certain cere-monies of Christian Church esp. Eucharist -sacrament'al a.

sa'cred a. dedicated, regarded as holy; revered; inviolable

sac'rifice n. giving something up for sake of something else; thing so given up; making of offering to a god; thing offered -vt. offer as sacrifice; give up -sacrifi'cial [-fish-] a.

sac'rilege [-lij] n. misuse, des-ecration of something sacred -sac'rilegious a.

sac'rosanct a. preserved by re-ligious fear against desecration or violence

sad a. sorrowful; unsatisfactory, de-plorable -sadd'en vt. make sad -sad'ly adv. -sad'ness n.

sad'dle n. rider's seat to fasten on horse, bicycle etc.; joint of meat -vt.

put saddle on; lay burden on -sadd'ler n. maker of saddles *etc.*

sa'dism n. love of inflicting pain **-sa'dist** n. **-sadist'ic** a.

s.a.e. stamped addressed envelope

safar'i n. (party making) overland (hunting) journey, *esp.* in Africa

safe a. secure, protected; uninjured, out of danger; not involving risk; trustworthy; sure -n. strong lockable container **-safe'ly** adv. **-safe'ty** n. **-safe'guard** n. protection -vt. protect

saff'ron n. crocus; orange coloured flavouring obtained from it; the colour -a. orange

sag vi. sink in middle; curve downwards under pressure; hang loosely (-gg-) -n. droop

sag'a [sahg'ə] n. legend of Norse heroes; any long (heroic) story

saga'cious a. wise **-sagac'ity** [-gas'-] n.

sage[1] n. very wise man -a. wise

sage[2] n. aromatic herb

sa'go n. starchy cereal from powdered pith of sago palm

said [sed] pt./pp. of SAY

sail n. piece of fabric stretched to catch wind for propelling ship *etc.*; act of sailing; ships collectively; arm of windmill -vi. travel by water; move smoothly; begin voyage -vt. navigate **-sail'or** n. seaman; one who sails

saint n. (title of) person formally recognized (*esp.* by R.C. Church) after death, as having gained by holy deeds a special place in heaven; exceptionally good person **-saint'liness** n. **-saint'ly** a.

sake n. cause, account; end, purpose **-for the sake of** on behalf of; to please or benefit

sal'ad n. mixed vegetables, or fruit, used as food without cooking -a.

salam'i [-lahm'-] n. variety of highly-spiced sausage

sal'ary n. fixed regular payment to persons employed usu. in nonmanual work **-sal'aried** a.

sale n. selling; selling of goods at unusually low prices; auction **-sale'able** a. capable of being sold **-sales'man** n. one travelling to sell goods **-sales'manship** n. skill in selling

sa'lient a. prominent, noticeable; jutting out

sa'line a. containing, consisting of a

chemical salt, *esp.* common salt; salty **-salin'ity** n.

sali'va n. liquid which forms in mouth, spittle

sall'ow a. of unhealthy pale or yellowish colour

sall'y n. rushing out, *esp.* by troops; witty remark -vi. rush; set out (-led, -ying)

salm'on [sam'-] n. large silvery fish with orange-pink flesh valued as food; colour of its flesh -a. of this colour

salon' n. (reception room for) guests in fashionable household; commercial premises of hairdressers, beauticians *etc.*

saloon' n. public room on passenger ship; public room for specified use; *e.g.* billiards; closed car with 2 or 4 doors and 4-6 seats **-saloon bar** first-class bar in hotel *etc.*

sal'sify [-fi] n. purple-flowered plant with edible root

salt [sawlt] n. white powdery or crystalline substance consisting mainly of sodium chloride, used to season or preserve food; chemical compound of acid and metal -vt. season, sprinkle with, preserve with salt **-salt'y** a. of, like salt **-old salt** sailor **-salt'cellar** n. small vessel for salt at table

salu'brious [-lōō'-] a. favourable to health, beneficial

sal'utary a. wholesome, beneficial

salute' [-lōōt'] vt. greet with words or sign; acknowledge with praise -vi. perform military salute -n. word, sign by which one greets another; motion of arm as mark of respect to superior *etc.* in military usage; firing of guns as military greeting of honour **-saluta'tion** [-yoo-tā'-] n.

sal'vage n. act of saving ship or other property from danger of loss; property so saved -vt.

salva'tion n. fact or state of being saved, *esp.* of soul

salve [or sahv] n. healing ointment -vi. anoint with such, soothe

sal'ver n. (silver) tray for presentation of food, letters *etc.*

sal'vo n. simultaneous discharge of guns *etc.* (pl. -vo(e)s)

same a. identical, not different, unchanged; uniform; just mentioned previously **-same'ness** n. similarity; monotony

sam'ovar n. Russian tea urn

sam'pan n. small oriental boat

sam'ple [sah'-] n. specimen -vt.

take, give sample of; try **-sam'pler** *a.* beginner's exercise in embroidery **-sam'pling** *n.*

sanator'ium *n.* hospital, *esp.* for chronically ill; health resort *(pl.* **-riums, -ria)**

sanc'tify *vt.* set apart as holy; free from sin **(-fied, -fying) -sanc'tification** *n.* **-sanc'tity** *n.* saintliness; sacredness **-sanc'tuary** *n.* holy place; place of refuge; nature reserve **-sanc'tum** *n.* sacred place or shrine; person's private room

sanc'tion *n.* permission, authorization; penalty for breaking law **-pl.** boycott or other coercive measure *esp.* by one state against another **-vt.** allow, authorize

sand *n.* substance consisting of small grains of rock or mineral, *esp.* on beach or in desert **-pl.** stretches or banks of this **-vt.** polish, smooth with sandpaper; cover, mix with sand **-sand'y** *a.* like sand; sand-coloured; consisting of, covered with sand **-sand'bag** *n.* bag filled with sand or earth as protection against gunfire, floodwater *etc.* and as weapon **-vt.** beat, hit with sandbag **-sand'paper** *n.* paper with sand stuck on it for scraping or polishing **-sand'piper** *n.* various kinds of shore birds **-sand'-stone** *n.* rock composed of sand

san'dal *n.* shoe consisting of sole attached to straps

sand'wich [san'wij] *n.* two slices of bread with meat or other substance between **-vt.** insert between two other things

sane *a.* of sound mind; sensible, rational **-san'ity** *n.*

sang *pt.* of SING

san'guine [-ng'gwin] *a.* cheerful, confident; ruddy in complexion **-san'guinary** *a.* accompanied by bloodshed; bloodthirsty

san'itary *a.* helping protection of health against dirt *etc.* **-sanita'tion** *n.* measures, apparatus for preservation of public health

sap' *n.* moisture which circulates in plants **-sap'ling** *n.* young tree

sap' *v.* undermine; weaken

sapph'ire [saf-] *n.* (*us.* blue) precious stone; deep blue **-a.**

sar'casm *n.* bitter or wounding ironic remark; (use of) such remarks **-sarcas'tic** *a.* **-sarcas'tically** *adv.*

sarcoph'agus [-kof'-] *n.* stone coffin

sardine' [-dēn] *n.* small fish of herring family

sardon'ic *a.* characterized by irony, mockery or derision

sartor'ial *a.* of tailor, tailoring, or men's clothes

sash' *n.* decorative belt, ribbon, wound around the body

sash' *n.* wooden window frame opened by moving up and down in grooves

Sask. Saskatchewan

Sa'tan *n.* the devil **-satan'ic(al)** *a.* devilish

satch'el *n.* small bag, *esp.* for school books

sate *vt.* satisfy a desire or appetite fully or excessively

sat'ellite *n.* celestial body or man-made projectile orbiting planet; person, country *etc.* dependent on another

sa'tiate [-shi-āt] *vt.* satisfy to the full; surfeit **-sa'tiable** *a.* **-sati'ety** [sǝ-tī'-] *n.*

sat'in *n.* fabric (of silk, rayon *etc.*) with glossy surface on one side

sat'ire *n.* use of ridicule or sarcasm to expose vice and folly **-satir'ic(al)** [-ti'ri-] *a.* **-sat'irist** *n.* **-sat'irize** *vt.* make object of satire

sat'isfy *vt.* content, meet wishes of; pay; fulfil, supply adequately; convince **(-fied, -fying) -satisfac'tion** *n.* **-satisfac'tory** *a.*

sat'urate *vt.* soak thoroughly **-satura'tion** *n.* act, result of saturating

Sat'urday *n.* seventh day of week

sat'urnine *a.* gloomy

sat'yr [-ǝr] *n.* woodland deity, part man, part goat; lustful man **-satyr'ic** [-ti'ri-] *a.*

sauce *n.* liquid added to food to enhance flavour **-vt.** add sauce to **-sauc'y** *a.* impudent **-sauce'pan** *n.* cooking pot with long handle

sau'cer *n.* curved plate put under cup; shallow depression

sault [soō] *n.* C rapids

saun'ter *vi.* walk in leisurely manner, stroll **-n.** leisurely walk or stroll

saus'age [sos'-] *n.* minced meat enclosed in thin tube of animal intestine or synthetic material **-sausage roll** pastry cylinder filled with sausage

sav'age *a.* wild; ferocious; brutal; uncivilized, primitive **-n.** member of savage tribe, barbarian **-vt.** attack ferociously **-sav'agery** *n.*

save *vt.* rescue, preserve; keep for

future; prevent need of -vi. lay by money -prep. except -sa'ving a. delivering from sin; excepting -prep. excepting n. economy -pl. money put by for future use

sa'viour n. person who rescues another; (S-) Christ

sa'vour [-vər] n. characteristic taste or smell -vi. have particular taste or smell -vt. give flavour to; have flavour of; enjoy -sa'voury a. attractive to taste or smell; not sweet

savoy' n. variety of cabbage

saw' n. tool with toothed edge for cutting wood etc. -vt. cut with saw -vi. make movements of sawing (sawed, sawn) -saw'yer n. one who saws timber -saw'dust n. fine wood fragments made in sawing

saw² pt. of SEE

sax'ifrage n. Alpine or rock plant

sax'ophone n. keyed wind instrument

say vt. speak; pronounce; state; express; take as example or as near enough; form and deliver opinion (said pt./pp., say'ing pr.p., says 3rd pers. sing. pres. ind.) -n. what one has to say; chance of saying it; share in decision -say'ing n. maxim, proverb

scab n. crust formed over wound; skin disease; disease of plants -scabb'y a.

scabb'ard n. sheath for sword or dagger

sca'bies [skā-] n. contagious skin disease

scaff'old n. temporary platform for workmen; gallows -scaff'olding n. (material for building) scaffold

scald [skawld] vt. burn with hot liquid or steam; heat (liquid) almost to boiling point -n. injury by scalding

scale¹ n. one of the thin, overlapping plates covering fishes and reptiles; thin flake; incrustation which forms in boilers etc. -vt. remove scales from -vi. come off in scales

scale² n. (chiefly in pl.) weighing instrument

scale³ n. graduated table or sequence of marks at regular intervals used as reference or for fixing standards, as in making measurements, in music etc.; ratio of size between a thing and a model or map of it; (relative) degree, extent -vt. climb -a. proportionate

scall'op [skol-] n. edible shellfish; edging in small curves like edge of

scallop shell -vt. shape like scallop shell; cook in scallop shell

scalp n. skin and hair of top of head -vt. cut off scalp of

scal'pel n. small surgical knife

scamp n. mischievous person

scam'per vi. run about; run hastily -n.

scan vt. look at carefully; measure or read (verse) by metrical feet; examine, search using radar or sonar beam; glance over quickly -vi. (of verse) conform to metrical rules (-nn-) -n. scanning -scann'er n. device, esp. electronic, which scans

scan'dal n. something disgraceful; malicious gossip -scan'dalize vt. shock -scan'dalous a.

scant a. barely sufficient or not sufficient -scant'ily adv. -scan'ty a.

scape'goat n. person bearing blame due to others

scar n. mark left by healed wound, burn or sore; change resulting from emotional distress -v. mark, heal with scar (-rr-) -scarred a.

scarce [skārs] a. hard to find; existing or available in insufficient quantity; uncommon -scarce'ly adv. only just; not quite; definitely or probably not -scarce'ness, scarc'ity n.

scare [skār] vt. frighten -n. fright, sudden panic -scar'y a. inf. -scare'crow n. thing set up to frighten birds from crops; badly dressed or miserable looking person

scarf n. long narrow strip, large piece of material to put round neck, head etc. (pl. scarfs or scarves)

scar'let n. a brilliant red colour; cloth or clothing of this colour, esp. military uniform -a. of this colour; immoral, esp. unchaste -scarlet fever infectious fever with scarlet rash

sca'thing [-ᴀ́ᴛʜ-] a. harshly critical

scatt'er vt. throw in various directions; put here and there; sprinkle -vi. disperse -n.

scav'enge v. search for (anything usable) usu. among discarded material -scav'enger n. person who scavenges; animal, bird which feeds on refuse

scene [sēn] n. place of action of novel, play etc.; place of any action; subdivision of play; view; episode; display of strong emotion -sce'nery n. natural features of district; constructions used on stage to represent a place where action is happening -**sce'nic** a. picturesque; of or on the stage

scent [sent] n. distinctive smell, *esp.* pleasant one; trail; perfume -vt. detect or track (by smell); sense; fill with fragrance

scep'tic [sk-], US **skep'tic** n. one who maintains doubt or disbelief -**scep'tical** a. -**scep'ticism** n.

scep'tre [sep'tə] n. ornamental staff as symbol of royal power

sched'ule [sh-] n. plan of procedure for a project; list; timetable -vt. enter in schedule; plan to occur at certain time -on schedule on time

scheme [sk-] n. plan, design; project; outline -v. devise, plan, *esp.* in underhand manner -**sche'mer** n.

schis'm [sizm] n. (group resulting from) division in political party, church *etc.* -**schismat'ic** n./a.

schizophre'nia [skit-sŏ-frē'-] n. mental disorder involving deterioration, of confusion about personality -**schizophren'ic** a.

school[1] [sk-] n. institution for teaching children or for giving instruction in any subject; buildings of such institution; group of thinkers, writers, artists *etc.* with principles or methods in common -vt. educate; bring under control, train -**schol'ar** n. learned person; one taught in school -**schol'arly** a. learned -**schol'arship** n. learning; prize, grant to student for payment of school or college fees -**scholas'tic** a. of schools or scholars, or education

school[2] [sk-] n. shoal (of fish, whales *etc.*)

schoon'er [sk-] n. fore-and-aft rigged vessel with two or more masts; tall glass

sci'ence [sī'-] n. systematic study and knowledge of natural or physical phenomena; any branch of study concerned with observed material facts -**scientif'ic** a. of the principles of science; systematic -**scientif'ically** adv. -**sci'entist** n. one versed in natural sciences

scin'tillate [sin'-] vi. sparkle; be animated, witty, clever

sci'on [sī'-] n. descendant, heir

scis'sors [siz'-] pl.n. (*esp.* pair of scissors) cutting instrument of two blades pivoted together

scoff [sk-] vt. express derision for -n. -**scoff'er** n.

scold [skō-] v. find fault; reprimand

scone [skon] n. small plain cake baked on griddle or in oven

scoop [-ōō-] n. shovellike tool for ladling, hollowing out *etc.* -vt. use scoop

scoot'er n. child's vehicle propelled by pushing on ground with one foot; light motorcycle also motor scooter

scope n. range of activity or application; room, opportunity

scorch v. burn, be burnt, on surface -n.

score n. points gained in game, competition; group of 20; a lot (*esp. pl.*); musical notation; mark or notch, *esp.* to keep tally; reason, account; grievance -vt. gain points in game; mark; cross out; arrange music (for) -vi. keep tally of points

scorn n. contempt, derision -vt. despise -**scorn'ful** a.

scor'pion n. small lobster-shaped animal with sting at end of jointed tail

scotch vt. put an end to

scot-free' a. without harm or loss

scoun'drel n. villain, blackguard

scour[1] vt. clean, polish by rubbing; clear or flush out

scour[2] v. move rapidly along or over (territory) in search of something

scourge [skurj] n. whip, lash; severe affliction -vt. flog; punish severely

scout n. one sent out to reconnoitre -vi. act as scout

scowl vt./n. (make) gloomy or sullen frown

scrabb'le v. scrape at with hands, claws in disorderly manner

scrag n. lean person or animal; lean end of a neck of mutton -**scrag'gy** a. thin, bony

scram'ble vi. move along or up by crawling, climbing *etc.*; struggle with others (for) -vt. mix up; cook (eggs) beaten up with milk -n. scrambling; rough climb; disorderly proceeding

scrap n. small piece or fragment; leftover material; *inf.* fight -v. break up, discard as useless -vi. *inf.* fight (-pp-) -**scrap'py** a. unequal in quality; badly finished

scrape vt. rub with something sharp; clean, smooth thus; grate; scratch; rub with harsh noise -vt. act, sound of scraping -**scra'per** n. instrument for scraping

scratch vt. score, make narrow

surface mark or wound with something sharp; scrape (skin) with nails to relieve itching; remove, withdraw from list, race *etc.* -*vi.* use claws or nails, *esp.* to relieve itching -*n.* wound, mark or sound made by scratching

scrawl *vt.* write, draw untidily -*n.* thing scrawled

scraw'ny *a.* thin, bony

scream *vi.* utter piercing cry, *esp.* of fear, pain *etc.* -*vt.* utter in a scream -*n.* shrill, piercing cry

scree *n.* loose shifting stones; slope covered with these

screech *vi./n.* scream

screed *n.* long (tedious) letter, passage or speech

screen *n.* device to shelter from heat, light, draught, observation *etc.*; blank surface on which photographic images are projected; windscreen -*vt.* shelter, hide; show (film); examine (group of people) for political motives or for presence of disease, weapons *etc.*

screw [-ōō] *n.* (naillike device or cylinder with) spiral thread cut to engage similar thread or to bore into material (wood *etc.*) to pin or fasten; anything resembling a screw in shape; propeller; twist -*vt.* fasten with screw; twist around -**screw'driver** *n.* tool for turning screws

scrib'ble *v.* write, draw carelessly; make meaningless marks with pen or pencil -*n.* something scribbled -**scrib'bly** *a.*

scribe *n.* writer; copyist -*v.* scratch a line with pointed instrument

scrimp *vt.* make too small or short; treat meanly -**scrim'py** *a.*

script *n.* (system or style of) handwriting; written text of film, play, radio or television programme

scrip'ture *n.* sacred writings; the Bible -**scrip'tural** *a.*

scroll [-ōl] *n.* roll of parchment or paper; ornament shaped thus

scrounge *v. inf.* get without cost, by begging -**scroun'ger** *n.*

scrub[1] *vt.* clean with hard brush and water; scour (**-bb-**) -*n.* scrubbing

scrub[2] *n.* stunted trees; brushwood -**scrubb'y** *a.*

scruff *n.* nape (of neck)

scrum(mage) *n. Rugby* restarting of play in which opposing packs of forwards push against each other to gain possession of the ball

scru'ple *n.* doubt or hesitation

about what is morally right -*vi.* hesitate -**scru'pulous** *a.* extremely conscientious; thorough -**scru'pulousness** *n.*

scru'tiny *n.* close examination; critical investigation -**scru'tinize** *vt.* examine closely

scud *vi.* run fast; run before wind (**-dd-**)

scuff *vi.* drag, scrape with feet in walking -*vt.* scrape with feet; graze -*n.* act, sound of scuffing

scuf'fle *vi.* fight in disorderly manner; shuffle -*n.*

scull *n.* oar used in stern of boat; short oar used in pairs -*v.* propel, move by means of scull(s)

scull'ery *n.* place for washing dishes *etc.*

sculp'ture *n.* art of forming figures in relief or solid; product of this art -*vt.* represent by sculpture -**sculp'tural** *a.* of sculpture -**sculp'tor** *n.* (**sculp'tress** *fem.*)

scum *n.* froth or other floating matter on liquid; waste part of anything; vile person(s) -**scumm'y** *a.*

scurf *n.* flaky matter on scalp, dandruff

scurr'ilous *a.* coarse, indecently abusive -**scurril'ity** *n.*

scurr'y *vi.* run hastily (**scurr'ied, scurr'ying**) -*n.* bustling haste; flurry

scur'vy *n.* disease caused by lack of vitamin C

scut'tle[1] *n.* fireside container for coal

scut'tle[2] *vi.* rush away; run hurriedly -*n.*

scut'tle[3] *vt.* make hole in ship to sink it

scythe [sīTH] *n.* manual implement with long curved blade for cutting grass -*vt.* cut with scythe

sea *n.* mass of salt water covering greater part of earth; broad tract of this; waves; vast expanse -**sea'board** *n.* coast -**sea'faring** *a.* occupied in sea voyages -**sea'gull** *n.* gull -**sea horse** fish with bony-plated body and horselike head -**sea'man** *n.* sailor -**sea'sickness** *n.* nausea caused by motion of ship -**sea'sick** *a.* -**sea'weed** *n.* plant growing in sea -**sea'worthy** *a.* in fit condition to put to sea

seal[1] *n.* piece of metal or stone engraved with device for impression on wax *etc.*; impression thus made (on letters *etc.*); device, material preventing passage of water, air, oil *etc.* (also **seal'er**) -*vt.* affix seal to ratify, authorize; mark with stamp as evidence of some quality; keep close or secret; settle; make watertight, airtight *etc.*

seal[1] *n.* amphibious furred carnivorous mammal with flippers as limbs -**seal'skin** *n.* skin, fur of seals

seam *n.* line of junction of two edges, *eg* of two pieces of cloth, or two planks; thin layer, stratum -*vt.* mark with furrows or wrinkles -**seam'less** *a.* -**seam'y** *a.* sordid

sear *vt.* scorch

search [-ur-] *v.* look over or through to find something -*n.* act of searching; quest -**search'ing** *a.* thorough

seas'on [sēz-] *n.* one of four divisions of year; period during which thing happens *etc.* -*vt.* flavour with salt, herbs *etc.*; make reliable or ready for use; make experienced -**seas'onable** *a.* appropriate for the season; opportune -**seas'onal** *a.* varying with seasons -**seas'oning** *n.* flavouring

seat *n.* thing for sitting on; buttocks; base; right to sit (*eg* in council *etc.*); place where something is located, centred; locality of disease, trouble *etc.*; country house -*vt.* make to sit; provide sitting accommodation for

sec'ateurs [*or* -turz'] *pl.n.* small pruning shears

secede' [si-sēd'] *vi.* withdraw formally from federation, Church *etc.* -**seces'sion** *n.*

seclude' *vt.* guard from, remove from sight, view, contact with others -**seclu'ded** *a.* remote; private -**seclu'sion** *n.*

sec'ond[1] *a.* next after first; alternate, additional; of lower quality -*n.* person or thing coming second; attendant; sixtieth part of minute -*vt.* support -**second-hand** *a.* bought after use by another; not original

second'[2] *vt.* transfer (employee, officer) temporarily

sec'ondary *a.* of less importance; developed from something else; *Education* after primary stage

se'cret *a.* kept, meant to be kept from knowledge of others; hidden -*n.* thing kept secret -**se'crecy** *n.* keeping or being kept secret -**se'cretive** *a.* given to having secrets

sec'retary *n.* one employed to deal with papers and correspondence, keep records *etc.*; head of a state

department -**secreta'rial** *a.* -**secreta'riat** *n.* body of secretaries

secrete' *vt.* hide; conceal; (of gland *etc.*) collect and supply particular substance in body -**secre'tion** *n.*

sect *n.* group of people (within religious body *etc.*) with common interest; faction

sec'tion *n.* division; portion; distinct part; cutting; drawing of anything as if cut through

sec'tor *n.* part or subdivision

sec'ular *a.* worldly; lay, not religious; not monastic

secure' [-kyoor'] *a.* safe; firmly fixed; certain -*v.* gain possession of; make safe; make firm -**secur'ity** *n.* state of safety; protection; anything given as bond or pledge

sedate'[1] *a.* calm, serious

sedate'[2] *vt.* make calm by sedative -**seda'tion** *n.* -**sed'ative** *a.* having soothing or calming effect -*n.* sedative drug

sedge *n.* plant like coarse grass growing in swampy ground

sed'iment *n.* matter which settles to the bottom of liquid

sedi'tion [-dish-] *n.* stirring up of rebellion -**sedi'tious** *a.*

seduce' *vt.* persuade to commit some (wrong) deed, *esp.* sexual intercourse -**seduc'tion** *n.* -**seduct'ive** *a.* alluring -**sedu'cer** *n.* (**seduct'ress** *fem.*)

see[1] *v.* perceive with eyes or mentally; watch; find out; interview; make sure; accompany; consider (**saw, seen, see'ing**) -**see'ing** *conj.* in view of the fact that

see[2] *n.* diocese, office of bishop

seed *n.* reproductive germs of plants; one grain of this; such grains saved or used for sowing; sperm -*vt.* sow with seed -*vi.* produce seed -**seed'ling** *n.* young plant raised from seed -**seed'y** *a.* shabby; full of seed

seek *v.* make search or enquiry (for) (**sought** [sawt], **seek'ing**)

seem *vi.* appear (to be or to do) -**seem'ing** *a.* apparent but not real -**seem'ly** *a.* becoming and proper

seep *vi.* trickle through slowly

seer *n.* prophet

see'saw *n.* game in which children sit at opposite ends of plank supported in middle and swing up and down; plank used for this -*vi.* move up and down

seethe [-TH] *vi.* boil, foam; be very

agitated; be in constant movement (as living crowd *etc.*) (**seethed, see'thing**)

seg'ment *n.* piece cut off; section –*v.* [-ment'] to divide into segments

seg'regate *vt.* set apart from rest –**segrega'tion** *n.*

seine [sān] *n.* type of large fishing net

seize [sēz] *vt.* grasp; lay hold of; capture –*vi.* in machine, or bearing or piston, to stick tightly through overheating –**seiz'ure** *n.* act of taking; sudden onset of disease

sel'dom *adv.* not often, rarely

select' *vt.* pick out, choose –*a.* choice, picked; exclusive –**selec'tion** *n.* –**selec'tive** *a.* –**selec'tor** *n.*

self *pron.*, used reflexively or to express emphasis (*pl.* **selves**) –*a.* (of colour) same throughout, uniform –*n.* one's own person or individuality –**self'ish** *a.* concerned unduly over personal profit or pleasure; greedy –**self'less** *a.* unselfish

self- (*comb. form*) of oneself or itself, as in the list that follows

   self-addressed
   self-centred
   self-confident
   self-contained
   self-control
   self-defence
   self-indulgent
   self-interest
   self-pity
   self-raising
   self-sacrifice
   self-satisfied

self-con'scious *a.* unduly aware of oneself

self-made' *a.* having achieved wealth, status *etc.* by one's own efforts

self-respect' *n.* proper sense of one's own dignity and integrity

self-right'eous *a.* smugly sure of one's own virtue

self'same *a.* very same

self-serv'ice *a./n.* (of) shop or restaurant where customers serve themselves

self-suffi'cient *a.* sufficient in itself; independent

self-will' *n.* obstinacy; wilfulness –**self-willed** *a.*

sell *vt.* hand over for a price; stock, have for sale; make someone accept; *inf.* betray, cheat –*vi.* find purchasers (**sold, sell'ing**) –*n. inf.* disappointment; *inf.* hoax –**sell'er** *n.*

sem'aphore *n.* system of signalling by human or mechanical arms

sem'blance *n.* (false) appearance; image, likeness

se'men *n.* fluid carrying sperm of male animals; sperm

semi- (*comb. form*) half, partly, not completely, as in *semicircle*

sem'icircle *n.* half of circle

semico'lon *n.* punctuation mark (;)

semidetached' *a./n.* (of) house joined to another on one side only

semifi'nal *n.* match, round *etc.* before final

sem'inal *a.* capable of developing; influential; of semen or seed

sem'inar *n.* meeting of group (of students) for discussion

sem'inary *n.* college for priests

semipre'cious [-presh'-] *a.* (of gemstones) having less value than precious stones

semoli'na [-lē'-] *n.* hard grains left after sifting of flour, used for puddings *etc.*

sen'ate *n.* upper council of state, university *etc.* –**sen'ator** *n.*

send *vt.* cause to go or be conveyed; despatch; transmit (by radio) (**sent, send'ing**)

se'nile *a.* showing weakness of old age –**senil'ity** *n.*

se'nior *a.* superior in rank or standing; older –*n.* superior; elder person –**senior'ity** [-o'ri-] *n.*

sensa'tion *n.* operation of sense, feeling, awareness; excited feeling, state of excitement; exciting event –**sensa'tional** *a.* producing great excitement

sense *n.* any of bodily faculties of perception or feeling; ability to perceive; consciousness; meaning; coherence; sound practical judgment –*vt.* perceive; understand –**sense'-less** *a.* –**sense'lessly** *adv.*

sen'sible *a.* reasonable, wise; aware –**sensibil'ity** *n.* ability to feel *esp.* emotional or moral feelings –**sen'sibly** *adv.*

sen'sitive *a.* open to, acutely affected by, external impressions; easily affected or altered; easily upset by criticism; responsive to slight changes –**sensitiv'ity, sen'sitiveness** *n.*

sen'sory *a.* relating to organs, operation, of senses

sen'sual *a.* of senses only and not of mind; given to pursuit of pleasures of sense –**sensual'ity** *n.*

sen'suous a. stimulating, or apprehended by, senses esp. in aesthetic manner

sen'tence n. combination of words, which is complete as expressing a thought; judgment passed on criminal by court or judge -vt. pass sentence on, condemn

sent'iment n. tendency to be moved by feeling rather than reason; mental feeling; opinion -sentiment'al a. given to indulgence in sentiment and in its expression -sentimental'ity n.

sent'inel n. sentry

sen'try n. soldier on watch

sep'arate [-āt] vt. part; divide -vi. [-it] withdraw, become parted from -a. [-it] disconnected, distinct, individual -sep'arable a. -separa'tion n. disconnection

se'pia n. reddish-brown pigment -a. of this colour

sep'sis n. presence of pus-forming bacteria in body

Sept. September

Septem'ber n. 9th month

septet(te) n. (music for) group of seven musicians

sep'tic a. of, caused by, sepsis; (of wound) infected

sep'ulchre [-kǝr] n. tomb; burial vault

se'quel n. consequence; continuation, eg of story

se'quence n. arrangement of things in successive order

se'quin n. small ornamental metal disc on dresses etc.

sequoi'a [si-kwoi'ǝ] n. giant Californian coniferous tree

serenade' n. sentimental song addressed to woman by lover esp. at evening -v. sing serenade (to someone)

serene' a. calm, tranquil; unclouded -seren'ity n.

serf n. one of class of medieval labourers bound to, and transferred with, land -serf'dom n.

Serg. Sergeant

serge n. strong hard-wearing twilled worsted fabric

serg'eant [sahrj'ǝnt] n. noncommissioned officer in army; police officer above constable -sergeant major highest noncommissioned officer in regiment

se'ries n. sequence; succession, set (eg of radio, TV programmes etc.) (pl. se'ries) -se'rial n. story or play

produced in successive episodes

se'rious a. thoughtful, solemn; earnest, sincere; of importance; giving cause for concern -se'riously adv.

ser'mon n. discourse of religious instruction or exhortation; any similar discourse

ser'pent n. snake -serp'entine a. twisting, winding like a snake

serra'ted a. having notched, saw-like edge

se'rum n. watery animal fluid, esp. thin part of blood as used for inoculation or vaccination

serve v. (mainly vt.) work for, under, another; attend (to customers) in shop etc.; provide; help to (food etc.); present (food etc.) in particular way; be member of military unit; spend time doing; be useful, suitable enough -ser'vant n. personal or domestic attendant -ser'vice n. the act of serving; system organized to provide for needs of public; maintenance of vehicle; use; department of State employ; set of dishes etc.; form, session, of public worship -pl. armed forces -vt. overhaul -ser'viceable a. in working order, usable; durable -ser'viceman n. member of the armed forces -service station place supplying fuel, oil, maintenance for motor vehicles

serviette' n. table napkin

ser'vile a. slavish, without independence; fawning -servil'ity n.

ser'vitude n. bondage, slavery

sess'ion [sesh'-] n. meeting of court etc.; continuous series of such meetings; any period devoted to an activity

set v. (mainly tr.) put or place in specified position or condition; make ready; become firm or fixed; establish; prescribe, allot; put to music; of sun, go down (set, sett'ing) -a. fixed, established; deliberate; unvarying -n. act or state of being set; bearing, posture; Radio, Television complete apparatus for reception or transmission; Theatre, Cinema organized settings and equipment to form ensemble of scene; number of associated things, persons -set'back n. anything that hinders or impedes -set up establish

settee' n. couch

sett'er n. various breeds of gun dog

sett'ing n. background; surroundings; scenery and other stage accessories; decorative metalwork holding precious stone *etc.* in position; tableware and cutlery for (single place at) table; music for song

set'tle *vt.* arrange; establish; decide upon; end (dispute *etc.*); pay –*vi.* come to rest; subside; become clear; take up residence **-set'tlement** *n.* act of settling; place newly inhabited; money bestowed legally **-set'tler** *n.* colonist

sev'en *a./n.* cardinal number, next after six **-sev'enth** *a.* the ordinal number **-sev'enteen** *a./n.* ten and seven **-sev'enty** *a./n.* ten times seven

sev'er *v.* separate, divide; cut off **-sev'erance** *n.*

sev'eral *a.* some, a few; separate; individual –*pron.* indefinite small number **-sev'erally** *adv.*

severe' [-êr'] *a.* strict; harsh; austere; extreme **-sever'ity** [-ve'ri-] *n.*

sew [sō] *v.* join with needle and thread; make by sewing (**sewed** *pt.,* **sewed, sewn** *pp.,* **sew'ing** *pr.p.*) **-sew'ing** *n.*

sew'age [sōō'ij] *n.* refuse, waste matter, excrement conveyed in sewer **-sew'er** *n.* underground drain

sex *n.* state of being male or female; males or females collectively; sexual intercourse –*a.* concerning sex –*vt.* ascertain sex of **-sex'ism** *n.* discrimination on basis of sex **-sex'ist** *n./a.* **-sex'ual** *a.* **-sexually** *adv.* **-sex'y** *a.* **-sexual intercourse** act of procreation in which male's penis is inserted into female's vagina

sex'tant *n.* navigator's instrument

sextet(te) *n.* (composition for) six musicians

sf science fiction

shabb'y *a.* faded, worn; poorly dressed; mean, dishonourable **-shab'b'ily** *adv.* **-shabb'iness** *n.*

shack *n.* rough hut

shac'kle *n.* metal ring or fastening for prisoner's wrist or ankle –*vt.* fasten with shackles; hamper

shade *n.* partial darkness; shelter, place sheltered from light, heat *etc.*; darker part of anything; depth of colour; screen; US windowblind –*vt.* screen from light, darken; represent shades in drawing **-sha'dy** *a.* shielded from sun; dishonest

shad'ow *n.* dark figure projected by anything that intercepts rays of light; patch of shade; slight trace –*vt.* cast shadow over; follow and watch closely **-shad'owy** *a.*

shaft [-ah-] *n.* straight rod, stem, handle; arrow; ray, beam (of light); revolving rod for transmitting power

shag *n.* long-napped cloth; coarse shredded tobacco **-shagg'y** *a.* covered with rough hair; unkempt

shah *n.* formerly, ruler of Iran

shake *v.* (cause) to move with quick vibrations; tremble; grasp the hand (of another) in greeting; upset; wave, brandish (**shook, sha'ken**) –*n.* act of shaking; jolt; *inf.* short period of time **-sha'kily** *adv.* **-sha'ky** *a.* unsteady, insecure

shale *n.* flaky fine-grained rock

shall *v. aux.* makes compound tenses or moods to express obligation, command, condition or intention (**should** *pt.*)

shall'ow [-ō] *a.* not deep; superficial –*n.* shallow place

sham *a./n.* imitation, counterfeit –*v.* pretend, feign (**-mm-**)

sham'ble *vi.* walk in shuffling, awkward way

sham'bles *pl.n.* messy, disorderly thing or place

shame *n.* emotion caused by consciousness of guilt or dishonour in one's conduct or state; cause of disgrace; pity, hard luck –*vt.* cause to feel shame; disgrace; force by shame (into) **-shame'ful** *a.* **-shame'less** *a.* with no sense of shame; indecent **-shame'faced** *a.* ashamed

shampoo' *n.* various preparations of liquid soap for washing hair, carpets *etc.*; this process –*vt.* use shampoo to wash

sham'rock *n.* clover leaf, *esp.* as Irish emblem

shank *n.* lower leg; shinbone; stem of thing

shan'ty' *n.* temporary wooden building; crude dwelling

shan'ty' *n.* sailor's song

shape *n.* external form or appearance; mould, pattern; *inf.* condition –*vt.* form, mould –*vi.* develop (**shaped, sha'ping**) **-shape'less** *a.* **-shape'ly** *a.* well-proportioned

share [shâr] *n.* portion; quota; lot; unit of ownership in public company –*v.* give, take a share; join with others in doing, using, something **-share'holder** *n.*

shark *n.* large usu. predatory sea fish; person who cheats others

sharp *a.* having keen cutting edge or fine point; not gradual or gentle; brisk; harsh; dealing cleverly but unfairly; shrill; strongly marked, esp. in outline –adv. promptly -**sharp'en** vt. make sharp -**sharp'ness** n. -**sharp'shooter** n. marksman

shatt'er v. break in pieces; ruin (plans etc.); disturb (mind etc.) greatly

shave v. cut close, esp. hair of face or head; pare away; graze; reduce (**shaved, sha'ven, sha'ving**) –n. shaving -**sha'vings** pl.n. parings

shawl n. piece of fabric to cover woman's shoulders or wrap baby

she pron. 3rd pers. sing. fem.

sheaf n. bundle, esp. corn; loose leaves of paper (pl. **sheaves**)

shear vt. clip hair, wool from; cut through; fracture (**sheared** pt. **-shorn, sheared** pp. **-shear'ing** pr.p.) -**shear'er** n. -**shears** pl.n. large pair of scissors

sheath n. close-fitting cover, esp. for knife or sword -**sheathe** vt. put into sheath

shed[1] n. roofed shelter used as store or workshop

shed[2] vt. (cause to) pour forth (eg tears, blood); cast off (**shed, shed'ding**)

sheen n. gloss -**sheen'y** a.

sheep n. ruminant animal bred for wool and meat -**sheep'ish** a. embarrassed, shy -**sheep'dog** n. dog of various breeds orig. for herding sheep

sheer[1] a. perpendicular; of material, very fine, transparent; absolute, unmitigated

sheer[2] vi. deviate from course

sheet[1] n. large piece of cotton etc. to cover bed; broad piece of any thin material; large expanse

sheet[2] n. rope fastened in corner of sail

shelf n. board fixed horizontally (on wall etc.) for holding things; ledge (pl. **shelves**)

shell n. hard outer case (esp. of egg, nut etc.); explosive projectile; outer part of structure left when interior is removed -vt. take shell from; take out of shell; fire at with shells -**shell'fish** n. mollusc; crustacean

shel'ter n. place, structure giving protection; protection; refuge -vt. give protection to -vi. take shelter

shelve vt. put on a shelf; put off -vi. slope gradually

shep'herd [shep'ərd] n. man who tends sheep (**shep'herdess** fem.) -vt. guide, watch over

sher'bet n. fruit-flavoured effer-

vescent powder, as sweet or in drink

sher'iff [sher'if] n. US law enforcement officer; in England and Wales, chief executive representative of the crown in a county; in Scotland, chief judge of a district; C municipal officer who enforces court orders etc. -**sher'iffdom** n.

sherr'y n. fortified wine

shield n. piece of armour carried on arm; any protection used to stop blows, missiles etc. -vt. cover, protect

shift v. (cause to) move, change position -n. relay of workers; time of their working; evasion; expedient; removal; woman's underskirt or dress -**shift'iness** n. -**shift'less** a. lacking in resource or character -**shift'y** a. evasive, of dubious character

shill'ing n. former Brit. coin, now 5p

shimm'er vi. shine with quivering light -n. such light

shin n. front of lower leg -vi. climb with arms and legs

shine vi. give out, reflect light; excel -vt. polish (**shone** [shon], **shi'ning**) -n. brightness, lustre; polishing -**shi'ny** a.

shing'le[1] [-ng'gl] n. wooden roof tile -vt. cover with shingles

shing'le[2] [-ng'gl] n. mass of pebbles

ship n. large seagoing vessel -vt. put on or send (esp. by ship) -pp.- -**ship'ment** n. act of shipping; goods shipped -**ship'ping** n. freight transport business; ships collectively -**ship'yard** n. place for building and repair of ships

shire n. county

shirk vt. evade, try to avoid (duty etc.) -**shirk'er** n.

shirr vt. gather (fabric) into parallel rows -n.

shirt n. garment for upper part of body

shiv'er[1] vi. tremble, usu. with cold or fear -n. act, state, of shivering

shiv'er[2] v./n. splinter

shoal[1] n. stretch of shallow water; sandbank or bar

shoal[2] n. large number of fish swimming together

shock[1] vt. horrify, scandalize -n. violent or damaging blow; emotional disturbance; state of weakness, illness, caused by physical or mental shock; paralytical stroke; collision; effect on sensory nerves of electric discharge

shock[1] n. group of corn sheaves placed together

shock[1] n. mass of hair

shod'dy a. worthless, trashy

shoe [shōō] n. covering for foot, not enclosing ankle; metal rim put on horse's hoof; various protective plates or undercoverings (pl. **shoes**) -vt. protect, furnish with shoes (**shod** pt./pt.p., **shoe'ing** pr.p.)

shoot v. wound, kill with missile fired from weapon; discharge weapon; send, slide, push rapidly; photograph, film -vi. hunt; sprout (**shot, shoot'ing**) -n. young branch, sprout; hunting expedition -**shoot'er** n.

shop n. place for retail sale of goods and services; workshop, works building -vi. visit shops to buy (-**pp**-) -**shop'lifter** n. one who steals from shop

shore[1] n. edge of sea or lake

shore[1] vt. prop up

short a. not long; not tall; brief; not enough; lacking; abrupt -adv. abruptly; without reaching end -n. drink of spirits; short film -pl. short trousers -**short'age** n. deficiency -**short'en** v. -**short'ly** adv. soon; briefly **short circuit** Electricity connection, often accidental, of low resistance between two parts of circuit -**short'coming** n. failing -**short'hand** n. method of rapid writing

shot n. act of shooting; missile(s); marksman; attempt; photograph; dose

shoul'der [-ōl-] n. part of body to which arm or foreleg is attached; anything resembling shoulder; side of road -vt. undertake; put on one's shoulder -vi. make way by pushing

shout n./v. (utter) loud cry

shove [-uv] vt./n. push

shov'el [-uv-] n. instrument for scooping earth etc. -vt. lift, move (as) with shovel (-**ll**-)

show [-ō] vt. expose to view; point out; explain; prove; guide -vi. appear; be noticeable (**showed, shown, show'ing**) -n. display; entertainment; ostentation; pretence -**show'y** a. gaudy; ostentatious -**show'down** n. confrontation -**show'man** n. one skilled at presenting anything effectively -**show off** exhibit to invite admiration; behave in this way -**show-off** n.

show'er n. short fall of rain; anything falling like rain; kind of bath in

which person stands under water spray -vt. bestow liberally -vi. take bath in shower

shrap'nel n. shell splinters

shred n. fragment, torn strip -vt. cut, tear to shreds (**shred or shred'ded, shredd'ing**)

shrew [-ōō] n. animal like mouse; bad-tempered woman

shrewd [-ōōd] a. astute; crafty -**shrewd'ness** n.

shriek n./v. (utter) piercing cry

shrill a. piercing, sharp in tone

shrimp n. small edible crustacean; inf. undersized person

shrine n. place of worship, usu. associated with saint

shrink vi. become smaller; recoil -vt. make smaller (**shrank** pt., **shrunk'en, shrunk** pp., **shrink'ing** pr.p.) -**shrink'age** n.

shriv'el vi. shrink and wither (-**ll**-)

shroud n. wrapping for corpse; anything which envelops like shroud -vt. put shroud on; veil

shrub n. bush -**shrubb'ery** n.

shrug v. raise (shoulders) as sign of indifference, ignorance etc. (-**gg**-) -n. shrugging

shuck n. shell, husk, pod

shudd'er vi. shake, tremble violently -n. shuddering

shuf'fle vi. move feet without lifting them; mix (cards) -n. shuffling; rearrangement

shun vt. keep away from (-**nn**-)

shunt vt. push aside; move (train) from one line to another

shut v. close; forbid entrance to (**shut, shutt'ing**) -**shutt'er** n. movable window screen; device in camera admitting light as required

shut'tle n. bobbin-like device to hold thread in weaving, sewing etc.; plane, bus etc. travelling to and fro

shy[1] a. timid, bashful; lacking -vi. start back in fear; show sudden reluctance (**shied, shy'ing**) -n. start of fear by horse

shy[1] v./n. throw (**shied, shy'ing**)

SI Fr. Système Internationale (d'Unités), international system of units of measurement

sib'ilant a./n. hissing (sound)

sib'ling n. brother or sister

sib'yl n. prophetess

sick a. inclined to vomit; not well or healthy; inf. macabre; inf. bored; inf. disgusted -**sick'en** v. make, become, sick; disgust -**sick'ly** a. unhealthy; inducing nausea -**sick'ness** n.

sic'kle n. reaping hook

side n. one of the surfaces of object; part that is to right or left; aspect; faction -a. at, in, the side; subordinate -vi. take up cause of (usu. with with) -**si'ding** n. short line of rails from main line -**side'board** n. piece of dining room furniture -**side'burns** pl.n. man's side whiskers -**side'long** a. not directly forward -adv. obliquely -**side'track** v. deviate from main topic -**side'ways** adv. to or from the side

si'dle vi. move in furtive or stealthy manner; move sideways

siege [-j] n. besieging of town

siest'a [si-est'ə] n. rest, sleep in afternoon

sieve [siv] n. device with perforated bottom -v. sift; blends

sift vt. separate coarser portion from finer

sigh [sī] v./n. (utter) long audible breath

sight [sīt] n. faculty of seeing; thing seen; glimpse; device for guiding eye; spectacle -vt. catch sight of; adjust sights of gun etc.

sign [sīn] n. mark, gesture etc. to convey some meaning; (board bearing) notice etc.; symbol; omen -vt. put one's signature to -vi. make sign or gesture

sig'nal n. sign to convey order or information Radio etc. sequence of electrical impulses transmitted or received -a. remarkable -vt. make signals to -vi. give orders etc. by signals (-ll-)

sig'natory n. one of those who sign agreements, treaties

sig'nature n. person's name written by himself

sig'net n. small seal

signif'icant a. revealing; designed to make something known; important -**signif'icance** n.

sig'nify vt. mean; indicate; imply -vi. be of importance (**sig'nified**, **sig'nifying**)

Sikh [sēk] n. member of Indian religious sect

si'lage n. fodder crop stored in state of partial fermentation

si'lence n. absence of noise; refraining from speech -vt. make silent; put a stop to -**si'lent** a.

silhouette' [-lŏō-] n. outline of object seen against light

sil'ica n. naturally occurring dioxide of silicon

sil'icon n. brittle metalloid element found in sand, clay, stone -**sil'icone** n. synthetic substance used in chemistry, industry, medicine

silk n. fibre made by larvae (**silkworm**) of certain moth; thread, fabric made from this -**silk'en** a. -**silk'y** a.

sill n. ledge beneath window

sill'y a. foolish; trivial

si'lo n. pit, tower for storing fodder (pl. -**los**)

silt n. mud deposited by water -v. fill, be choked with silt

sil'ver n. white precious metal; silver coins; cutlery -a. made of silver; resembling silver or its colour -**sil'very** a.

sim'ilar a. resembling, like -**similar'ity** n. likeness

sim'ile [-i-li] n. comparison of one thing with another

simil'itude n. likeness

simm'er v. keep or be just below boiling point

sim'per vi. smile, utter in silly or affected way -n.

sim'ple a. not complicated; plain; not complex; ordinary; stupid -**sim'pleton** n. foolish person -**simplic'ity** [-lis-] n. -**sim'plify** vt. make simple, plain or easy (-**plified**, -**plifying**) -**sim'ply** adv.

sim'ulate vt. make pretence of; reproduce

simulta'neous a. occurring at the same time

sin n. transgression of divine or moral law -vi. commit sin (-nn-) -**sin'ful** a. -**sin'ner** n.

since prep. during period of time after -conj. from time when; because -adv. from that time

sincere' a. not hypocritical; genuine -**sincere'ly** adv. -**sincer'ity** [-seʹri-] n.

si'necure n. office with pay but minimal duties

sin'ew n. tough, fibrous cord joining muscle to bone

sing v. utter (sounds, words) with musical modulation; hum; ring; celebrate in song (**sang, sung, singing**) -**sing'er** n. -**sing'song** n. informal singing session -a. monotonously regular in tone, rhythm

singe [-nj] vt. burn surface of (**singed, singe'ing**)

sin'gle [-ng'gl] a. one only; unmarried; for one; denoting ticket for outward journey only -n. single thing

-vt. pick (out) **-sin'gly** adv. **-single file** persons in one line **-single-handed** a. without assistance

sing'let n. sleeveless undervest

sin'gular a. remarkable; unique; denoting one person or thing

sin'ister a. threatening; evil-looking; wicked

sink vi. become submerged; drop; decline; penetrate (into) **-vt.** cause to sink; make by digging out; invest (**sank** pt., **sunk**, **sunk'en** pp., **sink'-ing** pr.p.) **-n.** fixed basin with waste pipe

sin'uous a. curving

si'nus n. cavity, esp. air passages in bones of skull **-sinusi'tis** n. inflammation of sinus

sip v. drink in very small portions (**-pp-**) **-n.**

si'phon, sy'phon n./v. (device to) draw liquid from container

sir n. polite term of address for a man

sire n. male parent, esp. of horse or domestic animal **-v.** beget

si'ren n. device making loud wailing noise

sir'loin n. prime cut of beef

si'sal n. (fibre of) plant used in making ropes

sis'sy a./n. weak, cowardly (person)

sis'ter n. daughter of same parents; woman fellow-member; senior nurse **-sis'terly** a. **-sister-in-law** n. sister of husband or wife; brother's wife

sit v. (mainly intr.) rest on buttocks, thighs; perch; pose for portrait; hold session; remain; take examination; keep watch over baby etc.

sitar' n. stringed musical instrument, esp. of India

site n. place; space for a building

sit'uate v. place **-situation** n. position; state of affairs; employment

six a./n. cardinal number one more than five **-sixth** a. ordinal number **-n.** sixth part **-six'teen** n./a. six and ten **-six'ty** n./a. six times ten

size' n. dimensions; one of series of standard measurements **-vt.** arrange according to size **-siz(e)'able** a. quite large

size' n. gluelike sealer, filler

siz'zle v./n. (make) hissing, spluttering sound as of frying

skate' n. steel blade attached to boot **-vi.** glide as on skates **-skate'-board** n. small board mounted on roller-skate wheels

skate' n. large marine ray

skein [-ā-] n. quantity of yarn, wool etc. in loose knot

skel'eton n. bones of animal; framework **-a.** reduced to a minimum

sketch n. rough drawing; short humorous play **-v.** make sketch (of) **-sketch'y** a.

skew'er n. pin to fasten (meat)

ski [skē] n. long runner fastened to foot for sliding over snow or water (pl. **skis** [-z]) **-v.** slide on skis (**skied, ski'ing**)

skid v. slide (sideways) (**-dd-**) **-n.** instance of this

skidoo' n. C snowmobile

skiff n. small boat

skill n. practical ability, cleverness, dexterity **-skilled** a. **-skil'ful** a.

skil'let n. small frying pan

skim vt. remove floating matter from surface of liquid; glide over lightly and rapidly; read thus **-vi.** move thus (**-mm-**)

skimp vt. give short measure; do imperfectly **-skimp'y** a. scanty

skin n. outer covering of body; animal hide; fruit rind **-vt.** remove skin of (**-nn-**) **-skin'less** a. **-skinn'y** a. thin **-skin'flint** n. miser

skip' vi. leap lightly; jump a rope **-vt.** pass over, omit (**-pp-**) **-n.** act of skipping

skip' n. large open container for builders' rubbish etc.

skipp'er n. captain of ship

skirm'ish n. small battle **-vi.** fight briefly

skirt n. woman's garment hanging from waist; lower part of dress, coat etc. **-vt.** border; go round

skit n. satire, esp. theatrical

skitt'ish a. frisky, frivolous

skit'tles pl.n. ninepins

skive v. evade work

skuldugg'ery n. inf. trickery

skulk vi. sneak out of the way

skull n. bony case enclosing brain

skunk n. small N Amer. animal which emits evil-smelling fluid

sky n. expanse extending upwards from the horizon; outer space (pl. **skies**) **-sky'light** n. window in roof or ceiling **-sky'scraper** n. very tall building

slab n. thick, broad piece

slack a. loose; careless; not busy **-n.** loose part **-v.** be idle or lazy **-slack'en** v. become looser; become slower

slacks pl.n. inf. trousers

slag n. refuse of smelted metal

slake vt. satisfy (thirst)

slam v. shut noisily; bang (-mm-) -n. (noise) of this action

slan'der [-ah-] n./v. (utter) false or malicious statement about person -**slan'derous** a.

slang n. colloquial language

slant [-ah-] v. slope; write, present (news etc.) with bias -n. slope; point of view -a. oblique

slap n. blow with open hand or flat instrument -vt. strike thus; (inf. put down carelessly) (-pp-) -**slap'stick** n. boisterous knockabout comedy

slash vt./n. gash; lash; cut

slat n. narrow strip

slate n. stone which splits easily in flat sheets; piece of this for covering roof -vt. cover with slates; abuse

slatt'ern n. slut

slaugh'ter [slaw'-] n. killing -vt. kill

slave n. captive, person without freedom or personal rights -vi. work like slave -**sla'very** n. -**sla'vish** a. servile

slav'er vi./n. (dribble) saliva from mouth

slay vt. kill (slew, slain, slay'ing)

sleaz'y a. sordid

sledge[1], **sled** n. carriage on runners for sliding along on snow; toboggan -v.

sledge[2], **sledge'hammer** n. heavy hammer with long handle

sleek a. glossy, smooth, shiny

sleep n. unconscious state regularly occurring in man and animals; slumber, repose -vi. take rest in sleep (slept, sleep'ing) -**sleep'er** n. one who sleeps; beam supporting rails; railway sleeping car -**sleep'less** a. -**sleep'y** a.

sleet n. rain and snow falling together

sleeve n. part of garment which covers arm

sleigh [slā] n. sledge

sleight [slīt] n. -**sleight of hand** (manual dexterity in) conjuring

slen'der a. slim, slight

sleuth [-ōō-] n. detective

slice n. thin flat piece cut off; share -vt. cut into slices

slick a. smooth; glib; smart -vt. make glossy, smooth -n. slippery area; patch of oil on water

slide v. slip smoothly along; glide; pass (slid pt., slid, slidd'en pp., sli'ding pr.p.) -n. sliding; track for sliding; glass mount for object to

be viewed under microscope; photographic transparency

slight [-īt] a. small, trifling; slim -vt. disregard -n. act of discourtesy

slim a. thin; slight -v. reduce weight by diet and exercise (-mm-)

slime n. thick, liquid mud -**sli'my** a.

sling n. loop for hurling stone; bandage for supporting wounded limb; rope for hoisting weights -vt. throw (slung, sling'ing)

slink vi. move stealthily, sneak (slunk, slink'ing)

slip v. (cause to) move smoothly; pass out of (mind etc.) -vi. lose balance by sliding; fall from person's grasp; make mistake (usu. with up) -vt. put on or take off easily, quickly (-pp-) -n. act or occasion of slipping; mistake; petticoat; small piece of paper -slipp'ed a. slovenly, careless

slipp'er n. light shoe for indoors

slipp'ery a. so smooth as to cause slipping or to be difficult to hold; unreliable

slit v. make long straight cut in (slit, slitt'ing) n.

slith'er [-TH-] vi. slide unsteadily (down slope etc.)

sliv'er n. splinter

slobb'er v./n. slaver

slog vt. hit vigorously -vi. work doggedly; plod (-gg-) -n.

slo'gan n. distinctive phrase

sloop n. small one-masted vessel

sloot n. SA ditch for irrigation

slop v. spill, splash (-pp-) -n. liquid spilt; liquid food -pl. liquid refuse -**slop'py** a.

slope v. be, place at slant -n. slant

slosh v. splash; hit

slot n. narrow hole; slit for coins -vt. put in slot; inf. place in series (-tt-)

sloth [-ō-] n. S Amer. animal; sluggishness -**sloth'ful** a.

slouch vi. walk, sit etc. in drooping manner -n.

slough[1] [-ow] n. bog; C hole where water collects

slough[2] [-uf] v. shed (skin); drop off

slov'en [-uv-] n. dirty, untidy person -**slov'enly** a./adv.

slow [-ō-] a. lasting a long time; moving at low speed; dull -v. slacken speed

slug[1] n. land snail with no shell; bullet -**slug'gard** n. lazy person -**slugg'ish** a. slow; inert; not functioning well

slug[1] v. hit, slog -n. heavy blow; portion of spirits

sluice [-ōōs] n. gate, door to control flow of water

slum n. squalid street or neighbourhood

slum'ber vi./n. sleep

slump v. fall heavily; relax ungracefully; decline suddenly -n. sudden decline

slur vt. pass over lightly; run together (words); disparage (-rr-) -n. slight

slush n. watery, muddy substance

slut n. dirty (immoral) woman

sly a. cunning; deceitful -**sly'ly** adv.

smack[1] n. taste, flavour -vi. taste (of); suggest

smack[2] vt. slap; open and close (lips) loudly -n. slap; such sound; loud kiss -adv. inf. squarely

small [-awl] a. little, unimportant; short -n. small slender part esp. of the back -**small'pox** n. contagious disease

smarm v. inf. fawn -**smarm'y** inf. a.

smart a. astute; clever; well dressed; causing stinging pain -v. feel, cause pain -n. sharp pain

smash vt. break violently; ruin; destroy -vi. break up heavy blow; collision

smatt'ering n. slight superficial knowledge

smear vt. rub with grease etc.; smudge -n. mark made thus; slander

smell vt. perceive by nose -vi. give out odour; use nose (**smelt** or **smelled, smell'ing**) -n. faculty of perceiving smell; anything detected by sense of smell -**smell'y** a.

smelt vt. extract metal from ore

smile n. curving or parting of lips in pleased or amused expression -v. wear, assume a smile

smirch vt. dirty; disgrace -n. stain; disgrace

smirk n. smile expressing scorn, smugness -v.

smite vt. strike; afflict (**smote, smitt'en, smi'ting**)

smith n. worker in iron, gold etc. -**smith'y** [-TH-] n. blacksmith's workshop

smock n. loose, outer garment

smog n. mixture of smoke and fog

smoke n. cloudy mass that rises from fire etc. -vi. give off smoke; inhale and expel tobacco smoke -vt. use (tobacco) by smoking; expose to

smoke -**smo'kily** adv. -**smo'ky** a.

smooth [-TH] a. not rough, even; calm; plausible -vt. make smooth

smoth'er [-UTH-] v. suffocate

smoul'der [-ō-] vi. burn slowly; (of feelings) be suppressed

smudge v./n. (make) smear, stain

smug a. self-satisfied, complacent

smug'gle vt. import, export without paying customs duties -**smugg'ler** n.

smut n. piece of soot; obscene talk etc. -**smutt'y** a.

Sn Chem. tin

snack n. light, hasty meal

snag n. difficulty; sharp protuberance; hole, loop in fabric; obstacle -vt. catch, damage on snag

snail n. slow-moving mollusc with shell

snake n. long scaly limbless reptile -v. move like snake -**sna'ky** a.

snap v. break suddenly; make cracking sound; bite (at) suddenly; speak suddenly, angrily -n. act of snapping; fastener; inf. snapshot -a. sudden, unplanned -**snapp'y** a. irritable; sl. quick; sl. fashionable -**snap'dragon** n. plant with flowers than can be opened like a mouth -**snap'shot** n. photograph

snare n./vt. trap

snarl n. growl of angry dog; tangle -vi. utter snarl

snatch vt. make quick grab (at); seize, catch -n. grab; fragment

snazz'y a. inf. stylish, flashy

sneak vi. move about furtively; act in underhand manner -n. petty informer

sneer n. scornful, contemptuous expression or remark -v.

sneeze vi. emit breath through nose with sudden involuntary spasm and noise -n.

sneeze'wood n. S Afr. tree yielding very hard wood

snide a. malicious, supercilious

sniff vi. inhale through nose with sharp hiss; (with at) express disapproval etc. -vt. take up through nose, smell -n. -**snif'fle** vi. sniff noisily esp. when suffering from a cold

snigg'er n. sly, disrespectful laugh, esp. partly stifled -v.

snip vt. cut, cut bits off (-pp-) -n. bit cut off; inf. bargain

snipe n. wading bird -v. shoot at enemy from cover; (with at) criticize -**sni'per** n.

sniv'el vi. sniffle to show distress; whine (-ll-)

snob n. one who pretentiously judges others by social rank etc. -**snobb'ery** n. -**snobb'ish** a.

snoo'ker n. game played on billiard table

snoop v. pry, meddle; peer into

snoot'y a. sl. haughty

snooze vi./n. (take) nap

snore vi. breathe noisily when asleep -n.

snor'kel n. tube for breathing underwater

snort vi. make (contemptuous) noise by driving breath through nostrils -n.

snout n. animal's nose

snow n. frozen vapour which falls in flakes -v. fall, sprinkle as snow; let fall, throw down like snow; cover with snow -**snow'y** a. -**snow'ball** n. snow pressed into hard ball for throwing -v. increase rapidly; play, fight with snowballs -**snow'drift** n. bank of deep snow -**snow'drop** n. small, white, bell-shaped spring flower -**snow goose** white N Amer. goose -**snow'mobile** [-bēl] n. C motor vehicle with caterpillar tracks and front skis -**snow'shoes** pl.n. shoes like rackets for travelling on snow

snub vt. insult (esp. by ignoring) intentionally (-bb-) -n. -a. short and blunt -**snub-nosed** a.

snuff' n. powdered tobacco

snuff' v. extinguish (esp. candle)

snuff'le v. breathe noisily

snug a. warm, comfortable -**snug'gle** v. lie close to, nestle

snye n. C side channel of river

so adv. to such an extent; in such a manner; very -conj. therefore; in order that; with the result that -interj. well! -**so-called** a. called by but doubtfully deserving that name

soak v. steep; absorb; drench; lie in liquid -n. soaking

soap n. compound of alkali and oil used in washing -vt. apply soap to

soar [sawr] vi. fly high; increase

sob vi. catch breath, esp. in weeping (-bb-) -n. sobbing -**sob story** tale of personal distress told to arouse sympathy

so'ber a. not drunk; temperate; subdued; dull; solemn -v. make, become sober -**sobri'ety** n.

Soc. Society

socc'er n. game of football, with spherical ball

so'ciable a. friendly; convivial -**sociabil'ity** n. -**so'ciably** adv.

so'cial a. living in communities; relating to society; sociable -n. informal gathering -**so'cialize** v. -**so'cially** adv.

so'cialism n. political system which advocates public ownership of means of production -**so'cialist** n./a.

soci'ety n. living associated with others; those so living; companionship; association; fashionable people collectively

sociol'ogy n. study of societies

sock' n. cloth covering for foot

sock' sl. vt. hit -n. blow

sock'et n. hole or recess for something to fit into

sod n. lump of earth with grass

so'da n. compound of sodium; soda water -**soda water** water charged with carbon dioxide

sodd'en a. soaked

so'dium n. metallic alkaline element -**sodium bicarbonate** baking soda

sod'omy n. anal intercourse

so'fa n. upholstered seat with back and arms

soft a. yielding easily to pressure, not hard; mild; easy; subdued; quiet, gentle; (too) lenient -**soft'en** [sof'n] v. make, become soft or softer -**soft'ly** adv. -**soft drink** one that is nonalcoholic -**soft'ware** n. computer programs, tapes etc.

sogg'y a. damp and heavy

soil' n. earth, ground

soil' v. make, become dirty

soir'ee [swah'rā] n. private evening party esp. with music

so'journ [soj'urn] vi. stay for a time -n. short stay

sol'ace n./v. comfort in distress

so'lar a. of the sun

sol'der n. easily-melted alloy used for joining metal -vt. join with it -**soldering iron**

sol'dier [sōl'jar] n. one serving in army -vi. serve in army; (with on) persist doggedly

sole' a. one and only -**sole'ly** adv. alone; only; entirely

sole' n. underside of foot, boot etc. -vt. fit with sole

sole' n. small edible flatfish

sol'emn [-əm] a. serious; formal -**solem'nity** n. -**sol'emnize** vt. celebrate, perform

sol'fa n. Mus. system of syllables sol, fa etc. sung in scale

solic'it [-lis'] vt. request; accost -**solic'itor** n. lawyer who prepares documents, advises clients -**solic'itous** a. anxious; eager -**solic'itude** n.

sol'id a. not hollow; composed of one substance; firm; reliable -n. body of three dimensions; substance not liquid or gas -**solidar'ity** [-da'ri-] n. unity -**sol'idify** v. harden (-ified, -ifying)

solil'oquy [-ǝ-kwi] n. (esp. in drama) thoughts spoken by person while alone

sol'itary a. alone, single -**solitaire'** [or sol'-] n. game for one person; single precious stone set by itself -**sol'itude** n. state of being alone

so'lo n. music for one performer (pl. **so'los**) -a. unaccompanied, alone -**so'loist** n.

sol'stice [-is] n. shortest (winter) or longest (summer) day

solve vt. work out; find answer to -**sol'uble** a. capable of being dissolved in liquid; able to be solved -**solu'tion** [-lōō-] n. answer; dissolving; liquid with something dissolved in it -**sol'vable** a. -**sol'vency** n. -**sol'vent** a. able to meet financial obligations -n. liquid with power of dissolving

som'bre a. dark, gloomy

sombre'ro [-â'-] n. wide-brimmed hat (pl. **-ros**)

some [sum] a. denoting an indefinite number, amount or extent; one or other; certain -pron. portion, quantity -**some'body** n. some person; important person -**some'how** adv. by some means -**some'thing** n. thing not clearly defined -**some'time** adv. at some (past or future) time -a. former -**some'times** adv. occasionally -**some'what** adv. rather -**some'where** adv.

som'ersault [sum'-] n. tumbling head over heels

somnam'bulist n. sleepwalker

son n. male child -**son-in-law** n. daughter's husband

sonat'a [-naht'-] n. piece of music in several movements

song n. singing; poem etc. for singing

son'ic a. pert. to sound waves

sonn'et n. fourteen-line poem with definite rhyme scheme

sonor'ous a. giving out (deep) sound, resonant

soon [-ōō-] adv. in a short time; before long; early, quickly

soot [oo] n. black powdery substance formed by burning of coal etc. -**soot'y** a.

soothe [-ōōTH] vt. make calm, tranquil; relieve (pain etc.)

sop n. piece of bread etc. soaked in liquid; bribe -vt. steep in water etc.; soak (up) (-pp-)

sophis'ticated a. worldly wise

soporif'ic a. causing sleep

sopran'o [-rahn'-] n. highest voice in women and boys (pl. **-os**)

sor'bet [or -bā] n. (fruit-flavoured) water ice

sor'cerer n. magician (**sor'ceress** fem.) -**sor'cery** n.

sor'did a. mean, squalid; base

sore a. painful; causing annoyance -n. sore place -**sore'ly** adv. greatly

sorr'ow [-ō] n./vi. (feel) grief, sadness -**sorr'owful** a.

sorr'y a. feeling pity or regret; miserable, wretched

sort n. kind, class -vt. classify

sort'ie n. sally by besieged forces

SOS n. international code signal of distress; call for help

so-so' a. inf. mediocre

sot n. habitual drunkard

souf'flé [sōō'flā] n. dish of eggs beaten to froth, flavoured and baked

soul [sōl] n. spiritual and immortal part of human being; person -**soul'ful** a.

sound¹ n. what is heard; noise -vi. make sound; seem; give impression of -vt. cause to sound; utter

sound² a. in good condition; solid; of good judgment; thorough; deep -**sound'ly** adv. -**sound'ness** n.

sound³ v. find depth of, as water; ascertain views of; probe

sound⁴ n. channel; strait

soup [sōōp] n. liquid food made by boiling meat, vegetables etc. -**soup'y** a.

sour a. acid; gone bad; peevish; disagreeable -v. make, become sour -**sour'ly** adv. -**sour'ness** n.

source [-aw-] n. origin, starting point; spring

souse v. plunge, drench; pickle -n. sousing; brine for pickling

south n. point opposite north; region, part of country etc. lying to that side -a./adv. (that) is; towards south -**south'erly** [suTH-] a. towards south -n. wind from the south -**south'ern**

[suth'] a. in south -**south'wards** a./adv.

souvenir' [soo-və-nēr'] n. keepsake, memento

sov'ereign [sov'rin] n. king, queen; former gold coin worth 20 shillings -a. supreme; efficacious -**sov'ereignty** n.

sow¹ [sō] vi. scatter, plant seed -vt. scatter, deposit seed (**sowed** pt., **sown** or **sowed** pp., **sow'ing** pr.p.) -**sow'er** n.

sow² n. female adult pig

spa [spah] n. medicinal spring; place, resort with one

space n. extent; room; period; empty place; area; expanse; region beyond earth's atmosphere -vt. place at intervals -**spa'cious** a. roomy, extensive

spade¹ n. tool for digging

spade² n. leaf-shaped black symbol on playing card

span n. space from thumb to little finger as measure; extent; space; stretch of arch etc. -vt. stretch over, measure with hand -**nn-**)

span'gle [-ng'gl] n. small shiny metallic ornament -vt. decorate with spangles

span'iel n. breed of dog with long ears and silky hair

spank vt. slap with flat of hand, esp. on buttocks -n. -**spank'ing** n.

spann'er n. tool for gripping nut or bolt head

span'spek n. SA sweet melon

spar¹ n. pole, beam, esp. as part of ship's rigging

spar² vi. box; dispute, esp. in fun (-**rr-**) -n. sparring

spare [-ār] vt. leave unhurt; show mercy; do without; give away -a. additional; in reserve; thin; lean -n. spare part (for machine) -**spar'ing** a. economical, careful

spark n. small glowing or burning particle; flash of light produced by electrical discharge; trace -v. emit sparks; kindle

spar'kle vi. glitter; effervesce -n. glitter -**spar'kling** a. glittering; (of wines) effervescent

sparr'ow n. small brownish bird -**sparr'owhawk** n. hawk that hunts small birds

sparse a. thinly scattered

spasm [-zm] n. sudden convulsive (muscular) contraction; sudden burst of activity etc. -**spasmod'ic** a.

spas'tic a. affected by spasms, suffering cerebral palsy -n.

spate n. rush, outpouring; flood

spa'tial a. of, in space

spatt'er v. splash, cast drops over -vi. be scattered in drops -n.

spat'ula n. utensil with broad, flat blade for various purposes

spawn n. eggs of fish or frog; oft. offens. offspring -vi. (of fish or frog) cast eggs

speak vi. utter words; converse; deliver discourse -vt. utter; pronounce; express; communicate in (**spoke**, **spo'ken**, **speak'ing**) -**speak'er** n. one who speaks; speech maker; loudspeaker

spear n. long pointed weapon -vt. pierce with spear -**spear'head** n. leading force in attack -vt.

spear'mint n. type of mint

spe'cial [spesh'əl] a. beyond the usual; particular -**spe'cialist** n. one who devotes himself to special subject -**spe'ciality** n. special product, skill, characteristic etc. -**spe'cialization** n. -**spe'cialize** vt. be specialist -vt. make special -**spec'ially** adv.

spe'cies n. [-shēz] n. sort, kind, class; animals etc. (pl. **spe'cies**)

specif'ic a. exact in detail; characteristic of a thing or kind -**spe'cif'ically** adv. -**spec'ify** vt. state definitely or in detail (-**ified, -ifying**) -**specifica'tion** n. detailed description of something

spec'imen [-es'-] n. part typifying whole; individual example

spe'cious a. deceptively plausible, but false

speck n. small spot, particle -vt. spot -**spec'kle** n./vt. speck

spec'tacle n. show; thing exhibited; ridiculous sight -pl. pair of lenses for correcting defective sight -**spectac'ular** a. impressive; showy -**specta'tor** n. one who looks on

spec'tre n. ghost; image of something unpleasant

spec'trum n. band of colours into which beam of light can be decomposed eg by prism (pl. **spec'tra**)

spec'ulate vi. guess, conjecture; engage in (risky) commercial transactions -**specula'tion** n. -**spec'ulative** a. -**spec'ulator** n.

speech n. act, faculty of speaking; words, language; (formal) talk given before audience -**speech'less** a. dumb; at a loss for words

speed n. swiftness; rate of progress -vi. move quickly; drive vehicle at high speed -vt. further (**sped** or **speed'ed** pt./pp.) -**speed'ing** n. driving at high speed, esp. over legal limit -**speed'ily** adv. -**speed'y** a. -**speedom'eter** n. instrument to show speed of vehicle -**speed'well** n. plant with small usu. blue flowers

spell[1] vt. give letters of in order; indicate, result in (**spelled** or **spelt** pt./pp.), **spell'ing** pr.p.) -**spell'ing** n.

spell[2] n. magic formula; enchantment -**spell'bound** a. enchanted; entranced

spell[3] n. (short) period of time, work

spend vt. pay out; pass (time); use up completely (**spent** pt./pp., **spen'ding** pr.p.) -**spen'der** n. -**spend'thrift** n. wasteful person

sperm n. male reproductive cell; semen

spew v. vomit

sphere [sfēr] n. ball, globe; field of action; status -**spher'ical** [sfe'ri-] a.

sphinx n. statue in Egypt with lion's body and human head (pl. **-es**)

spice n. aromatic or pungent vegetable substance; spices collectively; anything that adds relish, interest etc. -vt. season with spices -**spi'cy** a.

spick-and-span a. neat, smart, new-looking

spi'der n. small eight-legged creature which spins web to catch prey -**spi'dery** a.

spig'ot n. peg or plug

spike n. sharp point; long flower cluster with flowers attached directly to the stalk -vt. pierce, fasten with spike; render ineffective -**spi'ky** a.

spill v. (cause to) pour from, flow over, fall out, esp. unintentionally; upset; be lost or wasted (**spilt** or **spilled** pt./pp.) -n. fall; amount spilt -**spill'age** n.

spin v. (cause to) revolve rapidly; twist into thread; prolong (**spun** pt., **spun** pp., **spin'ning** pr.p.) -n. spinning -**spin'ning** n. act, process of drawing out and twisting into threads

spin'dle n. rod, axis for spinning -**spin'dly** a. long and slender

spine n. backbone; thin spike, esp. on fish etc.; ridge; back of book -**spi'nal** a. -**spine'less** a. lacking spine; cowardly

spinn'ey n. small wood

spin'ster n. unmarried woman

spi'ral n. continuous curve drawn at ever increasing distance from fixed point; anything resembling this -a. -**spi'rally** adv.

spire n. pointed part of steeple; pointed stem

spir'it n. life principle animating body; disposition; liveliness; courage; essential character or meaning; soul; ghost; alcohol -pl. emotional state; strong alcoholic drink -vt. carry away mysteriously -**spir'ited** a. lively -**spir'itless** a. listless, apathetic -**spir'itual** a. given to, interested in things of the spirit -n. negro sacred song, hymn -**spir'itualism** n. belief that spirits of the dead communicate with the living -**spir'itualist** n. -**spirituality** n. -**spir'itually** adv.

spit[1] vt. eject saliva -vt. eject from mouth (**spat**, **spit** pt./pp., **spitt'ing** pr.p.) -n. spitting, saliva -**spit'tle** n. saliva

spit[2] n. sharp rod to put through meat for roasting; sandy point projecting into the sea -vt. thrust through (**-tt-**)

spite n. malice -vt. thwart spitefully -**spite'ful** a. -**spite'fully** adv. -**in spite of** prep. regardless of; notwithstanding

splash v. scatter liquid about or on, over something -n. sound of this; patch, esp. of colour; (effect of) extravagant display

splatt'er v./n. spatter

splay v. spread out; turned outwards -vt. spread out; twist outwards

spleen n. organ in the abdomen

splen'did a. magnificent, excellent -**splen'dour** n.

splice v. join by interweaving strands; join (wood) by overlapping -n. spliced joint

splint n. rigid support for broken limb etc.

splint'er n. thin fragment -vi. break into fragments

split v. break asunder; separate; divide (**split**, **splitt'ing**) -n. crack, fissure

splutt'er v. make hissing, spitting sounds; utter incoherently with spitting sounds -n.

spoil vt. damage, injure; damage manners or behaviour of (esp. child) by indulgence -vi. go bad (**spoiled** or **spoilt** pt./pp., **spoil'ing** pr.p.)

spoke n. radial bar of a wheel

spokes'man n. one deputed to speak for others

sponge [-unj] n. marine animal; its skeleton, or a synthetic substance like it, used to absorb liquids; type of light cake -vt. wipe with sponge -**spong'y** a. spongelike; wet and soft

spon'sor n. one promoting something; one who agrees to give money to a charity on completion of specified activity by another; godparent -vt. act as sponsor -**sponsorship** n.

sponta'neous a. voluntary; natural -**spontane'ity** [or -ā'-] n. -**sponta'neously** adv. -**sponta'neousness** n.

spool [-ōō] n. reel, bobbin

spoon [-ōō] n. implement with shallow bowl at end of handle for carrying food to mouth etc. -vt. lift with spoon -**spoon'ful** n.

spoor n. trail of wild animals

sporad'ic a. singly, in scattered instances -**sporad'ically** adv.

sport n. game, activity for pleasure, competition, exercise; enjoyment; cheerful person, good loser -vt. wear (esp. ostentatiously) -vi. frolic; play (sport) -**sport'ing** a. of sport; behaving with fairness, generosity -**sports'man** n. one who engages in sport; good loser

spot n. small mark, stain; blemish; pimple; place; (difficult) situation; inf. small quantity -vt. mark with spots; detect; observe (-tt-) -**spot'less** a. unblemished; pure -**spot'ty** a. with spots; uneven

spouse n. husband or wife

spout v. pour out -n. projecting tube or lip for pouring liquids; copious discharge

sprain n./vt. wrench or twist (of muscle etc.)

sprat n. small sea fish

sprawl vi. lie or sit about awkwardly; spread in rambling, unplanned way -n. sprawling

spray[1] n. (device for producing) fine drops of liquid -vt. sprinkle with shower of fine drops

spray[2] n. branch, twig with buds, flowers etc.; ornament like this

spread [-ed] v. extend; stretch out; open out; scatter; distribute; unfold; cover (**spread**, **spread'ing**) -n. extent; increase; ample meal; food which can be spread on bread etc. -**spread-eagle(d)** a. with arms and legs outstretched

spree n. session of overindulgence; romp

sprig n. small twig; ornamental design like this; small nail

spright'ly [-rīt'-] a. lively, brisk -**spright'liness** n.

spring vi. leap; shoot up or forth; come into being; appear; grow; become bent or split -vt. produce unexpectedly; set off (trap) (**sprang**, **sprung**, **spring'ing**) -n. leap; recoil; piece of coiled or bent metal with much resilience; flow of water from earth; first season of year -**spring'y** a. elastic

spring'bok n. S Afr. antelope

sprin'kle [-ng'kl] vt. scatter small drops on, strew -**sprin'kler** n. -**sprin'kling** n. small quantity or number

sprint vt. run short distance at great speed -n. such run, race -**sprint'er** n.

sprout vt. put forth shoots, spring up -n. shoot

spruce[1] n. variety of fir

spruce[2] a. neat in dress

spry a. nimble, vigorous

spume n./vi. foam, froth

spur n. pricking instrument attached to horseman's heel; incitement; stimulus; -vt. ride hard (-rr-)

spurge n. plant with milky sap

spur'ious [spyoor'-] a. not genuine

spurn vt. reject with scorn

spurt v. send, come out in jet; rush suddenly -n. jet; short sudden effort

sputt'er v. splutter

spy n. one who watches (esp. in rival countries, companies etc.) and reports secretly -vi. act as spy -vt. catch sight of (**spied**, **spy'ing**)

Sq. Square

squab'ble [-ob'-] vi. engage in petty, noisy quarrel -n.

squad [-od] n. small party, esp. of soldiers -**squad'ron** n. division of cavalry regiment, fleet or air force

squal'id [-ol'-] a. mean and dirty -**squal'or** n.

squall [-awl] n. harsh cry; sudden gust of wind; short storm -vi. yell

squan'der [-on'-] vt. spend wastefully

square [-ār] n. equilateral rectangle; area of this shape; in town, open space (of this shape); product of a number multiplied by itself; instrument for drawing right angles -a. square in form; honest; straight; even; level, equal -vt. make square; find square of; pay -vi. fit, suit

squash [-osh] vt. crush flat; pulp;

suppress -n. juice of crushed fruit; crowd; game played with rackets and soft balls in walled court

squat [-ot] vi. sit on heels (-tt-) -a. short and thick

squawk n. short harsh cry, esp. of bird -v. utter this

squeak v./n. (make) short shrill sound

squeal n. long piercing squeak -vi. make one

squeam'ish a. easily made sick; easily shocked; overscrupulous

squeeze vt. press; wring; force; hug -n. act of squeezing

squid n. type of cuttlefish

squint vi. have the eyes turned in different directions; glance sideways -n. this eye disorder; glance

squire n. country gentleman

squirm vi. wriggle; be embarrassed -n.

squir'rel n. small graceful bushy-tailed tree animal

squirt v. (of liquid) force, be forced through narrow opening -n. jet

Sr. Senior

SRN State Registered Nurse

SS steamship

St. Saint; Strait; Street

st. stone (weight)

stab v. pierce, strike (at) with point-ed weapon (-bb-) -n. blow, wound so inflicted; sudden sensation, eg of fear; attempt

sta'bilize v. make or become stable -**sta'bilizer** n. device to maintain equilibrium of ship, aircraft etc.

sta'ble¹ n. building for horses; racehorses of particular owner, es-tablishment; such establishment -vt. put into stable

sta'ble² a. firmly fixed; steadfast, re-solute -**stabil'ity** n. steadiness; abil-ity to resist change -**sta'bly** adv.

stack n. ordered pile, heap; chimney -vt. pile in stack

sta'dium n. open-air arena for ath-letics etc. (pl. -s, -ia)

staff n. [-ah-] n. body of officers or workers; pole -vt. supply with per-sonnel

stag n. male deer

stage n. period, division of devel-opment; (platform of) theatre; stop-ping-place on road, distance between two of them -vt. put (play) on stage; arrange, bring about -**sta'gy** a. theatrical

stagg'er vi. walk unsteadily -vt. astound; arrange in overlapping or

alternating positions, times; distri-bute over a period -n. act of stagger-ing

stag'nate [or -nāt'] vi. cease to flow or develop -**stag'nant** a. sluggish; not flowing; foul, impure -**stagna'-tion** n.

staid a. of sober and quiet character, sedate

stain v. spot, mark; apply liquid col-ouring to (wood etc.) -n. -**stain'less** a. -**stainless steel** rustless steel alloy

stairs pl.n. set of steps, esp. as part of house -**stair'case, stair'way** n. structure enclosing stairs; stairs

stake n. sharpened stick or post; money wagered or contended for -vt. secure, mark out with stakes; wager, risk

stale a. old, lacking freshness; lacking energy, interest through monotony -**stale'mate** n. deadlock

stalk¹ [-awk] n. plant's stem; any-thing like this

stalk² [-awk] v. follow stealthily; walk in stiff and stately manner -n. stalking

stall [-awl] n. compartment in stable etc.; erection for display and sale of goods; front seat in theatre etc. -v. put in stall; (motor engine) unin-tentionally stop; delay

stall'ion n. uncastrated male horse, esp. for breeding

stal'wart [-awl-] a. strong, brave; staunch in spirit -n. stalwart person

stam'ina n. power of endurance

stamm'er v. speak, say with rep-etition of syllables -n. habit of so speaking -**stamm'erer** n.

stamp vi. put down foot with force -vt. impress mark on; affix postage stamp -n. stamping with foot; im-printed mark; appliance for marking; piece of gummed paper printed with device as evidence of postage etc.

stampede' n. sudden frightened rush, esp. of herd of cattle, crowd; C rodeo -v.

stance n. manner, position of stand-ing; attitude

stanch [-ah-] see STAUNCH

stand v. have, take, set in upright position; be situated; remain firm or stationary; endure; offer oneself as a candidate; be symbol etc. of -vt. inf. provide free, treat to (stood, stand'ing) -n. holding firm; position; halt; something on which things may be placed; structure from which spectators watch sport *etc.*; stop made by pop group *etc.* **-stand'ing** *n.* reputation, status; duration *-a.* erect; lasting; stagnant

stand'ard *n.* accepted measure of something against which others are judged; degree, quality; flag; **SA** school form or grade *-a.* usual; of recognized authority; accepted as correct **-standardiza'tion** *n.* **-stan'dardize** *vt.* regulate by a standard

stand'point *n.* point of view

stan'za *n.* group of lines of verse (*pl.* **-zas**)

sta'ple *n.* U-shaped piece of metal used to fasten; main product *-a.* principal *-vt.* fasten with staple **-sta'pler** *n.*

star *n.* celestial body, seen as twinkling point of light; asterisk (*); celebrated player, actor *-a.* adorn with stars; mark (with asterisk) *-v.* feature as star performer **(-rr-)** *-a.* most important **-starr'y** *a.* covered with stars **-star'fish** *n.* small starshaped sea creature

star'board *n.* right-hand side of ship, looking forward *-a.*

starch *n.* substance forming the main food element in bread, potatoes *etc.*, and used mixed with water, for stiffening linen *etc.* *-vt.* stiffen thus **-starch'y** *a.* containing starch; stiff

stare *vi.* look fixedly at; gaze with wide-open eyes *-n.* staring gaze

stark *a.* blunt, bare; desolate; absolute *-adv.* completely

star'ling *n.* glossy black speckled songbird

start *vt.* begin; set going *-vi.* begin, *esp.* journey; make sudden movement *-n.* beginning; abrupt movement; advantage of a lead in a race **-start'er** *n.* electric motor starting car engine; competitor in, supervisor of, start of race

star'tle *vt.* give a fright to

starve *v.* (cause to) suffer or die from hunger **-starva'tion** *n.*

state *n.* condition; politically organized people; government; pomp *-vt.* express in words **-state'ly** *a.* dignified, lofty **-state'ment** *n.* expression in words; account **-states'man** *n.* respected political leader **-states'manship** *n.* his art

stat'ic *a.* motionless, inactive *-n.* electrical interference in radio reception

sta'tion *n.* place where thing stops or is placed; stopping place for railway trains; local office for police force, fire brigade *etc.*; place equipped for radio or television transmission; bus garage; post; position in life *-vt.* put in position **-sta'tionary** *a.* not moving; not changing

sta'tioner *n.* dealer in writing materials *etc.* **-sta'tionery** *n.*

statist'ics *pl.n.* (with *sing. v.*) numerical facts collected systematically and arranged; the study of them **-statist'ical** *a.* **-statisti'cian** [-tish-] *n.* expert in statistics

statue *n.* solid carved or cast image **-statuesque'** [-esk'] *a.* like statue; dignified

stat'ure *n.* bodily height; greatness

sta'tus *n.* position, rank; prestige; relation to others **-status quo** existing state of affairs

stat'ute *n.* law

staunch [-aw-] *vt.* stop flow (of blood) from *-a.* trustworthy, loyal

stave *n.* one of the pieces forming barrel *-vt.* break hole in; ward (off) **(stove, staved** *pt./pp.*, **sta'ving** *pr.p.*)

stay¹ *vi.* remain; sojourn; wait; endure *-vt.* stop; postpone **(stayed, stay'ing)** *-n.* remaining, sojourning; check; postponement

stay² *n.* support, prop

STD subscriber trunk dialling

stead [-ed] *n.* place **-in stead** in place (of)

stead'y *a.* firm; regular; temperate *-vt.* make steady **-stead'ily** *adv.* **-stead'iness** *n.* **-stead'fast** *a.* firm, unyielding

steak [stāk] *n.* thick slice of meat

steal [-ēl] *vi.* rob; move silently *-v.* take without right or leave **(stole, sto'len, steal'ing)**

stealth [stelth] *n.* secret or underhand procedure, behaviour **-stealth'ily** *adv.* **-stealth'y** *a.*

steam *n.* vapour of boiling water *-vi.* give off steam; move by steam power *-vt.* cook or treat with steam **-steam'er** *n.* steam-propelled ship **-steam-engine** *n.* engine worked by steam

steel *n.* hard and malleable metal made by mixing carbon in iron; **C** railway track *-vt.* harden **-steel'y** *a.*

steep¹ *a.* sloping abruptly; (of prices) very high

steep² *v.* soak, saturate *-n.*

stee'ple *n.* church tower with spire **-stee'plechase** *n.* race with obstacles to jump **-stee'plejack** n. one who builds, repairs chimneys etc.

steer[1] vt. guide, direct course of vessel, motor vehicle etc. -vi. direct one's course

steer[2] n. castrated male ox

stell'ar a. of stars

stem[1] n. stalk, trunk; part of word to which inflections are added; foremost part of ship

stem[2] vt. check, dam up (-mm-)

stench n. evil smell

sten'cil n. thin sheet pierced with pattern which is brushed over with paint or ink, leaving pattern on surface under it; the pattern -vt. (-ll-)

step n. move and set down foot; proceed (in this way) -vt. measure in paces (-pp-) -n. stepping; series of foot movements forming part of dance; measure, act, stage in proceeding; board, rung etc. to put foot on; degree in scale

step'child n. child of husband or wife by former marriage **-step'-brother** n. **-step'father** n. **-step'-mother** n. **-step'sister** n.

stereophon'ic a. (of sound) giving effect of coming from many directions **-ster'eo** a./n.

ster'eotype [ste'ri-] n. something (monotonously) familiar, conventional

ster'ile [ste'rīl] a. unable to produce fruit, crops, young etc.; free from (harmful) germs **-steril'ity** n. **-ster'ilize** vt. render sterile

ster'ling a. genuine, true; of solid worth; in British money -n. British money

stern[1] a. severe, strict **-stern'ness** n.

stern[2] n. rear part of ship

steth'oscope n. instrument for listening to action of heart, lungs etc.

ste'vedore n. one who loads or unloads ships

stew n. food cooked slowly in closed vessel -v.

stew'ard n. one who manages another's property; official managing race meeting, assembly etc.; attendant on ship or aircraft **(-ess** fem.)

stick n. long, thin piece of wood; anything shaped like a stick -vt. pierce, stab; place, fasten, as by pins, glue; protrude -vi. adhere; come to stop, jam; remain **(stuck** pt./pp.) **-stick'er** n. esp. adhesive label, poster **-stick'y** a. covered with, like ad-

hesive substance; (of weather) warm, humid

stic'kleback [-kl-b-] n. small fish with sharp spines on back

stick'ler n. person who insists on something

stiff a. not easily bent or moved; difficult; thick, not fluid; formal; strong or fresh, as breeze **-stiff'en** v. **-stiff'ness** n.

sti'fle vt. smother, suppress

stig'ma n. mark of disgrace (pl. **-mas, -mata)**

stile n. arrangement of steps for climbing a fence

stilet'to n. small dagger

still[1] a. motionless, noiseless -vt. quiet -adv. to this time; yet; even -n. photograph esp. of film scene **-still'-ness** n. **-still'born** a. born dead

still[2] n. apparatus for distilling

stilt n. pole with footrests for walking raised from ground; long post supporting building etc. **-stilt'ed** a. stiff in manner, pompous

stim'ulus n. something that rouses to activity; incentive (pl. **-uli** [-lī, -lē]) **-stim'ulant** n. drug etc. acting as a stimulus **-stim'ulate** vt. rouse up, spur **-stim'ulating** a. **-stimula'tion** n. **-stim'ulative** a.

sting vt. thrust sting into; cause sharp pain to -vi. feel sharp pain **(stung, sting'ing)** -n. (wound, pain, caused by) sharp pointed organ, often poisonous, of certain creatures

stin'gy [-ji] a. mean; niggardly

stink vi. give out strongly offensive smell; sl. be abhorrent **(stank, stunk, stink'ing)** -n. such smell, stench

stink'wood S Afr. tree yielding hard wood

stint vt. be frugal, miserly to (someone) or with (something) -n. allotted amount of work or time; limitation, restriction

stip'ulate vi. specify in making a bargain **-stipula'tion** n. proviso; condition

stir v. (begin to) move; rouse; excite (-rr-) -n. commotion, disturbance

stirr'up n. loop for supporting foot of rider on horse

stitch n. movement of needle in sewing etc.; its result in the work; sharp pain in side; least fragment of (clothing) -v. sew

stoat n. small mammal with brown coat and black-tipped tail

stock n. goods, material stored, esp.

for sale or later use; financial shares in, or capital of, company *etc.*; standing, reputation; farm animals (livestock); plant, stem from which cuttings are taken; handle of gun, tool *etc.*; liquid broth produced by boiling meat *etc.*; flowering plant; lineage *-a.* kept in stock; standard, hackneyed *-vt.* keep, store; supply with livestock, fish *etc.* **-stock'y** *a.* thickset **-stock'broker** *n.* agent for buying, selling shares in companies **-stock exchange** institution for buying and selling shares **-stock'pile** *v.* acquire and store large quantity of (something) **-stock'taking** *n.* examination, counting and valuing of goods in a shop *etc.*

stockade' *n.* enclosure of stakes, barrier

stock'ing *n.* close-fitting covering for leg and foot **-stock'inged** *a.*

stodg'y *a.* heavy, dull

stoep [-oop] *n.* SA verandah

sto'ic *a.* capable of much self-control, great endurance without complaint *-n.* stoical person **-sto'ical** *a.* **-sto'icism** *n.*

stoke *v.* feed, tend fire or furnace **-sto'ker** *n.*

stole *n.* long scarf or shawl

stol'id *a.* hard to excite

stom'ach [-um'ək] *n.* sac forming chief digestive organ in any animal; appetite *-vt.* put up with

stone *n.* (piece of) rock; gem; hard seed of fruit; hard deposit formed in kidneys, bladder; weight, 14 lbs. *-vt.* throw stones at; free (fruit) from stones **-sto'nily** *adv.* **-sto'ny** *a.* of, like stone; hard; cold

stook [-ŏŏ-] *n.* group of sheaves set upright in field to dry

stool [-ŏŏ-] *n.* backless chair

stoop [-ŏŏ-] *vi.* lean forward or down; abase, degrade oneself *-n.* stooping carriage of the body

stop *vt.* bring to halt; prevent; desist from; fill up an opening *-vi.* cease, come to a halt; stay **(-pp-)** *-n.* stopping or becoming stopped; punctuation mark, *esp.* full stop; any device for altering or regulating pitch; set of pipes in organ having tones of a distinct quality **-stopp'age** *n.* **-stopp'er** *n.* plug for closing bottle *etc.* **-stop'watch** *n.* one which can be stopped for exact timing of race

store *vt.* stock, keep *-n.* shop; abundance; stock; place for keeping goods; warehouse *-pl.* stocks of goods, provisions **-stor'age** *n.* **-store cattle** cattle, sheep bought lean to be fattened for market

stor'ey *n.* horizontal division of a building

stork *n.* large wading bird

storm *n.* violent weather with wind, rain *etc.*; assault on fortress; violent outbreak *-vt.* assault; take by storm *-vi.* rage **-storm'y** *a.* like storm

story *n.* (book, piece of prose *etc.*) telling about events, happenings

stout *a.* fat; sturdy, resolute *-n.* kind of beer **-stout'ness** *n.*

stove *n.* apparatus for cooking, heating *etc.*

stow [stō] *vt.* pack away **-stow'age** *n.* **-stow'away** *n.* one who hides in ship to obtain free passage

strad'dle *vt.* bestride *-vi.* spread legs wide *-n.*

strag'gle *vi.* stray, get dispersed, linger **-strag'gler** *n.*

straight [strāt] *a.* without bend; honest; level; in order; (of spirits) undiluted; expressionless *-n.* straight state or part *-adv.* direct **-straight'en** *v.* **-straight'away** *adv.* immediately **-straightfor'ward** *a.* open, frank; simple

strain' *vt.* stretch tightly; stretch to full or to excess; filter *-vi.* make great effort *-n.* stretching force; violent effort; injury from being strained; great demand; (condition cause by) overwork, worry *etc.* **-strained** *a.* **-strain'er** *n.* filter, sieve

strain² *n.* breed or race; trace

strait *n.* channel of water connecting two larger areas of water *-pl.* position of difficulty or distress **-strait'jacket** *n.* jacket to confine arms of violent person **-strait-laced** *a.* prudish

strand' *v.* run aground; leave, be left in difficulties

strand² *n.* one single string or wire of rope *etc.*

strange [-ānj] *a.* odd; unaccustomed; foreign **-stran'ger** *n.* unknown person; foreigner; one unaccustomed (to) **-strange'ness** *n.*

stran'gle [-ng'gl] *vt.* kill by squeezing windpipe; suppress **-strangula'tion** *n.* strangling

strap *n.* strip, *esp.* of leather *-vt.* fasten, beat with strap **(-pp-)** **-strapp'ing** *a.* tall and well-made

strat'agem [-jəm] *n.* plan, trick **-strat'egy** *n.* art of war; overall plan **-strate'gic(al)** *a.* **-strat'egist** *n.*

strat'um [-aht-] n. layer, esp. of rock; class in society (pl. -ta) -strat'ify [-at'-] v. form, deposit in layers (-ified, -ifying) -stratifica'tion n.

straw n. stalk(s) of grain; long, narrow tube used to suck up liquid -straw'berry n. creeping plant producing a red, juicy fruit; the fruit

stray vi. wander; digress; get lost -a. strayed; occasional, scattered -n. stray animal

streak n. long line or band; element -vt. mark with streaks -vi. move fast -streak'y a.

stream n. flowing body of water or other liquid; steady flow -vi. flow; run with liquid -stream'er n. (paper) ribbon, narrow flag

stream'lined a. (of car, plane etc.) built so as to offer least resistance to air -stream'lining n.

street n. road in town or village, usu. lined with houses

strength n. quality of being strong; power -strength'en v. make stronger, reinforce

stren'uous a. energetic; earnest

stress n. emphasis; tension -vt. emphasize

stretch vt. extend; exert to utmost; tighten, pull out; reach out -vi. reach; have elasticity -n. stretching, being stretched, expanse; spell -stretch'er n. person, thing that stretches; appliance on which disabled person is carried

strew [-rōō] vt. scatter over surface, spread (strewed pt., strewn or strewed pp., strew'ing pr.p.)

strick'en a. seriously affected by disease, grief etc.; pp. of STRIKE

strict a. stern, not lax or indulgent; defined; without exception -strict'ness n.

stric'ture n. critical remark; constriction

stride vi. walk with long steps (strode, stridd'en, stri'ding) -n. single step; its length

stri'dent a. harsh, loud

strife n. conflict; quarrelling

strike v. hit (against); ignite; attack; sound (time) as bell in clock etc. -vt. affect; enter mind of -vi. cease work as protest or to make demands (struck pt., strick'en, struck pp., stri'king pr.p.) -n. act of striking -stri'ker n. -stri'king a. noteworthy, impressive

string n. (length of) thin cord or other material; series; fibre in plants -pl. conditions -vt. provide with, thread on string; form in line, series (strung, string'ing) -stringed a. (of musical instruments) furnished with strings -string'y a. like string; fibrous

strin'gent [-j-] a. strict, binding -strin'gency n. -strin'gently adv.

strip vt. lay bare, take covering off -vi. undress (-pp-) -n. long, narrow piece -stripp'er n. -strip(tease)' n. cabaret or theatre act in which person undresses

stripe n. narrow mark, band -striped, stri'py a. marked with stripes

strive vi. try hard, struggle (strove, striv'en, stri'ving)

stroke n. blow; sudden action, occurrence; apoplexy; chime of clock; completed movement in series; style, method of swimming; act of stroking -vt. pass hand lightly over

stroll [-ōl] vi. walk in leisurely or idle manner -n.

strong a. powerful, robust, healthy; difficult to break; noticeable; intense; emphatic; not diluted; having a certain number -strong'ly adv. -strong'hold n. fortress

struc'ture n. (arrangement of parts in) construction, building etc.; form -struc'tural a.

strug'gle vi. contend; fight; proceed, work, move with difficulty and effort -n.

strum v. strike notes of guitar etc. (-mm-)

strut vi. walk affectedly or pompously (-tt-) -n. rigid support; strutting walk

stub n. remnant of anything, eg pencil; counterfoil -vi. strike, as toes, against fixed object; extinguish by pressing against surface (-bb-) -stubb'y a. short, broad

stub'ble n. stumps of cut grain after reaping; short growth of beard

stubb'orn a. unyielding, obstinate -stubb'ornness n.

stucc'o n. plaster

stud' n. nail with large head; removable double-headed button -vt. set with studs (-dd-)

stud' n. set of horses kept for breeding -stud farm

stu'dio n. workroom of artist, photographer etc.; building, room where film, television or radio shows are made, broadcast (pl. -s)

stud'y *vi.* be engaged in learning –*vt.* make study of; scrutinize (**stud'ied, stud'ying**) –*n.* effort to acquire knowledge; subject of this; room to study in; book, report *etc.* produced as result of study; sketch –**stu'dent** *n.* one who studies –**stud'ied** *a.* carefully designed, premeditated –**stu'dious** *a.* fond of study; painstaking; deliberate

stuff *v.* pack, cram, fill (completely); eat large amount; fill with seasoned mixture; fill (animal's skin) with material to preserve lifelike form –*n.* material; any substance –**stuff'ing** *n.* material for stuffing –**stuff'y** *a.* lacking fresh air; *inf.* dull, conventional

stum'ble *vi.* trip and nearly fall; falter –*n.*

stump *n.* remnant of tree, tooth *etc.*, when main part has been cut away; one of uprights of wicket in cricket –*vt.* confuse, puzzle –*vi.* walk heavily, noisily –**stump'y** *a.* short and thickset

stun *vt.* knock senseless; amaze (**-nn-**) –**stunn'ing** *a.*

stunt[1] *vt.* check growth of

stunt[2] *n.* feat of dexterity or daring

stu'pefy *vt.* make insensitive, lethargic; astound (**-efied, -efying**) –**stupefac'tion** *n.*

stupen'dous [styoo-] *a.* astonishing; amazing; huge

stu'pid *a.* slow-witted; silly –**stupid'ity** *n.*

stu'por *n.* dazed state

stur'dy *a.* robust, strongly built; vigorous –**stur'dily** *adv.*

stur'geon [-jən] *n.* fish yielding caviare

stutt'er *v.* speak with difficulty; stammer –*n.*

sty[1] *n.* place to keep pigs in

sty[1], **stye** *n.* inflammation on eyelid

style *n.* manner of writing, doing *etc.*; sort; elegance; design –*vt.* design –**sty'lish** *a.* fashionable –**sty'list** *n.* one cultivating style in literary or other execution; designer

sty'lus *n.* (in record player) tiny point running in groove of record (*pl.* **-li** [-lī], **-luses**)

sty'mie *vt.* hinder, thwart

suave [swahv] *a.* smoothly polite –**suav'ity** *n.*

sub short for subeditor, submarine, subscription, substitute

sub'altern [-əl-tən] *n.* army officer below rank of captain

subcon'scious *a.* acting, existing without one's awareness –*n.* *Psychology* that part of the human mind unknown, or only partly known to possessor

subdivide' *vt.* divide again –**subdivi'sion** [-vizh'-] *n.*

subdue' *v.* overcome –**subdued'** *a.* cowed, quiet; not bright

sub'ject *n.* theme, topic; that about which something is stated one under power of another –*a.* owing allegiance; dependent; liable (to) –*vt.* [-jekt'] cause to undergo; subdue –**subjec'tion** *n.* act of bringing, or state of being, under control –**subject'ive** *a.* based on personal feelings, not impartial; existing in the mind –**subjectiv'ity** *n.*

sub'jugate *vt.* force to submit; conquer –**subjuga'tion** *n.*

sublet' *vt.* (of tenant) let whole or part of what he has rented to another (**sublet', sublett'ing**)

sublime' *a.* elevated; inspiring awe; exalted –**sublim'ity**, **sublime'ness** *n.*

sub'marine [or -rēn'] *n.* (war)ship which can travel and (attack) from) below surface of sea and remain submerged for long periods –*a.* below surface of sea

submerge' *v.* place, go under water –**submer'sion** *n.*

submit' *vt.* surrender; put forward for consideration –*vi.* surrender; defer (**-tt-**) –**submiss'ion** *n.* –**submiss'ive** *a.* meek, obedient

subnor'mal *a.* below normal

subor'dinate [-it] *n./a.* (one) of lower rank or less importance –*vt.* [-āt] make, treat as subordinate –**subordina'tion** *n.*

subscribe' *vt.* pay, promise to pay (contribution); write one's name at end of document –**subscri'ber** *n.* –**subscrip'tion** *n.* subscribing; money paid

sub'sequent *a.* later, following or coming after in time

subser'vient *a.* submissive, servile

subside' *vi.* abate; sink –**subsi'dence** [or sub'-] *n.*

subsid'iary *a.* supplementing; secondary –*n.*

sub'sidize *vt.* help financially; pay grant to –**sub'sidy** *n.* money granted

subsist' *vi.* exist, sustain life –**sub-**

sist'ence n. the means by which one supports life

sub'stance n. (particular kind of) matter; essence; wealth -**substan'tial** a. considerable; of real value; really existing -**substan'tially** adv. -**substan'tiate** vt. bring evidence for, prove

sub'stitute v. put, serve in exchange (for) -n. thing, person put in place of another -**substitu'tion** n.

sub'terfuge n. trick, lying excuse used to evade something

subterra'nean a. underground

subt'le [sut'l] a. not immediately obvious; ingenious; crafty; making fine distinctions -**subt'lety** n. -**subt'ly** adv.

subtract' vt. take away, deduct -**subtrac'tion** n.

sub'urb n. residential area on outskirts of city -**suburb'an** a.

subvert' vi. overthrow; corrupt -**subver'sion** n. -**subver'sive** a.

sub'way n. underground passage; US underground railway

succeed' vi. accomplish purpose; turn out satisfactorily; follow -vt. follow, take place of -**suc'cess'** n. favourable accomplishment, attainment, issue or outcome; successful person or thing -**success'ful** a. -**success'fully** adv. -**succes'sion** n. following; series; succeeding -**success'ive** a. following in order; consecutive -**succes'sor** n.

succ'our vt./n. help in distress

succ'ulent a. juicy; (of plant) having thick, fleshy leaves -n. such plant -**succ'ulence** n.

succumb' [-kum'] vi. give way

such a. of the kind or degree mentioned; so great, so much; so made etc.; of the same kind

suck vt. draw into mouth; hold (dissolve) in mouth; draw in -n. sucking -**suck'er** n. person, thing that sucks shoot coming from root or base of stem of plant

suck'le v. feed from the breast -**suck'ling** n. unweaned infant

suc'tion n. drawing or sucking of air or fluid; force produced by difference in pressure

sudd'en a. done, occurring unexpectedly; abrupt -**sudd'enness** n.

suds pl.n. froth of soap and water

sue v. prosecute; seek justice from -vi. make application or entreaty

suede [swād] n. leather with soft, velvety finish

su'et [sōō'it] n. hard animal fat

suff'er v. undergo, endure, experience (pain etc.) -**suff'erance** n. toleration -**suff'erer** n.

suffice' v. be adequate, satisfactory (for) -**suffi'ciency** n. [-fish'-] adequate amount -**suffi'cient** a. enough, adequate

suff'ix n. letter or word added to end of word

suff'ocate v. kill, be killed by deprivation of oxygen; smother -**suffoca'tion** n.

suff'rage [-rij] n. vote or right of voting

suffuse' vt. well up and spread over -**suffu'sion** n.

sug'ar [shoog'-] n. sweet crystalline vegetable substance -vt. sweeten, make pleasant (with sugar) -**sug'ary** a.

suggest' [-j-] vt. propose; call up the idea of -**suggestibil'ity** n. -**suggest'ible** a. easily influenced -**sugges'tion** n. hint; proposal; insinuation of impression, belief etc., into mind -**suggest'ive** a. containing suggestion, esp. of something indecent

su'icide [sōō'-] n. (act of) one who kills himself -**suici'dal** a.

suit [sōōt] n. set of clothing; garment worn for particular event, purpose; one of four sets in pack of cards; action at law -v. make, be fit or appropriate for; be acceptable to (someone) -**suitability** n. -**suit'able** a. fitting, convenient, -**suit'ably** adv. -**suit'case** n. flat rectangular travelling case

suite [swēt] n. matched set esp. furniture; set of rooms; retinue

suit'or [sōōt'-] n. wooer; one who sues

sulk vi. be silent, resentful, -n. this mood -**sulk'ily** adv. -**sulk'y** a.

sull'en a. unwilling to talk or be sociable, morose

sull'y vt. stain, tarnish (-led, -ying)

sul'phur [-fər] n. pale yellow nonmetallic element -**sulphur'ic** [-fyoor'-] a. -**sul'phurous** a.

sul'tan n. ruler of Muslim country -**sultan'a** [-tahn'ə] n. kind of raisin

sul'try a. (of weather) hot, humid; (of person) looking sensual

sum n. amount, total; problem in arithmetic -v. add up; make summary of main parts (-mm-)

summ'ary n. brief statement of chief points of something -a. done quickly **-summ'arily** adv. speedily; abruptly **-summ'arize** vt. make summary of **-summa'tion** n. adding up

summ'er n. second, warmest season **-summ'ery** a.

summ'it n. top, peak

summ'on vt. demand attendance of; bid witness appear in court; gather up (energies etc.) **-summ'ons** n. call; authoritative demand

sump'tuous a. lavish, magnificent **-sump'tuousness** n.

sun n. luminous body round which earth and other planets revolve; its rays -vt. expose to sun's rays **-sun-** **-sun'less** a. **-sun'ny** a. like the sun; warm; cheerful **-sun'bathing** n. exposure of whole or part of body to sun's rays **-sun'beam** n. ray of sun **-sun'burn** n. inflammation of skin due to excessive exposure to sun **-sun'down** n. sunset **-sun'flower** n. plant with large golden flowers **-sun'stroke** n. illness caused by prolonged exposure to hot sun

sun'dae [-dā] n. ice cream topped with fruit etc.

Sun'day n. first day of the week; Christian Sabbath **-Sunday school** school for religious instruction of children

sun'der vt. separate, sever

sun'dry a. several, various **-sun'-** **dries** pl.n. odd items not mentioned in detail

sup vt. take by sips -vi. take supper (-pp-) -n. mouthful of liquid

su'per [sōō'-] a. inf. very good

super- (comb. form) above, greater, exceeding(ly), as in **superhu'man** a., **su'pertanker** n.

superannua'tion n. pension given on retirement; contribution by employee to pension

superb' a. splendid, grand, impressive **-superb'ly** adv.

supercil'ious a. displaying arrogant pride, scorn **-supercil'iousness** n.

superfi'cial [-fish-] a. of or on surface; not careful or thorough; without depth, shallow **-superficial'ity** n.

super'fluous a. extra, unnecessary **-superflu'ity** [-flōō-] n.

superintend' v. have charge of; overlook; supervise **-superintend'ence** n. **-superintend'ent** n. esp. senior police officer

supe'rior a. greater in quality or quantity; upper, higher in position, rank or quality; showing consciousness of being so **-superior'ity** [-o'ri-] n.

super'lative a. of, in highest degree or quality; surpassing; Grammar denoting form of adjective, adverb meaning most -n.

su'permarket n. large self-service store

supernat'ural a. being beyond the powers or laws of nature; miraculous

supersede' vt. take the place of; set aside, discard

superson'ic a. denoting speed greater than that of sound

superstit'ion [-stish-] n. religion, opinion or practice based on belief in luck or magic **-supersti'tious** a.

su'perstructure [sōō-] n. structure above foundations; part of ship above deck

su'pervise [sōō-] vt. oversee; direct; inspect and control; superintend **-supervi'sion** [-vizh'-] n. **-su'pervisor** n. **-supervi'sory** a.

supine' [or sōō'-] a. lying on back with face upwards; indolent -n.

supp'er n. (light) evening meal

supplant' [-ahnt'-] vt. take the place of

supp'le a. pliable; flexible **-supp'ly** adv.

supp'lement n. thing added to fill up, supply deficiency, esp. extra part added to book etc. -vt. add to; supply deficiency **-supplement'ary** a.

supply' vt. furnish; make available; provide **-plied'**, **-ply'ing** -n. supplying; stock, store

support' vt. hold up; sustain; assist -n. supporting, being supported; means of support **-support'er** n. adherent **-support'ing** a. (of film etc. role) less important **-support'ive** a.

suppose' [-ōz'-] vt. assume as theory; take for granted; accept as likely; (in passive) be expected, obliged; ought **-supposed'** a. **-suppos'edly** [-id-li] adv. **-supposi'tion** [-zish'-] n. assumption; belief without proof; conjecture **-supposi'tious** a.

suppress' vt. put down, restrain; keep or withdraw from publication **-suppress'ion** [-presh-] n.

supp'urate vi. fester, form pus

supreme' a. highest in authority or

rank; utmost -**suprem'acy** n. position of being supreme

sur'charge vt./n. (make) additional charge

sure [shoor] a. certain; trustworthy; without doubt -adv. inf. certainly -**sure'ly** adv. -**sure'ty** n. one who makes himself responsible for another's obligations

surf n. waves breaking on shore

sur'face [-fis] n. outside face of body; plane; top; superficial appearance -a. involving the surface only -v. (cause to) come to surface

sur'feit [-fit] n. excess; disgust caused by excess -v. feed to excess

surge n. wave; sudden increase -vi. move in large waves; swell

sur'geon [-jən] n. medical expert who performs operations -**sur'gery** n. medical treatment by operation; doctor's, dentist's consulting room -**sur'gical** a.

sur'ly a. gloomily morose; ill-natured; cross and rude -**sur'lily** adv. -**sur'liness** n.

surmise' v./n. guess, conjecture

surmount' vt. get over, overcome -**surmount'able** a.

sur'name n. family name

surpass' [-ahs'] vt. go beyond; excel; outstrip -**surpass'ing** a. excellent

sur'plus n. what remains over in excess

surprise' [-fz'] vt. cause surprise to; astonish; take, come upon unexpectedly; startle (someone) into action thus -n. what takes unawares; something unexpected; emotion aroused by being taken unawares

surren'der vt. hand over, give up -vi. yield; cease resistance -n. act of surrendering

surrep'titious [-tish'-] a. done secretly or stealthily; furtive

surround' vt. be, come all round, encompass; encircle -n. border, edging -**surround'ings** pl.n. conditions, scenery etc. around a person, place, environment

surveill'ance [sur-vāl'-] n. close watch, supervision

survey' vt. view, scrutinize; inspect, examine; measure, map (land) -n. [sur'-] a surveying; inspection; report incorporating results of survey -**survey'or** n.

survive' vt. outlive; come alive through -vi. continue to live or exist -**survi'val** n. continuation of existence -**survi'vor** n. one who survives

suscep'tible [sə-sep'-] a. yielding readily (to); capable (of); impressionable -**susceptibil'ity** n.

suspect' vt. doubt innocence of; have impression of existence or presence of; be inclined to believe that -a. [sus'-] of suspected character -n. suspected person

suspend' vt. hang up; cause to cease for a time; keep inoperative; sustain in fluid -**suspend'ers** pl.n. straps for supporting stockings

suspense' n. state of uncertainty, esp. while awaiting news, an event etc.; anxiety, worry -**suspen'sion** n. state of being suspended; springs on axle of body of vehicle

suspi'cion [-spish'-] n. suspecting, being suspected; slight trace -**suspi'cious** a.

sustain' vt. keep, hold up; endure; keep alive; confirm -**sus'tenance** n. food

swab [-ob] n. mop; pad of surgical wool etc. for cleaning, taking specimen etc. -vt. clean with swab (-bb-)

swad'dle [-od'-] vt. swathe

swagg'er vi. strut; boast -n. strutting gait; boastful manner

swall'ow' [-ol'ō] vt. cause, allow to pass down gullet; engulf; suppress -n. act of swallowing

swall'ow' [-ol'ō] n. migratory bird with forked tail

swamp [-omp] n. bog -vt. entangle in swamp; overwhelm; flood -**swamp'y** a.

swan [-on] n. large, web-footed water bird with graceful curved neck

swap [-op], **swop** inf. n./v. exchange; barter (-pp-)

swarm' [-aw-] n. large cluster of insects; vast crowd -vi. (of bees) be on the move in swarm; gather in large numbers

swarm' [-aw-] vi. climb (rope etc.) by grasping with hands and knees

swar'thy [-aw-] a. dark-complexioned

swat [swot] vt. hit smartly; kill, esp. insects (-tt-)

swath [-awth] n. line of grass or grain cut and thrown together by scythe; whole sweep of scythe

swathe vt. cover with wraps or bandages

sway v. swing unsteadily; (cause to) vacillate in opinion etc. -vt. influence opinion *etc.* -n. control; power; swaying motion

swear [-âr] *vt.* promise on oath; cause to take an oath -*vi.* declare; curse (**swore, sworn, swearing**)

sweat [swet] *n.* moisture oozing from, forming on skin -*v.* (cause to) exude sweat; toil (**sweat** *or* **sweated** *pt./pp.,* **sweating** *pr.p.*) -**sweaty** *a.*

sweat'er *n.* woollen jersey

swede *n.* variety of turnip

sweep *vi.* effect cleaning with broom; pass quickly or magnificently; extend in continuous curve -*vt.* clean with broom; carry impetuously (**swept, sweeping**) -n. act of cleaning with broom; sweeping motion; wide curve; one who cleans chimneys -**sweep'ing** *a.* wide-ranging; without limitations

sweet *a.* tasting like sugar; agreeable; kind, charming; fragrant; tuneful; dear, beloved -*n.* small piece of sweet food; sweet course served at end of meal -**sweet'en** *v.* -**sweet'ish** *a.* -**sweet'ly** *adv.* -**sweet'heart** *n.* lover -**sweet pea** plant of pea family with bright flowers -**sweet william** garden plant with flat flower clusters

swell *v.* expand -*vi.* be greatly filled with pride, emotion (**swelled, swollen, swelling**) -n. act of swelling or being swollen; wave of sea

swelt'er *vi.* be oppressed with heat

swerve *vi.* swing round, change direction during motion; turn aside (from duty *etc.*) -n. swerving

swift *a.* rapid, quick -*n.* bird like a swallow -**swift'ly** *adv.*

swig *n.* large swallow of drink -*v.* drink thus

swill *v.* drink greedily; pour water over or through -n. liquid pig foods; rinsing

swim *vi.* support and move oneself in water; float; be flooded; have feeling of dizziness -*vt.* cross by swimming; compete in by swimming (**swam, swum, swimming**) -n. spell of swimming -**swim'mer** *n.*

swin'dle *n./v.* cheat -**swind'ler** *n.* -**swind'ling** *n.*

swine *n.* pig; contemptible person (*pl.* **swine**)

swing *v.* (cause to) move to and fro; (cause to) pivot, turn; hang -*vi.* be hanged; hit out (at) (**swung** *pt./pp.*) -n. act, instance of swinging; seat

hung to swing on; fluctuation (*esp.* in voting pattern)

swipe *v.* strike with wide, sweeping or glancing blow

swirl *v.* (cause to) move with eddying motion -n. such motion

swish *v.* (cause to) move with hissing sound -n. the sound

switch *n.* mechanism to complete or interrupt electric circuit *etc.*; abrupt change; flexible stick or twig; tress of false hair -*vi.* shift, change; swing -*vt.* affect (current *etc.*) with switch; change abruptly; strike with switch -**switch'board** *n.* installation for establishing or varying connections in telephone and electric circuits

swiv'el *n.* mechanism of two parts which can revolve the one on the other -*v.* turn (on swivel) (-ll-)

swoop [-ōō-] *vi.* dive, as hawk -n. act of swooping

swop *vt. see* SWAP

sword [sawrd] *n.* weapon with long blade -**sword'fish** *n.* fish with elongated sharp upper jaw

swot *inf. v.* study hard (-tt-) -n. one who works hard at lessons

syc'amore [sik-] *n.* tree allied to plane tree and maple

syc'ophant [sik'-] *n.* one using flattery to gain favours

syll'able *n.* division of word as unit for pronunciation

syll'abus *n.* outline of a course of study (*pl.* -**es, -bi** [-bī])

syll'ogism [-j-] *n.* form of logical reasoning consisting of two premises and conclusion

sylph [silf] *n.* slender, graceful woman; sprite

syl'van *a.* of forests, trees

sym- *see* SYN-, used before labial consonants

sym'bol *n.* sign; thing representing or typifying something -**symbol'ic** *a.* -**sym'bolism** *n.* -**sym'bolize** *vt.*

symm'etry *n.* proportion between parts -**symmet'rical** *a.*

sym'pathy *n.* feeling for another in pain *etc.*; compassion, pity; sharing of emotion *etc.* -**sympathet'ic** *a.* -**sympathet'ically** *adv.* -**sym'pathize** *vt.*

sym'phony *n.* composition for full orchestra

sympo'sium *n.* conference

symp'tom *n.* change in body indicating disease; sign -**symptomat'ic** *a.*

syn- [sin-, sing-] (*comb. form*) with, together, alike

syn'agogue [-gog] *n.* (meeting place of) Jewish congregation

syn'chromesh *a.* (of gearbox) having device that synchronizes speeds of gears before they engage

syn'chronize *vt.* make agree in time –*vi.* happen at same time

syn'copate *vt.* accentuate weak beat in bar of music –**synco'pa'tion** *n.*

syn'dicate *n.* body of persons associated for some enterprise –*v.* form syndicate –*vt.* publish in many newspapers at the same time

syn'drome *n.* combination of several symptoms in disease

syn'od *n.* church council

syn'onym *n.* word with same meaning as another –**synon'ymous** *a.*

synop'sis *n.* summary, outline

syn'tax *n.* arrangement of words in sentence

syn'thesis *n.* putting together, combination (*pl.* **-theses** [-ēz]) –**syn'thesize** *v.* –**synthet'ic** *a.* artificial; of synthesis

syph'ilis *n.* contagious venereal disease –**syphilit'ic** *a.*

syr'inge [si'rinj] *n.* instrument for drawing in liquid and forcing it out in fine spray –*vt.* spray, cleanse with syringe

syr'up [si'rap] *n.* thick solution obtained in process of refining sugar; any liquid like this

sys'tem *n.* complex whole; method; classification –**systemat'ic** *a.* methodical –**system'ic** *a.* affecting entire body or organism

T

ta [tah] *interj. inf.* thank you

taal [tahl] *n.* SA language, *esp.* Afrikaans

tab *n.* tag, label, short strap

tabb'y *n./a.* (cat) with stripes on lighter background

tab'ernacle *n.* portable shrine of Israelites

ta'ble *n.* flat board supported by legs; facts, figures arranged in lines or columns –*vt.* submit (motion *etc.*) for discussion –**ta'bleland** *n.* plateau –**ta'blespoon** *n.* spoon for serving

food –**table tennis** ball game played on table

tab'leau [-lō] *n.* group of persons representing some scene (*pl.* **-leaux** [-lōz])

table d'hôte [tahb'l-dōt'] *Fr.* meal, with limited choice of dishes, at a fixed price

tab'let *n.* pill of compressed powdered medicine; cake of soap *etc.*; inscribed slab of stone, wood *etc.*

taboo' *a.* forbidden –*n.* prohibition resulting from social conventions *etc.*

tab'ular *a.* arranged like a table –**tab'ulate** *vt.* arrange (figures *etc.*) in tables

tachom'eter [-kom'-] *n.* device for measuring speed, *esp.* of revolving shaft (in car)

tac'it [tas'-] *a.* implied but not spoken –**tac'iturn** *a.* habitually silent

tack[1] *n.* small nail; long loose stitch; *Naut.* course of ship obliquely to windward –*vt.* nail with tacks; stitch lightly; append; sail to windward

tack[2] *n.* riding harness for horses

tac'kle [-kol] *n.* equipment, *esp.* for lifting; *Sport* physical challenge of opponent –*vt.* undertake; challenge

tack'y *a.* sticky; not quite dry –**tack'ie** *n.* SA plimsoll

tact *n.* skill in dealing with people or situations –**tact'ful** *a.* –**tact'less** *a.*

tac'tics *pl.n.* art of handling troops, ships in battle –**tac'tical** *a.*

tac'tile *a.* of sense of touch

tad'pole *n.* immature frog

taff'eta *n.* stiff silk fabric

tag[1] *n.* label identifying or showing price of (something); hanging end –*vt.* add (on) (**-gg-**)

tag[2] *n.* children's game where one chased becomes the chaser upon being touched –*vt.* touch

tail *n.* flexible prolongation of animal's spine; hindmost, lower or inferior part of anything –*pl.* reverse side of coin –*vt.* remove tail of; *inf.* follow closely –**tail'back** *n.* queue of traffic stretching back from an obstruction –**tail'board** *n.* hinged rear board on lorry *etc.* –**tail coat** man's evening dress jacket –**tail'light** *n.* light at rear of vehicle –**tail'spin** *n.* spinning dive of aircraft –**tail off** diminish gradually

tail'or *n.* maker of clothing, *esp.* for men –**tailor-made** *a.* well-fitting

taint *v.* affect or be affected by pollution *etc.* –*n.* defect; contamination

take *vt.* grasp; get; receive, assume; accept; understand, consider; carry; use; capture; consume; subtract; require *-vi.* be effective; become (took, ta'ken, ta'king) *-ta'kings* n.pl. earnings, receipts *-take-off* n. commencement of flight *-take after* resemble in face or character *-take in* understand; make (garment *etc.*) smaller; deceive *-take off* (of aircraft) leave ground; *inf.* go away; *inf.* mimic

tal'cum powder powder, *usu.* scented, to absorb body moisture

tale n. story, narrative

tal'ent n. natural ability *-tal'ented* a. gifted

tal'isman [-iz-] n. object supposed to have magic power

talk [tawk] vi. express, exchange ideas *etc.* in words *-vt.* express in speech, utter; discuss *-n.* lecture; conversation; rumour *-talk'ative* a. *-talk'er* n.

tall [tawl] a. high; of great stature

tall'ow [-ō] n. melted and clarified animal fat

tall'y vi. correspond one with the other (tall'ied, tall'ying) *-n.* record, account

tal'on n. claw

tambourine' [-rēn'] n. flat half-drum with jingling discs of metal attached

tame a. not wild, domesticated; uninteresting *-vt.* make tame

tamp vt. pack down by repeated blows

tamp'er vi. interfere (with)

tam'pon n. plug of lint, cotton inserted in wound *etc.*

tan a./n. (of) brown colour of skin after exposure to sun *etc. -v.* (cause to) go brown; (of animal hide) convert to leather (-nn-) *-tann'in* n. vegetable substance used as tanning agent *-tan'bark* n. bark of certain trees, yielding tannin

tan'dem n. bicycle for two

tang n. strong pungent taste or smell *-tang'y* a.

tan'gent [-j-] n. line that touches a curve *-tangen'tial* a.

tangerine' [-rēn'] n. (fruit of) Asian citrus tree

tan'gible a. that can be touched; real *-tangibil'ity* n.

tan'gle [-ng'gl] n. confused mass or situation *-vt.* confuse

tan'go n. dance of S Amer. origin (pl. -gos)

tank n. storage vessel for liquids or gas; armoured motor vehicle on tracks *-tank'er* n. ship, lorry for carrying liquid

tank'ard n. large drinking cup

Tann'oy R type of public-address system

tan'talize vt. torment by appearing to offer something

tan'tamount a. equivalent, equal (to)

tan'trum n. outburst of temper

tap v. strike lightly but with some noise (-pp-) *-n.*

tap n. valve with handle, plug *etc.* to regulate or stop flow of fluid *-vt.* put tap in; draw off with tap; make secret connection to telephone wire to overhear conversation on it (-pp-)

tape n. narrow strip of fabric, paper *etc.*; magnetic recording *-vt.* record (speech, music *etc.*) *-tape measure* tape marked off in centimetres, inches *etc. -tape recorder* apparatus for recording sound on magnetized tape *-tape'worm* n. long flat parasitic worm

ta'per vi. become gradually thinner *-n.* thin candle

tap'estry n. fabric decorated with woven designs

tapio'ca n. beadlike starch made from cassava root

ta'pir [-pə] n. Amer. animal with elongated snout

tapp'et n. in internal combustion engine, short steel rod conveying movement

tar n. thick black liquid distilled from coal *etc. -vt.* coat, treat with tar (-rr-)

taran'tula n. large (poisonous) hairy spider

tar'dy a. slow, late

tar'get n. thing aimed at

tar'iff [ta'rif] n. tax levied on imports *etc.*; list of charges

Tar'mac R mixture of tar *etc.* giving hard, smooth surface to road *etc.*

tar'nish v. (cause to) become stained or sullied *-n.* discoloration, blemish

tarpaul'in n. (sheet of) heavy hardwearing waterproof fabric

terr'agon n. aromatic herb

tar'ry vi. linger, delay; stay behind (tarr'ied, tarr'ying)

tar'sier n. nocturnal tree-dwelling mammal of Indonesia

tart n. small pie or flan filled with fruit, jam *etc.*

tart[1] a. sour; sharp; bitter

tar'tan n. woollen cloth woven in pattern of coloured checks

tar'tar n. crust deposited on teeth -tartar'ic [-ta'rik] a.

task [-ah-] n. piece of work (esp. unpleasant or difficult) set or undertaken -task'master n. overseer -take to task reprove

tass'el n. ornament of fringed knot of threads etc.; tuft

taste n. sense by which flavour, quality of substance is detected by the tongue; (brief) experience of something; small amount; liking; power of discerning, judging -v. observe or distinguish the taste of a substance; take small amount into mouth; experience -vi. have specific flavour -taste'ful a. with, showing good taste -ta'sty a. pleasantly flavoured -taste bud small organ of taste on tongue

tatt'er v. make or become ragged -n. ragged piece

tatt'ing n. type of handmade lace

tatt'le vi./n. gossip, chatter

tattoo[1] n. beat of drum and bugle call; military spectacle

tattoo[2] vt. mark skin in coloured patterns etc. by pricking (tattooed', tattoo'ing) -n.

tatt'y a. shabby, worn out

taunt vt. provoke with insults etc. -n. scornful remark

taut a. drawn tight; under strain

tav'ern n. inn, public house

taw'dry a. showy, but cheap and flashy

taw'ny a./n. (of) light (yellowish) brown

tax n. compulsory payments imposed by government to raise revenue; heavy demand on something -vt. impose tax on; strain -taxa'tion n. levying of taxes -tax return statement of income for tax purposes

tax'i(cab) n. motor vehicle for hire with driver (pl. tax'is [-iz]) -vi. (of aircraft) running along ground under its own power (tax'ied pt./pp., tax'i-ing, tax'iing prp.) -taxi rank

tax'idermy n. art of stuffing animal skins -tax'idermist n.

TB tuberculosis

tea n. dried leaves of plant cultivated esp. in (sub)tropical Asia; infusion of it as beverage; tea, cakes etc. as afternoon meal -tea'spoon n. small spoon for stirring tea etc. -tea tree Aust., N.Z. tree

teach vt. instruct; educate; train (taught, teach'ing) -teach'er n.

teak n. (hard wood from) East Indian tree

team n. set of animals, players of game etc. -vi. (usu. with up) (cause to) make a team -team'ster n. driver of team of draught animals -team'work n. co-operative work by team

tear[1] [tēr] n. drop of fluid falling from eye -tear'ful a. inclined to weep; involving tears -tear'drop n. -tear gas irritant gas causing temporary blindness

tear[2] [tār] vt. pull apart -vi. become torn; rush (tore, torn, tear'ing) -n. hole or split

tease vt. tantalize, torment, irritate -n. one who teases

teat n. nipple of breast; rubber nipple of baby's bottle

tech'nical a. of, specializing in industrial, practical or mechanical arts; belonging to particular art or science; according to letter of the law -technical'ity n. point of procedure -techni'cian n. one skilled in technique of an art -technique' [-nēk'] n. method of performance in an art; skill required for mastery of subject -technical college higher educational institution

Tech'nicolor [tek'-] R colour photography, esp. in cinema

technol'ogy [tek-] n. application of practical, mechanical sciences; technical skills, knowledge -technolog'ical a. -technol'ogist n.

ted'dy (bear) child's soft toy bear

te'dious a. causing fatigue or boredom -te'dium n. monotony

tee n. Golf place from which first stroke of hole is made; small peg supporting ball for this stroke

teem vi. abound with; swarm; rain heavily

teens pl.n. years of life from 13 to 19 -teen'age a. -teen'ager n. young person between 13 and 19

tee'ter vi. seesaw, wobble

teeth n. pl. of TOOTH

teethe [-TH] vi. (of baby) grow first teeth -teeth'ing troubles problems, difficulties at first stage of something

teeto'tal a. pledged to abstain from alcohol

tel. telephone

tele- (comb. form) at a distance

tel'ecast v./n. (broadcast) television programme

tel'ecommunica'tions *pl. n.* (with *sing. v.*) communications by telephony, television *etc.*

tel'egram *n.* message sent by telegraph

tel'egraph *n.* electrical apparatus for transmitting messages to a distance –*v.* –**telegraph'ic** *a.* –**tel'egraphist** *n.* one who works telegraph –**teleg'raphy** *n.*

telep'athy *n.* action of one mind on another at a distance –**telepath'ic** *a.*

tel'ephone *n.* apparatus for communicating sound to hearer at a distance –*v.* communicate, speak by telephone –**teleph'onist** *n.* person operating telephone switchboard

telepho'to *a.* (of lens) producing magnified image

tel'escope *n.* optical instrument for magnifying distant objects –*v.* slide together –**telescop'ic** *a.*

tel'etext *n.* electronic system which shows information, news on subscribers' television screens

tel'evision *n.* system of producing on screen images of distant objects, events *etc.* by electromagnetic radiation; device for receiving this; programmes *etc.* viewed on television set –**tel'evise** *vt.* transmit by television; make, produce television programme

tel'ex *n.* international telegraph service –*v.*

tell *vt.* let know; order; narrate, make known; discern; distinguish –*vi.* give account; be of weight, importance (**told**, **tell'ing**) –**tell'er** *n.* narrator; bank cashier –**tell'ing** *a.* effective, striking –**tell'tale** *n.* sneak –*a.* revealing

tell'y *n. inf.* television (set)

temer'ity [-me'ri-] *n.* boldness, audacity

temp *n. inf.* one employed on temporary basis

temp. temperature

temp'er *n.* frame of mind; anger, oft. noisy; mental constitution; degree of hardness of steel *etc.* –*vt.* restrain, moderate; harden

temp'erament *n.* natural disposition; emotional mood –**temperament'al** *a.* moody; of, occasioned by temperament

temp'erate *a.* not extreme; showing moderation –**temp'erance** *n.* moderation; abstinence, *esp.* from alcohol

temp'erature *n.* degree of heat or

coldness; *inf.* high body temperature

temp'est *n.* violent storm –**tempest'uous** *a.* turbulent; violent

tem'ple *n.* building for worship

tem'ple *n.* flat part on either side of forehead

tem'po *n.* rate, rhythm

temp'oral *a.* of time; of this life or world

temp'orary *a.* lasting, used only for a time –**temp'orarily** *adv.*

tempt *vt.* try to persuade, entice, *esp.* to something wrong or unwise –**tempta'tion** *n.* –**tempt'er** *n.* (**tempt'ress** *fem.*) –**tempt'ing** *a.* attractive, inviting

ten *n./a.* number next after nine –**tenth** *a./n.* ordinal number

ten'able *a.* able to be held, defended, maintained

tena'cious *a.* holding fast; retentive; stubborn –**tenac'ity** [-nas'-] *n.*

ten'ant *n.* one who holds lands, house *etc.* on rent or lease –**ten'ancy** *n.*

tend [1] *vi.* be inclined; be conducive; make in direction of –**tend'ency** *n.* inclination –**tenden'tious** *a.* controversial

tend [2] *vt.* take care of –**tend'er** *n.* small boat carried by ship; carriage for fuel and water attached to steam locomotive; one who tends, eg bar tender

tend'er [1] *a.* not tough; easily injured; gentle, loving; delicate –**tend'erize** *vt.* soften meat

tend'er [3] *vt.* offer –*vi.* make offer or estimate –*n.* offer or estimate for contract to undertake specific work

tend'on *n.* sinew attaching muscle to bone *etc.*

tend'ril *n.* slender curling stem by which climbing plant clings

ten'ement *n.* building divided into separate flats

ten'et [or tē'-] *n.* belief

tenn'er *n. inf.* ten pound note

tenn'is *n.* game in which ball is struck with racket by players on opposite sides of net

ten'or *n.* male voice between alto and bass; general course, meaning

tense [1] *n.* modification of verb to show time of action

tense [2] *a.* stretched tight; taut; emotionally strained –*v.* make, become tense –**ten'sile** *a.* of, relating to tension –**ten'sion** *n.* stretching; strain when stretched; emotional strain; suspense; *Electricity* voltage

tent n. portable shelter of canvas

tent'acle n. flexible organ of some animals (eg octopus) used for grasping etc.

tent'ative a. experimental, cautious

tent'erhooks pl.n. **-on tenterhooks** in anxious suspense

ten'uous a. flimsy; thin

ten'ure n. (length of time of) possession of office etc.

te'pee n. N Amer. Indian coneshaped tent

tep'id a. moderately warm

term n. word, expression; limited period of time; period during which schools are open **-pl.** conditions; relationship **-vt.** name

term'inal a. at, forming an end; (of disease) ending in death **-n.** terminal part or structure; point where current enters, leaves battery etc.; device permitting operation of computer at distance

term'inate v. bring, come to an end **-termina'tion** n.

terminol'ogy n. set of technical terms or vocabulary

term'inus n. finishing point; railway station etc. at end of line (pl. **-ni** [-nī])

ter'mite n. wood-eating insect (also called **white ant**)

tern n. sea bird like gull

terr'ace n. raised level place; row of houses built as one block; (oft. pl.) unroofed tiers for spectators at football stadium **-vt.** form into terrace

terr'a cott'a n. hard unglazed pottery; brownish-red

terr'ain [or -ān'] n. area of ground, esp. with reference to its physical character

terr'apin n. type of aquatic tortoise

terres'trial a. of the earth; of, living on land

terr'ible a. serious; dreadful; causing fear

terr'ier n. small dog of various breeds

terrif'ic a. very great; inf. good; awe-inspiring

terr'ify vt. frighten greatly

terr'itory n. region; geographical area, esp. a sovereign state **-terri-tor'ial** a.

terr'or n. great fear; inf. troublesome person or thing **-terr'orism** n. use of violence to achieve ends

-terr'orist n./a. **-terr'orize** vt. oppress by violence

terr'y n./a. (pile fabric) with the loops uncut

terse a. concise; abrupt

ter'tiary [-shər-i] a. third in degree, order etc.

Ter'ylene [te'ra-] R synthetic yarn; fabric made of it

test vt. try, put to the proof; carry out test(s) on **-n.** examination; means of trial **-test'ing** a. difficult **-test case** lawsuit viewed as means of establishing precedent **-test match** one of series of international sports contests **-test tube** tube-like glass vessel

test'ament n. Law will; (T-) one of the two main divisions of the Bible

test'icle n. either of two male reproductive glands (also **test'is**)

test'ify v. declare; bear witness (to) (**-ified, -ifying**)

test'imony n. affirmation; evidence **-testimo'nial** n. certificate of character etc.; gift expressing regard for recipient

test'y a. irritable

tet'anus n. acute infectious disease (also called **lockjaw**)

teth'er [-TH-] n. rope for fastening (grazing) animal **-vt.** tie up with rope

tet'ragon n. figure with four angles and four sides **-tetrahe'dron** n. solid contained by four plane faces

text n. (actual words of) book, passage etc.; passage of Scriptures etc. **-text'ual** a. **-text'book** n. book of instruction on particular subject

tex'tile n. any fabric or cloth, esp. woven

tex'ture n. structure, appearance; consistency

thalid'omide n. drug found to cause abnormalities in developing foetus

than [TH-] conj. introduces second part of comparison

thank vt. express gratitude to; say thanks **-thanks** pl.n. words of gratitude

that [TH-] a. demonstrates or particularizes (pl. **those**) **-dem'onstrative** pron. particular thing meant (pl. **those**) **-adv.** as **-relative** pron. which, who **-conj.** introduces noun or adverbial clauses

thatch n. reeds, straw etc. used as roofing material **-vt.** to roof (a house) with this

thaw v. melt; (cause to) unfreeze -n. a melting (of frost etc.)

the [THǝ, THĒ] is the definite article

the'atre [-tǝr] n. place where plays etc. are performed; drama, dramatic works generally -**theat'rical** a. of, for the theatre; exaggerated

thee [TH-] pron. obs. form of THOU used after verb or preposition

theft n. stealing

their [THâr] a./pron. of THEM; possessive of THEY -**theirs** poss. pron. belonging to them

them pron. form of THEY used after verb or preposition; those persons or things -**themselves'** pron. emphatic and reflexive form of THEY

theme n. main topic of book etc.; subject of composition; recurring melody -**themat'ic** a.

then [TH-] adv. at that time; next; that being so

thence [TH-] obs. adv. from that place etc.

theod'olite n. surveying instrument for measuring angles

theol'ogy n. systematic study of religion(s) and religious belief(s) -**theolog'ical** a. -**theolo'gian** n.

the'orem n. proposition which can be demonstrated

the'ory n. supposition to account for something; system of rules and principles, esp. distinguished from practice -**theoret'ical** a. based on theory; speculative -**the'orist** n. -**the'orize** vi. form theories, speculate

ther'apy [the'ra-] n. healing treatment: usu. in compounds as RADIOTHERAPY -**therapeu'tic** [-pyōō-] a. of healing; serving to improve health -**ther'apist** n.

there [TH-] adv. in that place; to that point -**thereby'** adv. by that means -**there'fore** adv. that being so -**thereupon'** conj. immediately

therm n. unit of measurement of heat -**ther'mal**, **ther'mic** a.

thermo- (comb. form) related to, caused by or producing heat

thermodynam'ics pl.n. (with sing. v.) science that deals with the interrelationship of different forms of energy

thermom'eter n. instrument to measure temperature

thermonu'clear a. involving nuclear fusion

Ther'mos R vacuum flask

ther'mostat n. apparatus for regulating temperature

thesau'rus [-aw'-] n. book containing synonyms and antonyms

these [TH-] pron., pl. of THIS

the'sis n. written work submitted for degree, diploma; theory maintained in argument (pl. **the'ses** [-sēz])

Thes'pian a. theatrical -n. actor, actress

they [THā] pron. the third person plural pronoun

thick a. fat, broad, not thin; dense, crowded; viscous; (of voice) throaty; inf. stupid -n. busiest part -**thick'en** v. make, become thick; become complicated -**thick'ness** n. dimensions of anything measured at right angles to length and breadth; layer -**thick'et** n. thick growth of small trees -**thick'set** a. sturdy, stocky

thief n. one who steals (pl. **thieves**) -**thieve** v. steal

thigh [thī] n. upper part of leg

thim'ble n. cap protecting end of finger when sewing

thin a. of little thickness; slim; of little density; sparse; fine; not close-packed -v. make, become thin -**thin'ness** n.

thine [THīn] pron./a. obs. belonging to thee

thing n. (material) object

think vi. have one's mind at work; reflect, meditate; reason; deliberate; hold opinion -vt. consider in the mind; believe (thought [thawt], **think'ing**) -**think'able** a. able to be conceived, possible -**think'er** n.

third a. ordinal number corresponding to three -n. third part -**third party** Law, Insurance etc. person involved by chance in legal proceedings etc.

thirst n. desire to drink; feeling caused by lack of drink; craving -v. -**thirst'y** a.

thir'teen a./n. three plus ten -**thir'ty** n./a. three times ten

this a. demonstrative a./pron. denotes thing, person near, or just mentioned (pl. **these**)

this'tle [-sl] n. prickly plant

thith'er [THITH'-] adv. obs. to or towards that place

thong n. narrow strip of leather, strap

thor'ax n. part of body between neck and belly

thorn n. prickle on plant; bush noted

thor'ough [thur'ō] a. careful, methodical; complete **-thor'oughbred** n. purebred animal, esp. horse **-thor'oughfare** n. road or passage; right of way

those [TH-] pron., pl. of THAT

thou [TH-] pron. obs. the second person singular pronoun (pl. **ye, you**)

though [THŌ] conj. even if —adv. nevertheless

thought [thawt] n. process, product of thinking; what one thinks; meditation **-thought'ful** a. considerate; showing careful thought; attentive **-thought'less** a. inconsiderate

thou'sand [-z-] n./a. ten hundred

thrash vt. beat; defeat soundly —vi. move in wild manner

thread [-ed] n. yarn; ridge cut on screw; theme —vt. put thread into; fit film etc. into machine; put on thread; pick (one's way etc.) **-thread'bare** a. worn; shabby

threat [-et] n. declaration of intention to harm etc.; dangerous person or thing **-threat'en** vt. utter threats against

three n./a. one more than two **-three-ply** a. having three layers or strands

thresh v. beat to separate grain from husks; thrash

thresh'old [-ōld] n. bar of stone forming bottom of doorway; entrance; starting-point

thrice adv. three times

thrift n. saving, economy **-thrift'y** a. economical

thrill n. sensation of excitement and pleasure —v. (cause to) feel a thrill; tremble **-thrill'er** n. suspenseful book, film etc.

thrive vi. grow well; prosper (**throve, thrived** pt., **thriv'en, thrived** pp., **thri'ving** pr.p.)

throat n. front of neck; either or both of passages through it

throb vi. quiver strongly, pulsate (-**bb**-) —n. pulsation

throes [-ōz] pl.n. violent pangs, pain etc. **-in the throes of** inf. in the process of

thrombo'sis n. clot of blood in blood vessel or heart

throne n. ceremonial seat, powers of king —vt. place on throne

throng n./v. crowd

throt'tle n. device controlling amount of fuel entering engine —vt. strangle; restrict

through [throō] prep. from end to end; in consequence of; by means of —adv. from end to end; to the end —a. completed; inf. finished; continuous; (of transport, traffic) not stopping **-throughout'** adv./prep. in every part (of) **-through'put** n. quantity of material processed **-carry through** accomplish

throw [-ō] vt. fling; cast; move, put abruptly, carelessly; cause to fall (**threw, thrown, throw'ing**) —n. act or distance of throwing **-throw'back** n. one who, that which reverts to character of an ancestor

thrush n. songbird

thrust v. push, drive; stab (**thrust, thrust'ing**) —n. lunge, stab; propulsive force or power

thud n. dull heavy sound —vi. make thud (-**dd**-)

thug n. violent person

thumb [-m] n. shortest, thickest finger of hand —vt. handle with thumb; signal for lift in vehicle

thump n. (sound of) dull heavy blow —vt. strike heavily

thun'der n. loud noise accompanying lightning —v. make noise of or like thunder **-thun'derbolt, thun'derclap** n. lightning followed by thunder; anything unexpected **-thun'derstruck** a. amazed

Thurs'day n. fifth day of the week

thus [TH-] adv. in this way; therefore

thwack vt./n. whack

thwart [-awt] vt. foil, frustrate —adv. obs. across

thy [THĪ] a. obs. belonging to thee **-thyself'** pron. emphasized form of THOU

thyme [tīm] n. aromatic herb

thy'roid gland endocrine gland controlling body growth

tib'ia n. shinbone (pl. **-biae** [-bi-ē], **-bias**)

tic n. spasmodic twitch in muscles, esp. of face

tick¹ n. slight tapping sound, as of watch movement; small mark (√); inf. moment —vt. mark with tick —vi. make the sound **-ticker tape** continuous paper ribbon

tick² n. small insectlike parasite living on blood

tick'et n. card, paper entitling holder to admission, travel etc.; label —vt. attach label to

tick'ing n. material for mattress covers

tic'kle *vt.* touch, stroke (person *etc.*) to produce laughter *etc.*; amuse –*vi.* itch –*n.* act, instance of this; C narrow strait –**tick'lish** *a.* sensitive to tickling; requiring care

tidd'ly *inf.* a. tiny; slightly drunk

tidd'lywinks *pl.n.* game of trying to flip small plastic discs into cup

tide *n.* rise and fall of sea happening twice each lunar day –**ti'dal** *a.* –**tidal wave** great wave, *esp.* produced by earthquake –**tide over** help someone for a while

ti'dings *pl.n.* news

ti'dy *a.* orderly, neat –*vt.* put in order

tie *v.* equal (score) of –*vt.* fasten, bind; restrict (**tied, ty'ing**) –*n.* that with which anything is bound; restraint; piece of material worn knotted round neck; connecting link; contest with equal scores; match, game in eliminating competition –**tied** *a.* (of public house) selling beer *etc.* of only one brewer; (of cottage *etc.*) rented to tenant employed by owner

tier [tēr] *n.* row, rank, layer

tiff *n.* petty quarrel

ti'ger *n.* large carnivorous feline animal

tight [tīt] *a.* taut, tense; closely fitting; secure, firm; not allowing passage of water *etc.*; cramped; *inf.* mean; *inf.* drunk –**tights** *pl.n.* one-piece garment covering body from waist to feet –**tight'en** *v.* –**tight'rope** *n.* taut rope on which acrobats perform

ti'ki [tē'-] *n.* amulet, figurine of Maori cultures

tile *n.* flat piece of ceramic, plastic *etc.* used for roofs, floors *etc.* –*vt.* cover with tiles

till¹ *prep./conj.* until

till² *vt.* cultivate –**till'er** *n.*

till³ *n.* drawer for money in shop counter; cash register

till'er *n.* lever to move rudder of boat

tilt *v.* slope, slant –*vi.* take part in medieval combat with lances; thrust (at) –*n.* slope; *Hist.* combat for mounted men with lances

tim'ber *n.* wood for building *etc.*; trees –**tim'bered** *a.* made of wood; wooded –**timber limit** C area to which rights of cutting trees are limited; timber line –**timber line** limit beyond which trees will not grow

tim'bre [-bər, tam'brə] *n.* distinctive quality of voice or sound

time *n.* existence as a succession of states; hour; duration; period; point in duration; opportunity; occasion; leisure –*vt.* choose time for; note time taken by –**time'ly** *a.* at opportune time –**ti'mer** *n.* person, device for recording or indicating time –**time bomb** bomb designed to explode at prearranged time –**time-lag** *n.* period between cause and effect –**time'table** *n.* plan showing times of arrival and departure *etc.* –**Greenwich Mean Time** world standard time

tim'id *a.* easily frightened; shy –**tim-id'ity** *n.* –**tim'orous** *a.* timid; indicating fear

tim'pani, tym'pani *pl.n.* set of kettledrums

tin *n.* malleable metal; container made of tin –*vt.* put in tin, *esp.* for preserving (**-nn-**) –**tinn'y** *a.* (of sound) thin, metallic

tinc'ture *n.* solution of medicinal substance in alcohol; colour, stain –*vt.* colour

tin'der *n.* dry easily-burning material used to start fire

tine *n.* spike of fork, antler *etc.*

tinge [-j] *n.* slight trace –*vt.* colour, flavour slightly

tin'gle [-ng'gl] *vi.* feel thrill or pricking sensation –*n.*

tin'ker *n.* formerly, travelling mender of pots and pans –*vi.* fiddle, meddle (with)

tin'kle [-ng-k-] *v.* (cause to) give out sounds like small bell –*n.* this sound or action

tin'sel *n.* glittering decorative metallic substance

tint *n.* (shade of) colour; tinge –*vt.*

ti'ny *a.* very small, minute

tip¹ *n.* slender or pointed end of anything; small piece forming an extremity –*vt.* put a tip on (**-pp-**)

tip² *n.* small present of money given for service rendered; helpful piece of information; warning, hint –*vt.* give tip to (**-pp-**)

tip³ *vt.* tilt, upset; touch lightly –*vi.* topple over (**-pp-**) –*n.* place where rubbish is dumped

tip'ple *v.* drink (alcohol) habitually –*n.* drink

tip'sy *a.* (slightly) drunk

tip'toe *vi.* walk on ball of foot and toes; walk softly

tiptop' *a.* of the best quality *etc.*

tirade' [tī-rād'] *n.* long angry speech or denunciation

tire *vt.* reduce energy of, weary; bore

-vi. become tired, bored **-tire'some** a. irritating, tedious

tiss'ue n. substance of animal body, plant etc.; soft paper handkerchief etc.

tit n. small bird

titan'ic [tī-] a. huge, epic

tit'bit n. tasty morsel of food; scrap (of scandal etc.)

tithe [-ᴛʜ] n. tenth part **-vt.** exact tithes from

tit'ian [tish'-] a. (of hair) reddish-gold

tit'illate vt. stimulate agreeably

ti'tle n. name of book; heading; name, esp. denoting rank; legal right or document proving it; Sport championship **-title deed** document as proof of ownership

titt'er vi./n. snigger, giggle

tit'tle-tattle n./vi. gossip

tit'ular a. pert. to title; nominal

T.N.T. see TRINITROTOLUENE

to prep. denoting direction, destination; introducing comparison, indirect object, infinitive etc. **-adv.** to fixed position, state

toad n. animal like large frog **-toad'y** n. servile flatterer **-toad'stool** n. fungus like mushroom

toast n. slice of bread browned on both sides by heat; tribute, proposal of health etc. marked by people drinking together; one toasted **-vt.** crisp and brown (as bread); drink toast to; warm at fire **-toast'er** n. electrical device for toasting bread

tobacc'o n. plant with leaves used for smoking (pl. **-cos**) **-tobacc'onist** n. one who sells tobacco products

tobogg'an n. sledge for sliding down slope of snow

today' n. this day **-adv.** on this day; nowadays

tod'dle vi. walk with unsteady short steps **-todd'ler** n. child beginning to walk

to-do' n. inf. fuss, commotion (pl. **-dos**)

toe n. digit of foot; anything resembling this **-toe the line** conform

toff'ee n. chewy sweet made of boiled sugar etc.

togeth'er [-ᴛʜ'-] adv. in company, simultaneously

tog'gle n. small peg fixed crosswise on cord etc. and used for fastening

togs inf. pl.n. clothes

toil n. heavy work or task **-vi.** labour

toi'let n. lavatory; process of washing, dressing; articles used for this

to'ken n. sign; symbol; disc used as money; gift card, voucher exchangeable for goods **-a.** nominal

tol'erate vt. put up with; permit **-tol'erable** a. bearable; fair **-tol'erance** n. **-tol'erant** a. forbearing; broad-minded **-tolera'tion** n.

toll¹ [tōl] v. (cause to) ring (bell) slowly at regular intervals

toll² [tōl] n. tax, esp. for the use of bridge or road

toll'ie n. SA steer calf

tom n. male cat

tom'ahawk n. fighting axe of N Amer. Indians

tomat'o [-aht'-] n. plant with red fruit; the fruit (pl. **-toes**)

tomb [tōōm] n. grave; monument over one **-tomb'stone** n.

tome [tōm] n. large book

tomorr'ow [-ō] adv./n. (on) the day after today

tom'-tom n. drum associated with N Amer. Indians

ton n. measure of weight, 1016 kg (2240 lbs.) (long ton); US measure of weight, 907 kg (2000 lbs.) (short ton) **-tonn'age** n. carrying capacity; ships collectively

tone n. quality of musical sound, voice, colour etc.; general character **-vt.** blend, harmonize (with) **-to'nal** a. **-tonal'ity** n.

tongs [-z] pl.n. large pincers, esp. for handling coal, sugar

tongue [tung] n. organ inside mouth, used for speech, taste etc.; language; speech

ton'ic n. medicine to improve bodily condition; Mus. first keynote of scale **-a.** invigorating, restorative **-tonic (water)** mineral water oft. containing quinine

tonight' [-nīt'] n. this (coming) night **-adv.** on this night

tonne [tun, tun'i] n. metric ton, 1000 kg

ton'sil n. gland in throat **-tonsilli'tis** n. inflammation of tonsils

ton'sure n. shaving of part of head as religious practice; part shaved

too adv. also, in addition; overmuch

tool [-ōō-] n. implement or appliance for mechanical operations; means to an end **-vt.** work on with tool **-tool'ing** n. decorative work; setting up etc. of tools

toot [-ōō-] n. short sound of horn, trumpet etc.

tooth [-ōō-] n. bonelike projection in gums of upper and lower jaws of vertebrates; prong, cog (pl. **teeth**)

top¹ n. highest part, summit; highest rank; first in merit; garment for upper part of body; lid, stopper of bottle etc. -vt. cut off, pass, reach, surpass top; provide top for (-pp-) -**top'most** a. highest -**top'dress** vt. spread soil, fertilizer etc. on surface of land -**top hat** man's hat with tall cylindrical crown -**top-heavy** a. unbalanced -**top notch** a. excellent, first-class -**top-secret** a. needing highest level of secrecy; security -**top'soil** n. surface layer of soil

top² n. toy which spins on tapering point

to'paz n. precious stone of various colours

top'ic n. subject of discourse, conversation etc. -**top'ical** a. up-to-date, having news value

topog'raphy n. (description of) surface features of a place -**topog'rapher** n. -**topograph'ic** a.

top'ple v. (cause to) fall over

top'sy-tur'vy a. in confusion

torch n. portable hand light containing electric battery; burning brand etc.; any apparatus burning with hot flame

torment¹ n. torture in body or mind; afflict; tease -n. [tor'-] suffering, agony of body or mind -**torment'or, -er** n.

torna'do n. whirlwind; violent storm (pl. **-does**)

torpe'do n. self-propelled underwater missile with explosive warhead (pl. **-does**) -vt. strike with torpedo

tor'pid a. sluggish, apathetic -**tor'por** n. torpid state

torr'ent n. rushing stream -**torren'tial** a. resembling a torrent

torr'id a. parched; highly emotional

tor'sion n. twist, twisting

tor'so n. (statue of) body without head or limbs (pl. **-sos, -si** [-sē])

tor'toise [-təs] n. four-footed reptile covered with shell of horny plates -**tor'toiseshell** n. mottled brown shell of turtle

tor'tuous a. winding, twisting; involved, not straightforward

tor'ture n. infliction of severe pain -vt.

Tor'y n. member of Brit., Canad. conservative party

toss vt. throw up, about -vi. be thrown, fling oneself about -n.

tot¹ n. very small child; small quantity, esp. of drink

tot² v. add (up); amount to (-tt-)

to'tal n. whole amount; sum -a. complete, absolute -vi. amount to -vt. add up (-ll-) -**total'ity** n. -**to'talizator** n. machine to operate system of betting on racecourse

totalita'rian a. of dictatorial, one-party government

to'tem n. tribal badge or emblem -**totem pole** carved post of Amer. Indians

tott'er vi. walk unsteadily; begin to fall

touch [tuch] n. sense by which qualities of object etc. are perceived by touching; characteristic manner or ability; touching; slight contact, amount etc. -vt. come into contact with; put hand on; reach; affect emotions of; deal with -vi. be in contact; (with on) refer to -**touch'ing** a. emotionally moving -prep. concerning -**touch'y** a. easily offended -**touch'line** n. side line of pitch in some games -**touch'stone** n. criterion

tough [tuf] a. strong; able to bear hardship, strain; difficult; needing effort to chew; violent -n. inf. rough, violent person -**tough'en** v.

tour [toor] n. travelling round; journey to one place after another -v. -**tour'ism** n. -**tour'ist** n.

tour'nament [toor'-] n. competition, contest esp. with several stages -**tour'ney** n. Hist. knightly tournament

tour'niquet [toor'ni-kā] n. bandage, surgical instrument to stop bleeding

tou'sle vt. tangle, ruffle -n.

tow [tō] vt. drag along behind, esp. at end of rope -n. towing or being towed

towards' [tə-] prep. in direction of; with regard to; as contribution to (also **toward'**)

tow'el n. cloth for wiping off moisture after washing -**tow'elling** n.

tow'er n. tall strong structure esp. part of church etc.; fortress -vi. stand very high; loom (over)

town n. collection of dwellings etc. larger than village and smaller than city -**town'ship** n. small town; C land-survey area

tox'ic a. poisonous; due to poison -**toxae'mia** [-sē'-] n. blood poisoning -**toxic'ity** [-is'-] n. strength of a poison

toy n. something designed to be played with -a. very small -vi. trifle

trace n. track left by anything; indication; minute quantity -vt. follow course of; find out; make plan of; draw or copy exactly -**tra'cing** n. -**trace element** chemical element occurring in very small quantity -**tracing paper** transparent paper placed over drawing, map etc. to enable exact copy to be taken

trache'a [-kē-] n. windpipe (pl. **trache'ae** [-kē-ē]) -**tracheot'omy** n. incision into trachea

track n. mark left by passage of anything; path; rough road; course; railway line; jointed metal band as on tank etc.; course for running or racing; separate section on gramophone record -vt. follow trail or path of -**track events** athletic sports held on a track -**track record** past accomplishments

tract' n. wide expanse, area

tract' n. pamphlet, esp. religious one

tract'able a. easy to manage

trac'tion n. action of pulling

trac'tor n. motor vehicle for hauling, pulling etc.

trade n. commerce, business; buying and selling; any profitable pursuit -v. engage in trade -**tra'der** n. -**trade** in n. used article given in part payment for new -**trade'mark, trade'name** n. distinctive legal mark on maker's goods -**trades'man** n. -**trade union** society of workers for protection of their interests -**trade wind** wind blowing constantly towards equator in certain parts of globe

tradi'tion [-dish-] n. unwritten body of beliefs, facts etc. handed down from generation to generation; custom, practice of long standing -**tradi'tional** a.

traff'ic n. vehicles passing to and fro in street, town etc.; (illicit) trade -vi. trade (**traff'icked, traff'icking**) -**traffic lights** set of coloured lights at road junctions etc.

trag'edy [-aj-] n. sad event; dramatic, literary work dealing with serious, sad topic -**trage'dian** n. actor in, writer of tragedies -**trag'ic** a. of, in manner of tragedy; disastrous; appalling

trail vt. drag behind one -vi. be drawn behind; hang, grow loosely -n. track or trace; rough path -**trail'er** n. vehicle towed by another vehicle

train vt. educate, instruct; cause to grow in particular way -vi. follow course of training -n. line of railway vehicles joined to locomotive; succession, esp. of thoughts etc.; procession; trailing part of dress -**train'ing** n. -**trainee'** n. one training to be skilled worker

trait [trāt, trā] n. characteristic feature

trait'or n. one who is guilty of treason -**trait'orous** a.

trajec'tory n. line of flight

tram n. vehicle running on rails laid on roadway -**tram'car** n.

tramp vi. travel on foot; walk heavily as (homeless) person who travels about on foot; walk; tramping; cargo ship without fixed route

tram'ple vt. tread on and crush under foot

tram'poline [-lin] n. tough canvas sheet stretched horizontally with elastic cords etc. to frame

trance [-ah-] n. unconscious or dazed state; state of ecstasy or total absorption

tran'quil [-ng'kw-] a. calm, quiet; serene -**tranquill'ity** n. -**tran'quillize** vt. make calm -**tran'quillizer** n. drug which induces calm state

trans- (comb. form) across, through, beyond

transact' vt. carry through; negotiate -**transac'tion** n. performing of any business; single sale or purchase -pl. proceedings

transcend' vt. rise above; surpass -**transcend'ent** a. -**transcend'ence** n. -**transcenden'tal** a. surpassing experience; supernatural

transcribe' vt. copy out; record for later broadcast -**tran'script** n. copy

tran'sept n. transverse part of cruciform church

transfer' vt. move, send from one person, place etc. to another (-rr-) -n. [trans-] removal of person or thing from one place to another -**transfer(r)'able** a. -**transfer'ence** n. transfer

transfig'ure vt. alter appearance of

transfix' vt. astound, stun

transform' vt. change shape, character of -**transforma'tion** n. -**transform'er** n. Electricity apparatus for changing voltage

transfuse' vt. convey from one to another, esp. blood from healthy to ill person -**transfu'sion** n.

transgress' vt. break (law); sin -**transgres'sion** n. -**transgres'sor** n.

tran'sient [-z-] a. fleeting, not permanent

transis'tor n. Electronics small, semi-conducting device used to amplify electric currents; portable radio using transistors

tran'sit n. passage, crossing from one place to another -**tran'sitive** a. (of verb) requiring direct object -**tran'sitory** a. not lasting long

translate' vt. turn from one language into another; interpret -**transla'tion** n. -**transla'tor** n.

translu'cent [-loo'-] a. letting light pass through, semitransparent

transmit' vt. send, cause to pass to another place, person etc.; send out (signals) by means of radio waves -**transmis'sion** n. gear by which power is communicated from engine to road wheels

transmute' vt. change in form, properties, or nature -**transmuta'tion** n.

transpar'ent [-pa'rent] a. letting light pass without distortion; that can be seen through -**transpar'ence** n. -**transpar'ency** n. quality of being transparent; photographic slide

transpire' vi. become known; inf. happen; (of plants) give off water vapour through leaves

transplant' vt. move and plant again in another place; transfer organ surgically -n. [trans'-] surgical transplanting of organ

transport' vt. convey from one place to another -n. [trans'-] means of conveyance eg ships, aircraft etc. used in transporting stores, troops etc.; a ship etc. so used -**transporta'tion** n. transporting; Hist. deportation to penal colony

transpose' vt. change order of; put music into different key

transverse' a. lying across; at right angles

trap n. device for catching game etc.; anything planned to deceive, betray etc.; arrangement of pipes to prevent escape of gas; movable opening -vt. catch (-pp-) -**trapp'er** n. one who traps animals for their fur -**trap'door** n. door in floor or roof

trapeze' n. horizontal bar suspended from two ropes for acrobatics etc.

trapp'ings pl.n. equipment, ornaments

trash n. rubbish; nonsense

traumat'ic [-aw-] a. shocking, distressing

trav'ail vi./n. labour, toil

trav'el v. go, move from one place to another (-ll-) -n. act of travelling -pl. (account of) travelling -**trav'eller** n. -**trav'elogue** [-log] n. film etc. about travels

traverse' vt. cross, go through or over -n. anything set across -a. lying across

trav'esty n. grotesque imitation -vt. make, be a travesty of (-estied, -estying)

trav'ois [-voi'] n. C sled for dragging logs

tray n. flat board, usu. with rim, for carrying things

treach'ery [trech'-] n. deceit, betrayal -**treach'erous** a. disloyal; unreliable

trea'cle n. thick syrup produced when sugar is refined

tread [tred] v. walk; trample (on) (trod pt., trodd'en or trod pp.) -n. treading; fashion of walking; upper surface of step; part of tyre in contact with ground

tread'le [tred'l] n. lever worked by foot to turn wheel

trea'son [-z-] n. violation by subject of allegiance to sovereign or state; treachery -**trea'sonable** a.

treas'ure [trezh'-] n. riches; stored wealth -vt. prize, cherish -**treas'urer** n. official in charge of funds -**treas'ury** n. place for treasure; government department in charge of finance

treat n. pleasure, entertainment given -vt. deal with, act towards; give medical treatment to -**treat'ment** n. method of counteracting a disease; act or mode of treating

treat'ise [-iz] n. formal essay

treat'y n. signed contract between states etc.

treb'le [treb'l] a. threefold; Mus. high-pitched -n. soprano voice -v. increase threefold

tree n. large perennial plant with woody trunk

trek vi./n. (make) long difficult journey

trell'is n. lattice or grating of light bars

trem'ble vi. quiver, shake; feel fear -n. involuntary shaking

tremen'dous a. vast, immense; *inf.* exciting; *inf.* excellent

trem'or n. quiver; shaking

trem'ulous a. quivering slightly

trench n. long narrow ditch -**trench coat** double-breasted waterproof coat

trench'ant a. cutting, incisive

trend n. direction, tendency

trepida'tion n. fear, anxiety

tres'pass vi. intrude (on) property etc. of another -n. wrongful entering on another's land; wrongdoing

tress n. long lock of hair

tres'tle [-sl] n. board fixed on pairs of spreading legs

tri- (comb. form) three

tri'ad n. group of three

tri'al n. test, examination; Law investigation of case before judge; thing, person that strains endurance or patience

tri'angle n. figure with three angles -**triang'ular** a.

tribe n. race; subdivision of race of people -**tri'bal** a.

tribula'tion n. trouble, affliction

tribu'nal n. lawcourt; body appointed to inquire into specific matter

trib'utary n. stream flowing into another

trib'ute n. sign of honour; tax paid by one state to another

trick n. deception; prank; feat of skill or cunning; knack; cards played in one round -vt. cheat; hoax; deceive -**trick'ery** n. -**trick'ster** n. -**trick'y** a. difficult

tric'kle v. (cause to) run, flow, move in thin stream or drops

tri'cycle n. three-wheeled cycle

tri'fle n. insignificant thing or matter; small amount; pudding of spongecake, whipped cream etc. -vi. toy (with)

trigg'er n. catch which releases spring esp. to fire gun -vt. (oft. with off) set in action etc. -**trigger-happy** a. tending to be irresponsible

trigonom'etry n. branch of mathematics dealing with relations of sides and angles of triangles -**trigonomet'rical** a.

trill v./n. (sing, play with) rapid alternation between two close notes

trill'ion n. one million million million, 10^{18}; US one million million, 10^{12}

trill'ogy [-ji] n. series of three related (literary) works

trim a. neat, smart; slender; in good order -vt. shorten slightly by cutting; prune; decorate; adjust (-**mm-**) -n. decoration; order, state of being trim -**trimm'ing** n. (oft. pl.) decoration, addition

tri'maran n. three-hulled vessel

trinitrotol'uene n. a high explosive

trin'ity n. the state of being threefold; (**T-**) the three persons of the Godhead

trink'et n. small ornament

tri'o [-ē'ō] n. group of three; music for three parts (pl. **-s**)

trip n. (short) journey for pleasure; stumble; inf. hallucinatory experience caused by drug -v. (cause) to stumble; (cause) to make mistake -vi. run lightly (-**pp-**) -**tripp'er** n. tourist

tripe n. stomach of cow as food; inf. nonsense

trip'le [tripl] a. threefold -v. treble -**trip'let** n. one of three offspring born at one birth

trip'licate [-it] a. threefold -vt. [-āt] make threefold -n. state of being triplicate; one of set of three copies

tri'pod n. stool, stand etc. with three feet

trite a. hackneyed, banal

tri'umph n. great success; victory; exultation -vi. achieve great success or victory; prevail -**triumph'al** a. -**triumph'ant** a. victorious

triv'ia pl.n. petty, unimportant things -**triv'ial** a. of little consequence -**trivial'ity** n.

troll [-ō-] n. supernatural being in Scandinavian mythology and folklore

troll'ey n. small wheeled table for food and drink; wheeled cart for moving goods etc.; US tram -**trolley bus** bus deriving power from overhead electric wire

troll'op n. promiscuous woman

trombone' n. deep-toned brass instrument -**trombo'nist** n.

troop n. group of persons -pl. soldiers -vi. move in a troop -**troop'er** n. cavalry soldier

tro'phy n. prize, award

trop'ic n. either of two lines of latitude N and S of equator -pl. area of earth's surface between these lines -**trop'ical** a. pert. to, within tropics; (of climate) very hot

trot vi. (of horse) move at medium pace; (of person) run easily with short strides (-**tt-**) -n. trotting, jog

-trott'er n. horse trained to trot in race; foot of pig etc.

trou'ble [trubl] n. state or cause of mental distress, pain, inconvenience etc.; care -vt. be trouble to -vi. be inconvenienced; be agitated; take pains

trough [trof] n. long open vessel, esp. for animals' food or water; hollow between waves

trounce vt. beat thoroughly, thrash

troupe [-ōō-] n. company of performers -troup'er n.

trou'sers pl.n. two-legged outer garment with legs reaching to the ankles

trous'seau [trōō'sō] n. bride's outfit of clothing

trout n. freshwater fish

trow'el n. small tool like spade

troy weight system of weights used for gold, silver and gems

tru'ant [trōō-] n. one absent without leave -a. -tru'ancy n.

truce n. temporary cessation of fighting

truck[1] n. wheeled (motor) vehicle for moving goods

truck[2] n. dealing, esp. in have no truck with

truc'ulent a. aggressive, defiant

trudge vi. walk laboriously -n.

true [trōō] a. in accordance with facts; faithful; correct; genuine -tru'ism n. self-evident truth -tru'ly adv. -truth [-ōō-] n. state of being true; something that is true -truth'ful a. accustomed to speak the truth; accurate

trump n. card of suit ranking above others -vt.

trum'pet n. metal wind instrument like horn -vi. blow trumpet; make sound like one -vt. proclaim

truncate' vt. cut short

trun'cheon n. short thick club

trun'dle vt. roll, as a thing on little wheels

trunk n. main stem of tree; person's body excluding head and limbs; box for clothes etc.; elephant's snout -pl. man's swimming costume -trunk call long-distance telephone call -trunk line main line of railway etc. -trunk road main road

truss vt. fasten up, tie up -n. support; medical supporting device

trust n. confidence; firm belief; reliance; combination of business firms; care; property held for another -vt. rely on; believe in; expect, hope;

consign for care -trustee' n. one legally holding property for another -trust'ful a. -trust'worthy a. -trust'y a.

try v. attempt -v.t. test, sample; afflict; examine in court of law; refine (as metals) (tried, try'ing) -n. attempt, effort; Rugby score gained by touching ball down over opponent's goal line -tried a. proved -try'ing a. upsetting

tsar n. see CZAR

T-shirt, tee-shirt n. informal (short-sleeved) sweater

TT teetotal; tubercular tested

tub n. open wooden vessel like bottom half of barrel; small round container; bath

tu'ba n. valved brass wind instrument of low pitch

tube n. long, narrow, hollow cylinder; flexible cylinder with cap to hold pastes; underground electric railway -tu'bular a.

tu'ber n. fleshy underground stem of some plants

tuberculo'sis n. communicable disease, esp. of lungs -tuber'cular a. -tuber'culin n. bacillus used to treat tuberculosis

TUC Trades Union Congress

tuck vt. push, fold into small space; gather, stitch in folds -n. stitched fold; inf. food

Tu'dor a. of the English royal house ruling 1485-1603

Tues'day n. third day of the week

tuft n. bunch of feathers etc.

tug vt. pull hard or violently (-gg-) -n. violent pull; ship used to tow other vessels

tui'tion [tyōō-ish'ən] n. teaching, esp. private

tu'lip n. plant with bright cup-shaped flowers

tulle [tyōōl] n. kind of fine thin silk or lace

tull'ibee n. Canad. whitefish

tum'ble v. (cause to) fall or roll, twist etc.; rumple -n. fall -tum'bler n. stemless drinking glass; acrobat -tumble-down a. dilapidated

tumm'y n. inf. stomach

tu'mour n. abnormal growth in or on body

tu'mult n. violent uproar, commotion -tumult'uous a.

tu'na n. see TUNNY

tun'dra n. vast treeless zone between ice cap and timber line

tune n. melody; quality of being in

pitch; adjustment of musical instrument –*vt.* put in tune; adjust machine to obtain efficient running; adjust radio circuit –**tune'ful** *a.*

tung'sten *n.* greyish-white metal

tu'nic *n.* close-fitting jacket forming part of uniform; loose hip-length garment

tunn'el *n.* underground passage, *esp.* as track for railway line –*v.* make tunnel (through) (**-ll-**) –**tunn'eller** *n.*

tunn'y *n.* any of various large marine food and game fish

tu'pik [töö-] *n.* C tent used as summer shelter by Eskimos

tuque [took] *n.* C knitted cap with tapering end

tur'ban *n.* in certain countries, man's headdress, made by coiling length of cloth round head

tur'bid *a.* muddy, not clear

tur'bine *n.* rotary engine driven by steam, gas, water or air playing on blades

tur'bot *n.* large flatfish

tur'bulent *a.* in commotion; swirling; riotous –**tur'bulence** *n.*

tureen' *n.* serving dish for soup

turf *n.* short grass with earth bound to it by matted roots (*pl.* **turfs, turves**) –*vt.* lay with turf –**turf ac'countant** bookmaker –**the turf** horse racing

tur'gid *a.* swollen, inflated; bombastic

tur'key *n.* large bird reared for food

tur'moil *n.* commotion, confusion

turn *v.* move around, rotate; change, alter position or direction (of); (*oft.* with into) change in nature –*vt.* make, shape on lathe –*n.* act of turning; inclination *etc.*; period; turning; short walk; (part of) rotation; performance –**turn'er** *n.* –**turn'ing** *n.* road, path leading off main route –**turn'out** *n.* number of people appearing for some purpose –**turn'over** *n.* total sales made by business; rate at which staff leave and are replaced –**turn'stile** *n.* revolving gate for controlling admission of people –**turn'table** *n.* revolving platform –**turn down** refuse

tur'nip *n.* plant with globular root used as food

tur'pentine *n.* oil from certain trees used in paints *etc.* –**turps** *n. short for* turpentine

tur'pitude *n.* depravity

tur'quoise *n.* bluish-green precious stone; this colour

turr'et *n.* small tower; revolving armoured tower on tank *etc.*

tur'tle *n.* sea tortoise

tusk *n.* long pointed side tooth of elephant *etc.*

tus'sle *n./v.* fight, wrestle, struggle

tu'telage *n.* act, office of tutor or guardian

tu'tor *n.* one teaching individuals or small groups –*v.* –**tutor'ial** *n.* period of instruction

TV television

twang *n.* vibrating metallic sound; nasal speech –*v.* (cause to) make such sounds

tweak *vt.* pinch and twist or pull –*n.*

tweed *n.* rough-surfaced cloth used for clothing

tweez'ers *pl.n.* small forceps or tongs

twelve *n./a.* two more than ten –**twelfth** *a.* the ordinal number

twen'ty *n./a.* twice ten –**twen'tieth** *a.* the ordinal number

twice *adv.* two times

twid'dle *v.* fiddle; twist

twig *n.* small branch, shoot

twi'light *n.* soft light after sunset

twill *n.* fabric with surface of parallel ridges

twin *n.* one of two children born together –*a.* –*v.* pair, be paired

twine *v.* twist, coil round –*n.* string, cord

twinge *n.* momentary sharp pain; qualm

twin'kle *vi.* shine with dancing light, sparkle –*n.* twinkling; flash –**twink'ling** *n.* very brief time

twirl *vt.* turn or twist round quickly; whirl; twiddle

twist *v.* make, become spiral, by turning with one end fast; distort, change; wind –*n.*

twit *n. inf.* foolish person –*vt.* taunt (**-tt-**)

twitch *v.* give momentary sharp pull or jerk (to) –*n.* such pull; spasmodic jerk

twitt'er *vi.* (of birds) utter tremulous sounds –*n.*

two [töö] *n./a.* one more than one –**two-faced** *a.* deceitful

tycoon' [tī-] *n.* powerful, influential businessman

type *n.* class; sort; model; pattern; characteristic build; specimen; block bearing letter used for printing –*vt.* print with typewriter –**type'script** *n.*

typewritten document -**type'write** v. -**type'writer** n. keyed writing machine -**ty'pist** n. one who operates typewriter

ty'phoid n. acute infectious disease esp. of intestines -**ty'phus** n. infectious disease

typhoon' n. violent tropical storm

typ'ical a. true to type; characteristic

typ'ify vt. serve as model of (-**ified**, -**ifying**)

typog'raphy [tī-] n. art of printing; style of printing -**typograph'ical** a. -**typog'rapher** n.

ty'rant [tī-] n. oppressive or cruel ruler -**tyrann'ical** [ti-] a. despotic; ruthless -**tyr'annize** v. exert ruthless or tyrannical authority (over) -**tyr'annous** a. -**tyr'anny** n. despotism

tyre n. (inflated) rubber ring over rim of road vehicle

U

ubiq'uitous [yoo-bik'w-] a. everywhere at once

udd'er n. milk-secreting organ of cow etc.

UDI Unilateral Declaration of Independence

UFO unidentified flying object

ug'ly a. unpleasing to the sight, hideous; threatening -**ug'liness** n.

UHF ultrahigh frequency

UHT ultra heat treated

UK United Kingdom

ukule'le [yoo-kə-lā'li] n. small four-stringed guitar

ul'cer n. open sore on skin -**ul'cerate** v. -**ul'cerous** a.

ult. ultimate; ultimo

ulte'rior a. lying beneath, beyond what is revealed

ult'imate a. last; highest; fundamental -**ultima'tum** n. final terms (pl. -**s**, -**ta**) -**ult'imo** adv. in last month

ultra- (comb. form) beyond, excessively, as in ultramod'ern a.

ultrahigh frequency (band of) radio waves of very short wavelength

ultravi'olet a. of electromagnetic radiation beyond limit of visibility at violet end of spectrum

umbil'ical a. of navel -**umbilical**

cord cordlike structure connecting foetus with placenta of mother

um'brage n. offence, resentment

umbrell'a n. folding circular cover of nylon etc. on stick, carried in hand to protect against rain

u'miak [oo'-] n. Eskimo boat made of skins

um'pire n. person chosen to decide question, or to enforce rules in a game -v. act as umpire

UN United Nations

un- (comb. form) indicating not, reversal of an action The list that follows contains some of the more common compounds

unaccount'able a. that cannot be explained

unan'imous [yoo-] a. in complete agreement -**unanim'ity** n.

unassu'ming a. modest

unaware' a. not aware -**unawares'** adv. unexpectedly

unbos'om [-booz'-] vt. tell or reveal one's secrets etc.

uncann'y a. weird, mysterious

un'cle n. brother of father or mother; husband of aunt

uncon'scious a. insensible; not aware; of thoughts, memories etc. of which one is not normally aware -n. these thoughts

uncouth' [-kooth'] a. clumsy, boorish

unc'tion [ungk'shən] n. anointing; excessive politeness; soothing words -**unc'tuous** a. greasy; oily in manner

un'der prep. below, beneath; included in; less than; subjected to -adv. in lower place or condition -a. lower

under- (comb. form) beneath, below, lower, as in underground

un'derarm a. from armpit to wrist; Sport with hand swung below shoulder level

undergo' vt. experience, endure, sustain (-**went'**, -**gone'**, -**go'ing**)

undergrad'uate n. student member of university

un'derground a. under the ground; secret -adv. secretly -n. secret but organized resistance to government in power; railway system under the ground

un'derhand a. secret, sly

underline' vt. put line under; emphasize

un'derling n. subordinate

undermine' vt. wear away base, support of; weaken insidiously

underneath' adv. below -prep. under -a. lower -n.

understand' v. know and comprehend; realize -vt. infer; take for granted (-stood', -stand'ing) -understand'ing n. intelligence; opinion; agreement -a. sympathetic

un'derstudy n. one prepared to take over theatrical part -vt.

undertake' vt. make oneself responsible for; enter upon; promise (-took', -ta'ken, -ta'king) -un'dertaker n. one who arranges funerals -un'dertaking n.

un'dertone n. dropped tone of voice; underlying suggestion

un'derwear n. garments worn next to skin (also un'derclothes)

un'derworld n. criminals and their associates; Myth. abode of the dead

underwrite' vt. agree to pay; accept liability in insurance policy (-wrote, -written, -writing) -un'derwriter n.

undo' [-dōō'] vt. untie, unfasten; reverse; cause downfall of (undid', -done', -do'ing)

un'dulate [-dyoo-] v. move up and down like waves

unearth' vt. dig up; discover

uneas'y a. anxious; uncomfortable

unemployed' a. having no paid employment, out of work -unemploy'ment n.

ungain'ly a. awkward, clumsy

uni- (comb. form) one, as in unicorn, uniform etc.

u'nicorn n. mythical horselike animal with single long horn

u'niform n. identifying clothes worn by members of same group eg soldiers, nurses etc. -a. not changing; regular -uniform'ity n.

u'nify v. make or become one (-ified, -ifying) -unifica'tion n.

unilat'eral [yōō-] a. one-sided; (of contract) binding one party only

un'ion n. joining into one; state, result of being joined; federation; trade union -u'nionize v. organize (workers) into trade union

unique' [yōō-nēk'] a. being only one of its kind; unparalleled

u'nison n. Mus. singing etc. same note as others; agreement

u'nit n. single thing or person; standard quantity; group of people or things with one purpose

unite' [yōō-] vt. join into one; associate -vi. become one; combine -u'nity n. state of being one; harmony; agreement -United Empire Loyalist American colonist who settled in Canada in War of Amer. Independence from loyalty to Britain -United Nations Organization organization formed in 1945 to promote peace and international cooperation

u'niverse n. all existing things considered as constituting systematic

unaccept'able	unfamil'iar	unoffi'cial
unaccom'panied	unfeel'ing	unpaid'
unaccus'tomed	unfeigned'	unpleas'ant
unattached'	unfin'ished	unpop'ular
unauth'orized	unfound'ed	unprepared'
unbear'able	ungra'cious	unrealis'tic
unbeliev'able	unhap'py	unrea'sonable
unbi'as(s)ed	unharmed'	unrelent'ing
unbreak'able	unhurt'	unri'valled
uncer'tain	unhygie'nic	unroll'
uncharacteris'tic	unimpor'tant	unruf'fled
uncom'fortable	uninhab'ited	unsatisfac'tory
uncommit'ted	unin'teresting	unsolic'ited
uncondi'tional	uninvit'ed	unsuccess'ful
undeci'ded	unla'belled	unsuit'able
undeserved'	unlaw'ful	unu'sable
undesi'rable	unlim'ited	unu'sual
unearned'	unlocked'	unutt'erable
une'qualled	unluck'y	unwant'ed
unequiv'ocal	unmar'ried	unwarr'anted
unexpect'ed	unmistak(e)'able	unwhole'some
unexplained'	unnamed'	unwill'ing
unfail'ing	unnec'essary	unwise'
unfair'	unno'ticed	unwrap'

whole; the world -univer'sal a. relating to all things or all people

univer'sity [yōō-] n. educational institution that awards degrees

unkempt' a. slovenly

unless' conj. if not, except

UNO United Nations Organization

unrav'el vt. undo, untangle

unru'ly [-rōō-] a. badly behaved, disorderly

unsa'voury a. distasteful

unsightly a. ugly

unthink'able a. out of the question; inconceivable; unreasonable

until' conj. to the time that; (with a negative) before -prep. up to the time of

un'to prep. obs. to

untoward' a. awkward, inconvenient

untram'melled a. not confined, not constrained

unwell' a. not well, ill

unwieldy a. awkward

unwitt'ing a. not knowing; not intentional

up prep. from lower to higher position; along -adv. in or to higher position, source, activity etc.; indicating completion (upp'er comp., upp'ermost sup.) -up'ward a./adv. -up'wards adv.

up- (comb. form) up, upper, upwards as in uproot, upgrade etc.

upbraid' vt. scold, reproach

up'bringing n. rearing and education of children

upgrade' vt. promote to higher position; improve

upheav'al n. sudden or violent disturbance

uphold' vt. maintain, support etc. (upheld', uphold'ing)

upholst'er [-ō-] vt. fit springs, coverings on chairs etc.

up'keep n. act, cost of keeping something in good repair

upon' prep. on

upp'er a. higher, situated above -comp. of UP -n. upper part of boot or shoe -upp'ermost a. sup. of UP

up'right a. erect; honest, just -adv. vertically -n. thing standing upright, eg post in framework

up'rising n. rebellion, revolt

up'roar n. tumult, disturbance -uproar'ious a. rowdy

upset' vt. overturn; distress; disrupt; make ill (upset', upsett'ing) -n. [up'-] unexpected defeat; confusion

up'shot n. outcome, end

up'start n. one suddenly raised to wealth, power etc.

uptight' inf. a. tense; repressed

ura'nium [yoo-] n. white radioactive metallic element

ur'ban a. relating to town or city

urbane' a. elegant, sophisticated -urban'ity n.

urch'in n. mischievous, unkempt child

urge vt. exhort earnestly; entreat; drive on -n. strong desire -ur'gency n. -ur'gent a. needing attention at once

u'rine n. fluid excreted by kidneys to bladder and passed as waste from body -u'rinate vi. discharge urine

urn n. vessel like vase; large container with tap

US, USA United States (of America)

us pron. pl. form of WE used after verb or preposition

use [yōō] vt. employ; exercise; exploit; consume -n. [yōōs] employment; need to employ; serviceableness; profit; habit -u'sable [-z-] a. fit for use -u'sage [-s-] n. act of using; custom -used [-z-] a. secondhand, not new -use'ful [-s-] a. of use; helpful; serviceable -use'less a. -used to [-s-] a. accustomed to -vt. did so formerly

ush'er n. doorkeeper, one showing people to seats etc. (usherette' fem.) -vt. introduce, announce; inaugurate

USSR Union of Soviet Socialist Republics

u'sual a. habitual, ordinary -u'sually adv. as a rule

usurp' [yōō-z-] vt. seize wrongfully

u'sury [-zho-] n. lending of money at excessive interest -u'surer n. -usu'rious [-zhoor'-] a.

uten'sil [yōō] n. vessel, implement, esp. in domestic use

u'terus n. womb (pl. u'teri [-ī]) -u'terine a.

utili'dor n. C above-ground insulated casing for pipes

utility [yōō] n. usefulness; benefit; useful thing -a. made for practical purposes -utilita'rian a. useful rather than beautiful -u'tilize vt.

ut'most a. to the highest degree; extreme, furthest -n. greatest possible amount

Uto'pia [yōō-] n. imaginary ideal state -uto'pian a.

utt'er[1] vt. express, emit audibly, say -**utt'erance** n.

utt'er[2] a. complete, total

utt'ermost a. farthest out; utmost -n. highest degree

V

v volt

v. versus

va'cant a. without thought, empty; unoccupied -**va'cancy** n.

vacate' vt. quit, leave empty -**vaca'tion** n. time when universities and law courts are closed; US holidays; act of vacating

vac'cinate [vak's-] vt. inoculate with vaccine -**vaccina'tion** n. -**vac'cine** [-sēn] n. any substance used for inoculation against disease

vac'illate [vas'-] vi. fluctuate in opinion; waver; move to and fro -**vacilla'tion** n.

vac'uum [-yoom] n. place, region containing no matter and from which all, or most air, gas has been removed (pl. -**uums**, -**ua**) -**vacuum cleaner** apparatus for removing dust by suction -**vacuum flask** double-walled flask with vacuum between walls, for keeping contents hot or cold

vag'abond n. person with no fixed home; wandering beggar or thief -a.

va'gary [or və-gā'-] n. something unusual, erratic; whim

vagi'na [-jī'-] n. passage from womb to exterior

va'grant n. vagabond, tramp -a. -**va'grancy** n.

vague [vāg] a. indefinite or uncertain; indistinct; not clearly expressed

vain a. conceited; worthless; unavailing

vain'glory n. boastfulness, vanity -**vainglor'ious** a.

val'ance n. short curtain round base of bed etc.

vale n. Poet. valley

valedic'tion n. farewell -**valedic'tory** a.

val'entine n. (one receiving) card, gift, expressing affection, on Saint Valentine's Day

val'et [or -ā] n. gentleman's personal servant

val'iant a. brave, courageous

val'id a. sound; of binding force in law -**valid'ity** n. -**val'idate** vt. make valid

vall'ey n. low area between hills; river basin

val'our [-ər] n. bravery -**val'orous** a.

val'ue n. worth; utility; equivalent; importance -pl. principles, standards -vt. estimate value of; prize -**val'uable** a. precious; worthy -n. (usu. pl.) valuable thing -**valua'tion** n. estimated worth -**value added tax** tax on difference between cost of basic materials and cost of article made from them

valve n. device to control passage of fluid etc. through pipe; Anat. part of body allowing one-way passage of fluids

vamp'ire n. (in folklore) corpse that rises from dead to drink blood of the living -**vampire bat** one that sucks blood of animals

van[1] n. covered vehicle, esp. for goods; railway carriage for goods and use of guard

van[2] n. short for VANGUARD

van'dal n. one who wantonly and deliberately damages or destroys -**van'dalism** n. -**van'dalize** vt.

vane n. weathercock; blade of propeller

van'guard n. leading, foremost group, position etc.

vanill'a n. tropical climbing orchid; its seed(pod); essence of this for flavouring

van'ish vi. disappear

van'ity n. excessive pride or conceit

van'quish vt. conquer, overcome

van'tage [vahn'-] n. advantage

vap'id a. flat, dull, insipid

va'pour [-ər] n. gaseous form of a substance; steam, mist -**va'porize** v. convert into, pass off in, vapour -**va'porizer** n.

va'riable see VARY

var'icose [va'ri-] a. of vein, swollen, twisted

vari'ety n. state of being varied or various; diversity; varied assortment; sort or kind

va'rious a. diverse, of several kinds

var'nish n. resinous solution put on a surface to make it hard and shiny -vt. apply varnish to

va'ry v. (cause to) change, diversify, differ (**va'ried**, **va'rying**) -**varia-bil'ity** n. -**va'riable** a. changeable; unsteady or fickle -n. something subject to variation -va'riance n. state of discord, discrepancy -va'riant a. different -n. difference in form; alternative form of reading -varia'tion n. alteration; extent to which thing varies; modification -va'ried a. diverse; modified

vase [vahz] n. vessel, jar as or-nament or for holding flowers

Vas'eline [-ēn] n. R jellylike pet-roleum product

vast [-ah-] a. very large -vast'ly adv. -vast'ness n.

VAT value added tax

vat n. large tub, tank

vault¹ n. arched roof; cellar; burial chamber; place for storing valuables

vault² v. spring, jump over with the hands resting on something -n. such jump

vaunt v./n. boast

VC Victoria Cross

VD venereal disease

VDU visual display unit

veal n. calf flesh as food

veer vi. change direction; change one's mind

veg'etable [vej'-] n. plant, esp. edible one -a. of, from, concerned with plants -vegetable marrow plant with long, green-striped fruit, eaten as vegetable

vegeta'rian n. one who does not eat meat -a. -vegeta'rianism n.

veg'etate [vej'-] vi. (of plants) grow, develop; (of person) live dull, unproductive life -vegeta'tion n. plants collectively

ve'hement [-vē'im-] a. marked by intensity of feeling -ve'hemence n.

ve'hicle [vē'ikl] n. means of con-veying -vehic'ular [vi-hik'-] a.

veil [vāl] n. light material to cover face or head -vt. cover with, as with, veil

vein [vān] n. tube in body taking blood to heart; fissure in rock filled with ore; streak

veld, veldt [velt] n. elevated grass-land in S Afr. -veld'skoen [-skoon] n. SA ankle-length boot

veloc'ity [-os'-] n. rate of motion in given direction; speed

vel'vet n. silk or nylon fabric with thick, short pile -velveteen' [-] n. cotton fabric resembling velvet -vel'vety a. of, like velvet; soft and smooth

vend vt. sell -vend'or n. -vending machine n. one that automatically dis-penses goods

veneer' n. thin layer of fine wood; superficial appearance -vt. cover with veneer

ven'erable a. worthy of reverence -ven'erate vt. look up to, respect, reverence -venera'tion n.

vene'real a. (of disease) trans-mitted by sexual intercourse

vene'tian blind window blind made of thin horizontal slats

ven'geance n. revenge; retri-bution for wrong done -venge'ful a. -venge'fully adv.

ven'ison n. flesh of deer as food

ven'om n. poison; spite -ven'om-ous a. poisonous

vent n. small hole or outlet -vt. give outlet to; utter

ven'tilate vt. supply with fresh air -ventila'tion n. -ven'tilator n.

ventril'oquist n. one who can so speak that the sounds seem to come from some other person or place -ventril'oquism n.

ven'ture vt. expose to hazard; risk -vi. dare; have courage to do some-thing or go somewhere -n. risky undertaking -ven'turesome a.

ven'ue n. meeting place; location

Venus's flytrap insect-eating plant

vera'cious a. truthful; true -ver-ac'ity [-as'-] n.

veran'da(h) n. open or partly enclosed porch on outside of house

verb n. part of speech used to ex-press action or being -verb'al a. of, by, or relating to words spoken rather than written -verba'tim adv./a. word for word, literal

verd'ant a. green and fresh

verd'ict n. decision of a jury; opin-ion reached after examination of facts

verd'igris n. green film on copper

verge n. edge; brink; grass border along a road -vi. come close to; be on the border of

ver'ify vt. prove, confirm truth of; test accuracy of (-ified, -ifying) -verifica'tion n.

ver'itable [ver'i-] a. actual, true

ver'ity [ver'i-] n. truth

vermil'ion a./n. (of) bright red col-our or pigment

ver'min pl.n. injurious animals, parasites etc. -ver'minous a.

vernac'ular n. commonly spoken language or dialect of particular country or place -a. of vernacular; native

ver'satile a. capable of or adapted to many different uses, skills etc. **-versatil'ity** n.

verse n. stanza or short subdivision of poem or the Bible; poetry **-versed in** skilled

ver'sion n. description from certain point of view; translation; adaptation

ver'sus prep. against

vert'ebra n. single section of backbone (pl. **-brae** [-brē]) **-vert'ebrate** n. animal with backbone -a.

vert'ical a. at right angles to the horizon; upright; overhead

vert'igo n. giddiness

verve n. enthusiasm; vigour

ver'y [ve'ri] a. exact, ideal; same; complete; actual -adv. extremely, to great extent

ves'pers pl.n. evening church service; evensong

vess'el n. any object used as a container, esp. for liquids; ship, large boat; tubular structure conveying liquids (eg blood) in body

vest n. undergarment for the trunk -vt. place; confer **-vest'ment** n. robe or official garment

vest'ibule n. entrance hall, lobby

vest'ige [-ij] n. small trace, amount

vest'ry n. room in church for keeping vestments, holding meetings etc.

vet n. short for VETERINARY SURGEON

vet'eran n. one who has served a long time, esp. in fighting services -a. long-serving

vet'erinary a. of, concerning the health of animals **-veterinary surgeon** one qualified to treat animal ailments

ve'to n. power of rejecting piece of legislation; any prohibition (pl. **-toes**) -vt. enforce veto against

vex vt. annoy; distress **-vexa'tion** n. cause of irritation; state of distress

VHF very high frequency

VI Vancouver Island

vi'a adv. by way of

vi'able a. practicable; able to live and grow independently **-viabil'ity** n.

vi'aduct n. bridge over valley for a road or railway

vi'al n. same as PHIAL

vibrate' v. (cause to) move to and fro rapidly and continuously; give off (light or sound) by vibration -vi. oscillate; quiver **-vi'brant** a. throbbing; vibrating; appearing vigorous

-vibra'tion n. a vibrating **-vi'bra-tory** a.

vic'ar n. clergyman in charge of parish **-vic'arage** n. vicar's house

vica'rious a. obtained, enjoyed or undergone through sympathetic experience of another's experiences; suffered, done etc. as substitute for another

vice[1] n. evil or immoral habit or practice; criminal immorality esp. prostitution; fault, imperfection

vice[2] n. appliance with screw jaw for holding things while working on them

vice'roy [vīs'-] n. ruler acting for king in province or dependency **-vicere'gal** a.

vi'ce ver'sa [-si-] Lat. conversely, the other way round

vicin'ity n. neighbourhood

vi'cious [vish'əs] a. wicked, cruel; ferocious, dangerous

viciss'itude n. change of fortune -pl. ups and downs of fortune

vic'tim n. person or thing killed, injured etc. as result of another's deed, or accident, circumstances etc.; person cheated; sacrifice **-vic-timiza'tion** n. **-vic'timize** vt. punish unfairly; make victim of

vic'tor n. conqueror; winner **-victo'rious** a. winning; triumphant **-vic'tory** n. winning of battle etc.

vicu'na n. S Amer. animal like llama

vi'de Lat. see

vide'licet [-li-set] Lat. namely

vid'eo a. relating to or used in transmission or production of television image

vie [vī] vi. (with with or for) contend, compete against or for someone, something (**vied, vy'ing**)

view [vyōō] n. survey by eyes or mind; range of vision; picture; scene; opinion; purpose -vt. look at; survey; consider **-view'er** n. one who views; one who watches television; optical device to assist viewing of photographic slides **-view'point** n. way of regarding a subject; position commanding view of landscape

vig'il [vij'-] n. a keeping awake, watch; eve of feast day **-vig'ilance** n. **-vig'ilant** a. watchful, alert

vig'our [-ər] n. force, strength; energy, activity **-vig'orous** a. strong; energetic; flourishing

vile a. very wicked, shameful; disgusting; despicable **-vile'ness** n.

vill'a *n.* large, luxurious, country house; detached or semidetached suburban house

vill'age *n.* small group of houses in country area –**vill'ager** *n.*

vill'ain [-ən] *n.* wicked person –**vill'ainous** *a.* –**vill'ainy** *n.*

vin'dicate *vt.* clear of charges; justify –**vindica'tion** *n.*

vindic'tive *a.* revengeful; inspired by resentment

vine *n.* climbing plant bearing grapes –**vine'yard** [vin'-] *n.* plantation of vines –**vin'tage** *n.* gathering of the grapes; the yield; wine of particular year; time of origin –*a.* best and most typical –**vint'ner** *n.* dealer in wine

vin'egar *n.* acid liquid obtained from wine and other alcoholic liquors –**vin'egary** *a.* like vinegar; sour; bad-tempered

vi'nyl *n.* plastic material with variety of domestic and industrial uses

vio'la¹ *n. see* VIOLIN

vi'ola² *n.* single-coloured variety of pansy

vi'olate *vt.* break (law, agreement *etc.*), infringe; rape; outrage; desecrate –**viola'tion** *n.* –**vi'olator** *n.*

vi'olent *a.* marked by, due to, extreme force, passion or fierceness; of great force; intense –**vi'olence** *n.*

vi'olet *n.* plant with small bluish-purple or white flowers; the flower; bluish-purple colour –*a.* of this colour

violin' *n.* small four-stringed musical instrument –**vio'la** *n.* large violin with lower range –**violin'ist** *n.*

VIP very important person

vi'per *n.* venomous snake

vir'gin *n.* one who has not had sexual intercourse –*a.* without experience of sexual intercourse; unsullied, fresh; (of land) untilled –**vir'ginal** *a.* –**virgin'ity** *n.*

vir'ile [vi'rīl] *a.* (of male) capable of copulation or procreation; strong, forceful –**viril'ity** *n.*

vir'tual *a.* so in effect, though not in appearance or name –**vir'tually** *adv.* practically, almost

vir'tue *n.* moral goodness; good quality; merit –**vir'tuous** *a.* morally good; chaste –**vir'tuously** *adv.*

virtuo'so [-zō] *n.* one with special skill, *esp.* in a fine art (*pl.* -**sos**, -**si** [-sē]) –**virtuos'ity** *n.*

vir'ulent *a.* very infectious, poisonous *etc.*; malicious

vi'rus *n.* infecting agent that causes disease

vi'sa [vē'zə] *n.* endorsement on passport permitting the bearer to travel into country of issuing government

vis'age [viz'ij] *n.* face

vis'count [vī'-] *n.* Brit. nobleman ranking below earl and above baron (**vis'countess** *fem.*)

vis'cous *a.* thick and sticky

vis'ible [viz'-] *a.* that can be seen –**visibil'ity** *n.* degree of clarity of atmosphere, *esp.* for navigation –**vis'ibly** *adv.*

vis'ion [vizh'ən] *n.* sight; insight; dream –**vis'ionary** *a.* marked by vision; impractical –*n.* mystic; impractical person

vis'it [viz'-] *v.* go, come and see, stay temporarily with (someone) –*n.* stay; call at person's home *etc.* –**visita'tion** *n.* formal visit or inspection; affliction or plague –**vis'itor** *n.*

vi'sor, **vi'zor** [-z-] *n.* movable front part of helmet; eyeshade, *esp.* on car; peak on cap

vis'ta *n.* view, *esp.* distant view

vis'ual [viz'-] *a.* of sight; visible –**visualiza'tion** *n.* –**vis'ualize** *vt.* form mental image of

vi'tal *a.* necessary to, affecting life; lively, animated; essential –**vital'ity** *n.* life, vigour –**vi'talize** *vt.* give life to; lend vigour to

vit'amin *n.* any of group of substances occurring in foodstuffs and essential to health

vi'tiate [vish'-] *vt.* spoil; deprive of efficacy

viva'cious *a.* lively, gay, sprightly –**vivac'ity** [-as'-] *n.*

viv'id *a.* bright, intense; clear; lively –**viv'idness** *n.*

vivisec'tion *n.* dissection of, or operating on, living animals

vix'en *n.* female fox

viz. *short for* VIDELICIT

viz'ier *n.* high Muslim official

vi'zor *see* VISOR

vlei [flā] *n.* SA low, marshy ground

vocab'ulary *n.* list of words, usu. in alphabetical order; stock of words used in particular language *etc.*

vo'cal *a.* of, with, or giving out voice; outspoken, articulate –**vo'calist** *n.* singer

voca'tion *n.* (urge, inclination, predisposition to) particular career, profession *etc.* –**voca'tional** *a.*

vocif'erate *v.* exclaim, cry out

-vocif'erous a. shouting, noisy

vogue [vōg] n. fashion, style; popularity

voice n. sound given out by person in speaking, singing etc.; quality of the sound; expressed opinion; (right to) share in discussion -vt. give utterance to, express

void a. empty; destitute; not legally binding -n. empty space -vt. make ineffectual or invalid; empty out

vol. volume

vol'atile a. evaporating quickly; lively; changeable -volatil'ity n.

volca'no n. hole in earth's crust through which lava, ashes, smoke etc. are discharged; mountain so formed (pl. -no(e)s) -volcan'ic a.

vole n. small rodent

voli'tion [-ish'-] n. exercise of the will

vol'ley n. simultaneous discharge of weapons or missiles; rush of oaths, questions etc.; Sports kick, stroke etc. at moving ball before it touches ground -v. discharge; fly, strike etc. in volley

volt [-ō-] n. unit of electric potential -volt'age n. electric potential difference expressed in volts

vol'ume n. space occupied; mass; amount; power, fullness of voice or sound; book; part of book bound in one cover -volu'minous a. bulky, copious

vol'untary a. having, done by free will; done without payment; supported by freewill contributions -vol'untarily adv. -volunteer' n. one who offers service, joins force etc. of his own free will -v. offer oneself or one's services

volup'tuous a. of, contributing to pleasures of the senses; sexually alluring because of full, shapely figure

vom'it v. eject (contents of stomach) through mouth -n. matter vomited

voo'doo n. practice of black magic, esp. in W Indies, witchcraft

voor'kamer [foor'kah-mǝ] n. SA front room of a house

vora'cious a. greedy, ravenous -vora'ciously adv. -vorac'ity [-as'-] n.

vote n. formal expression of choice; individual pronouncement; right to give it; result of voting -v. express, declare opinion, choice, preference etc. by vote -vo'ter n.

vouch vi. (usu. with for) guarantee -vouch'er n. document to establish facts; ticket as substitute for cash -vouchsafe' vt. condescend to grant or do something

vow n. solemn promise, esp. religious one -vt. promise, threaten by vow

vow'el n. any speech sound pronounced without stoppage or friction of the breath; letter standing for such sound, as a, e, i, o, u

voy'age n. journey, esp. long one, by sea or air -vi. make voyage

VSO Voluntary Service Overseas

vul'canize vt. treat (rubber) with sulphur at high temperature to increase its durability -vulcaniza'tion n.

vul'gar a. offending against good taste; coarse; common -vulgar'ity n.

vul'nerable a. capable of being physically or emotionally wounded or hurt; exposed, open to attack, persuasion etc. -vulnerabil'ity n.

vul'ture n. large bird which feeds on carrion

W

W watt

wad [wod] n. small pad of fibrous material; thick roll of banknotes -vt. line, pad, stuff etc. with wad (-dd-) -wad'ding n.

wad'dle [wod'l] vi. walk like duck -n. this gait

wade vi. walk through something that hampers movement, esp. water -wa'der n. person or bird that wades

wa'fer n. thin, crisp biscuit

waf'fle [wof'l] n. kind of pancake

waft [-ah-] vt. convey smoothly through air or water -n. breath of wind; odour, whiff

wag v. (cause to) move rapidly from side to side (-gg-) -n. instance of wagging -wag'tail n. small bird with wagging tail

wage n. payment for work done (oft. in pl.) -vt. carry on

wa'ger n./vt. bet

wag'gle vt. wag -wag'gly a.

wag(g)'on n. four-wheeled vehicle for heavy loads; railway freight truck -wag(g)'oner n.

waif n. homeless person, esp. child

wail v./n. cry, lament

wains'cot n. wooden lining of walls of room

waist n. part of body between hips and ribs; various narrow central parts **-waist'coat** n. sleeveless garment worn under jacket or coat

wait v. stay in one place, remain inactive in expectation of (something); be prepared (for something); delay **-vi.** serve in restaurant etc. **-n.** act or period of waiting **-wait'er** n. attendant on guests at hotel, restaurant etc. (**wait'ress** fem.); one who waits

waive vt. forgo; not to insist on **-waiv'er** n. (written statement of) this act

wake[1] v. rouse from sleep; stir up (**woke**, **wo'ken**, **wa'king**) **-n.** vigil; watch beside corpse **-wa'ken** v. wake **-wake'ful** a.

wake[2] n. track or path left by anything that has passed

walk [wawk] v. (cause, assist to) move, travel on foot at ordinary pace **-vt.** cross, pass through by walking; escort, conduct by walking **-n.** act, instance of walking; path or other place or route for walking

wall [wawl] n. structure of brick, stone etc. serving as fence, side of building etc.; surface of one; anything resembling this **-vt.** enclose with wall; block up with wall **-wall'paper** n. paper, usu. patterned, to cover interior walls

wall'aby [wol'-] n. Aust. marsupial similar to and smaller than kangaroo

wall'et [wol'-] n. small folding case, esp. for paper money, documents etc.

wall'op [wol'-] inf. vt. beat soundly; strike hard **-n.** stroke or blow

wall'ow [wol'ō] vi. roll (in liquid or mud); revel (in) **-n.**

wal'nut [wawl'-] n. large nut with crinkled shell; the tree; its wood

wal'rus [wawl'-] n. large sea mammal with long tusks

waltz [wawls] n. ballroom dance; music for it **-v.**

wan [won] a. pale, pallid

wand [wond] n. stick, esp. as carried by magician etc.

wand'er [won'-] v. roam, ramble **-vi.** go astray, deviate **-n.** **-wand'-erer** n.

wane vi./n. decline; (of moon) decrease in size

want [wont] v. desire; lack **-n.** desire; need; deficiency **-want'ed** a. being sought, esp. by the police **-want'ing**

a. lacking; below standard

want'on [won'-] a. dissolute; thoughtless; unrestrained **-n.** wanton person

war [wawr] n. fighting between nations; state of hostility; conflict, contest **-vi.** make war (-rr-) **-war'like** a. of, for war; fond of war **-warr'ior** [wo'ri-] n. fighter **-war'fare** n. hostilities **-war'head** n. part of missile etc. containing explosives **-war'monger** n. one fostering, encouraging war **-war'ship** n. vessel armed, armoured for naval warfare

war'ble vi. sing with trills **-war'bler** n. any of various kinds of small songbirds

ward [-aw-] n. division of city, hospital etc.; minor under care of guardian **-ward'er** n. jailer (**ward'-ress** fem.) **-ward off** avert, repel

ward'en [-aw-] n. person in charge of building, college etc.

ward'robe n. piece of furniture for hanging clothes in; person's supply of clothes

ware n. goods; articles collectively **-pl.** goods for sale **-ware'house** n. storehouse for goods

warm [-aw-] a. moderately hot; serving to maintain heat; affectionate; hearty **-v.** make, become warm **-warmth** n. mild heat; cordiality; vehemence, anger

warn [-aw-] vt. put on guard; caution; give advance information to **-warn'-ing** n.

warp [-aw-] v. (cause to) twist (out of shape); pervert or be perverted **-n.**

warr'ant [wo'rant] n. authority; document giving authority **-vt.** guarantee; authorize, justify **-warr'anty** n. guarantee of quality of goods; security

warr'en [wo'ran] n. (burrows inhabited by) colony of rabbits

warr'ior [wo'ra] n. see WAR

wart [-aw-] n. small hard growth on skin **-wart hog** kind of Afr. wild pig

wa'ry a. watchful, cautious, alert **-wa'rily** adv.

was pt. first and third person sing. of BE

wash [wosh] v. clean (oneself, clothes etc.) esp. with water, soap etc. **-vi.** be washable **-vt.** move, be moved by water; flow, sweep over, against **-n.** act of washing; clothes washed at one time; sweep of water, esp. set up by moving ship **-wash'-able** a. capable of being washed without damage etc. **-wash'er** n. one who, that which, washes; ring put under a nut **-wash'ing** n. clothes to be washed

wasp [wosp] n. striped stinging insect resembling bee

waste [wāst] vt. expend uselessly, use extravagantly; fail to take advantage of -vi. dwindle; pine away -n. act of wasting; what is wasted; desert -a. worthless, useless; desert; wasted **-waste'ful** a. extravagant

watch [woch] vt. observe closely; guard -vi. wait expectantly (for); be on watch -n. portable timepiece for wrist, pocket etc.; state of being on the lookout; spell of duty **-watch'ful** a. **-watch'man** n. man guarding building etc., esp. at night **-watch'word** n. password; rallying cry

wat'er [wawt'-] n. transparent, colourless, odourless, tasteless liquid, substance of rain, river etc.; body of water; river; lake; sea; tear; urine -vt. put water on or into; irrigate or provide with water -vi. salivate; (of eyes) fill with tears **-wat'ery** a. **-water closet** sanitary convenience flushed by water **-wat'ercolour** n. pigment mixed with water, painting in this **-wat'ercress** n. plant growing in clear ponds and streams **-wat'erfall** n. perpendicular descent of waters of river **-water lily** plant that floats on surface of fresh water **-wat'erlogged** a. saturated, filled with water **-wat'erproof** a. not letting water through -v. make waterproof **-wat'ershed** n. line separating two river systems; divide **-wat'ertight** a. so fitted as to prevent water entering or escaping

watt [wot] n. unit of electric power **-watt'age** n. electric power expressed in watts

wat'tle [wot'-] n. frame of woven branches etc. as fence

wave v. move to and fro, as hand in greeting or farewell; signal by waving; give, take shape of waves (as hair etc.) -n. ridge and trough on water etc.; act, gesture of waving; vibration, as in radio waves; prolonged spell; upsurge; wavelike shapes in the hair etc. **-wa'vy** a.

wa'ver vi. hesitate, be irresolute; be, become unsteady

wax¹ n. yellow, soft, pliable material made by bees; this or similar substance used for sealing, making candles etc.; waxy secretion of ear -vt. put wax on **-wax'y** a. like wax

wax² vi. grow, increase

way n. manner; method; direction; path; passage; route; progress; state or condition **-way'farer** n. traveller, esp. on foot **-waylay'** vt. lie in wait for and accost, attack (**-laid'**, **-lay'ing**) **-way'side** n. side or edge of a road -a. **-way'ward** a. capricious, perverse, wilful

WC water closet

we pron. first person plural pronoun

weak a. lacking strength; feeble; fragile **-weak'en** v. **-weak'ling** n. feeble creature **-weak'ly** a. weak; sickly -adv. **-weak'ness** n.

weal n. streak left on flesh by blow of stick or whip

wealth [welth] n. riches; abundance **-wealth'y** a.

wean vt. accustom to food other than mother's milk; win over, coax away from

weap'on [wep'n] n. implement to fight with

wear [wār] vt. have on the body; show; produce (hole etc.) by rubbing etc.; harass or weaken -vi. last; become impaired by use (**wore**, **worn**, **wear'ing**) -n. act of wearing; things to wear; damage caused by use; ability to resist effects of constant use

wear'y [wēr'i] a. tired, exhausted, jaded; tiring; tedious -v. make, become weary (**wear'ied**, **wear'ying**) **-wear'ily** adv. **-wear'iness** n. **-wear'isome** a.

weas'el [wēz'-] n. small carnivorous mammal with long body and short legs

weath'er [weTH'-] n. day-to-day meteorological conditions, esp. temperature etc. of a place -vt. affect by weather; endure; resist; come safely through **-weath'ercock** n. revolving vane to show which way wind blows

weave vt. form into texture or fabric by interlacing, esp. on loom; construct; make one's way, esp. with side to side motion (**weaved** pt.) -vi. practise weaving (**wove**, **wo'ven**, **weav'ing**)

web n. woven fabric; net spun by spider; membrane between toes of waterfowl, frogs etc.

wed vt. marry; unite closely (**-dd-**) **-wed'ding** n. nuptial ceremony

wedge n. piece of wood, metal etc., tapering to a thin edge -vt. fasten, split with wedge; stick by compression or crowding

Wednes'day [wenz'-] n. fourth day of the week

wee a. small; little

weed n. plant growing where undesired -vt. clear of weeds -**weed'y** a. full of weeds

week n. period of seven days -**week'ly** a./adv. happening, done, published etc. once a week -**week'day** n. any day of week except Sunday and usu. Saturday -**week'end'** n. Saturday and Sunday

weep v. shed tears (for); grieve (wept, weep'ing) -**weep'y** a.

wee'vil n. small beetle harmful to grain etc.

weft n. cross threads in weaving, woof

weigh [wā] vt. find weight of; consider -vi. have weight; be burdensome -**weight** n. measure of the heaviness of an object; quality of heaviness; heavy mass; object of known mass for weighing; importance, influence -vt. add weight to

weir [wēr] n. river dam

weird [wērd] a. unearthly, uncanny; strange, bizarre

wel'come a. received gladly; freely permitted -n. kindly greeting -vt. greet with pleasure; receive gladly (-comed, -coming)

weld vt. unite metal by softening with heat; unite closely -n. welded joint -**weld'er** n.

wel'fare n. wellbeing

well¹ adv. in good manner or degree; suitably; intimately; fully; favourably, kindly; to a considerable degree -a. in good health; suitable (**better** comp., **best** sup.) -interj. exclamation of surprise, interrogation etc. -**well'be'ing** n. state of being well, happy, or prosperous -**well'mannered** a. having good manners -**well-off** a. fairly rich -**well-read** a. having read much

well² n. hole sunk into the earth to reach water, gas, oil etc.; spring -vi. spring, gush

wellingto'nia n. the giant sequoia

well'ingtons pl.n. high waterproof boots

welt n. raised, strengthened seam; weal

welt'er vi. roll or tumble -n. turmoil, disorder

wen n. cyst, esp. on scalp

wend v. go, travel

went pt. of GO

were pt. of BE, used with you, we, and they

west n. part of sky where sun sets; part of country etc. lying to this side -a. that is toward or in this region -adv. to the west -**west'erly** a. -**west'ward** a./adv. -**west'wards** adv. towards the west -**west'ern** a. of, in the west

wet a. having water or other liquid on a surface or being soaked in it; rainy; not yet dry (paint, ink etc.) (wett'er comp., wett'est sup.) -vt. make wet (wett'ed, wett'ing) -n. moisture, rain

whack vt. strike with sharp resounding blow -n. such blow

whale n. large fish-shaped sea mammal -**wha'ler** n. man, ship employed in hunting whales -**whale'bone** n. horny elastic substance from upper jaw of certain whales

wharf [-awrf] n. platform at harbour, on river etc. for loading and unloading ships

what [wot] pron. which thing; that which; request for statement to be repeated -a. which; as much as; how great, surprising etc. -**whatev'er** pron. anything which; of what kind it may be

wheat n. cereal plant yielding grain from which bread is chiefly made -**wheat'en** a.

whee'dle v. coax, cajole

wheel n. circular frame or disc (with spokes) revolving on axle; anything like a wheel in shape or function; act of turning -v. (cause) to turn as if on axis; (cause) to move on or as if on wheels; (cause) to change course, esp. in opposite direction -**wheel'barrow** n. barrow with one wheel -**wheel'chair** n. chair mounted on large wheels, used by invalids

wheeze vi. breathe with difficulty and whistling noise -n. this sound -**wheez'y** a.

whelp n. pup, cub -v. produce whelps

when adv. at what time -conj. at the time that; although; since -pron. at which (time) -**whenev'er** adv./conj. at whatever time

whence adv./conj. obs. from what place or source

where adv./conj. at what place; at or to the place in which -**where'abouts** adv./conj. in what, which place -n. present position -**whereas'** conj. considering that; while, on the contrary -where·upon' conj. at which point -wher·ev'er adv. at whatever place -where'with·al n. necessary funds, resources etc.

whet vt. sharpen; stimulate (-tt-) -whet'stone n. stone for sharpening tools

wheth'er [WETH⌐] conj. introduces the first of two alternatives

whey [wā] n. watery part of milk left after cheese making

which a. used in requests for a selection from alternatives -pron. which person or thing; the thing "who" -which·ev'er pron.

whiff n. brief smell or suggestion of; puff of air

while conj. in the time that; in spite of the fact that, although; whereas -vt. pass (time, usu. idly) -n. period of time

whim n. sudden, passing fancy -whim'si·cal a. fanciful; full of whims

whim'per vi. cry or whine softly; complain in this way -n. such cry or complaint

whine n. high-pitched plaintive cry; peevish complaint -vi. utter this

whin'ny vi. neigh softly (whinn'·ied, whinn'ying) -n.

whip vt. strike with whip; beat (cream, eggs) to a froth (-pp-) -n. lash attached to handle for urging or punishing

whir v. (cause to) fly, spin etc. with buzzing sound (-rr-) -n. this sound

whirl v. swing rapidly round; move rapidly in a circular course; drive at high speed -n. whirling movement; confusion, bustle, giddiness -whirl'·pool n. circular current, eddy -whirl'wind n. wind whirling round while moving forwards -a.

whisk v. brush, sweep, beat lightly; move, remove, quickly; beat to a froth -n. light brush; egg-beating implement

whisk'er n. any of the long stiff hairs at side of mouth of cat or other animal; any of hairs on a man's face

whis'ky n. spirit distilled from fermented cereals (Irish, C, US whis·key)

whis'per v. speak in soft, hushed tones, without vibration of vocal cords; rustle -n. such speech; trace or suspicion; rustle

whis'tle [-sl] vi. produce shrill sound by forcing breath through rounded, nearly closed lips; make such a sound -vt. utter, summon etc. by whistle -n.

such sound; any similar sound; instrument to make it -whis'tler n.

white a. of the colour of snow; pale; light in colour; having a light-coloured skin -n. colour of snow; white pigment; white part; clear fluid round yolk of egg; white person -whi'ten v. -white'ness n. -whi'tish a. -white'wash n. substance for whitening walls etc. -vt. apply this; cover up, gloss over

whith'er [WITH⌐] adv. obs. to what place; to which

whi'ting n. edible sea fish

whit'tle vt. cut, carve with knife; pare away

whizz(z) n. loud hissing sound -v. move with such sound, or make it (-zz-)

WHO World Health Organization

who [hōō] pron. what or which person or persons; that -who·ev'er pron. who, any one or every one that

whole [hōl] a. complete; containing all elements or parts; not defective or imperfect; healthy -n. complete thing or system -who'lly adv. -whole·heart'ed a. sincere; enthusiastic -whole'sale n. sale of goods by large quantities to retailers -a. dealing by wholesale; extensive -whole'some a. producing good effect, physically or morally

whom [hōōm] pron. form of WHO used as object in a sentence

whoop [wōōp] n. shout or cry expressing excitement etc.

whooping cough [hōōp'-] n. infectious disease marked by convulsive coughing with loud whoop or indrawing of breath

whore [h-] n. prostitute

whose [hōōz] pron. belonging to whom or to which

why adv. for what cause or reason

wick n. strip of thread feeding flame of lamp or candle with oil, grease etc.

wick'ed a. evil, sinful; very bad -wick'ed·ness n.

wick'er(work) n. woven cane etc., basketwork

wick'et n. small gate; Cricket set of three stumps and bails; cricket pitch

wide a. having a great extent from side to side, broad; having considerable distance between; spacious; vast; far from the mark; opened fully -adv. to the full extent; far from the intended target -wi'den v. -width. -wide'ness n. breadth -wide'-

spread a. extending over a wide area

wid'ow [-ō] n. woman whose husband is dead and who has not married again -vt. make a widow of -**wid'ower** n. man whose wife is dead and who has not married again -**wid'owhood** n.

wield vt. hold and use

wife n. a man's partner in marriage, married woman (pl. **wives**) -**wife'ly** a.

wig n. artificial hair for the head -**wigged** a.

wig'gle v. (cause to) move jerkily from side to side -n. -**wig'gly** a.

wild [wīld] a. not tamed or domesticated; not cultivated; savage; stormy; uncontrolled; random; excited; rash -**wild'ly** adv. -**wild'ness** n. -**wild'cat** n. any of various undomesticated feline animals -**wild'life** n. wild animals and plants collectively

wil'debeest [-di-bēst] n. gnu

wil'derness a. desert, waste place

wild'fire n. raging, uncontrollable fire; anything spreading, moving fast

wile n. trick -**wi'ly** a. crafty, sly

wil'ful a. obstinate, self-willed; intentional -**wil'fulness** n.

will v. aux. forms moods and tenses indicating intention or conditional result (**would** pt.) -vi. have a wish -vt. wish; intend; leave as legacy -n. faculty of deciding what one will do; purpose; volition; determination; wish; directions written for disposal of property after death -**will'ing** a. ready; given cheerfully -**will'ingly** adv. -**will'ingness** n. -**will'power** n. ability to control oneself, one's actions, impulses

willow [-ō] n. tree with long thin flexible branches; its wood -**will'owy** a. slender, supple

willy-nilly adv./a. (occurring) whether desired or not

wilt v. (cause to) become limp, drooping or lose strength etc.

win vi. be successful, victorious -vt. get by labour or effort; be successful in (**won, win'ning**) -n. victory, esp. in games -**win'ner** n. -**win'ning** a. charming -**win'nings** pl.n. sum won in game, betting etc.

wince vi. flinch, draw back, as from pain etc. -n. this act

winch n. machine for hoisting or hauling using cable wound round

drum -vt. move (something) by using a winch

wind¹ n. air in motion; breath; flatulence -vt. render short of breath, esp. by blow etc. -**wind'ward** n. side against which wind is blowing -**wind'y** a. exposed to wind; flatulent -**wind'fall** n. unexpected good luck; fallen fruit -**wind instrument** musical instrument played by blowing or air pressure -**wind'mill** n. wind-driven apparatus with fanlike sails for raising water, crushing grain etc. -**wind'pipe** n. passage from throat to lungs -**wind'screen** n. protective sheet of glass etc. in front of driver or pilot

wind² [wīnd] vi. twine; meander -vt. twist round, coil; wrap; make ready for working by tightening spring (**wound** wownd, **wind'ing**) -n. act of winding; single turn of something wound; a turn, curve

win'dow [-ō] n. hole in wall (with glass) to admit light, air etc.; anything similar in appearance or function; area for display of goods behind glass of shop front

wine n. fermented juice of grape etc.

wing n. feathered limb a bird uses in flying; one of organs of flight of insect or some animals; main lifting surface of aircraft; side portion of building -vi. fly; move, go very fast -vt. disable, wound slightly -**wing'er** n. Sport player positioned on wing

wink vi. close and open (an eye) rapidly, esp. to indicate friendliness or as signal; twinkle -n. act of winking

win'kle n. edible sea snail -**winkle out** extract, prise out

win'ter n. the coldest season -vi. pass, spend the winter -**win'try** a. of, like winter; cold

wipe vt. rub so as to clean -n. wiping -**wi'per** n. one that wipes; automatic wiping apparatus (esp. **windscreen wiper**) -**wipe out** erase; annihilate; sl. kill

wire n. metal drawn into thin, flexible strand; something made of wire, eg fence; telegram -vt. provide, fasten with wire; send by telegraph -**wi'ring** n. system of wires -**wi'ry** a. like wire; lean and tough -**wire-haired** a. (of various breeds of terriers) with short stiff hair

wire'less n. old-fashioned term for radio, radio set -a.

wise [wīz] a. having intelligence and

knowledge; sensible -wis'dom n. (accumulated) knowledge, learning

wish vi. have a desire -vt. desire -n. desire; thing desired -wish'ful a. desirous; too optimistic

wisp n. light, delicate streak, as of smoke; twisted handful, usu. of straw etc.; stray lock of hair -wisp'y a.

wist'ful a. longing, yearning; sadly pensive

wit n. ingenuity in connecting amusingly incongruous ideas; person gifted with this power; intellect; understanding; humour -witt'icism n. witty remark -witt'ily adv. -witt'ingly adv. on purpose; knowingly

witch n. person, usu. female, believed to practise, practising, or professing to practise (black) magic; ugly, wicked woman; fascinating woman -witch'craft n. -witch doctor in certain societies, man appearing to cure or cause injury, disease by magic

with prep. in company or possession of; against; in relation to; through; by means of -within' prep./adv. in, inside -without' prep. lacking; obs. outside

withdraw' v. draw back or out (-drew', -drawn', -draw'ing) -withdraw'al n. -withdrawn' a. reserved, unsociable

with'er v. (cause to) wilt, dry up, decline -with'ering a. (of glance etc.) scornful

withhold' vt. restrain; refrain from giving (-held', -hold'ing)

withstand' vt. oppose, resist, esp. successfully (-stood', -stand'ing)

wit'ness n. one who sees something; testimony; one who gives testimony -vi. give testimony -vt. see; attest; see and sign as having seen

wiz'ard n. sorcerer, magician; conjurer -wiz'ardry n.

wiz'ened a. shrivelled, wrinkled

wob'ble vi. move unsteadily; sway -n. an unsteady movement -wob'bly a.

woe n. grief -woe'begone a. looking sorrowful -woe'ful a. sorrowful; pitiful; wretched -woe'fully adv.

wolf [woolf] n. wild predatory dog-like animal (pl. wolves) -vt. eat ravenously

wol'verine [woolvə-rēn] n. carnivorous mammal inhabiting Arctic regions

wom'an [woom-] n. adult human female; women collectively (pl. wom'en [wim'-]) -wom'anhood n. -wom'anish a. effeminate -wom'anize vt. (of man) indulge in many casual affairs -wom'ankind n. -wom'anly a. of, proper to woman

womb [woom] n. female organ in which young develop before birth

wom'bat n. Aust. burrowing marsupial with heavy body, short legs and dense fur

won [wun] pt./pp. of WIN

won'der [wun-] n. emotion excited by amazing or unusual thing; marvel, miracle -vi. be curious about; feel amazement -won'derful a. remarkable; very fine -won'drous a. inspiring wonder; strange

woo vt. court, seek to marry -woo'er n. suitor

wood n. substance of trees, timber; firewood; tract of land with growing trees -wood'ed a. having (many) trees -wood'en a. made of wood; without expression -wood'y a. -wood'land n. woods, forest -wood'pecker n. bird which searches tree trunks for insects -wood pigeon large pigeon of Europe and Asia -wood'wind a./n. (of) wind instruments of orchestra -wood'worm n. insect larva that bores into wood

woof [-ōō-] n. the threads that cross the warp in weaving

wool n. soft hair of sheep, goat etc.; yarn spun from this -wooll'en a. -wooll'y a. of wool; vague, muddled -n.

word [wurd] n. smallest separate meaningful unit of speech or writing; term; message; brief remark; information; promise; command -vt. express in words, esp. in particular way

wore pt. of WEAR

work [wurk] n. labour; employment; occupation; something made or accomplished; production of art or science -pl. factory; total of person's deeds, writings etc.; mechanism of clock etc. -vt. cause to operate; make, shape -vi. apply effort; labour; operate; be employed; turn out successfully; ferment -work'able a. -work'er n. -working class social class consisting of wage earners, esp. manual -working-class a. -work'man n. manual worker -work'manship n. skill of workman; way thing is finished -work'shop n. place where things are made

world [wurld] n. the universe; the planet earth; sphere of existence; mankind, people generally; society -world'ly a. earthly; absorbed in the pursuit of material gain, advantage

worm [wurm] n. small limbless creeping snakelike creature; anything resembling worm in shape or movement -pl. (disorder caused by) infestation of worms, esp. in intestines -vi. crawl -vt. work (oneself) in insidiously; extract (secret) craftily; rid of worms

worn pp. of WEAR

worr'y [wur'i] vi. be (unduly) concerned -vt. trouble, pester, harass; (of dog) seize, shake with teeth (worr'ied, worr'ying) -n. (cause of) anxiety, concern -worr'ier n.

worse [wurs] a./adv. comp. of BAD or BADLY -worst a./adv. sup. of BAD or BADLY -vt. defeat -wors'en v. make, grow worse

wor'ship [wur'-] vt. show religious devotion to; adore; love and admire (-pp-) -n. act of worshipping -wor'shipful a. -wor'shipper n.

wors'ted [woos'tid] n. woollen yarn -a. made of woollen yarn

worth [wurth] a. having or deserving to have value specified; meriting -n. excellence; merit, value; usefulness; quantity to be had for a given sum -wor'thy [-THi] a. virtuous; meriting -n. one of eminent worth -wor'thily adv. -wor'thiness n. -worthwhile' a. worth the time, effort etc. involved

would [wood] v. aux. expressing wish, intention, probability; pt. of WILL -would-be a. wishing, pretending to be

wound[1] [woond] n. injury, hurt from cut, stab etc. -vt. inflict wound on, injure; pain

wound[2] [wownd] pt./pp. of WIND[2]

wove pt., wo'ven pp. of WEAVE

wran'gle [-ng'gl] vi. (noisily); dispute -n. noisy quarrel; dispute

wrap v. cover, esp. by putting something round; put round (-pp-) -wrap, wrapp'er n. loose garment; covering -wrapp'ing n. material used to wrap

wrath [roth] n. anger -wrath'ful a.

wreak vt. inflict (vengeance); cause

wreath [rēth] n. something twisted into ring form, esp. band of flowers etc. as memorial or tribute on grave etc. -wreathe [rēTH] vt. form into wreath; surround; wind round

wreck n. destruction of ship; wrecked ship; ruin; something ruined -vt. cause the wreck of -wreck'age n. -wreck'er n.

wren n. kind of small songbird

wrench vt. twist; distort; seize forcibly; sprain -n. violent twist; tool for twisting or screwing; spanner

wrest vt. take by force; twist violently

wres'tle [-sl] vi. fight (esp. as sport) by grappling and trying to throw down; strive (with); struggle -n. -wrest'ler n. -wrest'ling n.

wretch n. despicable person; miserable creature -wretch'ed a. miserable, unhappy; worthless -wretch'edness n.

wrig'gle v. move with twisting action; squirm -n. this action

wring v. twist; extort; squeeze out (wrung, wring'ing)

wrin'kle n. slight ridge or furrow on skin etc. -v. make, become wrinkled

wrist n. joint between hand and arm

writ n. written command from law court or other authority

write vi. mark paper etc. with the symbols which are used to represent words or sounds; compose; send a letter -vt. set down in words; compose; communicate in writing (wrote, writt'en, wri'ting) -wri'ter n. one who writes; author

writhe [rīTH] v. twist, squirm in or as in pain etc. (writhed pt., writhed pp., wri'thing pr.p.)

wrong a. not right or good; not suitable; incorrect; mistaken; not functioning properly -n. that which is wrong; harm -vt. do wrong to; think badly of without justification -wrong'ful a. -wrong'ly adv.

wrote pt. of WRITE

wrought [rawt] pt./pp. of WORK -a. (of metals) shaped by hammering or beating

wrung pt./pp. of WRING

wry a. turned to one side, contorted; dryly humorous

X

X Christ; Christian; Cross; Roman numeral, 10; mark indicating something wrong, a choice, a kiss, signature etc. -n. unknown, mysterious person, factor

x Maths. unknown quantity

xenopho'bia n. dislike, hatred, fear, of strangers or aliens

xerog'raphy n. photocopying process –Xe'rox **R** xerographic copying process, machine

X'mas [eks'məs] n. short for CHRISTMAS

x-rays pl.n. radiation capable of penetrating solid bodies –x-ray v. photograph by x-rays

xy'lophone n. musical instrument of wooden bars which sound when struck

Y

yacht [yot] n. vessel propelled by sail or power –yachts'man n.

yak n. ox of Central Asia

yam n. large edible tuber, sweet potato

yank v. jerk, tug; pull quickly –n. quick tug

Yank, Yank'ee a./n. sl. American

yap vi. bark (as small dog); talk idly (-pp-) –n.

yard[1] n. unit of length, .915 metre –yard'stick n. formula or standard of measurement or comparison

yard[2] n. piece of enclosed ground, oft. adjoining building and used for some specific purpose

yarn n. spun thread; tale –vi. tell a tale

yawl n. two-masted sailing vessel

yawn vi. open mouth wide, esp. in sleepiness; gape –n. a yawning

yd. yard

ye [ye] pron. obs. you

yea [ya] interj. obs. yes

year n. time taken by one revolution of earth round sun, about 365 days; twelve months –year'ling n. animal one year old –year'ly adv. every year, once a year –a. happening etc. once a year

yearn [yern] vi. feel longing, desire –yearn'ing n.

yeast n. substance used as fermenting agent, esp. in raising bread

yell v./n. shout, scream

yel'low [-ō] a. of the colour of lemons, gold etc.; inf. cowardly –n. this colour –yellow fever acute infectious disease of (sub)tropical climates –yel'lowwood n. SA type of conifer; its rich yellow wood

yelp vi./n. (produce) quick, shrill cry

yen[1] n. inf. longing, craving

yeo'man [yō'-] n. Hist. farmer cultivating his own land

yes interj. affirms or consents, gives an affirmative answer

yes'terday n. day before today; recent time –adv.

yet adv. now, still, besides, hitherto; nevertheless –conj. but, at the same time, nevertheless

yew n. evergreen tree with dark leaves; its wood

yield v. give or return; produce; give up, surrender –n. amount produced

YMCA Young Men's Christian Association

yo'del, yo'dle vi. warble in falsetto tone (-ll-) –n.

yo'ga n. Hindu philosophical system of certain physical and mental exercises

yog(h)'urt [yog'ət] n. thick, custard-like preparation of curdled milk

yoke n. wooden bar put across the necks of two animals to hold them together; various objects like a yoke in shape or use; fitted part of garment, esp. round neck, shoulders; bond or tie; domination –vt. put a yoke on, couple, unite

yo'kel n. (old-fashioned) country dweller

yolk [yōk] n. yellow central part of egg

yon a. obs. or dial. that or those over there –yon'der a. yon –adv. over there, in that direction

yore n. Poet. the distant past

you [yōō] pron. referring to person(s) addressed, or to unspecified person(s)

young [yung] a. not far advanced in growth, life or existence; not yet old; immature; vigorous –n. offspring –young'ster n. child

your [yawr] a. belonging to you –yours pron. –yourself' pron. (pl. -selves')

youth [-ōō-] n. state or time of being young; state before adult age; young man; young people –youth'ful a.

yowl v./n. (produce) mournful cry

YST US, C Yukon Standard Time

Y.T. C Yukon Territory

Yule n. the Christmas festival or season

YWCA Young Women's Christian Association

Z

za'ny a. comical, funny in unusual way

zeal [zēl] n. fervour; keenness; enthusiasm **-zeal'ot** [zel'-] n. fanatic; enthusiast **-zeal'ous** a.

zeb'ra n. striped Afr. animal like a horse

zen'ith n. point of the heavens directly above an observer; summit; climax

zeph'yr [zef'ər] n. soft, gentle breeze

ze'ro n. nothing; figure 0; point on graduated instrument from which positive and negative quantities are reckoned; the lowest point (pl. **-ro(e)s**)

zest n. enjoyment; excitement, interest, flavour

zig'zag n. line or course with sharp turns in alternating directions **-vi.** move along in zigzag course **(-zagged** pt./pp., **-zagging** pr.p.)

zip n. device for fastening with two rows of flexible metal or nylon teeth, interlocked and opened by a sliding clip (also **zipp'er, zip fastener**); short whizzing sound; energy, vigour **-vt.** fasten with zip **-v.** move with zip

zir'con n. mineral used as gemstone and in industry

zith'er n. flat stringed instrument

zo'diac n. imaginary belt of the heavens along which the sun, moon, and chief planets appear to move

zom'bi(e) n. person appearing lifeless

zone n. region with particular characteristics or use; any of the five climate belts of the earth

zoo n. place where wild animals are kept, studied, bred and exhibited (in full **zoological gardens**)

zool'ogy [zō-ol'- or zōō-ol'-] n. scientific study of animals; characteristics of particular animals or of fauna of particular area **-zoolog'ical** a. **-zool'ogist** n.

zoom v. (cause to) make loud buzzing, humming sound; (cause to) go fast or rise, increase sharply **-vi.** (of camera) use lens of adjustable focal length to make subject appear to move closer or further away